Encyclopedia of Retirement and Finance

Encyclopedia of Retirement and Finance

VOLUME I: A–I

Lois A. Vitt, *Editor-in-Chief*

Consulting Editors
E. Craig MacBean and Jurg K. Siegenthaler

Associate Editors
Jamie Losikoff-Kent, Candace D. Jenkins,
Mary Helen McSweeney, Julie Overton, Sandra L. Reynolds,
M. Shelton Smith, Denise Talbot-White

Managing Editors
Ingrid Carlson
Jay Schweig

Foreword by Yung-Ping Chen
Introduction by Dallas L. Salisbury

Published under the Auspices of the Institute for Socio-Financial Studies

GREENWOOD PRESS
Westport, Connecticut • London

Library of Congress Cataloging-in-Publication Data

Encyclopedia of retirement and finance / Lois A. Vitt, editor-in-chief ; consulting editors, E. Craig MacBean and Jurg K. Siegenthaler ; associate editors, Jamie Losikoff-Kent . . . [et al.] ; foreword by Yung-Ping Chen ; introduction by Dallas L. Salisbury.
p. cm.
Includes bibliographical references and index.
ISBN 0–313–32495–6 (2 vols. : alk. paper)
1. Old age—Economic aspects—United States—Encyclopedias. 2. Retirement planning—United States—Encyclopedias. 3. Retirement income—United States—Law and legislation—Encyclopedias. 4. Aged—Finance, Personal—Encyclopedias. 5. Retirement—Economic aspects—United States—Encyclopedias. I. Vitt, Lois A. II. MacBean, E. Craig. III. Siegenthaler, Jürg K., 1939– IV. Institute for Socio-Financial Studies. V. Encyclopedia of financial gerontology.
HQ1064.U5E524 2003
305.26'03—dc22 2003058417

British Library Cataloguing in Publication Data is available.

Library of Congress Catalog Card Number: 2003058417
ISBN: 0–313–32495–6

First published in 2003

Greenwood Press, 88 Post Road West, Westport, CT 06881
An imprint of Greenwood Publishing Group, Inc.
www.greenwood.com

Printed in the United States of America

The paper used in this book complies with the Permanent Paper Standard issued by the National Information Standards Organization (Z39.48–1984).

10 9 8 7 6 5 4 3 2 1

Contents

The Editors vii

The Contributors xiii

Core Topics xxi

Foreword xxvii

Preface xxxi

Introduction xxxv

THE ENCYCLOPEDIA 1

Appendix A: Chronological Summary of Post-ERISA Benefit Legislation 803

Appendix B: Major Post-ERISA Benefit Legislation 813

Appendix C: Organizations and Resources 817

Appendix D: Types of Benefits by Tax Treatment and by Function 831

Index 835

The Editors

EDITOR-IN-CHIEF

LOIS A. VITT, Ph.D., is Chair and Founding Director of the Institute for Socio-Financial Studies (ISFS), Middleburg, Virginia. Dr. Vitt has a background in business and finance for both entrepreneurial companies and investment banking firms, and she is a consultant to financial services companies and community organizations. She has conducted research on consumer decision making, financial literacy education, consumer health finances, the finances of retirement and aging, and financial instruments and organizations. Dr. Vitt has conducted studies for the Employee Benefit Research Institute (EBRI) and the Consumer Health Education Council (CHEC) on Consumer Health Care Financial Education and Consumer Health Values, and she also directed *Personal Finance and the Rush to Competence: Financial Literacy Education in the U.S.* for the Fannie Mae Foundation. She has developed interdisciplinary curricula and taught undergraduate and certificate courses in the social psychology of money and finance and the finances of aging for American University and Catholic University of America. Dr. Vitt pioneered the development of real estate financing vehicles for the capital markets, and her research on the beneficial effects of homeownership has been presented to audiences around the world. She received an Executive M.B.A. from Pace University, New York, and M.A. and Ph.D. degrees in Sociology at the American University in Washington, D.C.

CONSULTING EDITORS

E. CRAIG MacBEAN is a financial gerontologist with expertise in financial life planning, frailty planning, long-term care insurance, annuities, and life and health insurance. He is skilled in sales management and marketing financial products and is a consultant on long-term care issues. Mr. MacBean has broad knowledge of aging policy and the finances of aging and is a member of the Board of Directors of the National Council on Aging (NCOA). He also serves on the Board of Advisors of the National Institute on Financial Services for Elders (NIFSE). He is an author of *Thriving after 55: Your Guide to Fully Living the Rest of Your Life* (2000) and is an accomplished columnist, speaker, and educator on topics that span the finances and inner-life experiences of aging. Mr. MacBean is a senior fellow of the Institute for Socio-Financial Studies. He is a graduate of Wesleyan University, Middletown, Connecticut, and completed three years of study at Union Theological Seminary, Richmond, Virginia.

JURG K. SIEGENTHALER, Ph.D., is Professor Emeritus of Sociology at American University. His research and teaching earlier—at Cornell, the University of California at Los Angeles (UCLA), and Rutgers—have encompassed the sociology of work and organizations as well as social policy analysis. Interests in work and retirement issues connected his previous specializations with social-gerontological topics. Among his studies in recent years are an international comparison of rights of older adults, a review of innovations in different social security systems in response to population aging and other social changes, an examination of how systems of social protection provide for older single women, and a review of flexible work schedules and older workers. He has been a visiting researcher with the International Social Security Association and the U.S. Social Security Administration. A special interest of his is the relationship between aging research, policy, and professional practice as the field of financial gerontology develops.

ASSOCIATE EDITORS

JAMIE LOSIKOFF-KENT is a Senior Research Associate and Administrative Officer with the Institute for Socio-Financial Studies. She is a contributing researcher and author of the study *Personal Finance and the Rush to Competence: Financial Literacy Education in the U.S.* (2000), published by the Fannie Mae Foundation, and *Consumer Health Care Finances and Education: Matters of Values* (2000), published by the Employee Benefit Research Institute (EBRI). Ms. Losikoff-Kent has over 20 years of experience in project administration, planning, and resource development with local governments, regional agencies, and nonprofit organizations in the areas of community and economic development. Ms. Losikoff-Kent has a special interest and expertise in community and housing development issues, having worked as Executive Director of Habitat for Humanity in Charleston, South Carolina, and in Virginia and as Senior Project Director for the Christmas in April Program of Northern Virginia. Ms. Losikoff-Kent received her undergraduate degree from Antioch University. She earned her M.A. at the Danish National School of Design in Kolding, Denmark.

CANDACE D. JENKINS is a research associate at the Institute for Socio-Financial Studies. She edits and manages documentation for over 20 Department of Defense (DoD) and Veterans Health Administration (VHA) contracts for the Military Health System at Integic Corporation where she is the Manager and Editor in the Documentation Department. She is accomplished in training, auditing, and writing quality assurance policies and procedures. She graduated summa cum laude with a B.A. in English from Shenandoah University and is pursuing graduate education in English with a concentration in Professional Writing and Editing at George Mason University.

MARY HELEN McSWEENEY, Ph.D., is the Director of the Undergraduate Program in Health Administration and the Undergraduate Concentration in Long-Term Care at the University of Scranton in Scranton, Pennsylvania. Her professional expertise is in the areas of health care finance, long-term care issues, and employee benefits, and prior to her academic career, Dr. McSweeney served as an Economist and Consultant for Equitable Life's benefits division. She has written and researched extensively and is the author of the book *Long-Term Care: An Emerging Employer Benefit* (2002). She was a 1998 International Foundation of Employee Benefit Plans Research Fund recipient for her research on employer-sponsored long-term care insurance. Dr. McSweeney received a B.A. from Wellesley College and an M.I.A. and M.Phil. from Columbia University. She earned her Ph.D. in Economics from the Graduate Center, City University of New York. In addition, she is a Certified Employee Benefits Specialist (CEBS) and Certified Benefits Professional (CBP).

JULIE OVERTON, M.S.G, M.H.A., is the Program Manager of the National Resource Center on Supportive Housing and Home Modification at the University of Southern California (USC) Andrus Gerontology Center. She is a supportive housing and long-term care specialist whose primary expertise is in the area of home modification. Her most recent research has focused on analysis of state home modification efforts, specifically California, and ascertaining the environmental coping strategies of caregivers and care recipients via focus groups. Ms. Overton teaches two online courses—"Home Modification: The Basics and Beyond" and "Building Home Modification Awareness through Community Building"—as part of the Center's Executive Certificate Program in Home Modification. Ms. Overton has been the Program Manager for several Administration on Aging–funded National Resource Centers at the USC Andrus Gerontology Center over the past 14 years. She has published over 20 reports and articles including "The National Directory of Home Modification and Repair Programs" and "Critical Factors Affecting the Growth of Assisted Living" and presented over 50 workshops on home modification and accessibility issues to professionals, consumers, and caregivers. Ms. Overton has organized and led several local home modification coalitions in California, composed of professionals and consumers dedicated to improving the local housing stock. Ms. Overton is a founding member of the National Home Modification Action Coalition, a group of national associations and experts dedicated to increasing the availability and awareness of the importance of supportive home environments. She has a Master of Science in Gerontology and a Master of Health Administration from the University of Southern California.

SANDRA L. REYNOLDS, Ph.D., is Associate Professor of Gerontology at the University of South Florida in Tampa and an expert in banking and the finances of aging. She teaches sociocultural aspects of aging, and business management in an aging society. At the graduate level, she teaches research methods and population aging. Dr. Reynolds is a Fellow of the Gerontological Society of America and serves on the Board of Advisors of the National Institute on Financial Services for Elders (NIFSE). Her research has included disability among older adults, guardianship, advance directives, financial exploitation of older adults, health care trends for older adults, and working life expectancy for today's workforce. As a former Trust Banker, she acted as a guardian of the estate for many clients over the years. Dr. Reynolds received her undergraduate degree in Sociology from the University of Connecticut, a degree in Trust Banking from the New England School of Banking at Williams College, and her Ph.D. in Gerontology from the University of Southern California, Andrus Gerontology Center.

M. SHELTON SMITH, Ph.D., is a Senior Fellow at the Institute for Socio-Financial Studies and an Independent Consultant in Social and Health Psychology research. Dr. Smith has expertise in research design, measurement, and statistical analysis and has had extensive experience coordinating research programs and teams. Prior to starting her consulting practice, Dr. Smith taught Psychology at the University of Northern Iowa from 1992 to 2000, first as an Assistant Professor and then as an Associate Professor. She was the Coordinator of Research at Meharry Medical College's "I Have a Future" project, a longitudinal teenage pregnancy prevention study. Dr. Smith received her Ph.D. in Social Psychology, with an emphasis in Health Psychology, from Vanderbilt University in 1988.

DENISE TALBOT-WHITE, M.A., is the Gerontology Specialist at the Mature Market Institute at MetLife in Westport, Connecticut. The Mature Market Institute is MetLife's information and policy resource center for issues concerning aging, retirement, long-term care, and the mature market. The Institute provides research, training and education, consultation, and information to support MetLife and its business partners. Ms. Talbot-White is the editor of *QuickFacts*, the Institute's monthly newsletter, writes consumer publications that focus on caregiving and long-term care, and serves as a trainer on the mature market. She is currently on the West Hartford, Connecticut, Senior Citizen Advisory Commission and served on the Delegate Council for the National Institute on Financial Issues and Services for Elders (NIFSE), a constituent group of the National Council on the Aging. Ms. Talbot-White has been in the corporate environment for a number of years and prior to joining MetLife in October 1999 was employed as an Advertising Assistant for a major health insurance company, working in the Medicare/Health Maintenance Organization product area. She received her B.S. from Central Connecticut State University, New Britain, Connecticut, and her M.A. in Human Development and Gerontology from Saint Joseph College, West Hartford, Connecticut.

MANAGING EDITORS

INGRID CARLSON, M.S.F.S., is a Research Fellow, Project Director, and Strategic Development Consultant at the Institute for Socio-Financial Studies. Ms. Carlson has worked in strategic development and as a business planning associate for consulting firms and not-for-profit groups, including a foreign policy media program, a human rights media awareness group, and the United States Equestrian Team. Her expertise includes spearheading new initiatives, developing strategic business plans for organizations, heading project management teams, and streamlining operations. Ms. Carlson received her Master's from Georgetown University's School of Foreign Service, where she studied International Business-Government Relations and Foreign Policy. She received her B.A. in Psychobiology from Mount Holyoke College.

JAY SCHWEIG, formerly a Research Associate and Editor at the Institute for Socio-Financial Studies, is a doctoral student in the Mathematics Department at Cornell University. He was an administrator and assisted in the development of and taught three mathematics enrichment courses at George Mason University (GMU), where he also taught several additional math courses. Mr. Schweig earned his B.S. in Mathematics, summa cum laude, from GMU. He received the Mary K. Cabell Award to the Outstanding Mathematics Student and an Award for Academic Achievement in Mathematics. He was an editor and writer for the *Expulsion* newspaper at GMU.

The Contributors

The opinions expressed in the articles in this *Encyclopedia* are those of the author(s) and do not necessarily reflect those of the agencies or organizations with which they work or are affiliated.

W. Andrew Achenbaum, Ph.D., Professor of History and Social Work, University of Houston, Houston, TX

Laura Addington, C.F.M., M.S.F.S., Addington Financial Group, Greenville, TX

Michele C. Adler, M.P.H., Social Security Administration, Office of Disability and Income Security Programs, Office of Program Development and Research, Baltimore, MD

Linda Albert, Ph.D. Candidate, University of South Florida, Department of Gerontology, Tampa, FL

John Ameriks, Ph.D., TIAA-CREF Institute, New York, NY

Carol Anderson, M.S., President, Money Quotient, Inc., Poulsbo, WA

James A. Anderson, Ph.D., College of Weekend Studies, Jacksonville University, Jacksonville, FL

Sia Arnason, Ph.D., Codirector, Samuel Sadin Institute on Law, Brookdale Center on Aging of Hunter College, City University of New York, New York, NY

William Arnone, Partner, Ernst & Young LLP, New York, NY

Barry K. Baines, M.D., Medicare Medical Director, UCare Minnesota; Associate Medical Director, Hospice of the Twin Cities; CEO, The Legacy Center, Minneapolis, MN

Victor S. Barocas, Managing Director, Strategic Management Group, LLC, Chicago, IL

Thomas D. Begley, Jr., J.D., Begley & Bookbinder, PC, Morristown, NJ

Hubert Bermont, Consultant on Career Consulting, Princess Anne, MD

Leigh Bernstein, J.D., Fleming & Curti, Tucson, AZ

Robert H. Binstock, Ph.D., Professor of Aging, Health, and Society, School of Medicine, Case Western Reserve University, Cleveland, OH

Karen Brelsford, Adjunct Faculty, Financial Planning Division, Howard Community College, Columbia, MD

Kenneth A. Bretthorst, Chairman, First St. Louis Securities, St. Louis, MO

Clifton D. Bryant, Ph.D., Professor, Department of Sociology, Virginia Tech University, Blacksburg, VA

Veronica M. Bukowski, C.P.B.A., C.P.V.A., Bukowski-Stanton Associates, New Hope, PA

Jon E. Burkhardt, Senior Study Director, WESTAT, Rockville, MD

Cathleen Burnett, Ph.D., Department of Sociology/Criminal Justice and Criminology, University of Missouri, Kansas City, MO

Sean Cahill, Ph.D., Director, NGLTF Policy Institute, New York, NY

John W. Callinan, J.D., Attorney-at-Law, Wall, NJ

W. Donald Campbell, M.B.A., Consultant in Finance and Housing, Falls Church, VA

Kathleen Carlisle, Vice President of Marketing/Public Relations, Tech Federal Credit Union, Roanoke, VA

Andrew Carswell, Ph.D. Candidate, Visiting Assistant Professor, University of Georgia, Department of Housing and Consumer Economics, Athens, GA

Pinar Cebi, Ph.D., Research Associate, American Council for Capital Formation, Washington, DC

Susan M. Chambré, Ph.D., Professor of Sociology, Baruch College, City University of New York, New York, NY

Hong-Bin Chen, M.D., Ph.D., Assistant Director, State Data Center on Aging, Florida Policy Exchange Center on Aging, University of South Florida, Tampa, FL

Yung-Ping Chen, Ph.D., Frank J. Manning Eminent Scholar's Chair, Gerontology Institute, University of Massachusetts, Boston, MA

Zhan (Sandy) Chen, M.S., Ph.D. Candidate, Associate Professor, Department of Consumer Sciences and Retailing, Purdue University, West Lafayette, IN

Alfred J. Chiplin, Attorney-at-Law, National Senior Citizens Law Center, Washington, DC

Rachel Christensen, M.P.H., Employee Benefit Research Institute, Washington, DC

David L. Christopherson, Ph.D., C.L.U., G.R., St. Cloud State University, St. Cloud, MN

Elizabeth Clemmer, Ph.D., AARP Public Policy Institute, Washington, DC

Christine Cody, R.N.C., M.S.N., Vice President, Professional Education/Innovation, National Hospice and Palliative Care Organization, Alexandria, VA

John Collins, Ph.D., Professor of Religion, Wake Forest University, Winston-Salem, NC

Francis P. Conner, A.C.S.W., L.M.S.W., Department of Sociology, West Georgia College, Carrollton, GA

Fay Lomax Cook, Ph.D., Director, Institute for Policy Research, Professor of Human Development & Social Policy, Northwestern University, Evanston, IL

Stephanie Cory, M.S.G., Research Assistant, University of Southern California, Andrus Gerontology Center, Los Angeles, CA

Nancy J. Cox, M.S.W., Director, Partners in Caregiving, Department of Psychiatry & Behavioral Medicine, Wake Forest University School of Medicine, Winston-Salem, NC

Stephen Crystal, Ph.D., Research Professor and Chair, Division on Aging, Institute for Health, Health Care Policy and Aging Research, Rutgers University, New Brunswick, NJ

Neal E. Cutler, Ph.D., Boettner/Gregg Chair in Financial Gerontology, Widener University, Chester, PA

Teri Daniel, President & Owner, InsideOut HR Solutions PLLC, Ashland, KY, and Instructor, College of Business, Marshall University, Huntington, WV

Michele F. Davis, Associate Director of Education, TIAA-CREF Institute, New York, NY

Sharon A. DeVaney, Ph.D., Associate Professor, Department of Consumer Sciences and Retailing, Purdue University, West Lafayette, IN

Tracy Dietz, Ph.D., Department of Sociology & Anthropology, University of Central Florida, Orlando, FL

Patricia E. Dilley, Professor, University of Florida, Levin College of Law, Gainesville, FL

C.L. (Tim) Dimos, Attorney-at-Law, Middleburg, VA

Andrew Quang Do, Ph.D., Professor of Finance, Department of Finance, College of Business Administration, San Diego State University, San Diego, CA

Kenneth J. Doran, Attorney-at-Law, Doran Law Offices, Madison, WI

Karen Duggan, C.A., Canadian Institute of Chartered Accountants, Toronto, Ontario, Canada

Michael E. Edleson, Ph.D., Senior Vice President and Chief Economist, NASDAQ, Rockville, MD

Chip Eubank, C.F.P., Eubank Financial Group, Dallas, TX

Ann E. Fade, R.N., J.D., Choice in Dying, Inc., New York, NY

Mark Fagan, Ph.D., Department of Social Work, Jacksonville State University, Jacksonville, AL

Ronald A. Fatoullah, Esq., Ronald Fatoullah & Associates, Great Neck, Forest Hills, and Brooklyn, NY

Charles H. Fay, Ph.D., Professor of Human Resources, Chairman of HRM Department, School of Management and Labor Relations, Rutgers, The State University of New Jersey, Piscataway, NJ

Lucy Rose Fischer, Ph.D., Independent Consultant, St. Louis Park, MN

Paul Fronstin, Ph.D., Employee Benefit Research Institute, Washington, DC

Heather J. Gibson, Ph.D., Associate Professor, Department of Recreation, Parks and Tourism, University of Florida, Gainesville, FL

Stephen M. Golant, Ph.D., Department of Geography, University of Florida, Gainesville, FL

Jordan E. Goodman, President, Amherst Enterprises, Ltd., and Proprietor, www.moneyanswers.com, Scarsdale, NY

Roberta Gosier, Owner/Director, Help Unlimited, Inc., Silver Spring, MD

Mathew Greenwald, Ph.D., Mathew Greenwald & Associates, Inc., Washington, DC

Rebecca Gronvold-Hatch, Ph.D., Professor of Sociology, Mt. San Antonio College, Walnut, CA

Sherman D. Hanna, Ph.D., Professor, Consumer and Textile Sciences Department, Ohio State University, Columbus, OH

Sally Hass, Benefits Education Manager, Weyerhauser, Employee Benefits, Federal Way, WA

Catherine Hawes, Ph.D., Program on Aging and Long-Term Care, Social and Health Policy Research Center, Research Triangle Institute, Research Triangle Park, NC

Celia Ray Hayhoe, Ph.D., C.F.P.R., Family Financial Management, Cooperative Extension Specialist, Virginia Tech, Blacksburg, VA

Rona S. Henry, M.B.A., M.P.H., The Robert Wood Johnson Foundation, Princeton, NJ

Jean M. Hogarth, Ph.D., Consumer & Community Affairs, Federal Reserve Board, Washington, DC

Karen C. Holden, Ph.D., Professor of Public Affairs and Consumer Science, La Follette School of Public Affairs, University of Wisconsin, Madison, WI

Andrew Holmes, Ph.D., Assistant Professor, Business Management Department, Brigham Young University, Provo, UT

Harriet Howe, Ph.D., Visiting Assistant Professor of Sociology, University of North Florida, Jacksonville, FL

Donald A. Hunsberger, Esq., The Law Offices of Donald A. Hunsberger, Orange, CA

Kennes C. Huntley, C.L.U., Department of Finance, Insurance and Real Estate, Mankato State University, Mankato, MN

Gail A. Jensen, Ph.D., Professor, Institute of Gerontology, Wayne State University, Detroit, MI

David R. Johanson, Esq., Johanson Berenson LLP, Attorneys & Counselors at Law, Napa, CA

Marshall B. Kapp, J.D., M.P.H., Office of Geriatric Medicine & Gerontology, Wright State University School of Medicine, Dayton, OH

Enid Kassner, M.S.W., Senior Policy Advisor, AARP Public Policy Institute, Washington, DC

Mary Anne Keefer, B.A., M.A., Adjunct Professor, Lord Fairfax Community College, Middletown, VA

T. Erle Keefer, President, Belair Inc., Huntley, VA

Chris Kelly, Ph.D. Candidate, University of Southern California, Andrus Gerontology Center, Los Angeles, CA

Marilyn C. Kennedy, M.P.A., Public Administration, University of Arizona, Tucson, AZ

Eun-Jin Kim, Ph.D. Candidate, Department of Consumer and Textile Sciences, Ohio State University, Columbus, OH

Andrew S. Kochera, Senior Policy Advisor, AARP Public Policy Institute, Washington, DC

James E. Konlande, D.C., Life Chiropractic College West, San Lorenzo, CA

Janet L. Kuhn, Esq., Law Offices of Janet Kuhn, McLean, VA

Kevin J. Lamiman, Associate Editor, Better Investing Magazine, National Association of Investors Corporation, Madison Heights, MI

Thomas P. Langdon, J.D., Attorney-at-Law, Southington, CT

Jinkook Lee, Ph.D., Professor, Department of Consumer and Textile Sciences, Ohio State University, Columbus, OH

Jean D. LeMasurier, Deputy Director, Health Plan Benefits Group, Center for Beneficiary Services, Centers for Medicare and Medicaid Services, Baltimore, MD

Walter Leutz, Ph.D., Associate Professor, Schneider Institute for Health Policy, Heller School, Brandeis University, Waltham, MA

Phoebe Liebig, Ph.D., Associate Professor, University of Southern California Andrus Gerontology Center, Los Angeles, CA

Jo Ann Linck, Accredited Financial Counselor, Russell Resources and Instructor, Financial Planning, Howard Community College, Columbia, MD

Charles F. Longino, Jr., Ph.D., Reynolds Gerontology Program, Wake Forest University, Winston-Salem, NC

Jamie Losikoff-Kent, Senior Research Associate, Institute for Socio-Financial Studies, Middleburg, VA

E. Craig MacBean, Senior Research Fellow, Institute for Socio-Financial Studies, Middleburg, VA

Ronald J. Manheimer, Ph.D., Executive Director, North Carolina Center for Creative Retirement, and Research Associate, Professor of Philosophy, University of North Carolina, Asheville, NC

Robert D. Manning, Ph.D., Caroline Werner Gannett Professor of the Humanities, Rochester Institute of Technology, College of Liberal Arts, Rochester, NY

Jerry J. McCoy, LL.B., Attorney-at-Law, Law Offices of Jerry J. McCoy, Washington, DC

Christopher R. McDowell, Esq., Dinsmore & Shohl LLP, Cincinnati, OH

V. Karen McMahon, President/Owner, Telecommute-Now, Warrenton, VA

Mary Helen McSweeney, Ph.D., University of Scranton, Scranton, PA

Stacey Meshnick, Esq., Ronald Fatoullah & Associates, Great Neck, Forest Hills, and Brooklyn, NY

John N. Migliaccio, Ph.D., President, Maturity Mark Services Co., White Plains, NY, and American Institute of Financial Gerontology, Deerfield Beach, FL

Steven S. Miner, Research Director, Ragatz Associates, Eugene, OR

Scott A. Miskiel, M.S., Law Offices of Scott A. Miskiel, Cottonwood, AZ

Karlyn Mitchell, Ph.D., College of Management, North Carolina State University, Raleigh, NC

Harry R. Moody, Ph.D., Senior Associate, International Longevity Center—USA, New York, NY

Robert J. Morlock, Ph.D., Global Outcomes Research, Pfizer Pharmaceuticals Group, Ann Arbor, MI

Cyril Morong, Ph.D., Associate Professor of Economics, San Antonio College, San Antonio, TX

Nancy Morrow-Howell, Ph.D., School of Social Work, Washington University, St. Louis, MO

Phyllis H. Mutschler, Ph.D., Executive Director, National Center on Women and Aging, Heller School for Social Policy and Management, Brandeis University, Waltham, MA

Robert J. Myers, LL.D., International Actuarial Consultant, Silver Spring, MD

Rajesh Narayanan, M.B.A., Ph.D., Assistant Professor and Gardner Fellow of Finance, Department of Finance, Ohio University, Athens, OH

Robert Newcomer, Ph.D., Professor, University of California, San Francisco, CA

Brenda Watson Newmann, C.R.P.C., Financial Author/Writer and Chartered Retirement Planning Counselor, Half Moon Bay, CA

Christy Nishita, Ph.D. Candidate, Research Assistant, Andrus Gerontology Center, University of Southern California, Los Angeles, CA

John R. Nofsinger, Ph.D., Assistant Professor of Finance, Department of Finance, Insurance, and Real Estate, College of Business and Economics, Washington State University, Pullman, WA

Barbara O'Neill, Ph.D., Interim Extension Specialist in Financial Resource Management, Rutgers Cooperative Extension, Newton, NJ

Tonya M. Parrott, Ph.D., Professor of Sociology & Gerontology, Quinnipiac University, Hamden, CT

Mars A. Pertl, Ph.D., Fogelman College of Business and Economics, The University of Memphis, Memphis, TN

Ronald Peterson, M.S., President/CEO, Three Arrows Capital Corp., Bethesda, MD

Diane S. Piktialis, Ph.D., Work-Life Product Director, Ceridian, Boston, MA

Stephen L. Poe, Ph.D., Department of Business and Finance Administration, University of North Texas, Denton, TX

Nancy C. Porter, Ph.D., C.F.C.S., Interim Department Chair for Family and Youth Development, Interim State Program Leader for Family and Consumer Sciences, Clemson, SC

Janice K. Purk, Ph.D., State University of West Georgia, Department of Sociology, Anthropology, and Criminology, Carrollton, GA

Jon Pynoos, Ph.D., Andrus Gerontology Center, University of Southern California, Los Angeles, CA

Patricia Quigley, Ph.D., James A. Haley VA Hospital, Patient Safety Center, Tampa, FL

Ganas K. Rakes, Ph.D., Finance Department, Ohio University, Athens, OH

Sandra L. Reynolds, Ph.D., Associate Professor, Department of Gerontology, University of South Florida, College of Arts & Sciences, Tampa, FL

Suzanne Reynolds-Scanlon, Ph.D. Candidate, Department of Gerontology, University of South Florida, College of Arts & Sciences, Tampa, FL

Dorothy P. Rice, Sc.D. (Hon.), Professor Emeritus, University of California, San Francisco, CA

Jihane K. Rohrbacker, Communications Director, National Association of Professional Geriatric Care Managers, Tucson, AZ

Jeffrey I. Roth, M.A., J.D., Professor of Law, Touro College Law Center, Huntington, NY

Linda R. Rounds, Ph.D., School of Nursing, University of Texas Medical Branch, Galveston, TX

N. Lee Rucker, M.S.P.H., National Council on Patient Information and Education (NCPIE), Bethesda, MD

Thomas V. Rush, Ph.D., Social Security Administration, Office of Disability and Income Security Programs, Office of Program Development and Research, Baltimore, MD

Debra S. Sacks, R.N., J.D., Senior Staff Attorney, Samuel Sadin Institute on Law, Brookdale Center on Aging of Hunter College, City University of New York, New York, NY

Dallas L. Salisbury, M.P.A., A.B.D., Chief Staff Executive, Employee Benefit Research Institute, Washington, DC

Ann Elizabeth Sammon, Senior Manager, Membership Section, American Institute of Certified Public Accountants, New York, NY

Judith A. Sangl, Sc.D., Agency for HealthCare Research and Quality, Department of Health and Human Services, Rockville, MD

Kathleen K. Scholl, Ph.D., Consumer Economics, General Accounting Office, Washington, DC

Dennis G. Shea, Ph.D., Professor, Health Policy and Administration, Penn State University, University Park, PA

Jurg K. Siegenthaler, Ph.D., Professor Emeritus, Department of Sociology, American University, Washington, DC

Linda A. Siegenthaler, M.A., Consultant, Silver Spring, MD

Michael A. Smyer, Ph.D., Dean & Associate Vice President for Research, Graduate School of Arts and Sciences, Boston College, Chestnut Hill, MA

Ben J. Sopranzetti, Ph.D., Assistant Professor, Rutgers University, Department of Finance, Piscataway, NJ

Richard H. Stanton, C.P.B.A., C.P.V.A., Bukowski-Stanton Associates, New Hope, PA

Norman Stein, Ph.D., Visiting Professor, University of Maine School of Law, Portland, ME

Catherine M. Sullivan, M.P.A., The Brookings Institution, Washington, DC

Ralph B. Swisher, Ph.D., Department of Homeland Security, Washington, DC

Kenn Tacchino, J.D., LL.M., Professor of Taxation and Financial Planning, Accounting, Law & Taxation Department, Widener University, Chester, PA

Lynn Q. Taylor, Senior Policy Analyst, Institute for Health Policy Solutions, Washington, DC

Margo Thorning, Ph.D., Senior Vice President and Chief Economist, American Council for Capital Formation, Washington, DC

John H. Thornton, Ph.D., C.L.U., College of Business Administration, University of Texas, Denton, TX

Paul Thrasher, C.P.A., Halt, Jackson and Thrasher, Alexandria, VA

Sandra Timmermann, Ed.D., Director, Mature Market Institute, MetLife, Westport, CT

David J. Tolan, J.D., C.L.U., Tolan Schueller, Inc., Milwaukee, WI

Ronald Turner, J.D., George Butler Research Professor and Professor of Law, The University of Houston Law Center, Houston, TX

Peter Uhlenberg, Ph.D., Department of Sociology, University of North Carolina, Chapel Hill, NC

Jack L. VanDerhei, Ph.D., Department of Risk, Insurance, and Healthcare Management, The Fox School of Business and Management, Temple University, Philadelphia, PA

Valentine M. Villa, Ph.D., Adjunct Assistant Professor, UCLA Public Health–Community Health Sciences, Los Angeles, CA

Lois A. Vitt, Ph.D., Director and Founder, Institute for Socio-Financial Studies, Middleburg, VA

Anne S. Welch, M.A., Program in Human Development and Social Policy, School of Education and Social Policy, Northwestern University, Evanston, IL

Paul Westbrook, C.F.P., Westbrook Financial Advisers, Westfield, NJ

Robert Whaples, Ph.D., Department of Economics, Wake Forest University, Winston-Salem, NC

Monika White, President/CEO, Center for Healthy Aging, Santa Monica, CA

Joshua M. Wiener, Ph.D., The Urban Institute, Washington, DC

Steven Wilber, Ph.D., Research Associate, American Council for Capital Formation, Washington, DC

Bradley R. Williams, PharmD, Associate Professor, University of Southern California School of Pharmacy and Andrus Gerontology Center, Los Angeles, CA

Flora Williams, Ph.D., Consumer and Family Sciences, Purdue University, Lafayette, IN

David P. Willis, M.P.H., National Institute on Aging, Bethesda, MD

Louisa Woodville, M.A., M.B.A., Intersections Inc., Chantilly, VA

David L. Wray, President, Profit Sharing/401K Council of America, Chicago, IL

Bernadette Wright, Ph.D., Policy Research Analyst, AARP Public Policy Institute, Washington, DC

James D. Wright, Ph.D., Department of Sociology & Anthropology, University of Central Florida, Orlando, FL

Rui Yao, Ph.D., Assistant Professor, South Dakota State University, Brookings, SD

Sarah Zapolsky, M.S., Senior Research Advisor, Knowledge Management/Membership Group, AARP, Washington, DC

Core Topics

Advisors, Advice, and Support

Accountants
Agents and Brokers
Asset Allocation after Retirement
Banking Services for the Mature Market
Cash Flow Planning for Retirees
Corporate Eldercare Programs
CPA Eldercare Services
Credit Scores
Estate Planning
Ethics in Financial Planning
Financial Advisors
Financial Counseling for Mid- to Later Life
Financial Education for Seniors
Financial Literacy
Financial Planning Process
Financial Recovery in Later Life
Frailty Planning
Geriatric Care Managers (GCMs)
Gerontological Social Work
Investment Advice
Investment Clubs
Investor Education
Life Planning
Marketing to Mature Adults
Ombudsman
Physician–Older Patient Relationships

Retirement Expense Planning
Retirement Planning
Retirement Planning Software
State and Area Agencies on Aging

Economic and Income Security

Accelerated Death Benefits
Cost-of-Living Adjustments (COLAs)
Disability Programs, Federal and State
Economic Status of Older Men and Women
Means-Testing in Public Programs
Medicaid
Nutrition Programs
Old-Age Provisions and Economic Status
Social Security Privatization
Social Security Program of the United States
Supplemental Security Income (SSI)
Veterans' Benefits

Employment, Work, and Retirement

Age Discrimination in Employment Act (ADEA)
Attitudes about Retirement
Business Succession Planning
Cash Balance Pension Plans
Consulting in Retirement
Defined Benefit Pension Plan
Defined Contribution Plan
Early Retirement Incentive Plans (ERIPs)
Economic History of Retirement
Employee Benefits in the Public Sector
Employee Benefits in the United States
Employee Retirement Income Security Act (ERISA)
Employee Stock Ownership Plans (ESOPs)
Employer-Sponsored Long-Term Care Insurance
Entrepreneurship
Flexible Benefit Plans
Individual Retirement Account (IRA)
Job Lock
Keogh Plans
Life Planning in the Workplace

Pension Plans
Pension Plans for the Self-Employed
Phased Retirement and Retiree Skills Banks
Postretirement Health Coverage (PRHC)
Profit Sharing Plans
Retirement Plans—401(k)
Retirement Plans—403(b)
Workforce Patterns, Changes in
Working Retirees
Workplace Financial Education

Family and Intergenerational Issues

Cohabitation
Death Benefits
Divorce and Older Adults
Funerals and Funeral Finances
Inheritance
Intergenerational Conflict and Financial Issues
King Lear Syndrome
Marriage and Older Adults
Planning for Surviving Special Needs Children
Widowhood

Financial Investments and Insurance

Accident Insurance
Aging into Debt
Annuities
Bonds
Capital Gain
Charitable Contributions
Commodities
Consumer Credit
Daily Money Managers
Derivatives
Equity Securities
Federal Agency Securities
Growth Capital for Older Entrepreneurs
Influences on Retirement Investment Decisions
Liability Insurance
Life Insurance

Long-Term Care Insurance (LTCI)—A Consumer's Perspective
Long-Term Care Insurance: Individual Disability-Escalating Annuities (IDEAs)
Long-Term Care Insurance, Private
Medicare Supplemental Insurance
Mutual Funds
Predatory Lending
Real Estate Investments
Risk Tolerance
Savings Account Trusts
Savings Investments
Taxpayer Issues of Older Adults
U.S. Personal Saving Rates
U.S. Savings Bonds

Health Care and Health Coverage

Activities of Daily Living (ADLs)
Advance Directives
Assisted Living
Community-Based Care
Cost of Family Caregiving
Day Programs for Adults
Drugs and Senior Citizens
Geriatric Rehabilitation
Gerontological Nurse Practitioners (GNPs)
Health and Longevity
Health Benefits
Health Maintenance Organizations and Management Health Care for Older Adults
Home Care Services for Older Adults
Hospice Care
Medicaid Planning
Medical Savings Accounts (MSAs) and Medical IRAs
Medicare
Medicare + Choice
Mental Health among Older Adults
Mental Health Care Financing
Nursing Homes
Pharmacists

Housing and Housing Finance

Board and Care Homes
Condominiums

Continuing Care Retirement Communities (CCRCs)
Cooperative Ownership in Housing
Home Modifications Financing
Homelessness among Older Adults
Homeownership
Housing Counseling for Older Americans
HUD-Assisted Rental Housing
Life Estates
Mortgage Instruments
Retirement Migration
Reverse Mortgages
Seniors Housing Finance

Legal Issues

Attorneys
Bankruptcy
Durable Power of Attorney
Elder Law Practice
Ethical Will
Guardianship
Living Will
Probate
Titling Assets
Trusts
Wills
Zoning

Quality of Life and Well-Being

Aging America
Baby Boomers and Retirement
Consumer Protection for Older Adults
Crime Protection
Disaster Preparedness and Older Adults
Economic Hardship Measures in the Older Population
Education of Older Adults
Finances of Aging in the Gay Community
Financial Elder Abuse
Financial Gerontology, History of
Financial Security in Retirement
History of Retirement
Identity Theft

Internet Use by Seniors
Leisure
Minority Older Adults
Older Americans Act
Oldest Old
Religious Giving by Older Adults
Retirement Preparedness
Senior Discounts
Snowbird Checklist and Transborder Issues
Transportation
Vacation Homes and Recreational Property
Volunteering
Wealth Span

Foreword

During the coming decades, retirement of the 76 million baby boomers—those born from 1946 to 1964—will pose significant challenges for society as well as for boomers themselves. These challenges stem partly from the fact that the younger population cohorts have far fewer people available to work and pay taxes to defray the costs of public and private retirement benefits and health care. At the same time, increasing longevity compounds the problem. In short, lower fertility and greater longevity are making it more difficult for society as well as for individuals to prepare for retirement, both financially and nonfinancially.

In 2012, the oldest boomers will be 66 years old, the age at which Social Security will pay full retirement benefits to those who are eligible. In 2031, the youngest baby boomers will reach age 67, the age at which full Social Security retirement benefits will be due those who qualify. Medicare will cover the oldest boomers beginning in 2011 and the youngest in 2029 if the current eligibility age of 65 remains unchanged.

Financial needs during retirement are provided for privately by individuals and families or collectively by society, or by a combination of both. While individuals and families are responsible for satisfying their individual retirement needs, they need to operate in a basically sound and stable macroenvironment. In policy discussions, it is therefore important to understand the complementary roles of individual and collective responsibilities.

Individuals can and must do their part. Recognizing differences in individual preferences and within limits, one could argue that people can and should try, among other salutary lifestyle behaviors, to stay healthy in order to reduce expenses for themselves and to conserve health care resources for society at large. They should spend their income reasonably, save early and consistently, invest prudently, and diversify their investments. They should plan for the contingency of long-term care needs to avoid impoverishing themselves or their families or becoming a public charge.

Despite these and other like efforts, however, only the wealthiest may succeed, absent an overall social framework that encourages and supports individual efforts. We need a stable government and a well-functioning economy with ethical conduct by business, labor, and government. We need collective measures that are organized or facilitated by government, business, and labor, such as social insurance programs for income security and health care security that are solvent for the long term, work-based pensions that are secure and reliable, and a system of work and retirement that includes arrangements to accommodate those who seek work during older ages. And we need the support and assistance of civic, charitable, and religious organizations. Many such institutions and practices do exist today, but we also need to innovate more, strengthening what we already have and introducing new and better ways.

The challenge of policy development for ensuring greater old-age economic security in the new century lies, in my view, with seeking approaches that balance individual and collective responsibilities. Individual responsibility is expressed by what may be expected realistically of individuals and their families and friends. Collective responsibility is demonstrated by the array of public sector policies (i.e., federal, state, and local governments) and private sector policies (i.e., business, labor, and nonprofits, such as civic, religious, and charitable organizations). To embark on the task of reviewing and modernizing public and private retirement policies for the future, we have as a starting point the *Encyclopedia of Retirement and Finance*. This comprehensive inventory of policies, institutions, practices, and problems is another significant editorial contribution of Lois A. Vitt.

The relative roles of individual and collective responsibilities have undergone significant changes historically. For many decades before the Great Depression starting in 1929, the predominant opinion was that Americans could, by and large, provide for their own old age by individual savings and family assistance and by private philanthropy and public charity if all else failed.

The cataclysmic event of the Great Depression—stock market collapse, bank failures, and mass unemployment—uprooted the social mores of the time, as it exposed, more starkly than in previous business downturns, the hollow protective power of self-reliance, particularly in an industrial society. Mass unemployment for long years stripped many individuals of their ability to earn a living, let alone to save for future needs; a protracted period of financial crises simply swept away much of the life's savings of many people. Those financially catastrophic occurrences, which exacted untold human costs of ruined dreams and shattered lives, made it clear that, as President Franklin D. Roosevelt declared in his June 1934 message to Congress, it was necessary "to employ the active interest of the nation as a whole through government" to provide safeguards "against misfortune which cannot be wholly eliminated in this man-made world of ours."

Thus was ushered in an era of government intervention in the ensuing four decades (from the mid-1930s to the mid-1970s), witnessing passage of various major pieces of social legislation in pensions and health care—Social Security, Medicare, Medicaid, and the Employee Retirement Income Security Act (ERISA), to name the most significant.

Since the mid-1970s, however, political pressures have mounted to provide incentives for individuals to take more responsibility for their own future. By the 1990s, welfare reform, Medicare + Choice, and the continuing debate about Social Security privatization attested tellingly to changing attitudes. Ideology aside or in conjunction, those actual and proposed changes in policy direction reflected a confluence of factors. These factors juxtaposed diminished the fiscal capacity of the government (resulting from slackening productivity and economic growth) against the improved economic status of older people, rendering less compelling the advocacy for age-based social programs on their behalf.

Individuals are increasingly urged by politicians to assume more responsibility for their own retirement. Wittingly or unwittingly, some individuals also declare that they prefer to increase their self-responsibility. However, while individual responsibility is necessary and desirable, it has not proven sufficient. Not everyone has the financial sophistication or good luck to make winning investment choices. Collective responsibility is essential since many conditions in employment, pensions, investments, and health care that adversely affect individuals are occurring at the societal level through no fault of their own.

For example, in recent times, many workers and retirees have fallen victim to the business failures caused by corporate fraud, as illustrated by the notorious cases of Enron, WorldCom, Arthur Andersen, and their ilk. Stock market slumps have substantially shrunk the financial wealth of many individuals; they have also contributed to the large underfunding of many pension plans. Unemployment has sapped the ability of many individuals' ability to earn an income, let alone to save for their future. Bear stock markets have generated skepticism or reluctance about investing in equities among many investors and would-be investors. Medicare cuts to health care providers have put a large number of the program's participants at financial and health risks.

Development of public and private sector policies for the century that is unfolding must recognize that potential problems brought about by new and emerging demographic and economic realities carry with them new opportunities as well. For example, when the number and proportion of older people increase, a society is aging. Although an aging society could result in increasing scarcity of workers in the traditional age groups, it may also hold out the promising prospect that some older people, who would have retired under traditional rules and practices, may choose to work longer if conducive work environments are created. The outcome depends a great deal on whether we choose to live under the institutional arrangements that were once meaningful but have now become constraining or whether we venture to alter these arrangements in favor of new and more flexible work and pension systems in order to better utilize our human resources, including those represented by older people.

The world is what we collectively make of it. In designing and maintaining policies for future retirees, we must underscore the role of the government sector in fostering a supportive environment. We must understand how private sector policies of business, labor, and nonprofits may promote or hinder needed adjustments in our institutions and programs as demographic and economic circumstances change. And we must expect individuals and families to do what they can and should in service to themselves and to society. In short, to ensure greater old-age economic security, we need to balance individual and collective responsibilities, as we marshal our resources, private and public. Serving as a sourcebook, the *Encyclopedia of Retirement and Finance* will be valuable to concerned individuals as well as to specialists and policymakers in both the public and private sectors.

Yung-Ping Chen, Ph.D.
Frank J. Manning Eminent Scholar's Chair
Gerontology Institute
University of Massachusetts at Boston

Preface

The visibility of mid- to late-life finances as a major personal and national issue has increased significantly since the first edition of this *Encyclopedia* was published in 1996 as the *Encyclopedia of Financial Gerontology*. Whether readers' concerns are for the financial well-being of clients, colleagues, students, older relatives, or themselves, the times are vastly changed from just seven years ago. There is widespread uncertainty due to the changed nature of the country's national security and economic priorities. Employers continue to seek answers to the pressing problem of escalating employee benefits, particularly health benefits. Workplace trends that shift both risks and costs to employees continue as well. There is an anxious new tone audible in the voices of thought leaders, policymakers, employers, and financial advisors, all of whom are calling on Americans to take more responsibility for their future personal finances.

Research suggests that Americans *like* feeling responsible for themselves and their loved ones. After all, about 90% of the nation's infirm are cared for by family members. When they know what is expected of them, and when they are given the tools and the opportunity to become successful at whatever they undertake, Americans accept—and even seek—responsibility. Still, the sheer numbers of baby boomers who are aging into their retirement years is enough to ring alarm bells in every sector of the general economy, and most aging baby boomers today have neither the knowledge nor the savings required for successful retirement.

Americans today face changing trends and financial complexities unknown to their parents or grandparents. There is a bewildering array of decisions, planning goals, and choices to be made concerning work, health care, saving, investing, borrowing, family and intergenerational issues, plans for how to live in retirement, and plans even for approaching frailty and death. In short, Americans, in ever increasing numbers, must address financial issues that grow exponentially as people age in contemporary society. This revised and enlarged edition of the *Encyclopedia* was planned with these financial and social realities in mind.

This *Encyclopedia* is a multidisciplinary, authoritative, comprehensive, and readable mosaic of the financial topics, vehicles, services, advisors, costs, structures, programs, institutions, products, investments, issues, and social policies that impact nearly every aspect of people's everyday lives. One thing is certain: regardless of how much we think we know about the financial details of our approaching retirement and later years, we all could know a lot more. As a financial literacy educator, researcher, and advocate, I've seen the growing—and ubiquitous—hunger that Americans at all ages and life stages have for greater financial knowledge and for the confidence to apply it competently. What I've learned as well is that everyone needs help in finding resources that enhance their comprehension of modern finances—from asset allocation to the U.S. Tax Code to reverse mortgages, from Medicare to health maintenance organizations (HMOs) to caregiving options, from investments to consumer protection to retirement planning, from credit scores to 401(k)s to investor education.

When asked by colleagues, students, friends, and other seekers of information about the finances of aging, I have directed them first to the *Encyclopedia*, which I have often used myself. My experience in consumer financial education during the past several years led to this revised edition, which has been expanded to include many additional topics about preretirement and retirement issues. Included in the new edition are entries that span the array of employer-sponsored health and retirement benefits, which are increasingly central to working Americans and to their partners and family members. There is a great need for this financial knowledge to reach the many professionals who advise, support, sell products to, serve, assist, and teach mid-life and later-life clients. There is also a need for professionals and practitioners to help consumers themselves become educated about these topics.

Entries have been arranged to provide information at any alphabetical point. Readers are directed elsewhere by the references to other topics that appear at the end of each article. For teachers interested in using the *Encyclopedia* as a textbook, or advisors who are interested in specific life areas, a core set of articles under generic headings—e.g., "Advisors, Advice, and Support," "Economic and Income Security," "Employment, Work, and Retirement," "Family and Intergenerational Issues," "Financial Investments and Insurance," "Health Care and Health Coverage," and others—appear under "Core Topics" at the front of the book. Readers are also directed to Appendix C, Organizations and Resources, for the addresses, telephone numbers, and Internet addresses of the organizations referred to in many entries.

The contributions to this *Encyclopedia* have enriched these volumes with a breadth of research, knowledge, information, and perspectives on the finances of retirement and later life that have not before been collected into one reference. My debt to the Consulting Editors and to the Associate Editors who helped to weave the technical and varied language of many disciplines into a cohesive whole is gratefully acknowledged. Achieving this was a special challenge that was met so that professionals across the spectrum of aging and financial services, and consumers as well, could feel comfortable with the array of some otherwise difficult topics. Ingrid Carlson, Managing Editor of the *Encyclopedia*, and Jay Schweig, who managed the details of the contributions before Ingrid, kept the lines of communication open and running smoothly between the authors, editors, and the Greenwood Publishing Group.

Special thanks are due to production manager Karen McMahon, for her dedication and excellent administrative and technical assistance, and to John Donohue and Susan Badger for their superb project editing. We are grateful to Greenwood Publishing Group editors George Butler and Doug Goldenberg-Hart for their vision and Steven Vetrano for his valued assistance. Finally, we commend Greenwood Publishing Group for its commitment to the ideal of a public that is more knowledgeable—and thus less anxious—about the financial issues of later life. We are all in their debt.

Lois A. Vitt
Middleburg, VA

Introduction

Public and policymaker concern about retirement savings led to passage in 1974 of the Employee Retirement Income Security Act (ERISA) and to the Social Security Act Amendments of 1983. The Arthur Andersen, Enron, and WorldCom debacles of this new century have once again put retirement savings on the front pages of our news magazines and papers and as the headline story on television news. The *Encyclopedia of Retirement and Finance* is being published at a time of great need for basic information. This need encompasses the public, the media, and decision makers.

The *Encyclopedia* makes clear what a complex web of issues reformers must deal with as they seek to follow the lead of ERISA in strengthening retirement opportunity and retirement security. Needed reform once again surrounds Social Security, as projections make clear that the near-solvency crisis of 1983 will repeat itself within 20 years if action is not taken. Again, basic information for understanding is essential.

The first baby boomers will reach the magic Social Security age for full benefits at 66 (yes, 66 for the first wave and 67 for later waves) in 2012, less than a decade ahead. For them, it is time to focus on when and whether they can afford to retire at 66. Too many will not read this *Encyclopedia* and will sign up for Social Security when they reach age 62. They will not have learned that benefits are about 30% less if you take them at 62. Further, they will not have read that for the average earner that means an age 62 income replacement for a single individual at about 25% of final-year earnings (about $600 per month or $7,000 per year). While barely enough to live on, it is not the stuff that cruises and the "good life" are made of.

Too many will not read this *Encyclopedia* and will fail to ever open an Individual Retirement Account (IRA)—only 7% contributed in 2001 according to the Internal Revenue Service. Nor will they contribute to a savings or 401(k) plan at work—of those who could in 2001, the government reports that 24% chose not to do so, and over 80% chose to contribute less than the law allowed. Reading a few select articles within this *Encyclopedia* would give them a clear understanding of why they should open that IRA and contribute to that plan at work: it is tax effective; Social Security alone will not provide livable income; and as an average American, if I do not save, no one will do it for me.

Too many will not read this *Encyclopedia* and will think that "life expectancy" can be counted on to end before the money runs out. They will continue to miss the desired use of *average* in descriptions of life expectancy. They will focus on media reports that the "life expectancy" of a woman born today is 79, or a woman at 65 today is 85, without understanding that they must always assume the word *average* and understand that "*I have a 50% probability of living longer if I make it to that age.*" For myself, my dad turned 89 and my mom 87 in 2002. Both have now lived beyond multiple "average age specific life expectancies" and can now expect, on average, another 5 years. But it keeps rolling forward! The tables suggest that if I make it to 65, I, on average, can expect to live until 80, while my family and personal history suggest a number closer to 100. What if I retired at 62 with only an inadequate Social Security benefit and then lived to 100? A pretty financial picture it would not be. A reading of this *Encyclopedia*, however, would keep people from making that mistake as it guided them to knowledge about living longer and to retirement calculators that would make the numbers and the needs very clear.

Too many will not read this *Encyclopedia* and, as a result, will not have visited the many helpful articles or used the recommended retirement calculators. They will have missed the notations in the calculators and the knowledge offered here about "Health Benefits" and "Long-Term Care" and the savings needs that these represent during long years of retirement.

Too many will not read this *Encyclopedia* and will not have the information to help themselves and to advise and care for family members on issues ranging from accident insurance to accountants to assisted living to cash flow planning for retirees to drugs to reverse mortgages to salary reduction plans to titling assets to wills, and so much more.

Lois Vitt and the Greenwood Press are to be congratulated on this expanded new edition of the *Encyclopedia of Retirement and Finance*. This *Encyclopedia* should become a staple of gift giving as the baby boomers continue to age: from child to aging parent, to help them understand what they should be doing to prepare for the future; from parent to college-bound youth, to help them understand why they should seek to avoid high interest rate credit card debt and start saving early to enjoy the full magic of compound interest; from aged parent to graying adult children, as a means of sharing what they wish they had done to be better prepared for their ever-extending years; from employer to employee; or from financial advisor to client. As a transfer of information or as suggested reading, these volumes can literally help reduce pain and increase future economic security if they are read and absorbed.

Two-thirds of today's retirees live almost entirely on Social Security. The same is going to be true for the baby boom generation unless they begin to take action now. As this *Encyclopedia* documents, Social Security benefits will be paid at later ages and at the same time decline in the percentage of final earnings they pay. Even with that, the program will require either large tax increases or substantial benefit reductions in the decades ahead. Social Security is an antipoverty floor of income that will not be expanded for most Americans in any reform. The aging of the baby boomers will move the proportion of the population over the age of 65 from the current 13% to nearly 23%. This carries changes that are documented in this *Encyclopedia* for every generation alive today and for those yet to be born. The *Encyclopedia of Retirement and Finance* is a public service volume that will enhance economic and income security. The time for reading it and taking action is now!

Dallas L. Salisbury
President and CEO, Employee Benefit Research Institute
Washington, DC

Encyclopedia of Retirement and Finance

A

ACCELERATED DEATH BENEFITS, payment by an insurance company of part, or all, of a life insurance policy's death benefits before the insured's death in the event of certain qualifying events such as terminal illness. Availability of accelerated death benefits helps people who are facing death, life-threatening medical events, or confinement to a nursing home or extended care facility to access funds that would otherwise only be available to survivors. Familiarity with life insurance basics aids understanding of accelerated death benefits.

Normal Life Insurance Policy Benefits

An insurance company will pay the "face amount" (death benefit) of an in-force life insurance policy to the beneficiary when the insured dies. This is the case for all forms of life insurance, including term, endowment, whole life, universal life, and variable life. In term life policies, a promise to pay upon death while the policy is in force is the only policy benefit. In an endowment policy, the insurance company pays the face amount if the insured dies during the term of the endowment and also pays the face amount if the insured survives the policy's term. For example, in an Endowment at Age 65 policy, the death benefit is paid if the insured dies before age 65 or when the policy matures as an endowment if the insured lives to age 65. Whole life policies are really endowment at age 100 contracts and will pay the death benefit to the beneficiary if the insured dies before age 100 or to the insured if he or she lives to that age. Universal life and variable life policies may extend death benefit protection beyond age 100.

All forms of life insurance other than term also have a savings, or cash value, element. In whole life or endowment policies, premiums are set so that the cash value equals the face amount of the policy at the end of the policy term. In universal and variable life policies, the cash value is determined by the level of premium payments and the interest or investment results. The policy owner can borrow from this cash value, creating a debt against the policy's death benefit for the loan amount plus interest. Loans against life insurance policies do not have to be paid back but will be subtracted from the death benefit of the policy if not repaid before the insured's death. In universal and variable life policies, the cash value can also be withdrawn. In all cases, the policy can be completely or partially surrendered to get the cash value, but then the accompanying death benefit is also lost. A policy owner who borrows against the cash value or makes a partial withdrawal, or surrenders the policy to get all of the cash value, may use the money for any purpose, including costs associated with poor health. An insured's access to cash value is a "living benefit" available to the policy owner, often without incurring any income tax liability.

Other Living Benefits

Although funds provided under a life insurance policy's accelerated death benefit (ADB) option are sometimes called "living benefits," this term is also used to describe payments made by viatical settlement firms. A viatical settlement firm provides cash to terminally ill policy owners by purchasing their life insurance policies for some percentage of the death benefit. The less time the insured has to live, the higher the percentage. The firm then names itself as beneficiary, continues paying the policy premiums, and collects the policy proceeds upon the death of the insured. Viatical settlements (sometimes called "living settlements" or "senior settlements") are available to virtually anyone who has owned a life insurance policy for at least two years and is expected to live less than 12 years.

Accelerated death benefit options have been developed by life insurance companies as an alternative to viatical settlements, although they are not mutually exclusive. In many cases, life insurance policies with accelerated death benefit provisions make a viatical settlement unnecessary, although accelerated death benefit provisions of life insurance policies are generally much more restrictive than viatical settlements.

During the late 1980s, Canadian life insurers introduced accelerated death benefit options to help terminally ill AIDS (acquired immunodeficiency syndrome) patients, and they have become an increasingly popular product of U.S. life insurers. Though the original intent was to help AIDS victims, the accelerated death benefit option can be an important living benefit to anyone facing the costs associated with a terminal illness or other debilitating condition.

The Accelerated Death Benefit Option

There are, generally, four situations in which a life insurance company will advance payment of some of the death benefits of an in-force life insurance policy: (1) diagnosis of a terminal illness where the remaining life expectancy is six months or one or two years; (2) permanent confinement to a nursing care facility; (3) inability to perform activities of daily living; or (4) onset of a dread disease, such as cancer. Virtually all (more than 90%) policies that make provision for accelerated death benefits will accelerate for short life expectancy. At the time of the 1998 American Council of Life Insurance and the Life Insurance Marketing and Research Association (ACLI/LIMRA) *Accelerated Death Benefits* survey, 73% of companies offering ADB for terminal illness set the requirement at an expectation of death within 12 months. Now more use the definition of a terminally ill individual found in the Health Insurance Portability and Accountability Act (HIPAA) of 1996—someone "who has been certified by a physician as having an illness or physical condition that reasonably can be expected to result in death in 24 months or less from the date of certification"—as qualification for the benefit. When exercised due to terminal illness, the ADB payment typically is determined by discounting some or all of the death benefit. In most policies, some type of medical certification that a qualifying event has occurred must be provided to the insurer before the option may be exercised.

The ADB option is becoming an increasingly popular feature of life insurance policies. According to the 1998 survey by ACLI/LIMRA, the number of ADB option policies increased from about 1.13 million to at least 39.9 million from 1991 to 1997, and the number of insurers offering this feature increased from 113 to 245 during this same time period, despite the fact that the number of active life insurance companies dropped by 25% from 1994 to 1997. More employers include the ADB option as part of group life plans, given the low cost of providing this popular benefit to employees.

Terms of ADB options vary from insurer to insurer and can be offered as a feature of a new policy, added as a rider to an existing one, or made available by policy endorsement or administrative practice. Depending on policy terms and state laws, the maximum amount that can be accelerated ranges from 25% to 100% of a policy's face value. Often, minimum policy size and maximum benefit limitations are also imposed by companies. The policy owner may receive an ADB payment as a lump sum or in monthly installments, and no restriction is made on the use of such funds. In some policies, the ADB payment becomes a lien against the policy's death benefit, in which event access to the policy's cash value may be restricted by the amount of the lien.

Costs of ADB options also vary. Although some insurers charge an additional premium for the ADB option, many ADB policies do not carry an additional charge unless the option is exercised. Some insurers charge no additional premium for this feature. When the option is exercised, the insurer may charge a percentage of the policy's face value, an administrative fee, or both. Typically, the fee charged offsets interest lost by the insurer in paying the death benefit earlier than actuarially anticipated.

Prudential Insurance Company of America, in 1990, was the first major U.S. insurer to offer the ADB option and is among the top insurers in the nation in terms of ADB claims paid. From 1990 to 1994, Prudential paid more than $55 million on 680 claims for ADB payments, an average payment of more than $80,000 per claim (Armstrong 1994). About one-half of these payments went to cancer patients, about 27% went to AIDS victims, about 12% went to heart patients, and the remainder went to those diagnosed with other terminal illnesses. Under the Prudential ADB policy, insureds may accelerate up to 90% of the policy's face value if they are diagnosed with a terminal illness, and up to 70% or 80% of the policy's face value if they are confined to a nursing home.

ADB policies have been criticized on the grounds that this feature defeats the purpose of life insurance and usurps funds necessary to provide for family members after the insured's death. Unrestricted access to these funds, it can be argued, may save or prolong the life of the insured, which may not be in the best financial interests of the insured's dependents. As a result, many state laws limit the amount of the death benefit that may be accelerated and paid to the insured. Conversely, acceleration of the entire death benefit permits more of the insured's medical bills and other expenses to be paid prior to death, leaving more of the insured's other assets available to meet the needs of family and dependents.

Prior to January 1, 1997, uncertainty surrounding how accelerated benefit payments should be treated for income tax purposes was a major obstacle to their wider acceptance. Although life insurance proceeds usually are not taxable to the beneficiary, it was unclear whether receipt of an accelerated payment of the death benefit to the policy owner would be subject to income taxation. The Health Insurance Portability and Accountability Act of 1996 answered that question in the negative, effective on the first day of 1997, and both accelerated death benefit payments and viatical settlements are excluded from income for tax purposes if the insured is either a "terminally ill" or "chronically ill" individual. Terminally ill means that the insured can be reasonably expected to die within two years. Chronically ill means that an insured cannot perform at least two out of six activities of daily living without substantial assistance or requires substantial supervision to be protected from threats to health and safety due to severe cognitive impairment. Any policy owner who wishes to exercise the ADB option should consult a tax attorney or financial advisor prior to doing so.

Life insurance policies with the accelerated death benefits option offer a feasible, compassionate response to financial problems brought about by the onset of terminal illness. (See also ACTIVITIES OF DAILY LIVING [ADLs]; DEATH BENEFITS; ELDER LAW PRACTICE; FINANCIAL ADVISORS; LIFE INSURANCE; LONG-TERM CARE INSURANCE, PRIVATE.)

Organizations

American Council of Life Insurers
LIMRA International
Viatical Life Settlement Association

Suggested Readings

Shilling, Dana. 2000. *Financial Planning for the Older Client*. 5th ed. Erlanger, KY: National Underwriter.

Wolk, Gloria Grening. 1997. *Cash for the Final Days*. Laguna Hills, CA: Bialkin Books.

References

American Council of Life Insurance (ACLI). 2002. *Life Insurer's Fact Book 2002*. Washington, DC: Author.

American Council of Life Insurance (ACLI) and LIMRA International. 1998. *Accelerated Death Benefits*. Washington, DC: ACLI.

Armstrong, Sean. 1994. "AIDS and the Trusted Advisor: Accelerated Life Insurance Benefits for the Terminally Ill Patients." Best's *Review—Life Health Insurance Edition*. Oldwick, NJ: A.M. Best.

Stephen L. Poe, John H. Thornton, and Kennes C. Huntley
Updated by E. Craig MacBean

ACCIDENT INSURANCE, a form of insurance that is designed to cover expenses sustained as the result of an accident. This insurance generally applies to personal types of loss such as disability, death, medical expenses, and at times, loss of income. While the inclusion of accidental loss as a cause of loss in disability and Medicare Supplemental Insurance policies is important, the value of insurance policies that only cover losses caused by accidents is questionable.

As with any type of insurance, premiums paid should provide a needed benefit when loss occurs. Most experts question the value of accident insurance, especially if decisions to purchase such coverage are driven, as people age, by fear of increased vulnerability to accidents. The fact is that often an accident policy does not provide benefits beyond a certain age, and exclusions may include chronic conditions or illness that could contribute to or cause the insured to suffer an accident. A careful distinction must be made between an "accident" as a cause of loss and "accident insurance" as a type of protection. Most insurance covers accidents, but accident insurance typically covers only accidental death and dismemberment.

Accidents Only

An accident-only policy pays a stated benefit if an injury arises from an accident, sometimes under very specific conditions. These benefits may be a specified amount per day for a stated period if one is hospitalized, a death benefit if one dies because of an accident, or a stated benefit if one loses a limb, becomes paralyzed, loses hearing, or loses eyesight because of an accident. One appeal of accident insurance policies is the method of payment, which typically is made directly to the policyholder rather than to the hospital. While some may argue that the proceeds can be used to offset nonmedical expenses, accident policies pay only in the event of death or dismemberment from an accident, and most deaths occur because of illness. Further, since the benefits are payable only when an accident occurs, this type of policy does not provide substantial support for financial planning purposes.

Accidental Death and Dismemberment (AD&D)

This type of policy, or endorsement to life insurance or disability insurance, typically pays a benefit upon accidental death or loss of a limb, hearing, speech, or eyesight because of an accident. For example, the accidental death benefit may be a specified amount in the event of death by accident (e.g., $100,000). The dismemberment feature will also pay a specified amount upon loss of two limbs (e.g., $100,000) or a lesser amount in the event of the loss of one limb (e.g., $50,000).

The value of this policy, or endorsement, must be assessed relative to the need for such coverage. As people age, it is likely that some wealth has been accumulated, and the AD&D benefit may be a windfall and not needed. If one has not accumulated wealth, then the advisability of incurring costs for this type of insurance is also questionable. Another consideration is the occurrence of natural death or dismemberment caused by sickness. No benefit is provided for this latter case. Further, some AD&D policies provide coverage only until a specified age or under specific conditions.

Travel Accident

Travel accident policies pay a specified benefit if death occurs while traveling, sometimes on a specific carrier or if payment was made on a specific credit card. They typically cover business-related travel for employees who travel on business. They are also offered through credit card companies. They can be specially purchased for annual travel or bought as trip insurance at an airport or with a travel ticket. Travel accident insurance, when provided through a credit card, may well be sufficient to cover any need. A person should check the benefits provided by the credit card company supplying the card.

Accident insurance, as described in this section, is by itself seldom of substantial value. While accident as a cause of loss is important in health insurance, sickness as a cause of loss occurs with much more frequency. Whether a loss is caused by sickness or an accident, the premium outlay may be better applied toward regular life insurance or regular health insurance. When considering accident insurance alone, one should seriously consider the need for, and thus the value of, such coverage. (See also AGENTS AND BROKERS; LEISURE; LIABILITY INSURANCE; LIFE INSURANCE.)

References

Black, Kenneth, Jr., and Harold D. Skipper, Jr. 2000. *Life and Health Insurance*. 13th ed. Upper Saddle River, NJ: Prentice Hall.

Rejda, George E. 2001. *Principles of Risk Management and Insurance*. 7th ed. Boston, MA: Addison-Wesley.

Trieschmann, James S., and Sandra G. Gustavson. 1995. *Risk Management and Insurance*. 9th ed. Mason, OH: South-Western.

Vaughan, Emmett H., and Therese M. Vaughn. 1999. *Fundamentals of Risk and Insurance*. 8th ed. Hoboken, NJ: John Wiley and Sons.

Mars A. Pertl

ACCOUNTANTS, professionals who are trained for and work in the field of accounting. Accountants generally have extensive academic experience in accounting, but their degrees, including advanced degrees, may be in business administration, finance, or economics. Some accountants choose to work for organizations as employees, while others choose to provide accounting services to clients for a fee. An accountant who provides such services, in most states, must be registered and licensed as a "public accountant." Public accountants are entitled to call themselves certified public accountants (CPAs) when they have passed a rigorous examination, known as the Uniform Certified Public Accountant Examination, administered by the American Institute of Certified Public Accountants (AICPA).

CPAs and other public accountants practice as sole practitioners or affiliate into accounting firms, which range in size from small local firms to large national or international firms. Most organizations require accountants to be qualified as CPAs. Individuals, including seniors, usually are best served by sole practitioners or small- to mid-size firms where accountants specialize in providing personal service. Services usually fall into three areas: (1) accounting and audit, (2) tax planning and preparation of tax documents, and (3) consulting.

Accounting and auditing services are more commonly provided to businesses than to individuals, although business financial statements and reports are often utilized by business owners in their personal financial affairs. Services include reviewing books of account, assisting with the recording of transactions, and the preparation of financial statements and/or reporting on financial statements. There are three types of reports that CPAs issue, depending on the level of services that CPAs have performed on financial statements:

Compilation. The accountant takes the client's information and puts it in the form of financial statements without auditing, reviewing, or attempting to verify the accuracy or completeness of the information. These statements are usually prepared for a single purpose and may not follow generally accepted accounting principles.

Review. The accountant conducts a review of the financial information, using inquiry, analytical procedures, and discussion. The statements must follow generally accepted accounting principles.

Audit. This report is the highest form of assurance. The auditor follows generally accepted auditing standards to obtain reasonable assurance that the financial statements are free of material misstatement. Audit procedures include examining, on a test basis, evidence supporting the accounting principles and disclosures in the financial statements and also assessing the accounting principles used and significant estimates made by management as well as evaluating the overall financial statement presentation. The auditor can then give his or her independent opinion that the financial statements present fairly, in all material respects, the financial position of the company and the results of its operations in accordance with generally accepted accounting principles.

Accountants can also follow standards that allow them to provide assurance on certain nonfinancial items, such as whether a contract is being complied with or whether an individual or organization is following established policies and procedures.

Tax planning and preparing federal and state tax forms prompt most individuals to seek an accountant. Accountants are also usually well equipped to assist their clients in the event of a federal or state income tax audit. Some accountants are experienced in estate planning, including charitable contribution strategies, estate valuation services, Medicaid planning, preparation of wills, and business succession planning. These services are often provided in tandem with related legal services, and many accountants can recommend attorneys in these areas, if necessary.

Consulting services include financial planning, arbitration, eldercare or PrimePlus services, business advisory services, corporate and personal bankruptcy, due diligence and forensic investigation, litigation support, mergers and acquisitions, performance measurement, valuations for individuals and businesses, computer assistance and support, and information technology.

Some qualities to look for in the selection of an accountant are reputation, professional accreditation (academic degrees, certification), and professional affiliations (membership in the AICPA or relevant state societies). Experience is of paramount importance. The body of accounting information is immense; the accountant chosen should have a specialty in the client's area of interest or should be a member of an accounting firm large enough to embody several areas of specialization.

Personal chemistry is most important in establishing a relationship with an accountant where personal finances are discussed. A good rule of thumb is to interview three different accountants before choosing one, and a list of candidates can be developed by asking friends and relatives for suggestions. A personal banker or lawyer may also have suggestions. The local state society of CPAs will provide a list of CPAs in a specific state, and the state board of accountancy will check the licensing status of prospective CPAs. (See also CPA ELDERCARE SERVICES; FINANCIAL ADVISORS; GERIATRIC CARE MANAGERS [GCMs]; TAXPAYER ISSUES OF OLDER ADULTS.)

Organizations

American Institute of Certified Public Accountants
CPADirectory.com
National Society of Accountants

References

Bisk, Nathan M. 2002. *Financial Accounting and Reporting*. Tampa, FL: Bisk Publishing Co.

Magill, Harry T., Gary John Previts, and Thomas R. Robinson, 1997. *The CPA Profession: Opportunities, Responsibilities, and Services*. Upper Saddle River, NJ: Pearson Education.

Shim, Jae K., and Joel G. Siegel. 1989. *Encyclopedic Dictionary of Accounting and Finance*. New York: MJF Books.

Paul Thrasher
Updated by Ann Elizabeth Sammon

ACTIVITIES OF DAILY LIVING (ADLs), the core daily personal care activities that are necessary in order for people to be able to live independently. Loss of mental functioning is measured by other standardized tests and referred to as cognitive impairment. ADLs are particularly important because along with cognitive impairment, and in some cases "medical necessity," they are the mechanism used by the insurance industry to determine qualification for long-term care benefits and may also be used to determine qualification for admission to a nursing or assisted living facility. ADL dependence may be temporary, such as a need for assistance in bathing following surgery. When the aging process causes a loss in one or more ADLs, however, the loss is usually permanent and has an emotional impact that accompanies the physical limitation itself. Incomplete recovery from an accident or an acute episode of illness and deterioration of a chronic condition such as arthritis are common causes of the loss of independence.

The Katz Index of Independence in Activities of Daily Living—known as the Katz ADL scale—is the standard general measurement of an individual's ability to function independently in six areas: bathing, continence, dressing, eating, toileting, and transferring. In addition to an assessment of a person's ability to walk and get around (*ambulation*), the following ADLs are used to determine the amount and type of long-term care people may need. Subjects are scored yes or no on these sorts of definitions of independence:

- *Bathing*. Bathes self completely or needs help in bathing only a single part of the body such as the back, genital area, or disabled extremity. Long-term care insurance policies say this somewhat differently, generally referring to an ability to keep clean without assistance, including the ability to take a bath or shower safely. Bathing is usually the first ADL people fail.
- *Continence*. Maintains complete self-control over bowels and bladder.
- *Dressing*. Gets clothes from closets and drawers, puts them on, and fastens all buttons and other fasteners independently. Long-term care policies often specifically add the ability to put on a prosthesis without help as a measure of independence.
- *Eating*. Once prepared, gets food from plate into mouth without assistance. Preparation of food is not part of this measure.
- *Toileting*. Goes to toilet, gets on and off, arranges clothes, cleans genital area without help.
- *Transferring*. Moves in and out of bed or chair unassisted. This does not preclude the use of assistive devices such as handrails and supports.

As a memory aid, the seven ADLs (including ambulation) offer a sort of alphabetical mnemonic device ABCDE-TT when grouped by the first letter of each.

ADLs are not the only way loss of independence is measured and monitored, but because they describe the ability to manage self-care, they are the most basic. More refined ADL sets that are specific to diseases such as Alzheimer's are used by clinicians and caretakers where appropriate.

Other, less debilitating but nonetheless disconcerting losses are measured by instrumental activities of daily living (IADLs). Where ADLs measure the ability to function independently at a basic level, IADLs are used to measure ability to function in the community. What in other circumstances may be thought of as chores are in this setting the standard for whether or not a person needs caregiving assistance. There is not the standard measure of IADLs that the Katz scale provides for ADLs. The Mayo Clinic uses a scale that measures shopping, housework, accounting, food preparation, and transportation and goes by the unfortunate shorthand of SHAFT, based on the first letter of the five instrumental activities. Other lists often also include the ability to do laundry, use a telephone, manage money and medication, and participate in social activities.

People generally need help with IADLs before they need help with ADLs, and generally the loss of independence is not limited to one activity. Because the loss of independence is so frightening, exacerbated by the high value the U.S. culture places on independence, older people with IADL or ADL dependencies may try to hide their infirmity and may neither seek help nor accept it willingly. (See also EMPLOYER-SPONSORED LONG-TERM CARE INSURANCE; FRAILTY PLANNING; GERIATRIC CARE MANAGERS [GCMs]; LONG-TERM CARE INSURANCE, PRIVATE; LONG-TERM CARE INSURANCE: INDIVIDUAL DISABILITY-ESCALATING ANNUITIES [IDEAs]; LONG-TERM CARE INSURANCE [LTCI]—A CONSUMER'S PERSPECTIVE.)

References

Abrams, W.B., M.H. Beers, and R. Berkow. 1995. *The Merck Manual of Geriatrics*. White Station, NJ: Merck Research Laboratories.

Katz, S. 1983. "Assessing Self-Maintenance: Activities of Daily Living, Mobility and Instrumental Activities of Daily Living." *Journal of the American Geriatrics Society* 31(12): 721–26.

Katz, S., T.D. Down, H.R. Cash, et al. 1970. "Progress in the Development of the Index of ADL." *Gerontologist* 10: 20–30.

Katz, S., and M.W. Stroud. 1989. "Functional Assessment in Geriatrics: A Review of Progress and Directions." *Journal of the American Geriatrics Society* 37: 267–71.

Lueckenotte, A.G. 1990. *Pocket Guide to Gerontological Assessment*. Philadelphia, PA: C.V. Mosby.

E. Craig MacBean

ADULT DAY CARE. See Day Programs for Adults.

ADVANCE CARE PLANNING. See Accelerated Death Benefits; Advance Directives; Durable Power of Attorney; Living Will; Long-Term Care Insurance, Private.

ADVANCE DIRECTIVES, legal documents used to provide instructions about medical care, financial assistance, and organ and tissue donation, in the event of serious illness or incapacity. Advance directives enable a person to maintain control as death approaches; they are designed to relieve family members and loved ones of the burden of having to make difficult medical and financial decisions.

End-of-life medical treatment can be very costly. Approximately 27% of all Medicare expenditures occur in the last year of life (Emanuel 1996), and many fear that assets accumulated over a lifetime could quickly dissipate in unwanted medical treatment. Advance directives ensure that individuals receive their desired end-of-life treatment. While there is yet no evidence that using advance directives lowers health care costs, they can and do save individuals from receiving unwanted medical treatment and indirectly save medical expenses.

Types of Advance Directives

Types of advance directives include living wills, durable powers of attorney, and organ and tissue donation. There are two types of durable powers of attorney—the durable power of attorney, used for designating a surrogate to make financial decisions, and the durable medical powers of attorney, used to name a surrogate to make medical and health care decisions.

In contrast to the durable powers of attorney, living wills allow individuals to specify their end-of-life treatment wishes in writing. Subject to certain legal limitations, living wills include instructions concerning the use or withdrawal of artificial life support in end-of-life situations. Living will laws often require the attending physician, and sometimes an additional physician, to certify that the patient's condition is not expected to improve before the advance directive can be given effect.

Every state and the District of Columbia have at least one statute addressing advance directives. As of 2001, three states have a living will only (Pennsylvania, Louisiana, and Montana), three states have durable powers of attorney for health care only (Massachusetts, Michigan, and New York), 32 have both living wills and durable powers, and 13 states have a document that combines the living will and durable powers, called an advance health care directive (Gunter-Hunt, Mahoney, and Sieger 2001). The majority of these statutes require the agent to make health care decisions according to the patient's wishes, if known, or in the patient's best interests. The scope of an agent's authority is generally broader than the provisions contained in a living will. An agent is typically not limited to decisions about ending life support. These documents also address matters of health care management and grant the power to procure health care services and personnel. Medical power of attorney laws often set restrictions on who can serve as an agent. Frequently, health care providers and health care institutions are not permitted to act as agents for patients in their care.

Differences between state documents can create confusion for an older adult who may have an advance directive in one state, yet receive medical care in another state. Most states have laws that address the issue of reciprocity between states, but many states honor out-of-state documents only to the extent that they do not conflict with their own laws.

Historical Development

Advance directives were developed in response to the technological advances of modern medicine. The first living will was drafted at a 1967 meeting of the Society for the Right to Die, but nine years passed before the first living will law was enacted. In 1976, California became the first state to pass legislation that directly addressed the issue of end-of-life decision making. Also in 1976, the *Quinlan* case in New Jersey became the first right-to-die case to reach a state supreme court. Karen Ann Quinlan, a 21-year-old woman, was in a persistent vegetative state as a result of respiratory arrest. Her father sought court approval to remove her from the ventilator that was breathing for her. The court ruled that individuals have a constitutional right to refuse medical treatment and ordered the treatment stopped.

In 1990, the U.S. Supreme Court issued its landmark decision in the *Cruzan* case. In *Cruzan*, the Court recognized that every competent individual has a constitutional interest in being free from unwanted medical treatment. The case involved a young woman who was permanently unconscious after a car accident and whose life was being sustained by artificial tube feedings. The Missouri Supreme Court had ruled that tube feeding could not be stopped unless clear and convincing evidence of Ms. Cruzan's wish to refuse such treatment could be provided. Although the U.S. Supreme Court found a constitutional basis for the right to refuse medical treatment, the Court ruled that Missouri's clear and convincing evidence requirement was appropriate. One implication of the ruling is that verbal expressions of the desire to refuse medical treatment are not sufficient. Another implication is that individual states are free to define their own standards of evidence as they see fit. In general, this lack of specific guidance from the Supreme Court has led to increased impetus toward the allowance of advance directives, as state legislatures prefer to err on the side of caution.

The *Cruzan* decision also addressed the question of one's right to refuse artificial nutrition and hydration. Early right-to-die legislation frequently required that tube feeding be provided even when other types of life-sustaining treatment could be terminated. In the *Cruzan* decision, the Supreme Court explicitly rejected the idea that tube feeding is different from other forms of life support. Newer statutes generally recognize that nutrition and hydration may be refused but require that instructions for such refusal be explicitly set forth in the advance directive.

Responding to the rulings in the *Cruzan* case, in 1991 Congress passed the Patient Self Determination Act (PSDA), which requires federally funded health care institutions to provide patients with information about their rights to make advance directives. Health care facilities that receive Medicare funding must also provide staff and community education on the use of advance directives, although there has been no federal oversight on how well facilities have met such obligations. The PSDA leaves the substance of laws regarding advance directives to states, and it is too early to judge the impact PSDA will have on the use of advance directives.

Religion and Refusal of Treatment

Most religions do not specifically address the use of advance directives. Instead, they focus on two related issues: (1) when it becomes appropriate to withhold or withdraw medical treatment, and (2) how treatment termination is distinguishable from suicide and assisted suicide. In general, major religious traditions permit limits on medical treatment provided at the end of life.

Roman Catholic doctrine generally permits patients to refuse life-sustaining treatments. In the Church's statement on refusal of life-sustaining treatment, the *Declaration on Euthanasia* (1980), Pope John Paul II announced that medical treatments may be withdrawn if they impose on the patient

> strain or suffering out of proportion with the benefits which he or she may gain from such techniques. . . . [W]hen inevitable death is imminent in spite of the means used, it is permitted in conscience to take the decision to refuse forms of treatment that would only secure a precarious

and burdensome prolongation of life, so long as the normal care due to the sick person in similar cases is not interrupted.

This position of the Roman Catholic Church has been interpreted differently among individuals, groups, and clergy. The greatest disagreement centers on whether artificially administered nutrition and hydration may be withheld or withdrawn under the *Declaration*. Most mainline Protestant churches have taken positions that are generally consonant with those articulated by the Roman Catholic Church. In the Protestant religious tradition, there is no absolute authority or specific formula to guide end-of-life medical treatment. There is a rich tradition affirming the values of individual autonomy and responsibility toward others, however, that would argue in favor of a person's right to refuse unwanted medical treatment. Reformed and Conservative Judaism does not oppose withholding or withdrawing treatments that prolong the dying process, although there is disagreement among Conservative rabbis about whether artificial nutrition and hydration may be withheld or withdrawn. In Orthodox Judaism, all life-prolonging measures are required to be provided unless a person cannot be kept alive for more than three days.

Attitudes toward Executing or Implementing Advance Directives

While an overwhelming majority of adults agree that advance directives are important, the percentage of adults who have executed them remains low. For example, although it is estimated that only some 20% to 30% of older adults have advance directives (Greene 2002), a 1991 Gallup poll found that 84% of the public would wish to terminate life support if there was no hope for recovery, while only 9% would wish to continue life support. In the same survey, 75% of respondents said they wanted a written living will at some future time, while only 17% said they would not want one (Gallup and Newport 1991). Interestingly, a more recent study found that 93% of older adults specified no life-sustaining treatment in their treatment preferences, an additional 6% wanted no life-sustaining treatment if they were in an irreversible coma, and only 1% wanted everything possible done to prolong life (Gross 1998).

The portability of advance directives may be the greatest limitation on their use. It is unclear whether an advance directive written in one state must be honored in another. Increasingly, states guarantee reciprocity if out-of-state documents have been executed properly under either state's law, but many states still lack such reciprocity. Moreover, hospitals and nursing homes are risk averse and may be unwilling to honor an out-of-state advance directive even with the legislative authorization to do so.

Another institutional limitation of the recognition of advance directives—specifically the right to refuse unwanted treatment—consists of "conscience exclusions," which allow a health care facility to reject advance directive provisions on principle if honoring them would violate a religious or moral belief. Although facilities are required to give written notice of such a policy at the time of admission, many patients and families fail to read them thoroughly or to understand the importance of the materials they are given. Facilities that will not stop treatment must transfer a patient to one that will. In practice, it is difficult, however, to find facilities willing to admit patients solely for the purpose of terminating treatment so that death can occur.

Even where the law is clear that a competent adult may refuse medical treatment through an advance directive, many health care facilities remain reluctant to stop treatment. Reasons include misunderstanding of the law; conviction that what is medically appropriate is not consistent with personal, moral, or religious beliefs; the presence of family conflict or disagreement about end-of-life issues; and concern about potential liability.

Finally, there are personal barriers to discussions of end-of-life treatment preferences. Some of these barriers include cultural diversity, educational background, lack of familiarity with the health care system, and desire to delegate decisions entirely to family. For instance, discussions of end-of-life treatment options connote disrespect of the older adults in the Chinese American community. There are several studies published on the characteristics of those who execute advance directives but few regarding why individuals choose to do so.

Cultural issues can also strongly affect the end-of-life decision-making process. For example, Hopp and Duffy (2000) found that Whites were more likely than African Americans to execute advance directives. In addition, African Americans are more likely to opt for life-sustaining measures and prefer the involvement of multiple family members in treatment decision making. African Americans may also fear that the real agenda behind advance directives is to deny them needed care. Studies with Hispanic or Latino family caregivers have found that physicians are advised, for example, not to discuss autopsy decisions with families of dementia victims in order to avoid the appearance of giving up on the patient too soon. On the specific issue of end-of-life decision making, Mexican American families have indicated that when the medical establishment is respectful, empathic, and personal with the family, establishing a bond of mutual trust and goodwill, together they may be able to decide to terminate supportive care with *dignidad* (dignity).

Trends and Alternative Directives

Two new types of law permit end-of-life medical treatment decisions by others in the event of decisional incapacitation. The first involves surrogate decision making and provides that individuals, usually in order of priority, are empowered to make decisions for an incompetent patient who has no living will or durable medical powers of attorney. While these types of laws simply codify health care decisions traditionally made for incompetent patients, increasing medical regulation and oversight and fears of liability have made doctors reluctant to rely any longer on informal decision making without explicit legislative authorization, particularly after the rulings on *Cruzan*. Commonly, the surrogate (typically a family member or close friend) is required to consider the patient's personal, moral, or religious beliefs when making decisions. Surrogate decision making is often included as a provision within a living will statute. Twenty-three states and the District of Columbia currently provide for surrogate decision making (Choice in Dying 1994).

The second type of law is a nonhospital do-not-resuscitate (DNR) order. Emergency medical technicians, feeling trapped by laws that require aggressive treatment for individuals obviously near the end of life, have joined state medical associations and other organizations to develop and lobby for nonhospital DNR orders. DNR orders allow individuals to refuse emergency resuscitation in advance of an emergency. Usually a DNR order must be completed by an individual and his or her doctor. Some nonhospital DNR legislation provides for wallet-size versions of the official form or for identification bracelets or necklaces to indicate that the individual should not be resuscitated. In order to be effective, the individual must keep the form or other official notification on hand at all times so that it is available to emergency personnel. So far, 19 states have statutes authorizing nonhospital DNR orders, but more are likely to be passed (Choice in Dying 1994). Because both DNR laws and local policies are new, the public and many health care professionals remain unaware of them.

Beyond these legal developments, discussion and research focuses on the larger process of communication among patients, their health care providers, families, and others regarding appropriate care when a patient cannot make decisions. The goal of such advance care planning is to shape future clinical care to fit people's preferences and values. (See also DURABLE POWER OF ATTORNEY; ELDER LAW PRACTICE; FRAILTY PLANNING; HOSPICE CARE; LIVING WILL; NURSING HOMES.)

Organizations

American Academy of Family Physicians
Choice in Dying, Inc.

References

Allen-Burge, R., and W.E. Haley. 1997. "Individual Differences and Surrogate Medical Decisions: Different Preferences for Life-Sustaining Treatments." *Aging & Mental Health* 1: 121–31.

Choice in Dying. 1994. *Right-to-Die Law Digest*. New York: Author.

Cruzan v. Director, Missouri Department of Health. 1990. 110 S. Ct. 2841.

Declaration on Euthanasia. 1980. Adopted by the Sacred Congregation for the Doctrine of the Faith, approved by Pope John Paul II. Released to the public on June 26.

Emanuel, E. 1996. "Cost Savings at the End of Life." *Journal of the American Medical Association* 275: 1907–14.

Gallup, G., and F. Newport. 1991. "Mirror of America: Fear of Dying." *The Gallup Newservice* 55: 33.

Greene, K. 2002. "Many Consider a Living Will Important, But Wait Too Long." *Wall Street Journal Sunday*, April 21. Available online at http://online.wsj.com/public/us.

Gross, M.D. 1998. "What Do Patients Express as Their Preferences in Advance Directives?" *Archives of Internal Medicine* 158: 363–65.

Gunter-Hunt, G., J.E. Mahoney, and C.E. Sieger. 2001. "A Comparison of State Advance Directive Documents." *The Gerontologist* 42: 51–60.

Hill, T. Patrick, and David Shirley. 1992. *A Good Death*. New York: Addison-Wesley.

Hopp, F.P. 2000. "Preferences for Surrogate Decision Makers, Informal Communication, and Advance Directives among Community-Dwelling Elders." *The Gerontologist* 40: 449–57.

Hopp, F.P., and S.A. Duffy. 2000. "Racial Variations in End-of-Life Care." *Journal of the American Geriatrics Society* 48: 658–63.

In re Quinlan. 1976. 70 NJIO.

Sulmasy, D.P., P.B. Terry, C.S. Weisman, D.J. Miller, R.Y. Stallings, and M.A. Vettese. 1998. "The Accuracy of Substituted Judgments in Patients with Terminal Diagnoses." *Annals of Internal Medicine* 128: 621–29.

Teno, Joan M., Hilda Lindermann Nelson, and Joanne Lynn. 1994. "Advance Care Planning: Priorities for Ethical and Empirical Research." *Hastings Center Report*, Special Supplement (November–December).

Vaughn, G., E. Kiyasu, and W.C. McCormick. 2000. "Advance Directive Preferences among Subpopulations of Asian Nursing Home Residents in the Pacific Northwest." *Journal of the American Geriatrics Society* 48: 554–57.

Wilber, K.H., and S.L. Reynolds. 1995. "Rethinking Alternatives to Guardianship." *The Gerontologist* 35: 248–57.

Ann E. Fade
Updated by Sandra L. Reynolds

AGE DISCRIMINATION IN EMPLOYMENT ACT (ADEA), a federal law prohibiting age discrimination in employment and promoting the employment of older persons based on ability rather than age. The ADEA protects working men and women who are at least 40 years of age or older and renders unlawful an employer's, employment agency's, or labor organization's failure or refusal to hire, discharge, or otherwise discriminate against any individual with respect to his or her compensation, terms, conditions, or privileges of employment because of age.

Enactment of the ADEA

In 1964 the U.S. Congress passed, and President Lyndon B. Johnson signed into law, the Civil Rights Act. Title VII of that law prohibits employment practices that discriminate on the basis of race, color, religion, sex, or national origin. Congress considered but ultimately rejected an amendment that would have added age to the list of protected categories covered by Title VII but did instruct the U.S. secretary of labor to investigate the problem of age discrimination in employment. Complying with that directive, the secretary issued a report that found and concluded, among other things, that many employers practiced age discrimination based on stereotypes about older persons; that age discrimination harmed the national economy by depriving it of productive workers; that this form of discrimination inflicted economic and psychological injury on older persons; and that federal revenues were diverted to the increasing costs of government benefits paid to those adversely affected by age discrimination in the workplace.

In 1967, President Lyndon Johnson submitted a bill to Congress with this message on age discrimination:

> In economic terms, age discrimination is a serious and senseless loss to a nation on the move. But the greater loss is the cruel sacrifice in happiness and well-being, which joblessness imposes on these citizens and their families. Opportunities must be opened up to the many [older] Americans who are qualified and willing to work. We must end arbitrary age limits on hiring.

Congress heeded the president's call, passing the ADEA in 1967 (see 29 U.S.C. Section 621 et seq). As initially enacted, the ADEA prohibited age discrimination only in the private sector and then only against employees ages 40 to 65. Congress subsequently extended protection to most federal and state employees and expanded the class of protected employees by lifting the age ceiling to 70 and then eliminated that ceiling altogether (with certain exceptions). Thus, the ADEA today covers most private sector and public employees who are 40 years of age or older. It exempts, however, small employers with fewer than 20 employees. In a significant decision dealing with the rights of employees to sue their state employers under the ADEA, *Kimel v. Florida Board of Regents* ([2000] 528 U.S. 62), the U.S. Supreme Court held that states enjoy immunity under the Eleventh Amendment to the U.S. Constitution from ADEA suits seeking money damages brought by private individuals. Recent cases have made clear that the states enjoy no such immunity in ADEA suits brought by the Equal Employment Opportunity Commission (EEOC), the federal agency created by Title VII and empowered to enforce that statute as well as the ADEA.

Most states have age discrimination legislation, and some of those laws are more expansive than the ADEA. The important distinction between the ADEA and some state laws is that action can be brought against an employer with less than 20 employees. In addition, the ADEA does not preempt state law.

Proving Violations of the ADEA

Two categories of claims can be brought under the ADEA: disparate treatment claims and disparate impact claims. Disparate treatment claims are those in which an individual or class of individuals contends that an employer intentionally refused employment, salary, or promotion or terminated an individual's employment or otherwise discriminated against a person or persons because of age. Disparate impact claims arise when an employee challenges an age-neutral employment practice that has a disproportionate impact on older employees, even when there is no proof that the employer had acted according to discriminatory intent or motive.

Disparate Treatment Claims

In proving a disparate treatment claim of age discrimination, an individual may present direct evidence that an employer refused to hire, retain, or promote that person because he or she was too old for the job. For example, direct evidence of discrimination would be found where an employer openly and unambiguously refused to hire a person on the ground that the company did not hire persons who were over age 40. Direct evidence of discrimination is also of significance in mixed-motive cases involving both legitimate *and* illegitimate factors in an employment decision, as in the Supreme Court's decision in *Price Waterhouse v. Hopkins* ([1989] 490 U.S. 228). Where a plaintiff establishes that his or her age was an unlawful motivating factor in the decision, the burden of persuasion shifts to the employer to show that the decision would have been the same absent consideration of age. Although the *Price Waterhouse* mixed-motive analysis, as applied to Title VII cases, was changed by Congress in the Civil Rights Act of 1991, some courts continue to apply the 1989 approach to cases arising under the ADEA.

Most employers are sufficiently sophisticated to avoid such direct discriminatory action, and when such proof is lacking, employees must prove disparate treatment and ADEA violations through inferential rather than direct evidence. Courts have developed an allocation of burdens scheme applicable to inferential employment discrimination cases. As first set forth in *McDonnell Douglas Corp. v. Green* ([1973] 411 U.S. 792) and other Supreme Court Title VII decisions, an aggrieved individual initially must prove a case of age discrimination that will generally be established if (1) the individual is a member of the class protected by the statute, (2) is qualified for the position in question, (3) was subjected to an adverse action by the employer, and (4) the job or position was given to a person outside the plaintiff's protected group. Applying the *McDonnell Douglas* framework to age discrimination claims, courts generally held that a prima facie case is established where (1) the employee was in the age group protected by the ADEA, (2) the employee was discharged or suffered an adverse job action (demotion, denial of promotion, etc.), (3) at the time of his or her discharge or other adverse employment action, the employee was performing the job at a level that met the employer's legitimate expectations, and (4) the employee was replaced by someone of comparable qualifications outside the protected class. (In its important 1996 decision in *O'Connor v. Consolidated Caterers Corp.* [(1996) 517 U.S. 308] the Supreme Court held that the fourth factor—replacement by someone outside the protected class—is not a required element of the ADEA prima facie case. In so holding, the Court reasoned that the fact that one person in the protected class has lost out to another person in the protected class is irrelevant, so long as he has lost out because of his age.)

If the individual proves a prima facie case, the employer must produce evidence rebutting the inference of discrimination. That burden is met by the employer's articulation of a legitimate, nondiscriminatory reason for its actions. Where the employer meets this burden of production, the burden of persuasion shifts back to the aggrieved individual who must prove that the employer's articulated reasons were pretextual, i.e., were not the true reasons and were unworthy of credence. A showing of pretext, combined with a plaintiff's prima facie case, may permit (but does not compel) a fact finder (a judge or jury) to conclude that an employer has engaged in unlawful discrimination. In other cases, as explained by the Supreme Court in *Reeves v. Sanderson Plumbing Products, Inc.* ([2000] 530 U.S. 133), more evidence may be required to satisfy the plaintiff's burden of establishing that the ADEA was violated.

Disparate Impact Claims

A different methodology, initially developed in Title VII cases, governs disparate impact cases. A plaintiff must first present a prima facie case of disparate impact and show, generally with statistical data, that an employer's facially neutral employment practices have a significant adverse effect on older employees. If the plaintiff meets his or her burden, the employer must then show that the challenged practice is job related or had a manifest relationship to the employer's business. The plaintiff can rebut the employer's showing by demonstrating either that the employer could have satisfied its legitimate business purposes in a less discriminatory manner or that the employer was using the practice as a pretext for discrimination.

In a 1993 Supreme Court case, *Hazen Paper Co. v. Biggins* ([1993] 507 U.S. 604), the Court declined to consider or answer the question whether the disparate impact theory is available under the ADEA, with three justices noting that there are substantial arguments that it is improper to carry over disparate impact analysis from Title VII to the ADEA. In its 2001–2002 term the Court announced that it would take up that question in a case involving ADEA claims brought by employees terminated by their employer during a series of company reorganizations. The Court later removed that case from its docket, however, leaving for another day a final resolution of this important ADEA issue.

Employer Defenses to ADEA Claims

The ADEA arms employers with a number of defenses against claims of age discrimination. The most important of these defenses is that age is a bona fide occupational qualification reasonably necessary to the normal operation of the particular business. For example, courts have permitted mandatory retirement ages for certain law enforcement officials. But one court struck down an airline policy of refusing entry-level employment to pilots over 35 years of age, while another court approved a bus company's policy of refusing entry-level employment to drivers over 40 years old. The ADEA also provides defenses for employers who can demonstrate that an employment decision was based on (1) reasonable factors other than age, (2) a bona fide seniority system, or (3) a bona fide employee benefit plan.

It is noteworthy that an employer may not adopt a policy of discharging employees over age 40 involuntarily in a corporate reorganization, nor adopt a seniority system that retires an employee over age 40 involuntarily. Prior to 1989, the EEOC and virtually all federal courts that considered the question took the position that older employees could be treated differently in an employee benefit plan only if the employer could demonstrate a cost justification for the disparate treatment. In a surprising decision, *Public Employees Retirement System v. Betts* ([1989] 492 U.S. 158), the Supreme Court rejected the cost justification approach and held that an employer could discriminate on the basis of age in employee benefits plans unless the employee could show that the plan actually intended to discriminate in some non–fringe benefit aspect of the employment relationship. Congress reacted to and expressly overruled the *Betts* decision with the Older Workers Benefit Protection Act (OWBPA) of 1990. Under that statute, an employee benefit plan is bona fide only where, for each benefit or benefit package, the actual amount of payment made or cost incurred on behalf of an older worker is no less than that made or incurred on behalf of a younger worker.

An employer can also defend against an age discrimination claim by showing that an employee relinquished his or her ADEA rights under a waiver agreement meeting the minimum statutory standards set forth in the OWBPA. The OWBPA provides that a waiver is not knowing and voluntary unless it is written in a manner calculated to be understood by the individual, specifically refers to rights and claims arising under the ADEA, applies only to claims in existence at the date of the execution of the waiver, is given in exchange for consideration in addition to anything of value to which the employee is already entitled, advises the employee to consult with an attorney before executing the agreement, gives the employee at least 21 days to consider the agreement, and provides for at least 7 days after the execution of the agreement for the employee to revoke the waiver. (Other provisions apply where waivers are asked of groups or classes of employees.) A release or waiver not in compliance with the OWBPA's requirements does not bar an ADEA claim. In *Oubre v. Entergy Operations, Inc.* ([1998] 522 U.S. 422) the Supreme Court so held and further held that an age discrimination suit could be pursued even though the employee did not return or offer to return to the employer the monies he or she received for signing the waiver and release.

The Supreme Court has allowed employers to limit their liability in ADEA cases where evidence of employee misconduct is discovered subsequent to the employee's termination. *McKennon v. Nashville Banner Publishing Company* ([1995] 513 U.S. 352) held that such after-acquired evidence of employee wrongdoing does not bar a valid ADEA claim but does bear on the remedy to be ordered. As a general rule, the Court concluded, neither reinstatement nor front pay is an appropriate remedy, and backpay should be calculated from the date of the unlawful discharge to the date of the employer's discovery of wrongdoing of such severity that the employee would have been fired if the employer had known of the misconduct at the time of the discharge.

Criticism of the ADEA

Some commentators have argued that the ADEA is unwise and inefficient legislation. In his 1992 book *Forbidden Grounds: The Case against Employment Discrimination Laws*, Richard Epstein argued that employment discrimination statutes serve no legitimate purpose and that, in the labor marketplace, employers and employees will agree to contracts where the contracts offer gains to each. Barring structural failures in the marketplace, it is expected that labor will move to jobs where it is most highly valued. For Epstein, the right policy in the labor and employment market is to keep all barriers as low as possible. The ADEA has precisely the opposite effect, in his view, since it raises barriers to entry. Concerns that older workers will face obstacles in the labor market can be addressed by the market itself, he argues, for a firm that passes over superior older workers in favor of inferior younger ones will find itself at a cost disadvantage that it cannot recoup in the market. Another prominent critic of the ADEA, Richard Posner, has argued that the ADEA was sold by means of emotional rhetoric concerning the plight of older workers and is at once inefficient, regressive, and harmful to them. These views ignore the economic and psychological harm inflicted by discriminatory employment practices in which age-based stereotypes are substituted and serve as proxies for relevant abilities and performance. Although the costs of age (and other workplace) discrimination may be hard to quantify, they are real and merit reflection. Any market failure addressed and corrected by the ADEA may have actually increased rather than decreased societal net wealth.

The Future of the ADEA

Judicial trends have narrowed the scope and efficacy of the ADEA and other civil rights legislation. Courts are increasingly calling on employment discrimination plaintiffs to meet substantial burdens and matters of proof in order to establish discriminatory intent and motive. The Supreme Court has insulated states from ADEA suits brought by private plaintiffs. Congress, which in the past amended the ADEA to make it more hospitable for employees, is less inclined to expand the reach of civil rights laws; as a result, plaintiffs increasingly seek redress under state laws where available.

These judicial and legislative trends come at a significant time. Members of the baby boom generation are now moving into protected status under the ADEA, and a majority of the workforce will soon have ADEA protection. Indeed, persons age 55 and older comprise the fastest-growing segment of the U.S. workforce, and the median age of all workers will be 40.6 years by the year 2010. These older workers may create and benefit from strong political pressures leading to the expansion of ADEA protection against those who would discriminate on the basis of age, while those who are not protected by the statute may resent and counteract such pressures. It is difficult to predict what this will mean in terms of age discrimination law and policy and the political, economic, and social forces that strengthen or weaken legal protections for older workers. (See also OLDER AMERICANS ACT; WORKFORCE PATTERNS, CHANGES IN; WORKING RETIREES.)

References

Barrier, Michael. 2002. "An Age-Old Problem." *HR Magazine* 47: 1047–49.

Epstein, Richard. 1992. *Forbidden Grounds: The Case against Employment Discrimination Laws*. Boston, MA: Harvard University Press.

Hazen Paper Co. v. Biggins. 1993. 507 U.S. 604.

Kimel v. Florida Board of Regents. 2000. 528 U.S. 62.

McDonnell Douglas Corp. v. Green. 1973. 411 U.S. 792.

McKennon v. Nashville Banner Publishing Company. 1995. 513 U.S. 352.

O'Connor v. Consolidated Caterers Corp. 1996. 517 U.S. 308.

Oubre v. Entergy Operations, Inc. 1998. 522 U.S. 422.

Price Waterhouse v. Hopkins. 1989. 490 U.S. 228.

Public Employees Retirement System v. Betts. 1989. 492 U.S. 158.

Reeves v. Sanderson Plumbing Products, Inc. 2000. 530 U.S. 133.

Rosen, Benson, and Thomas H. Jerdee. 1976a. "The Influence of Age Stereotypes on Managerial Decisions." *Journal of Applied Psychology* 61: 428–32.

Rosen, Benson, and Thomas H. Jerdee. 1976b. "The Nature of Job-Related Stereotypes." *Journal of Applied Psychology* 61: 180–83.

Rosner, Richard. 1995. *Aging and Old Age*. Chicago: University of Chicago Press.

U.S. Department of Labor. 1965. *The Older American Worker: Age Discrimination in Employment*. Washington, DC: Author.

Norman Stein and Ronald Turner
Updated by Ronald Turner

AGENTS AND BROKERS, persons authorized to represent others or to negotiate on their behalf, usually for compensation. Health and financial concerns of older people and their families bring them into contact with an array of professional agents and others who operate under the laws of agency: accountants, attorneys, financial advisors, attorneys-in-fact, real estate and insurance agents, trustees, and persons who have been authorized to make medical decisions under advance directives. There is little literature that distinguishes between agency and brokerage, and much confusion surrounds the practices and ethics of those who are engaged to act on the older person's behalf, especially those in fiduciary relationships.

An agent is a person or entity authorized by another (the "principal") to represent and to act on the principal's behalf. The agreement of agent and principal constitutes an agency relationship. The agent acts only with the principal's consent and is subject to his or her direction and control. When acting under an agency arrangement, the agent's chief obligations are (1) loyalty to the principal, (2) obedience to the principal's instructions, (3) diligence in the performance of duties, (4) accountability for the principal's funds or property, and (5) full disclosure to the principal of all material facts. Actions taken under an agency relationship bind the principal in third-party transactions. Thus, third parties dealing with agents must bear in mind that the first loyalty of the agent, by law, is owed to the principal. There are many types of agency appointments, but most fall under two broad categories of agency: general and special.

A broker is an agent employed to make bargains and contracts for compensation, according to *Black's Law Dictionary*. When a broker enters into a transaction as a middle person or negotiator to bring buyer and seller together, he or she is acting as a "dual agent." There are many different types of brokers, and the term extends to almost every area of business. The term *broker* is often misused and misunderstood by consumers when referring to real estate, insurance, and other types of persons who actually work in agency relationships under most state laws. Certain industries are often closely regulated—the real estate and legal industries, for example—and their members are required to disclose agency relationships, obligations, and fee arrangements and to avoid conflicts of interest. In other industries—such as insurance and securities and commission-based financial planning—advisors and counselors do not supervise closely the agency and disclosure practices of their representatives. As a result, securities brokers—even those who are well intentioned—often call themselves financial advisors or financial service representatives. The effect of this is to elevate their profession and obscure how they are compensated.

General and Special Agents

General agents have been delegated authority by a principal to handle all matters connected with a particular (personal or business-related) situation, trade, or employment. They may exercise extremely broad authority, without restriction or qualification, for a principal; this includes entering into several types of contracts; making decisions; buying and selling property, goods, and services; and entering into short- or long-term obligations and/or commitments. A *managing agent* may be vested with exclusive and general power to exercise complete judgment and discretion in all management matters for his or her principal (person or organization).

Special agents are appointed to act on behalf of their principals in a limited capacity, usually in a single transaction or a series of acts not involving a continuity of service. An example of special agency is a literary agent appointed to enter into publishing negotiations and contracting arrangements on an author's behalf. A purchasing agent is typically a special agent as well, authorized to act on behalf of a company concerning matters of purchasing special materials such as supplies or inventory. A purchasing or literary agent would not be authorized to bind his or her principal in any matter other than the transaction or series of acts explicitly specified in an agency agreement.

Whether dealing with a special or general agent, third parties who have contact with agents should determine the exact scope of authority and range of actual power that have been delegated by the principal to the agent. It is important for anyone who deals with an agent to know directly from the principal, in as clear a manner as possible, what the scope of authority is in order to make informed judgments as to the appropriateness of the transaction under consideration. Without this knowledge, the third party dealing with an agent runs the risk of entering into agreements that go beyond the scope of the agent's authority. When compensation is involved, it is important to become aware of the fees charged or commissions customarily paid in the particular agency arrangement.

Common Agency Arrangements

Insurance agents are agents of insurance companies who have been hired as (1) general agents to manage sales operations on either a local or a regional basis or (2) special agents authorized only to sell insurance. An insurance general agent is authorized to act on behalf of a specific insurance company with respect to nearly every business matter concerning sales operations. They may not make underwriting or premium determinations. Insurance special agents are authorized only to sell insurance and do not have the authority to modify any terms of existing insurance agreements. Insurance agents, who earn commissions based on the insurance they sell, may represent one or many different companies. Since the cost of insurance varies greatly from company to company, it is important to shop for comparable coverage and service. Not surprisingly, high-cost policies usually pay high commissions to agents.

Real estate agents usually represent the seller of real estate. If an agent acts as a buyer's agent, they are still compensated from the sales commission paid by the seller unless specific alternative compensation arrangements have been made. The loyalties of real estate agents may seem especially confusing to buyers, since they can be genuinely motivated to bring buyers and sellers into harmonious and satisfactory transactions. Under real estate agency agreements (listings), however, agents are hired to sell real estate, and it is the seller who is the principal in this agency relationship. Buyer brokerage arrangements, however, where agency and compensation are specified, are increasing in real estate transactions.

Financial advisors or *managers*, employed as agents to manage assets or purchase investments on behalf of principals, may be acting instead as dual agents or brokers, because they are compensated by commissions based on sales of the financial products sold in addition to fees based on a percentage of assets managed. Increasingly, to avoid such conflicts of interest, financial advisors are charging a fee only for the time spent on a client's behalf. It is always important to understand the exact relationship one has with a financial services professional, his or her motivation for recommending an investment, and the manner in which the financial representative is compensated.

Many uncompensated agency relationships may exist in the lives of older persons as well, but all agency agreements require great care and planning before entering into them. Among the more serious types of agency created are those in which persons are delegated authority under powers of attorney, durable power of attorney, and advance directives for health care in the event of incapacity. (See also ACCOUNTANTS; DURABLE POWER OF ATTORNEY; ETHICS IN FINANCIAL PLANNING; FINANCIAL ADVISORS; LIFE INSURANCE; LONG-TERM CARE INSURANCE [LTCI]—A CONSUMER'S PERSPECTIVE; REAL ESTATE INVESTMENTS.)

Organizations

Duff & Phelps
Institute of Certified Financial Planners
International Association of Financial Planners
International Board of Standards and Practices for Certified Financial Planners, Inc.
Moody's
National Association of Personal Financial Advisors
Standard & Poor's

Suggested Readings

Jaffe, Charles A. 2001. *The Right Way to Hire Financial Help: A Complete Guide to Choosing and Managing Brokers, Financial Planners, Insurance Agents, Lawyers, Tax Preparers, Bankers, and Real Estate Agents*. 2nd ed. Cambridge, MA: MIT Press.

Wilson, Ray, and Thomas Early. 1998. *Bought, Not Sold: Single Agency, Buyer's Brokers, Flat Fees, and the Consumer Revolution in Real Estate*. Greenfield, MA: Cogna Books.

Reference

Garner, Bryan A., Henry Campbell, and Henry L. Black, eds. 2000. *Black's Law Dictionary*. 7th ed. St. Paul, MN: West Group.

Donald A. Hunsberger

AGING AMERICA, the changing proportion of older adults in the overall U.S. population. The age structure of any population is affected by the rates of fertility, mortality, and migration. Increased life expectancies (LEs) of infants and children escalated during the first half of the twentieth century, caused principally by the elimination of poor hygiene and sanitation and by decreasing rates of infectious diseases. Throughout the twentieth century, however, reductions in mortality for children reached a floor, and reductions in mortality for older adults began to occur, in large part because of improvements in cardiac and other medical care. This trend resulted in the aging of the U.S. population during the latter half of the twentieth century. This factor was compounded by the declining fertility rate throughout the century, which would further increase the proportion of older people in the U.S. population. In the twenty-first century, the U.S. population will age further, due to the increased birthrate between 1946 and 1964 of the baby boom—the oldest baby boomers will be 65 in 2011.

It was not until the baby boom approached middle age that policymakers and the public took notice of this phenomenon. Population pyramids graphically portray the changing nature of the U.S. population, during 1900, 1970, 2000, and 2030 (Himes 2001). In 1900, the U.S. population can be characterized as a pyramid, with high birthrates and generally increasing mortality rates with increasing age. By 1970, the baby boom had begun to reshape the U.S. population, creating a bulge of people at the youngest ages. In 2000, the baby boom is in middle age, and the "pyramid" now looks more like a rectangle; this process is complete by the time we reach 2030, at which time the baby boomers reach old age. This phenomenon is referred to as the rectangularization of the population.

Size and Location of the U.S. Population

In 1990, adults aged 65 and older comprised approximately 12.5% of the U.S. population. By 2070, the 65+ group will constitute approximately 21% of the U.S. population (Figure 1). Of increasing interest, particularly to the service sectors of American business, is the explosive growth of those who are 85 and older. In contrast to the 65+ group, the 85+ group is expected to more than triple between 1990 and 2070, constituting approximately 5% of the U.S. population by 2070 (U.S. Census Bureau 1999).

Older adults live in virtually every state in the nation, but there are concentrations in certain areas. Table 1 displays the ten states in which older adults make up the highest proportion of the U.S. population for 1990 and 2000 (Hetzel and Smith 2001). Florida is first in both years (18.3% in 1990; 17.6% in 2000), followed by Pennsylvania. After that the order changes, but the states listed in the top ten are pretty much the same states at both times, with the exception of Missouri in 1990 and Connecticut and Maine in 2000. Table 2, on the other hand, shows the top ten and bottom ten states in terms of older adult growth rate between 1990 and 2000, with Nevada growing 72% over the decade and the District of Columbia losing 10%.

One of the most important components in current and projected growth in the older

Figure 1
Projected Growth of the Older Population: 65+ and 85+ between 1990 and 2070

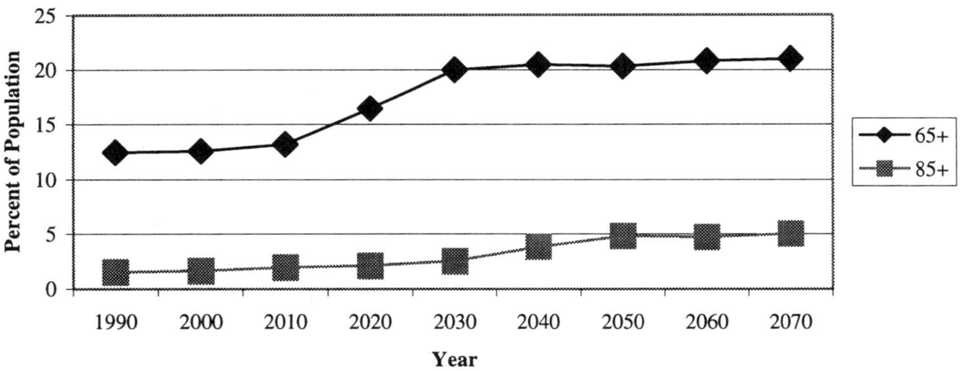

Source: U.S. Census Bureau 1999.

Table 1
Change in Oldest States between 1990 and 2000 in Rank Order

1990		2000	
Florida	18.3	Florida	17.6
Pennsylvania	15.4	Pennsylvania	15.6
Iowa	15.3	West Virginia	15.3
Rhode Island	15.0	Iowa	14.9
West Virginia	15.0	North Dakota	14.7
Arkansas	14.9	Rhode Island	14.5
South Dakota	14.7	Maine	14.4
North Dakota	14.3	South Dakota	14.3
Nebraska	14.1	Arkansas	14.0
Missouri	14.0	Connecticut	13.8

Source: Hetzel and Smith 2001.

population is increasing life expectancy during the twentieth century. In 1900, for example, the life expectancy for the U.S. population at birth was 47 years. By 1950, that figure had increased to 68, and by the year 2000, to nearly 77.

Differences in Life Expectancy

While life expectancy has increased for the total population, life expectancy for women has been higher than for men. Table 3 demonstrates that total life expectancy at birth rose from age 47.3 to 76.9 between 1900 and 2000. For men, however, the increase has been slower: in 2000, life expectancy for women is nearly 80, while for men, it is 74. At age 65 women can expect 19 more years of life, and men only 16 more. This differ-

Table 2
Top Ten and Bottom Ten in Growth of the Older Population, 1990 to 2000

Fastest Growing	Change 1990–2000	Slowest Growing	Change 1990–2000
Nevada	71.5	District of Columbia	−10.2
Alabama	59.6	Rhode Island	1.2
Arizona	39.5	Iowa	2.4
New Mexico	30.1	West Virginia	3.0
Hawaii	28.5	New York	3.6
Utah	26.9	North Dakota	3.8
Colorado	26.3	Kansas	4.0
Delaware	26.0	Nebraska	4.1
South Carolina	22.3	Illinois	4.4
Wyoming	22.2	Massachusetts	5.0

Source: Hetzel and Smith 2001.

Table 3
Life Expectancy at Birth and at Age 65 by Gender, in 1900, 1950, and 2000

Year	At Birth			At Age 65		
	Total	Male	Female	Total	Male	Female
1900	47.3	46.3	48.3	11.9	11.5	11.2
1950	68.2	65.6	71.1	13.9	12.8	15.0
2000	76.9	74.1	79.5	17.9	16.3	19.2

Source: Himes 2001.

ence is reflected in Figure 2, which shows the marital status of men and women age 65 and older. The two groups that most closely reflect the impact of this gender disparity in life expectancy are those who are married and widowed. Nearly 75% of men age 65 and older are married, compared to 44% of older women. Conversely, only 15% of men are widowed, while 45% of older women are widowed (Himes 2001).

Differences in life expectancy are more remarkable between racial/ethnic groups. In Figure 3, we examine data between 1940 and 1992 for Whites and African Americans. While good data were not available for African Americans until the 1970s, certain patterns can be observed. African Americans have lower life expectancy than Whites, but only when broken down by gender. Rates for White females are consistently highest, followed by African American females. African American female rates are similar to,

Figure 2
Marital Status, Ages 65 and Older

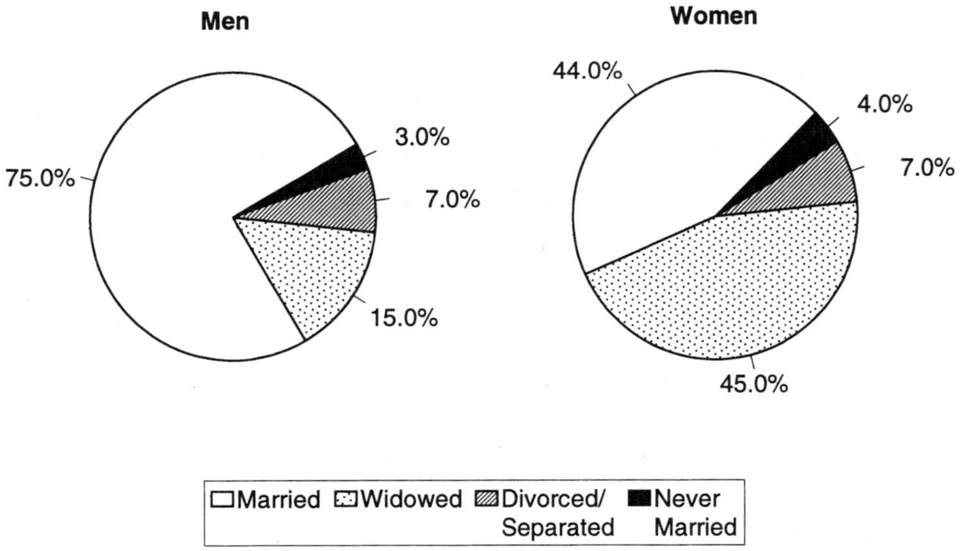

Source: Himes 2001.

Figure 3
Changing Life Expectancy for Whites and African Americans, 1940 to 1992

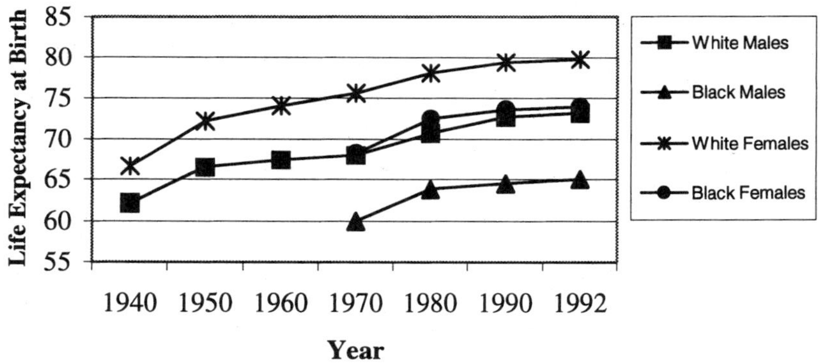

Source: Himes 2001.

but slightly higher than, those for White males. The lowest life expectancy rate is for African American males. The intraracial difference between the sexes, however, is approximately the same for African Americans as for Whites.

The impact of these differentials is not directly reflected in the current and projected racial composition of the older U.S. population. In Figure 4, the current proportion of all African Americans, Hispanics, and "other" races represents approximately 18% of the older adult population in the year 2000. By 2050, however, it is projected to represent 36% of the older adult population. This is due to the fact that the racial composition of the U.S. population is made up of other factors in addition to life expectancy. In the case

Figure 4
Older Americans by Race and Ethnicity, 2000 and 2050

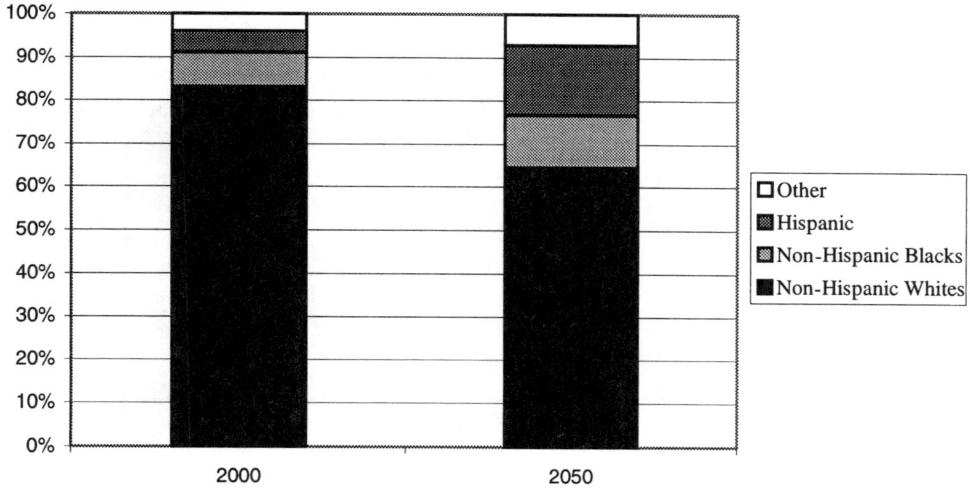

Source: Himes 2001.

Table 4
Poverty Rates among Older Men and Women, by Race/Ethnicity, 2000

	Percent in Poverty			
	Total	Non-Hispanic White	African American	Hispanic
Total, Ages 65+	10.2	8.3	22.3	18.8
Men	7.5	5.8	17.1	17.6
Women	12.2	10.2	25.8	19.6

Source: Himes 2001.

of the racial makeup of the U.S. population, non-White residents tend to have higher fertility than White residents. In addition, most migration into the United States is of young non-Whites in good health. These factors will account for the shift in the racial/ethnic proportion of the older adult 50 years from now.

In general, older adults in the United States are no more likely to be poor than the rest of the U.S. population, with approximately 10% living in poverty. Table 4, however, shows gender and racial differences in poverty rates. Rates for older women are 12.2% and 7.5% for older men. African American women have 151% the poverty rate of African American men, while Hispanic women have 11% higher poverty rates than Hispanic men.

Socioeconomic Status

The major difference is between the races: while Whites have poverty levels less than the average (8.3%), African Americans have 2.7 times and Hispanics have 2.3 times the

Table 5
Sources of Income among Americans Age 65 or Older, in Income Quintiles, 1998

	Income Level				
	1st Quintile	**2nd Quintile**	**3rd Quintile**	**4th Quintile**	**5th Quintile**
Total	100	100	100	100	100
Social Security	82	80	64	45	18
Asset Income	2	6	10	14	28
Pensions	3	7	15	24	21
Earnings	1	3	7	13	31
Public Assistance	10	2	1	1	1
Other	2	2	3	3	2

Source: Himes 2001.

poverty rate of Whites. There are also some marked gender differences. Both African American and Hispanic men have poverty rates three times that of White men, while Hispanic women have twice the poverty rate, and African American women have 2.5 times the poverty rate, of White women.

All but the top income quintile of older adults relies heavily on Social Security income (see Table 5 for sources of income for older Americans). For the two bottom quintiles, Social Security makes up 80% or more of total income, compared to 18% for the highest quintile of older citizens. Any new or revised policies regarding the preservation of the U.S. social welfare system for older adults (e.g., Social Security, Medicare, Medicaid) must take into account both the disproportionate number of non-White older Americans in the lower-income quintiles and the potential increase of older adults who will be highly dependent on Social Security for their future income.

Health Differences

The aging of the U.S. population will also have an impact on the U.S. health care system, particularly with the explosive growth of the 85+ group. Figure 5 presents information on the prevalence of chronic conditions among different age groups, and Figure 6 presents similar information for Whites, African Americans, and Hispanics (Himes 2001).

Figure 5 presents the prevalence of arthritis, hypertension, heart disease, cancer, diabetes, and stroke; in only one case do those who are 85+ have lower rates than those between 70 and 74—diabetes. Rates of hypertension and cancer appear to be relatively stable by age group, while arthritis, heart disease, and stroke are significantly more prevalent in the 85+ group. The reason diabetes goes in the reverse direction is probably one of selection, as people may be dying of diabetes prior to age 85.

For older Whites, African Americans, and Hispanics, prevalence rates also vary (Figure 6). Older African Americans have the highest rates of arthritis, hypertension, diabetes,

Figure 5
Chronic Health Conditions, by Age Group

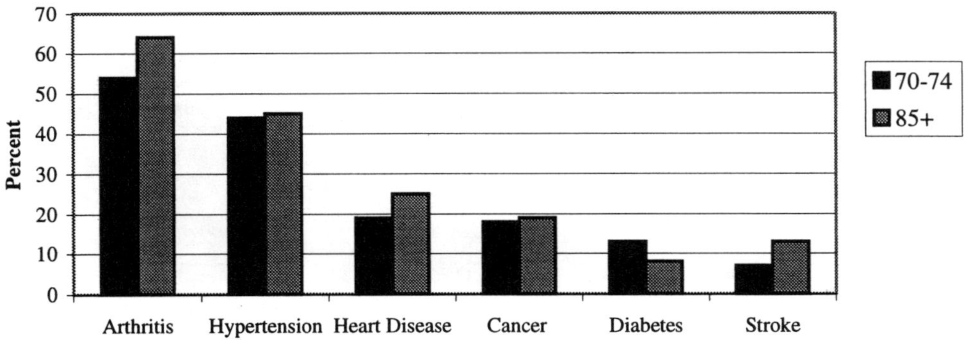

Source: Himes 2001.

Figure 6
Chronic Health Conditions, by Race/Ethnicity

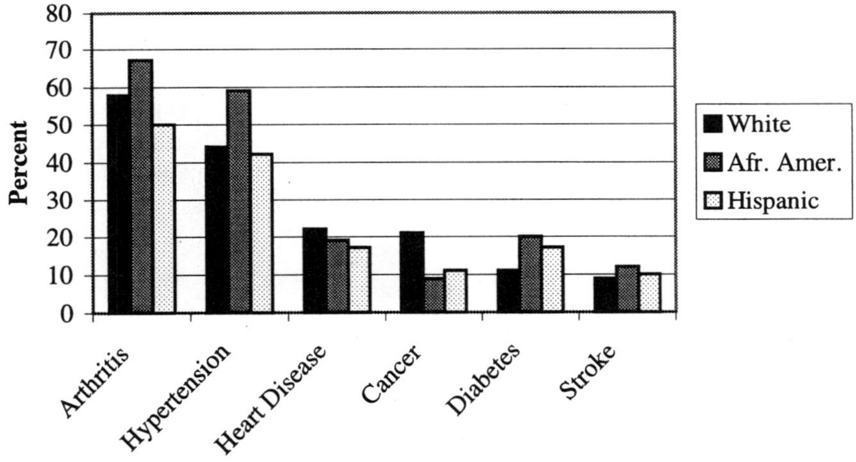

Source: Himes 2001.

and stroke, but they have significantly lower rates of cancer than Whites, and the racial differences in heart disease prevalence appear to be minor. Hispanics have the lowest levels of arthritis and hypertension, but differ little from African Americans on the other chronic conditions (Himes 2001). African Americans may have low rates of cancer due to one of two factors: (1) they may not be diagnosed as readily, because of relatively low participation in cancer screenings and preventive tests, or (2) they may not be receiving equally good cancer care, and thus more might be dying of cancer as compared to other groups.

These differences in health can translate into differential rates of functional limitation—basic activities of daily living (e.g., bathing, feeding, dressing, etc.) and instrumental activities of daily living (e.g., managing money, taking medications, preparing meals, etc.). When older adults become too impaired to perform many of these tasks,

Table 6
Percent of 60+ Population in the Oldest and Youngest Countries, 2000 and 2050

Oldest Countries				Youngest Countries			
2000		2050		2000		2050	
Country	%	Country	%	Country	%	Country	%
Italy	24.1	Spain	44.1	Niger	3.3	Niger	5.0
Greece	23.4	Slovenia	42.4	Yemen	3.6	Angola	5.2
Germany	23.2	Japan	42.3	Uganda	3.8	Yemen	5.3
Japan	23.2	Italy	42.3	Somalia	3.9	Somalia	5.7
Sweden	22.4	Austria	41.0	Burundi	4.3	Uganda	5.7
Belgium	22.1	Greece	40.7	Angola	4.5	Burkina Faso	6.5
Spain	21.8	Czech Rep.	40.1	Congo	4.5	Ethiopia	6.6
Bulgaria	21.7	Armenia	39.5	Zambia	4.5	Liberia	6.7
Switzerland	21.3	Switzerland	38.9	Burkina	4.8	Burundi	6.8
Latvia	20.9	Bulgaria	38.6	Chad	4.9	Mali	7.0

Source: United Nations Population Division 2002b.

assistance typically comes from a spouse, adult children, other relatives or friends, and paid care. While American long-term care policy has traditionally relied on the institutional solution of hospital, nursing home, or rehabilitation center, the vast majority of care for frail older adults is delivered in the community by family members.

International Perspective

How does the United States compare to the rest of the world? Life expectancy rates in the United States are similar to but not as strong as other developed nations, and they are clearly stronger than for developing countries. Table 6 displays the percentage of age 60 and older persons in the countries identified as the oldest and youngest for the year 2000 and projected for the year 2050 (U.N. Population Division 2002a). The United States makes neither list; in the year 2000, the 60+ population makes up approximately 14% of the U.S. population and in 2050 is projected to increase to 20%. The oldest countries today range between 21% in Latvia to 24% in Italy. By the year 2050, the oldest countries will range from 39% in Bulgaria to 44% in Spain. The youngest countries also show increases in their older populations, but not enough to approach the old-age proportions in the developed world. In 2000, the youngest countries had older populations ranging between 3% (Niger) and 5% (Chad), and by 2050, the youngest countries will have somewhere between 5% (Niger) and 7% (Mali).

These differences also are reflected in the relative life expectancy rates in the developed and developing world. Table 7 compares the United States to the ten countries with the highest rates—the developed world—and those with the ten lowest rates—the developing world (United Nations Population Division 2002b). In 1995, the United States ranked eleventh in the developed world. In contrast, the United States is clearly ahead of the ten countries with the lowest life expectancy rates in the developing world.

Table 7
Ten Highest and Lowest Countries in Life Expectancy at Birth, Ranked in 1995 and Compared to the United States

Highest LE Countries	**Life Expectancy 1995–2000**	**Life Expectancy 2045–2050**
Japan	80.5	88.0
Sweden	79.3	84.6
Iceland	78.9	83.1
Australia	78.7	83.0
Switzerland	78.6	82.9
Canada	78.5	82.8
Israel	78.3	83.5
France	78.1	84.0
Norway	78.1	83.7
Belgium	77.9	83.8
United States	76.5	82.6
Lowest LE Countries		
Sierra Leone	37.3	61.5
Rwanda	39.4	64.2
Zambia	40.5	66.0
Burundi	40.6	64.3
Mozambique	40.6	62.8
Malawi	40.7	64.0
Uganda	41.9	67.8
Afghanistan	42.5	62.4
Zimbabwe	42.9	66.3
Guinea-Bissau	44.1	66.0

Source: United Nations Population Division 2000b.

Conclusions

The U.S. population is getting older along with much of the rest of the world. This population will increase both in numbers and in diversity as the baby boom generation ages. The proportion of older U.S. adults in the twenty-first century projected to be female, minority, frail, poor, and highly dependent on Social Security for their economic survival is growing. In terms of planning, the nation must preserve and improve Social Security, Medicare, Supplemental Security Income (SSI), and Medicaid in order to maintain the safety and dignity of this population. For financial professionals, preserving and growing the assets of those fortunate enough to have resources and income outside of the social welfare system will become an increasingly critical factor for those numbers of older adults expected in the twenty-first century. (See also ATTITUDES ABOUT

RETIREMENT; ECONOMIC HARDSHIP MEASURES IN THE OLDER POPULATION; ECONOMIC HISTORY OF RETIREMENT; ECONOMIC STATUS OF OLDER MEN AND WOMEN; HISTORY OF RETIREMENT; U.S. PERSONAL SAVING RATE.)

Organizations

National Center for Health Statistics
Social Security Administration
U.S. Census Bureau

References

Hetzel, L., and A. Smith. 2001. *The 65 Years and Over Population: 2000.* U.S. Bureau of the Census, C2KBR/01-10. Washington, DC: U.S. Census Bureau.

Himes, C.L. 2001. "Elderly Americans." *Population Bulletin 56, No. 4.* Washington, DC: Population Reference Bureau.

United Nations Population Division. 2002a. *World Population Projects: The 2000 Revision.* Available online at http://www.geohive.com/charts/pop_age.php.

United Nations Population Division. 2002b. *World Population Projects: The 2000 Revision.* Available online at http://www.geohive.com/charts/pop_lifespan.php.

U.S. Census Bureau. 1999. *Population Projections Program, Population Division.* Available online at http://www.census.gov/population/www/projections/natsum-T3.html.

Sandra L. Reynolds

AGING INTO DEBT, the increasing numbers of midlife and older consumers indebted to banks, retailers, and credit card companies for the purchase of goods and services. The most rapid growth of consumer debt has been by Americans who are least able to pay it off, among them older workers and retirees. Between 1977 and 1986, the debt/income ratio rose only modestly for adults aged 35 to 44 (81.4% to 81.5%) and 45 to 54 (58.4% to 62.0%) but climbed dramatically for adults aged 55 to 64 (35.7% to 51.8%) and those aged 65 to 74 (19.4% to 41.2%). According to a recent study of household debt by SRI Consulting Business Intelligence, households under 65 years old reported a 95% increase in debt from 1992 to 2000, whereas households over 65 years old reported a 164% increase. Not surprisingly, the Consumer Bankruptcy Project at Harvard University (Sullivan 2001) found that the fastest growth in consumer bankruptcy in the 1990s was among the oldest households. Between 1991 and 1999, the study reports that bankruptcy filings increased 120% among households aged 55 to 64 years old and 119% among households over 65 years old. In 2001, the authors estimated that nearly 82,000 seniors filed for bankruptcy—up from almost 24,000 in 1991. Although medical expenses and the loss of a spouse are the most common reasons for bankruptcy among U.S. seniors, a growing factor is the rise of consumer loans—especially credit card debts—that are used to provide financial assistance to family members (particularly children and grandchildren).

The societal trend of rising consumer indebtedness is ominous as today's relatively debt-free retirement population is being replaced with more financially insecure segments of the baby boom generation. Indeed, boomers are much more tolerant of credit card debt than Depression Era seniors. This is illustrated by a 1998 U.S. Federal Reserve Board survey (based on respondents' self-reports) that includes questions on credit card payment practices. The following responded that they "Almost Always Pay Off Balance":

under 39 years old (39.0%), 35 to 44 years (46.5%), 45 to 54 years (48.2%), 55 to 64 years (61.0%), 65 to 74 years (74.0%), and over 75 years (86.3%). Significantly, the survey was conducted at the end of the longest economic expansion in U.S. history. This suggests that many members of the boomer groups (35 to 44 and 45 to 54 years old) opted to revolve their high-cost consumer debts even during their prime income-earning years; only 1.7% more older boomers paid off their credit card balances than younger boomers. Overall, this consumer debt pattern reflects greater financial obligations due to life-cycle needs, structural constraints (lower income, higher cost of living, employment disruptions) as well as cultural factors such as a preference for consumption over saving.

Credit card use among seniors is increasing. As younger cohorts of credit-dependent households age, they are replacing older adults without credit cards. As a result, the proportion of seniors with credit cards jumped sharply in the 1990s, from only 45% in 1992 to about 60% in 2000. Three out of every four U.S. households now possess universal credit cards. According to the SRI Consulting Business Intelligence study, the proportion of seniors with some consumer debt rose from 35% in 1992 to nearly 60% in 2000. This is consistent with the sharp escalation of credit card debt during this period and with the growing importance of consumer credit to America's older citizens.

In 2002, three out of five U.S. households revolved charges on their credit card accounts. On average, the cumulative net, outstanding credit card debt per "revolver" household was over $13,000 in 2002. This is instructive since those income groups least able to repay high-interest consumer loans have registered the greatest increase over the last decade. According to data from the Survey of Consumer Finances (SCF), the largest increase was reported by the working poor (annual income less than $10,000), followed by senior citizens (65 years and older). Between 1989 and 1998, average credit card debt among all households with an outstanding balance increased 66%, from $2,482 to $4,120. Among low-income households, it soared from $494 to $2,030 (311%) and it climbed from $1,497 to $3,608 (141%) among the oldest households.

The most striking differences in consumer credit card use among older Americans are associated with age and gender. Seniors in the United States are not a homogenous population as reflected in their different social activities and consumption patterns. The lifestyle of Americans 55 to 70 years old is distinct from those aged 70 to 75. The younger group is much more active, and its middle-class members are more able to enjoy and to afford travel and leisure activities such as entertainment, education programs, and cultural events. According to AARP, over two-thirds of its VISA cardholders are between 50 and 65 years old, and most of their purchases are for hotel accommodations, plane tickets, restaurant meals, and consumer catalog products. In response to the growing demand of its members, AARP offered its first fixed-rate VISA card in 1990 and added four "Classic" VISAs and a VISA Gold Card four years later. AARP's exclusive credit card marketing contract yields millions of dollars in annual royalties to the association. Members should examine the terms of their AARP "affinity" credit cards to determine whether they are receiving the most competitive benefits available.

The analysis of credit card use by the oldest seniors is more complex due to variations in family resources, cultural attitudes, and gender differences. The oldest age groups experience changing familial roles as well as the loss of a spouse, other family members, and friends. These groups are more likely to be composed of single women (especially widows) with fewer financial resources, and less experience and employment outside of the household. In addition, older senior women are more likely to be primarily dependent on the retirement and Social Security benefits of their husbands. They are least likely to have credit cards, since many lose them following the loss of an authorizing spouse, and they may lack an established credit history on their own.

Two other factors characterize the credit usage patterns of America's oldest seniors. First, those older than 70 are most likely to be culturally averse to using consumer credit due to harsh memories of the Great Depression and lack of familiarity with current consumer lending practices. Moreover, older seniors tend to pay for purchases with cash or checks. Lack of experience with revolving credit underlies the skepticism of many seniors to "amazing" credit card offers or fear that banks will charge exorbitant fees and interest rates. In fact, ignorance of these new bank lending practices is responsible for occasional inquiries from older AARP members about whether credit card purchases are free "gifts." In addition, many older seniors are lonely and look forward to the empowerment, entertainment, or companionship of discussing orders with catalog or home shopping salespeople, not to mention the excitement of the anticipated arrival of their purchases. AARP records indicate a high purchase-return cycle among the oldest cardholders, especially after they realize that credit purchases are returnable and refundable.

Corporate Policies and Consumer Issues

As U.S. longevity increases and health care costs soar, many older Americans face the prospect of outliving their retirement resources. Personal health and maintenance expenses are escalating, and more of America's older adults have little recourse but to use credit for purchasing necessary medicines and even groceries. Moreover, many seniors who had planned on living in a mortgage-free home are finding that rising tax assessments, escalating insurance premiums, and other home maintenance–related costs are claiming a growing portion of their fixed incomes. At the same time, difficult job markets, divorce, and life-cycle crises are leading adult children and grandchildren to seek help with living expenses or even to share the residences of older relatives. More recently, retirees on fixed incomes are encountering greater personal pressure to provide financial assistance to family members by borrowing from costly bank credit cards. This new access to financial resources is not only exacerbating stressful family relations but also leading to new forms of financial elder abuse and fraud. Many low-income seniors are being targeted for fraudulent financial schemes and financial (and physical) abuse because of the availability of bank credit cards. These range from impersonal telemarketing scams to improper "loans" to flagrant theft by nursing staff and even relatives and neighbors.

For most seniors, greater practical knowledge about credit can help ease some of the anxieties and burdens of consumer debt. First, the Equal Credit Opportunity Act (ECOA) of 1975 forbids discrimination in granting access to credit on the basis of race, color, religion, national origin, sex, marital status, or age. While minimum financial standards must be satisfied for credit approval, industry practices still exist that effectively evade antidiscrimination statutes such as credit score procedures that may impact credit applications based on the age, race, or gender of the applicant. Creditors cannot discriminate against persons receiving income from Social Security or public assistance and must establish clear criteria for their credit-scoring systems that evaluate income from annuities and pensions. Even so, creditworthiness standards can include age as a factor as long as the evaluation procedures are statistically defensible.

Various forms of indirect discrimination may be widespread, but they are hard to prove in the consumer credit industry. The reasons are that banks tend to initiate the credit card application process, many people are involved in the final approval, and a variety of formulas are used that are based on different interpretations of personal credit histories and other subjective factors. For example, seniors tend to have low income-to-asset ratios and few consumer debts. The credit-scoring system, however, favors consumers with higher incomes and a current history of repaying installment and revolving loans. As a result, debt-free seniors with low monthly incomes will tend to receive relatively lower, aggregate credit scores from consumer reporting agencies (CRAs). This subtle form of institutional discrimination is significant since consumer credit scores are the primary information used in the process of evaluating consumer loan applications.

Although the ECOA guarantees fair access to consumer credit, its purview does not include other sources of discrimination such as credit limits, interest rates, and financial penalties. Other federal laws such as the Truth in Lending Act (TILA) and the Fair Credit Reporting Act (FCRA) are concerned with the obligation of credit card companies to disclose the financial terms of their lending agreements and to explain the decision to reject an application for a consumer loan.

One problem with consumer credit practices involves the rise of deceptive "bait-and-switch" policies. That is, a favorable contract initially is offered to the consumer and is subsequently amended by fine-print inserts that can impose a higher interest rate and fee structure, force arbitration over disputes, reduce the "grace" period, give fewer membership benefits, and increase annual member fees as well as add other new contractual terms. Many companies will not explain specific reasons for raising an interest rate, which may be based on the payment history or outstanding loans with other financial institutions.

If the interest rate on a credit card has been suddenly increased and/or a consumer loan application has been denied, it is important that the consumer obtain a personal credit report from each of the three credit reporting agencies listed below. Each CRA receives information from different sources, and thus all three should be scrutinized. Under the FCRA, a consumer has the right to a free credit report each time an application for a loan has been rejected; some states require CRAs to offer one free credit report to their residents every 12 months. After examining the credit report(s), the consumer should immediately send a written request (by mail or fax) to change inaccurate information with any substantiating documentation. For example, errors typically encountered include loans that were mistakenly added to the file, old information still on file (negative information should be deleted after seven to ten years), debts from an ex-spouse or family members, and "phantom" loans due to bank mergers where the same debt is reported multiple times under the name of different financial institutions. Under the FCRA, the CRA must respond to the consumer's written request within 60 days.

Consumers must be vigilant in examining their monthly credit card statements for clerical errors and unknown charges so that they can be contested as soon as possible. This is due to the increase in telemarketing campaigns that are designed to confuse seniors while surreptitiously obtaining their permission to join a new or special membership program. In many cases, seniors do not understand that they have given their "oral consent" to a "trial period" since a formal contract was not signed and mailed to the company. Instead, they are shocked to learn that the membership and/or purchase costs are conveniently billed to their credit card accounts. This hard-sell tactic is used most commonly by companies selling magazine subscriptions, credit protection programs, and insurance products. This is the reason that telemarketers request permission to record the conversation with you as proof of a verbal contract.

In order to terminate these programs and rescind their fees, a letter disputing the charges must be written directly to the complaint department of the bank that issues the credit card (different from the address for sending the monthly payment) or directly to the company that provides the product or service. Calling the customer service department of the credit card company will not necessarily initiate the process for canceling past and future charges from the telemarketing company. In fact, a credit card account will continue to be charged at regular intervals—even indefinitely—and the right to dispute such charges, if a letter is not sent to the appropriate complaint department, may be inadvertently waived.

The primary reason for credit reporting agencies and credit card companies to compile detailed personal consumer histories is to assess individual creditworthiness. Unfortunately, these consumer profiles have become valuable resources for other companies to market their products. The result is an intensifying struggle over personal privacy. Indeed, financial institutions not only estimate the probability of expected consumer repayment of installment loans, but they are also interested in what a person is buying and where the products are purchased. Thus, creditors and mass marketers know much more about consumption and living patterns than could have been imagined only a couple of decades ago. This has important implications for future mass-marketing campaigns as well as the fraudulent use of consumer credit accounts.

Advocacy Groups Unsuccessful

Consumer advocacy groups have not been successful in enacting a federal "opt-in" provision that requires personal authorization for the selling or "sharing" of private consumer information to other commercial interests. As a result, the new financial services "conglomerates" such as Citigroup (merger of Citibank and Traveler's Group) are permitted by federal law to share individual background information with all of their subsidiaries. This explains how obtaining a Citibank credit card can lead to solicitations from its separate insurance and investment divisions. For example, a high savings account balance may produce unwanted solicitations for mutual funds from Citigroup's investment subsidiary (Salomon Smith Barney), while a medical condition may lead to a rejection for a Traveler's insurance policy and the subsequent denial of a Citibank loan application.

At present, the only recourse for consumers is to contact their individual credit card companies and request that they "opt out" from existing corporate marketing programs that share their personal consumer information with other corporations. This lack of protection of personal information has contributed to the unprecedented increase in "identity theft." This is the fraudulent procurement and use of credit by assuming another person's identity. Most people do not know that they have been victims until they are contacted by debt collectors or are rejected for new credit cards or other consumer loans. Further information on this important topic is available from the U.S. Federal Trade

Commission (a complaint can be filed from its Web site), the Consumers Union, and the U.S. Public Interest Research Group.

As the financial pain of consumer debt absorbs a growing proportion of household incomes, the appeal of home equity and debt consolidation loans has soared. The 1986 federal tax reform law phased out the deductibility of interest charges (over five years) on consumer debt such as credit cards and auto loans. As a result, one of the few options for reducing the effective cost of consumer credit is to convert credit card debt into home equity loans with fully deductible interest. Unfortunately, many families have learned the hard lesson that higher mortgage payments together with unforeseen economic crises (medical expenses, job loss, divorce) can result in the loss of their home through bank foreclosure and even bankruptcy. Another costly surprise may occur when consumer debts are purposefully hidden from household members. The unsuspecting spouse is astounded to learn that he or she is obligated to pay for one-half of all the consumer debts incurred during the marriage, regardless of the reasons for the loans and who benefited from them. This is relevant in the case of divorce but not in the case of death, since heirs cannot inherit the personal debts of the deceased unless they have cards issued in their own names. Of course, creditors do have the legal right to file claims on the financial assets of the estate while it is in probate.

Debt Consolidation Strategies

Increasingly, many financially desperate households have found that the encumbrances of consumer credit have pushed them to the precipice of bankruptcy and into the tangled web of debt consolidation companies. Not all "nonprofit" debt management companies serve the consumers' interest, and many are created merely to benefit the business founders. As a result, these companies must be selected with caution due to the large numbers of "upfront" fees that are required. In addition, most nonprofit enterprises receive a substantial amount of their operating expenses from the financial services industry and actually are created to serve the interest of creditors. These factors should be used as a guide for evaluating potential debt management companies. If a company is not certified by the National Foundation for Consumer Counseling (NFCC), the terms of the contract and its claims for negotiating lower payoff settlements should be examined with greater vigilance. Some reputable nonprofit agencies are listed below.

Lastly, many families have developed mutual aid strategies to help relatives who have found themselves overwhelmed with consumer debt. Some even cut up credit cards or freeze them in a glass of water. Psychologists suggest special care during the holidays and other meaningful social events when many people tend to overuse their credit cards. Suggested remedies range from managing a household fund for gift-giving expenses throughout the year to limiting the number of gifts or total cost of all holiday giving. Such suggested changes in personal behavior may not offer much help to the growing number of people who rely on their credit cards for necessities, although they may provide guidance for those who use them for discretionary purchases. The latter is important to those aging baby boomers who soon will be confronting their retirement with smaller nest eggs and greater personal indebtedness than their parents. Although older Americans have been more successful in resisting credit card debt, tomorrow's senior citizens may find it an unwelcome encumbrance in coping with the financial vagaries of their "golden years." (See also BABY BOOMERS AND RETIREMENT; BANKING

SERVICES FOR THE MATURE MARKET; BANKRUPTCY; CONSUMER CREDIT; CREDIT SCORES; EDUCATION OF OLDER ADULTS; FINANCIAL RECOVERY IN LATER LIFE; LEISURE; MARKETING TO MATURE ADULTS.)

Organizations

About, Inc.
Bank Rate
Card Rate
Card Web
Credit Card Nation

Consumer Credit Reporting Agencies

Equifax
Experian
TransUnion

Nonprofit Consumer Credit Counseling Services

Coalition for Responsible Lending
Consumer Counseling Centers of America, Inc.
Consumer Federation of America
Consumers Union
Council of Better Business Bureau
Debtors Anonymous

Federal Regulatory Agencies

Green Path Debt Solutions
National Consumer Law Center
National Foundation for Consumer Counseling

Nonprofit Consumer Action Organizations

Springboard, Consumer Credit Counseling Service
U.S. Federal Reserve System
U.S. Federal Trade Commission
U.S. House of Representatives, Committee on Financial Services
U.S. Public Interest Research Group
U.S. Senate, Committee on Banking, Housing, and Urban Affairs
U.S. Treasury, Office of the Comptroller of the Currency

Suggested Readings

Daskaloff, Alexander. 1999. *Credit Card Debt: Reduce Your Financial Burden in Three Easy Steps*. New York: William Morrow & Company.

DeGraff, John, David Wann, and Thomas H. Naylor. 2001. *Affluenza: The All-Consuming Epidemic*. Seattle, WA: Berrett-Koehler Publishers.

Enough! Center for a New American Dream, 6930 Carroll Avenue, #900, Takoma Park, MD 20912; (877) 683–7326. Available online at http://www.newdream.org/.

Matthews, Arlene Modica. 1993. *Your Money, Your Self: Understanding Your Relationship to Cash and Credit*. New York: Simon & Schuster.

Newtonian Finances Ltd. 2003. *Credit Card Nation*. Education Modules. Available online at www.creditcardnation.com/.

References

Drentea, Patricia. 2000. "Age, Debt and Anxiety." *Journal of Health and Social Behavior* 41 (December): 437–50.

Kennickell, Arthur B., Martha Starr-McCluer, and Brian J. Surette. 1998. "Summary Descriptions of 1998 Survey Results." *Federal Reserve Bulletin* 86: 1–29.

Mishel, Lawrence, Jared Bernstein, and Heather Boushey. 2003. *The State of Working America 2002–03.* Ithaca, NY: Cornell University Press.

Pollin, Robert. 1990. *Deeper in Debt: The Changing Financial Conditions of U.S. Households.* Washington, DC: Economic Policy Institute.

Seniors USA. 2002. "American Seniors Rack Up Debt Like Never Before." Available online at http://senrs.com.

SRI Consulting Business Intelligence. 2003. "Do You Have Too Much Debt?" Available online at http://www.SmartMoney.com/debt/calculator/index.cfm?story=debt-toomuch.

Sullivan, Teresa A., Deborah Thorne, and Elizabeth Warren. 2001. "Young, Old, and in between: Who Files for Bankruptcy?" *Norton Bankruptcy Law Adviser* 9A (September). Rochester, NY: West Group.

Sullivan, Teresa A., Elizabeth Warren, and Jay L. Westbrook. 2000. *The Fragile Middle Class: Americans in Debt.* New Haven, CT: Yale University Press.

Survey of Consumer Finances. 2000. "Recent Changes in U.S. Family Finances: Results from the 1998 Survey of Consumer Finances." Available online at http://www.hec.ohio-state.edu/scf/.

Robert D. Manning

ANNUITIES, the right to receive fixed, periodic payments, either for life or for a term of years. Annuity contracts purchased from insurance companies may start the payments right away (immediate annuities) or may start them at some future date (deferred annuities). Annuities can be purchased with either a lump sum of money (single premium annuity) or a series of payments (flexible premium annuity). Any money put into an annuity will earn a return. How it earns the return depends on whether it is a fixed annuity, an equity-indexed annuity, or a variable annuity. The money put into the annuity plus the earnings are the annuity account value. All annuities have both tax advantages and tax disadvantages, depending on perspective and the tax-triggering event. Annuities are the only financial instrument that can shift longevity risk—the risk of outliving assets—from an individual to an insurance company.

An annuity is a contract between the purchaser of the annuity and an insurance company on behalf of an annuitant or annuitants—the person or people who will receive the payments under the terms of the contract. Most commonly, the annuitant and the owner are one and the same person, but they do not have to be. The policyholder may also have a beneficiary to whom ownership of the annuity, or the right to receive payments, will pass in the event of the owner's death. The beneficiary is unlikely to be the same person as the annuitant but may be.

Fixed Annuities

In fixed annuities, the insurance company guarantees that the money deposited in the annuity will not decline in value. The insurance company will absorb any investment loss and retain any investment gain. The insurance company will also credit interest to the monies deposited in the annuity based on its investment experience and both market and marketing considerations. This has both positive and negative implications. Although insurance companies appear to assume all of the investment risk in fixed-rate fixed annuities, this is only true with regard to the principal investment, not with regard to return on the investment. The common objection to fixed annuities is that the rate of interest credited is variable at the insurance company's discretion, albeit within parameters stated in the policy. Because an insurance company's investment experience may fluctuate, relative to the market, rates of interest credited to a block of in-force policies may be less than competitive from time to time.

Equity-Indexed Annuities

Equity-indexed annuities (EIAs) were developed to respond to the concerns raised by the negative implications of fixed annuities. EIAs are fixed annuities that share the advantages of other fixed annuities—primarily, that the account value is guaranteed not to decline regardless of what happens in the stock and bond markets and that interest earnings are not subject to current income taxation—but they shift the determination of how much interest to credit to the annuity from the insurance company to an independent equity index such as the Standard & Poor's 500 (S&P 500). For example, if during a given year the S&P 500 index increases by 7.4%, then an EIA linked to it would be credited with 7.4% interest, regardless of how much the company actually earned. Different companies use different indexes, with the S&P 500 the most common, but the NASDAQ, NASDAQ 100, Russell 2000, and Dow Jones Industrial Average are also available. Some EIAs allow a choice as to the percentage of the annuity value to be indexed to each of a number of indexes, or a fixed account. There are also other variables (such as participation rate, cap, and measuring period) in the interest crediting formulas of equity-indexed annuities that differ from company to company and annuity to annuity, which make comparing EIAs more difficult.

Variable Annuities

Variable annuities represent the opposite end of the risk spectrum from fixed annuities. In variable annuities, the policyholder takes on the risk for both principal and interest by allocating deposits to the annuity among "subaccounts" that are similar to mutual funds and will rise and fall with market conditions. For example, if the underlying subaccounts decline 30% in value, then the policyholder's annuity account also declines 30% in value. Conversely, if the underlying subaccounts increase 20% in value, then the policyholder's account value increases at a like rate. Policyholders have the right to move their underlying investments among subaccounts with reasonable frequency, so that they can allocate their funds to the market sectors with which they feel most comfortable at a point in time. Variable annuities have mortality and expense risk charges and administrative fees on top of the loads and expenses in the subaccounts, so that performance is partially offset by expenses—which can be significant.

Withdrawals

It is generally not possible for an annuity owner to withdraw *all* of the money placed in an annuity without penalty for some period of time because of surrender charges. Surrender charges are imposed to protect the insurance company against loss of the use of funds paid in, or receipt of expenses and fees, before it has a chance to recuperate the costs it incurs in issuing the annuity. These costs include commissions and, in some cases, bonuses to the policyholder, along with the administrative costs associated with the policy. Surrender charges are usually only imposed during the first 6 to 12 years of a policy's existence. After surrender charges expire and before annuitization, all the monies in the account can be removed without penalty.

In addition, it is common for a policyholder to be able to withdraw some percentage—usually 10%—of either premiums paid or the account value (premiums paid plus interest credited) each year without penalty. Taking periodic payments (annuitizing the contract), even over a very short period of time, will often preempt imposition of surrender charges. Further, some policies waive surrender charges in the event of nursing home admission or similar life situations. Once periodic payments start and the annuity is "annuitized," there is almost no chance of stopping the payments and getting a lump sum instead, although that may be one of the annuity options.

Annuity Payouts

Subject to the kinds of restrictions or penalties noted, the owner of an annuity can receive money from an annuity in amounts that range from the full amount to whatever the insurance company will pay per period for a given length of time. This ability to convert assets to income is what annuities were designed to do. What sets them apart from other financial instruments are the guarantees available during payout, the most important being the guarantee to pay for the life of an annuitant. A common error in the financial community is to compare guaranteed annuity payouts with nonguaranteed rates of return on investment instruments, discounting the value of annuity guarantees. As the population's life expectancy extends toward age 100 and investment managers continue to experience volatile markets, these guarantees become increasingly valuable.

Whether purchasing an immediate annuity or annuitizing a deferred annuity, an owner has several choices for how frequently he or she wants payments made—monthly, quarterly, semiannually, or annually—and for how long they are to be guaranteed. While the owner makes the choices, it is the annuitant who receives the payments and whose life is used to measure life-term guarantees. The following classifications are the most common terms guaranteed under annuity payment obligations:

Term certain, also known as *period certain*, involves the promise of the insurance company to make payments for a specified number of years regardless of the number of years the annuitant survives. For example, with a 20-year period certain annuity, the insurance company commits to payments for 240 months, even if the annuitant dies prior to the end of the 20-year term (the balance of payments would be received by a named beneficiary). It should be noted that the longer the period certain, the lower the amount of money the insurance company guarantees to pay periodically for the term of the annuity payout.

Life contingencies are commitments by the insurance company to make payments until the annuitant, or the last survivor of two or more annuitants, dies. Life contingencies guarantee that the annuitant cannot outlive his or her money and thereby shift longevity risk from an individual to the population at large through the medium of the insurance company. There are three general categories of life contingencies: life only, life with minimum guarantees, and joint life (with or without minimum guarantees). *Life-only* annuities guarantee an amount of money will be paid periodically (usually monthly) to the annuitant for as long as the annuitant lives. Of the life contingency payouts, life only has the highest periodic payment and, depending on the age of the annuitant, life only may offer the highest of any annuity payout option.

Life with minimum guarantees. Although it is inherent in the nature of risk spreading that some people will appear to "win" by living a long time and others will appear to "lose" by dying relatively soon after payments commence, insurance companies offer optional minimum guarantees for those who are uncomfortable with this reality. The lowest form of guarantee, and therefore the least penalty to the amount of the monthly payout, is the guarantee to make payments for the life of the annuitant or at least until the amount of the premium (in an immediate annuity) or the account value (in a deferred annuity) has been paid out. This is known as *life with installment refund.* A variation is *life with immediate refund,* wherein the promise of the insurance company is to make periodic payments for the life of the annuitant and, should the annuitant die before the premium or account value has been paid out, refund the balance in a lump sum upon proof of death. The monthly payment in a life with installment refund will be slightly lower than the monthly payment in a life-only arrangement, and the monthly payment in a life with immediate refund will be lower than in a life with installment refund arrangement.

The next step away from life only is *life with a minimum period certain,* most commonly life with 10 or 20 years certain but available with a wide variety of minimum guarantee periods. In a life with 10 years certain arrangement ("life and 10"), the insurance company guarantees to make periodic payments for as long as the annuitant lives, but should the annuitant die before 120 monthly payments have been made, payments go to the beneficiary for the balance of the 120 months.

Joint life guarantees may be had with or without the kinds of guarantees covered above but primarily exist to make it possible for a couple to have the security of knowing neither partner can outlive their money. *Joint and survivor* (sometimes referred to as "joint and full survivor" or "joint and 100% survivor") refers to an annuity whose payments are based on the life expectancies of two or more individuals, most commonly the lives of a husband and wife. Under the terms of a joint and survivor annuity, the payout period is calculated based on the combined life expectancies of the husband and wife. The death of one spouse does not end the obligation of the insurance company to continue paying benefits to the surviving spouse. In fact, the entire basis of a joint and survivor annuity rests on the principle that payments will continue to be made regardless of which spouse survives the other. Payments under a joint and survivor annuity are lower than payments based on the life of one individual alone. Payments made under a *joint and X% survivor* arrangement would be less severely discounted because the insurance company's guarantee would be smaller than under a straight *joint and full survivor* arrangement. For example, a *joint and 50% survivor* arrangement would guarantee a certain amount to be paid periodically for as long as both of the annuitants are alive, then half that amount to be paid for as long as the survivor of them lives. This is obviously a less expensive guarantee than the promise to pay the same amount as long as either of two annuitants lives.

Annuity payments, regardless of whether from a fixed or variable deferred annuity or the purchase of an immediate annuity, are usually fixed from the point where they commence. Regardless of inflation, changes in bond and money instrument yields, or equity market performance, the amount determined at the point of annuitization is the amount that is paid out for the duration of the annuity, which may stretch into decades. In the late 1990s and early years of the twenty-first century, inflation has been an impediment to wider use of annuities for retirement income.

The insurance industry has begun to respond. It is now possible to link annuity payouts to the same financial indexes as equity-indexed annuities use during the deferral period. On the variable side, it is possible for annuity payouts to be linked to the underlying performance of stock, bond, and money market subaccounts, just as during the deferral period (variable annuitization). These relatively new developments are made possible by availability of options and financial derivatives that can be used to hedge or back up insurance companies' guarantees.

Tax Treatment of Annuities

The great attraction of deferred annuities, whether fixed or variable, is that all earnings that accrue during the deferral period are free from current income taxation. Depending on the length of a deferral period, and the income tax bracket of the owner, the effect of this tax deferral can double or even triple the value of an account at the point of surrender or annuitization. Advocates of variable annuities, especially, were able to portray this as an ideal solution to the problem of funding retirement income during the bull markets of the 1990s.

The payback is that every dollar of gain withdrawn from an annuity is treated as ordinary income rather than capital gain. While the logic of this is easy to grasp for fixed annuities, since interest is taxed as ordinary income, it can be harder for variable annuity advocates to explain (or to explain away) since it means giving up favorable capital gains treatment. As with every financial decision, the benefits of current income tax deferral must be weighed against the exposure to higher income taxation later.

Annuity payments are treated as partially excluded from income taxation, at least until the total investment in the contract has been recovered. The amount of each payment that can be excluded is determined by dividing the investment in the contract (generally, total premiums paid minus any prior nontaxable distributions) by the "expected return" under the contract and multiplying the payment by that ratio, known as the *exclusion ratio.* The expected return is determined by multiplying the amount of the payment by the remaining number of payments. That, in turn, is determined either by the terms of the contract (in the case of period certain arrangements) or by the use of life expectancy tables provided by the Internal Revenue Service. The effect of this is to spread the income tax burden over a much longer period of time than would be available with a lump-sum distribution.

As with other financial matters, tax considerations do not end with death. The full value of deferred annuities that have not been annuitized are includable in the estate of the owner at the time of the owner's death, and beneficiaries receive no stepped-basis on the gains in the contract. Some variable annuities have death benefits to accomplish the same result, however. In addition, deferral cannot continue unless the beneficiary is the spouse. In general, distributions must begin within one year of the owner's death and must be paid out over the greater of the life expectancy of the beneficiary or five years.

Private Annuities

By contrast to commercial annuities, private annuities are not paid by insurance companies but rather are arrangements between individuals by which property is exchanged for a series of payments, generally with a life contingency. Private annuities are frequently established where a property that is being exchanged is of importance to the parties (usually a parent and a child), and there is a desire to maintain control over the property at the same time that the property is being removed from the estate of the transferor. In other words, private annuities are often established where a parent removes property from his or her estate and passes it to a child in exchange for a promise to make periodic payments of an agreed amount to the parent. Fair and accurate valuation of the transferred property and amounts of the periodic payments are important to receiving desirable income tax treatment. (See also AGENTS AND BROKERS; ASSET ALLOCATION AFTER RETIREMENT; CASH FLOW PLANNING FOR RETIREES; FINANCIAL PLANNING PROCESS; WEALTH SPAN.)

Organization

National Association for Variable Annuities

References

Conners, Brian, and James W. Eckel. 1999. *Planning for the Golden Years with Variable Annuities.* Lexington, MA: Lexington House.

Shapiro, David, and J. Streiff. 2001. *Annuities.* Chicago: Dearborn Trade Publishing.

Williamson, Gordon K. 1999. *Getting Started in Annuities.* New York: John Wiley & Sons.

E. Craig MacBean

AREA AGENCIES ON AGING. See Older Americans Act.

ASSET ALLOCATION AFTER RETIREMENT, an approach to investment decision making under age-specific circumstances. During working years, when assets are most likely to be acquired, asset allocation tends to follow traditional views of portfolio structure. After some provision for liquidity or emergency funds, which (for example) could be three to nine months' cash flow needs, other financial assets normally can be considered long term, permitting the investor to take more risk with his or her portfolio. Most financial advisors agree that people in their twenties or thirties should structure their retirement portfolios into various asset classes that are diversified and that are likely over time to provide high returns (albeit with volatility), such as common stocks or equity (stock) mutual funds that do not have a fixed or stated rate of return (fixed income). Securities without fixed incomes have a higher expected rate of return and historically have outperformed fixed income assets (e.g., bonds) by about 5% per year over long periods of time. (In some years these variable return investments earn several times the returns of fixed income assets, and in other years they have negative comparable returns. But over a reasonably long period, these equity securities are expected to outperform fixed return assets.)

Many people feel that it is worth the risk of uncertain return and increased volatility in order to obtain a rate of return that approximates an additional 5% on average per year. Consider a 25-year-old saver deciding between a fixed account with a 7% return and a variable account expected to earn 12%. If this saver invests $100 per month until age 65, the fixed account will be worth $262,481. If the variable return account had been chosen, however, the account may have grown to $1,176,477, a difference of $913,996. Since year-to-year variations in the equities markets have historically averaged a higher return, it is easy to see why young savers are directed into variable return investments and why they are advised to buy and hold them for the longer term. However, there is a built-in fallacy to this kind of thinking. It is linear and assumes that the returns will be the same percentage year in and year out. As investors age, however, their ability to take advantage of the benefits of variable return securities diminishes. The nature of retirement requires liquidation of assets to provide current income, and when assets are sold, a commensurate decline in income based on a decreasing capital account also occurs.

Fear of reduced income prompts many retirees to invest in more predictable fixed return assets, but this investment strategy risks possible loss from inflation. Sixty-five-year-olds, on average, have 17.3 years left to live (15.2 years for men and 19.0 years for women). This means that 65-year-old retirees must plan for at least 20 years of retirement. If they invest only in fixed return assets, they will achieve little real portfolio growth, due to inflation. A $250,000 retirement nest egg, for example, invested in fixed accounts earning 7% will provide an income of approximately $2,000 per month for 20 years. While this may be adequate today, inflation may reduce the purchasing power of this income over time. By the twentieth year, assuming an inflation rate of 3%, the purchasing power of $2,000 will be $1,107. At 5% inflation, this monthly income would be worth only $754. Many retirees face this potential dilemma as they try to allocate their financial assets. Investment only in stocks yields no current fixed income, but investments in fixed income securities may fail to meet their needs for growth to offset the effects of inflation.

Mixed Allocations of Assets

A mixed allocation approach is called for, with some investments in fixed income assets and some portion invested in variable return assets. The question is, how much should be allocated to each type of investment, and how should this change as retirees grow older? Most retirees tend to worry more about market risk than inflation risk and tend to buy portfolios dominated by fixed return assets. Inflation effects must be considered, however, when the planning horizon is greater than five years. As a retiree ages, inflation risk becomes less important. Proper allocation, then, requires consideration of how time affects both market risk and inflation risk.

One common guideline that some advocate in this situation is to invest a percentage equal to 100 minus the retiree's age in variable return assets: for a 62-year-old, 38% (100 minus 62) of assets; the balance in fixed income assets. By the time one reaches age 75, this percentage will drop down to 25%. As individuals grow older, their expected planning horizon becomes shorter. This reduces the significance of inflation risk, making a more conservative approach appropriate. Healthy 60-year-olds may be justified in keeping more than 40% of their portfolios in variable return assets.

The basic principle underlying all retirement planning strategies regardless of the age of the planner is diversification. Individuals who have decided that they want to put 40% of their portfolio in variable return assets and 60% in fixed income assets still must decide how to invest within these asset classes. The overwhelming majority of people should invest through some type of mutual fund rather than trying to purchase individual securities. Mutual funds provide two essential elements not readily available to the purchasers of individual assets: diversification and low transaction cost. Mutual funds offer professional management for a management fee, which eliminates the need for constant analysis by savers but are generally a bargain for small investors.

With thousands of different mutual funds from which to choose, this can be complex. There are two approaches to this problem. First, savers can narrow the funds down independently. *Fortune* and *Forbes* magazines rank the performance history of many of the top funds on a yearly basis, and the rankings are done by category. As a place to start, investors should look at investment-grade bond funds for the fixed assets and the "growth and income" common stock funds for the variable assets. These rankings are complete with phone numbers that can be called to obtain additional information. A second approach would be to work with a professional financial advisor who can assist with portfolio selection.

Both of these approaches have pitfalls. By investing without an advisor to guide decision making, investors may miss valuable growth, income, and tax information. On the other hand, when professional financial advisors are contacted, advice may be motivated by self-interest rather than what is best for the retiree. Using a "fee-only" planner can mitigate this risk. In either case, it should be remembered that financial planning decisions rarely should be made in haste. One may simply put the money in a money market fund or certificate of deposit for a few weeks or even months during the decision-making period. Taking time to gather information from several sources before funds are invested is wise. If professional help is desired, several advisors may be contacted before making a decision as to who to retain. After the initial setup of the portfolio, changes will need to be made periodically in order to adjust for changes in the expected planning horizon and to rebalance the portfolio. A valuable guideline is to consider making changes at least once a year but not more than twice a year. The annual review is a time to consider changes.

Financial planning becomes more complicated prior to and during retirement. The need for current income invalidates the typical assumptions that long-range planners use. In order to balance the market risk and inflation risk associated with postretirement planning, a mixed approach must be employed. Assets must be allocated over both fixed income assets such as bonds and variable return assets such as common stock. As a retiree grows older, the balance of these two types of assets can change. However, these problems are not insurmountable. The guidelines suggested above provide a framework that will balance portfolios to provide for current income and allow for growth to overcome problems with inflation. (See also BONDS, CASH FLOW PLANNING FOR RETIREES; EQUITY SECURITIES; FINANCIAL ADVISORS; MUTUAL FUNDS; REAL ESTATE INVESTMENTS; RISK TOLERANCE; SAVINGS INVESTMENTS; WEALTH SPAN.)

References

Bernstein, William J., and David M. Darst. 2000. *The Intelligent Asset Allocator: How to Build Your Portfolio to Maximize Returns and Minimize Risk.* New York: McGraw-Hill.

Gibson, Roger C. 2000. *Asset Allocation: Balancing Financial Risk.* 3rd ed. New York: McGraw-Hill.

Andrew Holmes

ASSET PROTECTION. See Asset Allocation after Retirement; Cash Flow Planning for Retirees; Estate Planning; Financial Advisors; Financial Counseling for Mid- to Later Life; Medicaid; Trusts; Wills.

ASSISTED LIVING, living arrangements that promote the philosophy of personal control and responsibility for frail older persons within homelike group residences. Assisted living arrangements generally include:

- Group or congregate living situations that provide room and board as well as social and recreational opportunities
- Assistance to residents who need help with personal care needs and supportive services
- Protective oversight or monitoring
- Help available around the clock and on an unscheduled basis.

As of 1998, approximately 521,000 residents lived in 11,500 U.S. facilities that were marketed or described by the administrator as assisted living or that were similar in size and services to self-described assisted living facilities (Hawes, Rose, and Phillips 1999). However, only 4,693 of these facilities provided either or both the level of services or privacy consistent with the assisted living philosophy (Hawes, Phillips, and Rose 2000). These facilities served nearly 200,000 residents. In the assisted living setting, residents remain in charge of their own lives. They exert as much responsibility as their physical and mental capacities permit, including their right to make decisions about their care and safety.

Many facilities and states that do not use the term *assisted living* have programs that meet this definition. Conversely, this definition does not include facilities that offer little personal care assistance or privacy, or nursing homes that offer institutional care, even if they describe themselves as offering assisted living. Usually, residential facilities using the term *assisted living* espouse a philosophy of maximizing resident autonomy, providing a homelike environment, meeting residents' scheduled and unscheduled needs, and minimizing the need to move. However, the degree to which their management practices reflect the philosophy may vary.

Background

Prior to the growth of assisted living, much of the discussion about reforming long-term care had focused on institutional care and centered on nursing home financing and access—how to provide nursing home care to people without impoverishing them or depleting the public treasury. Since the late 1980s, however, private developers and administrators of state programs led by Oregon have offered assisted living as a way of providing support services in a group residential environment. Assisted living offers many frail older persons appropriate care while preserving their dignity and autonomy, and in many situations, it can do so at lower cost than nursing homes or home care. Frail older persons, fearing the institutional character and loss of independence associated with life in a nursing home, have embraced the arrangements and philosophy of assisted living.

The aim of assisted living is to enable frail older persons to live as independently as possible in a homelike atmosphere. This is accomplished through building design and care practices that facilitate independent functioning and reinforce residents' autonomy, dignity, privacy, and right to make choices. The philosophy of resident independence encompasses the concept of "the dignity of risk," also advocated by members of the disability community. It asserts the rights of residents to make decisions about their care and safety that others may consider risky. It is based on the notion that psychological health and well-being should be considered along with physical safety.

Living Arrangements and Assistance

In better facilities, the design of the building reflects the philosophy of promoting independence. Residents usually live either in private rooms with baths, individual temperature controls, and doors that lock or in small apartments with kitchenettes. They often bring their own furniture. The decor and scale are homelike throughout the building, often with one or more small sitting rooms that encourage residents to visit with each other and entertain guests. Many assisted living facilities explicitly avoid fluorescent lighting, long corridors, tile floors, and the nursing stations that are associated with nursing homes. The facilities, however, typically provide handrails, wide hallways, some type of emergency call system, and grab bars and other features in bathrooms, all of which help assure physical security and promote independence. The buildings also include a laundry, central kitchen, and other areas to support the delivery of services.

Assisted living buildings vary in size and type. They may be freestanding structures expressly designed to enhance the independence of frail older persons. Many continuing care retirement communities have a campus that includes three levels of housing and services: independent housing with some social and recreational services and perhaps one communal meal, an assisted living building to which residents move when they need personal care assistance or monitoring, and a separate building for nursing care. Other structures, including large private homes, schools, hotels, and nursing homes, have been remodeled to accommodate assisted living programs. The size of the buildings ranges from those in which 15 or fewer residents live (often in remodeled homes) to those with 100 or more residents. In building new structures, many developers choose to accommodate about 30 to 70 residents, which they believe is few enough to retain some residential character but large enough to allow economies of scale in providing services.

The typical program of assistance offers help with at least some activities of daily living (ADLs)—dressing, bathing, using the toilet, transferring to and from a chair, or eating—as well as supervision of medication and protective oversight. Before moving in, the resident or a family member describes the resident's needs and works with the staff to decide what help will be provided, how, and when. Most facilities offer a standard package of services, but they differ in what they "bundle" into these packages. They may also provide additional services "in-house," if needed, but at a higher fee, or help arrange for such services, including nursing care, from a third-party provider. Residents can also obtain assistance around the clock. Other services usually available include help with arranging doctor appointments, transportation for shopping and other excursions, social and recreational activities, housekeeping, nutrition counseling, and provision for special diets. Residents' preferences are taken into account in the scheduling of services, such as help with a bath. Residents often have the option of doing their own laundry, making their beds, cleaning their apartments, and fixing tea and coffee or light meals. Relatives are also encouraged to visit and join in these tasks.

Assisted Living Compared to Other Living Arrangements

While assisted living is similar to home care, congregate housing, board and care homes, and nursing homes, it differs from those programs in significant ways.

Home Care. The minimum time block for which home care usually can be scheduled is two hours. While this is ideal for help with dressing, bathing, housekeeping, and meal preparation, two-hour time blocks are inappropriate when assistance needs to be available throughout the day and evening. Assisted living can take advantage of economies of scale by using a core staff to offer both brief periods of assistance and general oversight to a much larger group of people than can home care. For this reason, assisted living is particularly appropriate for persons without friends or relatives to supplement assistance purchased from home health agencies.

Congregate Housing. Congregate housing programs usually offer support services such as a meal a day, transportation, and housekeeping to residents living in private apartment units. Although residents may be able to obtain assistance with some ADLs, even otherwise excellent congregate housing programs may not offer protective oversight and 24-hour assistance.

Board and Care Homes. Most board and care homes offer the protective oversight, homelike atmosphere, and some of the ADL assistance available in assisted living. However, board and care homes are generally smaller than assisted living facilities and typically do not provide the level of privacy or services found in assisted living. The board and care industry has been plagued with allegations of abuse and low quality, including putting residents at risk of harm from medications errors. Meager levels of public assistance available for the low-income residents who comprise about one-half of the population in board and care homes across the country exacerbate these problems (Hawes, Wildfire, and Luk 1993). In contrast, developers of assisted living have aimed their programs at moderate- and upper-income groups. However, many quality problems have recently been found in assisted living as well. These problems are most often due to low staffing levels, inadequate staff training, and high staff turnover.

Nursing Homes. Nursing homes usually care for persons with complex or unstable medical conditions who need continuing nursing supervision. Standardization of services in nursing homes and the assignment of two or more residents to a room, while encouraging quality care and cost control, have also contributed to nursing homes' institutional and regimented atmosphere. The requirement that a nurse always be on duty enables nursing homes to serve residents with various medical needs but adds a medical orientation to nursing home life and raises costs.

Studies comparing the costs of publicly subsidized nursing homes and assisted living have reached mixed conclusions. Cost data from Oregon, the only state to mandate assisted living to serve nursing home–eligible residents, do indicate some potential for savings. Rates for Oregon's assisted living residents who receive Medicaid, all of whom are nursing home–eligible, are about two-thirds as much as Medicaid rates for Oregon's nursing home residents (Hawes, Wildfire, and Luk 1993). That assisted living is serving persons with somewhat lower levels of service needs is illustrated by the fact that 20% of Oregon's assisted living residents eventually move to nursing homes. That 80% do not need to move to nursing homes, when many are nursing home–eligible, indicates the potential savings to both Medicaid programs and private-pay residents. Some studies, however, suggest that assisted living care does not save money, because many of the individuals served in assisted living would not have entered a nursing home in the absence of Medicaid funds for assisted living because family members would have continued to care for them at home.

Private Sector Fees and Public Assistance Programs

Developers have built and marketed assisted living primarily for middle- to upper-income older persons—those able to pay $2,000 a month or more—a cost prohibitive for many older persons. According to a survey of 300 assisted living facilities in 1998, only 20% of facilities charged a single rate. The other 80% charged varying rates, depending upon room sizes or apartments or for assistance beyond the facility's standard package of services. Most of the basic monthly rates ranged between $1,100 and $2,900 per month (Hawes, Phillips, and Rose 2000). Only 7% of the residents surveyed by the National Investment Center (NIC) and the Assisted Living Federation of America (ALFA) (1998) received public assistance for services (provided through Medicaid), and only 9% received public assistance for shelter costs (provided through the federal Supplemental Security Income program).

Public assistance for low-income persons is almost always inadequate to cover charges in typical assisted living programs. The federal government provides Supplemental Security Income (SSI) payments to impoverished older and disabled persons, but the federal benefit rate was only $545 a month in 2002. Although most states and some counties provide an additional amount, the total is far short of the typical base cost of $2,000 for assisted living arrangements.

Since it began in 1965, the federal Medicaid program has subsidized care in nursing homes. States pay varying proportions of the Medicaid rate, from 21% to 50%, depending on the cost of nursing home care in the state and the per capita income in the state. States have begun recognizing that assisted living can postpone or substitute for some nursing home admissions, offering states the potential to reduce their Medicaid expenditures. In a National Academy for State Health Policy survey in 2000, Robert Mollica found that 38 states reported having approval for at least one Medicaid-sponsored program to fund services for persons in assisted living or board and care. Usually, these programs serve relatively few people or are otherwise limited in scope, but there are a few exceptions. The percentage of licensed facilities participating in Medicaid varies from a low of 2% in New Mexico to a high of 93% in Oregon (Mollica 2000). Nationwide, only 11% of assisted living administrators report that they would accept Medicaid, if available (Hawes, Phillips, and Rose 2000).

Because the cost of assisted living often exceeds residents' incomes, many residents spend down their assets to pay for assisted living. A 1999 study by the National Investment Center (NIC) found that nearly two-thirds (64%) of assisted living residents reported an annual income of less than $25,000, an amount insufficient to cover a year's stay in most assisted living facilities. Residents who had been in assisted living longer had significantly fewer net assets than newer residents, suggesting that many residents are spending down their assets.

Financing Assisted Living Construction

Several efforts, both public and private, are helping assisted living become more affordable by lowering the cost of constructing assisted living facilities. The Department of Housing and Urban Development (HUD) has two programs that subsidize developers of affordable assisted living, allowing them to provide assisted living at a lower cost to consumers. Under the first program, the Assisted Living Conversion Program, HUD allocated $50 million per year from fiscal years 2000 to 2002 to provide grants to help owners of nonprofit low-income senior housing apartments to convert dwelling units into assisted living apartments (HUD 2001). The other HUD program, Section 232 of the Federal Housing Administration's (FHA) mortgage insurance program, was extended by the 1992 Housing Act to include assisted living facilities (Section 232 already covered nursing homes and board and care homes).

A private source of financing for the construction of affordable assisted living facilities is the Coming Home Program, a program of the National Cooperative Bank (NCB) Development Corporation in partnership with the Robert Wood Johnson Foundation. The Coming Home Program is providing three-year grants of up to $300,000 to nine states to foster affordable assisted living for low-income older persons. The program focuses on rural areas, where fewer assisted living facilities are available.

A few states have implemented programs that provide funds from the Medicaid program to help nursing home owners convert all or part of a nursing home to assisted living or other supportive service, such as adult day services, or to close the nursing home and construct a new assisted living facility. The first such program was instituted in Nebraska; the program provides grants or loan guarantees to nursing homes to convert wings or entire facilities. The state estimates that the Medicaid program will recover the costs of the program over a 13-year period through reduced Medicaid spending on nursing home care (Mollica 2000).

Changes around the Corner

Stakeholders, including regulators, providers, and consumers and their advocates, continue to discuss many issues presented by this relatively new combination of housing and supportive services. Some of the issues and questions are frailty level (how much "aging in place" is appropriate for assisted living before a very frail resident needs to move to a nursing home?); living arrangements (should private rooms with baths be mandatory?); risk and autonomy (to what extent can the resident make decisions about lifestyle and care, even if the decision increases the resident's risk of health or safety problems?); flexibility of regulations (how much leeway should providers have to determine procedures in their facility?); and financing (how to make the advantages of assisted living available to persons with low income). (See also BOARD AND CARE HOMES; COMMUNITY-BASED CARE; CONTINUING CARE RETIREMENT COMMUNITIES [CCRCs]; FRAILTY PLANNING; HOME CARE SERVICES FOR OLDER ADULTS; HUD-ASSISTED RENTAL HOUSING; MEDICAID; NURSING HOMES.)

Organizations

AARP
American Association of Homes and Services for the Aging (AAHSA)
American Senior Housing Association (ASHA)
Assisted Living Federation of America (ALFA)
Consumer Consortium on Assisted Living (CCAL)
National Center of Assisted Living (NCAL)
NCB Coming Home Project

References

Hawes, Catherine, Charles D. Phillips, and Miriam Rose. 2000. *High Service or High Privacy Assisted Living Facilities, Their Residents and Staff: Results from a National Survey*. Washington, DC: Department of Health and Human Services.

Hawes, Catherine, Miriam Rose, and Charles D. Phillips. 1999. *A National Study of Assisted Living for the Frail Elderly: Results of a National Survey of Facilities*. Washington, DC: Prepared for U.S. Department of Health and Human Services.

Hawes, Catherine, Judith Wildfire, and Linda Luk. 1993. "The Regulation of Board and Care Homes: Results of a Survey of the 50 States and the District of Columbia." *National Summary, State Summaries*. Washington, DC: AARP.

Lewin-VHI Inc. 1996. *National Study of Assisted Living for the Frail Elderly: Literature Review Update*. Washington, DC: Prepared for the Office of the Assistant Secretary for Planning and Evaluation & Administration on Aging, U.S. Department of Health and Human Services.

Lutzky, Steven, Lisa Maria B. Alecxih, Jennifer Duffy, and Christina Neill. 2000. *Review of the Medicaid 1915(C) Home and Community Based Services Waiver Program Literature and Program Data*. Washington, DC: Prepared for Department of Health and Human Services, Health Care Financing Administration.

Mollica, Robert. 2000. *State Assisted Living Policy: 2000*. Portland, ME: National Academy for State Health Policy.

National Investment Center (NIC). 1999. *Income Confirmation Study of Assisted Living Residents and the Age 75+ Population: A Follow-up to the NIC National Survey of Assisted Living Residents*. Annapolis, MD: Author.

National Investment Center (NIC) and Assisted Living Federation of America (ALFA). 1998. *National Survey of Assisted Living Residents: Who Is the Customer?* Annapolis, MD: Author.

NCB Development Corporation. 2001. *Affordable Assisted Living: Backgrounder*. Available online at http://www.ncbdc.org/.

Redfoot, Donald L. 1994. "Long-Term Care Reform and the Role of Housing Finance." *Housing Policy Debate* 4: 23–25.

Regnier, Victor A. 1994. *Assisted Living Housing for the Elderly: Design Innovations from the United States and Europe*. New York: Von Nostrand Reinhold.

U.S. Department of Housing and Urban Development (HUD). 2001. "Assisted Living Conversion Program (ALCP) for Eligible Multifamily Housing Projects." *Federal Register* 66(38): 12339–60.

U.S. General Accounting Office (GAO). 1999. *Assisted Living: Quality-of-Care and Consumer Protection Issues in Four States*. Washington, DC: GAO, GAO/HEHS-99-27.

Elizabeth Clemmer
Updated by Bernadette Wright

ATTITUDES ABOUT RETIREMENT. Retirement policies and pension systems were initially implemented as a means to move older workers out of the labor force. Retirement has since evolved into a normative, anticipated life stage, one that has become an institutionalized part of most modern societies (Brown 1996). Workers look forward to retirement, actively choose to retire as soon as it is financially feasible, and once retired report high levels of satisfaction with their lives (Schulz 1995).

However, labor force advantages and disadvantages tend to influence individual retirement experiences; thus attitudes toward retirement may vary based on a number of factors. Prospective health status and income are not only identified as concerns of those contemplating retirement, but they also consistently emerge as factors associated with retirement satisfaction. Poor health is often a precursor of early retirement, and individuals with health problems are more likely to report dissatisfaction with retirement. Those with adequate financial resources, obtained through pension benefits (public and private) and savings, and who are in good health, are most likely to express positive perceptions of retirement. These key resources enable retirees to more fully pursue activities associated with the retirement lifestyle—travel and leisure, education, volunteering, and other opportunities—free from the obligations of work life. Individuals with inadequate retirement income sources and/or poor health tend toward a more pessimistic attitude about retirement. Similarly, the state of the economy and its potential impact on retirement wealth can negatively or positively impact attitudes toward retirement.

Disparities in labor force experiences by gender and ethnicity affect attitudes toward retirement. Men are generally more likely to retire due to work circumstances or job characteristics, and women are more likely to retire for personal reasons. Women's experience of work often includes delayed entry into the labor force, interruptions in participation, lower occupational job status, and lower salaries, which result in lower levels of labor force attachment and, more important, decreased income benefits in retirement. As a result, retirement not may be as attractive an option for women. Additionally, the timing of women's retirement is not often actively chosen but rather dictated by the needs or actions of others, that is, assumption of a caregiving role or retirement in conjunction with that of a husband's.

Attitudes toward retirement may also be influenced by proximity to the retirement event; individuals approaching retirement are inclined to spend more time thinking about and planning for retirement. These activities tend to reinforce positive perceptions of a pending retirement experience and are associated with postretirement levels of life satisfaction. Estimates of persons who have not thought about or planned for retirement range from 10% to 40%. Individuals who strongly identify with their occupational status and exhibit high levels of attachment to the workforce are less likely to view retirement as a positive life event and may in fact forego retirement altogether in favor of continued labor force participation. (See also BABY BOOMERS AND RETIREMENT; HISTORY OF RETIREMENT; RETIREMENT PLANNING; RETIREMENT PREPAREDNESS.)

Organizations

AARP
Employee Benefit Research Institute

References

Brown, Arnold S. 1996. *The Social Processes of Aging and Old Age*. 2nd ed. Upper Saddle River, NJ: Simon & Schuster.

Cavanaugh, John C., and Fredda Blanchard-Fields. 2002. *Adult Development and Aging*. 4th ed. Belmont, CA: Wadsworth Group.

Ekerdt, D.J., J. Hackney, K. Kosloski, and S. DeViney. 2001. "Eddies in the Stream: The Prevalence of Uncertain Plans for Retirement." *Journal of Gerontology: Psychological Sciences* 56B: S162–70.

Morgan, Leslie A., and Suzanne Kunkel. 2001. *Aging: The Social Context*. 2nd ed. Thousand Oaks, CA: Pine Forge Press.

Schulz, James H. 1995. *The Economics of Aging*. 6th ed. Westport, CT: Auburn House.

Linda Albert

ATTORNEYS, individuals who advocate on behalf of or counsel others or are employed to prepare for trials in courts of law. While elder law practice is growing more important as the population ages, there are many areas or specialties within the practice of law. A specialty involves additional study, training, or experience. A patent attorney, for example, frequently has additional training as an engineer in order to perform within the specialty area of patent law. In seeking an attorney, a client should inquire about the attorney's background to determine the level of his or her expertise in the area of specialized need. Local bar associations can also refer attorneys by specialization.

Areas of Specialization

Appellate Law. Attorneys handling litigation matters that have progressed beyond the trial level are appellate attorneys. Courts of appeal include state and federal courts, as well as the supreme courts of the states and the federal government. Generally, the party who has lost a trial is the person who appeals, although either party may need to seek an attorney who specializes in the appeals process and has taken cases before courts of appeal in the past.

Bankruptcy Law. Bankruptcy law involves dealing with the federal bankruptcy statutes, which allow individuals to reorganize and/or terminate indebtedness by declaring bankruptcy. Under this law, the rights of the bankrupt and the creditors (entities owed money by the bankrupt) must be protected. In bankruptcy law, attorneys usually specialize in representing either the bankrupt or the creditors. It is not common practice in larger jurisdictions for attorneys to represent both creditors and bankrupt individuals, although it does happen on occasion. A person seeking a bankruptcy attorney should make an effort to find an attorney who customarily represents individuals in similar situations. When seeking protection against a bankruptcy proceeding by a debtor, one should seek a creditor's bankruptcy attorney.

Business and Corporate Law. Attorneys who specialize in the area of business and corporate law practice in a wide range of areas. They typically incorporate businesses; review contracts, leases, and loan documentation; consider matters of securities law; and in general, advise business owners and managers. Because of the broad area of practice within this specialty, practitioners of business law frequently have additional training or education such as a certified public accountant (CPA) or an individual with a Master of Business Administration (M.B.A.). Business and corporate attorneys need knowledge and familiarity in the areas of banking, finance, securities law, corporate law, and general management in order to serve the interests of their business and corporate clients. They usually do not go to trial and more frequently are transactional lawyers.

Business Litigation. Attorneys specializing in business and corporate litigation are trial lawyers rather than transactional attorneys in most cases. In this specialization, as with most areas of litigation, the most important asset of a business litigator is his or her litigation experience rather than knowledge of business and corporate law. Business litigators generally sue over matters such as collections, contract law, copyright or trademark infringement, unfair business practices, or other business matters.

Construction Law. Certain lawyers specialize in the area of law related to building, renovating, remodeling, and/or demolishing residences and commercial buildings. Lawyers practicing in the area of construction law must be familiar with municipal regulations, building codes, civil engineering, soil engineering, zoning, construction financing, and local building practices. As with many areas of the law, lawyers who practice in this field are important to seek out not just for their knowledge in the legal area but also for their knowledge of how construction practices work in their geographic regions. The problem of working with a general practitioner in matters of construction law arises from the fact that frequently attorneys not familiar with construction practice are similarly unfamiliar with practical problems of dealing with local governments and other bureaucracies in matters of seeking permits, gaining approval of plans, or obtaining other required clearances.

Copyright Law. Individuals who seek to publish magazine articles, books, music, poetry, or computer software programs should work with a copyright lawyer. Copyright lawyers protect the rights of their clients who have created any form of written or performed work. Copyright lawyers often also practice trademark and patent law (see below). Copyright law, like patent law, is highly specialized and requires detailed familiarity with pertinent federal statutes.

Criminal Law. Attorneys who practice criminal law work either as prosecutors on behalf of a government body or as defense counsel on behalf of individuals accused of criminal acts. When seeking the services of a criminal attorney, it is advisable to find someone who has dealt specifically with the alleged crime. An individual accused of violating a criminal statute against drunk driving, for example, should seek an attorney who regularly defends against drunk driving charges. Lawyers who defend against particular crimes are more familiar with jury responses and more knowledgeable about the particular criminal statute that may have been violated. Criminal lawyers are trial lawyers who should be able to demonstrate prior experience before the courts in question, whether municipal, state, or federal. A lawyer who has not had criminal trial experience in the past is not a good candidate to defend in a criminal law trial.

Elder Law. Attorneys who are engaged in elder law practice are experienced in working with state and federal statutes related to Medicaid and Medicare; state and federal social services programs; estate, probate, and trust law; as well as matters related to conservatorship and retirement law. Attorneys who practice in the area of elder law are not necessarily prepared to practice in every area of law in which an older person may require assistance. Rather, this area is specialized in the specific matters referenced above.

Estate, Probate, and Trust Practice. Estate planning lawyers (often elder law practitioners) must be experienced in matters of taxation, property law, and to some extent, family law. They assist their clients in drafting wills and trusts, and in other matters related to the ownership of property, in a fashion that will minimize the cost of probate and estate taxes and fees. Attorneys who are not experienced in estate planning should not be called upon to draft complicated testamentary documents, since the area is highly specialized and an inexperienced lawyer in this field can cause unexpected transfer fees to result at the time of death.

Family Law. Family attorneys handle adoptions, separations, and divorces and help alter or amend family status. Lawyers who have never tried a divorce case should advise prospective clients that they are unfamiliar with this area of the law. A client who is sued for divorce or who intends to sue for divorce should seek the advice and counsel of a family law attorney. Of all the areas of legal practice, few are more prone to misinformation than the area of family law practice. It is best to seek out the services of a family law attorney as soon as one is needed, rather than relying on the advice of friends. Family law attorneys must also be familiar with the effects of tax law as a result of divorce.

Immigration Law. Immigration attorneys assist clients in seeking visas to foreign countries and in seeking "Green Cards" that permit foreigners to reside in the United States. They also help clients from foreign nations obtain citizenship in the United States. Immigration law is largely federal, and it is highly important that an individual wishing to assist friends or family members in obtaining work permits or temporary visas in the United States seek an immigration law attorney. Since violations of immigration law are federal offenses that carry serious penalties, the assistance of an immigration attorney is crucial to assure smooth transition for individuals needing help in these matters.

Insurance Law. Lawyers who practice in the area of insurance law specialize in a subspecialty of business and corporate law. They represent two types of clients: (1) insurance companies who wish to protect their interests from claimants and (2) individuals who seek to enforce claims against their own insurance companies or those of individuals who caused them to suffer some loss. In both cases, insurance attorneys usually have a background in both business law and trial law, with the trial experience being the more important of the two areas.

International Law. Individuals who wish to conduct business outside the United States, or who seek to transact even a single matter in a foreign country, should seek the services of an international law practitioner. These attorneys, besides having experience in international law, should have experience with the particular foreign nation. International attorneys should be familiar with the legal aspects of international law, as well as cultural and social customs of the particular nations in which business is to be conducted.

Labor Law. Labor lawyers practice in two specific areas: They represent employers, and they represent employees. As with bankruptcy law, lawyers seldom practice on both sides of labor law. Someone seeking the services of a labor attorney, therefore, should determine whether the attorney has historically represented employers or employees and be guided accordingly to the type of representation needed. Labor lawyers work both as trial lawyers and as negotiators for their clients. Some labor lawyers also work with employers to create documents such as employee handbooks and employment contracts designed to protect the employer from lawsuits by employees. Labor law involves federal statutes, including the Americans with Disabilities Act (ADA), the Employee Retirement Income Security Act (ERISA), the National Labor Relations Act (NLRA), and state laws related to workers' compensation and unemployment insurance. Labor lawyers should also be familiar with such matters as sexual harassment, age discrimination, and wrongful termination.

Patent and Trademark Law. Lawyers who practice in the area of patent and trademark law strive to protect the property rights of their clients regarding new inventions and the business symbols that their clients may develop. Patent and trademark attorneys, like copyright attorneys, frequently conduct searches to determine whether inventions or trademarks have been previously claimed or discovered by other parties. Patent and trademark attorneys may be trained as engineers prior to becoming attorneys, as they are often required to examine blueprints or product designs. An individual who seeks to obtain a patent or trademark should deal only with a specialist in this area.

Personal Injury/Medical Malpractice. Attorneys who represent clients in lawsuits concerning accidental injuries or other physical harm, including medical malpractice claims, are referred to as personal injury attorneys. Attorneys defending against personal injury lawsuits are usually defense attorneys or insurance attorneys. Most personal injury attorneys enter into contingent fee agreements, where clients agree to pay a percentage of any judgment awarded in lieu of hourly fees. Lawyers who represent injured parties usually do not work as defense attorneys or insurance attorneys. In medical malpractice litigation, the plaintiff must establish (1) that a physician-patient relationship existed, (2) the applicable standard of care (a national standard), (3) violation of the standard of care, (4) that the injury is compensable, and (5) a causal connection exists between the violation of care and the harm. The plaintiff must produce appropriate expert witnesses to substantiate the claim. Medical malpractice lawyers' charges vary widely. A contingency fee may be based upon an increasing percentage, should a case extend over a long period of time, typically from one-fourth to two-thirds of the award, although some states regulate the amount of this percentage.

Real Estate Law. People who buy or sell property may do so without the assistance of an attorney, choosing instead to work with real estate agents and brokers until settlement, which usually involves lawyers skilled in the practice of real estate law. The cost of using an agent or broker, however, ranges from 3% to 6% of the total transaction cost and is primarily justified when the agent or broker finds a buyer for the property. When a buyer is already known to the seller, however, it is generally less expensive to obtain the services of a real estate attorney, who will typically charge by the hour, rather than a percentage of the transaction. People buying property, on the other hand, are well advised to use real estate attorneys who can assist them with both the legal and transactional complexities of contracting, title work, financing, and settlement.

Tax Law. One of the most highly specialized areas of legal practice is tax law. Many lawyers in this area have additional training beyond their law degrees, evident by such degrees or designations as CPA, M.B.A., or LL.M. Few lawyers are able to practice in the area of tax law while working in other fields because the tax law is quite complex. Tax attorneys assist clients in matters of personal income tax, estate tax, corporate tax, and real estate tax. Within these and other tax areas, lawyers are more particularly trained and highly specialized in civil or criminal tax court matters.

There are many other areas of specialization in the law besides those listed in this article. Any person seeking the services of an attorney should ask for a referral to an attorney who has performed these services in the past. (See also BANKRUPTCY; BUSINESS SUCCESSION PLANNING; DURABLE POWER OF ATTORNEY; ELDER LAW PRACTICE; ESTATE PLANNING; TRUSTS; WILLS.)

References

Jones, Vivian C. 1994. *Legal Research for Non-Lawyers: A Self-Study Manual*. Washington, DC: Special Libraries Association.

Roth, Bette J., Randall W. Wulff, and Charles A. Cooper. 1993. *The Alternative Dispute Resolution Practice Guide*. New York: Lawyers Cooperative Publishing.

Donald A. Hunsberger

B

BABY BOOMERS AND RETIREMENT, financial and other later-life issues facing an increasingly large group of future older adults, all born between 1946 and 1964. In developed countries around the world, the demographic balance of generations is shifting from dominance by the young toward hegemony of the mature. In the United States specifically, the top of the population pyramid is losing its members who were raised on thrift, economic depression, and world war; replacing them are those who were raised during times of increasing consumption and deficit spending. This shift has important implications for the future retirements of today's workers.

To project how this shift might shape the retirement landscape of the future, it is important to review a few points. First, the boomers will not change as they get older; the institution of retirement will. According to the General Social Survey opinions, levels of political and social liberality or conservatism and consumer-spending habits depend not so much upon a respondent's age as they do upon a person's cohort, or year of birth. To ask, "At what age will the boomers start behaving like their parents?" is the wrong question. If today one's grandparents are very conservative, it is because they were conservative when they were younger. We now realize that boomers are going to remain consistent with themselves as they age. Those who have always been liberal will remain liberal into their sixties and beyond. In 2003, the oldest boomers will be 57 years old with a life expectancy of about 25 more years (U.S. Bureau of the Census 1999). This implies a potential retirement lasting 15 years or more. A retirement of that length can be an expensive proposition, but how much is needed to finance it is dependent on a multitude of variables.

Factors Affecting the Retirements of Boomers—Positive

Several factors shape the paths that boomers may take as they age. Below are some of the issues that will strongly affect how successful this generation will be in reaching their retirement goals. Among the many positive factors potentially affecting the boomers' retirement are changing incentives to continue working, longer life with a potentially healthier lifestyle, evidence of increasing desire to continue working, and new career opportunities.

Removal of Income Limits for Social Security. Under prior law, beneficiaries of full retirement age but still under age 70 were subject to an annual earnings limit, which was

$17,000 in 2000, beginning with the year in which they attained full retirement age. For those in this age group, the deduction was $1 for every $3 of earnings over the exempt amount. Under new law effective January 1, 2000, these earnings limitations and deductions are eliminated for those of full retirement age, beginning with the month they attain full retirement age. Boomers, therefore, can continue working full-time once they reach full retirement age and start collecting their Social Security retirement benefits at the same time without losing any of their benefit amounts. If a boomer decides to keep working full-time after full retirement age while starting to collect benefits, this effectively is a raise. If a boomer wishes to switch careers, work part-time, work part of the year, or work in some other flexible situation, he or she may do so without a concurrent reduction in total income.

Another potential implication of the removal of earnings limits is that employers may be inclined to allow more schedule flexibility for persons of full retirement age in return for paying boomers somewhat less. Effectively, boomers could be seen as subsidized workers, and as such, they would pose less of a risk to hire than older adults are traditionally, though erroneously, thought to be.

Longer Life and the Chance for a Longer, Healthy, and Active Lifestyle. Given advances in medical technology and public health, and hoping that boomers take their health into their own hands through diet modification, better habits, and exercise, this generation may be able to maintain an active lifestyle far longer than most of today's older adults.

Boomer's Inclination to Continue Working. A new AARP study (Montenegro, Fisher, and Remez 2002) on multicultural work habits of persons aged 45 plus released in September 2002 shows conclusively that people work for more than just a paycheck. Even those surveyed who initially said they were not very engaged in their work went on to express a sense of purpose, involvement, social connection, and status that was provided by employment. Given this, it is unlikely that these engaged employees will find much to attract them to the traditional retirement paradigm that involves a sudden and complete stoppage of work. It is more likely that they will decrease their hours gradually, work part-time, or retire altogether from their career to volunteer or to work in another field of interest.

Generational Momentum Might Create New Career Opportunities. With the inclination to work, with good health, and with flexible work arrangements (if they are to be had), it is likely that boomers will want to redefine what it means to be retired. It is also likely that "retirement" will include more work for pay among older adults than is presently being seen among retirees today.

Factors Affecting the Retirements of Boomers—Negative

The vision above is a positive one, but boomers face many barriers to creating a new retirement paradigm. These may include unanticipated costs of aging, the economic cost of divorce, unrestrained consumption patterns, and uncertainty surrounding health and health care.

Unanticipated Costs of Aging. Given the low level of understanding about what Medicare does and does not cover (i.e., prescription drugs or nursing home care for themselves or their parents), retirement could become very unpleasant for some of the boomers who choose to live "just for today." Whether boomers are planning to fully retire and live on their savings and pensions, or whether they plan to spend more today and extend their working life, the costs of medical care and other personal consequences of illness are greatly underestimated by boomers. Professionals assisting aging baby boomers, as well as newly widowed older adults, would do well to raise this issue when planning for adequate retirement financing.

Economic Effects of Divorce in Older Age. In 2001, about 17% of all boomers were divorced or separated, and another 12% were never married (U.S. Bureau of the Census 1999). The financial effects of divorce will weigh heavily on women, especially when there are children in the family. While child support is a part of most divorce settlements involving children, pension benefits and rights to spousal benefits from Social Security are more often forfeited by divorcing women. If a boomer ex-wife has taken time out of the workforce to raise children, her primary insurance amount calculation for Social Security will contain a number of "zero years," or years in which no earnings were recorded by Social Security but which are factored into the average lifetime earnings amount. If pension and Social Security spousal benefits have not been negotiated in the divorce, or if the couple had been married for fewer than ten years, then the woman would get nothing for that period or would get a reduced Social Security benefit when she becomes eligible for retirement (Crittenden 2001).

Unrestrained Consumption, Debt, and Insufficient Savings. Baby boomers are enthusiastic consumers but traditionally poor savers, and they are not known for achieving balance between competing short-term wants and long-term goals. This first consumer generation has not been strong in balancing competing needs such as a desire for material goods against longer-term goals such as college tuition for children or retirement for themselves. Dream vacations and indulging in housing and automobile upgrades also detract from the more mundane task of saving for retirement.

Mind-set differences between today's older adults—the depression and World War II generation—and many aging baby boomers can hardly be overemphasized. Boomers carry more debt of all kinds than any other generation before it. Types of debt include relatively high levels of revolving credit, such as credit card debt, as well as large mortgage and home equity loans. This means that baby boomers have relatively less equity in their homes, a major asset for most of today's older adults.

Lack of Ability to Work or Opportunity to Work. Personal or family illness and disability may cut short the working or active lives of boomers who experience it. If they are adequately insured and have prepared for later life, chances are they will fare well even if they become disabled. If, however, they did not save for retirement and believed they could work during later life, they may experience disappointment if or when they become physically unable to work or to maintain their former lifestyle. This negative factor falls into a larger shadow falling over boomer retirement prospects—denial.

Barriers Boomers Face When Planning Ahead

Denial can manifest itself in the form of unwillingness to plan for retirement, ill health, or frailty. It may be a factor when making ill-advised long-term investment decisions or other failures to plan financially. If boomers are suddenly unable to work, or if the economy has not treated their retirement investments as well as hoped, the quality of later life can be severely impacted. The Employee Benefit Research Institute (EBRI) retirement confidence survey has consistently found a disconnect between current retirement reality and worker expectations for future retirement. For example, 57% of workers in the 2002 survey are planning to work to beyond age 65 or "never retire," but the same survey showed that only 24% of current retirees actually worked past age 65. More important, 45% of current retirees said they retired "earlier than planned," and many of them did so because of illness, a layoff, caring for a sick family member, or other reason largely beyond their immediate control. Some boomers may not be planning for retirement because they assume they will be able to keep working, either because they have to or because they want to. This may leave them vulnerable should they find themselves retired at 66 or earlier for unforeseen reasons.

Finally, boomers cannot save what they do not have. Ten percent (10%) of boomers were at or below 125% of the poverty level in 2001. Though official poverty is often a cyclical rather than a long-term state, boomers experiencing hard times are less likely to have pensions, 401(k) plans, or other savings. If they do, they usually have less income that they can feasibly set aside as savings.

Conclusion

As a large cohort of aging adults, baby boomers have the potential political clout to effect many changes that might enhance their ability to continue working, as well as to retire successfully. Changes to the health care system, particularly in the area of long-term care, will be essential to ensure continuing improvements in health, not only for the most affluent of baby boomers but for all. In addition, the baby boomers need to use their numbers to influence business and community leaders to further understand the creative and cost-effective contributions that retirees can have on the economy. First, however, they will need to understand it themselves. It is becoming increasingly important for the baby boomers to become more fiscally savvy—the comfort of their futures will depend on it. (See also AGING AMERICA; DIVORCE AND OLDER ADULTS; HISTORY OF RETIREMENT; PENSION PLANS; RETIREMENT EXPENSE PLANNING; RETIREMENT PLANNING; U.S. PERSONAL SAVING RATE.)

Organizations

AARP
American Savings Education Council (ASEC)
Employee Benefit Research Institute (EBRI)

References

Anderson, R.N., and P.B. DeTurk. 2002. *United States Life Tables, 1999. National Vital Statistics Reports*. Vol. 50, No 6. Hyattsville, MD: National Center for Health Statistics.

Crittenden, Ann. 2001. *The Price of Motherhood*. New York: Metropolitan Books.

Davis, James A. 2000. *Testing the Demographic Theory of Attitude Change: Secular Trends in Attitudes among U.S. Householders, 1972–1996*. Chicago: NORC.

Montenegro, Xenia, Linda Fisher, and Shereen Remez. 2002. "Staying ahead of the Curve: The AARP Work and Career Study." Washington, DC: AARP.

U.S. Bureau of the Census. 1999. "Statistical Abstract of the United States." Available online at http://www.census.gov/Press_Release/www/1999/cb99-238.html.

Sarah Zapolsky

BANK ACCOUNTS. See Banking Services for the Mature Market; Individual Retirement Account (IRA); Medical Savings Accounts (MSAs) and Medical IRAs; Savings Account Trusts; Savings Investments; Wealth Span.

BANKING SERVICES FOR THE MATURE MARKET. Banking services and products offered through banks that are of interest to seniors include checking and savings accounts, online banking, travel clubs, trusts, annuities, certificates of deposit, reverse mortgages, safety deposit boxes, money orders, traveler's checks, account information, direct deposit, automated teller machines (ATMs), check balancing, bill payment, and education on estate planning, probate, and financial management. In 2000 there were more than 35 million seniors; by 2030 that number is expected to grow to 70.3 million as baby boomers reach retirement age (Administration on Aging 2002). In a survey by AARP, 37% of boomers say that personal finance tops their list of things they would like to improve. Sixty percent (60%) of the boomers are looking to centralize all their accounts in a local bank rather than a brokerage house (Dullum 2003); however, brokerage firms are leading the way in offering these centralized services.

Most seniors live independently in the community; in 2000 only 4.5% of those over 65 lived in nursing homes (Administration on Aging 2002). This older population regularly conducts banking activities. Of families headed by someone aged 55 to 64, 14.4% owned CDs with a mean value of $12,000; 14.3% owned savings bonds with a mean value of $1,000; 6.1% owned bonds with a mean value of $60,000; 26.7% owned individual stocks with a mean value of $15,000; 21.3% owned mutual funds with a mean value of $60,000; and 59.1% owned retirement accounts with a mean value of $55,000. Of families headed by someone aged 65 to 74, 29.7% owned CDs with a mean value of $20,000; 11.3% owned savings bonds with a mean value of $2,000; 3.9% owned bonds with a mean value of $71,400; 20.5% owned individual stocks with a mean value of $85,000; 19.9% owned mutual funds with a mean value of $70,000; and 44% owned retirement accounts with a mean value of $60,000. Of families headed by someone aged 75 and older, 36.5% owned CDs with a mean value of $25,000; 12.5% owned savings bonds with a mean value of $3,000, 5.7% owned bonds with a mean value of $35,000; 21.8% owned individual stocks with a mean value of $60,000; 19.5% owned mutual funds with a mean value of $70,000; and 25.7% owned retirement accounts with a mean value of $46,000 (Aizcorbe, Kennickell, and Moore 2003). In fact, customers who are 50 years old or older use four times as many retail banking services as younger patrons (Sullivan 1990).

Over 93% of those aged 55 and older own transaction accounts. Those aged 55 to 64 have a mean balance in the account of $5,500; for those aged 65 to 74 the mean is $8,000; and for those aged 75 years and above the mean is $7,300 (Aizcorbe et al. 2003). Checking account customers visit banks about three times a month, while savings account customers visit only three times a year (Massie 1990). Major exceptions to this include minority group members, women, and the oldest old (those aged 85 and older), who often have few assets, little savings, and low security benefits.

New Trends in Banking Services

Seniors are looking for free services, preferred rates, and bonuses when they choose financial institutions. For example, in November 2002, Bank of America announced a new program with free banking services and preferred rates with no penalty for early withdrawal of up to $2,500 if the senior had laddered CDs. (Laddered CDs are CDs of the same amount that mature at different times [i.e., every six months for 3 years]. Thus you take advantage of interest rate movements if you think interest rates will rise in the near future and still have access to your money. A laddering CD calculator is available at http://bankofamerica.com to show how CD customers can use laddering to increase their earning power.) The program at Bank of America also offers security protection for debit and credit cards, financial education, and special customer service ("Bank of America" 2002).

While online banking is on the rise, many seniors still want personal contact (Dixon 2003). While 85% of those who say they will definitely not go online are seniors, the number of seniors who use the Internet is growing (15% of Internet users). Currently, the wealthier and better educated seniors go online. While 13% of seniors go online at work, most seniors (84%) were encouraged by their families to go online. Forty-four percent (44%) of seniors who use the Internet get financial information and 12% use it to sell stocks. Eight percent (8%) of senior Internet users have used online banking (Fox et al. 2002).

As baby boomers retire, more and more seniors will use the Internet for travel, medical information, games, chatting, e-mail, and banking. As their mobility decreases, seniors find that it is easier to do things on the Internet (Jenkins 2002). Of the seniors aged 50 to 64 who use the Internet, 16% use online banking, 50% get financial information, and 15% sell stocks (Fox et al. 2002). The majority of these cite convenience as the reason they switched to online banking (Fox 2002).

Travel services and investment services are offered by many banks to attract seniors. Those aged 50 and older made up 80% of the luxury travel market (White 2000). Travel services offer fully planned itineraries that are geared toward seniors for day trips as well as longer vacations with people of similar interest. These can range from a visit to a nearby outlet mall to a trip to England or a cruise to Alaska, and usually a travel club representative from the bank accompanies the group. Some banks offer senior VIP customers reduced fees for investment services; some also offer financial education and retirement planning. Seniors need to be aware that investment products bought through a bank are not covered by FDIC insurance. These investments carry the same risk as investments of a similar type bought through a brokerage firm; however, the bank does offer one-stop convenience that many seniors prefer. Banks are also starting to offer branch services at retirement communities to aid seniors.

High Fees to Receive Electronic Payments

As many low-income seniors are now required to receive Social Security and Supplemental Insurance payments electronically, they are paying high fees to be able to receive checks from payday lenders and other check cashing companies rather than from banks. For example, in 1999, Corus Bank in Chicago received $1.3 million in fees from 60,000 Social Security recipients who were not customers to have checks cut and sent to a check cashing company of their choice (Woker 2000). The bank says that the recipients signed disclosures that they understood the fees involved.

High Overdraft Fees

Another area of concern to seniors is fees for overdrafts. Many banks are not automatically linking savings and checking accounts to cover insufficient funds; instead they are charging fees of up to $35 to cover these overdrafts. Since a check can be put through several times before the consumer receives notice in the mail, it is easy to accumulate

$70 to $100 in fees with one check. Since the bank takes its fees out of any money in the account, other checks may bounce. Covering overdrafts with a line of credit is also expensive (interest rates can be as high as 20%). Besides a fee for this service, banks charge daily interest until the "loan" for the overdrafts is repaid. With most banks, putting funds in the account does not automatically repay the loan. The person must tell the bank to take funds to repay the overdraft. The least expensive way to have overdraft protection is for people to link a savings and a checking account. There is a fee of $7 to $15 to transfer the funds if there is an overdraft, which is minimal compared to the other ways of handling overdrafts.

Predatory Lending

Predatory lending is another problem that seniors face. Eighty percent (80%) of seniors own their own homes and have paid off their mortgage or are close to paying off their mortgage. A recent study found that seniors were three times more likely to have sub-prime mortgages than people under the age of 35 (Calhoun et al. 2001). Lenders that charge high fees, prepayment penalties, balloon payments, and high interest rates fall into the category of predatory lenders. They target low-income seniors with loans for home repairs and improvements or as home equity loans. Loan flipping, another type of predatory lending, is making a home loan that refinances an existing home loan when the new loan does not have a tangible net benefit to the borrower.

Another type of predatory lender is the payday or check cashing company that charges a fee, which is really a disguised interest rate for services. This loan has high fees and is made without regard to the borrower's ability to repay the amount, which can cause the borrower such financial hardship that it can be almost impossible to repay the loan. For example, it may cost $20 to cash a check for $100, so the borrower will receive $80.00. The company then holds the check for up to two weeks and then cashes it. Chances are that the borrower will not have an extra $100, as many people in this situation live from paycheck to paycheck, so the borrower must write a check for $120 to have the $100 to cover the first check, thereby paying another $20 fee. This works out to an annualized interest rate of 590%!

Banking Safety

Banking safety involves several issues. One is personal security when using an ATM machine. If seniors need to do banking after hours, they need to carefully inspect the area where the ATM is located. Users want to be sure that the area is well lit and that they can be seen easily by others. Other safety issues to consider are ensuring that parking is close to the ATM and that there are no places nearby where a person can hide. Check for security cameras and never go alone. Drive-up machines are the safest, and personal identification (PIN) numbers should always be safeguarded (Mizell 1994).

Elder Financial Exploitation

Financial abuse includes mishandling, fraud, or theft of a person's income, money, accounts, assets, or property by another person, such as a family member, a friend, a paid caregiver, a neighbor, a repair person, a bogus charity, or a con artist (Virginia Department of Social Services 2002b). It may include forgery, misappropriation of cash withdrawals and other money, abuse of joint bank accounts, abuse of powers of attorney, abuse of ATMs, fraudulent use of credit cards, and illegal transfers of property. According to a 1996 study, the most common types of abuse in order of prevalence are inability to handle finances due to self-neglect, financial abuse by a substance-abusing "roommate" or boarder, someone else living off the income of a frail or confused older person, abuse by a home care worker, misappropriation of cash, and abuse of power of attorney (Sacks 1996). A survey of three banking intuitions in New York found that the types of abuse most encountered by banks were forgery, misappropriation of funds, abuse of joint accounts, and abuse of powers of attorney. Most abusers were immediate family members or other relatives (Sacks 1996).

As cognitive impairment increases with age, the oldest old are the most vulnerable to financial abuse. Many states have added financial exploitation to their legislation on elder abuse. Some states, such as Virginia, while not making it mandatory for bank employees to report a suspicious transaction, free their employees from liability if they do make reports to Adult Protective Services. A bank employee may be the first to recognize unusual activity in a senior's account. Signs of abuse may be unusual activity on a senior's account through use of an ATM, debit, or credit card. Other signs of abuse may include checks for larger-than-usual amounts, several checks written to one person, or checks where the signature or amount may have been altered. New acquaintances who take up residence with the senior may indicate another sign of abuse, especially if the senior appears afraid of the person. Requests to notarize documents to change titles or other documents in favor of a new acquaintance may indicate abuse, especially if the senior cannot articulate why the changes are being made. Eviction notices, unpaid utility bills, or concern or confusion about missing funds may be another sign that seniors do not know where money is going. Missing documents and redirected mail may be another indication of abuse (Virginia Department of Social Services 2002a).

Seniors can protect themselves by taking some of the following steps: staying socially active, documenting their financial arrangements, not giving away property in exchange for promises of lifelong care, getting to know the staff at the financial institutions that they use, being cautious of the use of joint accounts, clearly stating their intentions, including any payment provisions in any power of attorney, never signing anything they do not understand, being aware of door-to-door scams, and planning ahead for the future control of assets. The more contact seniors have with others, the more likely someone will notice a problem before it gets out of hand (Virginia Department of Social Services 2002b).

By documenting the distribution and planning for financial issues in the event of incapacity, seniors can reduce the chance of abuse. However, seniors need to choose carefully and decide whether a family member or a third party may be the best person to handle their finances. Social service agencies in some states have people to assist seniors with financial issues. Many areas have legal services to assist seniors in executing the necessary documents. When these documents are brought to the senior's financial institution, bank employees should be aware of signs of abuse.

What Banks Can Do for Seniors

Seniors are looking for free services, preferred rates, and bonuses. They are starting to participate in online banking and this participation should grow as the baby boomers retire. However, as services increase to meet these needs, the opportunities to take advantage of seniors increase. Seniors need to watch for hidden fees, and they need to be aware of safety issues at ATMs. The banking industry can assist seniors by being mindful of these issues.

In addition, it is often the banking industry that can best spot financial abuse. Institutions need to train their personnel and their customers to spot abuse. Seniors should not give their PIN number to anyone or use it where others can see it. Banking staff need to watch for strangers who accompany seniors to the bank where withdrawals are made and the money is given to the stranger. Monitoring accounts for unusual activity is another way to stop financial abuse. Having a reputation of being senior friendly should assist the banking industry in participating in this expanding market. (See also ANNUITIES; ESTATE PLANNING; LIVING WILLS; PROBATE; REVERSE MORTGAGES; SAVINGS ACCOUNT TRUSTS; SAVINGS INVESTMENTS.)

References

Administration on Aging. 2002. "A Profile of Older Americans: 2002." Available online at: http://www.aoa.dhhs.gov/aoa/stats/profile/highlights.html.

Aizcorbe, Ana M., Arthur B. Kennickell, and Kevin B. Moore. 2003. "Recent Changes in U.S. Family Finances: Evidence from the 1998 and 2001 Survey of Consumer Finances." *Federal Reserve Bulletin* (January). Available online at http://www.federalreserve.gov/pubs/bulletin/2003/0103lead.pdf.

"Bank of America Launches 'Advantage to Seniors'." 2002. *PR Newswire*, November 21.

Calhoun, Mike, Margot Saunders, Elizabeth Renauart, Mark Benson, and Sharon Hermanson. 2001. "Home Loan Protection Act: A Model State Statute." AARP Stock Number D17346 (November).

Dixon, Guy. 2003, "Online Banking Is on the Rise, But Many Like the Personal Touch." *Globe and Mail, Metro*, January 23, B5.

Dullum, Justin. 2003. "Which Way to Boom Town." *Northwestern Financial Review* 188(3): 1042–1254.

Fox, Susannah. 2002. "Online Banking." *Pew Internet Project Data Memo. Pew Internet and American Life Project.* Available online at http://www.pewinternet.org.

Fox, Susannah, Lee Raine, Elena Larsen, John Horrigan, Amanda Lenhart, and Tom Spooner. 2002. "Wired Seniors." *Pew Internet and American Life Project.* Available online at http://www.pewinternet.org.

Jenkins, Henry. 2002. "Technology Review—The Aging Net." *MIT Technology Review*, December 11.

Massie, Marcy. 1990. "Package Deal for the Mature Market." *Bottomline* (March): 79–83.

Mizell, Louis R., Jr. 1994. *Street Sense for Seniors*. New York: Berkley Publishing Group.

Sacks, Debra. 1996. "Prevention of Financial Abuse, Focus of New Institute at Brookdale Center on Aging." *Aging Magazine* 367: 86–89.

Sullivan, Michael. 1990. "Seniors Today's Hottest Market." *U.S. Banker* (June): 16–22.

Virginia Department of Social Services. 2002a. *Prevent Financial Exploitation in Virginia: A Guide for Financial Institutions*. Richmond, VA: Author.

Virginia Department of Social Services. 2002b. *Prevent Financial Exploitation in Virginia: A Guide for Seniors and Adults with a Disability*. Richmond, VA: Author.

White, Sarah. 2000. "Why Overlooking Seniors Is Old-Time (& Expensive) Thinking." *Credit Union Journal* 4(26): 12.

Woker, Chris. 2000. "Bank Accused of Flaunting CRA Says It's Giving People What They Want." *American Banker* 165(63) (March 31): 1.

Celia Ray Hayhoe and Kathleen Carlisle

BANKRUPTCY, a set of legal procedures for dealing with severe debt problems and obtaining a financial fresh start. More than 1 million Americans each year file bankruptcy cases to seek relief from debts. Older persons file for bankruptcy in fewer numbers than younger adults. They tend to be better established financially and are less likely to be involved in aggressive or risky activities. Nevertheless, tens of thousands of older Americans file for bankruptcy every year. Having debt problems and being in poverty are not the same thing, although they can, of course, coincide. A person with substantial assets, income, and a comfortable lifestyle can become financially overextended, from either a precipitous drop in income or a surge in debt. On the other hand, a person with extremely limited means may be financially stable with few or no debts.

Bankruptcy can eliminate or modify debts so as to give the petitioning debtor a financial fresh start. There are two types of bankruptcy cases ordinarily applicable to individuals. They are commonly referred to by the chapters of the U.S. Bankruptcy Code that provide for them. The first is "straight bankruptcy," or "Chapter 7." The formal name is a "liquidation" case, which refers to the possible sale of the petitioning debtor's property to raise money to pay debts. In most cases, however, little or no property is actually sold. The primary effect of nearly all Chapter 7 cases is the discharge or cancellation of some or all debts. The second type is a "debt adjustment," or "Chapter 13," case. Under Chapter 13, a debtor makes at least partial payment on debts through the court, usually over three to five years. Chapter 13 provides a method for dealing with some types of debts that would not be resolved in a Chapter 7 case. Individuals are also eligible, under certain conditions, to file a Chapter 11. This bankruptcy proceeding, a reorganization option designed primarily for corporations and other businesses (also known as Chapter 12), applies only to farmers and is relatively rare.

Bankruptcy cases are governed by federal law (Title 11, U.S. Code) and are handled in a special branch of the federal courts. Each state has one or more federal court districts, and some districts have offices in more than one city or conduct hearings in cities other than where the court offices are located.

The Bankruptcy Process

A bankruptcy case starts with the filing at an office of the bankruptcy court of a petition, which is a short request for protection under the bankruptcy law. At the same time or soon after, the petitioner also files a prescribed set of disclosure forms. The forms include lists of debts and assets, statements of income and expenses, and certain other financial information. In a Chapter 13 case, the petitioner also files a specific plan for making payments through the court. A husband and wife can file a joint petition under either chapter.

The filing triggers a sweeping court order that protects the debtor from debt collection efforts while the bankruptcy case is pending. This prohibition, known as an "automatic stay," halts legal proceedings such as lawsuits, federal and state tax collections, wage garnishments, and foreclosures. It also stops collection letters and telephone calls. With regard to many creditors, this prohibition eventually becomes permanent through a "discharge of debts" court order at the end of the bankruptcy case. Meanwhile, even creditors who are not subject to permanent discharge are still temporarily restrained by the automatic stay from attempting to collect while the case is before the court. There is one mandatory court appearance, usually about a month after the filing. The hearing is formally called a meeting of creditors, although creditors need not attend and rarely do. At the hearing, a trustee who has been appointed to review the case asks the debtor to verify under oath that the information in the filing is accurate and requests additional information as necessary.

A routine Chapter 7 case may be essentially complete at that point. If no creditor objects and the trustee does not seek to sell any of the debtor's property, the court will issue the order discharging debts and close the case, sometimes fewer than four months from the filing. In a Chapter 13 case, the debt repayment plan is submitted after the meeting of creditors for approval, or "confirmation" by the judge. The trustee makes a recommendation for or against confirmation based on his or her analysis of the legality and financial feasibility of the plan. Creditors may also object, and a hearing is held by the judge, if necessary. If the plan is confirmed, payments are made to the trustee, to be passed on to creditors. If the judge rejects the plan, the petitioner usually has three choices: amend the plan and try again, switch to a Chapter 7, or dismiss the case and deal with the debts outside of bankruptcy law.

Dischargeable and Nondischargeable Debts

Many types of debts may be discharged and eliminated in a bankruptcy case if the debtor meets the tests and requirements of the law. There are two important groups of exceptions to that rule, however. First, bankruptcy law classifies certain types of debts as not able to be discharged. Second, most liens, including real estate mortgages and automobile purchase loans, remain valid after a bankruptcy, and that often forces the debtor to keep paying that account. Nondischargeable debts include most taxes, although income taxes that have been due for at least three years are usually dischargeable if no fraud has occurred. Alimony and child support payments (past or future) owed by the debtor are not dischargeable. A debt owed by one spouse to another to balance a divorce property settlement, however, may be discharged. Student loans are not dischargeable. This rule is usually interpreted also to apply to parents or others who have cosigned a student loan.

A debt is not discharged if the creditor proves it resulted from the use of a false financial statement by the debtor or from actual fraud. A debt arising from embezzlement, larceny, or deliberate injury to property is not dischargeable, nor are criminal fines and restitution. Claims or court awards for death or personal injury from an auto accident in which the debtor was driving while impaired by alcohol or other drugs is not dischargeable. Other auto accident claims involving property damage only, or based only on ordinary negligence, are dischargeable. The process for determining if a debt is not discharged varies. A creditor seeking to block discharge of a debt on ground of fraud, embezzlement, larceny, and injury to property must object in the bankruptcy court or lose its rights. Other exceptions, including taxes, student loans, and alimony or support, require no particular steps by the creditor. Virtually any other debt or financial obligation not covered by those exceptions can be discharged in bankruptcy.

Mortgages and Liens

Real estate mortgages, automobile liens, and other liens against property of the debtor are usually not affected by a bankruptcy filing. The creditor usually retains the right to go after the property for at least partial payment of the debt. The debtor can nearly always keep the property by paying the loan as before.

Liens on household goods or similar personal property, however, which have declined in value from the original purchase price of the collateral, usually are canceled outright in the bankruptcy. So are most liens that arise from lawsuits and court judgments. When a lien does survive a bankruptcy, the debtor generally has three choices for dealing with the situation afterward:

1. The debtor can keep the collateral and keep paying the loan; home mortgages and car loans are often handled in this way.
2. The debtor can surrender the collateral and discharge the debt.
3. The debtor can attempt to negotiate new payments based on the value of the collateral. When the amount of the debt exceeds the value of the collateral, creditors are often willing to negotiate a new deal.

Bankruptcy's Effects on Property

To obtain a discharge of debts in a Chapter 7 bankruptcy case, the petitioning debtor must disclose his or her property. This allows the trustee to review it for possible sale of some items to be applied toward the petitioner's debts. In fact, however, usually little or no property is sold this way. This is because two classes of property are not subject to sale, and these exceptions often cover everything the debtor owns.

The first exception is for property subject to a lien or mortgage. For example, a debtor owning a $100,000 home free of debt would, in most states, be forced to accept a sale of the house, and some or all of the proceeds would go to creditors. If the same home were subject to a $100,000 mortgage, however, the home and mortgage would ordinarily pass through the bankruptcy case unaffected. The mortgage ties up the value of the house for the mortgage holder, leaving no value for other creditors to go after. This principle generally applies as well to automobiles and other collateralized property.

The second exception involves "exempt property" laws. These laws protect some types of property from being seized by creditors, whether in bankruptcy or outside of it. The actual exempt property rules vary greatly from state to state. In bankruptcy, the debtor may keep specific property even while unpaid debts are permanently discharged. All values for such exemption purposes are based on net value, or "equity," above the amount of any liens and are doubled for a joint husband and wife filing.

Property values in the "federal" exemptions that apply in many states provide an illustration of what is protected. The federal exemptions protect $8,700 in homestead equity; $2,775 in a motor vehicle; $9,300 in household furnishings and personal apparel; $9,300 in life insurance cash value; all Social Security benefits and nearly all pension accounts; certain other small amounts or specialized items; and $9,650 in the debtor's choice of any property, including additional amounts of the specific categories just listed.

Exempt property laws in some states are more generous, including homestead exemptions that range up to $100,000, and in a few states have no dollar limit at all. Some states, however, have property exemptions that are more limited than the federal exemptions.

Causes of Bankruptcy

Every case is different, but some of a few basic themes recur in nearly all bankruptcies. The most frequent cause is unemployment. Illness and injury are often factors as well. A sudden drop in income is the fastest way for a reasonable debt load to become unmanageable, and a significant minority of the population is vulnerable to incurring medical expenses beyond insurance benefits and/or their ability to pay directly. For a person in the workforce, medical problems can also interfere with income. Divorce or separation usually increases expenses without increasing resources. Business failures often leave an owner with substantial debts. Poor planning and irresponsible use of credit are less pervasive causes of bankruptcy than is widely assumed, but they do occur. Regardless of the origin of debt problems, some individuals endure years of collection calls and letters, and even legal proceedings, without filing or even considering bankruptcy. Others realize they are headed for serious trouble and begin to take steps toward filing bankruptcy before they actually miss a payment.

Chapter 13 Repayment Plan

Many more Chapter 7 bankruptcy cases are filed each year than Chapter 13 debt repayment cases. This is not surprising, as a Chapter 7 bankruptcy produces a prompt discharge of debts, while a Chapter 13 requires a lengthy series of payments through the court, usually over three years. There are several reasons, however, why some people choose Chapter 13.

A debtor whose property would not be fully protected by exemption laws or liens, and so would lose some property in a Chapter 7, may be able to keep that property by filing under Chapter 13. Also, Chapter 13 rules allow a debtor to catch up on and reinstate a home mortgage, even if the lender has started foreclosure and refuses to negotiate. To make this process work, the debtor must be able to make both the required original payments plus catch-up payments. A Chapter 13 filing may be used by a debtor with a recent Chapter 7 discharge. The same debtor cannot receive another Chapter 7 discharge for six years, but it is possible to file again under Chapter 13. Multiple bankruptcy filings, however, often indicate that an individual has serious underlying problems and may be in need of financial or other counseling.

A few kinds of debts that are not dischargeable in a Chapter 7 bankruptcy (including some accident and injury claims) can be discharged in a Chapter 13, even if only a small percentage is paid through the court. A debtor can also sometimes use Chapter 13 to pay a debt while preventing the creditor from going after a cosigner. In practice, however, the same result can usually be achieved with voluntary payments after a Chapter 7 filing.

Bankruptcy and Credit Ratings

Most people considering bankruptcy are concerned about their credit rating, but this should usually not be a substantial factor in the decision-making process. If debt problems are serious enough to consider bankruptcy, resolving existing debts must be the first concern. A bankruptcy filing may actually improve access to credit. It removes much current debt, which is a key factor in new credit decisions. It also assures that there will be no new Chapter 7 filing for many years. Bankruptcy debtors should bear in mind, however, that if overextended credit was a cause of the problem, taking steps toward future borrowing may be unwise. It is often assumed that a Chapter 13 repayment filing is preferable from a future-credit perspective, but there is no good reason for this belief.

Hiring a Bankruptcy Attorney

Bankruptcy is a specialized area of law. Persons with debt problems should take care to locate attorneys who are experienced in bankruptcy law. Unless the matter is urgent, comparison shopping for a lawyer is highly recommended. While it is legally possible to file without the assistance of a lawyer, the law is complex enough to make that risky. If the debtor does not have enough property or income to pay the attorney's fees, the stakes may not justify bankruptcy either.

Changes in the Bankruptcy Laws

Bankruptcy law was rewritten in 1978 and was amended from time to time during the following years. From the late 1990s to 2003, discussions about bankruptcy in the U.S. Congress have been dominated by a series of proposals backed by many large banks and credit companies. These proposals have been designed to make it more difficult for consumers to walk away from their debts. Bankruptcy reform, which has come close to congressional passage only to fail several times during the past six years, may be passed during 2003. Consumer advocates have criticized the current bill for proposing changes that are intended to prevent individuals from filing Chapter 7, force full payment of all debts in Chapter 13, remove discretionary authority from judges and trustees, and empower creditors and their attorneys with many new legal presumptions. These groups charge that the new laws dramatically shift the burden of proof onto debtors seeking debt relief, thus increasing expense and legal difficulty for all filers. They add that it will punish ordinary taxpayers who have lost jobs, health insurance, or both and will be potentially detrimental to small businesses and their ability to reorganize, while producing few benefits. Nevertheless, the controversial H.R. 975, the Abuse Prevention and Consumer Protection Act of 2003, passed the House and was placed on the Senate legislative calendar (Senate Bankruptcy Reform Bill 2003) in March of 2003. Supporters of the reform legislation agree that the window of opportunity to get the bill through the Senate will narrow with the beginning of the 2004 election season. (See also AGING INTO DEBT; ATTORNEYS; CONSUMER CREDIT; ELDER LAW PRACTICE; FINANCIAL RECOVERY IN LATER LIFE.)

Suggested Reading

Snyder, Stephen. 2000. *Credit after Bankruptcy: A Step-by-Step Action Plan to Quick and Lasting Recovery after Personal Bankruptcy*. Fishers, IN: Bellwether, Inc.

References

Elias, Stephen, Albin Renauer, Robin Leonard, and Kathleen Micho. 2002. *How to File for Chapter 7 Bankruptcy*. 10th ed. Berkeley, CA: Nolo Press.

Epstein, David G. 2002. *Bankruptcy and Related Law in a Nutshell*. 6th ed. Florence, KY: West Wadsworth.

Tabb, Charles Jordan. 1977. *The Laws of Bankruptcy*. New York: Foundation Press.

Kenneth J. Doran

BOARD AND CARE HOMES, residential settings that provide more support services than boarding or rooming houses and most congregate apartments but less than the level of care that persons receive from many assisted living facilities and nursing homes. They are usually defined as nonmedical, community-based residential settings that house two or more unrelated adults and provide room, meals, protective oversight or supervision, and some type of assistance or personal care, such as medication supervision or reminders, help with bathing, dressing, and other daily activities, organized activities, and transportation to medical appointments. With some exceptions, board and care facilities are typically small and provide residential care in a more homelike environment than nursing homes. Many are actually private homes converted to several single or shared bedrooms, while others are large, multistory buildings.

Both policymakers and older people and their families have sought to expand the range of care alternatives for persons with chronic illnesses or disabilities and those who need assistance with basic activities of daily living. Families remain the major source of such care and assistance to older adults, providing an estimated 80% of long-term care. When more care is needed or no family is available, other supports are available including in-home help, respite care, caregiver services, adult day care programs, home health care, nursing homes, and a variety of residential settings including board and care homes.

Characteristics of Board and Care

There is considerable variation across the country in the regulation, costs, and types of people who reside in board and care homes. They are known by many different names, including personal care homes, rest homes, domiciliary care homes, residential care homes, adult congregate living facilities, adult foster homes, sheltered care homes, homes for the aged, adult foster care homes, and assisted living facilities. A study by the Research Triangle Institute (RTI), under contract with the U.S. Department of Health and Human Services (DHHS), estimates that about 34,000 licensed board and care facilities house more than 600,000 residents with an equal number of residents served in unlicensed homes (HHS Press Office 1995). Thus, more than 1 million older Americans and disabled and mentally ill individuals may be living in board and care homes. Unlicensed facilities also vary greatly and include personal residences, larger multiunit retirement facilities, and assisted living facilities.

Board and care homes vary greatly in size from 2 beds in private homes to more than 1,400 beds in high-rise buildings. Most are small, with 2 to 10 beds, but the majority of board and care residents live in larger facilities. According to the RTI study, while 67% of licensed homes have 10 or fewer beds, nearly two-thirds of residents are in homes with 11 or more beds (Hawes, Mor, and Brown 1994). Less than 25 residents reside in 87% of this type of facility (Damron-Rodriguez, Harada, and McGuire 2001). One-third reside in facilities with 51 or more beds. More than half reside in unlicensed homes with more than 51 beds. These larger unlicensed homes include assisted living facilities and retirement communities that provide meals, protective oversight, and some services. More than 80% of licensed homes are for-profit facilities. Eighty percent (80%) of unlicensed homes are for-profit facilities and 40% are nonprofit.

In addition to size, board and care homes differ in terms of physical environment, monthly charges, services, and mix of residents. They vary from three to four residents to a room in modest surroundings to private apartments with plush settings. Most have common areas with community or living rooms and outside sitting areas, although only about half allow residents access to a kitchen to fix a snack. Homes also vary in atmosphere, some being more institutional, and others more homelike. Some encourage residents to bring their own furniture, others only a few possessions.

Homes also vary in mix of residents. Some house mainly older residents. Data from the ten-state RTI study found that more than 60% of the 3,200 residents were 75 or older; more than 30% were 85 or older. Other homes, though not specifically licensed as such, mainly house persons with persistent mental illness or developmental disabilities. In states where the use of psychiatric hospitals has been reduced, board and care homes are an important alternative for the mentally ill. Other homes include frail older persons; persons with cognitive impairment; dementia, such as Alzheimer's disease; mental illness; and developmental disabilities.

Board and care homes are also coping with more complex problems. Forty-three percent (43%) report that they care for residents with alcohol abuse problems, and 14% report drug abuse problems. Some states also find that board and care homes are increasingly used to provide shelter for persons who have been homeless (Hawes, Mor, and Brown 1994). The care needs of the residents also vary. A recent study of two California board and care homes found that 75% of the residents required help with their medications, 52% used aids for walking, and 29% needed bathing assistance (Damron-Rodriguez, Harada, and McGuire 2001).

To meet the needs of this mix of residents, board and care homes offer a wide range of services. More than 90% of licensed homes report providing three meals a day, laundry, some personal care such as bathing and dressing, storage, and supervision and assistance with administration of medications. More than 80% of the licensed homes report providing organized activities, recreational trips, and transportation to medical appointments. Only 25% report providing nursing care by a licensed nurse, but half report that outside agencies provide nursing care. Homes vary on whether residents who need nursing care may stay in the home. Some states, such as Florida and Oregon, allow daily nursing care to be provided in some classes of board and care homes, while others limit the services such homes may provide.

One key characteristic of board and care homes is what Damron-Rodriguez and colleagues call "relatively open boundaries" (2001). Compared to nursing home placement, which typically follows hospitalization, residents can move in and out of board and care facilities from their own homes or from health and social services. This is partly due to the fact that reimbursement for this level of care is mostly private.

Payment and Regulation

Regulation of board and care homes is largely a state responsibility, and each state sets its own standards. Unlike nursing homes, no federal quality of care and life or safety standards exist for board and care homes, nor is there any federal policy on payment. As a result, in most states, care is paid by the residents or their families and, in some cases, the federal Supplemental Security Income (SSI) program. SSI, available to persons who are poor and aged, blind, or disabled, is the main source of public funds for board and care, although some states also use Medicaid funds to pay for some services to residents, usually through waiver programs with strict eligibility criteria.

The RTI study for DHHS found that, in 1993, 81% of the SSI rates with state supplements ranged from $400 per month to $700 per month. These monthly rates generally covered room, board, personal laundry, special diets, and assistance with eating, dressing, and toileting. However, in about one-fifth of the licensed homes, there was an additional charge if the resident needed a special diet or personal assistance with eating, dressing, and toileting, and three-fourths of the homes charged extra for incontinence supplies. Among unlicensed homes, almost half charged extra for special diets, 35% added charges for personal laundry, and 30% charged extra if the resident needed help with personal care. Private pay rates ranged from $600 per month to $4,200 per month; 74% of the rates were between $800 and $4,200 per month (Hawes, Mor, and Brown 1994). According to information on the AARP Web site, rates range from $350 to $3,000 per month (AARP 2003), but costs remain a function of location; for example, a board and care home in Santa Barbara, California, will cost significantly more than one in Lubbock, Texas. In any case, board and care homes cost approximately half of nursing homes and are considered quite cost-effective for those who need 24-hour supervision without skilled care.

Just as there is tremendous variability across homes and across states in terms of payment policies, considerable variation is found across the states in the nature of the regulatory system established to ensure resident safety, quality of care, and quality of life. In California, for example, board and care homes fall under the same regulations as assisted living facilities. There, board and care homes that house older adults (60 and older) are called residential care facilities (RCFs) or residential care facilities for the elderly (RCFEs). Inspection of homes ranges from monthly in one state to every 18 to 24 months in another, although a majority of states inspect homes once a year. Some notify homes in advance of inspection, while others conduct unannounced inspections. Some use nurses or social workers to inspect homes, while others rely on generalists or sanitarians. Fire departments inspect all licensed homes in all states. Since regulations and their enforcements differ so significantly from state to state, it is essential that consumers considering board and care as an option check with their state licensing office for local information.

Information for Consumers

The variability across homes and states offers many positive possibilities to consumers but also makes gathering and evaluating information prior to selecting a board and care home absolutely essential. Consumers can choose small homes with a more personal environment, large facilities offering a wide range of services, a shared room, or a private apartment. They can seek homes with a relatively homogenous set of residents or homes with a mix of younger and older persons having a range of conditions and needs. They can select homes that provide minimal assistance or a wide range of services that will address changes in the needs of the resident. Choices include homes with protective and specialized environments and homes that offer a less structured environment and greater autonomy.

Consumers and their families should consider what aspects of the environment—physical setting and amenities, services provided, and philosophy about care—are most important. They should also consider how the home will address changing needs over time and what will happen if private funds are exhausted and help from public programs, such as SSI or Medicaid, is needed to pay for care. Thus, the consumer and his or her family may wish to know the following information in advance:

- What range of services does the home offer, and is there an additional charge for any of them?
- What activities are available? Does the home arrange transportation to senior centers, shopping, entertainment, and medical appointments?
- What autonomy and choices are available? Do residents decide about bedtime? Can they fix a meal or eat a snack? Can residents close their door for privacy? Do staff knock on the door before entering the room? Is there assigned seating at meals? Must residents get permission to leave the facility for the day? What are the policies on visiting hours?
- Is there a residents' council that participates in setting policies and addressing problems or complaints? Is there a residents' bill of rights?
- How will a temporary illness or change in condition requiring more assistance or nursing care be handled?
- Does the home have an existing arrangement with a home health agency or temporary nursing service, and if so, what is the reputation of that agency?
- Will the home allow hospice care if the resident has a terminal illness and wishes to remain in the home until death?
- What is the home's policy and practice on the use of physical restraints?
- If the resident needs help taking medications, who in the home provides such assistance or supervision, and what are their qualifications?
- What does the home do to help residents maintain their maximum physical, social, and cognitive functioning?
- What is the resident mix?
- What is the monthly rate? What does it cover? What is extra? What happens if the resident changes from private pay to SSI or some other public payment?
- What is the home's policy on discharging residents?
- Who licenses or regulates the home? Who acts on complaints or helps resolve problems that may arise?

Other important considerations are suggested on the Seniors-site Web site (2003) and include the following:

- Will living in a board and care home provide residents with the independence, privacy, and security wanted?
- How often is housekeeping and laundry done? Does laundry service mean personal laundry as well as linen service?
- Is the home accessible to public transportation, places of worship, and shopping?
- Will the board and care home be able to meet special dietary needs?
- Can residents use their own furnishings?
- Is there a living room, TV room, or room for social activities?
- Are pets permitted?
- Is there just one telephone, or is there an option for a private phone?
- Are bathrooms private or shared?
- Is there a common area or extra bedroom for guests?
- Are there locks on the individual rooms?
- Is it possible to avoid climbing stairs, if difficult for you?

- Is the home in compliance with state and local standards for fire safety and health?
- To what extent does management assume responsibility for the security of personal belongings?

Several agencies or groups help consumers and their families evaluate homes and make choices, and they often have local chapters and guides. Long-term care ombudsmen, well known for their important and positive role in nursing homes, can be accessed through local or area agencies on aging and visit residents in board and care homes to help resolve problems or complaints. The National Citizens' Coalition for Nursing Home Reform (NCCNHR) has become increasingly active in helping consumers and their families with issues related to board and care. Finally, state licensing agencies and national- and state-level associations representing board and care homes can provide information and address complaints filed or problems brought before them.

Consumers can also find help on the Internet. There are numerous Web sites that provide information on varying residential care facilities and guides for older adults and families as they make important care decisions. For example, search for "housing," "residential care facilities," "board and care homes," "senior housing," or any similar term on global search engines such as Yahoo® or Google®. Or go directly to Web sites for organizations such as AARP, Alzheimer's Association, professional associations such as the American Association of Homes and Services for the Aging or the Assisted Living Federation of America, or government agencies such as the Department of Health and Human Services, State Aging Units, or local Area Agencies on Aging. Other organizations that will provide information and assistance include American Health Care Association, Assisted Living Facilities Association of America, National Association of State Long-Term Care Ombudsman Programs, National Citizens' Coalition for Nursing Home Reform, and Older Women's League. (See also ASSISTED LIVING; BABY BOOMERS AND RETIREMENT; COMMUNITY-BASED CARE; FRAILTY PLANNING; HUD-ASSISTED RENTAL HOUSING; NURSING HOMES.)

Organizations

AARP
Helpguide
Seniors-Site

References

AARP. 2003. "Housing Options for Older People." Washington, DC: Author. Available online at http://www.aarp.org/confacts/housing/housingoptions.html.

Clark, R.F., J. Turek-Brezina, C. Chu, and C. Hawes. 1994. "Licensed Board and Care Homes: Preliminary Findings from the 1991 National Health Provider Inventory." U.S. Department of Health and Human Services, Office of the Assistant Secretary for Planning and Evaluation, April 11, 1994.

Damron-Rodriguez, J.A., N. Harada, and J. McGuire. 2001. "Residential Care Facilities for the Elderly: Toward Understanding Their Place in Community Based Long–Term Care." *Journal of Housing for the Elderly* 15(1–2): 43–56.

Hawes, C., V. Mor, and F. Brown. 1994. "The Effect of Regulation on Quality of Care in Board and Care Homes: Results from a 10-State Study." Paper presented at the annual meeting of the Gerontological Society of America, Atlanta, GA.

HHS Press Office. 1995. "HHS Releases Report on Board and Care Regulations." Washington, DC: Author.

Seniors-site.com. 2003. "Board and Care Homes for Senior Citizens." Available online at http://seniors-site.com/housingm/boardcar.html.

Catherine Hawes
Updated by Monika White

BONDS, financial contracts between borrowers (issuers) and lenders (bondholders) in which the borrower agrees to repay a loan with interest according to a prearranged timetable. Bonds are medium- to long-term (7 to 30 years) negotiable debt securities. They provide funds to governments, government agencies, government bodies (states and municipalities), supranational organizations such as the World Bank, and corporations. Bonds differ from other loan contracts because they are brought to market by investment banks for issuers and are then traded in the financial markets. Bonds are well suited to retired investors wanting a steady cash income stream over long periods of time.

Until the 1970s, bond investing was uncomplicated, with most investors pursuing simple buy-and-hold strategies. Investors needing to sell their bonds benefited from stable bond prices. Defaults were rare because borrowers were of high-quality credit, and these factors combined to make bonds fairly safe investments. Since the 1970s, however, investing in bonds has become more complex due to greater price volatility, a decline in the credit quality of borrowers, and a spate of bond market innovations. While bonds can still be safe investments, greater care is needed in selecting them.

The Basic Bond Contract

The most common type of bond is a promise by the issuer to make payments of interest over the term of the bond and to repay the principal (face amount) of the bond when it becomes due. If the bond is purchased at a price below the face value, the yield to maturity (return on investment) is greater than the stated interest rate. If the bond is purchased at a price above the face value, the yield to maturity is less than the stated interest rate.

Additional bond features are provided in the bond indenture, the loan agreement between the issuer and those who buy the bonds. One feature is that a bond issue is secured by specific assets, or that it is unsecured and backed only by the earning power of the borrower. Another feature is seniority, that is, how far up in the queue of claimants the bondholder stands in the event of default. The borrower may have the right to pay off the bond before its maturity date, known as the call feature, or be obliged to repay the bond gradually, according to a timetable, rather than on the maturity date. In addition to these features, the indenture may include any number of protective covenants, which are detailed promises designed to protect lenders. Compliance with all terms of the indenture is monitored by the trustee, usually a bank.

Certain bond features do not typically appear in the indenture: tax treatment, credit quality, and marketability. Tax treatment depends on the characteristics of both the borrower and lender, making generalizations difficult. Interest income is usually taxed as ordinary income in the period received, although interest from bonds issued by some government units and in certain geographic areas may be exempt from taxes. Capital gain is taxed only if realized.

Higher rates of return are required from less creditworthy borrowers as compensation for bearing the risk of default. To aid investors in credit quality judgments, borrowers pay a bond-rating agency to assess the likelihood of default. The leading bond-rating agencies, Moody's and Standard and Poor's (S&P), use similar standards and rating schemes. Both agencies categorize bonds as either "investment grade" or "speculative grade," also known as junk bonds. Default is unlikely on the former, whereas default is more likely, or has already occurred, on the latter. Within these broad categories the agencies assign finer ratings. The agencies continually monitor borrowers for changes in credit quality and may upgrade or downgrade bonds as situations change.

A final bond feature not covered in the indenture is marketability. Although a few bond issues are traded on exchanges such as the New York Stock Exchange, most are traded in over-the-counter markets by bond dealers. A bond dealer stands ready to buy bonds at a price called the "bid price" and to sell bonds at a higher price called the "ask price." The difference, the "bid-ask spread," is the transaction cost a bondholder pays when buying or selling bonds. Whether a bond can be sold quickly at a fair price depends mainly upon the average daily trading volume in the bond issue. Trading volumes range from heavy to thin.

Bond Prices, Returns, and Risks

An investor who wants to sell a bond prior to maturity must be concerned with bond prices and how they relate to bond returns. Although the price, return, and risk properties of bonds cannot be fully detailed without the use of mathematics, the basics are easily described.

Bonds earn their returns in two ways: interest (the income yield) and value changes (the capital gains yield). Since interest payments are fixed, fluctuations are reflected in the current price an investor is willing to pay for the bond. A simplified illustration is useful. Suppose an investor buys a ten-year, $1,000 par-value bond with a 6% interest rate (coupon). If the market interest has increased from 6% to 8% since the bond was purchased, the bond's value (price) will decrease from $1,000 to $864.10. A decrease in market interest, for example, to 5%, will have the opposite effect. The $1,000 bond will become more valuable and increase to $1,135.90.

To use another example, if the market return of a 20-year, $1,000 bond with a 10% coupon declines from 10% to 8%, the bond's value (price) will rise from $1,000 to $1,197.93. The longer the term of a bond, as the example shows, the more sensitive is its price to changes in required return. Hence, a 2% change in required return produces a larger price change in the 20-year bond than the 10-year bond ($197.93 versus $135.90).

There are several risks of investment in bonds. Interest rate risk is the uncertainty in a bond's return due to uncertainty about future required market returns. An investor who buys a bond knows the interest income from the bond but faces the risk that future market increases could reduce the value of the bond. This is a problem if the investor needs to sell the bond unexpectedly. This form of interest rate risk is called price risk, which increases with a bond's term to maturity (duration). Although an investor can minimize exposure to price risk by investing in bonds with short durations, this strategy exposes the investor to another form of interest rate risk, reinvestment risk.

An investor in short-term bonds must find new bonds when old ones mature. Market changes may force the investor to accept new bonds with lower rates of interest. Unfortunately, an investor can minimize exposure to reinvestment risk only by investing in longer-term bonds and, thereby, increasing exposure to price risk.

Additionally, bonds are prone to inflation risk. Returns earned by bonds with given terms to maturity reflect a consensus forecast of the average annual rate of inflation expected during that term. Actual inflation rates may differ substantially from expectations, however. An unexpected increase in the inflation rate reduces the purchasing power of bond income and, hence, the effective (or real) return from a bond.

Default risk, that is, the risk that the borrower will fail to make a payment of interest or principal, is another type of risk. Borrowers more prone to default must offer bonds with higher coupons. Subsequent changes in the financial condition of the issuer, as tracked by bond rating agencies, may affect the return investors require to hold the bonds and, hence, their market price.

Most bonds are also subject to prepayment risk, the risk that the borrower will repay the loan early. Prepayments occur most often in the wake of a general decline in interest rates, when borrowers can obtain new loans at lower rates. Prepayments force bond investors to seek new investments at a time when bond returns are less favorable. A final form of risk is liquidity risk, the risk that an investor will be unable to sell a bond quickly at a fair price. Liquidity risk is inversely related to the volume of daily trading in the bonds and varies considerably by bond type and by issuer.

Major Bond Issuers

Major issuers of bonds held by private individuals include the U.S. Treasury, corporations, municipal governments, and specialized mortgage lenders. Bonds of these issuers differ mainly in their credit quality, tax treatment, and marketability.

The U.S. Treasury sells both marketable and nonmarketable bonds. Treasury bonds with terms of between two and ten years are called Treasury notes. The minimum denomination for marketable Treasury bonds is $1,000. Backed by the taxing power of the U.S. government, Treasury bonds are virtually free of default risk. Interest income is subject to federal income tax but not state and local income tax. Marketable Treasury bonds are actively traded in "thick" markets. Nonmarketable Treasury bonds include U.S. Savings Bonds, which are issued in eight denominations from $50 to $10,000 and typically are held by small investors.

Like the U.S. Treasury, corporations sell both marketable and nonmarketable bonds. (Mortgage bonds, debentures, subordinated debentures, and convertible bonds are special types of corporate bonds). In contrast to stockholders, bondholders are not owners, have no voice in corporate governance, and have no claim on corporate income beyond the interest and principal payments stipulated in the bond indenture. Most corporate bonds have $1,000 par values and their interest is subject to income tax. Most marketable corporate bonds trade relatively infrequently, making them less liquid than Treasury bonds.

Until the late 1970s, only large corporations with unblemished credit records could sell bonds, with the result that most corporate bonds were of investment grade. During the 1980s, however, bond investors became willing to accept greater default risk in return for higher coupons. This change in investor sentiment led to bond selling by corporations whose creditworthiness warranted speculative bond grades. The evolution of the so-called junk bond market was arguably the most important bond market innovation of the 1980s.

Until the October 1987 stock market crash, investors holding well-diversified junk bond portfolios enjoyed returns that more than compensated for the default risk of the bonds. Since then, returns have been substantially lower.

Municipal bonds are bonds sold by state and local governments to finance such projects as road building and school construction. Municipal bonds fall into two broad categories: general obligation bonds backed by the taxing powers of the issuing government, and revenue bonds backed by the projects financed. Municipal bonds sell in minimum denominations of $5,000. Interest income is exempt from federal income tax and is usually exempt from state income tax when the bondholder resides in the state of the issue. Municipal bonds are prone to default risk; consequently, municipalities pay to have their bonds rated. Daily trading volumes range from moderately high for recent, large offerings to low for older and smaller offerings.

Bonds backed by mortgages have become increasingly popular since their development in the 1970s. Pass-throughs and collateralized mortgage obligations, or CMOs, are special types of mortgage-backed bonds. Most mortgage-backed bonds are issued by one of three federal agencies: the Government National Mortgage Association, the Federal National Mortgage Association, and the Federal Home Loan Mortgage Corporation. These agencies buy mortgages and sell bonds whose payments are based on the mortgage payments. Thus, mortgage-backed bonds are much like shares in a mutual fund. Minimum denominations are $25,000. Interest income from mortgage-backed bonds is taxed as ordinary income. Because these three federal agencies have the implicit guarantee of the U.S. federal government, mortgage-backed bonds issued by them are virtually free of default risk. Mortgage-backed bonds issued by these agencies are actively traded.

Investment Strategies

The choice of an investment strategy hinges on the investor's investment objective. Three common investment objectives are income generation, total return maximization, and capital protection. Different objectives involve different trade-offs between the two components of bond return and the five types of risk.

Investors seeking stable incomes are more concerned with the income component of bond returns than with the capital gains component. Investors with this objective should probably favor a buy-and-hold strategy, buying and holding bonds with high coupons, low default risk, and low prepayment risk. In practical terms, this means gravitating toward longer-term, high-grade Treasury, corporate, municipal, and mortgage-backed bonds.

Investors seeking maximum total return give equal weight to the income and capital gains components of bond return. Total return maximization requires the assumption of substantial risks. Maximizing income return probably requires a willingness to consider high-coupon, speculative-grade corporate and municipal bonds, which subject the investor to default risk. Maximizing capital gains return probably requires a willingness to realize capital gains and cut capital losses by selling "winners" and "losers" at appropriate times, transactions that subject the investor to liquidity risk and reinvestment risk. Capital gains returns can sometimes be enhanced by altering the duration of a portfolio to take advantage of changes in investors' required returns on bonds. However, in light of the relatively low historical return on bond portfolios generally, especially in inflation-adjusted terms, investors seeking to maximize total return would do well to consider investing in common stocks instead of bonds.

Investors striving to protect the value of their portfolios are more concerned with the possibility of capital losses than with generating income. Investors with this objective should probably focus on high-quality, shorter-term bonds, thereby minimizing possible losses from default risk and the price component of interest rate risk. In practical terms, this probably means selecting shorter-term Treasury, corporate, municipal, and mortgage-backed bonds.

A relatively recent bond market development is the growth of bond mutual funds. Similar to equity mutual funds, bond mutual funds purchase bonds and sell shares representing proportional ownership in the underlying bonds. Bond funds tend to specialize in a particular type of bond (Treasury, corporate, municipal, or mortgage-backed) and a particular term to maturity (short-term, intermediate-term, or long-term). Bond funds aid in the construction of diversified bond portfolios, since shares in bond funds can be purchased for amounts far smaller than the minimum denominations of most types of bonds. Greater diversity also potentially reduces exposure to interest rate risk, default risk, and prepayment risk. Bond funds also tend to reduce liquidity risk, since shares of bond funds trade more actively than do the underlying bonds. Although bond funds offer investors new opportunities to reduce risk, these funds are by no means free of risk. Investors should select bond funds with investment objectives compatible with their own. (See also ASSET ALLOCATION AFTER RETIREMENT; INVESTOR EDUCATION; MUTUAL FUNDS; RISK TOLERANCE; U.S. SAVINGS BONDS; WEALTH SPAN.)

References

Fabozzi, Frank J., ed. 1991. *The Handbook of Fixed Income Securities*. 3rd ed. Homewood, IL: Dow Jones–Irwin.

Logue, Dennis E., ed. 1995. *The WG&L Handbook of Financial Markets*. Cincinnati, OH: South-Western Publishing.

Thau, Annette. 1995. *The Bond Book*. Chicago: Probus Publishing.

Karlyn Mitchell

BROKERS. See Agents and Brokers.

BUDGET TECHNIQUES. See Cash Flow Planning for Retirees; Financial Advisors.

BUSINESS SUCCESSION PLANNING, a process by which management and ownership of a business entity are transferred from one person or group to another, thus allowing the business to continue. The process may become complicated when transferors and transferees are members of the same family. Factors such as equality and fairness may prevail over business factors such as experience, technical ability, and accountability. Business succession has a gerontological component since a high percentage of businesses are transferred because the owner would like to retire, is concerned about obtaining funds for retirement, or wishes to transfer the responsibility to the next generation.

Only recently has the emotional aspect of business succession planning been recognized by practitioners. Since many problems in the construction of a successful business plan are legal and financial, successful technicians in this field tend to be attorneys and financial advisors. A client, especially the founder of the enterprise, tends to identify with the company. This strong identification may account for both the reluctance of entrepreneurs to retire and the observed, shortened life expectancy of those who do.

The business succession planning process involves two areas that should be considered separately: (1) family and ownership and (2) issues concerning business management. If ownership of the business will be transferred within the family, issues include stock distribution to children, equal stock rights, selling rights, and rights to employment. None of these, however, relates solely to the efficient, profitable operation of the enterprise. These issues concern continuation of a successful family relationship, but if not addressed as an integral part of the planning, the successful continuation of the business may be impossible.

Ownership succession raises other issues, including control of the business, the protection of nonvoting or minority shareholders, company philosophy regarding income distribution, compensation, and prerequisites for active versus inactive shareholders demanding high dividends. Transfer of ownership may require significant amounts of cash and sophisticated tax planning and other technical assistance. Within a family situation, the parties seeking to justify a low value for tax purposes but fair market value for interfamily transfers complicate the problem. Tax law is designed to frustrate efforts by entrepreneurs selling their businesses to family members for less than fair market value. If the business is to be sold to other than a family member, fair market value is, of course, the appropriate price. In either case, the source of cash and method of payment are critical to the success of a succession plan.

Another consideration in an ownership succession plan is time. Business owners frequently believe they have completed a succession plan when they have instead executed a "buy/sell" agreement. These agreements deal with ownership but in most cases do not address problems incident to the family or to ownership systems. Most important, buy/sell agreements are contingency plans, and they provide for the evolution of stock interests when some event (e.g., death, disability, or retirement) occurs. They do not address the more complex problems of transition necessary for a successful succession plan.

Management succession issues may conflict with family ownership arrangements. Successful management depends on accountability. Few family businesses establish job descriptions for family members or conduct performance evaluations or reviews. In today's competitive environment, management must have the power to establish performance criteria and to enforce these standards. In family businesses, questions arise regarding power to establish criteria and enforce standards. Compensation strategies for successful businesses will be based on accomplishments rather than on family ties.

Retirement Planning

A critical element in the decision by a business owner to devise a succession plan may be whether he or she has adequate sources of retirement income, independent of the enterprise. The retirement decision involves psychological and economic factors. For many entrepreneurs, their businesses are central to their lives; the mortality component associated with retirement planning may prevent effective business succession planning. Therefore, if the succession plan is designed to become effective when the business owner retires, instead of during working years when the business owner can plan to use the proceeds to acquire a new business or to diversify investments, the development of a retirement strategy may be essential for the succession plan itself.

The psychological component of this strategy must take into account the identification problem through a period of mentoring and task transferal. The time for actual transfer of management responsibilities (not necessarily simultaneous with the transfer of control) should be fixed, and the entrepreneur/founder should thereafter act only as counselor.

When the retiring party fails to create a new focus for the energies that have brought business success, internal conflict and crisis may result. It is recommended that retirees phase into retirement using volunteer work, politics, travel, sports, or education as replacement activities for work. The key is to avoid the shock of a sudden retirement.

Financial Aspects of Business Succession Plans

If the business is to be sold, a cash purchase presents fewest problems for the entrepreneur when the sum is sufficient to create adequate retirement cash flows. When ownership transfer is to be accomplished through gifts, installment payments, or sophisticated transfer arrangements, certain issues must be addressed. They include the cash flow needs of the entrepreneur, future inflation, and the extent to which other assets, income potential, and qualified plan investments exist.

A strategic plan for business succession overarches considerations of retirement security and psychological adjustment. Here, considerations of wealth transfer, family equity, management ability, accountability, and tax efficiency must be harmonized. The technical assistance of experienced tax and legal advisors is valuable. Where there are competing interests within a family, it may also be prudent to retain the services of a business psychologist to help the parties understand how they may best contribute to the success of the family enterprise.

In summary, addressing tax and technical legal issues is essential to the success of a business succession plan, but the parties must also recognize the emotional component that is frequently present in these transactions. Matters of control, asset balancing, retirement security, and personal identification can become threshold considerations that must be addressed before the process can begin. Beginning the process as early as possible can minimize the emotional concerns and allow development of the planning in a deliberative fashion. (See also ATTORNEYS; ENTREPRENEURSHIP; FINANCIAL ADVISORS; WORKING RETIREES.)

References

Alcorn, P. 1982. *Success and Survival in the Family-Owned Business.* New York: McGraw-Hill.

Chasman, Herbert D. 1983. *Who Gets the Business?* Rockville Center, NY: Farnsworth Publishing.

Cohn, Mike. 1992. *Passing the Torch.* New York: McGraw-Hill.

Danco, L. 1975. *Beyond Survival.* Cleveland, OH: Center for Family Business.

Drucker, P.F. 1985. *Innovation and Entrepreneurship.* New York: Harper & Row.

Hollander, B.S. 1983. "Family-Owned Business as a System: A Case Study of the Interaction of Family, Task, and Marketplace Components." Ph.D. dissertation, School of Education, University of Pittsburgh.

Lansberg, I. 1985. "The Succession Conspiracy: Mapping Resistances to Succession Planning in First-Generation Family Firms." Unpublished paper, Yale University.

Rosenblatt, P.C., L. de Mik, R.M. Anderson, and P.A. Johnson. 1985. *The Family in Business:*

Understanding and Dealing with the Challenges Entrepreneurial Families Face. San Francisco, CA: Jossey-Bass.
Ward, John L. 1987. *Keeping the Family Business Healthy*. San Francisco, CA: Jossey-Bass.

David J. Tolan

C

CAPITAL GAIN, positive change in the value of a capital asset over a specified time period. All assets owned, except for a few business assets, are termed capital assets. When an asset is sold and the owner receives income or profit in excess of the purchase price plus costs, capital gain is realized and taxes are paid. Under the most recent tax law, the Taxpayer Relief Act of 1997, the tax rate applied depends upon:

1. *Type of assets sold.* Qualifying for the lowest rates are stocks, bonds, mutual funds, and other securities. Taxed at a slightly higher rate are business or investment real estate, collectibles, and depreciation.
2. *Cost basis.* The original price paid for an investment in the capital asset (including commissions). If realized capital losses exceed realized capital gains, the excess can be offset against other income up to $3,000 per year.
3. *The length of time the assets are held before being sold and income level.* There are three holding periods for capital assets sold: those held for less than a year are considered *short term*, those held for more than a year but less than five years are considered *long term*, and those held for more than five years are considered *super long term*. Short-term capital gains are taxed at ordinary income tax rates, while long- and super-long-term capital gains receive preferential tax treatment. If an individual is in the 15% ordinary income tax bracket, long-term capital gains are taxed at a reduced rate of 10%, while super-long-term capital gains are taxed at an even more reduced rate of 8%. If an income tax bracket greater than 15% applies, then long-term and super-long-term capital gains are taxed at 20% and 18% rates, respectively. For the 18% tax rate to apply on super-long-term capital gains, the assets must have been purchased on or after January 1, 2001. For assets purchased before that date, the 20% tax rate applies.

Long-Term Capital Gain on Homes

For many people, the single largest capital gain transaction is usually the sale of a principal place of residence. This occurs when the home is sold for more than the original purchase price plus the cost of any improvements. For most homeowners, the Taxpayer Relief Act of 1997 effectively eliminates capital gains taxes on the sale of their homes by exempting from taxation gains of up to $500,000 for couples filing jointly ($250,000 if filing singly). To be eligible for the exemption, the home in question should be the principal place of residence and occupied for at least two years in the five years prior to the sale. This is not a one-time exemption. It is available once every two years. (See also BONDS; EQUITY SECURITIES; ESTATE PLANNING; FINANCIAL ADVISORS; MUTUAL FUNDS; REAL ESTATE INVESTMENT; RELIGIOUS GIVING BY OLDER ADULTS; TAXPAYER ISSUES OF OLDER ADULTS.)

References

Gitman, Lawrence J., and Michael D. Joehnk. 2002. *Fundamentals of Investing*. 8th ed. Boston, MA: Addison-Wesley.

Ho, Kwok, Grady Perdue, and Chris Robinson. 1999. *Personal Financial Planning*. North York, Ontario: Captus Press.

Keown, Arthur J. 2001. *Personal Finance*. Upper Saddle River, NJ: Prentice Hall.

Ganas K. Rakes

CASH BALANCE PENSION PLANS, employer-sponsored defined benefit pension plans in which the benefit is defined by account value rather than monthly lifetime retirement income. Cash balance plans are often referred to as "hybrids" because they have some of the characteristics of traditional "defined benefit" (DB) pension plans and some of the characteristics of "defined contribution" (DC) plans, such as 401(k). In general, traditional defined benefit plans promise qualified employees an income benefit for life (or some other period) starting at "normal retirement age," without regard to how much (or little) the employer must contribute to the plan to fund the benefit. Defined contribution plans, on the other hand, promise only how much the employer will contribute to a qualified employee's account from time to time until the employee retires but they make no promises with regard to investment earnings or results, let alone a monthly income benefit for life.

Cash balance plans have some of the characteristics of both. They promise a defined benefit but define it in terms of a hypothetical account balance rather than an income stream at retirement. As with a 401(k) defined contribution plan, cash balance plan benefits are typically expressed in terms of an individual pension account balance so that an employee can understand exactly what the employer is depositing toward his or her retirement annually and what the account value is after earnings have been credited. Cash balance plans, however, still meet the same Employee Retirement Income Security Act (ERISA) minimum funding, vesting, and participation standards that other defined benefit plans are required to meet. And like other traditional DB plans, they are guaranteed by the Pension Benefit Guaranty Corporation (PBGC), a protection that is generally highly valued by employees.

In addition to expressing benefits in terms of an account value, cash balance plans are like defined contribution plans in that they offer benefit portability through the availability of lump-sum payments or tax-free "roll-overs" to an Individual Retirement Account (IRA) or a subsequent employer's pension plan after changing jobs or retirement.

Two key attributes distinguish a cash balance plan from a defined contribution plan. One is that the investment decisions—and risks—are the responsibility of the employer, not individual employees. The investment earnings allocated each year are based on a formula defined by the plan document. These investment credits are not directly tied to actual investment results with plan assets. So, with respect to this portion of their retirement funds, employees are insulated from any investment gains or losses whatsoever. Employees will receive the stated investment credit each year, regardless of the performance of the market or the employer's actual investment results, whether better or worse than the plan formula.

The other factor that distinguishes cash balance plans from defined contribution plans is the availability of payouts as a series of monthly payments for life. Cash balance plans must offer employees the ability to convert their account balances to lifetime annuities, although nearly all employers offering such programs allow (and speak in terms of) single lump-sum distributions as well. While both defined benefit and cash balance plans are required to offer payment of an employee's benefit in a series of monthly payments for life, the emphasis on account balance as opposed to lifetime income can lead an employee retiring from a cash balance plan to take the lump sum and expose himself or herself to the risk that the money will not last as long as life does.

Since Bank of America pioneered the concept of a cash balance pension plan in 1985, there has been a growing trend toward the adoption of these "hybrid" retirement programs. Employers are continuing to move away from "paternalistic"-type employee benefits in which the ultimate payout takes the form of a life annuity. They are also eliminating historical policies that provide employees with retirement benefits for life.

For corporate-sponsored retirement plans, this has meant an increased emphasis on the payment of benefits in the form of lump-sum distributions (e.g., the payout of the total benefit in one single payment). It has also sparked the rethinking of retirement benefits offered by many employers, some of which have substituted cash balance pension plans for defined benefit plans. More than $330 billion in assets has been transferred from traditional pension programs to these hybrid-type plans over the past two decades (Williamson 1999). In fact, these plans have grown so popular that at least 22 of the Fortune 100 companies have implemented such a program for some or all of their employees (Williamson 1999). Another 300 or more firms are said to be waiting in line for approvals as soon as the Treasury Department issues new regulations and lifts its moratorium on plan approvals, which is scheduled to happen in 2003. That doesn't count those that have made the conversion without waiting for Internal Revenue Service (IRS) approval.

The need for new regulations came in the wake of high-profile corporate plan conversions. In such cases, employees cried "foul" after being informed of cuts in long-term employees' projected pension benefits. Some employees were told they would lose almost two-thirds of what they had been counting on for their retirement planning due to the conversion. This was further aggravated by "wear-away" periods—numbers of years after the conversion during which long-term employees would have to work without any additional contribution to their cash balance plan because their existing benefit, derived from the defined benefit plan in which they had been participating, was greater than what they would have accrued had the cash balance plan been in effect from the beginning of their employment. The ensuing congressional hearings, class action lawsuits (in which the courts ultimately backed employees over employers), and charges of age discrimination led the IRS to declare a moratorium on issuing new approvals of cash balance pension plans.

In December 2002, the U.S. Treasury Department issued some long-awaited guidance to employers about cash balance plans. These proposed regulations, issued under Internal Revenue Code Section 411 (b)(1)(H), prohibit age discrimination in benefit accruals and are fairly comprehensive in nature. Although a public hearing on the regulations was held in April 2003, the rules are not yet final as this article goes to press.

In essence, the regulations generally indicate that a company cannot directly or indirectly affect a participant's benefit accrual based on age. The result is that future conversions to cash balance plans will likely provide transition credits to older and longer-service workers to make up for any "lost" benefits created by the conversion to a cash balance plan. A secondary result is that employers will likely put more emphasis on eliminating the "wear-away" affect that sometimes occurs when the opening balance is calculated at the time of conversion. Not everyone is satisfied with the proposed regulations, however; over 200 members of Congress have signed a letter asking President George Bush to direct the Treasury to scrap them and start over again with more sensitivity to older workers.

The problem is not cash balance plans in and of themselves but rather what happens to employees—and especially middle-age to older employees with long service to an employer—in the event of a conversion from a traditional defined benefit pension plan to a cash balance plan. When a company decides to alter its retirement plan—or even considers doing so—employees can (and do) get nervous. The uncertainties surrounding a major change in company benefits are understandable, and companies themselves often have a lot of questions about the best way to make those changes. Cash balance conversions can be particularly complex and sensitive, especially when it comes to older employees. Changing benefits later in an employee's career can generate mistrust and suspicion. To successfully undertake the move to this new type of plan requires care, planning, and a great deal of communication among all parties concerned. All of that being said, however, there are structural differences between traditional defined benefit plans and cash balance plans that necessarily work against long-service, middle-age to older employees in the event of a conversion.

Given that a typical defined benefit pension formula is some factor times final compensation (or final average compensation) times *number of years of service*, it is apparent why this is so. The biggest variable is the number of years of service. An employee who stays with one employer for an entire career may have a multiplier as large as 25 or 30 or more. Further, an employee who stays with one employer for 25 or 30 years is likely to have received a lot of raises, and so the high multiplier for number of years of service is applied to a high compensation or average compensation number. For this reason, traditional defined benefit pension plans can be seen to favor older, long-term workers, and conversions of traditional plans to cash balance plans will result in real losses to those employees.

On the other hand, an employee who shifts jobs even only every 7 to 10 years or so will not have a very big multiplier in a traditional DB plan. According to statistics published by the Employee Benefit Research Institute, only 12% of employees work a complete career (e.g., 30 years or more) with a single company (EBRI 1999). For the 88% of Americans who do switch jobs, benefits are frozen each time they change jobs, and there are no subsequent increased results from the defined benefit pension formula due to long service or higher pay. As a result, a mobile employee who switches jobs just twice during a career will find that his or her defined benefit pension is significantly lower than that of a similarly situated employee who stays with the same employer for the long haul.

In contrast, a portable cash balance plan can be seen as the best of both worlds for both the mobile employee and his or her employer. The mobile employee gets benefit credits and investment credits every year, can see and identify them clearly, and take them along if (when) he or she changes jobs—all free of investment risk and backed by the Pension Benefit Guaranty Corporation. From the employer's perspective, no more keeping track of ex-employees for 20 or 30 years to pay them a relatively small monthly benefit when they reach normal retirement age. No more uncertainty about how long retired employees will live, which means no more guessing what their pension liability *really* is. Cash balance plans result in greater certainty of cost for employers, although they do not necessarily result in a reduction of real economic cost.

In the near term, many employers may see a temporary decrease in their pension expense as reported on their financial statements. These results are attributable to accounting anomalies affecting how pension expense is recorded for traditional and cash balance plans. This short-term accounting impact sometimes creates an erroneous impression that an apparently more generous plan is somehow less expensive. The reality is this: Better benefits cost more. The long-term economic impact is often an increase in employer costs but more predictable expenses. In summary, recent history indicates that cash balance conversions can be particularly complex and sensitive, especially when it comes to older employees. Changing benefits later in an employee's career can generate mistrust and suspicion. To successfully undertake the move to this new type of plan requires care, planning, and a great deal of communication among all parties concerned. How to take care of older, long-service employees in the wake of a conversion is where the controversy about cash balance pension plans can be found. (See also AGE DISCRIMINATION IN EMPLOYMENT ACT (ADEA), DEFINED BENEFIT PENSION PLAN; DEFINED CONTRIBUTION PLAN; PENSION PLAN; RETIREMENT PLANNING.)

References

Campbell, Sharon. 1996. *EBRI Special Report 32/Issue Brief Number 171*. Washington, DC: EBRI, March.

Daniel, Teresa A. 2000. *Cash Balance Pension Plans: A Practical Primer*. Washington, DC: International Foundation of Employee Benefit Plans.

Demby, Elayne Robertson. 1999. "Cash-Balancing Act." *Plan Sponsor* 7(1) (February). Washington, DC: EBRI. Available online at http://www.ebri.org.

Employee Benefit Research Institute. "Retirement Patterns and Bridge Jobs in the 1990s." Available online at http://www.ebri.org/ibex/ib206.htm.

Inglis, R. Evan, and Richard R. Joss. 1999. "Smoothing the Way for Cash Balance Plans." *HR Magazine* (December).

Maury, Mary, and Victoria Shoaf. 2001. "The Effects of Adopting Cash-Balance Pension Plans." *Business Horizons* (March).

McCarthy, E.I. 2000. "Staying Off the Cover of Time." *Journal of Accountancy* (February).

Quick, Carol. 1999. "An Overview of Cash Balance Plans." *EBRI Notes* 20(7) (July).

Williamson, Christine. 1999. "Cash Balance Catches Fire." *Pension & Investments* 27 (May): 11.

Teri Daniel

CASH FLOW PLANNING FOR RETIREES, the process by which the flow of income necessary to sustain a given standard of living in retirement is identified and financed.

It is perhaps the most critical part of retirement planning. Cash flow planning for retirees depends crucially on two factors: (1) the resource constraints a retiree faces in terms of assets and other sources of income and (2) the desires and needs a retiree has for spending in retirement. Both of these, in turn, depend to a great degree on when the planning is done.

While cash flow planning is of clear importance to retirees, it is of even greater importance to preretirees. By the time a person retires, the resource constraints he or she will face as a retiree are typically firmly in place. Some modification of these financial constraints may be possible in cases where a return to work is possible; however, in many cases this is not feasible. For preretirees, decisions with regard to saving or spending for current consumption will play a critical role in determining the constraints that will be faced later in retirement. Intelligent investing, asset allocation, and luck (good and bad) each have a role in determining financial constraints in retirement, but the determination of how much to save is the most critical variable. It is difficult, if not impossible, for preretirees to make optimal saving decisions without a firm idea of their cash flow needs in retirement. Without paying some attention to cash flow planning in retirement, preretirees may make decisions that result in resource constraints that are much more restrictive than they need to be or end up with constraints that are too slack, resulting in unnecessarily forgone spending when young and a waste of resources when old.

Identifying a Retirement Standard of Living

There are at least two schools of thought with regard to the basic principles involved in planning for retirement spending. The first, and most common, approach poses the problem as a seemingly simple determination of the income needs of a retiree relative to preretirement income. This is typically expressed as a "replacement rate," in which a retiree targets a given fraction of his or her preretirement income level as an amount adequate to sustain a desired lifestyle without working. Often, a particular level of income is given as a rule of thumb (e.g., 80% of preretirement income). While this rule appears to provide simple and easily communicated guidance, it masks several aspects of the complexity of the problem. At least two questions left unanswered by such rules of thumb are: (1) Why is 80% (or any other figure) the "right" number? and (2) How, exactly, does a dollar of accumulated assets get transformed into a stream of income at the point of retirement?

A second, perhaps preferable, approach to retirement cash flow planning attempts to rectify the first deficiency by being much more careful about the determination of the spending desires of retirees instead of spending being determined by income level. This approach involves a highly detailed determination of the spending needs and desires of the retiree and his or her household. While many financial professionals unfortunately consider such analysis unglamorous and unexciting work, it is perhaps the most basic and critically important form of financial planning. Such a determination of cash flow needs or desires typically includes a detailed estimation of living expenses, including items such as dining and groceries, mortgage or rental payments, health, life, and long-term care insurance premium payments, and predicable one-time expenditures (such as large planned gifts or outlays). Expected annual or lump-sum expenditures on other items, such as travel, clothing, and replacement of large durables, are also tallied and cataloged.

Additional Considerations

In addition, anticipated future rates of increase or decrease in living expenses (due to inflation or other considerations) must be estimated and described and the projected needed amounts "grossed up" to account for estimated future income tax rates. Sustaining the purchasing power of the income received—accounting for inflation—is the first variable that must be dealt with. Inflation will not be a major issue if death occurs shortly after retirement, but increasing life expectancies suggest this is a significant matter. Inflation can best be built into this projecting needs phase of cash flow planning rather than in the later process of determining sources and amounts of cash flow and an appropriate investment profile. What matters most is that it only be done once—and not accounted for twice.

Grossing up is the process of calculating how much gross income is needed at a projected effective tax rate to arrive at a needed amount of income. For example, it takes $1,250 at a 20% effective tax rate to have $1,000 to pay for living expenses. How one projects and coordinates the inflation and taxation factors is an important but inexact exercise, and often the advice of a financial advisor is especially desirable for this step.

Finally, another category of expense must be included: considerations such as providing a bequest to heirs, making a charitable donation to other beneficiaries, or creating a reserve for emergencies. This step will affect the calculation of assets that are available to supply the necessary income. To make an effective assessment of how to finance cash flow needs in retirement, a detailed description of all of these needs, and other planned expenditures, is critical. These calculations produce a detailed pattern of expected expenditures over the retiree's lifetime and that of his or her spouse and dependents.

Financing Projected Cash Flow Needs

Once the cash flows to be financed are determined, whether via a detailed version of the determination of planned expenditures or the simpler "rule of thumb approach," the question of how each $1 of assets will be turned into an income flow must be addressed. How much income will each dollar generate, and for how long? This is the basic issue of longevity risk (the risk that a person will live either beyond, or not until, their "life expectancy"). This source of uncertainty presents perhaps the most significant challenge for cash flow planning in retirement.

Fortunately, the most significant source of income for most retirees, Social Security, is structured to overcome both longevity risk and the eroding effects of inflation. Income payments continue as long as retirees or dependents are alive to receive them. In other words, longevity risk is not a factor in Social Security income flows. In addition, Social Security income payments are indexed to price inflation, and thus this income is not subject to erosion by high inflation. The second most common source of cash flow after retirement, traditional company pensions (called "defined benefit" pensions), also enable retirees to receive an income stream that will last at least until their death. In some cases, continuing income payments are made to dependents after the death of the covered worker. In most cases, the income payments available through employer-provided defined benefit pensions are not explicitly tied to inflation.

For some people, Social Security and traditional pension benefits provide the basic foundation from which most retirement expenditures will be funded. For those who are not able to fund their expenditures from these two sources alone, other resources saved for retirement must be tapped. Other assets, accumulated either inside a tax-preferred savings account such as an Individual Retirement Account (IRA) or a 401(k)-type pension plan, are increasingly necessary for financing retirement spending. Efficient use of these assets to fund an income stream is an important issue.

In much of the literature directed at financial planners and their more knowledgeable clients, the only mechanism considered for the liquidation of accumulated balances to finance expenditures is a process of systematic or periodic withdrawals (Bengen 1994; Pye 2000). Researchers have analyzed the sustainability of various patterns of withdrawals over long periods of time, and their results may be seen by many as surprising: while the sustainability of systematic income withdrawals varies with asset type, the rate at which one can safely liquidate such assets over a long period is far below that which is typically assumed by some individuals and even some financial advisors. For example, the study by Pye (2000) finds that a withdrawal rate of 4% over even a ten-year period has only a 92% chance of success.

Basically, these results suggest that if future rates of return on financial assets are similar to past returns, one must spend at low rates and conserve for the possibility of a long expenditure period and even modest rates of inflation in retirement. If a person lives a long time in retirement, the amount of assets left for bequests or other purposes will be substantially reduced.

If, on the other hand, a person does not live a long time in retirement, the consequences of longevity risk are that funds and assets will be left as unspent, unplanned (and in some cases constitute an undesired) bequest. It is important to note that this risk is entirely separate from financial, or market, risk. Choosing a combination of risky or risk-free assets in a portfolio will certainly affect total financial risk and total expected return on the level of assets available to a retiree, but such planning will not necessarily affect longevity risk. Even if a retiree could obtain a very high, guaranteed rate of return on accumulated assets, he or she could still spend too much, or too little, as a result of not knowing how long he or she may need to spend.

More recent research on retirement cash flow focuses on alternatives to systematic withdrawals for financing retirement cash flows and on immediate life annuities in particular. Immediate life annuities are an insurance product through which individuals can convert an asset or lump sum into an income stream that is paid to them (and/or to a spouse partner or other beneficiary) as long as they live. These vehicles enable those with 401(k) or other accumulated assets to obtain a benefit similar to that of a "traditional" company pension.

The basic rationale for the use of life annuities for this purpose is explained in an article that is now over 35 years old (Yaari 1965). This theoretical paper shows that in the absence of an overriding bequest motive, and even reasonable cost assumptions, rational, risk-averse individuals would exclusively use a life-contingent annuity arrangement to fund consumption expenditures. This results because under these assumptions as long as one is alive and continues to enjoy spending, the annuity vehicle effectively provides a higher rate of total return. When a bequest motive is introduced, the result changes, but it is not completely reversed. Because of the desire to leave a bequest, assets also have value when one is no longer alive. It follows that individuals then rationally hold back some assets from the life-contingent "annuity pool" in order to finance their bequests. As a consequence, they only "partially annuitize" a portfolio of assets.

Recent results, in particular those of Ameriks, Veres, and Warshawsky (2001), and more recently, Ibboston (2002), illustrate that given real-world assumptions and costs, the use of immediate life annuities (i.e., partial annuitization) can provide a means for hedging longevity risk, thereby increasing the likelihood and size of funds being left unannuitized while funding a retirement cash flow. Immediate life annuities can therefore provide a means for individuals to plan more effectively for the desired use and disposition of their assets for financing cash flow in retirement. Immediate life annuities can efficiently finance stable periodic income needs, while unannuitized assets can be set aside and managed appropriately for emergency or contingency planning and bequests.

There has as of yet been surprisingly little practical research related to the determination of the optimal level of annuitized and unannuitized assets for the financing of cash flows in retirement and the optimal management of those assets. Part of this is a result of the fact that there are many complex issues surrounding the use of annuities in retirement. These include the critical issue of cost. The cost issues are perhaps most clearly addressed in a recent article by Mitchell et al. (1999).

In addition, there is an issue of timing. Because immediate annuity purchases are irreversible, there may be a value to postponing their use, especially for younger individuals (Milevsky and Young 2002). As self-managed retirement account balances begin to account for more and more of the financial resources dedicated to generating cash flow in retirement, it seems clear that the appropriate use of annuities and other mechanisms of financing retirement will need to receive far greater attention.

Because there are few effective rules of thumb, in general, the cash flow planning for retirees is a challenge that can only be tackled by careful and thorough financial planning, judicious allocation and management of assets, and appropriate use of the vehicles available to hedge longevity risk. (See also ASSET ALLOCATION AFTER RETIREMENT; RETIREMENT EXPENSE PLANNING; RETIREMENT PLANNING; RETIREMENT PLANNING SOFTWARE; WEALTH SPAN.)

References

Ameriks, John, Robert Veres, and Mark J. Warshawsky. 2001. "Making Retirement Income Last a Lifetime." *Journal of Financial Planning* 14:60–76.

Bengen, William P. 1994. "Determining Withdrawal Rates Using Historical Data." *Journal of Financial Planning* 14–24.

Ibbotson Inc. 2002. "The Role of Immediate Annuities in Retirement." Available online at http://www.ibbotson.com/default.asp.

Milevsky, Moshe, and Virginia R. Young. 2002. "Optimal Asset Allocation and the Real Option to Delay Annuitization: It's Not Now or Never." Working Paper, York University.

Mitchell, Olivia S., James M. Poterba, Mark J. Warshawsky, and Jeffrey R. Brown. 1999. "New Evidence on the Money's Worth of Individual Annuities." *American Economic Review* 89: 1299–1318.

Pye, Gordon B. 2000. "Sustainable Investment Withdrawals." *Journal of Portfolio Management* (Summer): 73–83.

Yaari, Menahem E. 1965. "Uncertain Lifetime, Life Insurance, and the Theory of the Consumer." *Review of Economic Studies* 32: 137–50.

John Ameriks

CHARITABLE CONTRIBUTIONS, gifts made to eligible organizations consistent with existing laws and designed to benefit society from an educational, religious, moral, physical, or social standpoint.

One characteristic of American society is its array of nonprofit institutions. Writing nearly 200 years ago in *Democracy in America,* Alexis de Tocqueville observed upon visiting the United States:

> Americans of all ages, all stations in life, and all types of disposition are forever forming associations. . . . [They] combine to give fetes, found seminaries, build churches, distribute books, and send missionaries to the antipodes. Hospitals, prisons, and schools take shape in that way. . . . In every case, at the head of any new undertaking, where in France you would find the government or in England some territorial magistrate, in the United States you are sure to find an association.

Today, U.S. colleges and universities, hospitals, schools, zoos, museums, and other institutions are admired worldwide. One factor that makes these institutions unique is that so many of them are supported primarily by voluntary contributions of cash and property from private citizens. This system of voluntary support for nonprofit institutions is sometimes characterized as a parallel to the private enterprise economic system.

Why We Give

Contributions are encouraged by such widely varied motivations as the affection one feels for his or her college, the gratitude of a patient treated in a nonprofit hospital, the compassion of a person whose loved one has been lost to a dreaded disease for which a cure is being sought, or the deep feelings a churchgoer holds for his or her religion. While individual motivations differ, one important incentive encouraging charitable giving is the tax treatment of charitable contributions in the United States.

The most fundamental tax incentive is the income tax charitable deduction. Amounts given to qualified charitable organizations can be deducted from the donor's income in computing his or her income tax. There are a number of detailed limitations, but for most donors who itemize their deductions, amounts given to charity are deductible up to one-half of their income. Any excess over the amount deductible in a given year may be carried over and deducted in each of the five subsequent taxable years.

Contributors Must Have Receipts

All tax deductions must be proven since the Internal Revenue Service is understandably skeptical of the taxpayer who has no evidence to support a claimed deduction. Charitable contributions, however, are subject to even more stringent rules in this regard.

Donors' deductions for contributions of $250 or more may be disallowed unless they have timely receipts from their donees stating the amount contributed (or, in the case of property contributions, a description of the contributed property), plus a description and the estimated value of any goods or services provided to the donee in consideration of his or her contribution. If no goods or services are given to the donor, the receipt must state that fact. This latter rule is designed to prevent donors from claiming deductions for amounts that are really purchases rather than contributions. An example would be a payment of $1,000 to a symphony orchestra organization for a fund-raising event, where the donor received the right to attend a concert and a postconcert dinner; if the value of the concert and dinner totals $250, the donor's deduction is limited to $750, and the receipt must tell him so.

Many individuals give freely of their time, talents, and money. These contributions of services and other volunteer time are not deductible, although volunteers may deduct any out-of-pocket expenses incurred in rendering services to a charitable organization. Blood donors likewise receive no tax benefits.

Planned Giving: More for the Money

In addition to a straightforward gift of cash or property, there are other ways to structure charitable contributions so as to provide substantial benefits to the donor and the recipient. This approach, often referred to as planned giving, generally involves contributions that produce an income stream to the donor, followed by an eventual transfer to a charitable beneficiary. The term *planned giving* refers to gifts other than simple cash donations and is subject to a number of sophisticated rules. Planned giving transfers can offer particularly attractive benefits to persons who are either retired or planning for their retirement. Several planned giving vehicles are designed specifically for donors who, like retirees or prospective retirees, want to make a charitable gift but are also concerned about their income.

Charitable Remainder Trusts (CRTs)

These are trusts that make distributions to the donor or another beneficiary for life, or for a term of up to 20 years, then turn the remaining trust property to a charitable beneficiary. There are two types of CRTs. The charitable remainder unitrust pays a stated percentage (at least 5%) of the trust corpus to the donor or other beneficiary each year. Thus, if the value of the trust assets doubles, the current payout will also double, and if the value of the trust declines, the distributions likewise go down. The other type, the charitable remainder annuity trust, pays out a fixed amount to its current beneficiaries each year for as long as the trust continues. Some donors like the certainty of a fixed payout, while others prefer the potentially increasing income provided by the unitrust alternative.

Upon creating a CRT, the donor receives a current income deduction equal to the actuarial value of the charitable remainder interest in the trust. If the trust is funded with appreciated property (i.e., property that would produce a capital gain and hence a capital gain tax if the donor sold it instead of contributing it), an additional benefit is available. Because the CRT is exempt from income tax, this capital gain tax will be avoided if the property is transferred to the trust and then sold by the trustee. Since 1997, a CRT will not qualify for either of these benefits unless the value of the charitable remainder interest in the trust is at least 10% of the total trust assets.

Pooled Income Funds

The CRT can produce dramatic results but may be impractical for smaller gifts, since donors must create and maintain a trust with the help of attorneys knowledgeable in this area. There is annual upkeep as well, for the trust must file annual income tax returns and perhaps pay trustee's fees and other expenses as well. These expenses may be justified if the donor is contemplating a fairly large gift of $50,000 or more since the donor can customize the trust to fit his or her plans.

This expense is avoided when a donor uses a pooled income fund operated by a charity in lieu of creating a trust. The fund pools together the contributions of many donors into a single investment fund that pays income to the donors for life and at the donor's death distributes the donor's share to the charity that maintains it. As with the CRT, the donor receives a charitable tax deduction for the actuarial value of the charity's interest in the donor's contribution.

The expense of creating and maintaining a pooled income fund is borne by the fund's sponsoring charity. The donor signs a one-page instrument of transfer and sends it back to the charity with a contribution. Most funds have a minimum contribution, usually $5,000. The fund is usually managed by a skilled investment manager at no cost to the donor.

While the pooled income fund resembles a mutual fund, it is actually very different. Many planned giving vehicles resemble investments, but they are not investments, and this is important to remember. All of the tax benefits flow from the pooled fund or trust because the property contributed has been given irrevocably to a charitable organization. This is the opposite of an investment, which the purchaser owns and can sell or leave to children or other private beneficiaries.

Charitable Gift Annuities

The charitable gift annuity is a different arrangement that produces a result much like the CRT or the pooled income fund. Instead of a trust or fund, the charity and the donor enter into a private annuity arrangement. The donor gives the charity cash or property and receives in exchange the charity's promise to pay to the donor (and/or another beneficiary) a stated amount for life. The actuarial value of the annuity stream is less than the value of the cash or property given to the charity, and the difference is the amount of the donor's income tax charitable deduction.

In times when interest and dividend rates are low, the charitable gift annuity is generally favored over the pooled income fund for smaller gifts because the donor/beneficiary generally receives a larger income amount. In addition, a part of that income is generally tax free under the rules governing annuities.

Planning for Retirement—A Practical Example

Norris and Martha have some stock they bought ten years ago for $12,000. This stock is now worth $75,000 but pays them only $1,000 per year in dividends. If they sell the stock to reinvest in higher-income investments, they will have only about $52,000 left after capital gains taxes. At a 5% return, that would produce income of $2,600 per year. They would like to provide an eventual bequest to their church, but feel they will need their nest egg for retirement.

If Norris and Martha transfer the stock to a CRT, the trustee can sell the stock and have virtually the entire $75,000 available to reinvest; at 5%, that would produce annual income of $3,750, an increase of more than 40% over the dividends they now receive. The trust will provide Norris and Martha with an income stream that will continue for as long as either of them is alive, and upon the death of the last, the remaining trust property will pass to their church. If they want even more income, they can have their trust drafted with a higher payout, 7% or 8%, for example.

Additionally, Norris and Martha will be entitled to an income tax deduction in the year they create the trust. The amount of that deduction depends upon several variables—their ages, the terms of the trust (primarily its payout rate), and the IRS actuarial interest rate for the month in which they create the trust.

Although this example involved a CRT, Norris and Martha may receive similar benefits using a pooled income fund or a charitable gift annuity. Selecting the best vehicle may require the help of an experienced charitable gift planner. Most universities and larger charities have such planners on staff to help donors make this selection; even though a donor may prefer to have advice from an independent source rather than the potential donee organization, the donee's planned giving officer can still be an important (and free) source of information. Most donees will gladly provide such information but advise the donor to consult his or her own advisors for advice on the tax consequences of a proposed gift.

Other Charitable Arrangements

There are other ways to structure charitable contributions to cover particular financial circumstances. For example, a person might use a charitable lead trust to generate large estate and gift tax savings on large transfers. Such a trust operates much like the CRT except the positions of the parties are reversed. The charitable lead trust makes distributions to charity for a stipulated number of years, after which the remaining trust property is turned over to the donor's family. Such trusts are often established by means of a decedent's will. Newspaper accounts described the use of such an arrangement under Jacqueline Kennedy Onassis's will to virtually eliminate estate taxes on her large estate.

A bargain sale arrangement may be used to transfer property to charity by means of a sale, but the price is less than the full value of the property. For example, a school may want to acquire land adjacent to its campus; the owner is willing to sell it to the school for $40,000 even though it is worth $100,000. Thus, the "seller" is really a donor and has made a $60,000 charitable contribution. He or she has also made a sale and may have a capital gain tax to pay. On these facts, since the property was sold for only 40% of its full value, only 40% of the tax basis would be used in computing capital gain. Thus, if the donor/seller in this example had paid $40,000 for the land in question, he or she would realize a gain for tax purposes of $24,000 (sales proceeds of $40,000, less 40% of the $40,000 cost basis, or $16,000).

Finally, some donors are reluctant to make a contemplated charitable contribution because they do not want to deny their children or other beneficiaries the property they would be contributing to charity. For this situation, the donor might want to consider a wealth replacement trust. Although not an actual charitable device, such a trust is often used in conjunction with a sizable charitable transfer. For example, if a donor is considering making a contribution of $100,000 to a CRT, some of the distributions from the trust could be used to buy a $100,000 life insurance policy through an irrevocable life insurance trust. Such a trust is called a wealth replacement trust because it allows the donor to replace the wealth being given to charity. The CRT will provide the donor with an income stream for life, and upon the donor's death, the charity receives the property remaining in the CRT, and family beneficiaries receive the policy proceeds, with no estate tax payable on either amount.

A wealth replacement trust requires caution. If a donor has serious reservations about the amount of a proposed charitable contribution, the proposed contribution may be too large. No responsible charity, under normal circumstances, would encourage a donor to give away a major portion of the donor's estate while he or she was still alive and might potentially need the funds. Moreover, the purchase of insurance is entirely separate from the proposed charitable contribution, and the donor must decide whether such insurance is necessary or desirable.

Family Foundations and Alternatives

A person who is very charitably-minded may wish to consider creating his or her own charity to facilitate ongoing support for causes or organizations deemed important. If the amounts in question are large enough to warrant the cost, a *family foundation* can be created. This is a private charity (either a nonprofit corporation or a trust) that is qualified with the Internal Revenue Service as a charitable organization for tax purposes. Amounts transferred to a foundation are deductible for income tax purposes, and amounts left to it on the death of the donor are also deductible for federal estate tax purposes. The foundation can hold such amounts as an endowment fund to generate investment income that it can devote to its charitable purposes.

A family foundation can serve a number of nontax purposes as well. A donor who contributes funds to a family foundation can maintain ongoing control of the contributions as they are kept in the foundation or passed on to other charities. This provides institutionalized yet flexible giving and allows the donor and his or her family to maintain and endow an ongoing charitable giving program that even lasts past the donor's death. A foundation can offer a donor privacy and insulation from unwelcome charitable solicitations. In addition, the foundation serves as a family institution or memorial and can help with the personal development of younger family members—introducing them to philanthropy and to the basics of investments and money management.

Most family foundations operate primarily by making grants to other charitable organizations, as determined by its trustees or directors, but it may also have active charitable operations of its own. The tax rules governing foundations are quite complex—including limitations on the deductions allowed to donors and a series of operating restrictions. For this reason, a person contemplating creating a foundation should consult an attorney who is familiar with these rules.

Much of the advantage of a foundation can be accomplished without the cost and complication by using a *donor-advised fund*. Such funds are offered by community foundations in virtually every region of the United States and by a number of financial institutions and mutual fund firms—even by some colleges and national charities. A donor-advised fund may be maintained by a charity, or it may be a separate charitable organization in its own right.

The donor's gifts to the fund are charitable contributions, fully deductible for tax purposes. The fund uses those contributions to create an account for the donor from which distributions will be made to other charitable organizations. The donor and his or her family retain the right to make nonbinding recommendations or advice to the sponsoring charity as to what distributions will be made from their account, and the sponsoring charity is free to accept or reject that advice. Although the donor thus has no real legal control over his or her account, as a practical matter, the donor's advice is typically followed. So long as the donor and the family make recommendations for grants to recognized, publicly supported charities, the use of a donor-advised fund enables the donor to achieve almost the same effect as a family foundation but without the accompanying expense and complication. (See also ANNUITIES; ATTORNEYS; ELDER LAW PRACTICE; ESTATE PLANNING; RELIGIOUS GIVING BY OLDER ADULTS; TRUSTS; WILLS.)

References

Arthur Andersen and Co. 2003. *The Tax Economics of Charitable Giving*. Chicago: Arthur Andersen.

Bowen, William G. 1994. *The Charitable Non-profits: An Analysis of Institutional Dynamics and Characteristics*. San Francisco, CA: Jossey-Bass.

Colliton, James W. 1993. *Charitable Gifts*. Colorado Springs, CO: Shepard's/McGraw-Hill.

Internal Revenue Code (Title 26, U.S. Code). Section 170.

McCoy, Jerry J., and Kathryn W. Miree. 2001. *Family Foundation Handbook*. New York: Aspen Publishers. Available online at http://www.aspenpublishers.com/.

Nagai, Althea K., Robert Lerner, and Stanley Rothman. 1994. *Giving for Social Change: Foundations, Public Policy, and the American Political Agenda*. Westport, CT: Praeger.

Tocqueville, Alexis de. 2001. *Democracy in America*. Ed. Richard D. Heffner. New York: Signet.

U.S. Congress. 1994. Senate Committee on Commerce, Science, and Transportation. Subcommittee on the Consumer. *Charitable Solicitation Fraud: Hearing before the Subcommittee on the Consumer of the Committee on Commerce, Science, and Transportation*. Washington, DC: GPO.

Jerry J. McCoy

COHABITATION, heterosexual couples living together without legally being married. Although infrequent, cohabitation does occur among couples older than 65. As with marriage after age 65, availability of a partner plays a significant role in cohabitation trends. Since most men ages 65 and older are married, there is a shortage of men 65 and older for cohabitation. More women than men survive to older ages, but even so, older men cohabit at rates two to three times the rates for older women. This percentage varies with race/ethnicity and 5-year age groupings.

The U.S. Census Bureau identified 3.8 million households as unmarried-partner households of which 5.3% were opposite sex unmarried-partner households. The number of people 65 and over who are living together in a cohabiting household increased 7% from 1980 to 1990, and 60% from 1990 to 2000, for an overall increase of 71%. One of the difficulties in measuring the change in cohabitation over time is how this living arrangement is measured. Prior to 1990, the number of cohabiting couples was estimated using indirect methods of inferring cohabitation. When using these methodologies, some households are included that do not meet the Census Bureau's POSSLQ definition (roommates), and some "true" cohabitors in households are not included because of the presence of children aged 15 and over. In 1990, the Census Bureau added the category of unmarried-partner households in the Current Population Survey and the census.

At the present time, most general knowledge about cohabitation is based on data collected about the younger population (35 years old and younger). The availability of data that reflects self-reported cohabitational status in large public samples will make it easier for researchers to conduct studies of older cohabitants, of which there are few. However, cohabiting data taken from the census and Current Population Survey are likely to underrepresent the actual number of cohabiting households due to reluctance of many, especially seniors, to report nontraditional consensual unions. Older adults often are uncomfortable with cohabitation and may be reluctant to disclose their status as cohabitors. The ageism that persists in society, especially as it relates to sexuality in later years, is reflected in the behavior of older adults. While older people may accept children who cohabit, they may avoid cohabitation themselves due to concerns about what peers might say or think.

For many older people to consider cohabitation as an alternative to other living arrangements, they must have strong reasons that transcend their natural unwillingness to go against societal and familial customs. Economic factors may constitute the most important reason seniors have to consider cohabitation. The adage "two can live cheaper than one" is not without some truth, and economic incentives to cohabit may parallel economic theories of marriage. If both partners have resources to contribute to the household, there may be economic gains to cohabitation in retirement. Constraints to marriage for seniors may come in the form of federal taxes and Social Security or death benefits.

A marriage penalty or tax on marriage originates from the "breadwinner system," under which men earned income and women had no market earnings. One-earner couples in this system are equated with two-earner couples. Despite today's workplace realities, the marriage penalty still exists, and retired older persons are not necessarily exempt. Elevated Social Security income is now taxable, and other sources of income in retirement have always been taxable. In addition to potential loss of survivor's benefits under Social Security upon remarriage before age 60 and the lower rate paid for a spouse benefit than a widow benefit, the maximum allowable earned benefits for a two-earner couple are less than they would be if each were collecting benefits as individuals. Private pensions can be at risk upon remarriage as well. Eligibility for Medicaid benefits is another important economic consideration for those older persons who might wish to remarry. When an eligible person marries, Medicaid regulations require that the savings of the new partner must be exhausted before eligibility is reinstated.

Intergenerational inheritance transfers may also be a factor in decisions either to remarry or cohabit. Research indicates that adult children cite inheritance as the biggest concern in their opposition to remarriage of parents. Courts, however, are moving toward recognition of cohabitational relationships, and precohabitation contracts may become necessary to ensure that inheritance will pass directly to children. In addition, trends indicate an increase in bequests to nonfamily members, including cohabitants, which may spur adult children to contest wills that contain such bequests.

In research that focuses on the portion of the population that is 45 years old and older, several economic factors—job income, Social Security and Supplemental Security Income, investment income, and homeownership—have been found to increase the likelihood that an older person will cohabit. The lower the income at advanced ages, the higher the proportion of older people who cohabit. Seniors tend to cohabit if they no longer can work for health reasons or when they are eligible for entitlement income. The effects on cohabitation are not as clear for homeownership. Cohabitors are more likely to be renters than their married counterparts. However, cohabitors are more likely to be homeowners than older single persons who are not cohabiting.

There are several reasons to expect an increase in cohabitation among those 65 and older. First, decreased mortality rates will increase the population aged 65 and older who are available to cohabit. Second, because divorced persons are more likely to cohabit, an increase in divorce is likely to bring about a corresponding increase in cohabitation. Third, the population aged 45 to 64 has a higher propensity to cohabit than those aged 65 and older, and it is likely that as these persons age, they will continue to have higher proportions of persons cohabiting. Finally, those who came of age during the 1960s and later have embraced cohabitation as an acceptable alternative to marriage. They undoubtedly will reflect this acceptance in their own lives as they age into the twenty-first century. (See also ESTATE PLANNING; FINANCES OF AGING IN THE GAY COMMUNITY; MARRIAGE AND OLDER ADULTS; SOCIAL SECURITY PROGRAM OF THE UNITED STATES; TITLING ASSETS.)

References

Casper, Lynne M., and Philip N. Cohen. 2000. "How Does POSSLQ Measure Up? National Estimates of Cohabitation." *Demography* 37(2) (May): 237–45.

Eekelaar, John J., and Sanford N. Katz, eds. 1980. *Marriage and Cohabitation in Contemporary Societies: Areas of Legal, Social and Ethical Change*. Toronto: Butterworths.

Fields, Jason, and Lynne M. Casper. 2001. *America's Families and Living Arrangements: March 2000*. Current Population Reports, P20-537. Washington, DC: U.S. Census Bureau.

Gronvold-Hatch, Rebecca. 1995. *Aging and Cohabitation*. New York: Garland Publishing.

Smock, P. 2000. "Cohabitation in the United States: An Appraisal of Research Themes, Findings, and Implications." *Annual Review of Sociology* 26: 1–20.

Spanier, Graham B. 1985. "Cohabitation in the 1980s: Recent Changes in the United States." In *Contemporary Marriages: Comparative Perspectives on a Changing Institution*, ed. K. Davis with A. Grossbard-Schectman. New York: Russell Sage Foundation.

Rebecca Gronvold-Hatch

COMMODITIES, goods, produce, wares, and in general, all items that are bought and sold in commerce. Out of this large group, only certain items are traded as commodity future contracts, mainly due to their universal acceptance and marketability throughout the world. These include, but are not limited to, raw agricultural goods in the agricultural area, such as corn, wheat, soybeans, sugar, coffee, cocoa, and orange juice. Additional examples include the meat markets of cattle, pork bellies, and other food products; the energy complex of crude oil, heating oil, and unleaded gas; and the precious metals, such as gold and silver. Newer financial instruments traded as commodities are Treasury bonds and Treasury bills, eurodollar bonds, international currencies (the European euro, the Japanese yen, the Korean won), and more recently, stock index futures, weather futures, and electricity futures. Futures are contracts, standardized in quantity and quality, for the purchase or sale of a commodity at a specified future time and place. All transactions are placed through a commodity exchange by a member of the exchange.

Commodities investment is often considered the high-wire act of the investment arena. *Substantial risk* is the first key term associated with commodity trading. In the hands of knowledgeable and sophisticated professionals, commodities can be an investment that provides substantial gain or risk transfer. As a means of enhancing financial security for one's older years, the first rule for the individual investor is to understand thoroughly the investment tool and the risk of capital; the saying that 95% of commodity players lose contains some truth. Once thoroughly understood, however, commodities trading can enhance a diversified portfolio when sufficient risk capital exists to permit it.

Buyers or sellers must post collateral, or margin, which is a promise to perform when trades are made in order to show good faith in fulfilling their future obligations. The value of contracts is determined by the price of entry, or cost per unit, multiplied by the quantity. The transactions are contractual obligations to be satisfied prior to the designated date of delivery, either by taking or making physical delivery of the approved grade and quantity of the commodity.

The majority of commodities transactions are closed out prior to delivery by offsetting sales or purchases of the same commodity on the exchange for an equivalent quantity and delivery date. Contractual obligations of certain futures contracts, for example, a stock index future, are satisfied by offsetting sales or purchases or by cash settlements of the amount on the expiration date of the contract. The investor's profit or loss is the difference between the price at which the person acquired the futures contract and its value on the offsetting trade or, if held until expiration, its value on the expiration/settlement date.

Futures markets are organized by commodity futures exchanges. The exchanges standardize the terms of all contracts, oversee trading, and coordinate all payments. Only members of an exchange are permitted to trade. Historically future orders received by member firms were transmitted to the exchange floor for execution. This is achieved by an open outcry system where bids and offers are presented to all members of the pit or ring present at the time. While this open outcry system is still used, technology in the late 1990s brought the advent of computer screen–trading networks where buyers and sellers are matched electronically within a few seconds.

The two largest exchanges in the United States are the Chicago Board of Trade (CBOT) and the Chicago Mercantile Exchange (CME). Other exchanges include the New York Mercantile Exchange (NYMEX), the Commodity Exchange (COMEX), and the Kansas City Board of Trade (KCBOT). Foreign commodity exchanges include the London International Financial Futures Exchange (LIFFE), the Singapore International Financial Futures Exchange (SIMEX), and the Korean Futures Exchange (KOSPI).

In the United States, legislation by Congress was enacted to regulate trading, the exchanges, the brokers, brokerage houses, advisors, and pool operators. The controlling legislation, known as the Commodity Exchange Act (1974), is designed to promote the orderly and systematic marketing of commodities and commodity futures contracts, while preventing fraud, speculative excess, and price manipulations. The act is implemented by the rules and regulations set by the Commodity Futures Trading Commission (CFTC). The CFTC is the government agency responsible for regulating domestic commodity exchanges and commodity futures trading. The National Futures Association (NFA) is the self-regulatory body of commodity professionals. Any violations of the Commodity Exchange Act are subject to punishment including revocation of registration, civil fines, and imprisonment.

The two basic groups of participants in futures trading are "hedgers" and "speculators." Those individuals or companies directly involved with the production, marketing, or processing of certain commodities (the cash commodity or actuals market), such as farmers or mining companies, utilize futures markets primarily for hedging, a strategy designed to minimize losses from price fluctuations over a period of time. This generally covers the time between which merchandisers or processors contract to sell their raw or processed commodities and the time they must deliver. The objective of hedgers in the futures market is to protect the profit they expect to earn from their farming, merchandizing, or processing operations. Many hedge strategies share the basic concept of minimizing risk exposure to interim price fluctuations. Other examples of hedging include U.S. companies that rely on imported goods or parts for manufacturing. If the company requires 5 million European euros in three months to pay for parts, the company can lock in the exchange rate by using the currency futures market to offset devaluation over that period of time.

Unlike hedgers, speculators generally do not expect either to deliver or receive physical commodities, or to hedge against price volatility, but rather to profit from price fluctuations in the value of commodity futures contracts. Speculators, often derided as gamblers, provide an essential element in futures trading—liquidity. Hedgers tend to be all buyers or all sellers at a given time. Without speculators to sell to or buy from—in other words, to take the opposite side of the risk—futures markets could not function. The efficiency of any free market operation requires a fairly equal number of buyers and sellers, and imbalance of the buyer/seller ratio is similar to an imbalance in demand and supply of a given commodity. When corn crops are destroyed by natural forces, for example, the price of corn rises drastically because demand is greater than supply, not because of speculators in the futures market. Inflation worries may cause a rise in gold prices not due to lack of the supply of gold but rather to individual beliefs (correct or incorrect) that gold is a safer investment when inflation rises. Speculations in the commodity markets are essential to hedging and help achieve a stabilization of price.

Most trading for individual investors is through brokerage houses, whether individuals are making decisions or are part of pools or funds where managers handle trading strategies. Brokerage houses charge commissions for each trade enacted, and all trading transactions are made through members of a commodity exchange. Margin accounts are set up for the trading activities, and margin requirements (basically downpayments) range roughly from 5% to 20% of contract values.

In stock investments, investors are required to place a margin (downpayment) of 50% or more of the stock price, with the remainder amount loaned at a broker loan rate to fulfill 100% of the purchase obligation. Commodity margins are based on fixed minimums per unit or per contract, ranging from 5% to 20% of the actual cost of the futures contracts, and are good-faith performance bonds. There are no loans made to cover the additional costs of the contracts. This creates opportunities to leverage larger positions in commodities than in stocks, but price movements in commodities, relative to margin requirements, can create very large losses or profits, and it is in this area that investors must thoroughly familiarize themselves to fully comprehend the risk. Profits and losses are treated similarly to stocks in tax rules: both are capital items. However, there are no state or federal taxes involved in the purchase or sale of commodity positions.

The leap in volume of commodity trading during the last 30 years has been dramatic. Commodity trading is now global in nature, particularly in financial and stock index futures trading. The different levels of income-producing investments, whether personal or corporate, domestic or international, along with the shifting coalition of interest groups, keeps the financial structure in a constant state of change. Desires to preserve and increase capital motivates financial innovations around tax and regulatory restrictions imposed by government, and reactions can be transitory or lasting. The Eurodollar bond market, for example, was created by reaction to U.S. ceilings on the rate of interest commercial banks could offer on time deposits. With the volatility of interest rates in the 1960s and

1970s, U.S. commercial banks were aware that this restriction did not apply to dollar-denominated time deposits in their overseas branches, particularly in western Europe. Eurodollar financial futures were created and are still traded in the futures market despite subsequent regulation changes and interest rate retraction.

Index contracts, Eurodollar bonds, and financial futures are all part of a complex and creative international investment market so intertwined it appears incomprehensible to the average investor. These complex instruments can be daunting to the uninitiated, but like the challenges of modern medical and tax forms and procedures, choices to further financial gain through commodities can be sorted through with the assistance of knowledgeable specialists and a thorough understanding of risk for investors, whether they are in their middle years planning for retirement or have already retired. (See also AGENTS AND BROKERS; ASSET ALLOCATION AFTER RETIREMENT; EQUITY SECURITIES; FINANCIAL ADVISORS; RISK TOLERANCE.)

Organization

Commodity Futures Trading Commission (CFTC)

References

Bernstein, Jacob. 2000. *How the Futures Markets Work.* Upper Saddle River, NJ: Prentice Hall.
Chicago Board of Trade. 1999. *Commodity Trading Manual.* Ed. Frank Rose. New York: AMACOM.
Schwager, Jack D. 1984. *A Complete Guide to the Futures Markets.* New York: John Wiley & Sons.
Waldron, Richard E. 2000. *Futures 101: An Introduction to Commodity Trading.* North Quincy, MA: Squantum Publishing.

Mary Anne Keefer

COMMUNITY-BASED CARE, senior care services that include case management, home health care, homemaking, adult day care, transportation, home-delivered meals, and other.

Community-based long-term care covers a broad spectrum of services that vary in type, target population, intensity (level of skill, amount of care), duration, and cost. These programs are intended for people with chronic physical or mental disabilities. A defining and unifying characteristic of community-based long-term care is that the objective is to support the ability of the patient/client to remain living in the community rather than an institution.

Community-based services often entail services that take place in a person's home—for example, a visiting nurse, home health aide, homemaker, or various therapies provided at home. However, the service setting might be institutional if the overall purpose is to sustain independent living—for example, adult day care, respite care, or assisted living programs. Care coordination or case management is often an important component of community-based long-term care, especially when the target population is geographically dispersed and there are diverse sources and resources for services.

The Substitution Hypothesis

Does access to community-based long-term care prevent or postpone nursing home placement for at-risk older people? Research in the 1970s suggested that a substantial number of nursing home residents could be cared for at home if adequate community-based long-term care were available and that a modest amount of formal community-based services might reduce caregiver burden and burnout and thus prevent inappropriate institutionalization (Seidl et al. 1983; Williams et al. 1973).

The expectation that community-based services could substitute for institutional long-term care for disabled persons and frail older persons provided the rationale for a series of demonstration projects. The substitution hypothesis is built on the following premises:

- *Community-based long-term care is desirable.* There is ample evidence that people overwhelmingly prefer to remain in their own homes and avoid nursing home placement (Kane and Kane 1987). Long-term institutionalization tends to be a "last resort."
- *Nursing home placement can be prevented or substantially delayed.* This premise refers particularly to persons with moderate levels of impairment who either lack close relatives or whose care has exhausted their family caregivers. As numerous studies have shown, at-risk older people who lack informal caregivers are much more likely to be institutionalized than older adults who have comparable disabilities but who have spouses or adult children able and willing to care for them (Fischer and Hoffman 1984; Shanas and Maddox 1985). The implication is that, for these persons, nursing home placement may be inappropriate or premature.
- *Community-based long-term care is more cost-effective than institutional care.* This is a corollary to the previous point—that persons with moderate disabilities who do not require full-service facilities can be served instead with relatively inexpensive interventions.
- *Community-based long-term care improves quality of life for disabled persons and their caregivers.* Although the emphasis of the substitution hypothesis is often on the potential for cost savings, the benefit of community care is equally important. A substantial body of research literature, over many years, has documented the human cost for older adults and their caregivers of inadequate access to community-based services (Estes, Swan, and Associates 1993; Fengler and Goodrich 1979; Fischer and Hoffman 1984; Fischer et al. 1998).

Evaluations of Community Care Demonstration Projects

The substitution hypothesis has been tested in a number of community care demonstration projects, including several federally sponsored projects. Much of the policy interest in these demonstration projects has been on the cost benefits of community-based services compared to institutional care. Overall, however, most evaluations of the demonstrations have not supported the substitution hypothesis in terms of a cost-offset effect. The largest and most elaborate evaluation was the National Long Term Care Demonstration, the Channeling project. The Channeling project, as well as other demonstrations, failed to find a significant difference in nursing home placement or hospital utilization. In their review of community-based long-term care demonstrations, Kemper, Applebaum, and Harrigan (1987) concluded: "The demonstrations have shown that expanding publicly financed community care does not reduce aggregate costs, and it is likely to increase them—at least under the current long-term care service system." But they also reported that the demonstrations were associated with higher life quality, so they added: "It is wrong, therefore, to conclude that expanding public financing for community care is not cost effective. Costs are likely to go up, but so are benefits." Weissert, Cready, and Pawelak (1988) found a few projects saved money—but only those where the cost of the intervention was very modest.

PACE—Program of All-Inclusive Care for the Elderly—is another model for providing services to frail older people. The program began in the early 1970s in San Francisco's Chinatown and now has multiple sites around the United States. Each site serves 120 to 150 participants, most of whom come several times a week to adult day care centers, where they receive services from physicians, nurses, social workers, therapists, and others. Patients that are unable to leave their homes are eligible for home care (Eng et al. 1997; Shannon and Van Reenen 1998). A study of hospitalization rates for PACE participants found that short-term hospital utilization among PACE participants is low compared to hospital use for other older and disabled populations (Wieland et al. 2000).

The Social Health Maintenance Organization (S/HMO) is another federally sponsored demonstration project intended to substitute home and community-based services for more costly institutional care. The S/HMO model creates financing for a community-based long-term care benefit, a care management system that identifies members eligible for that benefit, and coordination mechanisms that integrate the delivery of long-term care within the medical care system. While most other long-term care demonstrations were designed to serve primarily or exclusively frail or disabled populations, the target population in the S/HMO is composed of an approximate cross section of the community-based population, with a subset eligible for long-term care services. The S/HMO concept was to add a "social" component to Medicare HMO services, in order to meet the non-medical/support needs of older enrollees with chronic conditions and disabilities.

A recent study used the closure of an S/HMO in Minnesota as a natural experiment to test the substitution hypothesis. The study followed a cohort of former Minnesota S/HMO enrollees and a cohort of enrollees in a comparable Oregon S/HMO, where the program continued to operate. The researchers compared the probability of long-term institutionalization or death, controlling for site effects, age, gender, and comorbid medical conditions. The research found that the loss of this community-based care program was associated with a 40% increased risk of institutionalization over the next five years (Fischer et al. 2001).

Community-Based Long-Term Care in Future Public Policy

Over the last 20 years or so, in almost every developed country, rates of institutionalization have dramatically decreased and community-based services have increased (Amaradio 1998; Melzer et al. 1999; Merlis 2000). In part, this has resulted from deliberate policy initiatives to support and facilitate community-based services. Undoubtedly, much of the increase in community-based care also reflects the preferences of frail older persons and their families.

Long-term care has been a particularly thorny issue in public policy in the United States—often not even making it to the table in recent debates on health care reform. Currently, Medicare and most private medical plans in the United States cover acute and postacute care but deny claims for long-term custodial care (Estes, Swan, and Associates 1993; Leutz 1999). Public programs, most notably Medicaid, finance a substantial proportion of long-term care, but these benefits are restricted to persons with very low incomes or assets (Amaradio 1998; Bodenheimer 1999; Feder, Komisar, and Niefield 2000). Thus, the very wealthy, who can afford to pay out of pocket, and the very poor, who are eligible for public benefits, are the most likely to have access to both institutional and community-based long-term care services (Fischer et al. 1998; Merlis 2000; Murtaugh et al. 1997).

The substitution hypothesis is appealing because of its win-win premise: that patients benefit *and* there could be a cost offset in terms of public monies. The lack of dramatic research evidence for a cost offset has disappointed gerontologists and policy planners. A commentary in *Gerontologist* argued that "there is no impact" so that "the original justifications for community based services, including respite care, are no longer valid" (Callahan 1989).

The aging of the baby boom generation portends a sharp increase in the numbers and proportions of people surviving into very old age and, almost inevitably, an increased demand for long-term care. Providing good-quality, cost-effective long-term care, including both community-based and institutional care, will be an ever-more-urgent national priority. (See also DAY PROGRAMS FOR ADULTS; FRAILTY PLANNING; GERIATRIC CARE MANAGERS [GCMs]; HOME CARE SERVICES FOR OLDER ADULTS; HOME MODIFICATIONS FINANCING; REVERSE MORTGAGES.)

References

Amaradio, L. 1998. "Financing Long-Term Care for Elderly Persons: What Are the Options?" *Journal of Health Care Finance* 25: 75–84.

Bodenheimer, T. 1999. "Long-Term Care for Frail Elderly People—The On Lok Model." *New England Journal of Medicine* 341: 1324–28.

Callahan, J.J. 1989. "Play It Again Sam—There Is No Impact." *Gerontologist* 29(1): 5–6.

Eng, C., J. Pedulla, G.P. Eleazer, R. McCann, and N. Fox. 1997. "Program of All-Inclusive Care for the Elderly (PACE): An Innovative Model of Integrated Geriatric Care and Financing." *Journal of American Geriatric Society* 45(2): 223–32.

Estes, C.L., J.H. Swan, and Associates. 1993. *The Long Term Care Crisis: Elders Trapped in the No-Care Zone*. Newbury Park, CA: Sage Publications.

Feder, J., H.L. Komisar, and M. Niefeld. 2000. "Long-Term Care in the United States: An Overview." *Health Affairs* 19: 40–56.

Fengier, L.R. et al. 2001. "Community-Based Care and Risk of Nursing Home Placement." Paper presented at the annual meetings of the Gerontological Society of America, Chicago, IL, November.

Fischer L.R. 1990. "Medicare HMOs and Home Health Care." *Journal of Aging Studies* 4(2): 171–93.

Fischer, L.R., C.A. Green, M. Goodman, M. Aickin, K.K. Brod, F. Wei, L.W. Phelps, and W.N. Leutz. 2001. "Community-Based Care and Risk of Nursing Home Placement." Paper presented at the annual meetings of the Gerontological Society of America, Chicago, IL, November.

Fischer, L.R., and C. Hoffman. 1984. "Who Cares for the Elderly: The Dilemma of Family Support." In *Research in Social Problems and Public Policy*, ed. M. Lewis and J. Miller. Vol. 2. Greenwich, CT: JAI Press.

Fischer, L.R., W. Leutz, A. Miller, T.L. von Sternberg, and J.M. Ripley. 1998. "The Closing of a Social HMO: A Case Study." *Journal of Aging and Social Policy* 10: 57–75.

Kane, R.A., and R.L. Kane. 1987. *Long-Term Care: Principles, Programs, and Policies*. New York: Springer Publishing Co.

Kemper, P., R. Applebaum, and M. Harrigan. 1987. "Community Care Demonstrations: What Have We Learned?" *Health Care Finance* 8(1): 87–100.

Leutz, W.N. 1999. "Five Laws for Integrating Medical and Social Services: Lessons from the United States and the United Kingdom." *Milbank Quarterly* 77: 7–110.

Leutz, W., M.R. Greenlick, and J. Capitman. 1994. "Integrating Acute and Long-Term Care." *Health Affairs* 13: 55–74.

Melzer, D., B. McWilliams, C. Brayne, T. Johnson, and J. Bond. 1999. "Profile of Disability in Elderly People: Estimates from a Longitudinal Population Study." *British Journal of Medicine* 318: 1108–11.

Merlis, M. 2000. "Caring for the Frail Elderly: An International Review." *Health Affairs* 19: 141–49.

Murtaugh, C.M., P. Kemper, B.C. Spillman, and B.L. Carlson. 1997. "The Amount, Distribution, and Timing of Lifetime Nursing Home Use." *Medical Care* 35: 204–18.

Seidl, F.W., R. Applebaum, C. Austin, and K. Mahoney. 1983. *Delivering In-Home Services to the Aged and Disabled: The Wisconsin Experiment.* Lexington, MA: Lexington Books.

Shanas, E., and G.L. Maddox. 1985. "Health, Health Resources, and the Utilization of Care." In *Handbook of Aging and the Social Sciences*, ed. R. Binstock and E. Shanas. 2nd ed. New York: Van Nostrand.

Shannon, K., and C. Van Reenen. 1998. "PACE (Program of All-Inclusive Care for the Elderly): Innovative Care for the Frail Elderly: Comprehensive Services Enable Most Participants to Remain at Home." *Health Program* 79(5): 41–45.

Weissert, W.G., C.M. Cready, and J.E. Pawelak. 1988. "The Past and Future of Home- and Community-Based Long-Term Care." *Milbank Quarterly* 66: 309–88.

Wieland, D., V.L. Lamb, S.R. Sutton, R. Boland, M. Clark, S. Friedman, K. Brummel-Smith, and G.P. Eleazer. 2000. "Hospitalization in the Program of All-Inclusive Care for the Elderly (PACE): Rates, Concomitants, and Predictors." *Journal of American Geriatric Society* 48(11): 1373–80.

Williams, T.F., J.G. Hill, M.E. Fairbank, and K.G. Knox. 1973. "Appropriate Placement of the Chronically Ill and Aged: A Successful Approach by Evaluation." *Journal of the American Medical Association* 226: 1332–35.

Lucy Rose Fischer

CONDOMINIUMS, a form of real estate ownership in which owners have full ownership rights to individual dwelling units consisting of all airspace found within the interior surfaces of walls, ceilings, and floors and an undivided interest in the common areas of the complex. The common areas include the land under the condominium unit, exterior walls, roof, lobbies, hallways, meeting rooms, elevators, and the surrounding areas such as parks, pools, tennis courts, and parking areas. Condominium ownership was legislated in the United States only in the 1960s, but this form of ownership dates back to ancient Rome. Many condominium developments today are located in popular retirement areas, such as California, Arizona, and Florida, appealing to retirees and to older adults seeking warm weather and carefree ownership.

Similar to other forms of ownership, the use of condominium units is privately restricted according to certain covenants, conditions, and regulations. Owners of condominium units inevitably become members of the condominium owner's association, which is usually an unincorporated association that governs the management of the property and its common areas. The purpose of the association is to determine and regulate conditions of ownership and occupancy and to maintain the common areas in the condominium building or complex. The condominium association is run by a board of directors elected by the owners, and the board usually hires a property manager and related staff to administer the complex. Subcommittees composed of residents are often charged with specific administrative responsibilities. A condominium association is responsible for various tasks, including interior and exterior building maintenance and repairs, safety, financial and budgetary topics, rules and regulations, and social functions. It also oversees insurance and tax matters and sets forth policies concerning delinquent fees or assessments from individual owners.

Association fees paid by owners fund routine maintenance of the condominium complex, including interior maintenance such as plumbing or electrical work and exterior maintenance such as roofing or landscaping. The association may also collect assessments to pay the property taxes for the common areas. Some portion of the fee is set aside in a building reserve fund in the event of large unexpected future maintenance expenses. Residents may still be charged one-time assessments to cover larger maintenance demands (e.g., new roof, new plumbing) when the condominium association reserve funds are insufficient. Most important, the condominium association has the responsibility of enforcing rules and regulations established for the complex. Responsibilities can range from handling a complaint from a disgruntled owner to having a lien levied against a unit because an individual owner has not paid the required fees or assessments.

Condominium ownership offers older adults a host of benefits, including a maintenancefree lifestyle, a relatively low-cost form of housing, and the use of common area facilities for social functions—typically holiday parties, swimming, tennis, or golf. Pets may be permitted by the condominium association's regulations in some complexes, and others have gates or employ full-time security guards for added safety. Since most neighbors live close together, theft is discouraged, and aid may be available in case of medical and other emergencies. The satisfaction of occupants will often depend on the regulations established for the complex and how well the management performs. Owners can voice opinions at association meetings, which are held at regular intervals and can cover such topics as association dues or necessary changes in current rules or regulations.

A condominium unit usually costs less than a single-family detached home. Mortgage payments on a condominium unit are typically comparable to rents paid for apartments, yet condominium ownership offers tax benefits, equity buildup, and the possibility of future appreciation in value. Unlike rentals, owners may decorate the interior of their unit as they wish, and they are free from anxieties such as fear of eviction, the need for negotiating lease terms, and future rent increases. Since management is employed and supervised by the condominium association, it is often particularly responsive to the unit owners. Older buyers, therefore, may find living environments that are quieter, more mature, and better suited to their specific needs.

Noticeable disadvantages associated with condominium unit ownership may include overcrowding, an overbearing condominium association, rules and regulations that are too restrictive, and limitations on financing the unit. The high land costs associated with today's real estate markets force many developers to maximize the density of units in condominium complexes in order to achieve a worthwhile profit. Noises from neighbors can become a nuisance, especially for older newcomers who may have lived in single-family detached residences. Dense living environments can limit the amount of privacy enjoyed by owners, and some housing complexes lack adequate visitor parking spaces to host guests.

Requests for needed maintenance may be mishandled or handled slowly by managers of some complexes, and this can be a burden for some older persons who may need expeditious repairs. An interested buyer should become aware of rules and regulations concerning the condominium complex and also seek out the opinions of residents on the efficiency and consideration of management. If there is disagreement between management and owners or among owners on how situations should be implemented or handled, tension may result. Improper or inefficient management, poor market conditions, or poor construction can cause condominium association fee increases.

Prospective owners should also consider pertinent financing and future refinancing of condominium units, since most lenders follow strict guidelines when considering such financing. For example, if the number of owner-absentee (rented) units in the complex reaches a certain percentage (typically 30% to 50%), it may be difficult for a potential buyer to arrange financing. Problems can also arise when the owner of a condominium unit wishes to obtain secondary financing, as some lenders refuse to make home equity loans on condominium units. Further, most lenders prefer to diversify their mortgage portfolio and will usually limit the number of units in any given complex. The financing restrictions on condominium units are not only applied to conventional mortgages but also to government agency mortgages such as Federal Housing Administration (FHA) and Veterans Administration (VA) loans. (See also AGENTS AND BROKERS; ASSET ALLOCATION AFTER RETIREMENT; CORPORATE ELDERCARE PROGRAMS; FINANCIAL ADVISORS; HOME CARE SERVICES FOR OLDER ADULTS; HOMEOWNERSHIP.)

Suggested Readings

Irwin, Robert. 1999. *Tips and Traps When Buying a Condo, Co-Op, or Townhouse*. New York: McGraw-Hill.

Shapiro, Sylvia. 1998. *The Co-Op Bible: Everything You Need to Know About Co-Ops and Condos: Getting In, Staying In, Surviving, Thriving*. New York: St. Martin's Griffin.

References

Freedman, Warren. 1992. *The Law of Condominia and Property Owners' Associations*. New York: Quorum Books.

Kiplinger's Personal Finance Magazine, eds. 2002. *Kiplinger's Buying & Selling a Home*. 7th ed. Washington, DC: Kiplinger Books.

Shilling, James D. 2002. *Real Estate*. 13th ed. Cincinnati, OH: South-Western/Thomson Learning.

Wiedemer, John P. 1990. *Real Estate Finance*. 6th ed. Englewood Cliffs, NJ: Prentice-Hall.

Andrew Quang Do

CONSERVATORSHIP. See Attorneys; Durable Power of Attorney; Elder Law Practice; Guardianship.

CONSULTING IN RETIREMENT, using expertise gained over a career, or through other life experience, to generate income after retirement. Everyone who has reached the stage of maturity where retirement is possible has acquired expertise of one sort or another, and it is expertise that consultants sell in blocks of time. Indeed, time and expertise are the only two inventories stored by consultants.

In letting government contracts, the U.S. government categorizes consultants as "experts." This is accurate; successful consultants are experts. By last count there were approximately 280 different fields of consulting expertise. So anyone who has retired and who feels that he or she does not wish to spend the rest of his or her life playing golf, gardening, surfing the Internet, or watching television has the potential to become an independent consultant. For some, this is a most productive period of life that permits work on projects that are of interest, and at times that are convenient, for the consultant.

A good current economic environment exists for independent consultants. Not only have the services industries far outstripped manufacturing in the gross national product (GNP), but both private and public organizations are resorting more and more to outsourcing their services requirements in order to keep their staffs to a minimum. Outsourcing, of course, means the retaining of consultants. All independent consultants combined earn as much as do the big international consulting firms such as Booz-Allen and McKinsey and Company—over $35 billion a year.

The life of a successful independent consultant has many advantages. There are no office politics with which to contend, and the consultant is not accountable to a superior. The client is seldom the consultant's "boss"; indeed, it is the client who is in need of assistance or has a problem to be solved, not the consultant. A consultant may have the opportunity to travel extensively at a client's expense. And losing a client seldom involves the financial tragedy of losing a job because there are usually other clients to step in and to pay a consultant's fees. Perhaps best of all, the consultant chooses the number of hours to work and the amount and time of days to take off. The client typically accommodates to the consultant's calendar.

The first issue is to clearly identify the expertise around which the consultancy will be established. For many people, this will be clear from the experience of having been a source of information to colleagues before retirement. For others, it will be a non-work-related field of interest that has always occupied leisure time and attention. For still others, it may be a field that has been a lifelong interest that can now be developed into expertise with the extra time available after retirement. However it has developed, the first step is to clearly identify the area of expertise that will be marketable to and required by a sufficient number of prospective clients. Yet expertise is not all that is required to set up a successful consultancy. Other important factors include a person's own makeup, personality, and character.

It typically takes six months to one year of marketing consulting expertise to make a consulting venture successful. Patience and perseverance are required by an aspiring consultant, or this career path may prove too frustrating to maneuver. Consulting will seldom produce a steady income but rather it typically has drought periods as well as very profitable ones. If an individual (and his or her spouse) cannot get used to going without a steady paycheck, then consulting is not a wise path to pursue. Further, a consultant must be self-motivated and not easily distracted. There will be no one pushing a consultant to accomplish tasks in the same way an employee has a superior directing his or her effort. Also, most consultants work out of their homes, and a disciplined approach to self-appointed tasks is imperative so that family affairs and household chores do not interfere. Finally, even though many potential clients will engage in conversations that do not lead to paying engagements, a beginning consultant cannot take this personally or develop contempt for his or her client universe.

There is a financial benefit to setting up a consultancy in one's home. Most retirees have few tax deductions, and the Internal Revenue Service (IRS) will allow a deduction for mortgage or rent and utilities for whatever percentage of space in one's home is used for an office. Education and training, insurance, health care, automobile, and other expenses in connection with the business may be allowable as well.

Ninety percent (90%) of beginning consultants do not make it past the first 12 months. This is not because they are not experts in their respective fields; most of them are. It is because they do not understand the business of consulting. And although consulting is considered a profession, it is also a business. Doctors, dentists, and accountants are also professionals who must acquaint themselves with good business principles and practices in order to succeed. This statistic is not presented to dissuade or discourage anyone from consulting but to reinforce the requisites of consulting success.

One factor that can lead to lack of success in consulting is the mistaken belief that as a "professional" salesmanship is not a requirement. Nothing could be further from the truth. In point of fact, a beginning consultant must sell the most difficult intangible thing of all: him- or herself.

Finally, some may be discouraged from entering the profession because of negative publicity in today's media about the misdeeds of a few large consulting firms or unflattering jokes about consultants. Some consultants are rethinking the use of the word *consultant* altogether and are calling themselves "counselors" or are changing the names of their businesses from consultancies to "advisories." A final obstacle in today's economic environment is the increasing numbers of middle managers who have been downsized or who have taken early retirement and now have calling cards as "consultants" but may not be taking consulting seriously. Nevertheless, consulting—when practiced by an expert who is honorable, helpful, ethical, and innovative—is a noble profession from which great rewards can be reaped during later life.

The best business practices of successful consultants are not optional and are devoted to the following areas:

- Marketing expertise to gain clients
- Representing oneself as a true professional
- Setting fees knowledgeably for client acceptance
- Writing winning proposals
- Avoiding risk when contracting with a client
- Conforming to the highest ethical standards of the consulting profession

There is no college or university that offers a degree in consulting. While some universities (notably Harvard Business School and the Wharton School) offer courses in consulting as part of their M.B.A. programs, the courses deal essentially with management consulting only. Business courses such as those outlined above are often available at local community colleges or extension programs, as well as on the Internet.

Finally, many independent consultants who have enjoyed a successful, profitable career may do so in a phased manner. The workload is always within the consultant's control, and they may enjoy the wonderful feelings accompanying the successful completion of a project well done for as long as they wish after normal "retirement." (See also BUSINESS SUCCESSION PLANNING; ENTREPRENEURSHIP; KEOGH PLANS; LIFE

PLANNING; PENSION PLANS FOR THE SELF-EMPLOYED; WORKING RETIREES.)

Reference

Bermont, Hubert. 1997. *How to Become a Successful Consultant in Your Own Field.* 3rd ed. Roseville, CA: Prima Publishing.

Hubert Bermont

CONSUMER CREDIT, credit extended by banks, credit card companies, other financial institutions, and retailers to older persons for the purchase of goods and services on a flexible payment schedule. Unlike traditional installment borrowing, which features a specified monthly payment over a fixed period of time (such as a traditional auto or home mortgage loan), the desirability of "revolving" consumer credit is its flexible terms of repayment. That is, the payment is interest only until the principal is due in full, such as in a "balloon payment" in some home equity loans, or the consumer can choose the size of the monthly payment (in most credit cards a minimum of 1% to 2% of outstanding principal) and thus the length of the repayment period that determines the total cost of the loan. This is significant since credit cards, in particular, are distinguished by whether they must be paid in full (charge cards) or in part (revolving accounts) at the end of the monthly billing cycle. An example of a charge account is *American Express*, and examples of revolving accounts are *VISA* and *Mastercard* on which an outstanding balance is financed over succeeding months. It is important to note that the *Discover* credit card is issued by a financial services company, while VISA and Mastercard are membership associations. The primary goals of VISA and Mastercard are marketing and improving the transaction processing technology for its member banks. Major financial institutions such as Bank of America issue individual credit card accounts.

Charge accounts typically do not impose interest charges (unless the payment is late), but they often require a membership fee. In comparison, credit cards levy a finance charge on the outstanding balance and on any new purchases during the billing cycle. Some also impose a membership fee and, in addition, charge a growing assortment of fees including those for late payment, exceeding credit limits, cash advances, and overdraft protection on personal checking accounts. With the exception of special reward programs, such as frequent airline travel accounts, annual membership fees may be waived as "a courtesy" to loyal customers simply by calling the customer service department of the credit card company.

Credit cards can be used without incurring finance charges or penalty fees by paying the entire balance in full before the end of the specified "grace" period. Extra fees, however, may be assessed for convenience services, especially when traveling out of state or in other countries. For instance, automated teller machines (ATMs) in shopping malls provide access to different information networks across the country, and a credit card may incur "user" fees if the ATM is not part of the card issuer's bank system.

Smart Cards

Also, there are new technologically sophisticated "smart" cards that feature computer chip "brains" that can be used in many different financial information networks throughout the United States. They can access a variety of financial services accounts (checking, savings, credit) as well as serve as a repository of purchasing information that can be transferred to different vendor systems for future marketing programs. If, for example, a consumer purchases groceries or medicines at the supermarket, the items purchased will be added to the consumer's credit card information file and will be downloaded to a shopping profile that is stored in the supermarket's computers as well.

There are certain variants of credit cards that offer atypical credit arrangements. People with poor credit histories, for example, may obtain "secured" credit cards that require a bank deposit equal to the extended credit amount. Such cards may also carry membership charges and very high interest rates (19% to 29%). Typically, charges are limited to the amount of the accountholder's deposit, although some companies may increase the credit limit by 50% to 300%, in accordance with the customer's payment record. Other products include check cashing cards from banks (that may include the VISA trademark) and that electronically pay for purchases from checking accounts at the "point of sale" (POS) and debit cards that immediately deduct purchases from a checking or savings account. Annual account and activation fees may be charged, and each POS carries certain transaction costs. Some banks offer their customers "overdraft" protection on check cashing and debit cards. This is essentially a loan or additional line of credit that usually incurs a transaction fee plus finance charges at the standard credit card interest rate.

Check cashing and *debit* cards may be used in the same financial transaction systems as bank credit cards, but they do not have the same benefits. For example, they do not include the generous fraud and purchase protection that are provided by bank credit cards. Many consumers learn this expensive lesson only after the theft of their checking, savings, and overdraft lines of credit. In comparison, the major credit card companies offer 100% protection against theft as long as unauthorized activities are reported within a reasonable period of time. This policy is designed to encourage shopping over the Internet without fear of financial liability from the fraudulent use of credit cards (Manning 2001).

Credit Cards in America: A Brief History

Although bank credit cards are a relatively recent innovation, typically marked by the establishment of the "businessman's *Diner's Club* card" in 1950, U.S. society has historically depended upon the availability of consumer credit. For example, farmers depended on store credit before the harvest of their crops in rural America, whereas industrial workers were issued "script" for purchases in the company store that were later deducted from their wages. Significantly, both forms of consumer credit often produced a form of debt/labor servitude. This common experience was recounted in the famous lyrics of Tennessee Williams, *"I owe my soul to the company store."*

Even in the mid-twentieth century, local merchants frequently extended informal or "open book" credit to their most reliable customers since it fostered customer loyalty and future business sales. Not surprisingly, strong social ties between merchants and consumers in small-town America reinforced the social control functions of debt (stigma and shame) and work discipline (dependence on future credit). Public scorn for failing to repay one's debts was an embarrassment to the debtor as well as to his or her extended family and was avoided whenever possible. As a result, persistent indebtedness often took on moral and religious overtones, and thrift was equated with godliness, self-discipline, and hard work. These social factors encouraged financial responsibility and limited the number of people who failed to repay their debts. When widespread violations of these Puritan-inspired values occurred in the early twentieth century, a calamitous loss of family homesteads and personal property resulted during the Great Depression. Today, these devastating experiences still constitute powerful intergenerational reminders of the social and economic consequences of failing to "save for a rainy day."

After World War II, the rising U.S. standard of living combined with the rapid proliferation of suburban residential communities encouraged new forms of consumer credit that were not based on personal relationships. Furnishings for new homes and the purchase of new automobiles required greater amounts of consumer credit than were traditionally available from local banks. The unprecedented geographic mobility of postwar America undermined informal credit networks, because small businesses were reluctant to offer informal credit to unknown or potentially transient customers. These factors contributed to the profound transformation of Main Street USA, from downtown business districts with primarily small shopkeepers to suburban shopping malls with their corporate retail "anchors." Large retail stores such as Sears, Roebuck and Montgomery Ward included formal consumer charge and proprietary credit card accounts. These credit programs were designed primarily to reinforce customer loyalty since they could not be used in other stores. Even with high annual finance charges, most proprietary credit card programs were not profitable due to high account management expenses.

U.S. Industrial Restructuring and Banking Deregulation: The Rise of the Universal Bank Credit Card

Only 25 years ago, today's ubiquitous use of "universal" bank credit cards might have seemed a futurist fantasy. Prior to the deregulation of the financial services industry in 1980, banks made consumer loans as "installment" credit. Loan approval was based on an assessment of the applicants' household income, personal assets, credit repayment history, and outstanding debt. Preferred clients had financial collateral and repaid their loans on a fixed time schedule. Similarly, financial companies and banks cautiously issued charge cards and revolving credit cards to low-risk clients, primarily upper- and some middle-income households, who used them for convenience or for business. Although the high inflation rates and stagnant real wages of the late 1970s encouraged greater levels of consumer borrowing, banks were reluctant at first to increase their lines of revolving credit. When they did, outstanding credit card debt increased from nearly $3 billion in 1970 to about $47 billion in 1980.

In the early 1980s, several factors contributed to the emergence of consumer financial services as a highly attractive market for banks: major losses from Third World loan delinquencies, a sharp rise in U.S. commercial real estate foreclosures, escalation of personal and corporate bankruptcies, decline in corporate borrowing, collapse of the junk bond market, and costly deregulation policies. The Reagan administration's deregulation of the banking industry was accompanied by an effective campaign against inflation, which fell from 18% in the late 1970s to 3% in the mid-1980s, but interest rates for consumer financial services remained high. With the restructuring of America's manufacturing industries, and the cost efficiencies of computer information technologies, banks turned to retail merchants and consumers to market their highly profitable consumer credit services.

Banks expanded their credit card portfolios and shifted their marketing focus from affluent "convenience" users to middle-income "revolvers." With interest rates stable at over 20%, banks soon realized that the economically stressed American middle classes were willing to accept increasing balances on their credit cards—even with inflation under 5%. As credit card profits spiraled, banks sought to sustain their growth by marketing to traditionally neglected groups: senior citizens, the working class, and college students. The success of mass-marketing campaigns, which generated billions of dollars in interest and fee revenues, contributed to a dramatic upsurge in credit card users and to the consolidation of the credit card industry.

Between 1980 and 1990, credit card debt jumped from $47 billion to almost $200 billion, and it nearly tripled again to over $570 billion in 2000. Whereas the top 50 banks accounted for about one-half of the consumer credit card market before 1980, today the top 10 banks control about 80% of outstanding credit card debt. Seventy-six million American households possess nearly 1.6 billion credit cards. Outstanding net credit card debt is in excess of $620 billion, while outstanding installment debt has crossed the $1.0 trillion threshold. In addition to retail purchases, credit cards can be used for most small business and consumer transactions, including the payment of taxes and purchases from the U.S. Postal Service and other federal and municipal governments. Credit cards, in fact, are all but required by airlines, hotels, auto rental, and other travel booking companies. They are the financial backbone of television home shopping clubs and Internet commerce. As Americans have struggled with intensifying spending pressures into the twenty-first century, credit cards have been used to launch new households and new businesses, to cushion domestic crises and survive periods of unemployment, to finance college tuition, medical emergencies, and even burial costs. With the innovation of cash advances and credit card checks or vouchers, revolving credit can now be used to buy or pay for anything. In addition, credit cards have created numerous conveniences such as detailed records of all transactions, free purchase protection and insurance benefits, instant access to cash (ATMs), and an immediate line of credit for entertainment, speculative, or investment transactions.

Some "affinity" or sponsored credit card programs enable consumers to accumulate points for a variety of gifts as well as free or discounted air travel, gasoline, long-distance telephone calls, and even the downpayment on an automobile. In sum, the universal credit card has revitalized the financial services industry with its high-cost products and created a plethora of valuable and innovative conveniences for American consumers. While credit cards have become a part of American culture, at issue are the significance and ramifications of their growing use by seniors.

Demographic and Economic Background

The number of Americans aged 65 years and older was 35.3 million in 2000 (12.8% of the U.S. population). Estimates by the U.S. Census Bureau, based on medium growth assumptions, are that this population will climb to 40.1 million in 2010 (13.1%), to 53.3 million in 2020 (16.4%), and then rise sharply to 70.1 million in 2030 (20.1%) as the baby boomer "bulge" enters retirement. By 2050, an estimated 80 million Americans will be at least 65 years old, and those aged 80-plus will increase significantly as well. American society will be composed of a growing proportion of nonworking seniors whose increased longevity will require greater resources for living and for medical care. As early baby boomers transition into retirement, consumer debt will play an increasingly important role in limiting the size of their financial "nest egg" as well as their ability to finance necessary or discretionary expenditures on high-interest consumer credit cards.

The prosperity of the post–World War II era has provided older adults with an increasing range of financial resources in retirement. Today, Social Security, Medicare, and private pensions supplement income from personal savings, investments, and family support. Compared with other developed nations, Americans have been only moderate savers, except during World War II when the U.S. savings rate exceeded 25%. During the next four decades, the personal savings rate was relatively stable at 8%, peaking at 10% in 1973. Over the last two decades, however, this rate has fallen precipitously—from about 7% in 1980 to zero at the end of 1999.

Some analysts argue that the U.S. personal savings measure substantially understates household wealth due to the appreciation of stock market investments in private pensions and 401(k)s in the 1990s. Although considerable stock market wealth was accumulated in this period, its unequal distribution tends to be overlooked. Between 1983 and 1998, an analysis of the national Consumer Finance Surveys (CFSs) reveals that the net worth of the bottom 40% of U.S. households actually declined (from $4,700 to $1,100), and the middle 20% rose by $5,500 (from $55,500 to $61,000). Even the next 20% of U.S. households, where significant stock gains would be expected, experienced only a moderate increase in net worth, from $133,600 to $161,300. Most stock market wealth is concentrated in the top 1%—especially the top one-tenth. These data, moreover, precede the $7+ trillion of losses in the equity markets over the last two years, which has intensified the pressure on U.S. households to increase personal savings. For many baby boomers, the sharp decline in their stock market investments will require an extension of their working careers or a lower standard of living in retirement, or both. Indeed, employment rates for older adults are rising, as is the proportion of seniors relying on Social Security for their primary income. This situation is exacerbated by the sharp decline in investment returns on low-risk certificate of deposits and public and corporate bonds.

For most Americans, the equity in their homes constitutes the bulk of their retirement assets. Between 1979 and 2001, the Federal Reserve Board reports that mortgage debt as a proportion of disposable household income soared from 46.6% to 73.2%. Families have extended the credit card repayment period and folded other forms of consumer debt into their primary home mortgages. Today, on average, total household debt is over 110% of disposable household income. For seniors with paid-off mortgages, their housing investment provides the potential for accessing home equity with reverse mortgages, but this possibility will not exist for the growing numbers of Americans entering retirement years with substantial outstanding mortgage debt on their homes.

These asset formation patterns are illustrative of a new and disturbing trend among baby boomer American households in the twenty-first century: spending rather than saving home equity for retirement. The Federal Reserve Board does not report any home equity loans in 1979. In 2001, on average, home equity accounts for 9.5% of disposable U.S. household income. Consequently, baby boomers are repaying higher interest credit card debt by obtaining larger home mortgages during the prime of their careers rather than accumulating retirement assets for what may otherwise have been their "golden years." (See also AGING INTO DEBT; BABY BOOMERS AND RETIREMENT; CREDIT SCORES, FINANCIAL COUNSELING FOR MID- TO LATER LIFE; FI-

NANCIAL EDUCATION FOR SENIORS; FINANCIAL RECOVERY IN LATER LIFE.)

References

Bilker, Scott. 2002. *How to Be More Credit Card and Debt Smart*. Vol. 1. Barnegat, NJ: Press One Publishers.

Drentea, Patricia. 2000. "Age, Debt and Anxiety." *Journal of Health and Social Behavior* 41 (December): 437–50.

Hall, Margaret. 2001. *Credit Cards and Checks (Earning, Saving, Spending)*. New York: Heinemann.

Manning, Robert D. 2001. *Credit Card Nation: The Consequences of America's Addiction to Credit*. New York: Basic Books.

Mishel, Lawrence, Jared Bernstein, and Heather Boushey. 2003. *The State of Working America 2002–03*. Ithaca, NY: Cornell University Press.

Pollin, Robert. 1990. *Deeper in Debt: The Changing Financial Conditions of U.S. Households*. Washington, DC: Economic Policy Institute.

Seniors USA. 2002. "American Seniors Rack Up Debt Like Never Before." Available online at http://www.senrs.com.

Sullivan, Teresa A., Elizabeth Warren, and Jay L. Westbrook. 2000. *The Fragile Middle Class: Americans in Debt*. New Haven, CT: Yale University Press.

Robert D. Manning

CONSUMER PROTECTION FOR OLDER ADULTS, federal, state, and local statutes enacted to protect older consumers. Legislation that protects older consumers includes the unfair and deceptive acts and practices statutes, the home solicitation sales acts, the Honesty in Sweepstakes Act, the Truth in Lending Act, the Fair Credit Reporting Act, and the Fair Debt Collection Practices Act. Unfair and deceptive acts and practices statutes exist in all 50 states and the District of Columbia. These statutes prohibit unfair, false, misleading, and deceptive acts or practices committed by sellers, not only in the sale of goods and services but also in advertising or soliciting the sale of goods and services. In 2000, the Protecting Seniors from Fraud Act (P.L. 106–534) was enacted, requiring the secretary of Health and Human Services (HHS) to disseminate information designed to educate senior citizens and raise awareness about the dangers of fraud. In addition, the act directs the attorney general to conduct a study that would provide assistance in developing new crime prevention strategies pertaining to crimes against seniors and to include statistics in the National Crime Victimization Survey on crimes that impact seniors.

The federal government's principal consumer protection agency is the Federal Trade Commission (FTC). Under the Federal Trade Commission Act, Congress has directed the commission to prohibit unfair or deceptive acts or practices. The recent FTC law enforcement initiatives that are of particular importance to older consumers include health care initiatives, financial practices initiative sales and promotional practices initiatives, and enforcement initiatives against fraud.

Older consumers are disadvantaged in the market due to their physical, psychological, and social frailty. Many fraudulent business activities are specifically targeting older people; in some scams, 80% or more of the victims are 65 or older. Older adults are often the deliberate targets because many older people have cash reserves or other assets to spend on seemingly attractive offers. However, they are frequently the least able to rebound from being victimized.

The frequency of occurrence and actual monetary loss are expected to be even greater than reported. Consumer abuse tends to be underreported, especially by older adults, because they are afraid of being considered incompetent or unintelligent (Friedman 1992; Lee, Soberon-Ferrer and Lee 1996; McGhee 1983). In addition to monetary loss, psychological costs including the emotional stress of being defrauded are also substantial (Friedman 1992; Lee and Soberon-Ferrer 1997).

Health Care Initiatives

Health Claims. Health care is of particular concern to older consumers, and older consumers may be particularly vulnerable to false or misleading claims about health care products and services because the marketing of such products and services often relates to conditions associated with aging (FTC 2003). Two federal agencies devote substantial resources to preventing the dissemination of unsubstantiated or otherwise deceptive claims about the health benefits of particular products or services. The Food and Drug Administration has a primary responsibility for the safety and labeling of over-the-counter (OTC) drugs, foods, and dietary supplements, and the Federal Trade Commission is responsible for making sure that advertising about the health benefits of OTC drugs, devices, foods, and dietary supplements is truthful, not misleading, and substantiated by solid scientific support. The most dramatic growth in health-related marketing has been in the dietary supplement industry, including vitamins, minerals, herbs, and hormones, with an estimated 100 million U.S. consumers using such supplemental products.

As a part of efforts to protect consumers against false or misleading claims, the FTC launched "Operation Cure.all," a comprehensive law enforcement and consumer education campaign directed at protecting consumers from Internet health fraud. The FTC has also provided continuing effort to ensure that consumers get accurate and reliable information about weight-loss products and programs through "Operation Waistline," a coordinated, long-term consumer education and law enforcement program.

Medicare Fraud. Another form of health care fraud is Medicare fraud, which refers to unnecessary service supply or low-quality service that does not satisfy the standard. Medicare fraud tends to accompany billing for services that were never rendered or billing for a service at a higher rate than is actually provided. The U.S. General Accounting Office estimates that $1 out of every $7 spent on Medicare is paid inappropriately due to fraud or abuse. Last year, Medicare lost nearly $13 billion to improper claims.

In 1995, Operation Restore Trust (ORT) was enacted. Through ORT, the Administration on Aging (AoA) joined with an antifraud plan in the Medicare and Medicaid programs. AoA trained approximately 2,500 staff and collected $187 million in fines, recoveries, and settlements. In 1996, Congress enacted the Health Insurance Portability and Accountability Act (HIPAA) to fund protecting Medicare program integrity. This reduced Medicare's payment error rate from 14% to 6.8% during 1990–2000. Health and Human Services and the Department of Justice coordinate federal, state, and local health care law enforcement programs. During the past four years, the federal government has conducted 1,291 criminal prosecutions and recovered a total of $3.4 billion in fines, judgments, and settlements. In addition, individuals and businesses who are convicted of

Medicare fraud may not receive payments from Medicare, Medicaid, and other federal health care programs. During fiscal year 2000, 3,350 individuals and businesses were excluded from doing business with Medicare and Medicaid.

The Office of Inspector General (OIG) monitors the Medicare and Medicaid programs at HHS through evaluating and criminal investigating. These activities help to improve quality of health care and reduce fraud and abuse. Also, OIG maintains an antifraud hotline against Medicare fraud. The hotline received over 500,000 calls in 2001 and has fielded over 1.5 million calls since 1995.

Sales and Promotional Practices Initiatives

Telemarketing. One of the most frequent types of elder consumer abuse occurs through telemarketing. More than a quarter (26%) of telemarketing fraud reports were from older consumers (NCL 2002). The top three telemarketing frauds toward older adults are sweepstakes and prize offers (average loss: $2,752), magazine sales (average loss: $98), and credit card loss protection plans (average loss: $229). Targeting consumers with financial problems, scammers guarantee a credit card regardless of bad credit history. Most credit card issuers do not charge in advance, but the free offers end up with monetary losses.

The Securities and Exchange Commission and the FTC provide protection from deceptive telemarketing through the Federal Securities Laws and Telemarketing Sales Rules (TSR), respectively. The state also may bring a civil action to enforce the rule of the commission and to obtain compensation for its residents. FTC's amended TSR includes a national "do not call" registry to stop unwanted sales calls. This rule also allows consumers to request to be put on the company's own "do not call" list. The law requires telemarketers to search the registry every 90 days and delete phone numbers on the registry from the list. A violation of this rule would fine the telemarketer up to $11,000 for each call.

Amended TSR also restricts unauthorized billing. Before billing, telemarketers should get a customer's consent to be charged. In the case of a "free-to-pay conversion" offer, a telemarketer should have a customer's permission to use a particular account number, confirm the number by repeating the last four digits, and record the entire phone transaction. The new sales rule also requires caller ID (identification) transmission to protect privacy and help in law enforcement efforts. Telemarketers must transmit their telephone numbers to caller ID services. Other continuing telemarketing sales rules are as follows: Calling times are restricted to the hours between 8 A.M. and 9:00 P.M. Telemarketers must make their identities clear before making a sales pitch. Telemarketers must disclose all material information about the goods or services they are offering and the terms of the sale.

Funeral Services. A funeral can cost $10,000 or more, and this expensive consumer purchase is often made at an emotionally difficult time, often a first-time purchase (FTC 2003). Under the Funeral Industry Practices Rule (16 CFR Part 453), funeral providers should provide consumers timely and clear information relating to the range of funeral goods and services offered and the prices charged. FTC, state attorneys general, and AARP have collaborated in their enforcement approaches since the rule became effective in 1984, including investigations and test shopping across various geographic areas and, since 1999, test shopping more vigorously.

Energy and Home Appliances. Older consumers often try to save on expenses by cutting down on energy use. The Appliance Labeling Rule requires the manufacturers of home appliances to provide consumers accurate information about energy usage levels for home appliances. The rule requires that manufacturers disclose specific energy information at the point of sale in the form of an Energy Guide label that is affixed to the covered product.

Home Improvement. Most elder homeowners periodically have repairs or maintenance work. Many home improvements are performed in inadequate or fraudulent home repair work. According to the National Association of Consumer Agency Administrators (NACAA) and the Consumer Federation of America (CFA), home improvement fraud is a highly ranked elder consumer crime. Among the common fraudulent home improvement practices are charging high prices for low-quality materials; misrepresenting the need for repairs, the work to be performed, or the materials to be used; and using deceptive pricing.

State statutes and their enforcement regarding home improvement scams differ among states. Some states have no applicable laws or regulations, while others have specific statutes regarding home improvement contractors. The enforcement of state laws that cover home improvement contractors plays a key role in protecting consumers. The AARP has developed a model statute for regulating home improvement contractors. This requires home improvement contractors to be licensed, to carry certain insurance coverage, and to grant consumers the recovery of damages and costs.

Enforcement Initiatives against Fraud

At the federal level, there are two important enforcement initiatives to identify fraudulent or deceptive schemes. First, in 1997, the FTC established the *Consumer Sentinel* as a Web-based law enforcement network, which allows law enforcement agencies in the United States, Canada, and Australia an immediate access to consumer complaints. Both public and private consumer organizations, including 64 local offices of the Better Business Bureaus across the nation, the National Consumers League's National Fraud Information Center, Project Phonebusters in Canada, and the U.S. Postal Inspection Services, contribute consumer complaints to the Consumer Sentinel database, from which law enforcement agencies can identity theft, telemarketing scams, and other consumer abuse in a timely manner.

Building on the Consumer Sentinel, the FTC works closely with foreign governments and launched a pilot project called *econosumer.gov*, a joint effort of the commission, agencies from 12 other countries, and the Organization for Economic Cooperation and Development (OECD) to gather and share cross-border e-commerce complaints. This project allows law enforcers from around the world to access a database of consumer complaints specifically about cross-border Internet transactions.

The growth of the Internet and e-commerce has been explosive, and not surprisingly, the boom in e-commerce has been accompanied by online fraud and deception. In 2000, roughly 26% of all fraud complaints reported to the Consumer Sentinel were related to online fraud and deception. The top ten Internet scams identified through an analysis of complaint data in the Consumer Sentinel database were Internet auction fraud, Internet service provider scams, Internet Web site design/promotions (Web cramming), Internet information and adult services, pyramid scams, business opportunities and work-at-home scams, investment schemes and get-rich-quick scams, travel/vacation fraud, telephone/pay-per-call solicitation frauds, and health care frauds.

Finally, identity theft is rapidly growing due to increasing e-commerce transactions, which allow the scammers to easily access personal information. An identity theft victim often realizes that he or she was defrauded after having a problem with using credit. The U.S. General Accounting Office reported a huge increase in identity theft, costing millions of dollars (Stana 2002). The Identity Theft Act (1998) made it a federal crime to misuse identification of another person. The crime is investigated by federal investigative agencies, such as the U.S. Secret Service, the Federal Burea of Investigation (FBI), and the U.S. Postal Inspection Service, and prosecuted by the Department of Justice. Also, privacy principles were set out in the 1980 OECD *Guidelines for the Protection of Privacy and Personal Data*, taking into account the OECD *Ministerial Declaration on the Protection of Privacy*. (See also CPA ELDERCARE SERVICES; CRIME PROTECTION; DISASTER PREPAREDNESS AND OLDER ADULTS; ELDER LAW PRACTICE; FINANCIAL ELDER ABUSE; OMBUDSMAN.)

References

AARP. 2002. "Talking to an Old Audience about Fraud: Information for Crime Prevention Officers." Washington, DC: AARP.

Federal Trade Commission (FTC). 2003. "Staff Summary of Federal Trade Commission Activities Affecting Older Consumers." Available online at http://www.ftc.gov/os/2001/10/agingrpt.htm.

Friedman, M. 1992. "Confidence Swindles of Older Consumers." *Journal of Consumer Affairs* 26 (1): 20–46.

Lee, J., and L.V. Geistfeld. 1999. "Elderly Consumers' Receptiveness to Telemarketing Fraud." *Journal of Public Policy & Marketing* 18(2): 208–17.

Lee, J., and H. Soberon-Ferrer. 1997. "Consumer Vulnerability to Fraud: Influencing Factors." *Journal of Consumer Affairs* 31(1): 70–89.

Lee, J., H. Soberon-Ferrer, and G. Lee. 1996. "The Elderly: Vulnerability to Deception and Fraud." *Consumer Interests Annual* 42: 423–28.

McGhee, J.L. 1983. "The Vulnerability of Elderly Consumers." *International Aging and Human Development* 17(3): 223–46.

National Consumer League (NCL). 2002. "One in Four Telemarketing Victims Age 60 and Older." Available online at http://www.natlconsumersleague.org/elderfraudweek.htm.

Stana, R.M. 2002. "Identity Theft: Available Data Indicate the Prevalence and Cost." *Justice Issues*. Washington, DC: GAO.

Jinkook Lee and Eun-Jin Kim

CONTINUING CARE RETIREMENT COMMUNITIES (CCRCs), residential communities distinguished by the presence of communal dining facilities and a range of nonacute medical care on campus. CCRCs are one of several types of planned residential communities that also include assisted living, congregate housing, and retirement communities/resorts (such as Del Webb's Leisure World). Characteristically CCRCs comprise a campus setting and three levels of care: independent living units, assisted living/personal care units, and a skilled nursing facility (SNF). Because CCRCs offer this continuum of shelter and care, they are considered one type of long-term care option (e.g., adult day care, assisted living, nursing homes). They usually include a service package of meals, activities, and transportation, as well as health care. They also constitute a housing option that, thanks to supportive services, enables residents to age in place within a community defined by the campus setting. Indeed, the median annual residence turnover (18%) for CCRCs is low compared to that for assisted living (60%) and independent living residences (39%) (American Seniors Housing Association [ASHA] 2002b).

A Brief History

Although CCRCs are regarded as a relatively new approach to caring for older adults, their roots go back to the Middle Ages. In Europe, medieval craft guilds developed housing to provide safe, secure environments for their members when they became old and no longer were able to work. In the latter part of the nineteenth century, some U.S. nonprofit church, fraternal, and community groups ran facilities that provided food, shelter, and health care for their older members for the rest of their lives, even if they were unable to pay. They were called "lifecare" or "total care" communities; an individual's estate was often surrendered in return for perpetual care. As the need for additional facilities emerged, larger pools of capital were required, giving rise to nonrefundable entrance fees that could be used as seed money for other projects.

There were about 25 lifecare communities in the early 1960s; 20 years later, their numbers had grown to about 400 facilities. In the mid-1980s, articles were published about lifecare communities going bankrupt, which gave rise to resident fears, underwriter unwillingness to finance facilities, and some state regulation (Scott and Maziarka 1987). One factor was the inability of communities to get nursing home licenses as states sought to control the number of SNFs, making it difficult for CCRCs to honor their guarantee of lifetime care. Other factors were the lack of access to low-cost capital and the need for more funds (e.g., monthly fees) as residents' longevity increased and their needs grew, as well as for more sophisticated actuarial calculations to project costs appropriately.

Despite these problems, the numbers of CCRCs continued to grow in the 1990s as more older adults sought freedom from the upkeep and maintenance of their single-family homes. They also looked for an option that provided continued care without their being a burden to their families, usually located within 25 miles of where they lived before entering the facility. The failure rate now is very low due to the greater sophistication of the investment community, more educated residents, improved actuarial techniques and better management, and strengthened regulation of the financial aspects of CCRCs. Today, the American Association of Homes and Services for the Aging (AAHSA) estimates slightly more than 2,000 CCRCs serve approximately 625,000 older adults in all 50 states and the District of Columbia and that more than 40% of all CCRCs are found in five states: California, Pennsylvania, Florida, Illinois, and Ohio. The average age of CCRC campuses is 25 years.

One recent trend is the emergence of for-profit CCRCs. Because relatively few communities have been built within the last decade, this has led to pent-up demand and more financing becoming available for for-profits. This group of CCRCs tends to be more upscale than those operated by nonprofits, although the higher-end market is limited.

Living Arrangements

CCRCs facilitate an independent lifestyle, combined with security. If residents become frail or ill, they know their needs will be met in a familiar environment, rather than having to relocate to a new place, as is true of those who live in their own homes and apartments or in stand-alone assisted living facilities (Golant 1992). However, in some CCRCs residents must move from one level of care to another, which often requires going to live in another wing or floor or perhaps a separate building. Most persons entering a CCRC, whether a single individual or a couple, reside in an apartment or cottage and move to a personal care unit or assisted living when, or if, their health declines. If their health status warrants 24-hour skilled nursing care, residents subsequently move to the SNF.

The average CCRC includes about 200 independent living units that can be studio or efficiency apartments and one-, two-, or three-bedroom apartments or cottages (Golant 1992). The larger units include a living room, a kitchen, and a bath; studios typically include a kitchen alcove and a bath. Apartments are decorated with the resident's own furniture and other belongings. Since the 1980s, two-bedroom units have become more popular; most CCRCs find it difficult to market studios and end up combining them into larger units, entailing substantial remodeling costs.

Residents usually retain use of their automobile, requiring the CCRC to provide adequate parking spaces, and typically eat some meals in their own units. Eating one meal a day in the congregate dining room supports residents' need for community and interaction. They are expected to be able to carry out most instrumental activities of daily living (IADLs) (e.g., shopping, cooking, money management, house cleaning, taking medications without supervision), as well as activities of daily living (ADLs), such as bathing, dressing, eating, toileting, and getting out of their unit without assistance. When a resident is unable to perform one or two ADLs or a combination of ADLs and IADLs, he or she moves to assisted living or a personal care unit, where help with these activities is provided. These units are often clustered together in a separate wing or floor or even a separate building. The likelihood of this kind of move occurring is greater today as the average age of a CCRC resident is 81, compared to age 79 just a decade ago (Golant 1992). These units are typically one room with a bath. Residents eat their meals in a congregate dining room that, in some instances, may be separate from the dining room serving the independent living units. Depending upon contract provisions, personal care is either provided by the CCRC or can be obtained on a fee-for-service (FFS) basis. In some CCRCs, personal care services may be provided in the independent living unit, especially if a spouse also resides there.

Should residents experience greater impairment in ADLs or cognitive function, they may be moved to the skilled nursing level of care. SNFs are usually housed in a separate building on a contiguous part of the CCRC. Sometimes a CCRC may contract with an SNF located next door to its campus. One advantage of the CCRC SNF for couples is that as one spouse needs a higher level of care, they may reside in separate care levels but are able to contact or be with each other with relative ease.

Services and Amenities

CCCRs offer a variety of services to residents. These include building and grounds maintenance, utilities, activity and recreational programs, light and/or heavy house cleaning, laundry, meals including special diets, transportation and parking, emergency call and security systems, home modifications (e.g., grab bars), and various kinds of exercise and therapy programs. Amenities include libraries, barber and beauty shops, game rooms and auditorium/chapel, private dining rooms (for family celebrations), overnight accommodation facilities for guests, arts and crafts programs, cable television, swimming and therapeutic pools, garden plots, woodworking shops, and small convenience stores. The most typical amenities offered by at least 80% of CCRCs include beauty and barber shops, activities, crafts and multipurpose rooms, laundry facilities, libraries, and private dining rooms (ASHA 2002a). Increasingly, residents are looking for services and amenities related to their interests in health and wellness and in technology. Computer training and hookups, putting greens, yoga and a health office for checkups, and health promotion classes are among the new kinds of activities being offered, especially by larger CCRCs. Some CCRCs also provide services to nonresidents, similar to European "service houses." These can include adult day care, respite care, meal services, and support groups. This is one strategy being used by lower-cost CCRCs that may also admit nonresident patients to the nursing care unit.

Payment Methods

The continuum of care offered by the CCRC is governed by a contract to which the resident agrees at the time of entry. Residents must abide by a variety of financial and legal obligations that are unique to this housing and care option. The contract governs both the financial and care relationship between the resident and the community. CCRC contracts take several forms. Knowledge of the various options offered under these contracts and how they are financed is important for those contemplating a move into a CCRC, as well as for those with primary responsibility for an older person's well-being and professionals who provide older adults with legal and financial advice or who provide retirement planning services to clients of all ages.

There are three general approaches to financing CCRC residency: entry fee, monthly fee only, and equity. Under an endowment or entry fee plan, the resident pays a lump sum upfront; this can cost from less than $100,000 up to more than $500,000, particularly in California. Such fees are often partially deductible as prepaid health care for income tax purposes. The entry fee is commonly in addition to monthly fees or other periodic fees that are payable during the time the individual or couple resides in the CCRC. These can increase over time.

The entry fee may be partially or totally refundable or nonrefundable to the resident upon leaving, death, or transfer. Under most contracts, the portion that is refundable decreases over time—typically, 2% per month over 50 months. Communities with more liberal refunds usually balance off that policy with higher monthly fees. CCRCs with large entry fees and less liberal refunds are likely to provide strong guarantees of lifetime care, accompanied by limits on how much monthly fees can be raised during the resident's tenure in the community. Communities with small or no entry fees and more generous refund policies are likely to have weaker lifecare guarantees, unless management has a "benevolence" or "endowment" program that helps pick up some of the costs. Entry fees and monthly fees vary greatly from CCRC to CCRC. The amounts depend on the type of unit occupied, the type of health care coverage, and the resident agreement and payment plan offered.

Two other approaches include the monthly fee only and the equity plan. The former is a rental arrangement with a service package and/or health care package, similar to many assisted living arrangements (http://www.aahsa.org/member/backgrd4.as). The latter plan is somewhat rare. It involves the purchase of the living unit as real estate, with the actual ownership of the unit being transferred upon sale to the resident. In equity contracts, the resident (owner) participates in any changes in the value of the unit from purchase. In this kind of contract, health-related service arrangements vary, but usually the resident is required to purchase service and/or health packages.

Within any of these general approaches there are three major types of contracts, primarily focused on health care coverage: extensive, modified, or fee-for-service. The *extensive* or all-inclusive contract includes housing, residential services and amenities, and unlimited long-term nursing care, usually without substantial increases in periodic payments except for normal operating cost and inflation adjustments. This arrangement combines a large health care insurance element with residential living. In essence, a resident shares the cost of SNF and catastrophic health care with all other residents.

Modified agreements include housing, residential services and amenities, combined with a substantial—but not unlimited—amount of long-term nursing care at no additional cost. For example, the contract may specify 30, 60, or 90 days, per lifetime or per year. Once the limit is reached, the resident who is availing him- or herself of these services pays a per diem or discounted per diem amount for additional nursing care.

By contrast, less than one-third of CCRCs offer a *fee-for-service* (FFS) contract. This arrangement includes housing, residential services, and amenities but does not cover assisted living or SNF costs. Residents are guaranteed access to health care service, but they must pay prevailing rates. In essence, they pay only for the long-term nursing care services actually used. Entry and monthly fees tend to be lowest under this kind of contract, but total monthly costs may not be; many FFS CCRCs require no advance or a minimal fee.

CCRCs allow older adults to make more efficient use of their financial resources by assuming the financial risk for housing, food, and care needs for the rest of their lives; by providing a form of long-term care insurance; by avoiding the need to pay for two types of housing at the same time (a home or apartment and an SNF); and providing economies of scale in the delivery of services such as home care. However, there are business risks associated with CCRCs. For example, while they function like insurance companies in assuming risk, especially the risk of the cost of providing long-term care, they have far fewer customers on which to base expected cost projections and over which to spread actual costs. CCRCs also may encounter adverse selection and, by providing quality care, may exacerbate their financial exposure by extending the lives of their residents if they do not also adjust for the financial risk of increased resident life spans.

Regulation

To counter some of these problems, policymakers focus on protecting residents' investments and ensuring that the terms of the contract with the CCRC are upheld. CCRC regulation can take three forms: self-regulation via an accreditation process; regulation via accounting protocols and procedures; and state regulation. AAHSA, through the Continuing Care Accreditation Commission (CCAC) founded in 1985, accredits both nonprofit and for-profit communities. Using a series of standards, the CCAC seeks to assure consumers that a CCAC-accredited provider has met specific predetermined standards of quality in three areas: governance, finance and strategy, and health and wellness. It also seeks to help providers develop, interpret, and evaluate all components of their organizations and to provide the commission with a reliable basis for making accreditation decisions.

Integrated strategic planning and a self-study are crucial aspects of this accreditation process. As of 1997, 246 CCRCs in more than 25 states were accredited by the CCAC (CCAC 2002). However, only three states accept this accreditation in lieu of a state review (ASHA 2002c).

To evaluate financial strengths and weaknesses of CCRCs, three rating agencies are active: Fitch Investors Service, Standard and Poor's, and Moody's Investor Service. Several organizations also provide benchmarking studies based on financial ratios and trends. Other factors such as management and board experience, facility location, and competitive pressures are equally important in evaluating the overall strength of a CCRC. Standards promulgated by the Financial Accounting Standards Board (FASB) also affect nonprofit CCRC financial ratios, including FASB #116, Accounting for Contributions Received and Made, and FASB #117, Financial Statements of Not-for-Profit Organizations. These reports can reassure consumers and their advisors about the viability of a CCRC to make good on its guarantees of lifelong care.

Finally, all states regulate a CCRC's health care unit in accordance with the Centers for Medicare & Medicaid Services (CMS) guidelines. In addition, 39 states regulate CCRCs on financial and other aspects, but with considerable variation. State insurance agencies have primary responsibility for CCRC oversight, followed by health and then aging agencies. Contract forms must be submitted to 30 of the 39 states for review. Not all states require disclosure of a CCRC's financial report to residents. One-third do require such disclosure before a contract is signed, but 17% only require it if the resident requests it. Other states require disclosure based on some combination of before or at signing and some additional time period (e.g., annually, semiannually), or on request. Thirty of the 39 states have some designated period in which residents can rescind their contract, ranging from 7 days to 1 year; the most frequent time periods are 7 days, 10 days, and 30 days (ASHA 2002c).

Given the focus of policymakers on preserving the residents' investment, it is a matter of some concern that not all 39 states with CCRC regulations have explicit requirements for reserves or for the escrow treatment of entry fees. Of a less serious nature, but related to the ability of residents to protect their investment, less than half of these states have enacted legislation enabling residents' rights to organize through an association.

Consumer Information

Caveat emptor—let the buyer beware—is a wise admonition for older adults who are contemplating a move into a CCRC. To determine if a CCRC is the right choice, prospective residents need to learn about the full range of services and amenities offered and to weigh the different senior housing options and the expenses of each. Two basic kinds of consumer information exist to help older consumers make good decisions: directories of different CCRCs (and often other housing options), often grouped by state or by region, and booklets or brochures that provide information and often worksheets to enhance decision making. AAHSA and an organization called Lifestyles provide the first kind of information to help prospective CCRC residents find a community to fit their needs. The AAHSA directory (AARP 2002c) profiles more than 500 CCRCs and also identifies accredited communities, while Lifestyles information focuses on all kinds of housing options in a given region.

Information provided by AARP, and other AASHA information, may be of greater relevance to a consumer trying to decide whether or not to enter a CCRC. The AARP, like one AAHSA brochure (AARP 2002b), features a range of housing options, including CCRCs, to enable consumers to make overall comparisons between CCRCs and other kinds of senior housing and care arrangements. AAHSA's guidebook for consumers (AARP 2002d) provides tips on how to conduct an initial search and emphasizes criteria to be addressed: services and ownership arrangements, location and management; common contract provisions; and specific services and charges, fee increases, and contract termination. Worksheets and consumer checklists are included.

Ultimately, the decision to enter a CCRC or not is likely to be a permanent decision, not only about housing and care but also about lifestyle preferences. Many seniors do not want to live in age-segregated housing or with large groups of other people. Many also want to age in place and, assuming that home care services are available, may just as easily be able to afford the costs of such care as to pay CCRC costs. Purchasing a long-term care insurance policy with an inflation-adjustment factor and with coverage for both home-based and SNF care is another option for those who can afford a CCRC. Additionally, those wishing to bequeath an estate to family members or a favorite charity may be less able to pursue that goal, unless they can find a CCRC with an equity contract or a liberal refund policy. Despite these cautions, the CCRC lifestyle, wide range of services and amenities, and peace of mind for both seniors and their families will continue to make this housing and care option attractive to many older people. (See also CPA ELDERCARE SERVICES; FINANCIAL ADVISORS; FINANCIAL PLANNING PROCESS; FRAILTY PLANNING; HOMEOWNERSHIP.)

Organizations

AARP
American Association of Homes and Services for the Aging (AAHSA)
American Seniors Housing Association (ASHA)
Continuing Care Accreditation Commission

Suggested Reading

Simmons, Henry C., and E. Craig MacBean. 2000. *Thriving after 55: Your Guide to Fully Living the Rest of Your Life*. Richmond, VA: Prime Press.

References

AARP. 2002a. *The Continuing Care Retirement Community: A Guidebook for Consumers*. Washington, DC: American Association of Homes and Services for the Aging.

AARP. 2002b. *The Continuing Care Retirement Community: A Life-Style Offering Security and Independence*. Washington, DC: American Association of Homes and Services for the Aging.

AARP. 2002c. *The Consumers' Directory of Continuing Care Retirement Communities*. Washington, DC: American Association of Homes and Services for the Aging.

AARP. 2002d. *Selecting Retirement Housing*. Washington, DC: American Association of Homes and Services for the Aging.

American Seniors Housing Association (ASHA). 2002a. *Non-profit Housing and Care Options for Elder People*. Washington, DC: Author (in English and Spanish).

American Seniors Housing Association (ASHA). 2002b. *Seniors Housing Statistical Handbook*. 3rd ed. Washington, DC: Author.

American Seniors Housing Association (ASHA). 2002c. *State of Seniors Housing 2001*. Washington, DC: Author.

Continuing Care Accreditation Commission. 2002. *Seniors Housing: State Regulatory Handbook*. Washington, DC: Author.

Golant, Stephen M. 1992. *Housing America's Elderly*. Newbury Park, CA: Sage Publications.

Golant, Stephen M. 2002. *Standards of Excellence*. Washington, DC: Continuing Care Accreditation Commission.

Scott, Terence J., and Robert F. Maziarka. 1987. *Elderly Housing Options*. Chicago: Pluribus Press.

Phoebe Liebig, Marilyn C. Kennedy, and Stephanie Cory

COOPERATIVE OWNERSHIP IN HOUSING, a form of ownership in which a corporation (or trust or partnership) holds title to a multiunit development and grants occupancy rights in specific units to shareholders under proprietary leases. Individuals do not hold title to their dwelling unit; instead, they own stock in a corporation that owns the building or development. The cooperative buyer becomes a shareholder in the corporation and enters into a "proprietary" lease for a particular dwelling unit. Cooperative owners thus have leasehold rights to their housing units and ownership rights in the cooperative housing corporation. The lease payment covers a pro rata share of the amounts needed to cover operating expenses, taxes, and the mortgage debt of the whole complex. Owners of cooperative housing are eligible for income tax deductions for their shares of the mortgage interest and property taxes paid by the cooperative corporation. This is in contrast to the owners of condominiums, who have ownership of their occupied units plus an ownership interest with all other owners in the common area. Owning a cooperative apartment can be significantly less expensive than renting an apartment because landlord profits are not found in cooperative housing.

Some of the advantages and disadvantages of condominium ownership also apply to cooperative housing. An important distinction is that individuals owning stock in a corporation that owns cooperative housing assume the additional financial responsibility of keeping the corporation solvent. When an owner defaults on payments in cooperative ownership, the remaining share owners are responsible for paying the defaulted portion of the mortgage, real estate taxes, and operating expenses. If there are large enough numbers of defaulted share owners, the financial burden may have a snowball effect, causing other share owners in the cooperative housing complex to default. This snowball phenomenon is less likely to occur in condominiums, since owners obtain their own financing and are responsible for their own mortgage payments and property tax assessments. Individual owners therefore are not liable for the default on any other owner's financing obligations.

Since mortgage lenders cannot take the dwelling unit itself as collateral, and many do not wish to make long-term loans that are collateralized by the shares in the cooperative corporation, obtaining financing or refinancing for a cooperative unit can be difficult. (An exception occurs where cooperatives are a common form of homeownership. In New York, for example, lenders readily make loans to purchasers of cooperatives.) This may be an important factor for prospective owners to consider, especially if the market should sour and shareholders become unable to sell their units. Then the only option is to sublet temporarily, but almost all cooperative apartment complexes impose subleasing restrictions on the owner. Additionally, the managing board of the cooperative can reject a prospective buyer, causing the sale of one's cooperative shares (and the dwelling unit) to take longer.

As rents continue to rise, and as the demographic profile in the United States changes to reflect an increasingly older population, easy-to-maintain homeownership options such as cooperatives are likely to increase in popularity. This trend will be encouraged by the current high costs associated with purchasing raw land and building materials, compelling developers to build more housing complexes with increased numbers of dwelling units per acre than before. The condominium and cooperative forms of ownership offer older buyers more affordable options, as well as an assortment of exterior amenities and opportunities for increased social activities. Efficiently managed cooperative and condominium projects may thus constitute excellent housing options for the U.S. older population. (See also CONDOMINIUMS; FINANCIAL ADVISORS; FRAILTY PLANNING; HOMEOWNERSHIP; HOUSING COUNSELING FOR OLDER AMERICANS.)

Organization

National Association of Housing Co-operatives

Suggested Readings

Irwin, Robert. 1999. *Tips and Traps When Buying a Condo, Co-op, or Townhouse*. New York: McGraw-Hill.

Kiplinger's Personal Finance Magazine, eds. 2002. *Kiplinger's Buying & Selling a Home*. 7th ed. Washington, DC: Kiplinger Books.

Shapiro, Sylvia. 1998. *The Co-op Bible: Everything You Need to Know about Co-Ops and Condos: Getting In, Staying In, Surviving, Thriving*. New York: St. Martin's Griffin.

References

Golant, Stephen M. 1992. *Housing America's Elderly: Many Possibilities/Few Choices*. Newbury Park, CA: Sage Publications.

Shilling, James D. 2002. *Real Estate*. 13th ed. Cincinnati, OH: South-Western/Thomson Learning.

Smith, Halbert C., and John B. Corgel. 1992. *Real Estate Perspectives*. Boston, MA: Irvin.

Taishoff, Lewis C. 1981. *Cooperative Housing Conversions*. New York: Praeger.

Andrew Quang Do

CORPORATE ELDERCARE PROGRAMS, a form of employee assistance for the benefit of employees' older relatives. Human resource professionals in U.S. companies have extended the meaning of eldercare to include a variety of innovative programs designed to help employees who care for an older member of the family.

Several rapidly converging factors have contributed to the growing numbers of corporate eldercare programs: the aging of America, costs of family caregiving, changes in family structure that have eroded traditional caregiving at home, increased employment of women outside the home, and changing societal values about the balance between work and family life. Because of the demands it places on an employed caregiver, the care of older adults has emerged as a bottom-line issue for leading companies. Caregiving can take a personal toll on a company's employees and impair their productivity on the job. It is estimated that caregiving costs U.S. businesses $11 to $29 billion each year.

Benefits of corporate eldercare programs accrue to several constituencies: employed caregivers, their companies, and older persons who are the indirect beneficiaries of the assistance their younger relatives receive by way of information and resources to help older individuals with their current needs.

Types of Corporate Eldercare Programs

Company eldercare programs vary widely. Some companies have recast existing benefits—flextime programs, leave benefits, work schedule adjustments, and financial benefits—to encourage their use for the dependent care needs of employees, including care of children, adolescents, and older adults. Others offer initiatives designed specifically for eldercare. A 1994 General Accounting Office survey found that medium and large companies who employ a combined 23 million workers offer at least flexible scheduling options that could be identified and actively supported as usable for eldercare. Of the total, 9 million people work for corporations that also provide assistance specifically designed for eldercare, such as information about long-term care services and support groups for caregivers. More than 8 million people work for companies planning to expand existing eldercare options or to offer new ones.

Publications

Substantial numbers of companies have published or distributed eldercare information to their workforce. These have ranged from comprehensive handbooks on issues associated with aging and the service system to information about specific topics such as Alzheimer's disease. Other firms have developed work and family resource libraries that include books, videos, and audiocassettes on popular eldercare issues.

Eldercare has also moved to online providers. Some company programs enable employees to download "tip sheets" and resource information and to order larger booklets and books online.

Fairs and Support Groups

Many companies have supplemented informational materials with workshops, seminars, and support groups for employees who are currently caring for an older relative. Numerous corporations employ outside experts or services to conduct these seminars. Topics can include financial concerns such as estate planning, paying for nursing home care, and understanding the insurance needs of older persons. Some companies have even begun to offer these events virtually through use of phone and computer technology.

Financial Assistance

Few companies provide direct financial assistance to employees or their relatives, but many offer dependent care assistance plans (DCAPs) under the Internal Revenue Code to employees. This benefit, however, can help only a small proportion of employed caregivers because DCAPs are limited to older adults who are legal dependents of the employee. Several companies offer long-term care insurance to their employees, and the employee can sometimes purchase a policy for a parent as well. In most cases, employees pay the full premium for coverage of a portion of nursing or home care costs for themselves or their older relatives, should long-term care be needed in the future.

Consultation and Referral Services

The most common response by large employers has been to take a broad approach to the range of eldercare problems employees face by offering them consultation and referral services. These services have been viewed as critical, since employees cannot come to work unless they have made care arrangements for their older relatives. Consultation and referral services have been designed to address specific issues including information, referrals to care providers, and individual counseling.

Eldercare consultation and referral services, when comprehensively delivered, include access to an eldercare professional. This professional provides expert counseling and helps the employee identify concerns and reach informed decisions, based on detailed knowledge of national and local community resources. The services also provide education through counseling and written materials that help employees select appropriate care. They can refer to providers as diverse as home health and transportation programs, elder law attorneys, and bill-paying services. Employees and their families remain responsible for selecting and paying for any services they choose. In 2001, a Hewitt Associates survey found 40% of companies in their sample now offer consultation and referral services.

Development of Services

Several companies have gone beyond consultation and referral programs to increase the supply and quality of eldercare (and child care) services in communities where employees, retirees, or older relatives live. IBM, in 1989, earmarked a portion of its Fund for Dependent Care Initiatives for eldercare projects such as respite care and development, recruitment, and training of in-home health and social service workers. Later, the American Business Collaboration, which used IBM funds to leverage investment by other companies with similar needs, continued some investment in the eldercare infrastructure. AT&T also announced, in 1989, a significant Family Care Development Fund of $10 million, jointly funded by its unions and management. This fund continues to provide seed money to encourage the development and improve the quality of child and eldercare programs.

Decision Making

There is no best way to select an eldercare program. Many companies, however, go through a series of steps in examining eldercare options. These include examining existing benefit programs, assessing employees' eldercare responsibilities and needs, examining costs, and selecting an approach to meet the needs of the broadest group of employees.

Care Management Services

The newest corporate eldercare response extends support to more involved caregivers by paying part of the cost of geriatric care management service, such as in-person assessments and professional evaluations of facilities, such as assisted living and nursing homes.

Improving employee productivity, retaining experienced workers, and responding to employee requests are the primary reasons corporations offer eldercare plans. Reasons given by companies not planning to introduce or expand eldercare benefits include concerns about costs, lack of a needs assessment, or being unaware of the issue (General Accounting Office 1994). However, the needs of employees with eldercare responsibilities are becoming more prevalent. Some of the impacts of caregiving include lost productivity in American corporations, loss of top performers, absenteeism, and tardiness. While corporate eldercare is still in its infancy, innovative programs already in place help companies achieve their business objectives and increase employee productivity, and older persons receive the information and care they need. As the numbers of aging Americans increase even more rapidly in the decades ahead, and as the baby boom generation moves into retirement age, demand for corporate eldercare programs is likely to increase, and even more innovative programs are likely to be developed. (See also CPA ELDERCARE SERVICES; EMPLOYEE BENEFITS IN THE UNITED STATES; GERIATRIC CARE MANAGERS [GCMs]; GERONTOLOGICAL SOCIAL WORK; HOME CARE SERVICES FOR OLDER ADULTS.)

Organizations

Bureau of National Affairs
Conference Board
National Alliance of Caregiving

References

General Accounting Office. 1994. *Long-Term Care: Private Sector Elder Care Could Yield Multiple Benefits*. Washington, DC: Author.

Hewitt Associates. 2002. "Spec Summary™: Work/Life Benefits 2001–2002 (U.S.)." Available online at http://was4.hewitt.com/hewitt/.

Neal, Margaret, Neal Chapman, and Berit Ingersoll-Dayton. 1988. *Eldercare, Employees and the Workplace: Findings from a Survey of Employees*. Portland, OR: Research Institute on Aging, Portland State University.

Rodgers, Francene, and Charles Rodgers. 1989. "Business and the Facts of Family Life." *Harvard Business Review* (November–December).

Diane S. Piktialis

COST OF FAMILY CAREGIVING, the estimated financial impact of caring for older and disabled persons. One out of four families in the United States is caring for an aging relative or other loved one, and as longevity rates increase, this number is likely to grow. Despite the changes in family structure that have seen the nuclear family disperse, a family member still provides an estimated 80% to 90% of all care to the frail older adults in our population. The strain on the family—with fewer siblings to care for aging parents than in previous generations, more women in the workforce, divorce and remarriage, and family members living in different parts of the country—can be great, but family members continue to take responsibility for their loved ones. While they provide care willingly, they also often pay a price emotionally, physically, and financially.

Financial Impact on Caregivers

Caregiving has a financial impact on caregivers, both in terms of the money they spend on behalf of their loved ones and, if they are employed, in real lost wealth over their lifetime. It is estimated that caregivers spend $95 to $357 per month to assist those they are caring for with groceries, medications, home modifications, and other out-of-pocket expenses; on a national basis this adds up to $1.5 billion per month (National Alliance for Caregiving/AARP 1997).

While these out-of-pocket expenses incurred by caregivers had been documented previously, until recently there were no calculations of the income and savings losses incurred by caregivers who were in the workforce. Employed caregivers, balancing work and caregiving responsibilities, often must pass up promotions or relocation possibilities, go from full-time to part-time work, take leaves of absence, or leave the workforce altogether as a result of the obligations to provide care. As a result, their income may be reduced and retirement savings may suffer as well. The MetLife (1999) Juggling Act Study estimated that the average loss in total wealth as a result of "free" caregiving is $659,139 over a lifetime. This includes lost wages ($566,443), lost Social Security benefits ($25,494) and for those who had them, lost pension benefits ($67,202).

Caregivers might also be called upon to pay for round-the-clock care at home or in a nursing home, resulting in an even greater financial burden for them or their loved ones. Neither Medicare nor private health insurance covers most long-term care costs. Nursing home care in 2002 averaged $61,000 per year, not including the costs of prescription drugs, medical care, and other expenses.

Financial Impact on Businesses and the Economy

The financial impact of caregiving does not fall solely on the caregiver. It lands heavily on other elements of the economy as well. Although a half a day here and an hour late getting to work there seem insignificant when taken individually, an estimate made in 1999 of the aggregate costs of caregiving in lost productivity to U.S business ranges from $11.4 billion to over $29 billion per year (MetLife 1997). These estimates were based on the costs of employee absenteeism, workday interruptions, supervisors' time, and replacing employees who move from full- to part-time, retire early, or leave the workforce altogether. There is no way to estimate the impact on noncaregiver employees' productivity due to their inability to rely on these employee caregivers.

A more recent report (Alzheimer's Association 2002) on the economic impact of Alzheimer's disease in the United States puts the cost to U.S. business at $61 billion—in 2002 alone. This was approximately equal to the net profits of the top ten Fortune 500 companies. Of the total cost, $24.6 billion is the cost of health care for those employees, spouses, and retirees who have Alzheimer's disease. The other $36.5 billion is the total cost to businesses of workers who are caregivers for people with Alzheimer's disease. This includes (in round numbers): absenteeism, $10 billion; productivity losses, $18 billion; worker replacement cost, $6 billion; continuing insurance for workers on leave and temporary worker replacement fees, $2 billion; and Employee Assistance Program usage, $64 million.

Both studies point to the dramatic real dollar costs of "free" family caregiving, and no one is projecting that these costs will decline.

Monetary Value of Caregiving

If family members suddenly stopped caring for their loved ones, who would pay for the care they provide? In 1997, the market value of care provided by unpaid family members and friends was estimated at $196 billion (Arno, Levine, Memmott 1999).

Updated figures for the year 2000 indicate that the value of "informal" uncompensated care is somewhere between $140 billion and $389 billion (Arno 2002). While impressive enough on their own, these figures are even more significant when compared to national spending for home health care ($32 billion) and nursing home care ($83 billion) (Arno 2002).

Public and Private Policy Implications

The financial burden on caregivers has come to the attention of policymakers, thanks to the growing influence of the caregiver advocacy movement and increased coverage of caregiver issues in the media. However, there are few federal or state policies in place to provide assistance to caregivers. The costs for services needed by the care recipient are not tax deductible unless the older person is a legal dependent. In the 107th session of Congress (2001–2002), legislation was introduced with bipartisan support to provide a tax credit for those who take care of a family member, but it was not passed. A few states have initiated programs that provide some financial support for caregivers, but for the most part, families bear the costs of care unaided.

While Medicaid provides a safety net and funds long-term care for individuals who have limited assets or who spend down and can no longer pay privately, governments in all our states are facing a fiscal crisis. The 2001 report on "The Role of Medicaid in State Budgets" by the Kaiser Commission on Medicaid and the Uninsured noted that the increased cost of caring for older and disabled Medicaid beneficiaries was the single largest factor behind the $12.4 billion increase in federal Medicaid spending between 2000 and 2001 (Kaiser Commission on Medicaid and the Uninsured 2001). Its authors also observe that, according to data gathered by the National Conference of State Legislatures, 44 states are reporting that revenues have come in below forecasted levels in fiscal year 2002, and a smaller—but still significant—number of states are reporting that their expenditures are exceeding budgeted levels. In these states, Medicaid is often cited as one of the programs that is growing most rapidly.

With state revenues down and the costs of care spiraling, state budgets are close to the breaking point, and their ability to fund the future long-term care needs of their impoverished citizens is in jeopardy. Public policies that can help caregivers continue to provide care for loved ones at home would have a positive impact on the caregiver, care recipient, and the nation. Programs such as day care for adults, respite care, and caregiver training may provide enough support to keep a loved one at home longer and thus avoid (or delay) placement in assisted living or a nursing home facility. While this will partially alleviate the financial burden on the Medicaid system, its real significance lies in the positive impact on the lives of the caregivers.

Today's caregivers also must plan for their own future long-term care needs and consider financial tools, such as long-term care insurance, to cover the costs of care for themselves, should it become necessary. It is likely that those who have had hands-on experience in providing care and who understand the costs involved will be more likely to plan ahead for themselves, but there can be no guarantees. The trends noted above will not abate any time soon, and neither will the financial impacts on individuals and both state and federal government. (See also COMMUNITY-BASED CARE; CORPORATE ELDERCARE PROGRAMS; CPA ELDERCARE SERVICES; DAY PROGRAMS FOR ADULTS; HOME CARE SERVICES FOR OLDER ADULTS;

LONG-TERM CARE INSURACE, PRIVATE; LONG-TERM CARE INSURANCE [LTCI]—A CONSUMER'S PERSPECTIVE.)

References

Alzheimer's Association. 2002. *Alzheimer's Disease: The Costs to U.S. Business in 2002*. Chicago: Alzheimer's Association.

Arno, P. 2002. "Economic Value of Informal Caregiving: 2000." Paper presented at the American Association for Geriatric Psychiatry, Orlando, FL, June.

Arno, P., C. Levine, and M. Memmott. 1999. "The Economic Value of Informal Caregiving." *Health Affairs* 18(2): 182–88.

Kaiser Commission on Medicaid and the Uninsured. 2001. "The Role of Medicaid in State Budgets." *The Henry J. Kaiser Family Foundation*, Policy Brief, October.

MetLife. 1997. *The MetLife Study of Employer Costs for Working Caregivers*. Warwick, RI: Author.

MetLife. 1999. *The MetLife Juggling Act Study: Balancing Caregiving with Work and the Costs Involved*. Warwick, RI: Author.

National Alliance for Caregiving/AARP. 1997. *Family Caregiving in the U.S.: Findings for a National Survey*. Bethesda, MD: NAC.

Sandra Timmermann

COST-OF-LIVING ADJUSTMENTS (COLAs), periodic additions to income payments that enable recipients to purchase the same amount and quality of goods and services over time despite inflation. As experienced by older Americans, COLAs are annual increases to Social Security benefits and other income payments that reflect the previous year's inflation rate in urban areas. Although a common perception is that older persons dependent on Social Security are protected from losing purchasing power, in actuality, after a few years they often cannot maintain the level of living they had upon retirement and experience increases in their cost of living greater than increases in their retirement income.

Understanding the reasons why COLAs fail to keep up with the cost of living as experienced by older Americans can be beneficial for planning a secure retirement. Financial advisors often advise their older clients to earn a return on retirement investments that is greater than the inflation rate, but their clients are often satisfied with conservative investments instead of those that outperform the current rate of inflation. The following provides information that financial advisors can use to explain to their clients why they are jeopardizing their financial future by being content with rates of return that only meet the current rate of inflation.

Why Do COLAs Fail to Keep Up?

Key points about COLAs that affect older Americans are as follows: (1) COLAs do not adjust for cost of living, (2) COLAs are introduced with a time lag and always reflect what happened in the previous year—not what is currently happening in the U.S. economy, (3) not all sources of retirement income have COLAs, and (4) COLAs are based on an inflation rate that older Americans do not necessarily experience.

First, COLAs are calculated with a measure that does not reflect the cost of living. The Consumer Price Index (CPI) is used to determine COLAs, but this index measures changes in prices only and does not incorporate other changes that may occur. Beef prices, for example, may increase more rapidly than other meat prices, and older persons may change their shopping patterns to substitute poultry for beef. Behavior changes that alter the cost of living are not reflected in the CPI and cause the CPI to overstate inflation as experienced by those who purchase lower-priced substitutions. The CPI is based on out-of pocket expenditures. However, it does not include taxes such as income and Social Security tax contributions. Therefore, changes in tax rates are not reflected in the CPI.

Second, by the nature of how the calculations are made, COLAs reflect inflation from the previous year. When rapidly rising inflation is experienced, COLAs do not compensate for the large price increases that retired persons see currently when they shop. The reverse is true when inflation occurs at a slower pace than the previous year and the COLA is greater than the rate of change in prices older persons are currently paying.

Third, not all retirement income has COLAs. Even benefits with COLAs, such as Social Security and federal Civil Service Retirement, have experienced COLA freezes, cuts, and delays.

Fourth, the CPI used to calculate COLAs for older Americans does not necessarily reflect the changes in prices for goods and services they buy. Social Security COLAs are determined by changes in the Consumer Price Index for Urban Wage Earners and Clerical Workers (CPI-W), an inflation index based on the spending patterns of households in which more than one-half of the income comes from clerical or wage occupations. The CPI-W represents about 32% of the total U.S. population, and it excludes retired persons. Another index, the Consumer Price Index for All Urban Consumers (CPI-U) is based on the expenditures reported by almost all urban residents. The CPI-U includes retired persons, professional employees, the self-employed, the poor, the unemployed, wage earners, and clerical workers (who are also in the CPI-W). It represents about 87% of the U.S. population. The CPI-W registered a lower rate of inflation in three of ten years from 1990 to 1999. Older Americans who are dependent on Social Security can lose the ability to maintain their level of living when their COLAs are based on the CPI-W.

Older Americans are thought to experience lower rates of inflation than the younger population, since older people buy different goods and services. This difference is important when the items purchased have different rates of price change. It has been suggested also that the broad use of senior citizen discounts lowers the cost of living for older adults.

Consumer Price Index for Older Adults

In the late 1980s, the U.S. Department of Labor's Bureau of Labor Statistics (BLS), the government agency that calculates the CPI, was directed by Congress to calculate an experimental Consumer Price Index for the Elderly (CPI-E). This experimental index for Americans 62 years old and older is based on existing data, reweighted to reflect expenditure patterns in the older population. A comparison with published CPIs found that older adults experienced a higher rate of inflation from 1983 through 1999 than the rates reported for either the CPI-W or the CPI-U. However, it is important to remember that the CPI-E is an experimental index and is not regularly published by the BLS.

In order to calculate a nonexperimental Consumer Price Index for the Elderly that could be used to determine COLAs, the measure must be designed to reflect the purchase behaviors of the older adults. The item and outlet samples surveyed for the index must represent the older population as well. Specifically, BLS must identify what should be tracked every month and where to gather prices for these items. The Consumer Expenditure Survey, used to determine the "market basket" of goods and services that consumers buy for the CPI-W and the CPI-U, does not include enough older persons to determine a CPI-E market basket. The Point-of-Purchase Survey is used to learn where consumers shop but does not include enough older adult buyers to determine which outlets should be surveyed each month.

Broadening the surveys to include a larger older adult household population would take years and would be costly and is unlikely under current budgetary constraints. Nonetheless, since an overstatement of the inflation rate could result in an overpayment of billions of dollars each year in Social Security, federal retirement, and military COLAs, the cost of developing a new index may be a good investment. If, however, a CPI-E demonstrates that COLAs understate inflation and Social Security COLAs increase, obviously more federal funds would be paid out in benefits. In the meantime, planning for a solvent retirement becomes a more difficult task. To keep up with the cost of living, retirement funds need to be placed in investments where they increase in value. Doing so, however, is likely to place the funds at a greater risk of loss.

Planned Changes for the CPI

In 1997, BLS Commissioner Katharine G. Abraham announced that a third CPI will be published in addition to the CPI-U and the CPI-W. Publication of the new index began in mid-2002 and will use a different "superlative" formula to calculate it. The term *superlative* has been associated with it, in part, because the formula is considered to provide a more accurate representation of the cost of living. It will be called "CCPI-U" because the formula "chains" price changes from one month to another in its calculation. In essence, it makes an adjustment for consumers who switch to different items as a result of price changes—those instances, for example, when consumers substitute poultry for more expensive beef products.

The uses of the CCPI-U will most likely be affected by the manner in which BLS will release the data. Critical expenditure information, such as how much more poultry and how much less beef was purchased in a month, is not immediately available to calculate the CCPI-U. Therefore, each month BLS will publish an "initial" CCPI-U index number, which will be revised and later finalized. In February each year, the prior year's initial index numbers will be revised and released as "interim" CCPI-U index numbers. Also, in February, the numbers for two years ago will be revised again before they are published as "final" CCPI-U index numbers. Until the CCPI-U is published and its uses are observed, it is not clear what the value will be, especially to older Americans and their financial advisors, of a more accurate measure of an annual rate of inflation that is two years old when it is published. (See also CASH FLOW PLANNING FOR RETIREES; DAILY MONEY MANAGERS; FINANCIAL ADVISORS; FINANCIAL PLANNING PROCESS; SOCIAL SECURITY PROGRAM OF THE UNITED STATES; WEALTH SPAN.)

References

Amble, Nathan, and Ken Stewart. 1994. "Experimental Price Index for Elderly Consumers." *Monthly Labor Review* 117 (May): 11–16.

Bureau of Labor Statistics. 1988. *An Analysis of the Rates of Inflation Affecting Older Americans Based on an Experimental Reweighted Consumer Price Index. A Study Prepared for the Senate Select Subcommittee on Aging.* Washington, DC: U.S. Department of Labor.

Bureau of Labor Statistics. 1998. *Understanding the Consumer Price Index: Answers to Some Questions.* Washington, DC: U.S. Department of Labor. Available online at http://www.bls.gov/cpi/cpi1998g.htm.

Bureau of Labor Statistics. 2000. "Experimental Consumer Price Index for Americans 62 Years of Age and Older, 1995–99." *CPI Detailed Report* (February): 5–7.

U.S. Senate. Special Committee on Aging. 1987. *Developing a Consumer Price Index for the Elderly.* Washington, DC: GPO.

Kathleen K. Scholl

CPA ELDERCARE SERVICES, also called CPA PrimePlus Services℠, cover a wide range of financial and lifestyle management services that certified public accountants (CPAs) provide to older adults or their families. CPAs who provide these services have training and experience that give them the knowledge and skills necessary to serve the unique concerns and needs of their clients. These services can range from assistance with day-to-day needs, such as assistance with money management, to assistance with evaluating living options and creating plans to fund those lifestyle choices. CPAs can act as the point person for the client or work as one part of a team of professionals, such as lawyers, insurance professionals, social workers, and nurses. Some CPAs have hired these other professionals as part of their firm in order to serve all of their clients' needs.

CPAs who provide CPA eldercare services consider all the needs of the client when providing services to them. They understand the nonfinancial as well as the financial aspects of providing services to mature clients. For example, they understand that the evaluation of future living options involves many issues—Where do you want to live? How do you want to live? How do you feel about the approaching move?—as well as whether different properties meet their needs and desires (criteria) or how the client can fund his or her ideal living option.

CPAs providing these services are bound by their professional ethics to act with objectivity and integrity, and the services they provide are also regulated by State Boards of Accountancy in their respective states.

Here is a list of the financial and nonfinancial services that a CPA can provide directly or with the assistance of other professionals to his or her eldercare clients:

Financial Services

- Planning for fiduciary needs
- Evaluation of health care and lifestyle financing options
- Receive, deposit, and account for client receipts
- Ensure expected revenues are received
- Make appropriate disbursements
- Submit claims to insurance companies
- Confirm accuracy of provider bills and appropriate reimbursements
- Protect client from predators by controlling checkbook and other assets
- Estate planning

- Income tax planning and preparation
- Gift tax return preparation
- Estate tax return preparation
- Preparation of employment tax returns for household help
- Read and analyze financial transactions
- Evaluate investments and trust activity
- Portfolio management
- Risk management and insurance planning
- Verify third-party calculations, such as pension payouts, insurance payouts, and annuity payouts
- Read and analyze reports from fiduciaries
- Snowbird issues

Nonfinancial Services

- Eldercare planning
- Plan for housing and support service needs
- Plan for declining competency
- Plan for death or disability of one or both spouses
- Evaluate alternative costs of retirement communities and other housing
- Evaluate housing and care alternatives
- Provide inventory of services available in the community
- Lifestyle management services
- Help arrange for transportation, housekeeping, and other services
- Manage real estate and other property
- Snowbird services
- Concierge services
- Coordinate support and health care services
- Needs assessment
- Help family monitor care (act as "eyes and ears" of the family)
- Establish standards of care expected
- Communicate expectations to care providers
- Evaluate and report on the performance of other outside parties, such as caregivers or contractors
- Family facilitation

Many but not all CPAs provide CPA eldercare services. If your CPA does not provide these services, he or she can refer you to a CPA who does.

Chartered accountants (CAs) in Canada also provide eldercare services under the name CA eldercare services (or CA PrimePlus Services™). For clients with assets in both the United States and Canada or who have extended stays in both countries, eldercare services can be provided throughout the year. (See also ACCOUNTANTS; FINANCIAL

ADVISORS; FINANCIAL PLANNING PROCESS; GERIATRIC CARE MANAGERS [GCMs]; GERONTOLOGICAL SOCIAL WORK.)

Ann Elizabeth Sammon

CREDIT SCORES, a three-digit number usually falling between 300 and 850 that indicates the credit risk posed by a consumer to a lending or other financial organization; the higher the score, the lower the risk. Credit bureau scores are often called "FICO® scores" because most credit bureau scores used in the United States are produced from software developed by Fair, Isaac and Company. FICO scores are provided to lenders by the three major credit reporting agencies: Equifax, Experian, and TransUnion. The score is a snapshot of a consumer's credit risk potential. It is used to make 25 billion credit decisions each year, including over 75% of mortgage loan originations. More than 40 of the nation's 50 largest financial institutions rely on the FICO score to determine an individual's creditworthiness. Although other financial institutions will calculate their own credit score, often they include the FICO score in addition to other information about the consumer.

The company's founders, William Fair, an engineer, and Earl Isaac, a mathematician, generated the first score in 1958, two years after establishing Fair, Isaac and Company. In the 1960s and 1970s, Fair Isaac coupled complex mathematical formulas with low-tech data-gathering methods to create their scoring system. By the mid-1980s, the company was using credit history that Equifax, Experian, and TransUnion gather on millions of people. Together, these three credit bureaus track 90% of the borrowing and payment histories of Americans. In 1989, Fair, Isaac and Company updated its credit scoring formula to predict consumer credit behavior, and the new scores were introduced in partnership with Equifax.

Credit scores today carry more weight than ever. Banks, mortgage companies, credit, and other financial institutions use credit scores to tell whether or not a consumer is a good credit risk. Insurance companies use a customized version of the credit score for underwriting purposes to predict future losses and to determine the level of individual policyholder risk. Many organizations and individuals rely on credit scores, from potential employers screening job applicants to landlords gauging a tenant's ability to meet his or her monthly rental payments.

FICO scores are calculated from mathematical formulas that rely upon four types of information:

1. Payment history accounts for 35% of the score. Timely payments are good; late payments lower the score. A mortgage is the most important bill to pay on time.
2. How much money is owed on all accounts, how much is paid and satisfied, and the percentage of the credit limit that is currently being used adds up 30% of the score. Using the full credit limit also lowers a score.
3. Length of credit history accounts for 15% of the score (long and solid is preferred over short and erratic). Lenders like to see a mix of debt beyond credit cards. Having a mortgage and auto loan, for example, shows that a person can obtain financing and handle money management activities. Borrowing from finance companies lowers the score.
4. The number of recently opened accounts and the mix of credit cards, installment loans, and mortgages are tallied in the score. Customers who shop around in an effort to secure the best

deal used to be penalized after a 7-day window, but today all loan requests within a 14-day period are counted as a single credit inquiry.

The key, however, is not any single piece of data but rather how the variables interact. A missed payment may weaken one score by as much as 100 points but may have a smaller effect on another. The models analyze outstanding debts, then compare credit history against the actual payment performance of Americans in numerous categories, from consumers with a lot of credit experience ("thick" files) and those with relatively little ("thin" files) to consumers with new credit accounts and those with delinquent records (*Consumer Reports* 2001a). In order for a FICO score to be calculated, the report must contain at least one account that has been open for six months or longer. In addition, the report must contain at least one account that has been updated in the past six months. This ensures that there is sufficient information, and enough recent information, on which to base a score.

Credit risk is the single most important factor that lenders look at in the credit process but the least understood by consumers. Many people have turned to third-party credit monitoring services in order to understand the ramifications of credit report blemishes and errors that deleteriously affect their score. It is estimated that revenue from such credit monitoring services will total $420 million in 2002 and will grow to $1 billion by 2007 (Online Banking Report 2003). Analysts claim that consumer sales of credit scores, credit reports, and related products should total roughly $600 million in 2003 and could easily reach $1 billion by 2005. Some suppliers of these products offer educational resources for consumers as well. Credit monitoring companies also help consumers contact credit bureaus to have misinformation in their reports corrected. In cases of potential fraud, consumers are helped to notify police and banking institutions.

Do Credit Scores Discriminate?

Credit reports, from which scores are calculated, must conform to the 1971 Fair Credit Reporting Act (FCRA) and subsequent 1996 amendments. The law gives consumers certain rights, such as access to their credit files and the right to dispute inaccurate information, which credit bureaus must correct or delete. Credit scores, however, are not subject to the FCRA, which specifically excluded them in the 1996 amendments, and as financial institutions have increased their reliance on the quick assessment these scores afford, they have become mired in controversy.

The FICO formula and scores were kept under wraps until mounting pressure from consumer advocacy groups and legislators forced the company and the credit depositories to rethink their policy to keep consumers in the dark. An upstart Internet lender, E-Loan, first gave consumers access to their scores, and as a result, Fair, Isaac and Company began selling scores through their online site (http://www.myfico.com/). Today, credit scores assess an individual's credit risk without relying on such discriminatory data as skin color, gender, or even income, according to Fair, Isaac.

Others disagree. While credit scoring is an apparently neutral and legal method of screening potential credit applicants, this screening device may encode subtle discriminatory criteria.

Discriminatory or not, use of credit scores is pervasive. Most lenders and brokers nationwide obtain credit risk scores that are calculated using proprietary Fair, Isaac and

Company software installed at each of the three national credit bureaus. FICO scores are generated when electronic credit files are ordered and run through the software. About one in three credit reports contains serious errors. Today's high-speed, automated underwriting environment emphasizes credit scores with little opportunity for review of the underlying files and records that produce the scores (Harney 2002a). Sixty percent (60%) of U.S. consumers have credit scores between 700 and 850, with the median score of 720. Twenty-seven percent (27%) of consumers' scores fall between 600 and 700 points, and inaccuracies in this range can be very costly. For example, a score between 620 and 640 is marginal and can result in a decision to extend a prime mortgage loan versus one that is "subprime." This decision will result in significant differences in interest rate and in the monthly payment a consumer must pay.

Mortgage industry experts estimate that 350,000 to 400,000 applicants are overcharged every year when lenders incorrectly label them high risk or subprime borrowers because of their credit score (Harney 2002b). A nationwide survey drives home the correlation between a good credit score and money saved. If, for example, a consumer is seeking a 30-year, $300,000 mortgage, with a FICO score of 500 to 599, she would qualify for a 10.2% loan, or $2,677.16 a month; at 620 to 674, she would be quoted 8.43%, or $2,291.87 a month; and at 700 to 719, the rate falls to 6.7%, or $1,935.83 a month. The added cost between the two extremes amounts to almost $9,000 annually.

Dealing with Credit Bureaus

Correcting mistakes in a credit report can be a frustrating process, according to people who have tried. Serious credit report errors can take more than six months to correct—credit bureaus average 23 weeks to correct errors—and in some cases, consumers will be able to obtain no results at all. Inaccuracies are not the only factors that negatively affect a score. It is estimated that 30 million Americans have accurate but blemished credit reports because of late payments, collections, judgments, bankruptcy filings, and the growing problem of identity theft.

Consumers can follow certain steps to improve their score, including:

- Limit shopping for credit to a 14-day window.
- Limit credit to 80% of available credit and pay more than the minimum payment.
- Pay bills on time.
- Apply only for credit that is needed.

Conclusion

Credit scores can give creditors an instantaneous assessment of a person's risk—an amazing feat when one considers the technological orchestration of the million bits of information that traverse the wires each day. Consumers move every year and three million last names change due to marriage or divorce. Six million or more U.S. consumers own second homes and often use both addresses. Tens of millions of consumers use a business address for at least one credit card. All those changes notwithstanding, the vast majority of information in the consumer reporting system is positive information. Credit scoring today is available to consumers who can have access to their score. Experts agree that consumers should make an effort to learn what is in their credit file and know their credit score. Knowing what's in a credit report and understanding the score is a critical part of financial management, according to Mitch Haws, vice president of public relations at Equifax, one of the big three national credit bureaus. (See also AGING INTO DEBT; CONSUMER CREDIT; FINANCIAL COUNSELING FOR MID- TO LATER LIFE; FINANCIAL RECOVERY IN LATER LIFE; HOMEOWNERSHIP; IDENTITY THEFT.)

Organizations

Equifax
Experian
FICO
TransUnion

References

Consumer Reports. 2001a. "New Assault on Your Credit Rating." January.
Consumer Reports. 2001b. "A Breakthrough for Borrowers." June.
Deagan, Brad. 2002. "Getting Your Credit History Doesn't Have to Be a Headache." *Wall Street Journal*, August 6.
Forster, Stacy. 2002. "If Credit Report Firms Can Flag Errors, Why Not Do It for All?" *Wall Street Journal*, July 26.
Harney, Kenneth R. 2002a. "Data Correction Services Help Borrowers Hurt by Wrong Scores." *Washington Post*, June 15.
Harney, Kenneth R. 2002b. "Mortgage Insurance Premiums Rise for Some Borrowers." *Washington Post*, August 17.
Online Banking Report. 2003. "Top 10 Industry Developments." January.

Louisa Woodville

CRIME PROTECTION, recognition of factors that increase vulnerability to crime and measurements and strategies to reduce possible victimization. According to the Bureau of Justice Statistics (2001), persons 65 years old or older are the least likely of all age groups in the United States to become victims of crime. In fact, crime victimization rates among older adults have generally been declining for more than 20 years. Personal safety, however, is a growing concern for older Americans, who as a group express a high fear of crime.

Like the general population, older adults are more likely to experience property crimes such as larceny, burglary, fraud, and vandalism and are least likely to be victimized by violent crimes (Bureau of Justice Statistics 2001). Assault was the most common of the violent crimes experienced by older victims (McCabe and Gregory 1998).

Alston (1986) describes who is likely to become a victim of crime by three characteristics: attractiveness, exposure, and guardianship. Attractiveness is related to "benefit," as some potential victims represent greater opportunity for gain than others. Wearing jewelry or carrying a purse usually can influence attractiveness. Exposure has to do with visibility and proximity. Visibility is a factor when persons are outside on the streets, and proximity suggests that it may be easier to victimize someone close by than having to travel to some distant suburb. Guardianship refers to forms of physical or social protection. Physical protection might involve staying home after dark, whereas social protection would include walking, or living, with a companion.

Purse snatching, like pocket picking, happens on public streets, where exposure and attractiveness combine with lack of guardianship to identify certain individuals as targets. It happens to persons who appear unstable and off guard. Purse snatching and pocket picking are exceptions to the negative relationship between age and victimization, as persons 65 years old and older are about as likely as those younger than 65 to be victims of personal larceny with contact. Home burglary most often victimizes older persons. In burglary, proximity, opportunity, and physical protection are key to selecting targets. Most burglars do not want to meet their victims and usually enter when no one is home. A Kansas City study of older Americans reported that most burglary victims had no outside lights burning, thus lowering their guardianship factor.

Attractiveness, exposure, and lack of guardianship are the characteristics of older persons most likely to become victims. Since older men are more likely to be on the streets, they are more likely to become victims. Blacks are more likely than Whites to be victims, due to their greater likelihood to reside in inner-city areas where crime is generally higher (exposure). Marriage provides guardianship, and married people enjoy the lowest victimization rates. Despite these patterns, there is no convincing evidence that older people are particularly sought out as targets for serious crimes.

Fear of Crime

Fear of victimization may be unrelated to actual crime rates, and extreme fear can be explained partially by media exaggeration of all violent crimes. A survey of Chicago residents, however, shows that fear of crime is positively correlated to victimization rates once rates are adjusted for exposure to risk. Thus, fear of crime should not be interpreted as irrational or unjustified and, in fact, can be reduced by lowering victimization rates (Stafford and Galle 1984). Fear among older persons is greatest when they lack social integration in the neighborhood and when they see neighborhood compositions changing, abandoned buildings becoming more widespread, and unsupervised teens loitering in their proximity. These community attributes add to a sense of loss of control, a characteristic strongly related to fear of crime (Donnelly 1989).

Costs of Crime

Personal contact with offenders during the crime is likely to produce greater fear, anxiety, and feelings of vulnerability as a result of the encounter. Those who already feel powerless and alienated find these feelings reinforced. Psychological costs to older victims, however, are not uniform and do not appear to differ from those of younger victims. Although burglary is a property crime, for example, it is perceived by young and old as a personal threat because it violates the idea of home as a safe place. Financially, older persons do not, in an absolute sense, lose more than younger persons, but if they are in a marginal economic position, those losses they do incur pose a greater source of hardship. Further, older persons are more likely to be injured when they are physically attacked (Bachman, Dillaway, and Lachs 1998). Ultimately, all costs of crime depend on the social, economic, and physical resources older persons possess; those of lesser means are more vulnerable to the consequences of criminal acts.

Reducing Risks of Victimization

Older persons can reduce risks by being alert and by keeping the three characteristics of victims in mind. Staying home, thus avoiding outside activities, tends to increase isolation and may increase suspicion and fear as well. A more effective strategy is to improve individual and community awareness of the risk factors.

In terms of attractiveness, older persons should look more alert and carry a purse tightly, if at all. With regard to exposure, traveling with companions helps substantially. Guardianship support includes locked doors, bright lights, and stronger window frames. Having adequate homeowner's or renter's insurance is important. Resources available in most communities assist individuals in victimization prevention programs. AARP has a wide range of pamphlets and brochures that outline practical strategies for personal safety.

Crime prevention also requires involvement at the community level. Rather than retreating into the home and becoming prisoners of fear, older persons should become involved in neighborhood and community activities. Knowing neighbors and participating in community programs are ways of staying connected. Safety programs include school safety programs, Safe House programs, escort services, Neighborhood Watch, and local dispute resolution. Being involved reintegrates citizens into a changing community and increases commitment to the physical and social environment. Seniors, having time and experience to offer, are invaluable to these efforts. (See also CONSUMER PROTECTION FOR OLDER ADULTS; ELDER LAW PRACTICE; ETHICS IN FINANCIAL PLANNING; FINANCIAL ELDER ABUSE; GUARDIANSHIP; OMBUDSMAN.)

References

Alston, Letitia. 1986. *Crime and Older Americans*. Springfield, IL: Charles C. Thomas.

Bachman, Ronet, Heather Dillaway, and Mark Lachs. 1998. "Violence against the Elderly." *Research on Aging* 20: 183–98.

Bureau of Justice Statistics. 2001. *Victim Characteristics*. Washington, DC: U.S. Department of Justice.

Donnelly, Patrick. 1989. "Individual and Neighborhood Influences on Fear of Crime." *Sociological Focus* 22: 69–85.

McCabe, Kimberly, and Sharon Gregory. 1998. "Elderly Victimization." *Research on Aging* 20: 363–72.

Stafford, Mark, and Omer Galle. 1984. "Victimization Rates, Exposure to Risk and Fear of Crime." *Criminology* 22: 173–85.

Cathleen Burnett

D

DAILY MONEY MANAGERS, a rapidly growing profession whose members provide personal finance and business management services, and some social support assistance, to seniors and to others requiring such services. Daily money managers (DMMs) manage personal monetary affairs, organize financial documents, keep financial records, monitor health insurance claims and payments, and maintain bank accounts. They can be a second pair of eyes and ears for their clients and act as a facilitator or an advocate on specific living and care issues. Daily money management has emerged and grown from both financial services and social services roots.

Daily money managers do not take the place of other professionals, such as attorneys, accountants, and social workers. Rather, their work complements and facilitates the work of other financial professionals. By handling day-to-day financial tasks, the information needed by these other professionals is more available and in good form when they receive it. For example, a DMM, by managing bank accounts and other financial affairs, can provide accurate bank records and other documents that are needed by a tax professional in order to file income taxes. Some DMMs are also qualified to prepare and file state and federal tax forms when they are due.

At this time, daily money management is an unregulated field. Practitioners have a variety of professional and educational backgrounds, including social work, accounting, financial planning, and general business experience. Persons seeking DMM services may contact the American Association of Daily Money Managers, their local Area Agency on Aging, or the Better Business Bureau or seek a referral to a DMM from someone they know and trust. Since involvement of an outsider in personal financial affairs may be a sensitive issue, it is strongly recommended that persons seeking this type of service interview more than one DMM and hire the one who best complements their values and style in the management of their day-to-day finances.

The American Association of Daily Money Managers (AADMM) was formed in 1996. The mission of this organization is to:

- Foster high standards of client services provided by practitioners.
- Support the growth of the profession.

- Provide members with education and support in their efforts to provide quality service.
- Pursue respect and recognition of the field of daily money management.

The AADDM has grown into a network of providers of daily money management services in most states around the country. Most daily money management is performed by sole proprietors of small businesses that serve a specific geographic area. A list of member practitioners and other information on the field is available on the AADMM Web site: http://www.aadmm.com/. (See also ACCOUNTANTS; BANKING SERVICES FOR THE MATURE MARKET; CASH FLOW PLANNING FOR RETIREES; CPA ELDERCARE SERVICES; FINANCIAL ADVISORS; GERIATRIC CARE MANAGERS [GCMs]; GERONTOLOGICAL SOCIAL WORK.)

Organization

American Association of Daily Money Managers (AADMM)

Suggested Reading

American Association of Daily Money Managers. "Daily Money Management: What Is It and How Can It Help Me?" Available by contacting the Association at (301) 593-5462 or Info@AADMM.com.

Roberta Gosier

DAY PROGRAMS FOR ADULTS (also known as adult day care; adult day centers; adult day services), community-based, nonresidential group programs designed to meet the needs of functionally and/or cognitively impaired adults through individualized care. Day programs are structured to provide a variety of health, social, and other related support services in a protective setting during any part of a day but less than 24-hour care. Adult day programs are designed to serve adults who need supervision, social interaction, and assistance with more than one activity of daily living (eating, walking, toileting, bathing, dressing). The adult day center environment recognizes and attends to emotional and intellectual needs, as well as to physical needs.

A national study of adult day services found that the majority of adult day centers are open Monday through Friday for eight or more hours a day. Some centers, however, offer extended hours of service during the week, are open on weekends, and provide overnight care. Twenty-one percent (21%) of centers are medical models, 37% are social models with no medical component, and 42% are a combination of the two. Day programs provide a vast array of services such as meals and snacks, therapeutic activities (e.g., exercise programs, art therapy, music therapy, pet therapy), health monitoring, nursing care, medication management, assistance with activities of daily living (e.g., walking, eating, toileting), personal care services (e.g., bathing, hair care, nail care), rehabilitative therapies (e.g., physical therapy, speech therapy, occupational therapy), medical services, social services, counseling, caregiver education and support groups, care management, and transportation.

Although adult day centers serve a population that ranges in age from 18 to over 100, the average age of persons attending them is 72 (Partners in Caregiving [PIC] 2003). The two most prevalent health conditions are 52% dementia (all forms) and 41% frail older persons who have no dementia but are in need of supervision and/or at risk of social isolation. Twenty-four percent (24%) of participants are diagnosed with mental retardation and/or developmental disabilities, and 23% are physically disabled but cognitively intact (e.g., stroke, Parkinson's disease, multiple sclerosis). Other health conditions include chronic mental illness, HIV/AIDS, and traumatic brain injury.

Most people attending an adult day center live with a spouse or an adult child, and the average length of stay is two years. The number one reason for discharge from the center is placement in a residential setting such as a nursing home, and the number two reason is death (PIC 2003). Adult day programs have become a practical and appealing part of the solution to long-term care needs—a viable, cost-effective, community-based service option that helps individuals in need of chronic care remain at home, in the community, and with family and friends for as long as possible.

Overview/Need

The model for adult day programs in the United States was the psychiatric day hospital started in the Soviet Union in the 1940s. Similar programs began in the 1950s in England. Experience showed that these programs reduced the need for in-patient beds. The first day program in the United States opened in the 1960s at Cherry Hill State Hospital in Goldsboro, North Carolina. Adult day programs subsequently expanded from medical services, transportation, and meals to offer supportive health and social services for marginally impaired and/or socially isolated individuals residing in the community.

Between 1969 and 1973, fewer than 15 adult day centers were in existence in the United States (Webb 1989). By 2002, over 3,400 centers had been established, of which 60% are located east of the Mississippi River (PIC 2003). Of these centers, over half have been operating for more than ten years. While a majority are not-for-profit and operate under the umbrella of a large parent organization (e.g., nursing home, hospital, senior service organization), there has been an increase in the number of for-profit adult day centers from 16% of centers open for ten years or more to 44% of centers opened within the last five years.

A minimum community population base of 20,000 is necessary to support an adult day center. It is estimated that 1% of that number, or about 200 people, are potential candidates for an average daily census of 20 to 30 people per day (Cox and Reifler 1994). Generally, two to three participants must be enrolled to support one daily slot, since many people use day center services on a part-time basis. Although the field is in flux, with centers opening and closing on a regular basis, growth is evident, with 26% of all adult day centers having opened during the past five years (PIC 2003). Growth, however, lags behind the need for adult day centers, with 1,770 of 3,141 counties nationwide currently underserved. With only 39% of requirements for adult day care being met, 5,415 new adult day centers are needed (PIC 2003).

Regulations/Funding

There are no federal regulations for adult day programs. Funding or other regulatory standards usually exist at the state level, but the type of state agency overseeing adult day programs varies widely. The majority of centers (79%) report being certified or licensed by their state, with only 6% accredited on a voluntary basis by the Commission on Accreditation of Rehabilitation Facilities (CARF), the national accrediting body of adult day programs (PIC 2003).

On average, adult day centers serve 25 people per day at a cost of $56 per day (PIC 2003). The average daily fee, however, is only $46 per day, or less than cost. Cost and daily fees vary by state and by center, depending on the range of services offered. Most centers have a sliding fee scale, offering discounts based on income.

Overall, the largest source of revenue (38%) comes from public third-party reimbursements, which includes federal and state funds coming into a center on a fee-for-service basis (PIC 2003). The number-one reimbursement source in this category is Medicaid Home and Community-Based Waiver dollars, reported by 60% of adult day centers as a source of revenue. In some states, however, this revenue stream is not available. And in some states in which it is, day centers cannot access these funds unless they are a medical model. Also, Medicaid eligibility varies by state, and there are limits on access to those participants meeting income criteria.

Private and out-of-pocket payments comprise 35% of total revenue—the second largest source of income for adult day centers (PIC 2003). Other operating revenue (from managed care contracts, private long-term care insurance, and ancillary services such as bathing) totals 13% of all revenue (PIC 2003). And although private long-term care insurance plays only a small role in financing adult day centers, there is an increasing trend for insurance companies to provide reimbursement for adult day programs in long-term care policies (Henry and Reifler 1997). The remaining income at 14% comes from nonoperating revenue, such as United Way dollars and money from donations/contributions, fund-raising events, and grants. And when looking at revenue compared to expenses, 44% of centers report operating at a deficit (PIC 2003).

National Initiatives

The financial viability of adult day centers was of primary interest to The Robert Wood Johnson Foundation when, in 1987, it created the first national adult day services demonstration program—the Dementia Care and Respite Services Program (1988–1992). With cofunding from the National Alzheimer's Association and the Federal Administration on Aging, the foundation sought to demonstrate that adult day centers could serve people with dementia and that they could do so in a financially viable manner. A particular emphasis was on fee-for-service payments, as opposed to philanthropy. The success of this program led to another foundation initiative, Partners in Caregiving: The Dementia Services Program (1992–1996), a four-year replication program that continued to demonstrate that adult day centers could effectively care for people with dementia in the community (versus nursing home placement) and could be financially viable at the same time.

Findings from the four-year demonstration program showed that adult day centers can be financially self-sufficient. Four factors proved to be statistically significant predictors of better financial performance (percentage of total expenses covered by net operating revenue): a higher ratio of daily fees to unit cost; staying open a full day (i.e., 7:30 A.M. to 6:00 P.M.); receiving government fee-for-service reimbursement in addition to private pay; and a higher average daily census (Reifler et al. 1997).

However, a higher ratio of daily fees to unit cost means giving consumers and funding sources the opportunity to pay the full cost of service. Because of their nonprofit status, and their mission to serve everyone who needs service, many day center boards and staff are often reluctant to charge the full costs for fear high fees will prevent people from using the service. One way to balance the tension between pursuing their mission while operating in a fiscally sound manner is for day centers to charge full cost but offer discounts on a case-by-case basis, depending upon need. Philanthropy can then be used to fund the discounts.

Increasing the number of people served per day results in economies of scale and lowers unit cost, since some large expenses (e.g., rent, administration) remain fixed regardless of the number of people served. Pursuing government reimbursement gives day centers a way to serve people who might not otherwise be able to afford services and provides another funding stream to help cover operating expenses. Being open a full day allows day centers to serve a wider range of participants, including those whose caregivers work. Being open a longer day also gives nonworking caregivers more choice in using the service.

Overall, the demonstration sites were able to meet 63% of their total expenses with net operating revenue (Reifler et al. 1997). During the four-year replication program, improvements were made, with the replication sites (overall) meeting 83% of their cash expenses through net operating revenue (Reifler et al. 1999). Today, 37% of adult day centers across the country do not track financial performance. The Dementia Care and Respite Services Program and Partners in Caregiving also showed gains that can be made through attention to marketing and other essentials for success (Henry et al. 1997). From a marketing perspective, the most successful adult day centers are those that show a willingness to adapt in order to fit the needs and wants of individual participants and their caregivers and to find creative solutions to problems. Solving the customer's problem helps centers become more competitive and thus more financially viable. Also, from the perspective of the caregiver and participant, the quality of a program can be judged further by the availability of transportation, a full day of engaging activities that offer choices, professional/trained staff, links with other community services, support services for caregivers, and a well-functioning board of directors.

With widespread needs existing in the community and the profile of services and financial support becoming solidified, adult day programs continue to grow in importance and strength as part of the continuum of care. (See also COMMUNITY-BASED CARE; CONTINUING CARE RETIREMENT COMMUNITIES, [CCRCs]; HOME CARE SERVICES FOR OLDER ADULTS; LONG-TERM CARE INSURANCE [LTCI]—A CONSUMER'S PERSPECTIVE; TRANSPORTATION.)

Organizations

Administration on Aging
Brookdale National Group Respite Program
National Adult Day Services Association
National Alzheimer's Association
National Association of Area Agencies on Aging
National Association of State Units on Aging
Partners in Caregiving: The Dementia Services Program

References

Cox, N.J., and B.V. Reifler. 1994. "Dementia Care and Respite Services Program." *Alzheimer Disease and Associated Disorders* 8 (Suppl. 3): 113–21.

Henry, R.S., N.J. Cox, B.V. Reifler, and C. Asbury. 2000. "Adult Day Centers." In *To Improve Health and Health Care 2000: The Robert Wood Johnson Foundation Anthology*, ed. S.L. Isaacs and J.R. Knickman. San Francisco: Jossey-Bass.

Henry, R.S., and B.V. Reifler. 1997. "Coverage of Adult Day Services in Long Term Care Insurance Policies." *Journal of Applied Gerontology* 16(2): 221–34.

National Adult Day Services Association. 2002. *Adult Day Services Fact Sheet*. McLean, VA: Author.

Partners in Caregiving (PIC). 1995. "The Dementia Services Program." In *Life after Diagnosis—Adult Day Services in America*. Winston-Salem, NC: Wake Forest University School of Medicine.

Partners in Caregiving (PIC). 2003. "The Adult Day Services Program." *National Study of Adult Day Services*. Winston-Salem, NC: Wake Forest University School of Medicine.

Reifler, B.V., N.J. Cox, B.N. Jones, J. Rushing, and K. Yates. 1999. "Service Use and Financial Performance in a Replication Program on Adult Day Centers." *American Journal of Geriatric Psychiatry* 7(2): 98–107.

Reifler, B.V., R.S. Henry, J. Rushing, K. Yates, N.J. Cox, et al. 1997. "Financial Performance among Adult Day Centers: Results of a National Demonstration Program." *Journal of the American Geriatrics Society* 45: 146–53.

Von Behren, R. 1986. *Adult Day Care in America: Summary of a National Survey*. Washington, DC: National Council on the Aging/National Institute on Adult Daycare.

Webb, L.C., ed. 1989. *Planning and Managing Adult Day Care: Pathways to Success*. Owings Mills, MD: National Health Publishing.

Nancy J. Cox and Rona S. Henry

DEATH BENEFITS, money and/or in-kind benefits paid to the survivors of the deceased (also called survivor benefits). These benefits are usually provided to eligible survivors of the deceased upon receipt of proof of death, such as a copy of the death certificate. Amounts may be paid in one lump sum, as in life insurance policies and the Social Security lump-sum burial expense payment, or they may be paid over time, as in Social Security survivor benefits.

Historically, death benefits go back at least to biblical times, when a person who killed or injured someone was required by law to pay an indemnity to the kin of the injured or deceased, and the person who killed or disabled a slave was required to reimburse the master. The practice of paying an indemnity in the case of wrongful death expanded over the years to include workers killed on the job and soldiers killed during war. In 1935, the Social Security Act established the practice in America of paying government benefits to dependent survivors of workers who died.

Public Death Benefits

Publicly paid death benefits come primarily from three programs: Social Security, the Veterans Administration, and Worker's Compensation. Of these, the most common is survivor's insurance under Old-Age, Survivors, and Disability Insurance (OASDI), paid to eligible dependents of deceased workers by the Social Security Administration. Eligible dependents include widows or widowers 60 years old or older, disabled widows or widowers age 50 or older, younger widows or widowers caring for children younger than 16 years old or disabled children, unmarried children younger than 18 years old (or up to 19 if they are attending elementary or secondary school full-time), unmarried children disabled before age 22, or dependent parents age 62 years and older. Survivor benefits under OASDI consist primarily of monthly payments based on earnings of the deceased if he or she was still working when death occurred. If the deceased had already retired or was receiving Social Security Disability payments at the time of death, survivor benefits are tied to the deceased's monthly payments. Under OASDI, survivors—a spouse living with the worker at the time of death, or dependent children—are also eligible for a lump-sum payment of $255.00 toward funeral expenses. (Information can be found at http://www.ssa.gov/).

The Veterans Administration pays two types of survivor benefits: (1) dependency and indemnity compensation (DIC) for dependent survivors of service persons who die of a service-connected injury or illness while on active duty; or (2) death pensions for spouses and children (18 years old or under or 18 to 23 years old and attending school) of veterans who died of non-service-connected illness or injury. Eligibility for death pensions may depend on the income of the dependents.

Dependent survivors of all honorably discharged wartime veterans are eligible for survivors benefits whether the death was service connected or not, while survivors of peacetime veterans are only eligible if death was service connected. "Wartime service" applies to all declared wars and undeclared wars such as the Korean and Vietnam conflicts. Burial allowances of $300 are available for veterans of wartime service and for peacetime veterans whose deaths are service connected. When death occurs while the veteran is in a Veterans Administration (VA) hospital or under contracted nursing home care, some of the costs for transporting the deceased's remains may also be reimbursed. When death is service connected, moreover, survivors may apply for a $2,000 lump-sum payment in lieu of the smaller allowance when they have surviving dependents.

Veterans who are honorably discharged are eligible for burial flags and internment in national cemeteries. Spouses and minor children may also be eligible for burial in national cemeteries. Information is available from funeral directors, local veterans affairs offices, and online at http://www.va.gov/.

Each state and territory pays benefits under Workers' Compensation laws to survivors of workers killed or fatally injured on the job. While state laws are similar, each state controls the manner of determining eligibility, amount of benefits, and length of time survivors receive payments. Under Workers' Compensation, spouses are eligible until remarriage, and dependent children are eligible until a specified age. Most states have Workers' Compensation boards or commissions that hear cases and award compensation; some states allow the court system to make these determinations. Burial allowances vary under Workers' Compensation.

Private Benefits

Survivor benefits are paid under life insurance policies and through pension plans offered by employers as part of employees' benefits. Life insurance pays a predetermined sum directly to beneficiary(ies) named in the policy or to the estate of the deceased, if so designated. While benefits are usually lump-sum payments, other options are available, such as lifetime income for the spouse or periodic payments for a specific length of time. Benefits may increase in cases of accidental death and may be denied in cases of suicide.

Life insurance held by a creditor to secure payment of a debt is paid directly to the mortgage or lien holder when death of the insured occurs. Most lending institutions require such credit insurance if a loan amount is substantial, and while this requirement protects the bank, it reduces survivors' financial burden as well.

Survivor benefits from pension plans are available under certain circumstances. If an employed spouse is vested in a pension plan but dies before retirement, a death benefit tied to the amount of retirement proceeds may be payable to the widowed spouse or other assigned beneficiary. When someone elects to continue payments to a spouse after death, a reduction in pension payments during lifetime is usually required. Death benefits under employee pension plans may be paid as a percentage of the employee's average pay, expected pension, or accrued pension. Pensions, life insurance, and similar accounts usually provide a death benefit that is not subject to probate.

Other death benefits are paid through fraternal organizations and through special life insurance plans for employees of the federal government. More specific information may be obtained from a local Social Security Administration office, VA office, Employment Security office (Workers' Compensation), or the financial office of an employer. (See also LIFE INSURANCE; PENSION PLANS; SOCIAL SECURITY PROGRAM OF THE UNITED STATES; VETERANS' BENEFITS.)

Organizations

Department of Veterans Affairs
Office of Worker's Compensation Programs
Social Security Administration

References

Quadagno, Jill. 1987. *The Transformation of Old Age Security*. Chicago: University of Chicago Press.

Quadagno, Jill. 2002. *Aging and the Life Course*. New York: McGraw-Hill.

Roy, F. Hampton, and Charles Russell, eds. 1992. *The Encyclopedia of Aging and the Elderly*. New York: Hamilton Printing.

Walker, Alexis, Margaret Manoogian-O'Dell, Lori McGraw, and Diana White. 2001. *Families in Later Life*. Thousand Oaks, CA: Pine Forge Press.

Francis P. Conner
Updated by Janice K. Purk

DEFINED BENEFIT PENSION PLAN, an employer-sponsored, formula-driven retirement plan that provides a fixed amount of pension benefit at the employee's normal retirement age (usually age 65). The amount of benefit received typically depends upon whether the benefit is a flat dollar amount or a percentage of pay, as well as the employee's length of service and earnings. For example, an employee might receive 1% of pay or a flat dollar amount for each unit of service provided to the organization. Defined benefit plans are typically noncontributory for employees but require an annual contribution from employers who offer the plan.

If the defined benefit plan provides for a pay-related benefit, the benefit may be calculated according to the total earnings of an employee (a career average approach) or the last few years of an employee's company service, such as three to five years (a final pay approach). The final pay approach benefits the employee by calculating a plan payout at the highest years of individual earnings. The career average approach, in contrast, calculates the mean earnings of the employee over every year of employment and may include years of low earnings. This calculation may produce a benefit that penalizes the employee for long years of service. In addition, the value of benefits under a final pay approach may provide for preretirement inflation protection, where the employer assumes the cost associated with that inflation.

The formula used in a defined benefit plan may provide for a full unit of benefit for each year of service, or there may be a maximum period over which benefits are credited. The design of the formula should reflect the employer's objectives as to income replacement levels (i.e., 50% to 70% of pay). Most defined benefit pay–related plans are integrated with Social Security benefits so that the total payout between the employer-sponsored plan and Social Security is less than 100% of pay. This approach recognizes that Social Security is of greater value to less highly compensated employees and helps the employer design a plan that contributes a reasonable amount toward an employee's retirement.

Any tax-qualified pension plan must provide that employee contributions to the plan are vested at all times and that accrued employer contributions are vested by normal retirement age. Two types of vesting schedules exist: (1) five-year "cliff" vesting, where all benefits vest after five years of service, and (2) graded vesting, where 20% of benefits vest after three years of service, and that percent increases in 20% increments until 100% vesting occurs after seven years. Defined benefit plans also provide that if an employee terminates his or her employment, the vested benefit is payable at retirement. However, many plans have a provision that small benefit amounts (less than $5,000) may be payable at the time of termination of employment.

The most common form of death benefit under a defined benefit pension plan is a joint and survivor benefit where some part of the employee's benefit is payable in periodic installments to the employee's spouse or other survivor. For a spouse, the benefit is payable for life, while for a child, benefits may be payable only until the child reaches a certain age. Defined benefit plans may also provide for disability benefits by treating the disability as a form of early retirement, or the plan may have a separately stated disability benefit with more liberal age and service requirements. Defined benefit plans are subject to the Employee Retirement Income Security Act (ERISA) plan termination requirements, and employers sponsoring these plans are required to pay annual Pension Benefit Guaranty Corporation (PBGC) premiums. If, for any reason, the plan is terminated with insured but unfunded benefits, the employer's net worth may also be exposed to liability.

Since the enactment of ERISA in 1975, the total number of private sector tax-qualified retirement plans more than doubled (from 311,000 to 730,000), but the number of defined benefit plans has decreased from an estimated 170,000 plans in 1985 to 56,000 plans in 1998. Suggested explanations for the decline include: (1) increased government regulation; (2) workplace trends that increasingly favor defined contribution plans; (3) business environment and risk associated with funding and managing pension plans; (4) firm size; (5) global competition faced by employers in recent years, which has increased the need for more flexibility in plan design; and (6) the successful marketing efforts of consultants and defined contribution plan service providers.

With recent changes in business investment conditions, many employers have introduced hybrid pension plan arrangements, that is, those that incorporate characteristics of both defined benefit and defined contribution pension plans. A popular type of defined benefit hybrid plan is the "cash balance plan," where the plan provides a determinable benefit, but the employee's accrued benefit is expressed as an account balance, and the annual "contribution" or credits paid to this account may be expressed as a percentage of the employee's current pay. However, actual employer contributions and return on plan assets may not be the same as the annual addition and increases credited to employee accounts.

There are many arguments for and against defined benefit pension plans. Employers seeking specific income replacement goals for their employees can achieve this through a defined benefit plan. Defined benefit plans favor long-service employees who are in turn protected from the effects of preretirement inflation. They are also a favorite plan choice for union leaders, who can influence an employer's choice of pension plans. Defined benefit plans require employers to commit to pay the cost of promised benefits, including any increases in inflation and despite any adverse investment results. However, during times of a booming stock market, employers may not need to make any annual plan contributions. Until recently, prior contributions plus investment returns alone provided sufficient plan funding for some large employers.

Defined benefit plans also have implications for plan participants. Since these plans are formula driven and noncontributing, employees may be unaware of accumulated earnings that exist within a plan. However, a defined benefit plan offers no direct investment risk to participants, and plan sponsor bankruptcy risk is limited to the risk of losing benefits not guaranteed by the PBGC, should an employer become insolvent. These factors have different meanings for each type of employer who must weigh the needs of employees against the reality of their financial structure and future economic performance. (See also CASH BALANCE PENSION PLANS; EARLY RETIREMENT INCENTIVE PLANS [ERIPs]; EMPLOYEE BENEFITS IN THE PUBLIC SECTOR; EMPLOYEE BENEFITS IN THE UNITED STATES; PENSION PLANS; PENSION PLANS FOR THE SELF-EMPLOYED.)

References

Rajnes, David. 2002. "An Evolving Pension System: Trends in Defined Benefit and Defined Contribution Plans." EBRI *Issue Brief*, September.

Rosenbloom, Jerry S. 2001. *The Handbook of Employee Benefits: Design, Funding and Administration*, 5th ed. New York: McGraw-Hill.

Mary Helen McSweeney

DEFINED CONTRIBUTION PLAN, an employer-sponsored retirement savings program that does not guarantee a fixed pension benefit but promises a specified contribution to an account into which an employee also makes contributions. The employer contribution may be a fixed percent or a flat dollar amount, or it may be related to profits. How much an employee receives in a benefit, therefore, depends upon the level and frequency of contributions, length of plan participation, as well as choices of investment vehicles. Consequently, the responsibility for accumulating a pension benefit under a defined contribution plan rests primarily in the hands of the employee.

There are various types of defined contribution plans. These include (1) money purchase plans, which require a fixed percentage of compensation to be contributed annually to each eligible employee; (2) deferred profit sharing plans, where the employer contribution is discretionary or related to profits; (3) Section 401(k) cash or deferred arrangements, where employees contribute up to legally allowable amounts and employers have the discretion to match these contributions; (4) savings or thrift plans that typically act as a supplement to another defined contribution plan such as a 401(k); and (5) employee stock ownership plans (ESOPs) that are either a qualified stock bonus plan or a stock bonus and money purchase plan qualified under Internal Revenue Code (IRC) Section 401(a). A brief explanation of each plan type will be provided below.

Money purchase plans require a fixed contribution from an employer, but employees may also contribute from after-tax income according to predetermined contribution rates stipulated in the plan and frequently expressed as a percentage of pay. An example of such an arrangement is a 3% employee contribution with an employer match of 50 cents for every dollar contributed.

Profit sharing plans typically have formula-driven contributions made only by an employer (i.e., noncontributory for the employee), which are allocated to employees in proportion to their level of compensation and possibly service with the organization. Employees may also supplement their account balances by making additional contributions on an after-tax basis. However, there is tremendous flexibility within the plan, since contributions need only be made if the level of corporate profits are sufficient, thereby containing plan costs.

Section 401(k) cash or deferred arrangements (CODAs) offer an employee the choice between cash or deferred employer contributions to a qualified retirement plan. In addition, employees can make elective contributions of amounts that could otherwise be received in cash on a pretax basis, which reduces their taxable income and helps to avoid federal income taxes until the point of distribution. CODAs may be part of a profit sharing plan or stock bonus plan (including thrift and savings plans) and may be subject to certain safe harbor contribution requirements. CODAs are subject to limits on elective deferrals ($11,000 maximum in 2002), a limit on compensation applicable for determining contributions and benefits, and IRC Section 415 limits ($25,000 of employee's compensation or $35,000, the latter being indexed to cost-of-living requirements). They are also subject to coverage tests under nondiscrimination requirements. Recent legislative changes created a small employer version of 401(k) plans, or SIMPLE (Savings Incentive Match Plan for Employees) 401(k)s. In these plans, employers are not subject to meeting nondiscrimination requirements in exchange for meeting specific contribution rules (100% of employee contributions equal to 3% of their compensation or nonelective contributions equal to 2% of compensation for each employee making over $5,000 in the year).

Thrift plans (which frequently accompany 401(k) plans) promote employee savings by requiring a minimum employee contribution to be credited with an employer match. Employee participation is voluntary, and the employee can determine his or her level of contributions subject to certain plan minimum and maximum levels. Contributions are generally made to a trust fund, and employees have the option of taking in-service withdrawals of their own monies or all or a part of employer vested contributions. Many employers instituted thrift plans as a vehicle for accumulation of supplemental retirement benefits, as well as meaningful benefits during years of active employment.

Employee stock option plans are similar to profit sharing plans but are different in that distributions are made in company stock. While it is an employee benefit plan, ESOPs are well known as a vehicle for companies to borrow based on their credit to finance purchases of company stock for the firm's employees. An ESOP must meet distribution, put option, nonallocation, and voting requirements.

From 1975 to 1998, the number of qualified private sector–defined contribution plans rose from 208,000 to 673,000, with growth concentrated in smaller firms. While assets in both defined benefit and defined contribution plans increased, defined contribution plan assets grew exponentially, from $74 billion in 1975 to almost $2.1 trillion in 1998 (Rajnes 2002). Although interest in defined benefit plans has been reported recently among employees, more employers prefer defined contribution approaches because of the flexibility of these plans, growing employee job mobility, and a need for employees to learn how to manage their own retirement income. Employers are also seeking new approaches to integrate the best aspects of defined benefit and defined contribution plans, which may be accomplished by offering both plans, or a hybrid such as a cash balance plan. An important factor for future defined contribution plan design is the passage of H.R. 1836, the Economic Growth and Tax Relief Reconciliation Act of 2001 (P.L.107-16), or EGTRRA. Key provisions of EGTRRA include increased limits on contributions to qualified retirement plans, faster vesting of employer matching contributions, and greater flexibility with respect to withdrawals, rollovers, and plan contributions. This legislation provides new incentives to encourage sponsorship of both defined benefit and defined contribution plans and may encourage workers to continue to earn vested rights in plans to protect their retirement income. (See also ANNUITIES; INDIVIDUAL RETIREMENT ACCOUNT [IRA]; PROFIT SHARING PLANS; RETIREMENT PLANS—401(k); RETIREMENT PLANS—403(b).)

References

Rajnes, David. 2002. "An Evolving Pension System: Trends in Defined Benefit and Defined Contribution Plans." EBRI *Issue Brief*, September.

Rosenbloom, Jerry S. 2001. *The Handbook of Employee Benefits: Design, Funding and Administration*. 5th ed. New York: McGraw-Hill.

Mary Helen McSweeney

DERIVATIVES financial instrument contracts having a value that is derived from the value of an underlying financial product. Examples of the underlying product or "basis" are equity securities, commodities, bonds, foreign currency, short-term negotiable debt securities, and money market products. Options and futures traded on exchanges are derivatives contracts, as are over-the-counter options and forwards sold by dealers and bought by investors.

As synthetic investment instruments, derivatives fashioned from currencies, stocks, bonds, commodities, and other underlying financial products are designed to manage the risks of doing business, conserve capital, and enhance earnings. They also provide a source of investment and speculation. Most age groups, including older persons, indirectly experience the effects of derivatives trading. Pension funds utilize them, and many companies in which older investors hold stocks, bonds, or shares in mutual funds use them as well. Some money market accounts allocate part of their funds using interest rate derivatives as yield stabilizers and enhancers. There are derivatives for interest rate risks, currency risks, commodity risks, credit risks, insurance risks, and many other purposes.

For the large majority of individual investors, derivatives are neither a common nor appropriate direct investment vehicle. Only those who are fully acquainted with derivative instruments and investment risks should consider them. Most derivatives require highly technical mathematical software to build, value, and keep fluctuating risk profiles updated. On Wall Street, the design of exotic derivatives has taken on a "rocket science" aura that requires personnel with high-level math skills and access to sophisticated computer technology. Large losses and possible financial market disruptions due to derivatives trading and investment have been widely publicized, such as the multibillion-dollar crisis with Long-Term Capital Management in 1998.

Older persons and their financial advisors should be familiar with the concept of derivatives, because these investments will continue as key financial tools for corporations, government bodies, pension funds, mutual funds, banks, and other institutional investors in the future. Any inducements given older individuals to use derivatives as a speculative investment, however, should be thoroughly investigated and understood, and at least one second opinion should be obtained before any such investment is made.

Types of Derivatives

Derivatives come in two basic forms: option type and forward type. Both types may be traded on an exchange, such as commodity futures and stock options. They may also be traded privately by an arrangement between interested parties over the counter (OTC). Option-type derivatives give buyers the right, but not the obligation, to buy or sell an asset at a specific price over defined periods of time. The price for this right is usually a small percentage of the underlying asset value. For example, corporate stock options allow employees to profit from a change in the firm's stock price without owning the underlying shares. Forward-type contracts commit buyers and sellers to trade a specific quantity of assets at a set price on a set future date. Forward types include futures, forwards, and swaps. Normally, no money exchanges hands until the delivery date, when the contracts are often settled in cash rather than by exchanging assets. When homeowners apply for a mortgage and lock in an interest rate for a future settlement date, typically 60 days, they have secured a privately traded forward derivative contract (commitment) from the mortgage lender. Like options, a relatively small performance margin deposit is required, which ranges from 1% to 20% of the value of the underlying assets covered by the contract. This is the *leverage effect* in the debate about derivatives.

Market Size and Leverage

The global derivatives market is estimated to be over $100 trillion, an amount greater than ten times the U.S. gross domestic product (GDP). The estimated market size is a notional value reflecting the full value of the underlying assets, but this overstates the economic value of derivative transactions. Industry estimates indicate that the replacement cost of most derivatives that would be lost upon default by the counterparty to the transaction ranges from 3% to 6% of the notional value. To place notional value in perspective, consider an insurance policy as a form of derivative. For $750 of insurance, the car owner covers the loss of a $25,000 car. The $25,000 car represents the notional value. It would cost $750, not $25,000, to obtain a replacement policy.

The great power of derivative instruments, and most of the controversy, results from this leverage. A $10,000 performance margin deposit might control, for example, $10 million in underlying bonds, and there is real concern that during chaotic trading or a financial crisis such leverage could trigger or accelerate a financial domino effect. Critics worry about a set of outcomes where too many participants could be overleveraged and unable to meet margin and loss calls, which would precipitate mass liquidations of portfolios with few, or no, buyers to cushion the liquidations. The result could trigger financial and stock market collapses.

On the other hand, there are significant members of the global financial community, including central bankers, who believe that the interlocking web of derivatives will act ultimately as a smoothing effect to forestall a domino effect. They believe derivatives can dampen the impact of a financial crisis. Derivatives could allow various entities to hedge in such a manner as to forestall mass liquidations and thereby ride out intermittent financial storms that might randomly erupt. Without derivatives, they would be forced to liquidate and might accelerate financial collapse instead.

Two Types of Investors

Two classes of derivative users are *hedgers* and *speculators*. Commercial interests are the primary hedgers, because hedging is designed to lock in a price and to minimize losses that can result from price fluctuations between the time contractual obligations are made and the time they are delivered. Business, for example, contracts to deliver a raw or processed material, financing, or a financial instrument at some future time. A firm will hedge by using derivatives to protect its anticipated profit against adverse price fluctuation over the time period from order receipt to final delivery and customer payment, thereby reducing uncertainty. Unlike the hedger, the speculator primarily seeks to profit from price fluctuations in the underlying securities or assets and assumes the risks associated with such fluctuations. For the hedger, the minimum deposit represents a low-cost avenue to insure against the risk of price movement over time. For the speculator, the power of leverage represents an opportunity to multiply a relatively small initial investment into a large profit. For both types of investors, derivatives represent the potential for large losses as well.

Such leverage is at the center of debates about the appropriateness of derivatives use by certain participants. Regulation is under consideration for certain industries, such as banking and pension funds, to prohibit certain types of derivatives as not appropriate while allowing other types of derivatives that are. The challenge facing legislative and regulatory agencies worldwide is to create an environment that would allow the positive effects of derivatives to continue without excessive regulation. To this end, steps are being taken to better display, explain, and account for these complex instruments with greater transparency. In the immediate future, more companies and financial institutions will disclose in annual reports, mutual fund offerings, and other information sources their use and degree of involvement in derivatives. This will better inform older investors, and their advisors, about the holdings and levels of risk within the investment portfolios of the corporations, banks, insurance companies, mutual funds, and other organizations in which they invest.

Why Derivatives Evolved

During the past 30 and particularly last 15 years, the global financial markets have witnessed an increasing demand for cost-efficient protection against the risks of large and volatile foreign exchange, interest rate movements, and even credit quality risks. Without better protection against future unpredictability, companies could not function, plan, compete, and grow efficiently in global markets. When a U.S. company receives an order from Germany or Japan to be delivered in three months, it needs to hedge in a cost-effective manner against fluctuations in currency exchange rates that could wipe out its profit when paid in Eurodollars or yen.

Derivatives have provided the ability to "unbundle" and transfer certain risks from entities not willing, or unable, to manage the risks to those who desire to do so. U.S. companies, for example, not wanting to bear the risk of foreign exchange are now able to hedge their exposure by purchasing an option that guarantees the future exchange rate price and amount. The counterparty, the seller of the option, is willing to take on the exchange rate risk for a price called the *premium paid.*

The financial shocks in the 1980s and 1990s, such as the 1987 stock market crash, the failures of major banks, hedge funds, insurance companies, and securities firms, and the savings and loan crisis, have continued to reinforce the need for better financial tools to anticipate and prevent future crises. As a result of major advances in finance the evolution of derivatives has accelerated. These advances include the speed and sophistication of information processing and communications technology. Derivatives have allowed the traditional financial risks—market, credit, legal, and operational—to be managed in new, innovative, low-cost ways. In the financial, regulatory, and media arenas since the 1990s, however, negative impressions of derivatives trading remains. But a different viewpoint suggests that derivatives are necessary financial tools to control future price and market volatility for the benefit of all consumers. Mediating these opposite viewpoints and making the disclosure, measurement, control, and use of derivatives more orderly and understandable are the challenges that face the global markets for these exotic investments. (See also AGENTS AND BROKERS; ETHICS IN FINANCIAL PLANNING; FINANCIAL ADVISORS; INVESTOR EDUCATION; RISK TOLERANCE.)

References

Crouhy, Michel. 2000. *Risk Management.* New York: McGraw-Hill Trade.

General Accounting Office. 2002. *Financial Derivatives.* Washington, DC: GAO. Available online at http://www.gao.gov/.

Global Derivatives Study Group. "Group of Thirty." Available online at http://www.group30.org/.

Hull, John C. 2000. *Options, Futures, and Other Derivative Security.* 4th ed. Englewood Cliffs, NJ: Prentice Hall.

Schwartz, Robert J. 1997. *Derivatives Handbook: Risk Management and Control.* Wiley Series in Financial Engineering. New York: John Wiley & Sons.

Wilmott, Paul. 1998. *The Theory and Practice of Financial Engineering.* New York: John Wiley & Sons.

T. Erle Keefer

DISABILITY PROGRAMS, FEDERAL AND STATE, programs that provide cash support, health care coverage, and direct supportive services to eligible people with disabilities. The Americans with Disabilities Act and eight major federal and two major state programs serve sizable proportions of the disabled population aged 50 or over. These programs are typically limited to people under age 65, and the specifics of enrollment vary with the individual agency involved.

Background

Federal disability programs serve people of all ages, but most disability programs target children or working adults ages 18 through 64. Since disabilities increase with age, many programs include large numbers of people aged 50 through 64 in their later working years. The eight federal programs are (1) Social Security Disability Insurance (SSDI); (2) Supplemental Security Income (SSI); (3) Medicare; (4) Medicaid; (5) Black Lung Program; (6) the Veterans Administration Disability Compensation Program; (7) the Veterans Administration Pension Program; and (8) the Veterans Administration Health Services Program. The two state programs are (1) Workers' Compensation and (2) Temporary Disability Insurance.

People may receive benefits from more than one program if they meet eligibility requirements. Specific eligibility requirements vary, depending on the program purpose, and requirements may change over time as the result of amendments to law, new regulations, or court decisions. Eligibility is determined by factors related to disability as well as to age, income, veteran status, or work experience. Federal and state offices administering specific disability programs should be contacted directly for the current eligibility requirements.

The concept of disability has generally shifted from diseases, conditions, and impairments to a focus on functional deficits caused by these factors. Disability measures used in clinical settings or research often underlie or are incorporated into program eligibility. Disability is defined in research as significant difficulty with or the inability to perform certain daily functions (i.e., working, keeping house, living independently) because of a health condition or medical impairment.

Some commonly used factors in assessing disability are:

- *Sensory Impairments.* Difficulty with or the inability to see, hear, or speak.
- *Cognitive/Mental Impairments.* The presence of or resulting disabilities from cognitive/mental impairments (e.g., Alzheimer's disease, mental illness, mental retardation).
- *Functioning of Specific Body Systems.* Capacity of specific body systems (e.g., climbing stairs, walking three blocks, lifting ten pounds).
- *ADLs/IADLs.* Difficulty with or the inability to perform the activities of daily living (ADLs) without assistance, typically including bathing, dressing, eating, toileting, getting in or out of a bed or chair, and walking; and/or the instrumental activities of daily living (IADLs), which generally include using the telephone, shopping, preparing meals, cleaning house, doing laundry, doing yardwork, managing personal finances, and managing medications.
- *Working.* Inability to work, limitations in the amount or kind of work, and/or ability to work only occasionally, irregularly, or part-time.

The Americans with Disabilities Act

The intent of the Americans with Disabilities Act (ADA) of 1990 is to protect the civil rights of persons with disabilities. Equal opportunity provisions pertain to employment, public accommodation, transportation, state and local government services, and telecommunications.

For purposes of the ADA, disability is present if an individual meets one of the following three tests: (1) There is a physical or mental impairment that substantially limits one or more major life activities; (2) there is a record of such an impairment; or (3) the individual is regarded as having an impairment. The ADA definition is identical to the one used in Section 504 of the Rehabilitation Act of 1973 and in the Fair Housing Amendments of 1988.

Major Federal Disability Programs

Social Security Disability Insurance

Social Security Disability Insurance (SSDI) is the primary social insurance program that protects workers from loss of income due to disability. SSDI provides monthly cash benefits to disabled workers under age 65 and to certain dependents. SSDI is intended for workers who stop working early (before age 65) because of a disability.

History. The 1935 Social Security Act established the federal Social Security system to provide old-age benefits for retired workers. The SSDI program was enacted in 1956 to provide benefits to disabled workers aged 50 through 64 years and disabled adult children of deceased or retired workers. Subsequent amendments widened SSDI coverage to include certain dependents and workers younger than age 50 (Social Security Administration [SSA] 2000).

Administration. SSDI is federally administered by the Social Security Administration.

Scope. In January 2002, 6.9 million persons received SSDI benefits: 5.3 million disabled workers under age 65; 204,100 disabled widows/widowers aged 50 to 59; and 672,100 adults under age 65 who were disabled in childhood. One-half of disabled workers were between the ages of 50 and 64. In January 2002, the average monthly benefit was $815 for disabled workers, $537 for disabled widows/widowers, and $542 for adults disabled in childhood. SSDI benefits end at age 65, when workers who stop working early due to disability are converted to regular retirement benefits (SSA 2002a).

Funding. Funding is provided through the Disability Insurance portion of the Social Security payroll tax on earnings. The payroll tax is 7.65% of earnings, of which 5.6% is for the Old-Age and Survivors Insurance (OASI) portion of Social Security, 0.6% for the SSDI portion, and 1.45% for the Hospital Insurance (HI) portion of Medicare. A matching 7.65% tax is borne by employers. For 2002, the OASI and Disability Insurance (DI) parts of the payroll tax are collected only for the first $84,900 of earnings, but there is no earnings limit for the HI payroll tax (SSA 2001).

Eligibility. In order to become eligible for SSDI, an individual must have worked the required number of Social Security–covered work quarters and must have a severe impairment that makes him or her unable to perform his or her previous work or any other kind of substantial gainful activity. Insured work quarters are credited annually for those years during which an individual works, is covered by Social Security, and earns a specified amount, which is adjusted upward each year. Only four quarters can be credited each year. In 2002, one quarter of coverage is credited for $870 of earnings (this figure is adjusted annually).

Workers over age 31 must be fully insured and have at least 20 quarters of coverage during the 40-quarter period up to time of disability to receive SSDI. Fully insured status means the person has 1 quarter coverage for every year after he or she attained age 21. Persons who have 40 quarters are fully insured for life. There are special rules for persons under age 32. Workers between the ages of 24 and 31 must be fully insured and have at least 1 quarter of coverage for every 2 quarters up to time of disability to receive SSDI. Persons aged up to 24 years must have at least 6 quarters coverage in the 12 quarters up to and including the quarter the disability began.

For SSDI, disability is defined as the inability to engage in any substantial gainful activity (earn more than $780 per month for disabled and $1,300 for blind persons in 2002) by reason of a medically determinable physical or mental impairment that can be expected to last for a continuous period of at least 12 months or result in death as stated in Social Security Act, Section 223(d) (Committee on Ways and Means 2000; SSA 2002b).

After a claimant is technically qualified, State Disability Determination Services examines medical evidence to determine if the claimant's mental or physical impairment is severe enough to have more than a minimal effect on the claimant's ability to work. If so, the claimant's medical condition is compared to the SSA Listing of Impairments, covering each major body system (SSA 2002a). Claimants whose medical conditions are at least as severe as those in the listing are considered disabled. Claimants who are not found disabled are evaluated at two additional steps. A determination is made regarding whether the claimant can do his or her past work, based on assessments of his or her physical and/or mental abilities.

If it is determined that claimants cannot do their past work, then a determination is made as to whether they can do other work that exists in the national economy. This assessment is based on the individual's residual functional capacity, age, education, and work experience. Jobs are said to exist in the national economy if there are significant numbers with requirements that are within the functional abilities and vocational qualifications of claimants.

Dependent coverage and survivor benefits are offered through SSDI. Disabled individuals can receive SSDI in three ways: on their own as disabled workers (described above), as widows or widowers (who are aged 50 to 59) of insured individuals, and as adults aged 18 to 64 who became disabled in childhood, whose parent(s) either receive SSDI, are Social Security retirees, or are deceased (but had been insured under Social Security).

Disability determination criteria for disabled widows/widowers is identical to those used for disabled workers and adults disabled in childhood. Dependent coverage is also provided to nondisabled family members (spouses who are either aged 60 or older or who care for one or more entitled children younger than 16). Survivor benefits are paid to the widowed aged 60 or older; to the widowed of any age if they are caring for a dependent child who is either younger than 16 or disabled; to unmarried children younger than 18 (or 19 if in elementary or secondary school); or to dependent parents aged 62 or more.

An SSDI beneficiary may, under certain circumstances, also receive SSI payments for their disability.

Supplemental Security Income

The Supplemental Security Income (SSI) program provides monthly cash payments to low-income aged, blind, and disabled persons.

History. The SSI program was established by the 1972 amendments to the Social Security Act, which replaced earlier federal grants to the states for old-age assistance and aid to the blind and to the permanently disabled. It began operation in January 1974.

Administration. The SSI program is administered by the Social Security Administration.

Scope. In January 2002, 5.4 million blind or disabled persons received SSI, with monthly payments averaging about $423. Approximately 39% of those receiving SSI because of blindness or disability are aged 50 or over (SSA 2002b).

Funding. Funding comes from federal general revenues. Many states have chosen the option to supplement federal SSI payments with their own funds.

Eligibility. Unlike SSDI, people receiving SSI because of blindness or other disability have no prior work requirements but must meet a financial means test. Persons under age 65 must meet disability and financial criteria, whereas those aged 65 or over need only meet the financial means test. SSI payments may be received by individuals or couples. Both members of a couple must be aged, blind, or disabled and must meet the financial means test in order to collect payments. There are no dependent or survivor benefits under SSI. Disability determination is the same as in the SSDI program. Under certain circumstances, an SSI recipient may also receive SSDI benefits because of disability.

Medicare

Medicare, enacted in 1965, provides health insurance coverage to persons 65 or older, certain disabled persons under age 65, and individuals of any age with end-stage renal disease.

History. Medicare was established by the Social Security Amendments of 1965 under Title XVIII. As part of the 1972 amendments to the Social Security Act, Medicare was extended, under certain circumstances, to persons receiving SSDI and to those with kidney disease (SSA 2001). Until the passage of the Balanced Budget Act (BBA) of 1997 (P.L. 105–33), Medicare consisted of two parts: Part A, or Hospital Insurance (HI), and Part B, or Supplementary Medical Insurance (SMI). Under the BBA, a new provision, Part C, more commonly known as the Medicare + Choice program, expanded beneficiaries' options for participation in private sector health care plans (SSA 2001). Because HI (Part A) is financed through the Social Security payroll tax, HI is automatically extended to individuals eligible for Social Security. SMI (Part B) is a voluntary program available only by paying monthly premiums (Committee on Ways and Means 2000).

Administration. The Medicare program is administered by the Centers for Medicare & Medicaid Services (CMS) in the Department of Health and Human Services. CMS was formerly known as the Health Care Financing Administration (HCFA).

Scope. As of July 2000, over 39.6 million persons were enrolled in some part of the Medicare program: 34.3 million were aged 65 or over and 5.3 million were under 65.

Of these, almost 292,000 persons (of all ages) were reported to have end-stage renal disease (ESRD) (CMS 5% Denominator File). There were $236.5 billion in Medicare payments made during fiscal year 2001, of which $31.9 billion were for persons under 65 years of age receiving SSDI. In July 2000, approximately 3.7 million disabled individuals between the ages of 45 and 64 were enrolled in Medicare. During 2001, of the total Medicare beneficiaries (aged and disabled), approximately 15.6% were enrolled in Medicare + Choice and other prepaid health plans (USDHHS 2002).

Funding. Funding for Part A of Medicare comes from the HI portion of the Social Security payroll tax and is automatically deposited in the HI Trust Fund. In 2002, the HI payroll tax was 1.45% of earnings for employees and 1.45% for employers. Self-employed persons are taxed 2.9% of earnings for HI. The SMI part of Medicare is financed by a combination of monthly premiums, which generally cover about 25% of program expenditures, and federal general revenues, which cover the remaining 75% (Committee on Ways and Means 2000). In 2002, the monthly SMI premium was $54 (USDHHS 2002). Financing for Medicare + Choice comes from the HI and SMI Trust Funds (SSA 2001).

Medicare beneficiaries are responsible for charges not covered by Medicare. These charges can include noncovered services, deductibles, coinsurance, copayments, limits, premiums for Part B and voluntary Part A, and premiums for supplemental insurance (i.e., Medigap). Payments can be made out of pocket, through a health insurance plan (often referred to as "Medigap" insurance), or through Medicaid.

Services. Traditional fee-for-service Medicare coverage has two parts. Part A, or HI, is subject to deductibles, coinsurance, and limits and generally covers all Medicare beneficiaries. Part A covers inpatient hospital care, skilled nursing and/or rehabilitative post-hospital care in a skilled nursing facility (generally only within 30 days of a hospital stay of at least 3 days), home health care (which can also be covered under SMI), and hospice care (for terminally ill persons who are expected to live for less than six months). Part B, or SMI, has deductibles and monthly premiums. Part B covers physicians' and surgeons' services, outpatient services from certain other medical providers, emergency room and outpatient clinic services (including same-day surgery), ambulance services, home health care not covered by Part A, laboratory tests, x-rays, diagnostic radiological services, certain preventive screening services (e.g., tests for breast cancer, cervical cancer, prostate cancer, bone mass, diabetes monitoring, immunizations for influenza, pneumonia, and Hepatitis B), ambulatory surgical center services, certain physical and occupational therapy and speech pathology services, outpatient rehabilitation services, certain mental health care services, radiation therapy, dialysis, certain transplants, approved durable medical equipment and supplies for home use, and drugs that cannot be self-administered (Committee on Ways and Means 2000; SSA 2001; USDHHS 2000a). Medicare + Choice plans provide Part A and B services at a minimum (except for hospice care) and may offer expanded services, such as routine examinations, dental care, and prescription drugs (SSA 2001).

Eligibility. Persons aged 65 or over who are entitled to Social Security, federal employees covered under HI, and certain employees of state and local governments and nonprofit organizations are enrolled in Medicare. There are two ways that persons under age 65 can be eligible for Medicare: (1) SSDI beneficiaries are enrolled in Medicare 24 months after receiving SSDI benefits (the 24-month waiting period is waived for persons with amyotrophic lateral sclerosis), and (2) persons in the ESRD program are enrolled in Medicare after three months. Medicare recipients who are eligible because of SSDI are aged 20 to 64. Former SSDI beneficiaries under age 65 who are no longer entitled because they have earnings that exceed the substantial gainful activity amount can exercise the option to purchase Medicare Part A and B premiums (SSA 2001).

A Medicare beneficiary, under certain circumstances, may also be covered by Medicaid.

Medicaid

Medicaid is a joint federal and state program that pays for the health care of low-income and medically indigent individuals.

History. Medicaid was established, along with Medicare, by the Social Security Amendments of 1965. Medicaid replaced earlier programs that provided medical payments for needy individuals.

Administration. Medicaid is jointly administered by the states and territories and the federal Centers for Medicare & Medicaid Services. CMS was formerly known as the Health Care Financing Administration (HCFA).

Scope. During fiscal year 2000, $194.7 billion in Medicaid payments were made for an estimated 41.7 million persons. Nearly 18% of Medicaid recipients who were blind or disabled accounted for 38% of payments. During that time, $39.5 billion of all Medicaid expenditures went for nursing facilities, $9.9 billion for intermediate care facilities for the mentally retarded (ICF-MRs), and $18.3 billion for community-based long-term care. Altogether, 20.3% of all Medicaid expenditures were spent on nursing facilities, 5.1% on ICF-MRs, and 9.4% on community-based long-term care (USDHHS 2002).

Funding. Medicaid is funded by the federal and state governments. Federal dollars come from general revenues. The federal-to-state match rate is derived annually by comparing the states' average per capita income to national figures. The federal share of total Medicaid spending was 56.8% in 2000. By law, this share can range from 50% to 83% in these states. During 2000, the federal match rate was 50% for ten states. Mississippi had the highest federal match rate at 76.8% (USDHHS 2002).

Services. Medicaid covers required and optional services. Required services include inpatient hospital services, outpatient hospital services, physician services, nursing facility services for those aged 21 or over, rural health clinic services, home health care for those eligible for skilled nursing services, laboratory and x-ray services, federally qualified health center services, and many services for prenatal care and pediatrics. Optional services include diagnostic services, clinic services, intermediate care facilities for the mentally retarded, prescribed drugs and prosthetic devices, optometrist services and eyeglasses, nursing facility services for those under age 21, transportation services, rehabilitation and physical therapy services, and home and community-based care to certain persons with chronic impairments. Additional services provided under the home and community-based care may include personal care services, chore services, respite care services, and adult day care. Three Medicaid services that are important for people with disabilities are (1) nursing facilities, (2) home health services, and (3) personal care services. Nursing facilities are mandatory for people aged 21 or over who receive cash payments from SSI or Temporary Assistance to Needy Families (TANF) but are optional services for others. Home health services are mandatory for the same Medicaid recipients for whom nursing facility services are provided. Personal care services are provided in a person's home by a qualified person under the guidance of a registered nurse (SSA 2001).

Eligibility. Medicaid coverage is generally extended to persons receiving cash assistance under TANF and to those who receive SSI. Medicaid coverage is mandatory for many pregnant women and children near the poverty level and persons in specially protected groups, such as persons who lost cash assistance from SSI due to increased earnings or Social Security benefits but who may be covered by Medicaid for a certain time. Medicaid coverage is also mandatory for certain low-income Medicare beneficiaries who receive help from Medicaid in paying their Medicare premiums, deductibles, coinsurance, and other cost-sharing features. Those Medicare beneficiaries under age 65 who no longer receive SSDI due to increased earnings may also be eligible for Medicaid to purchase Medicare premiums for a period of time.

Eligibility for Medicaid is complex and varies from state to state. People with comparable illnesses, disabilities, and incomes may be eligible for Medicaid in one state but not in another.

Many of the disabled who are eligible for Medicaid also receive SSI cash assistance. However, there are a number of optional state programs through which ill or disabled persons who do not receive SSI can receive Medicaid.

Receipt of SSI typically guarantees eligibility for Medicaid in most states. As of December 2000, 11 states had exercised their authority to impose more restrictive eligibility criteria for Medicaid than SSI uses: Connecticut, Hawaii, Illinois, Indiana, Minnesota, Missouri, New Hampshire, North Dakota, Ohio, Oklahoma, and Virginia. These states permit individuals to deduct their medical expenses from their incomes when determining eligibility. Under this system, known as "spend down," if an otherwise eligible applicant's income exceeded the state's income standard for Medicaid eligibility, applicants would become eligible after incurring sufficient medical expenses to reduce their income below the standard. States must extend Medicaid eligibility to certain groups of disabled people who may not receive SSI but who are deemed to meet SSI income and resource standards.

States can elect to establish a medically needy program, under which disabled individuals whose income exceeds SSI standards but who need assistance with medical expenses can obtain eligibility by spending down. The medically needy option is exercised by most states.

The home and community-based care waiver program, elected in every state except Arizona, where the entire Medicaid program operates under a demonstration waiver, will aid in keeping certain disabled persons in the community rather than in institutions.

Under certain circumstances, Medicaid recipients may also be covered by Medicare. Approximately 6 to 7 million persons have some level of coverage in both programs (USDHHS 2002).

Black Lung

Black Lung benefits are paid to coal miners who are totally disabled as a result of pneumoconiosis (i.e., Black Lung disease), to widows of miners who died from Black Lung disease, and to their dependents (SSA 2001). The legal definition of pneumoconiosis is "a chronic dust disease of the lung and its sequelae, including respiratory and pulmonary impairments, arising out of coal mine employment" (USC 902 (b)). Both surface and underground coal miners are covered. Medical expenses for treating pneumoconiosis are also covered.

History. The Black Lung Program was established by the Federal Coal Mine Health Safety Act of 1969 (SSA 2001).

Administration. The Black Lung Program is administered by the Department of Labor. There are two programs: Part B and Part C. Part B covers miners, widows, and dependents whose payments are based on claims filed before July 1, 1973. Part C covers claims filed after that date (Committee on Ways and Means 2000).

Scope. About 70,900 persons were paid Part B benefits in December 2001, of whom only 9,900 were coal miners. The remainder were widows (55,900) or dependents (5,100). During that same time period, approximately 47,500 persons were paid under Part C, of whom 14,500 were coal miners, 31,600 were widows, and 1,400 were dependents. About 92% of people receiving Part B and Part C Black Lung benefits are aged 65 or over. Altogether, in December 2001, $37.7 million was spent for Part B and $26.4 million for Part C beneficiaries. During 2001, approximately $52.4 million was spent on medical care for Black Lung beneficiaries (U.S. Department of Labor 2002).

Funding. Part B is funded through federal general revenues, and Part C of the Black Lung Program is funded by an excise tax on coal of $1.10 per ton of coal from underground mines (55 cents from surface mines), with a cap of 4.4% of the coal's selling price.

Eligibility. A miner must meet three general conditions: (1) have (if deceased, had) pneumoconiosis; (2) be totally disabled by the disease (or have been totally disabled at the time of death); and (3) the pneumoconiosis must have been caused by coal mine employment.

VA Disability Compensation Program

The VA (Veterans Affairs) Disability Compensation Program provides cash assistance to veterans with service-connected disabilities, that is, illness or injury incurred or aggravated while in military service. Employment is not a factor; veterans can be employed and still receive benefits.

History. Veterans' health, disability, and pension programs have grown out of a long history of benefits provided to veterans. Disability pensions were provided to veterans of the Revolutionary War by the Continental Congress. In 1789, Congress enacted a veterans pension program.

Administration. The VA Disability Compensation Program is administered by the Department of Veterans Affairs (VA).

Scope. In fiscal year 2001, 2.3 million veterans with service-connected disabilities and survivors of 294,000 deceased veterans received $19.7 billion through this program. The largest share of veterans receiving benefits for service-connected disabilities served in the Vietnam era (32.9%). Another 19% served in World War II and 16.9% in the Gulf War. Altogether, approximately 30.3% of veterans with a service-connected disability were aged 70 or over in fiscal year 2001 (U.S. Department of Veterans Affairs 2002b).

Funding. Funding is provided from federal general revenues.

Eligibility. An individual must have a partial or total impairment by injury or disease incurred or aggravated during military service. A VA Rating Board employs criteria developed by the VA to rate the extent of a disability, and the illness, injury, or disease manifestations must have arisen during service. Dishonorably discharged veterans are not eligible. While the SSDI, SSI, and Black Lung Programs have an "all or nothing" disability determination process, wherein a person either is or is not determined to be eligible to receive benefits, a range or band of eligibility exists in the VA Disability Compensation Program. This range is contained in the disability ratings system, from 0% to 100%, and is based on the presumed reduction in income caused by the disability. Dependent allowances and survivor benefits are paid under certain circumstances.

VA Disability Pension Program

The VA Disability Pension Program pays cash benefits to older, low-income war veterans who have become permanently and totally disabled from non-service-connected causes or who have attained the age of 65. Certain low-income requirements must be met. This program is similar to SSDI because there are employability standards.

Administration. The VA Disability Compensation Program is administered by the Department of Veterans Affairs.

Scope. In fiscal year 2001, this program served 557,000 pensioners, including surviving spouses, at a cost of $2.3 billion (U.S. Department of Vetrans Affairs 2002b).

Funding. Funding is provided from federal general revenues.

Eligibility. A veteran must be permanently and totally disabled or must have attained the age of 65. Surviving spouses need not be disabled to qualify; however, they must meet more strenuous income limitations. An individual must have an injury or disease sustained outside of military service rendering a veteran permanently and totally impaired. Impairment is determined based on the veteran's ability to function at work and at home. Persons with dishonorable discharges are not eligible. Low-income criteria are based on income and family size. In 2002, income limits were $9,556 for a veteran living alone and $12,516 for a veteran living with one dependent (U.S. Department of Veterans Affairs 2002b). Benefits are paid to surviving spouses and children if the veteran served in specified wartime periods. Survivors must meet the same conditions as for the VA Disability Compensation Program.

Veterans Health Services

The Veterans Health Administration (VHA) administers a nationwide health care network that provides medical care services to eligible veterans.

Administration. The Veterans Health Services programs are administered federally by the Department of Veterans Affairs. (For further details, contact the nearest VA health care facility or call 1-877-222-8387.)

Scope. During fiscal year 1999, the Veterans Health Services programs cost $18 billion and were provided to 3.6 million persons. There were approximately 752,000 inpatient episodes and 38 million outpatient visits (Committee on Ways and Means 2000).

Funding. Funding is provided from federal general revenues.

Eligibility. To receive hospital and outpatient medical care, veterans must generally be enrolled with the VA. They may apply for enrollment at any time. Veterans do not have to be enrolled if they (1) have a "service-connected" disability of 50% or more, (2) want care for a disability that the military determined was incurred or aggravated in the line of duty but that the VA has not rated, during the 12-month period following discharge; or (3) want care for a service-connected disability only.

Services. Nursing home care in VA or private nursing homes may be provided for veterans who are not acutely ill and who are not in need of hospital care. Veterans generally must have received care in a VA facility for transfer to a private nursing home. VA will provide nursing home care to veterans whose service-connected disability requires such care and to veterans with a service-connected disability rated at 70% or more who need this type of care. Most other veterans are eligible for nursing home care on a space and resource available basis.

Hospital Care and Outpatient Medical Services. Certain non-service-connected and 0% noncompensable service-connected veterans receiving care for non-service-connected conditions must provide income information to establish eligibility for VA health care. Veterans whose income exceeds established thresholds are required to participate in the cost of their care through the medical care copayment program.

Extended Care Services. Certain veterans are required to agree to pay a copayment for extended care services. The following veterans are exempt from copayment requirements for extended care services: (1) veterans who were receiving extended care services on or before November 30, 1999, and who have been continuously receiving these services since that date; (2) veterans with a compensable service-connected disability; and (3) veterans whose annual income is less than a single veteran non-service-connected disability pension income amount in effect under title 38 U.S.C. 1521(b).

Medications. Certain veterans are required to pay a copayment for each 30-day or less supply of medication provided on an outpatient basis (other than medication administered during treatment) for treatment of a non-service-connected disability. The following veterans are exempt from copayment requirements for outpatient medications: veterans who (1) have a service-connected disability of 50% or more; (2) require outpatient medication for a service-connected disability; (3) have an annual income that does not exceed the maximum annual rate of VA pension that would be payable to them if they were eligible for a VA pension under 38 U.S.C. 1521; (4) require medication necessary to treat conditions related to military service such as exposure to Agent Orange, ionizing radiation, or environmental contaminants; (5) experienced sexual trauma while in the military; or (6) have head and neck cancer resulting from nasopharngyl radium treatment (U.S. Department of Veterans Affairs 2002).

Major State Disability Programs

Workers' Compensation

Workers' Compensation provides cash payments to workers (or their survivors) and medical and rehabilitation services to workers who have disabilities or who have died because of accidents on the job or occupational diseases.

History. The first Workers' Compensation law was enacted in 1908 to cover federal employees in certain hazardous occupations. By 1916, all federal workers were covered, and by 1920, Workers' Compensation programs had been established in all but seven states and the District of Columbia. By 1949, all states had Workers' Compensation programs (SSA 2001).

Administration. There are 53 separate Workers' Compensation programs administered by the states, the District of Columbia, the Virgin Islands, and Puerto Rico. The U.S. Department of Labor administers Workers' Compensation programs for federal civil servants, Longshore and Harbor Workers, the Black Lung Program (see above), and programs under the recently enacted Energy Employees Occupational Illness Compensatory Program of 2000. (The Energy Employees Occupational Illness Compensatory Program of 2000 went into effect on July 31, 2001. Persons covered under this program and who are eligible for benefits and medical expenses include Department of Energy employees and contractors and subcontractors (and certain survivors) of the Department of Energy who were exposed to beryllium and who contracted chronic beryllium disease or who have chronic silicosis and worked at least 250 days in mining tunnels for underground nuclear weapons sites in Nevada and Alaska. Benefits are also provided to uranium miners and other individuals covered under the Radiation Exposure Compensation Act. [Committee on Ways and Means 2000; SSA 2001]).

Scope. In 2000, $45.9 billion in benefits were paid. Approximately 56% of these benefits were cash payments, and 44% of benefits were for medical and rehabilitation services for these individuals. Workers' Compensation benefits are second only to the SSDI and Medicare programs for providing cash benefits and medical coverage. Weekly cash payments for workers vary by state but are typically limited to no more than two-thirds of a state's average weekly wage. There are no national figures on the number of people receiving Workers' Compensation benefits.

Funding. Workers' Compensation benefits are financed almost entirely by employers. Employers' costs averaged 1.25% of payroll in 2000 (Mont et al. 2002). Many employers have private insurance, some large employers are self-insured, and others operate in states that have state funds allotted for Workers' Compensation. Workers' Compensation coverage for most jobs in private industry is compulsory. Nationwide, about 97% of the labor force is covered by Workers' Compensation.

Eligibility. Disabilities or death can be caused by work-related injuries or occupational diseases, though the impact of the latter is often difficult to establish. Employer negligence is not an issue. However, Workers' Compensation benefits are generally not paid if the cause of the injury was intoxication of the worker, willful misconduct, or gross negligence. Unlike the SSDI and SSI programs, where eligibility is limited to those with permanent total disabilities, Workers' Compensation can provide for four types of disability: temporary total disability, temporary partial disability, permanent total disability, and permanent partial disability. Most cases involve temporary total disability.

Benefits vary by the type of disability. Temporary total and temporary partial disability benefits are paid to the worker while he or she is recovering (unable to perform regular job). Temporary partial disability benefits are uncommon. Permanent total disability benefits are paid to the worker, with survivor benefits being paid to his or her dependents when the worker dies from an occupational illness or injury. Permanent partial disability benefits are paid to the worker to compensate for his or her permanent loss of earnings (or permanent impairment).

Temporary Disability Insurance

Temporary Disability Insurance (TDI) provides workers with cash benefits for temporary nonoccupational disability or maternity. Five states (California, Hawaii, New Jersey, New York, and Rhode Island), Puerto Rico, and the railroad industry provide these benefits.

History. Federal law does not provide for a federal-state system of short-term disability comparable to the federal-state system of unemployment insurance, but in 1946 the Federal Unemployment Tax Act was amended to permit some states to use some of these funds for disability benefits. Railroad workers receive TDI under the Railroad Unemployment Insurance Act, as amended in 1946.

Administration. Program administration within the state is mostly done in the same state agency that administers unemployment insurance, but some states have private plan administration.

Scope. In general, the benefit amount is intended to be at least one-half of the weekly wage loss; however, minimum and maximum payment amounts are specified. Payment duration ranges from 26 to 52 weeks.

Funding. Authority to provide these disability benefits under the Federal Unemployment Tax Act does not provide for payment for administration. Employees may be required to contribute to the cost of TDI, with the exception of the Railroad Program. In most programs employers also are required to contribute. In general, the state government does not contribute.

Eligibility. A worker should be unable to perform his or her regular or customary job due to a mental or physical condition, but some states have more strict disability requirements. In all states a pregnant worker receives full benefits. Vesting eligibility for benefits differs, with some plans providing for immediate eligibility and others requiring some probationary work period (SSA 2001). (See also ELDER LAW PRACTICE; MEDICAID; MEDICARE; SOCIAL SECURITY PROGRAM OF THE UNITED STATES; SUPPLEMENTAL SECURITY INCOME [SSI]; VETERANS' BENEFITS.)

Organizations

Centers for Medicare & Medicaid Services
Social Security Administration

References

Adler, Michele. 1991. "Programmatic Definitions of Disability: Policy Implications." *Proceedings of the American Statistical Association.* Government Statistics Section. Alexandria, VA: ASA.

Adler, Michele. 1996. "Disability Programs, Federal." In *Encyclopedia of Financial Gerontology*, ed. Lois A. Vitt and Jurg K. Siegenthaler. Westport, CT: Greenwood Press.

Burwell, Brian, Bonnie Preston, and Sarah Bailey. 1990. *Task II: Federal Programs for Persons with Disabilities.* Washington, DC: U.S. Government Printing Office.

Committee on Ways and Means. U.S. House of Representatives. 2000. *2000 Green Book (Background Material and Data on Programs within the Jurisdiction of the Committee on Ways and Means).* Washington, DC: U.S. Government Printing Office.

Mont, Daniel, John F. Burton, Jr., Virginia Reno, and Cecili Thompson, with the advice of the Study Panel on National Data on Workers' Compensation and the Steering Committee on Workers' Compensation. 2002. *Workers' Compensation: Benefits, Coverage and Costs, 2000 New Estimates.* Washington, DC: National Academy of Social Insurance, May.

Social Security Administration. 1995. *Disability Evaluation under Social Security.* Baltimore, MD: Author.

Social Security Administration. 1997. "Social Security Programs in the U.S." Pub. 13-11758.

Social Security Administration. 2000. *A Brief History of Social Security, Issued on Social Security's 65th Anniversary, August 2000*. Baltimore, MD: Author.
Social Security Administration. 2001. *Annual Statistical Supplement to the Social Security Bulletin 2001*. Baltimore, MD: Author.
Social Security Administration. 2002a. *Program Operations Manual System*. Baltimore, MD: Author.
Social Security Administration. 2002b. Unpublished program statistics.
U.S. Department of Health and Human Services. Centers for Medicare & Medicaid Services. 2002. *2002 CMS Statistics*. CMS Pub. No. 03437. April.
U.S. Department of Health and Human Services. Health Care Financing Administration. 2000a. *Medicare and You*. Washington, DC: Author.
U.S. Department of Health and Human Services. Health Care Financing Administration. 2000b. *A Profile of Medicaid, Chartbook 2000*. Washington, DC: Author, September.
U.S. Department of Labor. 2000. *Black Lung Program Regulations, 2000 Amendments: Employment Standards Administration, Regulations Implementing the Federal Coal Mine and Safety Act of 1969, as amended 20 C.F.R. Parts 718, 722, 725, 726, 727, 65 Fed. Reg. 79919*. Washington, DC: Author.
U.S. Department of Labor. Black Lung Program. 2002. Unpublished data.
U.S. Department of Veterans Affairs. 2002a. *Federal Benefits for Veterans and Dependents. 2002 Edition*. Washington, DC: Author.
U.S. Department of Veterans Affairs. 2002b. *Internal Review*. Washington, DC: Author.

Michele C. Adler and Thomas V. Rush

DISASTER PREPAREDNESS AND OLDER ADULTS, emergency preparedness, disaster response, financial assistance, and social services provided to older adults during a widespread disaster and to assist them in recovery. Typical disasters are earthquakes, hurricanes, riverine floods, flash floods, tornadoes, severe thunderstorms, power failures, residential fires, large-scale industrial accidents, and wildfires. Less typical, but of increasing concern, are terrorist attacks.

Managing the problems posed by disasters can be complex because each hazard—natural, technological, or national security—brings a different combination of effects, and disasters of any kind may range from difficult to catastrophic in intensity and scope. Emergency management is commonly organized into four phases: (1) preparedness; (2) prevention (mitigation); (3) response; and (4) recovery. Assessing the financial implications will be easier after reviewing both the costs that might be incurred and the assistance that may be available for items or actions identified in each phase.

Preparedness

Preparedness steps can be grouped into four sets: (1) Know the hazards. (2) Develop plans: determine evacuation routes; have the contents of an evacuation kit ready to "grab and go"; have a plan for getting back together with family or caregivers; prepare checklists for emergency stock of personal, medical, and household supplies; list emergency telephone numbers. (3) Obtain emergency supplies, including cash, and make financial provisions for expenses if it is necessary to leave home for a week or more. (4) Rehearse or practice plans. Personal financial planning should provide for any emergency with the recognition that most governmental disaster assistance is for presidentially declared major disasters only. Preparedness measures should include available cash and credit resources, protection of valuable papers, and access to important supplies such as food, water, medications, and prescriptions.

Preparedness steps begin by obtaining information about the hazards that are likely to be in the area and what to expect in the event of a disaster—information that can be obtained from the local office of emergency management or Red Cross chapter. Recent catastrophic events have helped increase the knowledge and awareness of emergency managers and disaster services as to the specific needs of the older adults and the disabled in emergency situations. More attention is now paid to preparedness measures designed to ensure the adequacy, promptness, and effective manner of delivery of financial assistance and social services. Advance arrangements for helping older persons evacuate, get to shelters, and receive the care they need once they are in shelters have become common.

Older persons living independently should know where to go if evacuation is necessary. Planning may include making advance arrangements for transportation to a safe shelter and arranging evacuation assistance for those who need physical help, including immediate assistance in case of fire. Service agencies providing evacuation assistance should know how to locate individuals needing help and have information about where they can go.

The likelihood of disability increases with age, and the need for awareness of the special needs of older adults with disabilities in disaster situations is critical not only to survival but also to their successful recovery. For example, those with impaired mobility should know in advance what help they will need if evacuation should become necessary, including special assistance available in public shelters, and who will provide it. Making necessary arrangements provides assurance that assistance will arrive promptly when needed.

Older adults are more affected by major stress, such as the dislocations caused by disaster, than are younger adults. Evacuation to public shelters is a particularly difficult adjustment for many, especially if they are in a shelter without family or acquaintances. Long-term or permanent relocations actually shorten the remaining life span of some. Staying with friends, family, or other acquaintances is less stressful. If that is not possible and it is financially feasible to make standby arrangements for public lodging, advance arrangements can be made with hotels or motels out of the disaster area (for example, when planning a community evacuation in the event of a hurricane). If such standby arrangements are made, the stress is further reduced if the older person has a chance to visit the lodging at some point in the context of a vacation or recreational visit, so that it is more familiar if they return.

Flood insurance, underwritten by the U.S. government, is available through many insurance carriers and will pay for all covered losses, not just those in areas covered by major disaster declarations. Flood insurance is not covered by general household policies. Some insurance against specific hazards, such as earthquake insurance, is also available.

Prevention

Mitigation measures, such as strengthening the physical protections provided by a residential, commercial, or public property, and community facilities available where such properties are located, usually require at least a modest investment, but they are the most important means of reducing the total costs of disasters.

Either relocation to a safer area or other physical mitigation measures to avoid disaster impact should be investigated and may be necessary to protect both buildings and occupants against the force and effect of floods, high winds, earthquakes, fires, or other disasters.

Response

Response steps are those taken at the time a disaster threatens or occurs. Hurricanes and riverine floods afford plenty of warning time. Flash flood and tornado warnings may not be possible until little time remains. While they cannot yet be predicted, when earthquakes do occur, public warnings give instructions from local authorities about aftershocks, fire hazards, and damaged roads, bridges, and water and sewer systems. Individuals should be prepared to follow the instructions of officials and to adapt the actions from their plan to fit the situation. It may be necessary, for instance, to go to the "safe room" in one's home in the event of tornado or hurricane force winds if evacuation is not a feasible option. An unexpected evacuation may be necessary in these or other types of dire emergency.

Immediate emergency needs for shelter, food, clothing, personal items, first aid, medical care, and emergency financial assistance are available from local social service agencies and volunteer and humanitarian organizations such as the American Red Cross, Salvation Army, and a host of other organizations, whether or not the event is a presidentially declared major disaster or a state governor formally declares a disaster.

Recovery

Recovery begins with returning home to clean up and make repairs. One of the most important objectives of the Federal Emergency Management Agency (FEMA) and state and local governments after any disaster is to inform individuals of the assistance available and to help them with the application and delivery process. Information outlining available aid programs is disseminated by FEMA through radio, television, newspapers, mass distribution of pamphlets, community relations teams, and toll-free telephone help lines. Recovery includes elements of prevention and preparedness against the next disaster. The recovery process may also lead to a decision to relocate, away from hazardous areas such as floodplains, coastlines, or unstable slopes. Individual assistance from Federal Disaster Relief and from state and local assistance is made available at this point. Disaster relief programs are designed to help people get back on their feet and to make recovery possible. They do not restore all losses and are only available in areas identified in formally declared disasters.

Disaster victims can get information and apply for disaster assistance in a number of ways. Toll-free numbers are available for disaster victims to apply for certain types of disaster programs and obtain information about others. Federal, state, and local emergency management agencies and other social service organizations have substantially improved the help they provide for older persons in establishing eligibility for various kinds of assistance.

A presidential declaration of a major disaster can make a broad range of assistance available to victims. This may include the following:

- Disaster housing, until alternative housing is available, for disaster victims whose homes are uninhabitable. Home-repair funds may be given to owner-occupants in lieu of other forms of disaster housing assistance, so that families can quickly return to their damaged homes.
- In areas covered by disaster declarations, FEMA may provide technical assistance and hazard mitigation grants that can provide up to 75% of the cost of FEMA-approved projects to reduce the severity of future disasters.
- Disaster unemployment assistance and job placement assistance for those unemployed as a result of a major disaster.
- Individual and family grants to help meet disaster-related necessary expenses or serious needs when those affected are unable to meet such expenses or needs through other programs or means.
- Legal services to low-income families and individuals.
- Crisis counseling and referrals to appropriate mental health agencies to relieve disaster-caused mental health problems.
- Loans to individuals, businesses, and farmers for repair, rehabilitation, or replacement of damaged real and personal property and some production losses not fully covered by insurance.
- Assistance in handling flood insurance claims.
- Agricultural assistance, including technical assistance; payments covering a major portion of the cost to eligible farmers who perform emergency conservation actions on farmland damaged by the disaster; and provision of federally owned feed grain for livestock and herd preservation.
- Veterans' assistance, such as death benefits, pensions, insurance settlements, and adjustments to home mortgages held by the Department of Veterans Affairs (VA) if a VA–insured home has been damaged.
- Tax relief, including help from the Internal Revenue Service, in claiming casualty losses resulting from the disaster, and state tax assistance.
- Waiver of penalties for early withdrawal of funds from certain time deposits.
- The Cora Brown Fund, to assist victims of natural disasters for those disaster-related needs that have not been or will not be met by government agencies or private organizations that have programs to address such needs.

Disaster Assistance and Long-term Care Facilities

When considering long-term care facilities, such as nursing homes, independent living, or assisted living facilities for older persons, it is wise to inquire about the type of disaster insurance they carry and the type of disaster arrangements they will provide for the safety of their residents in the event of an actual disaster. The situation of older adults in such settings, both before and after the trauma of disaster, is characterized by general potential vulnerability. Even though the basics of shelter and food are provided, it is more difficult for older adults to recover. Since recovery depends in part on having sufficient financial resources for support and care, and because of the exceptional costs incurred when major disasters do occur, the quality of life for the older adults—and life itself—may be threatened substantially. Institutions must be in a position to evacuate residents to another facility and care for them adequately, should a disaster occur.

Psychological Consequences

Disasters often leave victims feeling disoriented and helpless. Although this applies to disaster victims of all ages, the severity increases when individuals are physically incapable of rebuilding, especially older and disabled persons. For older persons, damage to their homes or personal property, financial losses, new surroundings, strange faces, and disruptions of daily routine may cause great psychological stress. Some stress can be ameliorated by preparedness measures that instill feelings of confidence and success in coping with disaster. Mental preparedness, therefore, may be as important as financial and property preparedness in preventing feelings of helplessness among older victims. The important point to remember is that all elements of preparedness are mutually supportive and reinforcing, in older victims as with everyone. (See also FINANCIAL ADVISORS; FINANCIAL RECOVERY IN LATER LIFE; FRAILTY PLANNING; HOMELESSNESS AMONG OLDER ADULTS; HOME MODIFICATIONS FINANCING.)

Organization

Federal Emergency Management Agency.

Suggested Readings

Federal Emergency Management Agency. 1983. *Tips on Handling Your Insurance Claim*. Washington, DC: U.S. GPO.

Federal Emergency Management Agency. 1991. *Your Family Disaster Plan* (L-191). Washington, DC: Author, September.

Federal Emergency Management Agency. 1992. *Your Family Disaster Supplies Kit* (L-189). Washington, DC: Author, rev. March.

Federal Emergency Management Agency. 1993. *Emergency Preparedness Checklist* (L-154 English and Spanish). Washington, DC: Author, rev. August.

Federal Emergency Management Agency. 1995. *Preparing for Emergencies: A Checklist for People with Mobility Problems* (L-154M). Washington, DC: Author, rev. September.

Federal Emergency Management Agency. 1997a. *Before Disaster Strikes: How to Make Sure You're Financially Prepared to Deal with a Natural Disaster* (FEMA 291). Washington, DC: Author, rev. May.

Federal Emergency Management Agency. 1997b. *A Guide to Federal Aid in Disasters* (FEMA 262). Washington, DC: Author, June.

Federal Emergency Management Agency. 2002. *Are You Ready? A Guide to Citizen Preparedness* (H-34). Washington, DC: Author, rev. June.

Federal Emergency Management Agency. 2003. *Action Guidelines for Senior Citizens (for Hurricanes)*. Washington, DC: Author.

Reference

American Institute for Certified Public Accountants (AICPA), American Red Cross (ARC), National Endowment for Financial Education (NEFE). 2003. *Disaster Recovery: A Guide to Financial Issues*. Published jointly by AICPA, ARC, and NEFE. Available online at http://www.redcross.org/services/disaster/beprepared/financeprep.html.

Ralph B. Swisher

DIVORCE AND OLDER ADULTS, dissolving a marriage, or already having dissolved a marriage, after age 65. Early in this century, divorce was uncommon and difficult to obtain. In 1900, only one divorce occurred in 13 marriages, but by the 1990s, divorce was commonplace, with one divorce for every two marriages. The most dramatic increase in divorces occurred between 1965 and 1980, when the divorce rate more than doubled. Since 1980, divorce rates have persisted at high levels, and the increased incidence of divorce over time has important implications for all segments of the U.S. population, including older adults.

Few studies have focused on the significance of divorce for older adults; one reason for this neglect among researchers may be the relatively small proportion of divorces that occur within the older adult population. In 1990, for example, fewer than 2% of the 2.3 million persons becoming divorced were over age 65. (The National Center for Health Statistics [NCHS] has not published detailed divorce data since 1990. The NCHS ceased collecting these data for budgetary reasons and because some states ceased collecting detailed information.) Further, a relatively small number (fewer than 7%) of all older persons currently are divorced. Despite these statistics, a growing proportion of older persons is affected by divorce, and divorce has significant consequences for the older adult population.

Changes in the Divorce Rate over Time

One way to view the impact of divorce trends on older adults is to observe changes over time in the proportion of ever-married persons who have experienced a divorce before reaching older age. Since the majority of divorces occur in the early years following marriage, the most critical determinant of divorce for people entering later life is the divorce rate that existed 30 or 40 years earlier. The majority of divorces experienced by persons reaching age 65 in 1990, for example, occurred between 1945 and 1960 (when they were between ages 20 and 35). About 20% of persons reaching age 65 in 1960 had divorced, compared to 30% of those reaching age 65 in 1990 and 40% of those reaching age 65 in 2000. For those reaching age 65 in 2020, it is expected that nearly 50% will have divorced. Thus, only in recent years has the upsurge in divorces that occurred after 1965 begun to have an impact on the marital history of older adults. However, rapid changes will occur over the next several decades as those baby boomers, who married after 1965 and experienced high divorce rates over their adult lives, enter later life stages and become an increasingly large proportion of the older population.

The Currently Divorced

A second perspective on divorce in later life looks at the proportion of people who are currently divorced when reaching later life. Due to remarriages, the proportion who are currently divorced is significantly lower than the proportion who have ever divorced. The percentage of women who were divorced when they reached age 65 more than quadrupled between 1960 and 2000, but this only meant a growth from 2% to 9% of the relevant population. Projections by the Social Security Administration suggest that 20% of women entering later life around 2025 will be divorced. The actual percentage could exceed this projection, however, if divorced persons in the future remarry at lower rates than this projection anticipated. Changing marriage, divorce, and remarriage experiences of the baby boomers will lead to large changes in the marital and family characteristics of future older populations.

Divorce and Well-Being

The significance of divorce for well-being in later life has been demonstrated in three areas of study—mortality and morbidity, economics, and intergenerational support. A number of studies have examined the relationship between marital status and mortality.

These studies consistently find that both men and women who are married experience lower death rates than their unmarried counterparts. Among the unmarried, the divorced have higher death rates than the widowed or the never-married.

The survival disadvantage of divorced compared to married persons is greater among men than women. Marital status differences in mortality are greater among middle-aged than older persons, but divorced older people still have significantly higher death rates than the married older person. The high death rate of those divorced is especially strong for causes of death related to lifestyle and psychological state—suicide, homicide, accidents, and cirrhosis of the liver. Studies of morbidity also find that divorced persons are the least healthy of any marital status category and are more likely to suffer from both acute illnesses and chronic diseases.

Financial Consequences of Divorce

Cross-sectional studies of divorced older adults reveal they have the lowest income of any marital status category. Divorced females over age 65 are more than four times as likely to be in poverty than married females (24% versus 5%), and divorced males are about three times as likely to be in poverty than married males (17% versus 5%). The disadvantaged economic status of the divorced persists in multivariate analyses, which control for factors correlated with poverty, such as race and education level. The divorced also are relatively disadvantaged with respect to assets. For example, about 80% of married and widowed older women live in homes they own, compared to 50% of divorced women.

Most older persons who are divorced experienced their divorce earlier in life. Longitudinal analyses shed light on why the negative consequences of divorce tend to persist into their older years, especially for women. At the time of divorce, both partners usually experience a loss of wealth (frequently associated with loss of home equity). Following the divorce, men are often able to recover their former standard of living within a few years. Women, however, tend to have lower earning potential and are much less likely to experience economic recovery. Upon reaching later life, they are less likely to have accumulated significant assets and are less likely to have adequate pension incomes.

The Social Security program, technically sex neutral, also contributes to the lower economic status of older divorced women. At retirement, any worker retains the right to the primary benefit he or she earned as a covered worker. Social Security benefits for most men are unaffected by divorce, but for women who have depended on their husband's income after marriage, divorce can have a significant impact. If the marriage lasted for less than ten years, a divorced spouse is not entitled to any spousal benefit. If the marriage lasted for more than ten years, a divorced spouse (at age 65) is entitled to 50% of her former spouse's primary benefit (or 100% of her own primary benefit if it is greater), while her former spouse receives 100% of the benefit. Thus, a divorced woman who has not had earnings equal to her former spouse's will receive a smaller Social Security benefit. In many cases, there is also an unequal splitting of private pension benefits that were accumulated prior to divorce.

Research documents the important role that adult children play in the lives of most older persons. Those who have a high level of contact and interaction with their adult children receive much of their instrumental assistance and emotional support from their children. Divorced persons do not experience the same quality of intergenerational relationships as the nondivorced. Whether or not they have remarried, older men who are divorced from the biological mother of their children are much less likely to maintain contact with these children. Also, divorced men are less likely to receive help from these children or to view their adult children as a potential source of support in case of need. Further, stepchildren do not fill this vacuum, since divorced men do not have stronger ties with their stepchildren than with their biological children. Divorce also negatively affects mother-child relationships in later life, although the effect is not as striking for mothers as fathers.

The proportion of older persons who are divorced or who have experienced an earlier divorce is increasing and will continue to increase for several decades. Approximately one-half of baby boomers who will enter old age between 2010 and 2030 will have experienced a divorce from their first marriage. As discussed above, evidence suggests that divorce has negative consequences for well-being in later life. Compared to those who are married, those divorced on average experience greater poverty, have higher death rates, and receive less support from adult children. Negative effects of divorce on economic status are greater for women than men, while negative effects on social support networks are greater for men. If the current relationship between divorce and well-being persists, divorce will play an increasingly important role in shaping aging experiences, and a growing number of older people will experience adverse consequences associated with marital instability. (See also CASH FLOW PLANNING FOR RETIREES; ECONOMIC HARDSHIP MEASURES IN THE OLDER POPULATION; ECONOMIC STATUS OF OLDER MEN AND WOMEN; FINANCIAL SECURITY IN RETIREMENT; INTERGENERATIONAL CONFLICT AND FINANCIAL ISSUES; MARRIAGE AND OLDER ADULTS.)

Suggested Reading

AARP. 1994. *Women, Pensions and Divorce: Small Reforms That Could Make a Big Difference.* Washington, DC: Author.

References

Butrica, Barbara A., and Howard M. Iams. 2000. "Divorced Women at Retirement: Projections of Economic Well-being in the Near Future." *Social Security Bulletin* 63: 3–12.

Cherlin, Andrew J. 1992. *Marriage, Divorce, Remarriage.* Rev. and enlarged ed. Cambridge, MA: Harvard University Press.

Cooney, Teresa M., and Peter Uhlenberg. 1990. "The Role of Divorce in Men's Relations with Their Adult Children after Mid-Life." *Journal of Marriage and the Family* 52: 677–88.

Fethke, Carol C. 1989. "Life-Cycle Models of Saving and the Effect of the Timing of Divorce on Retirement Economic Well-Being." *Journal of Gerontology* 44: S121–28.

Holden, Karen C., and Hsiang-Hui Daphne Kuo. 1996. "Complex Marital Histories and Economic Well-being: The Continuing Legacy of Divorce and Widowhood as the HRS Cohort Approaches Retirement." *The Gerontologist* 36: 383–90.

Pezzin, Liliana E., and Barbara Steinberg Shone. 1999. "Parental Marital Disruption and Intergenerational Transfers: An Analysis of Lone Elderly Parents and Their Children." *Demography* 36: 287–97.

Uhlenberg, Peter, Teresa Cooney, and Robert Boyd. 1990. "Divorce for Women after Mid-Life." *Journal of Gerontology* 45: S3–S11.

Peter Uhlenberg

DRUGS AND SENIOR CITIZENS, the utilization of prescription medications by older adults. Persons aged 65 years and older account for 12.0% of the U.S. population (U.S. Census Bureau 2002). In 2000, the mean number of annual prescriptions for this age group was 25.5, versus only 7.1 for persons under 65 (Thomas, Ritter, and Wallack 2001). Of the 35 million older people enrolled in the Medicare program, 83% (29 million) file at least one prescription drug claim. Medicare, however, lacks an outpatient prescription drug benefit (hospital prescription medications are covered).

The utilization of prescription medicines by older adults is driven by many factors, including:

- Changing health status due to natural forces of aging, preventive measures, availability of new medicines
- Market forces such as the restructuring of retiree health benefits
- Expanding sources for health information, particularly the Internet
- Public policy focus on improving patient safety and reducing medication errors

Changing Health Status

In 2000, persons aged 65 to 74 represented 53% (18.4 million) of the older adult population. Those aged 75 to 84 represented 35% (12.4 million), and those aged 85 and older accounted for 12% (4.2 million). From 1990 to 2000, the fastest growing segment was those aged 85 and older, which increased by 30%. A survey of adults age 65 and older found that 76% take at least three medications, and one-third take eight or more (American Society of Health-System Pharmacists 2001). The National Ambulatory Medical Care Survey (1999 Summary, released July 2001) found that 66% of visits to office-based physicians resulted in at least one prescription being written. Among patients aged 65 to 74, over one-fifth (21.6%) had visits with physicians that resulted in at least four drug "mentions." For patients 75 years and over, nearly one-quarter (24.6%) had office visits with at least four drug mentions (Cherry, Burt, and Woodwell 2001).

Overall, only 4.5% of older adults resided in nursing homes in 2000; of those 85 and over, 18.2% were in nursing homes. However, this is considerably less than the 24.5% of the oldest old in nursing homes during 1990. This may be due in large part to the rapid proliferation of alternate care options, such as assisted living facilities and continuing care retirement communities that offer multitiered levels of care.

Among nursing home residents, there was an average of 6.7 routine medication orders and 2.6 "as-needed" orders (Tobias and Sey 2001). However, among all residents, 27% took nine or more regularly scheduled medications. This is a significantly higher number than the same survey found in 1997.

A study examining drug utilization among assisted living facility (ALF) residents found the mean number of medications to be 6.2 (Armstrong, Rhoads, and Meiling 2002). The similarity to the average number of routine medications in nursing home residents may change with further study of ALF residents (a growing but understudied population) and with medication reviews by specially trained geriatric pharmacists that are becoming more common.

Overall, the utilization of prescription medications by older people is expected to increase due to (1) clinical literature and medical practice guidelines that recommend additional medications for disorders common to older adults, such as heart failure and diabetes; (2) enhanced treatment of previously undertreated conditions, such as depression and pain; and (3) an increased focus on wellness and preventive health, with pharmacologic treatment for conditions such as osteoporosis (Tobias and Sey 2001).

According to the Food and Drug Administration (FDA), most drug-related problems in the older adult population are due to pharmacokinetic differences related to age itself (e.g., drug absorption or excretion) or to age-associated conditions such as renal impairment, congestive heart failure, or multiple drug therapy (FDA 1994). Since 1998, the FDA has required specific labeling for geriatric patients on certain classes of medicines. Priority classes for implementing the geriatric labeling were antidepressants; nonsteroidal anti-inflammatory drugs; digoxin, antiarrhythmics, and calcium channel blockers; oral hypoglycemic agents; anticoagulants; and quinolones.

Market Forces

Because Medicare does not provide outpatient prescription drug coverage, many seniors incur high out-of-pocket drug costs. In 1999, retail outpatient prescription drug spending increased 18.4%, and in 2000 the rate of growth slowed slightly to 14.5%. Overall health care spending rose 7.2% from 1999 to 2000, the largest jump in a decade (Strunk, Ginsburg, and Gabel 2001). Of the 9,900 prescription drugs on the market, 23 of the 50 top sellers accounted for 50% of the increase in drug spending (Jacob 2001). For older adults, mean total drug spending rose from $827 in 1997 to $1,378 in 2000, an 18.5% annual increase (Thomas, Ritter, and Wallack 2001).

The primary factor in this growth was the number of prescriptions per person. This grew from 20.7 in 1997 to 25.5 in 2000 (or 7.1%) for older adults versus from 6.2 to 7.1 prescriptions (or 4.7%) for younger populations. Historically, "high-cost" seniors (those who incur greater total pharmaceutical expenditures) use more brand-name drugs, treat more conditions, and use more medications overall. To obtain prescription drug coverage, seniors have several options. Many purchase a "Medigap" insurance plan that covers outpatient medicines. Some retirees retain employer-sponsored health insurance that have deductibles and require copayments for drugs. Low-income Medicare beneficiaries with few assets may qualify for state-sponsored pharmaceutical assistance programs. In 2001, 20 states offered such programs (Tilly and Wiener 2001). Further, some older people may enroll in "Medicare + Choice" managed care or fee-for-service plans, if locally available. In 2001, 5.6 million Medicare beneficiaries chose these plans, which represents a 12% decline since 1999 (Centers for Medicare & Medicaid Services 2001). Historically, these plans included outpatient drug coverage, but this is changing. In 1999, 78% of Medicare + Choice enrollees had such coverage; by 2001, only 35% of enrollees were in plans that featured drug coverage.

Insurance coverage for prescription drugs is a significant factor in the access to and appropriate use of medicines by older adults. Researchers who studied a nationally representative sample of Medicare beneficiaries with coronary heart disease found that use of statins—relatively expensive medications that improve survival—ranged from only 4.1% in Medicare patients with no supplemental outpatient drug coverage to 27.4% in those with employer-sponsored coverage. Nitrate use also occurred less frequently in persons with Medicare coverage only (Federman et al. 2001).

Access to Health Information

Another trend affecting drug utilization by seniors is expanding sources of drug information. First, since 1997, the Food and Drug Administration has permitted the pharmaceutical industry to advertise their products "direct to consumers" (DTC) much more aggressively, particularly on television. The pharmaceutical industry spent over $2 billion on DTC ads in 2000 versus $1.3 billion in 1998—the first full year after the FDA relaxed the guidelines.

Many of these broadcast DTC ads (whose companion pieces usually appear in newspapers and magazines) promote drugs used to treat chronic conditions common in older adults, such as hypertension, cholesterol reduction, diabetes, arthritis, and depression. These ads often feature grandparents playing with their grandchildren, thus reinforcing the pitch to seniors. An AARP study (Foley and Gross 2000) of consumers' familiarity with printed DTC ads found that those age 60 and older appear to obtain less information from the ads, and they are less likely than younger consumers to understand whether the advertised product requires a prescription. Further, AARP found that only 48% of older consumers notice the small print in the ads (containing indication, directions, and risk information) versus 66% of persons aged 18 to 39. Older consumers also tended to talk with their pharmacists and physicians about their medications less than younger consumers. Thus, older consumers "may be more vulnerable than others to the 'medication information gap,' " AARP notes.

One way that older adults are fighting this vulnerability is by turning to the Internet for health and medicine information. (Internet users age 65 and older represent the fastest-growing segment of new users.) Most of the DTC broadcast and print ads have an electronic component—product-specific Web sites developed by pharmaceutical manufacturers to provide more information for consumers and health care professionals. Such Web sites may feature online consumer health newsletters geared to the relevant health conditions as well as coupons or rebates. Still other Web sites allow consumers to conduct an electronic medicine review where they type in the names of their prescription and nonprescription medicines and can receive warnings about possible drug-drug or drug-food interactions.

Unfortunately, the unregulated Internet is also home to unsubstantiated health claims, to online pharmacies that bypass direct health professional evaluation (completing a short questionnaire is all a consumer may need to obtain a prescription medicine via these disreputable Web sites), and to drug information for which risks and benefits may not be presented clearly, if at all. Homebound older adults who surf the Internet for health information, others who do not have regular access to a licensed health care professional, and those without high reading levels may be most at risk (Berland et al. 2001). To encourage safe online shopping for pharmaceuticals, the FDA and the National Council on Patient Information and Education formed the CyberSmart Safety Coalition (see http://www.fda.gov/).

Patient Safety and Appropriate Use of Medicines

Two reports from the Institute of Medicine (IOM) (Washington, DC), *To Err is Human* (1999) and *Crossing the Quality Chasm* (2001), brought the term *patient safety* into the public health lexicon. The first IOM study found that medication errors were the most common type of medical error. Consequently, there has been a growing research focus on the appropriate use of medicines in the older adult population. (Much of this is driven by the anticipation that a Medicare outpatient prescription drug benefit will be enacted this decade.)

One examination of a Medicare managed care population found that nearly one in four such beneficiaries potentially used medication inappropriately (Fick et al. 2001) This subset had a substantially higher number of providers prescribing their medicines, significantly higher total health care costs, and a higher mean number of inpatient, outpatient, and emergency room visits. The authors judged the "prevention and recognition of drug-related problems" in this population to be the "principal challenge in patient safety in the next decade."

In 2001, the Agency for Healthcare Research and Quality (AHRQ) awarded $50 million worth of grants for patient safety, with over $38 million devoted to promoting safe medicine use (AHRQ 2001). Many of these research projects are specific to improving medicine use and reducing errors in the older adult population. The following organizations develop and maintain timely consumer messages regarding the safe use of medicines:

- National Council on Patient Information and Education (NCPIE) (Bethesda, MD)—http://www.talkaboutrx.org/
- Alliance for Aging Research (Washington, DC)—http://www.agingresearch.org/
- United States Pharmacopeia (Rockville, MD)—http://www.usp.org/
- SMART Coalition (Sacramento, CA)—http://www.smartcoalition.org/

To reduce risk of medication errors, NCPIE recommends that older adults and/or their caregivers:

1. Ask questions of the physician, nurse, and/or pharmacist about what a medicine is for, exactly how to use a new medicine, what side effects to watch for, and when the medicine will no longer be needed.
2. Tell all health care professionals about all other prescribed and over-the-counter medicines being taken, including dietary supplements (keep an updated, written list).
3. Learn what other medicines, drinks, and activities to avoid when taking a new medicine.
4. Ask if any monitoring tests (such as for blood count or liver or kidney function) are required while on a medicine; keep all appointments for such monitoring; and share results with all health care professionals involved in all facets of health care.

Older adults play an important role in managing their own care, particularly when medicines are involved. Incorporating the above points into each health care visit can help ensure safe, appropriate medicine use. (See also MEDICARE + CHOICE; MEDICARE SUPPLEMENTAL INSURANCE; NUTRITION PROGRAMS; PHARMACISTS; PHYSICIAN–OLDER PATIENT RELATIONSHIPS; RETIREMENT PREPAREDNESS.)

Organization

CyberSmart Safety Coalition

References

AHRQ. 2001. "New Research Projects Awarded to Improve Patient Safety." Available online at http://www.ahrq.gov/qual/newgrants/index.html.

American Society of Health-System Pharmacists. 2001. "New Study Reveals One-Third of Seniors Take Medications Prescribed by Two or More Physicians." August 6. Available online at http://www.ashp.org/.

Armstrong, E.P., M. Rhoads, and F. Meiling. 2002. "Medication Usage Patterns in Assisted Living Facilities." *The Consultant Pharmacist* 16(1): 65–69.

Berland, G.K. et al. 2001. "Health Information on the Internet." *Journal of the American Medical Association* 285(20): 2612–21.

Centers for Medicare & Medicaid Services. 2001. "The Medicare + Choice Program in 2001 and 2002." Fact Sheet, August 29. Available online at http://www.hcfa.gov/facts/fs010829.htm.

Cherry, D.K., C.W. Burt, and D.A. Woodwell. 2001. *National Ambulatory Medical Care Survey: 1999 Summary. Advance Data from Vital and Health Statistics*. No. 322. Hyattsville, MD: National Center for Health Statistics, July 10.

FDA. 1994. "Guideline for Industry Studies in Support of Special Populations: Geriatrics." Available online at http://www.fda.gov/cder/guidance/iche7.pdf.

Federman, A.D., et al. 2001. "Supplemental Insurance and Use of Effective Cardiovascular Drugs among Elderly Medicare Beneficiaries with Coronary Heart Disease." *Journal of the American Medical Association* 286(14): 1732–39.

Fick, D.M., et al. 2001. "Potentially Inappropriate Medication Use in a Medicare Managed Care Population: Association with Higher Costs and Utilization." *Journal of Managed Care Pharmacy* 7(5): 407–13.

Foley, L.A., and D.J. Gross. 2000. "Are Consumers Well-Informed about Prescription Drugs? The Impact of Printed Direct-to-Consumer Advertising." *AARP Public Policy Institute*, April. Available online at http://research.aarp.org/.

Institute of Medicine. 1999. *To Err Is Human*. Washington, DC: Author.

Institute of Medicine. 2001. *Crossing the Quality Chasm*. Washington, DC: Author.

Jacob, Julie A. 2001. "A Few Drugs Spark Rise in Prescription Costs." *American Medical News*, October 1.

National Council on Patient Information and Education. 2000. *Medicine: Before You Take It, Talk About It*. Bethesda, MD: Author.

Strunk, B.C., P.B. Ginsburg, and J.R. Gabel. 2001. "Tracking Health Care Costs." *Health Affairs*. Available online at http://www.healthaffairs.org/.

Thomas, C.P., G. Ritter, and S. Wallack. 2001. "Growth in Prescription Drug Spending among Insured Elders." *Health Affairs* 20(5): 265–77.

Tilly, J., and J.M. Wiener. 2001. "State Pharmaceutical Assistance Programs for Older and Disabled Americans." *Health Affairs* 20(5): 223–32.

Tobias, D.E., and M. Sey. 2001. "General and Psychotherapeutic Medication Use in 328 Nursing Facilities: A Year 2000 National Survey." *The Consultant Pharmacist* 16(1): 54–64.

U.S. Census Bureau. 2002. "March 2002 Current Population Survey." Available online at http://www.census.gov/population/socdemo/age/ppl-167/tab01.pdf.

N. Lee Rucker

DURABLE POWER OF ATTORNEY, a legal document in which an individual (the "principal") appoints and authorizes another to act as his or her agent ("attorney-in-fact"). The power of attorney is durable because it remains in effect if the principal becomes ill or mentally incapacitated. The power can be general or specific to a certain transaction such as an authorization to sign on another person's behalf in a real estate settlement. A general durable power of attorney (DPOA) is typically very broad, authorizing the attorney-in-fact to make medical decisions if necessary, sign checks, cash in savings or investment accounts, buy or sell a home or other asset, and in general do anything that the principal could do. Other DPOAs are more narrowly drawn, such as a durable power of attorney for health care, a type of advance directive for use in a medical emergency.

As in all powers of attorney, the power is revoked upon the death of the principal. Nondurable powers of attorney automatically become invalid upon the death or incapacity of the principal, but DPOAs remain effective if the principal becomes completely incapacitated. "This power of attorney . . . shall not terminate on disability of the principal" effectively distinguishes a nondurable power of attorney from one that is durable.

Assuming a person is fortunate enough to have a completely trustworthy person to act on his or her behalf, a DPOA is an excellent way to plan for the management of financial, medical, and practical affairs in the event of temporary or permanent disability. It can spare loved ones trauma, expense, and the red tape of a guardianship or conservatorship proceeding. The choice of attorney-in-fact (not necessarily professional attorneys) is typically a spouse, adult child, or close friend. In drafting a DPOA, critical issues arise and must be considered carefully. It may be inappropriate, for example, to grant fiduciary powers to the same person empowered to make medical decisions.

Nondurable powers of attorney did not contemplate the types of functions today's guardianship-avoidance instruments may usefully permit. It took more than three decades for every jurisdiction to enact legislation permitting DPOAs, and until every jurisdiction had taken such action, most nationwide organizations refused to accept them. Today, the DPOA has become an essential part of estate planning, but acceptance of DPOAs by financial institutions and other organizations can still pose practical problems. Some financial institutions will request an affidavit executed by the attorney-in-fact that states the power of attorney has not been revoked and that the principal is still living. In an increasing number of jurisdictions, problems have been resolved by statutes that indemnify against the risks of persons relying in good faith on a DPOA after revocation of the DPOA or after the death of the principal.

Generally, any power of attorney will be construed narrowly and should contain an explicit recitation of the powers granted by the document. Gifts might be designated as "$11,000 per year, per donee 'annual exclusion' " and recipients limited to "children and grandchildren." Or a DPOA may be drafted broadly so that all assets may be given in the sole judgment of the attorney-in-fact to someone else, including the attorney-in-fact. Broad powers are often essential for married couples when planning for the possibility of long-term illness or incapacity. A spouse, acting as attorney-in-fact for an institutionalized spouse, needs a broad power of attorney in order to take advantage of laws permitting the "community spouse" (the non-ill spouse) of an institutionalized Medicaid recipient to preserve assets and protect against impoverishment. Gift-giving power under a DPOA should be carefully considered in light of the specific potential needs of the individual who will grant such power.

Whether estate planning, planning for charitable contributions, or for Medicaid eligibility, careful consideration must be given to defining the extent of the power and the class of donees. DPOAs may be beneficial for estate tax and Medicaid planning purposes. In the case of a wealthy individual, removing assets from the principal's taxable estate while he or she is incapacitated may save otherwise unnecessary estate taxes. If someone is a candidate for care under Medicaid, it is essential to consider whether authorization of asset divestment is appropriate. Anyone considering granting a DPOA must realize, however, that a power of attorney in the wrong hands is an invitation for financial elder abuse.

Depending on who is serving as attorney-in-fact, an individual may wish to include protective language requiring record-keeping and reporting. If one adult sibling is serving as attorney-in-fact, other siblings may wish to require a copy of the DPOA and all copies of financial and other records periodically. When a nonrelative is named as attorney-in-fact, he or she may have to account to the principal's family members. Particularly when asset divestment powers are included, an agent must be trusted to act in the same manner in which the principal himself or herself would act under the circumstances. Keeping everything "out in the open" may help avoid potential abuse and animosity among family members. Finally, even the most beloved adult child may not be a good candidate for attorney-in-fact if he or she has problems such as drug or alcohol abuse or is frequently on the edge of financial problems.

Although most forms of DPOA do not include provisions for compensation, payment may be appropriate in certain cases. Compensation may protect the principal, for example, by providing an incentive to the attorney to handle duties that become burdensome. For principals who are also parties to recoverable trusts, parallel provisions should be included in both the trust document and the DPOA to accomplish the coordination of objectives.

A Case Illustration

Drafted properly, the DPOA can be the single most important legal instrument anyone can execute. The following example illustrates its usefulness. Mrs. Murphy's husband has been in a nursing home with Alzheimer's disease for four years. Two years ago, Mr. Murphy qualified for Medicaid, after most of their savings had been spent on his care. Mrs. Murphy is now in bad health and wishes to move to a continuing care retirement community. In order to afford her new living arrangement, Mrs. Murphy must sell her house and invest the proceeds from the equity to supplement her income. She and her husband are both owners of the house as "tenants by the entirety," however, so the house cannot be sold without her husband's signature. But he is not competent to sign the required legal papers. If Mrs. Murphy had obtained a broadly drafted DPOA from her husband while he was still capable of executing one, she could proceed with the sale. If she does not have a power of attorney, she must spend thousands of dollars in legal fees obtaining the permission of a court to sell the house. Because her husband has been receiving Medicaid in the nursing home, and depending on the state in which she resides, the court might order that one-half of the proceeds from the sale of the house be turned over to Medicaid and/or the nursing home, leaving her with inadequate resources. The importance of a carefully drafted durable power of attorney simply cannot be overstated. (See also ADVANCE DIRECTIVES; ELDER LAW PRACTICE; FINANCIAL ADVISORS; FRAILTY PLANNING; HEALTH AND LONGEVITY.)

References

Alexander, George J. 1988. *Writing a Living Will: Using a Durable Power-of-Attorney*. New York: Praeger.

Berg, Adriane G. 1993. *Financial Planning for Couples*. New York: Newmarket Press.

Cohen, Elias. 1984. *Durable Power of Attorney: An Important Alternative to Guardianship, Conservatorship, or Trusteeship*. Washington, DC: U.S. Department of Health and Human Services.

Haman, Edward A. 1994. *The Power of Attorney Handbook: With Forms*. Clearwater, FL: Sphinx Publishers.

Levitin, Nancy. 1994. *Retirement Rights: The Benefits of Growing Older*. New York: Avon Books.

Janet L. Kuhn

E

EARLY RETIREMENT. See Corporate Elder Care Programs; Early Retirement Incentive Plans (ERIPs); History of Retirement; Individual Retirement Account (IRA); Keogh Plans; Pension Plans; Working Retirees.

EARLY RETIREMENT INCENTIVE PLANS (ERIPs), plans that extend the benefits offered to workers or give additional financial inducements that motivate employees to retire prior to the age or time they otherwise would retire. Early retirement incentive plans first appeared on the employee benefit landscape in the late 1970s and early 1980s. The nation was struggling with "stagflation," and many firms sought to reduce their labor costs without resorting to layoffs. At the same time, the long-term trend toward earlier retirements was proceeding unabated. Many workers expressed a desire to enjoy the "leisure" that could be secured through the early retirement provisions of many companies' defined benefit plans. ERIPs offered enhancements to these benefits, allowing employees to retire earlier than they had planned. They proved popular among salaried and hourly workers alike and were smiled on by unions. No wonder, then, that a study of Fortune 100 firms in 1989 found that eight out of ten had offered such programs (BNA 1989).

When first offered, firms could not reliably predict how many or which workers would accept them. Especially when ERIPs were generous, and their eligibility criteria quite broad, firms lost many workers they would have wished to retain. Sometimes they found they had to hire back these new retirees as consultants or independent contractors. For example, a survey of 232 private and public employers by Mercer Human Resource Consulting found that 35% hired back retirees as consultants or independent contractors, and 37% brought back retirees as temporary or part-time employees. In the past two decades, however, firms have become much more sophisticated in targeting offers to avoid such outcomes.

During the past several years, the popularity of ERIPs has been on the wane. Several factors are involved in their diminished use. First, the ranks of potential retirees have been thinned by two decades of offering such programs. In addition, many employers have faced the need for substantial reductions in their workforce or the need for cutting particular jobs in response to a merger—goals that were unlikely to be achieved with ERIPs alone.

Moreover, while earlier programs had been able to call on the ample funds available in defined benefit plans, newer retirement plans were likely to take the form of defined contribution plans, which are not readily useful in creating ERIPs. Indeed, many firms making layoffs today are in the service industry, where workers may not be covered by *any* retirement plan. And with declining stock values, many defined benefit plans are finding that they now must add funds to pension reserve funds in order to cover their obligations for current and future retirees. Companies must annually report the actual—not just the estimated—value of their pension funds. Under federal law, if a firm's loss exceeds 10% of the greater of a pension's liability or the fair market value of assets, it must by law begin making contributions to the plan (Kerchoff 2002).

Finally, rapidly rising health care costs and the legal issues raised in interpretations of Employee Retirement Income Security Act (ERISA) or the Older Workers Benefit Protection Act (OWBPA) legislation served to dampen the enthusiasm of firms regarding ERIPs. Although retiree health benefits—at least helping to bridge a worker until (s)he was eligible for Medicare—were a standard part of earlier ERIP packages, firms now find the costs of such benefits prohibitive. Without a guarantee of protection from rising health care costs, potential early retirees find ERIPs much less attractive.

Despite these influences, ERIPs continue to exist. In fact, they have been widely adopted within higher education and are being offered by states and local communities to achieve downsizing objectives. A 2001 article by the *Chronicle of Higher Education* reported that since 1994 "nearly half of all colleges have offered financial incentives to encourage faculty members to retire early" (Fogg 2001). Before describing the most recent set of ERIPs offered by corporations, academic institutions, or government, a review of the basic characteristics of such programs is in order.

First, participation in ERIPs is voluntary. Firms are careful to target an entire class of employees, or a particular location; this protects them from charges of age discrimination. Second, these programs are short term. They are often called "open window plans" because offers are made and must be accepted during a limited time period, typically one to two months, though the range may run from one day to one year. Finally, these plans provide *one-time* cash and/or pension plan adjustments. Some also provide continuation of other benefits (e.g., health and life insurance) for a specified period. The range of benefits offered is described below, but, as already noted, firms have gained a good deal of experience in the design of ERIPs and are able to be more selective in setting eligibility requirements. They also have become less generous in the benefits packages being offered.

While firms and employee benefit consultants agree that, to be most effective, an offer should occur only once, many firms do offer such plans periodically—some nearly every year. A Hewitt Associates 1992 survey of nearly 700 companies, for example, found that one-fifth had offered two programs since 1988; 7% had offered three, and 3% had offered four or more (Hewitt Associates 1992). A 1999 report by Watson Wyatt found that 31% of firms had offered more than one window plan. Unfortunately, workers exposed to frequent ERIPs come to believe that they will be able to postpone retirement and still receive an offer "when the right time comes." Indeed, in 1998, 81% of retirements from employers with pension plans took place prior to retirees' sixty-fifth birthdays (*Employee Benefit Plan Review* 1999).

Prevalence

Because ERIPs are not as widespread as they had been a decade or two ago, there are fewer reports detailing their dimensions. Price Waterhouse Coopers (2001) surveyed 114 firms in 2001 and reported that 12.3% had made such an offer to employees. Watson Wyatt surveyed 75 large companies in 1998–1999, finding that 61% had offered at least one ERIP in the previous ten years. In 2002, however, Watson Wyatt's survey found that only 17% of U.S. firms had offered such plans in the prior three years.

In 1997, Spencer and Associates surveyed 221 private and 68 public/nonprofit employers; 10% of the former and 13% of the latter provided ERIPs for employees. Of those offering ERIPs in 1995, half of the private employers had made prior offers, while only one-third of the public firms had done so. Seventy percent (70%) of the private firms not offering a 1995 ERIP had offered one in the past. In 1998, Spencer and Associates reported:

> A booming economy over the 1994-1998 period creating a tight labor market, witnessed a sharp decline in the proportion of early retirements attributable to early retirement window offers and "sweeteners." In 1992, following two years of ferocious recession-induced downsizing, 37.6% of early retirements that year were the result of such offers. That proportion dropped to 14.5% in 1994, 6.12% in 1996, and 4.89% in 1998. ("Robust Economy" 1999)

In addition to reports from employee benefit consulting firms, there is a national survey that studies retirement decision making, the Health and Retirement Survey. Since 1992, every two years, the federal government has collected information about retirement plans of respondents. In 1992, the sample for the survey ranged from 51 to 61 years of age. In both Wave 1 (1992) and Wave 2 (1994), any of these men and women who had worked in the past 20 years were asked about window plans they had been offered. Nearly 9 % (8.8%) had been offered at least one such plan; three out of ten who received one offer received more than one, usually from the same employer.

Eligibility

The majority of firms offering ERIPs use a combination of years of age and service to define those eligible for a window plan offer. Or they may have a "magic number" that can be reached by different combinations of age and service. For example, if the number is 75, then a person aged 55 with 20 years of service and another aged 60 with 15 years of service would both be eligible. Eighty-nine percent (89%) of the plans surveyed by Hewitt Associates in 1997 used a combination of age and service criteria to define which workers would be eligible for ERIPs; only 8% used age alone, and only 3% relied solely on service years to define eligibility (Hewitt Associates 1997). Watson Wyatt's 1999 survey also showed age 55 as the minimum age requirement for 20 firms, while 13 companies reported that they required employees to have 10 years' tenure in order to qualify for an ERIP. In 2002, Watson Wyatt reported that 45% of firms surveyed used the criteria defining early retirement in their defined benefit plan, while 41% included younger workers and 12% restricted the offer by job class and another 25% restricted it to workers in certain locations.

What Is Offered

For ERIPs within a defined pension plan, the most common incentive is the addition of age or service credits in calculating pension benefits. Typically, "5 and 5"—adding five years to age and/or five years to length of service—is offered. Other incentives may reduce or eliminate the penalty for early retirement, provide cash supplements until an employee is eligible for Social Security (in the main, at age 62, though some plans bridge payments to age 65), provision of life insurance, outplacement assistance, and less often, retiree health benefits (Hewitt Associates 1997).

When a defined benefit plan is not extant—if instead a firm has a defined contribution plan, for example—or when an employer wishes to design incentives that would not be permitted under ERISA rules, other incentives are utilized. Watson Wyatt (2002) reports that a cash payment/severance pay was offered to 43% of targeted employees. Cash offers varied; for example, some workers are offered one to two weeks per year of service, while others may be offered an additional 5% of pay. Lump-sum options also are attractive to employees:

> As a special supplement to the retirement benefit, you can give people the option to take the present value of the supplement in lump sum and roll over into an individual retirement account—if the defined benefit plan normally doesn't give a lump sum option—making one available in window is so attractive you may not have to sweeten the pension at all. (Richard Koski, quoted in Brenner 1998)

The economic environment in 1998 appeared much rosier than it did in 2002, however. After several years of recession, potential retirees were far less sanguine about their chances of finding another job if they accepted an employer's ERIP offer.

Acceptance Rates

It is important to note *when* the window plans are offered in evaluating acceptance rates. Hewitt Associates (1997) reported that participation rates varied from 1% to 79%, while Watson Wyatt (1999) found that rates ranged from 1% at Dow Chemical (in 1995) to 100% at American Home Products (in 1998). Allstate (1994), J.C. Penney (1997), Motorola (1998), Nationwide Insurance (1995), and Texas Utilities (1997) all reported acceptance rates of 80% or higher (Watson Wyatt 1999). Spencer Associates (1998) reported that in 1995, 42.4% of those eligible in private firms accepted these offers; by 1997 that proportion rose to 52.3%.

Price Waterhouse Coopers (2001) reported that of the firms that offered ERIPs in the form of unreduced benefits, over half (57.1%) of employees accepted these offers. Watson Wyatt's 2002 report also shows that 55% of eligible employees accepted ERIPs, noting that acceptance rates were highest when age and service credits *and* cash payments were provided.

In looking at the Health and Retirement Survey sample, Charles Brown (1996) reports that those accepting a window plan were more likely to anticipate that layoffs would occur and that wage growth would slow or halt. Interestingly, they are also less likely to have a spouse who works outside the home and more likely to have a health condition that limits the kind or amount of work they can do. He notes: "A subtler implication is that window offers may be accepted precisely because they are a sign that employer stability and traditional wage increases are less certain if one remains."

In fact, focus groups of state employees in Connecticut—both those who had accepted and those who had rejected an early buyout—showed that most thought the ERIPs and the way they were offered were commendable. However, those who had rejected the offers spoke of the "deterioration in the work environment" because of the increased workload (Rix 1997).

Not everyone observing these plans believes them to be benign. Some worry that the overall reduction in benefits, particularly when one considers the decline in the value of a 401(k) or 403(b) portfolio, may mean that there will not be sufficient assets to provide a reasonable standard of living in retirement. "Other analysts wonder whether . . . [ERIPs] are not just a new way of turning American veteran employees into contingent workers" (Walsh 2001, 1).

ERIPs in the Halls of Ivy

On January 1, 1994, an amendment to the Age Discrimination in Employment Act (ADEA) became law, ending mandatory retirement at age 70 for tenured faculty. In 1998, Ashenfelter and Card (Clark and Hammond 2000) conducted a study of faculty at 37 institutions and found that the end of mandatory retirement had, indeed, led to marked declines in the proportion retiring. There were no significant differences by gender or race, but faculty with higher salaries as well as those teaching at research universities were much less likely to retire before or at the age of 70. The consequence was that with no, or very small, increases in budgets, colleges and universities found it difficult to hire any of the Ph.D.s who had received their degrees in the prior 10 years. Achieving increased diversity among faculty members was also a challenge.

Universities and colleges scrambled to find ways to induce aging faculty members to retire. A survey in 2000 by the American Association of University Professors (AAUP) Committee on Retirement found that among 608 public and private institutions with 75 or more full-time faculty members, there were widely varying retirement plans, some with structures that contained early retirement incentives (Fogg 2001). A little more than one-third of the institutions offered a buyout, though these were twice as common at private institutions. In about half of the cases in which buyouts were offered, all tenured faculty members were automatically eligible if they met the age and years-of-service requirements. At about 90 of the institutions there was an increase in annual retirement benefits (Fogg 2001). Some institutions also offered phased-retirement programs; they were especially useful for public institutions and community colleges since they are able to keep experienced teachers while allowing them to reduce their workload. Uncertainty regarding the legality of setting an upper age limit for incentives caused institutions to shy away from using ERIPs, but recent cases have allowed their use. And because public sector plans are not subject to ERISA, age-based formulas are available for use in those settings.

Conclusion

The recent economic downturn, widespread downsizing and restructuring of many firms in corporate America, and the increased use of defined contribution or cash balance pension plans has diminished the use of ERIPs in the late 1990s and the beginning of the twenty-first century. There has also been a change in people's expectation of work. No longer do men and women believe that they will have a lifetime career with one firm. And many firms no longer believe they must play a paternalistic role in their worker's retirement planning. Retirement security has become the individual's responsibility. (See also FINANCIAL PLANNING; HEALTH BENEFITS; JOB LOCK; LIFE PLANNING; RETIREMENT EXPENSE PLANNING.)

References

Brenner, Lynn. 1998. "Quitting Time." PLANSPONSOR, May. Available online at http://www.assetpub.com/archive/ps/98-05psmay/may98ps32.html.

Brown, Charles. 1996. "Early Retirement Windows." Presented as part of the Health and Retirement Study for the National Bureau of Economic Research, Cambridge, MA.

Bureau of National Affairs, Inc. (BNA). 1989. "Despite Legislative Encouragement, Workers Reluctant to Stay on the Job." *BNA Pension Reporter* 16 (May 15): 854.

Charles D. Spencer and Associates, Inc. 1998. "Early Retirement Incentives in 1995 and 1997. Fewer Offers, More Takers, in Private Sector." *Spencer's Resource Report* (June 26).

Clark, Robert, and Brett Hammond. 2000. "Implications of Changing Retirement Policies and Patterns in Higher Education." PRC #P2000-6. University of Pennsylvania, Wharton School, Pension Research Council.

Fogg, Piper. 2001. "Early Retirement Offers to Faculty Members Are Common, a Study Finds." *Chronicle of Higher Education* (August 10).

Hewitt Associates. 1992. *Early Retirement Windows, Lump Sum Options, and Postretirement Increases in Pensions*. Lincolnshire, IL: Author.

Hewitt Associates. 1997. *Employer Approaches to Workforce Reduction*. Lincolnshire, IL: Author.

Kerchoff, Sue. 2002. "Pensions Squeeze." *Boston Globe*, October 25.

LaRock, Seymour. 1996. "Early Retirement Incentives in 1995: More Takers for Fewer Offers." *Employee Benefit Plan Review* 3 (September): 54.

Price Waterhouse Coopers. 2001. *Severance and Retention Practices*. New York: Author.

Rix, Sara E. 1997. "Update on the Older Worker: 1997 Participation Rises and Unemployment Falls." *Data Digest* 33 (AARP Public Policy Institute, April 1998): 1–2.

"Robust Economy Sends Early Retirement Soaring to 81% of 1998 Retirements." 1999. *Employee Benefit Plan Review* 54(5) (November): 50–51.

Walsh, Mary Williams. 2001. "No Time to Put Your Feet Up as Retirement Comes in Stages." *New York Times*, Business/Financial Desk Section 1 (April 15), 1.

Watson Wyatt. 1999. *Survey of Early Retirement Windows and Postretirement Benefit Increases Provided by Large U.S. Companies as of January 1, 1999*. Washington, DC: Author.

Watson Wyatt. 2002. "Employers' Report on Early Retirement Windows." *Insider*. Available online at http://www.watsonwyatt.com/us/pubs/insider/.

Phyllis H. Mutschler

ECONOMIC HARDSHIP MEASURES IN THE OLDER POPULATION, measures used to assess either the lack of basic material necessities or the experience of serious financial difficulties of older adults. Unlike the official poverty threshold, which is based on household income, measures of economic hardship use nonincome items to determine levels of privation. Economic hardship measures probe such things as whether individuals have adequate food, housing, access to medical and dental care, and clothing; whether they can pay for their necessities each month; and how satisfied they are with their financial situation. The study of economic hardship is still fairly new in the United States, and the corresponding body of literature is small and exploratory.

Determining the level of economic hardship among older persons is important because many of the major social welfare programs available provide in-kind benefits rather than income, such as food, medical care, housing, and utilities. Economic hardship measures give a more accurate indication than income of the success with which these public programs provide for persons age 65 and older. As the work of Holden and Smeeding (1990) has shown, there are older persons whose incomes are too high to qualify for public programs but too low to provide security against potentially devastating life events.

Economic hardship measures are a purer measure of the factors associated with standards of living than income-based measures. The amount of food families can buy, the kind of housing they can afford, or the extent to which they can access medical care and transportation can only be approximated from income. With economic hardship measures, however, these capacities can be measured directly.

Reports of income and living standards are particularly disparate among the older population. Comparing reports of hardship in a number of economic areas to official poverty thresholds, Mayer and Jencks (1989) found that a family's official income-to-needs ratio explains less than one-fourth of the variance in material hardship. Similarly, there was little overlap between level of income and level of satisfaction with financial well-being in this population. Income and financial assets explain only about 25% of older adults' reports of financial satisfaction (George 1993). The apparent discrepancies between income and perceptions of financial well-being, and between the poverty line and the consumption patterns of older adults, emphasize the need for alternative measures of economic well-being.

Economic Hardship Measures versus the Official Poverty Threshold

Economic hardship measures and the official poverty threshold both try to determine what proportion of society is marginalized by a low standard of living. Both attempt to define a minimum standard below which hardship occurs, and both measure resources; however, the similarities end there.

Economic hardship measures typically define *minimum standard* as lacking adequate levels of certain necessities, such as inability to purchase needed food. Minimum standard definitions may vary, however, depending on the survey and the domain studied. Measures of economic hardship use reports of consumption and consumptive capacity to determine *resources*. For example, respondents are asked if there were times they had no food or were unable to pay bills. In contrast, the official poverty threshold is set at a minimum standard, three times the amount of money the U.S. Department of Agriculture (USDA) estimates is required for a family to purchase a minimally nutritious diet. This minimum standard calculation is adjusted for household size and for heads of households age 65 and older. Household income is then compared to the minimum standard, and households with incomes less than the minimum standard are considered to be living below the poverty threshold.

There are several problems with the poverty threshold as a measure of economic well-being among older adults. Originally, adjustments in the official poverty threshold for age of household head were justified on the basis that older persons had fewer dietary requirements, thus lower food costs, and a lower minimum standard. This assumption is problematic for several reasons. Studies of consumption have found that persons age 65 and older spend the same or greater proportions of their income on food than younger households (Cook and Settersten 1995). Additionally, these studies have found that persons over age 64 spend a higher proportion of their income on housing, health care, and utilities than younger households, even when controlling for income levels.

The present poverty measure was criticized in a National Academy of Sciences (NAS) review in 1995 for its noninclusion of in-kind benefits, as well as its failure to take account of the ways in which the cost of various goods, such as food, housing, and medical care, has changed relative to other goods since it was developed in the early 1960s (Citro and Michael 1995). In response, the Census Bureau calculated four experimental alternative measures, one of which generally follows the NAS recommendations (Short et al. 1999). This alternative measure adjusts poverty thresholds by geographical differences in cost of living, counts noncash benefits as income, and subtracts from income some work-related, housing, and child care expenses.

While not proposing measures of self-perceived hardship such as those discussed above, the Census Bureau also calculated three other alternative poverty measures that vary in their treatment of family composition and residence. These included a Different Child Care (DCM) measure that assigns fixed amounts of child care expenses to working families with children, based on number and age of the children; a Difference Equivalence Scale (or DES) measure that uses a new method for adjusting for changes in expenses as family size increases; and a No Geographic Adjustment (or NGA) measure that, unlike the NAS measure, does not adjust thresholds for geographic differences in cost of living. The alternative measures were standardized to the 1997 official poverty lines in such a fashion that each produced the same overall U.S. poverty rate as the official rate and applied to income data for 1999, according to the U.S. Bureau of the Census. Interestingly, the 65+ poverty rate was considerably higher for each of the alternative measures than for the current official measure, while the child poverty rate was lower (there was little change for working-age persons). For example, while the 1999 poverty rate for persons 65 and over was 9.7% by the official measure, it was 13.3%, 13.0%, 13.7%, and 13.6%, respectively, for the four alternative measures. By contrast, information from the U.S. Bureau of the Census states that the poverty rate for persons under 18 years of age was 16.9% under the official measure, but was 14.8%, 15.5%, 14.3%, and 14.6% for the four alternative measures. These results have been taken to support the argument that the official poverty lines underestimate the real prevalence of poverty among older people.

In contrast to both the official and alternative measures of poverty, which are based on income adjusted in various ways for objectively measurable proxies for need, "economic hardship" measures reflect a concept based on consumption—whether individuals have, or think they have, access to adequate levels of goods and services. The poverty threshold measures income, or resources, which is at best only an indirect measure of consumption. Persons may be able to consume beyond their income by borrowing, drawing on savings, or using nonmonetary exchanges. Conversely, those who have adequate income may choose not to spend it on necessities, thereby ending up with inadequate levels of consumption. Finally, households also have different needs, tastes, priorities, and levels of efficiency that may alter the relationship between income and consumption. Since income is only an indirect indicator of consumption, alternative measures of economic well-being that are not income based are needed.

Measuring Economic Hardship

Although alternative measures have been part of the European statistical literature for almost 30 years, they have only recently been used in the United States, and the empirical literature in the United States is still surprisingly limited. Some studies of economic hardship measure material hardship or lack of needed goods and services. Other studies look at "level of living," which includes nonmaterial components, such as access to education, working conditions, family relations, and measures of material needs. Still other studies focus on subjective financial well-being and measure how satisfied people are with their financial situation. Though the methodology differs, all of these studies have a common goal: to determine levels of hardship and deprivation through the use of nonincome measures.

Finding measures of economic hardship that compare households of different sizes and different needs is difficult. Although it is obvious that people of different ages and health statuses have different needs, it is not obvious what kinds of measures can be used to standardize the ratio of resources to consumption. The first major study to use nonincome measures of economic well-being, the Swedish Level of Living Survey, outlined nine areas of living conditions: (1) health and access to care, (2) employment and working conditions, (3) economic resources, (4) knowledge and educational opportunities, (5) family and social integration, (6) recreation and culture, (7) housing and neighborhood facilities, (8) security of life and property, and (9) political resources. Most work on *material hardship* has concentrated on basic necessities—food, housing, clothing, access to medical and dental care, and transportation—while recognizing that there are other items that contribute to quality of life, the lack of which may also cause considerable hardship.

To determine adequate levels of these factors, *hardship* is defined differently depending on the survey questions asked. Most surveys question whether respondents could afford what they needed. Other surveys ask if there was a time in the past year when respondents had to go without items that they needed, could not afford to buy needed food, or could not afford to pay the rent or mortgage; if they had no access to medical insurance; or if there were times when they had to go without needed medical attention. Some researchers look at housing conditions, such as levels of disrepair, or at the presence of durable goods such as dishwashers, automobiles, and air conditioners, as indicators of well-being. Some studies also use subjective assessments of economic well-being, which generally ask the respondents about their levels of satisfaction with income, financial resources, and current living standards or the extent to which they worry about making ends meet.

Empirical Data

Studies consistently have found that persons over the age of 64 report fewer material hardships than younger adults. For example, Mayer and Jencks (1989) reported findings from the Chicago Hardship Study showing that, on average, families with heads age 65 and older had 36% as much income as younger families of the same size who reported the same number of hardships.

Also using Chicago Hardship Study data, Cook and Kramek (1986) found that households with heads age 65 and older were the least likely age group to report experiencing one or more hardships in the areas of food, rent, housing conditions, medical, dental, or utilities. Fewer adults age 65 and older said grocery spending was inadequate, and less than one-half as many adults over 65 as those under 65 reported a time when they needed food but could not afford it. Very few age 65 and older reported a time they could not afford to pay the rent, they had been evicted, or had utilities discontinued. The 65 and older sample was less than half as likely as younger age groups to report having two or more physical housing problems.

Lower levels of hardship among older adults, however, do not mean they are universally better off than younger adults. Without controlling for income, Cook and Kramek also found that older adults spent less on groceries than those aged 50 to 64, and a higher percentage of adults over age 65 spent less than the USDA minimum than adults aged 50 to 64. Older persons in the Chicago Hardship Study reported more medical problems than younger adults. They were as likely to say they had been sick and needed help but were less likely than younger adults to say they went without medical care or dental care because of lack of money. The data show that the domains in which persons age 65 and older are most likely to experience hardship are medical care, food, and housing. Similarly, national survey data indicate that the risk of hardship related to medical care is substantial among low-income older adults, with about 40% of beneficiaries with incomes below the poverty level, in fair or poor health, with ADL (activities of daily living) limitations, reporting difficulty paying their medical bills or getting needed health care (Neuman et al. 1999). In a Baltimore survey, 50% of disabled minority women, and 13% of disabled White women, reported financial difficulty acquiring food, and such difficulty was associated with symptoms of depression (Klesges et al. 2001).

Subjective assessments of economic well-being were measured in the Chicago Hardship Study by asking respondents to express feelings about their standard of living and making ends meet. Without controlling for income, those aged 65 and older were less satisfied with their standard of living than those aged 18 to 49, but more satisfied than those aged 50 to 64. Similarly, of persons reporting no hardships, those aged 65 and older were less satisfied with their standard of living than those aged 18 to 49, but slightly more satisfied than those aged 50 to 64. However, persons aged 65 and older who had experienced at least one hardship had the lowest satisfaction with their standard of living of any age group. Members of the oldest group were the least likely to be worried about making ends meet, regardless of whether they had experienced a hardship. Reviewing the literature on subjective assessments of economic well-being, George (1992) found that even though older adults had lower income on average than younger adults, older adults consistently reported higher levels of satisfaction with their income, financial resources, and standard of living than younger adults. Thus, both financial satisfaction measures and material deprivation measures appear to provide quite a different perspective on age differences in economic disadvantage than do the alternative poverty measures discussed above, one that places older people in a relatively more favorable light.

Although the poverty threshold adjusts over time for changes in consumer prices, it does not account for changes in consumption habits and priorities of society. Changing priorities in society are not captured by a poverty threshold based on income alone. In 1963, when the poverty line was being developed, it was considered unnecessary for households to have a telephone, whereas now this need is seen differently. Thus, alternative measures of deprivation that are based directly on consumption are important supplements to the poverty thresholds. Several studies suggest that widely used economic indicators may be misleading in terms of the overall living conditions in society. For example, although conventional wisdom has maintained that the U.S. standard of living declined in the 1970s, measures in four areas (health, housing, transportation, and food) have shown that conditions in these areas actually improved (Jencks 1984).

The relationship between changes in income and objective and subjective measures of economic hardship over the past three decades is less clear. Objective income levels of older persons have increased since 1973, while there has not been a concomitant increase in financial satisfaction. This may reflect differences in expectations between cohorts. For example, recent cohort analyses of financial satisfaction trends from 1972 to 1996, using data from the General Social Survey, indicate that perceived financial satisfaction did increase within cohorts as they aged but that satisfaction was markedly lower in the younger cohorts, leading to an overall reduction in financial satisfaction over time due to cohort succession (Hsieh 2000, 2002).

Explaining Levels of Economic Hardship in Older Adults

Although age differences in reports of material hardship have been found consistently, little work has attempted to untangle the effects of age and other factors on reports of economic hardship. The factors that put some older adults at risk for economic hardship and those that make others resilient to it have also not been explored in detail. Studies asking individuals to state an amount of money they perceive as a "just sufficient" level of income or "enough income to make ends meet" may provide some clues to the reasons for age differences in reports of economic hardship. These studies have found that older adults have lower expectations of their economic resources, which suggests that they may report fewer economic hardships than younger adults because their idea of a sufficient level of income is lower than younger adults. Perceptions of poverty may change little over a lifetime, and older persons experiencing lower incomes in the 1920s, 1930s, and 1940s may have unchanged criteria for what constitutes an adequate standard of living, consistent with the findings by Hsieh discussed above.

Some researchers suggest that older adults may report fewer hardships because they are more likely to have assets than younger adults. They are more likely to own their homes, and older homeowners are less likely to have mortgages (Keister 2000). Several studies have found that, in general, older adults underreport income and assets, making them seem objectively less well-off than they are (Crystal and Shea 1990, 2002; Smith 2002). Other possible explanations are more speculative. Some suggest that older adults are better managers of money, or that they have different tastes, but these explanations have not been investigated empirically. Others propose that measures of past hardships do not capture the economic worries of the older population, which may have more to do with future ability to pay bills, especially large medical expenses, as their health deteriorates (George 1992; Holden and Smeeding 1990). These worries are shared with those who have not yet reached age 65. For example, in the 2001 Health Confidence Survey sponsored by the Employee Benefit Retirement Institute, 49% of respondents reported lacking confidence that they would be able to afford health care without financial hardship in retirement, and 51% lacked confidence that they would be able to afford prescription drugs that they need without financial hardship (Employee Benefit Research Institute 2002).

Since the study of economic hardship is a new field, there is simply not an adequate amount of research to understand specifically why older persons report different levels of economic hardship from those reported by younger adults. Yet this focus of inquiry has been valuable in bringing to light some of the complexity of the levels of well-being across age categories. (See also ECONOMIC STATUS OF OLDER MEN AND WOMEN; FINANCIAL COUNSELING FOR MID- TO LATER LIFE; FINANCIAL EDUCATION FOR SENIORS; FINANCIAL LITERACY; MEANS-TESTING IN PUBLIC PROGRAMS; MINORITY OLDER ADULTS.)

References

Allen, Susan M., and Vincent Mor. 1997. "The Prevalence and Consequences of Unmet Need. Contrasts between Older and Younger Adults with Disability." *Medical Care* 35(11): 1132–48.

Citro, Constance F., and Robert T. Michael, eds. 1995. *Measuring Poverty: A New Approach*. Washington, DC: National Academy Press.

Cook, Fay Lomax, and Lorraine M. Kramek. 1986. "Measuring Economic Hardship among Older Americans." *The Gerontologist* 26: 38–47.

Cook, Fay Lomax, and Richard A. Settersten, Jr. 1995. "Expenditure Patterns by Age and Income among Mature Adults: Does Age Matter?" *The Gerontologist* 35: 10–23.

Crystal, Stephen, and Dennis Shea. 1990. "Cumulative Advantage, Cumulative Disadvantage, and Inequality among Elderly People." *The Gerontologist* 30(4): 437–43.

Crystal, Stephen, and Dennis Shea. 2002. "Cumulative Advantage, Public Policy, and Late-Life Inequality." In *Focus on Economic Outcomes in Later Life*, ed. Stephen Crystal and Dennis Shea. Public Policy, Health, and Cumulative Advantage. Vol. 22 of *Annual Review of Gerontology and Geriatrics*. New York: Springer.

Employee Benefit Retirement Institute. 2002. "Health Confidence Survey, 2001 Results: Confidence in Health Care System." *EBRI*. Available online at http://www.ebri.org/hcs/2001/index.html.

George, Linda K. 1992. "Economic Status and Subjective Well-Being: A Review of the Literature and an Agenda for Future Research." In *Aging, Money and Life Satisfaction: Aspects of Financial Gerontology*, ed. Neal E. Cutler et al. New York: Springer.

George, Linda K. 1993. *Financial Security in Later Life: The Subjective Side*. Philadelphia, PA: Boettner Institute of Financial Gerontology.

Holden, Karen C., and Timothy M. Smeeding. 1990. "The Poor, the Rich, and the Insecure Elderly Caught in Between." *Milbank Quarterly* 68: 191–219.

Hsieh, Chang-ming. 2000. "Trends in Financial Satisfaction among Middle-Age and Old-Age Americans, 1972–1996." *International Journal of Aging and Human Development* 51(2): 105–13.

Hsieh, Chang-ming. 2002. "Trends in Financial Satisfaction: Does Poverty Make a Difference?" *International Journal of Aging and Human Development* 54(1): 15–30.

Jencks, Christopher. 1984. "The Hidden Prosperity of the 1970s." *Public Interest*. 77: 37–61.

Keister, Lisa A. 2000. *Wealth in America: Trends in Wealth Inequality*. New York: Cambridge University Press.

Klesges, L.M., M. Pahor, R.I. Shorr, J.Y. Wan, J.D. Williamson, and J.M. Guralnik. 2001. "Financial Difficulty in Acquiring Food among Elderly Disabled Women: Results from the Women's Health and Aging Study." *American Journal of Public Health* 91(1): 68–75.

Mayer, Susan E., and Christopher Jencks. 1989. "Poverty and the Distribution of Material Hardship." *Journal of Human Resources* 24: 88–114.

Neuman, Patricia, Diane Rowland, Michelle Kitchman, Drew Altman, Catherine Schoen, Karen Davis, and E. Puleo. 1999. "Understanding the Diverse Needs of the Medicare Population: Implications for Medicare Reform." *Journal of Aging and Social Policy* 10(4): 25–50.

Short, Kathleen, Thesia Garner, David Johnson, and Patricia Doyle. 1999. "Experimental Poverty Measures: 1990 to 1997." *Current Population Reports, Consumer Income Series*. No. P60-205. Washington, DC: U.S. Census Bureau.

Smith, James. 2002. "Measurement of Late-Life Income and Wealth." In *Focus on Economic Outcomes in Later Life*, ed. Stephen Crystal and Dennis Shea. Vol. 22 of *Annual Review of Gerontology and Geriatrics*. New York: Springer.

Fay Lomax Cook and Anne S. Welch
Updated by Stephen Crystal and Fay Lomax Cook

ECONOMIC HISTORY OF RETIREMENT. Retirement is often difficult to measure, so economic historians have focused on the labor force participation rate. The current definition of *labor force participation* includes those who are employed and those who are unemployed (actively searching for a job). Before 1940, the census used the concept of gainful employment, which included all those who claimed to have had an occupation in the past year, whether or not they worked. Table 1 gives labor force participation rates from 1850 to 2000 for older men in the United States, using both definitions. (For an international comparison, see Table 2.) The retirement rate can be approximated by subtracting the labor force participation rate from 100%. The data show that retirement was fairly rare in the mid- and late 1800s. After 1880 retirement rates began to climb, generally rising from decade to decade—with a few interruptions.

Why have retirement rates generally risen over time? The earliest theory stressed the effects of the "modernization" of the economy. It argued that the shift from an agricultural economy to an industrial economy between about 1880 and 1930 pushed older men out of the workforce. During this period new production processes increasingly prohibited workers from laboring at their own paces, rapid technological change and shifts in the occupational mix made some older workers' skills obsolete, higher capital-to-labor ratios raised the cost of using less efficient workers, the rationalization of big business and the scientific management movement sought efficiency at every margin and created mandatory retirement schedules and policies against hiring workers over a certain age, and stiff competition came from the young and immigrants who were willing to adopt a relentless work pace. According to this argument, changes such as these worsened the employment prospects of older workers, pushing them onto the "industrial scrap heap." An additional concern was that attitudes about the abilities of older persons changed between the Civil War and the Great Depression, so that they may have been increasingly viewed as peripheral, less capable members of society.

Most economic historians now reject these views, however. Carter and Sutch (1996), for example, show that at the beginning of the twentieth century it was farmers and other self-employed workers who were most likely to retire. They conclude that the shift out of agriculture would tend to *lower* retirement rates, rather than pushing men into early retirement. Costa (1998) concurs, finding that declines in part-time work, nonfarm self-

Table 1
Labor Force Participation Rates of Older Men in the United States, 1850–2000

Year	Age 65 and over		Age 55–64	
	Gainful (%)	Current (%)	Gainful (%)	Current (%)
1850	76.6		92.2	
1860	76.0			
1870				
1880	78.0		95.2	
1890	73.8			
1900	65.4		91.0	
1910	58.1		91.1	
1920	60.1		89.1	
1930	58.0			
1940	43.5	41.8	82.2	86.1
1950	47.0	41.4	88.1	85.8
1960	40.8	30.5	83.8	84.8
1970	35.2	24.8	86.7	81.5
1980	24.7	19.9	77.4	71.9
1990	18.4	16.3	67.0	67.6
2000		17.5		67.3

Notes: This table only includes rates for men because the negative relationship between labor force participation and retirement has not existed historically for women. From 1950 to 2000, the participation rate of women below age 65 climbed very strongly, while the rate for older women showed little long-term trend, falling slightly from 1955 to 1985 and then rising slightly. The rates for women 65 to 69, for example, have been 15.5% (1950), 17.8% (1960), 17.3% (1970), 15.1% (1980), 17.0% (1990), and 19.4% (2000) (Gendell and Siegel 1992). The labor force participation rate of Black males over 65 was originally much higher than the overall rate but fell below it after 1950. The Black male rate was 87.3% in 1880, then fell to 84.1% (1900), 76.8% (1920), 54.6% (1940), 37.3% (1960), and 15.7% (1990).

Source: Costa 1998.

employment, and farming cannot explain the rise of retirement and showing that about half of older Union Army veterans who had been common laborers in 1900 were able to move upward to jobs as farmers (20%), professionals/proprietors (16%), and artisans (15%) by 1910. Whaples (1991) shows that gainful employment rates of older men were not generally affected by the configuration of occupations in local labor markets, nor by the size and capital intensity of firms. Haber and Gratton (1994) argue that mandatory retirement was adopted jointly with seniority plans (and sometimes pensions) that protected older workers, even as they made it more difficult for some older men to find jobs. In addition, Range and Vinovskis (1981) find little change in the images of older adults in a content analysis of popular magazines and question the claim that ageist attitudes worsened during this period. Rather than being ejected from the labor market, many older industrial workers in the late 1800s and early 1900s seem to have been able to "retire" more gradually. In jobs that required substantial brawn, many retired "on the job" by switching to less physically intense occupations (Ransom and Sutch 1986).

The new consensus is that rising levels of wealth and lifetime income have been the

Table 2
International Comparisons of Labor Force Participation Rates of Men Aged 65 and Over

Year	Percentages			
	United States	Britain	France	Germany
c. 1890	73.8	65.5	54.1	58.0
c. 1910	58.1	56.9	51.1	52.0
c. 1930	58.0	47.9	48.1	29.7
c. 1950	47.0	31.1	36.2	26.8
c. 1970	35.2	18.6	10.6	17.2
c. 1990	18.4	8.2	3.5	5.1

Note: This table compares labor force participation rates of older men in the United States to those in Britain, France, and Germany. It shows that the American experience of a long-term rise in retirement rates has been similar to that in Europe but that the retirement rate in the United States has generally been 10 to 20 percentage points lower.

Source: Costa 1998.

driving force behind increasing retirement rates in the United States, particularly before 1940. Costa (1998) shows that the retirement of Union Army veterans in 1900 and 1910 was strongly linked to the size of their pensions. In 1900, for example, 39% of veterans under 70 in good or fair health who received monthly pensions of $15 or more were retired, while only 22% of those with smaller pensions were retired. Likewise, among those in poor health the retirement rates were 54% for those with larger pensions and 36% for those with smaller pensions. Overall, she finds that a 1% increase in pension amount, controlling for health and other factors, increased retirement by 0.73% in 1900 and 0.47% in 1910. Costa then uses the 1910 pension-retirement relationship to project the retirement trend in light of the fact that wealth levels rose considerably during the twentieth century. This procedure implies that about 90% of the rise in retirement rates in the decades before 1930 can be explained by rising wealth and that up to 60% of the retirement rise before 1990 may be similarly explained. These rising wealth levels counteracted the effects of improved health among older adults. Advances in medical technology, lessened occupation hazards, and better early life health and nutrition improved the health of older persons substantially over the course of the twentieth century, which would otherwise have increased older men's labor force participation rates. The rising wealth of older Americans is also reflected in their housing and household arrangements. In 1880, 46% of all retired men age 65 and older were living in a household headed by their children or other relatives. By 1920 this fraction had fallen to 32%, then to 13% in 1960 and 5% in 1990. Costa also argues that the falling price of leisure goods and the increase in the variety of recreational activities (such as television) have made leisure more attractive to older people and played an important role in increasing retirement rates.

Finally, there is the role of government in fostering the increase in retirement rates. In the late 1800s and early 1900s nearly 1 million people (mostly older Americans) received Civil War pensions. They covered over half of older native-born Northern males, made up 42% of the federal budget at their peak, and are probably largely responsible for the large drop in older men's labor force participation rates from 1890 to 1910 and the slight rebound to 1920 as the post–Civil War generation reached retirement age. However, the United States was later than most western European nations in instituting a state-sponsored old-age pension system covering the general population when it passed the Social Security Act in 1935. In its early years, Social Security's welfare component, Old Age Assistance (OAA), dominated the Old Age Insurance (OAI) component, which bases monthly benefits on the amount of taxes workers have paid into the system. Disability Insurance was added to the package in 1956. As the decades have progressed the fraction of older persons receiving Social Security benefits and the level of these benefits have increased. In 1940, only 23% of the population 65 years and older received Social Security benefits. A decade later this rose to 40%, then 73% (1960) and 89% (1970), as coverage was extended to groups initially excluded, including farmers, domestics, professionals, and the self-employed. Meanwhile, the inflation-adjusted average monthly benefits of retired workers more than doubled between 1950 and 1975 (Myers 1981).

Before the long-run historical trend in retirement rates became understood, some observed the post-1940 trend and concluded that Social Security had played the key role in driving the retirement rate upward. However, recent studies emphasize that Social Security's influence on the retirement trend has been "modest." Leonesio (1993) summarizes recent research by saying that while "the social security system has contributed to the popularity of retirement at ages 62 and 65, [it] appears to be a minor force in the long post–World War II trend to retire at earlier ages" Parsons (1991), however, estimates that Old Age Assistance was responsible for the unusual trend in retirement rates between 1930 and 1950, with a huge drop from 1930 to 1940 and a slight rebound from 1940 to 1950. OAA was available only to those who had no regular employment and provided a strong incentive for low-paid and unemployed older workers to retire. Parsons estimates that the new availability of OAA combined with its earnings restrictions increased the retirement rate for men 65 and over by about 6 percentage points in 1940.

While the forces behind the adoption of Social Security are manifold and complex, most historians argue that Social Security was ultimately enacted because of society's desire for economic security. Beginning around 1900, reformers launched a campaign to solve the "problem of old age." They echoed and amplified the fear that old age would inevitably mean dependency, poverty, and worst of all, a trip to the poorhouse. Poorhouses were tax-supported residential institutions to which people were required to go if they could not support themselves in the 1800s and early 1900s (Crannel 2000). Interestingly, much of the reformers' rhetoric (and perhaps public perception) was out of touch with economic reality. For example, Haber and Gratton (1994) estimate that despite the misrepresentation of reformers the proportion of older adults in the poorhouse remained constant at about 2% throughout the late nineteenth and early twentieth centuries. Families adopted many strategies to avoid old-age poverty during this era, including savings, pensions, working, and relying on the wages of children. Average annual household incomes of those 60 and over were only modestly lower than those in their forties and fifties, and Gratton (1996) shows that real wages of older workers rose sharply from 1890 to 1950, with positive age-earnings profiles across the life cycle. However, the Great Depression changed everything. With it the savings and wealth of many older people evaporated and unemployment among this population and those supporting them became a serious problem. "It took the Great Depression to launch social security in the United States" (Achenbaum 1986); without it the country might never have adopted Social Security.

Social Security was designed to solve poverty and dependency by transferring wealth to older adults and to combat unemployment among the young by luring the old out of the labor market. Its goal was to induce retirement. Initially, there was a limit of only $15 per month that retirees could earn in the labor market. If they earned more, they lost their Social Security benefits. This "retirement test," a legacy of the Great Depression, has been gradually eased over time. In 1950, the income threshold was raised to $50, and the retirement test was eliminated for those aged 75 and older. In 1960, for the first time, earnings over the exempt amount did not produce total loss of benefits, instead—for income in a certain range—benefits were reduced $1 for every $2 in earnings. In 1990, this rate was cut to $1 for every $3 in earnings for workers above the normal age of retirement. In 2000, as unemployment reached its lowest rate in over 30 years, both houses of Congress unanimously voted to eliminate the retirement earnings test for workers above Social Security's normal retirement age.

At the same time that Social Security was conceived, established, and expanded, private pensions grew tremendously. American Express adopted the nation's first corporate pension in 1875, and by the early twentieth century pensions had become widespread among railroads. It is estimated that by 1913 about 9% of the non–farm labor force was covered by a pension (Craig and Trawick 1993). This grew to nearly 14% in 1929 but collapsed to 4% during the depression, before rebounding to 25% in 1950. By 1988 about 58% of middle-aged full-time, private sector workers were covered by private pensions.

Before employer-based pensions became widespread, many workers purchased annuities, called tontines, directly from insurance companies.

> However, in 1906, after a public scandal of alleged mismanagement and impropriety in the insurance industry and an extensive investigation which exposed abuses in the handling of tontine insurance funds, the State of New York prohibited any further issue of tontine insurance. Other states quickly followed suit and the individually-purchased pension disappeared. (Ransom, Sutch, and Williamson 1993)

Company pensions arose to fill this void. The use of pensions was also accelerated by the federal government's creation of tax breaks for them, beginning in 1938. Thus, workers who desired to save for retirement found that their best option was a company pension. (See also EMPLOYEE BENEFITS IN THE PUBLIC SECTOR; HEALTH BENEFITS; HISTORY OF RETIREMENT; PENSION PLANS; RETIREMENT MIGRATION; SOCIAL SECURITY PROGRAM OF THE UNITED STATES.)

References

Achenbaum, W. Andrew. 1986. *Social Security: Visions and Revisions*. New York: Cambridge University Press.

Carter, Susan, and Richard Sutch. 1996. "Myth of the Industrial Scrap Heap: A Revisionist View of Turn-of-the-Century American Retirement." *Journal of Economic History* 56: 5–38.

Costa, Dora. 1998. *The Evolution of Retirement: An American Economic History, 1880–1990*. Chicago: University of Chicago Press.

Craig, Lee, and L. Michelle Trawick. 1993. "Federal Regulation and the Growth of Private-Sector Pensions, 1913–1950." Paper presented at the annual meeting of the Gerontological Society of America, New Orleans.

Crannel, Linda M. 2000. *Poorhouse Story*. Available online at http://www.poorhousestory.com/.

Gendell, Murray, and Jacob S. Siegel. 1992. "Trends in Retirement Age by Sex, 1950–2005." *Monthly Labor Review* 115: 22–29.

Graebner, William. 1980. *A History of Retirement: The Meaning and Function of an American Institution, 1885–1978*. New Haven, CT: Yale University Press.

Gratton, Brian. 1996. "The Poverty of Impoverishment Theory: The Economic Well-Being of the Elderly, 1890–1950." *Journal of Economic History* 56: 39–61.

Haber, Carole, and Brian Gratton. 1994. *Old Age and the Search for Security: An American Social History*. Bloomington: Indiana University Press.

Leonesio, Michael. 1993. "Social Security and Older Workers." In *As the Workforce Ages: Costs, Benefits, and Policy Challenges*, ed. Olivia Mitchell. Ithaca, NY: ILR Press.

Myers, Robert J. 1981. *Social Security*. 2nd ed. Homewood, IL: Irwin.

Parsons, Donald. 1991. "Male Retirement Behavior, 1930–1950." *Journal of Economic History* 51: 657–74.

Range, Jane, and Maris Vinovskis. 1981. "Images of Elderly in Popular Magazines: A Content Analysis of Littell's Living Age, 1845–1882." *Social Science History* 5: 123–69.

Ransom, Roger, and Richard Sutch. 1986. "The Labor of Older Americans: Retirement of Men on and off the Job, 1870–1937." *Journal of Economic History* 46: 1–30.

Ransom, Roger, Richard Sutch, and Samuel Williamson. 1993. "Inventing Pensions: The Origins of the Company-Provided Pension in the United States, 1900–1940." In *Societal Impact on Aging: Historical Perspectives*, ed. K. Warner Schaie and W. Andrew Achenbaum. New York: Springer.

Whaples, Robert. 1991. "The Shortening of the American Work Week: An Economic and Historical Analysis of Its Context, Causes, and Consequences." *Journal of Economic History* 51: 454–57.

Robert Whaples

ECONOMIC SECURITY. See Pension Plans; Pension Plans for the Self-Employed; Social Security Program of the United States; Supplemental Security Income (SSI); Wealth Span.

ECONOMIC STATUS OF OLDER MEN AND WOMEN. Within the last 20 years, the economic status of older adults in the United States has improved, but there are still disadvantaged subgroups among the older population. An excellent source of data on the economic status of Americans is the Survey of Consumer Finances. The surveys are collected every three years under the sponsorship of the Federal Reserve Board of Governors (Kennickell, Starr-McCluer, and Surette 2000). A unique feature of the surveys is that information is collected on the assets and liabilities of a household, and the random sampling design of the surveys allows researchers to generalize the results to all American households.

Measures of Economic Status. Income is the most commonly used measure of economic status, but other measures such as net worth and homeownership are also useful. For instance, income is a measure of the amount that a household receives on a regular basis, but income may be insufficient to cope with unexpected expenses. If an emergency occurs, it is important to know the net worth of the household. Furthermore, many older Americans are homeowners, and the home may be their most valuable asset. Unfortunately, it may take several months to sell a home and convert its value to a stream of income. Therefore, three measures of economic status must be evaluated: household income, net worth, and homeownership.

The components of household income include earned income, asset income, government payments, and so forth. Net worth is the value of total assets minus the value of total liabilities. It includes the market value of the home minus the total amount of the mortgage on the home.

Instead of presenting the average values of income and net worth, the median value will be presented. The median represents the midpoint, so 50% of households will be above the median and 50% will be below the median. In 1998, the median value of household income was $33,000, and the median net worth for all American households was $73,800.

Age and Economic Status. Examining the Survey of Consumer Finance data for 1998 revealed that the median value of income peaked before retirement and declined as households aged. The relationship between age and income is consistent with life cycle stage theories (Ando and Modigliani 1963; DeVaney and Zhang 2001). Households headed by an individual aged 34 or younger had a median income of $27,000, while those aged 35 to 49, 50 to 64, 65 to 74, and 75+ had a median income of $44,000, $42,000, $24,000, and $17,000, respectively. The Social Security Administration reported that the major sources of income for those 65 and over in 2002 were Social Security (reported by 90% of older persons), income from assets (reported by 59%), public and private pensions (reported by 41%), and earnings (reported by 22%) (Administration on Aging 2003).

The values for median net worth for the same age categories (less than 34, 35 to 49, 50 to 64, 65 to 74, and 75 and older) were $9,300, $73,800, $128,090, $150,900, and $129,100, respectively. The noticeable increase in median value of net worth between the youngest category (less than 34) and the age 35 to 49 category is probably due to the purchase of a home by households age 35 to 49 and increased saving as households become more well established. The decline in net worth for the oldest category (75 and over) suggests that some older households may be spending down their savings in retirement (Ando and Modigliani 1963). Reasons for this could include the older adults' ineligibility for a pension, little or no asset income, or dependence on Social Security (Bieker, DeVaney, and Chen 2001; DeVaney and Zhang 2001). Other reasons might be a lack of knowledge in investing one's pension (DeVaney and Kim 2003), having a low tolerance for risk (DeVaney and Chien 2001), or increased spending on health care costs (Rubin and Nieswiadomy 1997).

Homeownership and Economic Status. Examining the amount of household income and net worth by homeownership of households of all ages in 1998 revealed that the median income of homeowners of all ages was twice that of renters ($46,000 compared to $22,000). However, the median value of net worth for homeowners of all ages was 21 times greater than the net worth of renters ($152,170 compared to $7,200).

Race and Economic Status. When households were categorized by race, White households had higher income and higher net worth in 1998. Median income for White households was one and one-half times greater than median income for non-White households

Table 1
The Influence of Age and Race on Income and Net Worth

Age	Race	Variable	Median
65 to 74	White	Income	$ 26,000
		Net worth	$179,200
	Non-White	Income	$ 11,000
		Net worth	$ 25,000
75 and over	White	Income	$ 18,000
		Net worth	$146,700
	Non-White	Income	$ 8,100
		Net worth	$ 35,490

Source: Federal Reserve Board 1998.

($37,000 compared to $23,000). In contrast, median net worth was almost six times greater for White households compared to non-White households ($97,250 compared to $16,600).

Table 1 shows median income and net worth in 1998 for White and non-White households headed by an individual who was age 65 to 74 and for those aged 75 and over. The age group 75 and over non-White households had less income, but they had more net worth.

Marital Status and Economic Status. Another perspective considers the amount of income and net worth of those who are married compared to those who are unmarried. The term *married* includes those who cohabit as partners in addition to those who are legally married. The term *unmarried* includes those who have never married and those who are separated, divorced, or widowed. As might be expected, the married couples were more well off than unmarried men, who in turn were more well off than unmarried women. Median income in 1998 for all couples was $50,000, followed by $27,000 for all unmarried men and $17,000 for all unmarried women. Median net worth for couples in 1998 was $124,120, while it was $25,540 for unmarried men and $30,280 for unmarried women.

Table 2 shows median income and net worth in 1998 by marital status and age category. Income declined with age for couples, unmarried men, and unmarried women. There was no consistent pattern for the change in net worth and age. Some households may have encountered large expenses for health care (Rubin and Nieswiadomy 1997), or some other situation may be affecting the amount of net worth.

Several conclusions can be drawn about economic status. When all ages are considered, homeowners were better off than renters, couples were better off than unmarried men, who were better off than unmarried women, and Whites were better off than non-Whites; however, those in the oldest age category were less well off than were those in younger categories and some changes occur. (See also AGING AMERICA; DIVORCE AND OLDER ADULTS; ECONOMIC HARDSHIP MEASURES IN THE OLDER POPULATION; FINANCES OF AGING IN THE GAY COMMUNITY; MARRIAGE AND OLDER ADULTS.)

Table 2
The Influence of Age and Marital Status on Income and Net Worth

Age	Marital Status	Variable	Median
65 to 74	Couple	Income	$ 37,000
		Net worth	$226,000
	Unmarried man	Income	$ 22,000
		Net worth	$ 94,400
	Unmarried woman	Income	$ 15,000
		Net worth	$ 90,930
75 and over	Couple	Income	$ 26,000
		Net worth	$260,400
	Unmarried man	Income	$ 18,000
		Net worth	$141,000
	Unmarried woman	Income	$ 13,000
		Net worth	$ 87,420

Source: Federal Reserve Board 1998.

References

Administration on Aging. 2003. Washington, DC. Available online at http://www.aoa.gov/aoa/stats/profile/highlights.html.

Ando, A., and F. Modigliani. 1963. "The Life Cycle Hypothesis of Saving: Aggregate Implications and Tests." *American Economic Review* 53(1): 55–84.

Bieker, R., S.A. DeVaney, and Z. Chen. 2001. "Determinants of Employment among Older Americans." *Financial Counseling and Planning* 12(2): 33–42.

DeVaney, S.A., and Y. Chien. 2001. "A Model of Savings Behavior and the Amount Saved in Retirement Accounts." *Journal of Financial Service Professionals* 57 (March): 72–80.

DeVaney, S.A., and H. Kim. 2003. "Women's Knowledge of Their Pension Plans." *Journal of Family and Consumer Sciences* 95(2): 19–25.

DeVaney, S.A., and T.C. Zhang. 2001. "A Cohort Analysis of the Amount in Defined Contribution and Individual Retirement Accounts." *Financial Counseling and Planning* 12(1): 89–104.

Federal Reserve Board. 1998. "Survey of Consumer Finances." Washington, DC: Author. Available online at http://www.federalreserve.gov/pubs/oss/oss2/98/scf98home.html.

Kennickell, A.B., M.S. Starr-McCluer, and B.J. Surette. (2000). "Recent Changes in U.S. Family Finances: Results from the 1998 Survey of Consumer Finances." *Federal Reserve Bulletin* 86 (January): 1–29.

Rubin, Rose M., and Michael L. Nieswiadomy. 1997. *Expenditures of Older Americans*. Westport, CT: Praeger.

Sharon A. DeVaney and Zhan (Sandy) Chen

EDUCATION OF OLDER ADULTS. In the United States, older adult education is shaped more by consumer demand and the rise of a multitude of nonprofit educational organizations than by state-run institutions or government policies. Fueling the demand is a new generation of retirees who are more affluent, better educated, and healthier than any previous generation in American history. Thirty or 40 years ago, only a tiny fraction of the population, the wealthy and healthy, could really enjoy a robust Third Age. Now leisure time has become democratized, giving millions of ordinary citizens more options than they had ever imagined (Laslett 1991). And since prior education remains a main determinant of demand for education in the later years (Snyder, Hoffman, and Geddes 1997), this combination of factors has generated a growing population of older learners.

Responding to meet this demand, community-based, nonprofit organizations as well as for-profit educators have supplemented traditional providers such as adult education programs at colleges and universities. Some of the new players that have come upon the U.S. scene in the last 20 to 30 years include Elderhostel, a travel-learning program offering those 50 and over one- or two-week-long residencies at educational centers in the United States and abroad and reaching about 300,000 annually; Institutes for Learning in Retirement (ILRs), largely run by participants who help to develop curricula, teach, and govern some 300 programs connected to college and universities, involving about 100,000 annually; a department store–based senior center–type program called OASIS (Older Adult Service and Information Systems) at some 30 shopping center locations across the country and serving approximately 300,000 annually; SeniorNet, a senior-user computer network with over 100 centers where courses on computer use are taught by members to members; and Shepherd's Centers, religious organization–sponsored, volunteer-run community service and education centers located at churches and synagogues (Manheimer, Snodgrass, and Moskow-McKenzie 1995).

In addition, there are 15,000 community-based senior centers supported by local municipalities, usually also receiving some federal and state funds that, in addition to social services and low-cost or free meals, offer a variety of recreational and educational programs. And in addition, there are 1,200 community colleges, many that attract older learners to free or low-fee programs in subjects ranging from crafts to foreign languages. Publicly funded American colleges and universities in many states offer tuition-free enrollment in regular college classes for those 62 or 65 and over on a space-available basis. Educational programs are also offered free or for a fee through college and university alumni organizations, hospitals, banks, investment companies, museums, labor organizations, recreation centers, and the Internet. There has also been a surge of outdoor education programs ranging from inexpensive hiking and biking clubs to businesses offering deluxe adventure trips to exotic places (Manheimer 1998).

Most of the organizations described offer nonformal or noncredit courses, seminars, workshops, and learning tours and depend on user fees to operate. Others, such as colleges and universities, also offer credit and degree-generating courses, though participation rates remain relatively low for people over 55 or 60. Workplace- or workforce-related education and training is offered by many companies and businesses, but, as we shall see, the private sector is slow to see the value of enhancing the skills of older workers. The most recent national survey of how and where senior adults participate in continued learning shows the largest growth in nonformal, community-based programs.

According to the National Household Education Surveys (NHES), during the 1990s, the percentage of people in the United States aged 66 to 74 who took at least one adult education class in the previous year more than doubled—from 8.4% in 1991 to 19.9% in 1999. The biggest growth in participation of individuals aged 55 to 74 was in community-provided, nonformal education. This includes not-for-credit courses, workshops, and seminars offered by churches, libraries, department stores, senior centers, and so on, where the rate went from 4.6% in 1991 to 11.6% in 1999. This compares to rates of 5.5% taking courses in a school or university in 1991 and 8.6% in 1999. The increase among the "young-old" surpassed that of any other age group.

Age-related role expectations still seem to be a defining factor for workplace educational participation. Participation rates for job-related education reveal modest increases compared to younger age groups. For example, between 1991 and 1999, the rate of those ages 48 to 56 participating in educational programs offered by business or industry rose from 12.6% to 19.6%, while for the age group 66 to 74, the rate rose from 2.0% to 4.8%. This reflects a continuing trend as business and industry prefer to invest their training dollars in the younger workforce.

Degree of prior education remains the chief predictor of educational participation for adults of all ages. But greater visibility of educational opportunities and a growing acceptance of the value of lifelong learning were also factors. In all likelihood this trend will continue as an even better educated American baby boom population enters the retirement period and since the average age of retirement in the United States holds fairly steady at about 63. However, another strong trend, a desire to return to the workforce after formal retirement in both full- and part-time second careers, may alter this pattern (AARP 1999). If the high percentage of today's baby boomers actually do seek postretirement careers, there should be a huge increased demand for continuing education.

Unprecedented participation rates of older adults in adult education confirm an overall pattern—emergence of a so-called lifelong learning society. It is estimated that almost half of the entire adult population in the United States participates in organized education in a given year (Belanger 1999; Belanger and Tuijnman 1997). With regard to older adults, the United States is in what might be called a "rehearsal stage." While the United States is certainly an "aging society" with a median age of 36 that will rise to 39 by the year 2010, it is the aging of the huge baby boomer population (born between 1946 and 1964) that will truly challenge cultural and educational institutions. Currently, those 65+ make up 13% of the U.S. population, and those 60+ comprise about 1%. The United States actually saw little growth in the percentage of its 65+ population during the 1990s because of the low birthrate for the cohort born during the era of the Great Depression of the 1930s and into the early part of the 1940s. But by the year 2020, those 65 and over will comprise 18% of the U.S. population, and that percentage will continue to rise until the 2050s (23%). The percentage of college-educated older adults will rise from the current 12% to 20% by 2010 and continue to rise dramatically thereafter (Manheimer 1994). Moreover, this rising percentage applies to a numerically vastly larger cohort.

In the current rehearsal stage, we have seen demand for education growing as education in the later years is viewed as valuable for everything from preparation for second or third careers, personal enrichment and psychological growth, prevention or delay in the onset of cognitive decline, and aiding in adjustment to life beyond or after work. In all likelihood, the demand for educational opportunities will overwhelm current providers in terms of both numbers and range of curricular diversity. People in every industry in the United States have been trying to predict what baby boomers will want in their role as consumers. And this is no less true for providers of lifelong learning opportunities. But thinking only in terms of consumers may be a big mistake. What is called for is new leadership and vision.

Currently, organizational leadership in older adult education is fragmented and decentralized in the United States. There is no organized group lobbying Congress or state governments for increased funding to educational programs primarily serving older adults. There are a number of national associations with subcommittees or affinity groups focused on older learners. For example, the American Society on Aging has its Lifetime Education and Renewal Network (LEARN), which is composed of about 250 individuals whose work (usually only in part) is associated with some form of older adult education. And the American Association of Higher Education has its division of Older Adult Education. The American Association for Gerontology in Higher Education (AGHE) focuses primarily on professional-level teaching of gerontology and only to a slight extent on education for seniors. Most individuals associated with the Institute for Learning in Retirement are also members of a consortium, the Elderhostel Institute Network (EIN), affiliated with the Elderhostel organization. EIN's main activities consist of biennial regional conferences and maintenance of an informative Web site. After 11 years, EIN is still struggling for survival.

Professionally speaking, older adult education has no real independent standing. As a field, it is a subject of peripheral concern to both aging and educational organizations. The field lacks monetary significance since it is not a major revenue source for institutions of higher education. Only a few nonprofit organizations, Elderhostel perhaps the most significant, derive their main income from offering services and programs to seniors. Education for seniors, however, is seen as an important marketing tool for investment companies, banks, hospitals, and cultural organizations, which regard it as a mechanism to attract potential clients, contributors, and members. In the sphere of higher education, affiliated ILR programs have proven to be an entrée to successfully solicit major donors.

Even in the area of research, where millions of dollars are spent on the causes of and potential remedies for cognitive decline as related to aging, hardly any research looks at the potential impact of older adult education on sustaining cognitive functioning. And little research involves applying what has been learned in cognitive science to better ways to educate or foster older adult learning.

Having presented this largely negative view, how can one argue that older adult education has a positive future?

The key lies in understanding the larger framework of an aging society and the growing ranks of members of the so-called Third Age. The modern phenomenon of retirement as an expanding segment of the life course has been shaped by private and public sector policies emerging in the middle to late part of the twentieth century. For the United States, these include government Social Security, private pension plans, public health care insurance, and federal anti-age discrimination laws. Meanwhile, social attitudes toward retirement continue to change. Major national studies show that 75% to 80% of today's baby boomers plan to extend their working years (AARP 2000) by engaging in postretirement employment. The majority of middle-aged adults regard later life not simply as a period for rest and relaxation but as a time for personal growth through acquiring new skills, exploring new leisure activities, and expanding involvement in current ones. Community service among older adults has been rising as seniors view volunteering as both a way to give back to society and as a mechanism for establishing new friendships to offset those lost when exiting the workforce.

The media further reflect these changes. Books about getting the most out of the retirement years are flooding bookstores, and articles on new roles for older adults fill the pages of magazines and newspapers. New books are appearing each year on the progressive role older people will play in improving the quality of life in society. And major popular films keep appearing showing older people as both socially redeemable and redeeming of those of younger generations.

Nor can one underestimate the antiaging, stay-young ethos so prevalent in the United States, where billions of dollars are spent on cosmetic surgery. Critics are probably correct that preoccupation with youthfulness may cloak a denial of the aging process and fear of death. But the quest to extend youthfulness may also involve the desire to stay socially engaged and connected to productive roles that garner social approval and produce self-esteem.

Given the positive respect for education in American society and for the long tradition of education serving as a mechanism for economic advancement, personal growth, and an indicator of social stature, older adult education should fare well in the coming years. However, the question remains: What are the characteristics of future successful programs, and will everyone benefit? Here are my predictions.

A rapidly growing pool of competent, college-educated adults will soon reach their retirement years. Even though many will choose to work part-time, they will also seek out continued learning opportunities. Many of these individuals will be attracted to educational organizations that allow them to play active roles by helping to shape curricula, teach by drawing on both their expertise and life experiences, organize courses, participate in governing the organization, and serve in a multitude of ways that satisfy their desire for a renewed sense of community. They will be prepared to pay sufficient fees and to volunteer their time to make these organizations financially viable.

Those educational organizations that can generate an image of creative or productive aging, either by being associated with institutions primarily serving younger generations such as colleges and universities or by linking to age-neutral organizations such as museums and cultural groups, will attract seniors who seek continued learning but who shun identification with being old, infirm, or needy. Opportunity to learn together with younger people through formal courses and informal exchange will be attractive to a subset of these older learners who prefer intergenerational and age-integrated experience.

Programs that offer hands-on experiences rather than passive, traditional classroom learning will attract the growing legions of experiential learners ranging from those seeking courses in the arts, environmental sciences, fitness, outdoor study, and adventure.

Flexible scheduling of learning opportunities including evening or weekend programs, and intensive short courses will appeal to those continuing to work full- or part-time and to those who want to mix education with myriad other activities such as travel, family involvement, and recreation. Education via the Internet and through computer user groups should continue to grow but will supplement, not replace, face-to-face learning experiences. Older learners will increasingly expect telecommunications to be utilized in their learning experiences.

Given continued rapid technological changes and a highly unstable and unpredictable global political situation, those educational organizations that can help learners assimilate new knowledge will enjoy increased participation rates.

Again, because older adult education does not fall into one academic discipline but overlaps several and is marginal to all, opportunities to prepare for professional careers in the field are lacking. There is a great need for curricula to help prepare planners, administrators, and educational facilitators of older adults that incorporates the latest research findings on cognitive and emotional development in midlife and old age. The pedagogy of older persons, sometimes called andragogy or "gerontagogy," needs to be infused into both adult education degree programs and social gerontology. Ensuring high-quality programs remains limited to counting enrollments rather than utilizing professional assessment techniques.

The downside of this optimistic picture of the future of older adult education is that it will leave many behind. Those privileged by earlier college education who can afford user fees and tuition will discover a wealth of opportunities, while those with lesser levels of prior formal education, who lack skills for accessing educational programs and/or cannot afford to pay for them, will have few resources to draw on. There have been few signs, even during the economically heady years of American affluence of the 1990s, that the federal or state governments plan to become major players in leveling the playing field. The era of government support to bring free or low-cost educational opportunities to working-class and underserved people (including minorities) is long past. Unless large advocacy organizations such as AARP start lobbying for an expanded role for lifelong learning that includes older adults, this situation is unlikely to change. The United States does not enjoy a long tradition of government-sponsored adult education programs such as is found in the Scandinavian countries.

Older adult education in the United States is such that it will take a wide range of private and public organizations to develop innovative programs for older learners and compete for their time, energy, and money. This ensures a wide diversity of programs, curricula, and delivery formats (e.g., in person, via the Internet) and lets participants "vote with their feet" as far as which programs succeed and which fail. Moreover, the American tradition of voluntary service supports an increasing number of senior adults to take leadership roles in older learner programs. In this sense, older adult education can be highly emancipatory and empowering. Too often government-designed and -managed educational programs, even innovative ones, become resistant to change and entrenched in bureaucracies that seek to perpetuate themselves, or funding priorities change and programs disappear overnight.

The negative side is that recruitment and access to these programs are limited to the well educated, well off, and well connected. There are few cultural and educational organizations that have the resources or ability to reach underserved populations. When they do, it is usually episodic and often based on the whims of outside funding sources such as private foundations and government agencies. Perhaps older adults who are themselves leaders and organizers of educational programs will take it upon themselves to develop outreach programs to the underserved. (See also ATTITUDES ABOUT RETIREMENT; FINANCIAL EDUCATION FOR SENIORS; LEISURE; LIFE PLANNING; VOLUNTEERING.)

References

AARP. 1999. *Baby Boomers Envision Their Retirement*. An AARP Segmentation Analysis. Washington, DC: Author.

AARP. 2000. *A Profile of Older Americans: 2000*. Washington, DC: U.S. Department of Health and Human Services, Administration on Aging.

Belanger, P., ed. 1999. *The Silent Revolution of Adult Learning Societies: Who Participates in Adult Learning?* New York: Elsevier Science, Ltd.

Belanger, P., and Albert Tuijnman, eds. 1997. *New Patterns of Adult Learning: A Six-Country Comparative Study*. New York: Elsevier Science, Ltd.

Laslett, Peter. 1991. *A Fresh Map of Life: The Emergence of the Third Age*. Cambridge, MA: Harvard University Press.

Manheimer, R.J. 1994. "Life Enrichment Opportunities." Unpublished paper.

Manheimer, R.J. 1998. "The Promise and Politics of Older Adult Education." *Research on Aging* 20: 391–414.

Manheimer, Ronald J., Denis D. Snodgrass, and Diane Moskow-McKenzie. 1995. *Older Adult Education: A Guide to Research, Programs, and Policies*. Westport, CT: Greenwood Press.

Snyder, T.D., C.M. Hoffman, and C.M. Geddes. 1997. *Digest of Educational Statistics, 1997*. Washington, DC: U.S. Department of Education, National Center for Educational Statistics.

Ronald J. Manheimer

ELDER LAW PRACTICE, the legal practice of counseling and representing older persons or their representatives. It is the only area of law that is described by the clientele that is served rather than by the substantive area of law involved. Most clients are aged 55 and older. They range from the worker about to take early retirement to the older persons who are frail. The elder law attorney assists the senior citizen in a wide range of financial concerns, from basic estate planning to asset protection for long-term care.

Health and Personal Care Planning

Elder law attorneys advise clients about, and help prepare, advance directives for health care. These documents are also known as medical powers of attorney, living wills, or health care declarations. All 50 states and the District of Columbia have laws permitting advance directives, based on the constitutional right to privacy. Through an advance directive a person sets forth his or her intentions regarding medical treatment in the last stages of life. An advance directive is usually accompanied by the appointment of a health care representative to act on behalf of the person. Elder law attorneys also counsel health care representatives and families about medical and life-sustaining choices. It is sometimes necessary to go to court to enforce an advance directive or to obtain an order to terminate life in the absence of an advance directive.

Premortem Legal Planning and Fiduciary Representation

This area of elder law, commonly called estate planning, includes giving advice and preparing documents concerning wills; trusts; durable, general, or financial powers of attorney; charitable giving; and the financial and tax implications of proposed actions. The attorney's role is to assist in the development of a plan for distribution of a person's assets to plan for avoidance of federal and state taxes upon the transfer of assets, to avoid probate where appropriate, and to provide protective measures for the client that may be triggered upon disability.

Fiduciary representation includes seeking the appointment of, giving advice to, and representing persons serving as executor, personal representative, attorney-in-fact, trustee, guardian, conservator, representative payee, or other formal or informal fiduciary. An elder law attorney gives such legal advice as may be necessary to the fiduciary in performing his or her duties. Advance care planning for the appointment of and instruction to fiduciaries adds to flexibility and reduces costs in carrying out the wishes of the older person who may no longer be able to care for himself or herself. In the absence of a power of attorney, a guardian may have to be appointed to manage the affairs of an incompetent adult.

Legal Capacity Counseling and Protective Arrangements

Unfortunately, some older persons become incompetent and incapable of understanding the nature and consequences of particular acts or decisions. The medical community has developed client capacity screens that can be helpful in identifying whether a person is competent to act. The legal community also has developed a number of tests or standards to determine what level of capacity is needed for various acts.

On occasion, a person may seek guardianship for a parent or other older person over that person's objection. If the older person is competent, it is inappropriate to appoint a guardian. Another concern is whether the person applying to be appointed guardian is best suited to act as such. A close living relative, for example, is not always the best choice to handle the affairs of the older person. The elder law attorney may be called upon to represent the person who is the subject of the guardianship proceeding or other family member. In the case of guardianship or conservatorship, an elder's financial resources should be protected.

Public Benefits and Insurance Advice

One of the most dynamic areas of elder law involves devising plans for assisting older people in obtaining or dealing with Medicare, Medicaid, Social Security, Supplemental Security Income (SSI) benefits, veterans benefits, and food stamps. Perhaps the largest single area in public benefits advice for elder law attorneys involves protecting the family's assets in situations requiring long-term care.

The elder law attorney designs a plan that may involve the use of trusts, annuities, or transfers of assets within the framework of the Medicaid law that makes a nursing home patient eligible for benefits. Usually the family depletes some of its own assets prior to Medicaid eligibility, but the spouse remaining at home is able to save some assets, and assets can also be protected for children. Elder law attorneys also advocate for clients in obtaining Medicare benefits or assist in dealing with the administrative apparatus when problems arise.

Older adults have special needs relating to insurance that range from health and life insurance to long-term care, home care, Medicare supplemental insurance (Medigap), and long-term disability insurance. Clients often call upon elder law attorneys to analyze the various types of policies that are available and to make recommendations about what is needed and affordable.

Resident Rights Advocacy

Patients and residents in hospitals, nursing facilities, continuing care retirement communities, assisted living facilities, adult day care facilities, and those cared for in their homes by others have certain rights. On occasion, the rights of the patient are ignored by the hospital or the nursing home. Problems may involve financial elder abuse, or range from the use of unlawful restraints to sexual abuse by members of a nursing home staff. Older persons entering continuing care retirement communities often require the assistance of an elder law attorney to review the contract and occasionally to resolve disputes that arise between the community and the resident. An elder law attorney may be called upon to interpret the contract and help enforce the rights of the resident.

Nursing homes and other elder facilities may become aggressive in attempting to discharge patients when the insurance available to pay for a patient's care expires. The elder law attorney enforces the rights of the patient to prevent unlawful discharge. The financial issue of who will pay—the patient, a public assistance program, or the institution—is typically the issue to resolve.

Housing Counseling

Most older persons prefer to live in their own homes. Unfortunately, many do not have sufficient income to pay taxes, insurance, and maintenance and sustain a lifestyle that affords dignity. Elder law attorneys often are able to assist such clients in obtaining reverse annuity mortgages. Under a reverse mortgage, the homeowner receives a monthly check from the lender and can continue to live at home. The amount of the check is based on an appraisal of the property, the prevailing rate of interest, and the life expectancy of the borrower. The mortgage contract calls for repayment of the mortgage only when the borrower moves from the home or upon his or her death. The attorney must review the documents to be sure the homeowner is protected. A reverse mortgage holds the potential for helping the older person be financially independent.

Many communities have loan programs available to older homeowners for purposes of rehabilitating their homes. The programs often provide that after a certain period of years the loan is forgiven. Other programs do not forgive the loan but make funds available at a below-market rate of interest. An attorney can be helpful in assisting a client in obtaining such loans. Many communities have subsidized senior citizen housing available, which an elder law attorney can assist low-income older persons to obtain.

Employment and Retirement Advice

At the time of retirement, questions arise about options relating to employee benefits, pension funds, retiree health benefits, and unemployment benefits. There are often substantial tax consequences and significant financial considerations involving the retiree and the retiree's spouse. An elder law attorney is in a position to advise retirees on the options available and how they will financially impact the retiree and spouse.

Income, Estate, and Gift Tax Advice

A substantial amount of advice that elder law attorneys give their clients relates to passing assets from one generation to another. Federal estate tax, inheritance tax, and gift tax affect these transfers. Elder law attorneys develop plans for transferring assets in such a manner as to minimize or, if possible, eliminate transfer taxes. Proper income, estate, and gift tax advice can enable older persons to stretch their dollars to remain independent and pass assets on to future generations.

Tort Claims against Nursing Homes

On occasion, patients in nursing homes are illegally restrained or neglected, or they fall or are injured in some other way. They may be subjected to mental, physical, sexual, or financial abuse by nursing home staff. These cases are difficult because often the only witness is the older person, and in some cases the capacity of the older person is diminished and his or her testimony may be suspect. Litigation can be successful in protecting the rights of nursing home patients and in gaining compensation for physical and mental injuries suffered. An elder law attorney is often able to represent the nursing home patient or family members in this regard. Tort claims against nursing homes may result in compensation or even punitive damages.

Advocacy

Elder law attorneys advocate for their clients not only in the traditional judicial forums but also in the halls of state and federal legislatures and before state and federal regulatory agencies. As public entitlement programs are squeezed, the older and disabled are often affected adversely. Elder law attorneys and their allies in the aging community are often effective voices on behalf of those unable to help themselves.

Discrimination in Employment and Housing

As American businesses downsize and restructure, the victims are often aging workers. In many cases early retirement programs are structured in such a way as to compensate older workers for the rights they are relinquishing. Those who accept early retirement packages usually sign a written waiver of any rights they have based on age. However, older persons may be discriminated against through early termination or failure to hire, based solely on age. There are a number of elder law attorneys who specialize in age discrimination cases.

Elder law is a relatively new area of law, and most people are not aware of it. The National Academy of Elder Law Attorneys was established in 1988. The organizations listed below can provide help in learning about and obtaining an elder law attorney. (See also ADVANCE DIRECTIVES; DURABLE POWER OF ATTORNEY; LIVING WILL; TITLING ASSETS; TRUSTS; WILLS.)

Organizations

AARP Legal Counsel for the Elderly
Commission on Legal Problems of the Elderly
National Academy of Elder Law Attorneys
National Senior Citizens Law Center

Suggested Reading

Regan, John J. 1989. *Your Legal Rights in Later Life*. Washington, DC: AARP.

References

Margolis, Harry S. 1995. *The Elder Law Portfolio Series*. Boston, MA: Little, Brown.

Mezzullo, Louis A., and Mark W. Wolpert. 1992. *Advising the Elderly Client*. New York: Clark, Boardman and Calaghan.

Regan, John J. 1982. *Tax, Estate and Financial Planning for the Elderly*. New York: Matthew Bender.

Thomas D. Begley, Jr.

EMPLOYEE BENEFITS IN THE PUBLIC SECTOR, benefits available to federal, state, and local government employees. In 2001, there were about 19 million government employees in all three groups. While these government workers have much in common

Table 1
Numbers and Union Representation of Private and Public Sector Unions, 2001

	Total Employed	Represented by Unions
Private Wage and Salary Workers	101,605,000	9.7%
Government Workers	19,155,000	41.8%
Federal	3,284,000	36.6%
State	5,677,000	34.5%
Local	10,195,000	47.5%

Source: U.S. Bureau of Labor Statistics (BLS) 2002.

with private sector workers, there is one key characteristic in which they are very different: the degree of unionization. Higher union membership among federal employees has a pronounced effect on both traditional and nontraditional benefits. Table 1 shows the number of workers in the public and private sectors and the degree of unionization in each sector.

Because of the heavy degree of unionization, government employers are less able to reduce or drop current benefits and are reluctant to introduce new benefits programs. Thus, government benefits programs look much more like earlier private sector programs. A second general factor impacting public sector employee benefits is the degree of political activity by employee unions and individual employees. Legislators and officials depending on the votes of public sector employees for winning margins are reluctant to cut benefits levels for fear of being targeted by unions or other public activists.

The following description of public sector benefits is of necessity broad; exceptions will occur in many public jurisdictions. Five different benefit areas are considered: retirement and capital accumulation programs, income protection plans, medical and other health benefits, paid time off, and services and miscellaneous benefits.

Retirement and Capital Accumulation Programs

There are three basic types of these programs, all designed to allow an employee and his or her spouse to live in relative comfort after they reach some retirement age. Mandated programs include Social Security. The second type of capital accumulation program includes organization-supported individual accumulation programs. The third program type is the company pension plan, whether a defined benefit plan (the traditional pension), a defined contribution plan such as a 401(k) or the equivalent public sector 403(b), or a hybrid plan such as a cash balance plan.

Social Security did not apply to federal employees until P.L. 98-21 was passed in 1983. This placed all federal employees hired after January 1, 1994, under the provisions of the Social Security Act and also prevented states from terminating Social Security coverage for state and local government employees if they were already covered. About one-fourth of state and local workers are still not covered by Social Security in the sample studied by Rajnes (2001). Thus, some state and local pension programs are the sole source (aside from personal savings) of retirement income for many public sector em-

Table 2
Incidence of Income Protection Plans in Medium and Large Private Establishments, in State and Local Governments, and in the Federal Government

	Medium and Large Private Establishments	State and Local Governments	Federal (Civilian Workforce)
Life Insurance	87%	89%	100%
Multiple of Earnings	1.5	1.6	~ 1
Flat Dollar Amount	$16,947	$18,922	Pay (rounded up to nearest $000) + $2,000
Accidental Death and Dismemberment	68%	58%	100%
Long-Term Disability Insurance	43%	34%	100%
Survivor Income Coverage	5%	1%	Annuitant option

Sources: BLS 1998; OPM 1997, 1998 data.

ployees, and this has had the effect of an upward bias on pension levels. Many provisions of the Employee Retirement Income Security Act (ERISA) do not apply to public sector retirement programs.

State and local government workers generally receive retirement benefits as well; 98% get retirement of one kind or another, with 90% getting defined benefit pensions and 14% participating in defined contribution plans. About 22% of all plans require no employee contribution. Using a much larger sample than Rajnes, the Bureau of Labor Statistics (BLS) found only 10% of employees are not covered by Social Security, and an additional 82% of employees have plans that are not integrated with Social Security.

Income Protection Plans

Income protection programs are designed to protect the employee and his or her family in the event the employee becomes unable to work. They are typically mandated at some base level (if they exist at all), but organizations often supplement one or more of these programs. Typical income protection plans include workers' compensation, unemployment insurance, disability coverage, and life insurance. Table 2 shows the incidence of various income protection plans in the private sector, state and local governments, and the federal government. Data series are available online from the Bureau of Labor Statistics, and the data are from that source. Private sector data are from 1997; public sector data are from 1998. Federal civilian workforce data are from the Congressional Budget Office (1998) and the Office of Personnel Management's (OPM) Web site.

Medical and Other Health Benefits

These programs cover the range of health care requirements of workers. Hospitalization and surgery/major medical are the two largest (and most expensive) categories of health

Table 3
Incidence of Medical and Other Health Benefits in Medium and Large Private Establishments, in State and Local Governments, and in the Federal Government

	Medium and Large Private Establishments	State and Local Governments	Federal (Civilian Workforce)
Medical Care Benefits	76%	86%	100%
Employee Premium Contribution Required	80%	75%	100%
% in HMOs	33%	39%	n.a.
% in PPOs	40%	35%	n.a
Prescription Drug Coverage	100%	100%	100%
Dental Care	59%	60%	100%
Vision Care	26%	43%	Through HMO/PPO
Sickness/Accident Insurance	55%	20%	100%
Drug Treatment	97%	99%	100%
Alcohol Treatment	96%	99%	100%
Wellness Programs	36%	35%	% unknown

Sources: BLS; OPM; Congressional Budget Office (CBO) 1997, 1998 data.

benefits, although health maintenance organizations (HMOs), preferred provider organizations (PPOs), and other managed care solutions have been substituted for them. Other benefits in this category include long-term care insurance, prescription drug plans, and coverage for vision and hearing care.

Analyzing actuarially adjusted data from a sample of public and private sector employers, Long and Marquis (1999) concluded that public sector employees are more likely to be covered than private sector workers (79% to 60%), although this difference largely disappears for private sector employers of 500 or fewer employees. State and local government employers pay the highest share of premiums for single coverage, followed by private sector employers; the lowest share is paid by federal employers. Family coverage is just the opposite, with federal employers paying a higher share for dependent coverage than either private sector employers or state and local government employers, who pay about the same share.

A comparison of specific health benefits offered by private sector employers, state and local government employers, and the federal government is shown in Table 3.

Paid time-off programs vary widely across sectors. Traditionally, the largest paid time-off programs are vacation and holidays. Other categories are personal days, special-purpose days (jury duty, bereavement, military service, etc.), family leave, sabbaticals, rest and meal times, and community service leave. The value of paid time off is frequently ignored, since there are no out-of-pocket costs involved. However, if the average paid time off in an organization includes 3 weeks of vacation and 11 holidays, 10% of payroll (52 weeks × 5 days = 260 days work per year/26 paid days off) is devoted to

Table 4
Incidence of Paid Time Off in Medium and Large Private Establishments, in State and Local Governments, and in the Federal Government

	Medium and Large Private Establishments	State and Local Governments	Federal (Civilian Workforce)
Vacation	95%	67%	100%
Vacation days at 1 year	9.6	12.6	13
Vacation days at 5 years	13.8	15.6	n.a.
Vacation days at 10 years	16.9	18.6	n.a.
Vacation days at 20 years	20.3	22.3	26
Holidays	89%	73%	100%
Number of paid holidays	9.3	11.4	10
Personal days	20%	38%	n.a.
Sick leave	56%	96%	100%
Military leave	47%	76%	100%
Jury duty	87%	95%	100%
Funeral leave	81%	65%	100%

Sources: BLS; OPM 1997, 1998 data.

paid time off. Private sector data are from 1997; public sector data are from 1998. Federal civilian workforce data are from OPM's Web site.

Paid Time Off

A comparison of paid time off as shown in Table 4 provides a mixed picture. Vacation and holiday time is more generous in the public sector when it is offered. Sick leave has a much higher incidence in the public sector. Other paid time off is generally more prevalent in the public sector but not for every type of leave. Federal paid time off is the most generous except for number of paid holidays.

Services and Other Miscellaneous Benefits

A variety of miscellaneous benefits are given by organizations. These include Christmas and related bonuses, dependent care (both child and elder care), family leave programs, employee assistance programs, legal services, financial planning, property and liability insurance, paid or subsidized meals, discounts on products and services, parking, and gym and other health/recreation services.

Table 5 shows the incidence of selected miscellaneous benefits in the private sector, state and local governments, and the federal government. Data series are available online from the Bureau of Labor Statistics, and the data are from that source. Private sector

Table 5
Incidence of Miscellaneous Benefits in Medium and Large Private Establishments, in State and Local Governments, and in the Federal Government

	Medium and Large Private Establishments	State and Local Governments	Federal (Civilian Workforce)
Child Care	7%	8%	Agencies may use appropriated funds to support childcare for low-income federal workers.
Job-Related Education	67%	63%	Agencies may support.
Non-Job-Related Education	20%	22%	No support, but agencies may make accommodating work schedule adjustments.
Employee Assistance Programs	63% (1992)	95%	100%

Sources: BLS; OPM 1997, 1998 data.

data are from 1997; public sector data are from 1998. Federal civilian workforce data are from OPM's Web site.

Summary

The Congressional Budget Office (1998) estimates that the overall value of federal government employee benefits is well above that of typical private sector employees, and in selected age/service categories may be as high as 7.2%. Online data from the Bureau of Labor Statistics (Employer Cost for Employee Compensation) shows that state and local governments paid an average of $8.73 per employee per hour for benefits, compared to the private sector's cost of $5.63 per employee per hour. While some of this difference may be due to different demographic profiles in the two groups, it appears that public sector employees receive a higher level of benefits overall than do private sector employees. (See also ANNUITIES; EMPLOYEE BENEFITS IN THE UNITED STATES; RETIREMENT PLANS—403(b), SOCIAL SECURITY PROGRAM OF THE UNITED STATES; VETERANS' BENEFITS.)

Organizations

American Federation of Government Employees
American Federation of State, County, and Municipal Employees
Council of State Governments
Employee Benefit Research Institute
Government Finance Officers Association
International Personnel Management Association
U.S Bureau of Labor Statistics
U.S. Office of Personnel Management

Suggested Reading

Mitchell, Olivia, and Michael Hustead, eds. 2001. *Pensions in the Public Sector*. Philadelphia: University of Pennsylvania Press.

References

Bureau of Labor Statistics. 1998. "National Compensation Survey—Benefits." Available online at http://www.bls.gov/ncs/ebs/home.htm.

Bureau of Labor Statistics. 2000. *Employee Benefits in State and Local Governments, 1998*. Washington, DC: Government Printing Office.

Bureau of Labor Statistics. 2002. "Union Members in 2002." Washington, DC. ftp://146.142.4.23/pub/news.release/union2.txt.

Congressional Budget Office. 1998. *CBO Memorandum: Comparing Federal Employee Benefits with Those in the Private Sector*. Washington, DC: Author.

Long, Stephen S., and M. Susan Marquis. 1999. "Comparing Employee Health Benefits in the Public and Private Sector, 1997." *Health Affairs* November–December: 183–93.

Office of Personnel Management (OPM). n.d. "Information for Federal Benefits Officers." Available online at http://www.opm.gov/asd/.

Rajnes, David. 2001. *State and Local Retirement Plans: Innovation and Renovation*. EBRI Issue Brief Number 235. Washington, DC: Employee Benefit Research Institute.

Charles H. Fay

EMPLOYEE BENEFITS IN THE UNITED STATES, benefits intended to promote financial security of employees by insuring against uncertain events and to raise living standards by providing targeted services. Employee benefit programs also add to economic stability by helping to secure the income and welfare of American families, which helps the economy as a whole.

The U.S. employee benefit system is a partnership among businesses, individuals, and the government. Most employment-based benefits, such as pensions and health insurance, are provided voluntarily by businesses. The government supports these voluntary employment-based benefits by granting them favorable tax treatment. Other benefits, including Social Security, unemployment insurance, workers' compensation, and family and medical leave, are mandatory. The government also supports individual financial security programs through individual retirement accounts, favorable taxation of life insurance contracts, and tax-free death benefits.

A Brief History

Employee benefit programs have existed in the United States since colonial times. Early programs include the Plymouth Colony settlers' military retirement program in 1636; Gallatin Glassworks' profit sharing plan in 1797; American Express Company's private employer pension plan in 1875; Montgomery Ward's group health, life, and accident insurance program in 1910; and Baylor University Hospital's formalized prepaid group hospitalization plan in 1929. The federal government's involvement in the provision of such benefits further expanded coverage. In 1935, Congress mandated basic retirement income protection under the Social Security program; in 1956, it added income protection for disabled workers and their dependents; and in 1965, it added health insurance for older and disabled Americans under the Medicare program. Moreover, voluntary employment-based benefit programs became more prevalent as federal tax preferences for employee benefits coincided with rising tax rates, strengthening incentives to provide private benefits.

The Role of Employee Benefits

Today's employment-based benefit programs represent a national commitment to provide some measure of income security and access to certain services (especially medical care) to active workers, displaced and disabled workers, retirees, and their families.

Income Security. A family's income security can be threatened if a wage earner dies or becomes disabled. Group life insurance and long-term disability insurance, often provided voluntarily by employers, can help to alleviate such unexpected financial losses. Employment-based pension and savings plans can also help to provide economic security for workers who look forward to a period of voluntary retirement in old age. Mandatory government programs also address the need for income security. The Social Security Old-Age, Survivors, and Disability Insurance (OASDI) program provides an income base, in the form of a lifetime annuity, to nearly all retired and disabled workers and their surviving spouses. Workers who become unemployed or disabled may qualify for temporary unemployment insurance or workers' compensation payments, respectively.

Nearly all Americans will benefit from one or more private and public income security programs during their lifetime. In February 2001, 74.3 million workers (67.8% of wage and salary workers) worked for an employer that sponsored a retirement plan. Of these 74.3 million workers, 90.7% participated in an employment-based retirement plan (Copeland 2001). In 2001, 34.9% of all older adult (age 65 and over) married couples and 34.8% of all unmarried older individuals had income from employment-based pensions according to Employee Benefit Research Institute (EBRI) estimates from the March 2002 Current Population Survey (Fronstin 2002).

Mandatory government programs provide nearly universal coverage. In 1999, the Social Security system covered 151.8 million employees and self-employed persons, and 44.6 million persons, including the older disabled and their dependents and survivors, were receiving benefits. An estimated 92.9% of older married couples and 93.0% of older unmarried individuals received income from Social Security in 2001 according to EBRI estimates of data from the March 2002 Current Population Survey (Fronstin 2002).

Access to Important Services. The U.S. employee benefit system also seeks to provide American workers and their families with access to certain vital services, especially medical care. Many American workers participate in group health insurance programs sponsored voluntarily by their employers or negotiated by employers and unions. Coverage may be limited to acute hospital care or may include such routine services as dental exams and physician visits. Often, an employee's dependents are covered. Of the civilian population under age 65, 65.6%, or 162.3 million persons, were covered by employment-based health insurance in 2001 (Fronstin 2002). Among workers age 18 to 64, 73.7% had employment-based coverage.

Some employers and unions make health insurance benefits available to retired employees. The Agency for Health Care Quality and Research reports that 12% of employing establishments in the United States provide access pre-65 and 11% access post-65 for retirees. The 44% of the workforce with employers of 500 or more employees are more likely to have access than those working for small firms. In 2001, 96.1% of the older population received health insurance coverage through the Medicare program. However, Medicare does not cover all medical services; for example, it does not cover maintenance prescription drugs.

Employee benefit programs are not limited to income security and health insurance. Specialized benefit programs help provide access to a wide range of important services, including ongoing education and training, child care, long-term care, and legal assistance. Other employee benefits, such as subsidized parking, product discounts, and relocation expense reimbursement, can provide convenience and cost savings for employees. Employee benefits also include paid sick leave, holidays, vacations, and maternity or paternity leave.

Tax Treatment

The Federal Internal Revenue Code has provided tax incentives since 1921 for employment-based pension plans, since 1939 for compensation received for injuries or sickness, and since 1942 for health plans. The Social Security program, as initially enacted in 1935, provided retirement income to workers and their spouses; in 1956, the program was extended to provide income to disabled workers (their dependents were included in the program in 1958); and in 1965, the program was extended again to provide health insurance coverage to the older, disabled, and low-income individuals as Medicare and Medicaid.

The general tax treatment of employee benefit programs has remained relatively consistent over the years. Employer contributions to health insurance remain tax exempt to employees and tax deductible to employers; in addition, the benefits received under employment-based health plans are not treated as taxable income. Taxes on most retirement programs are deferred until benefit receipt. Other benefits, such as life insurance, dependent care, and educational assistance, are tax exempt up to specified dollar limits. Vacations and other time-off benefits, bonuses and awards, and severance pay are fully taxable.

Meeting Changing Needs

Given such a wide range of options, compensation packages can be tailored to achieve employer and employee goals and can change in response to workers' needs and preferences. Demographic changes in the American workforce and general population have influenced, and are likely to continue influencing, the provision and design of employee benefit programs.

An Aging Population. One change in progress is the shift in the U.S. population's age distribution. Members of the large baby boom cohort (individuals born between 1946 and 1964) currently compose a disproportionately large part of the overall workforce, especially in new and fast-growing industries. As this cohort ages, and the smaller baby bust cohort (individuals born between 1965 and 1975) enters the labor force, the age distribution of the workforce will shift toward older workers, whose needs and preferences may differ from those of younger workers. As the baby boom cohort begins to retire, an increasing proportion of Americans will be older and living longer and will depend on sources other than employment for income and vital services. These forces will affect both income security and health care insurance programs.

Developments in the retirement plan market may in part represent a response to workforce changes. It has been well documented that, in the private sector, participation in defined contribution plans (which promise a specified contribution to an employee's account) is growing faster than participation in traditional defined benefit pension plans (which promise a specified benefit at retirement). The number of active participants in a defined benefit plan where the defined benefit plan was the primary plan declined slightly between 1975 and 1998 (from 27 million to 23 million), while the number of active participants in a defined contribution plan where the defined contribution plan was the primary plan grew during those years (from 4 million to 29 million) (U.S. Department of Labor 2002).

Defined contribution plans historically have offered faster vesting than defined benefit plans, and defined contribution lump-sum benefits are more portable than defined benefit plan deferred annuities. Thus, younger workers may anticipate future job changes and therefore place a higher value on faster vesting and benefit portability common to defined contribution plans. In addition, young families may be attracted to defined contribution plan provisions that allow access to money in the account prior to retirement in cases of financial hardship and on termination of employment (although preretirement and hardship withdrawals are generally subject to a 10% excise tax and regular income tax). However, as the baby boom cohort ages and the workforce becomes weighted more toward older workers, preferences may shift again toward defined benefit plans, which are generally characterized as providing more secure retirement protection than defined contribution plans for long-tenure employees working at the same company until retirement. Also, it is possible to save more money in the last several years before retirement in a defined benefit plan than in a defined contribution plan.

The effects of the aging population on retirement programs can already be seen in the Social Security Old-Age and Survivors Insurance (OASI) program. Partly as a result of increased life expectancies, past population shifts are reflected in a decrease in the ratio of OASI-covered workers to OASI beneficiaries from 16.5 in 1950 to 3.7 in 1970 to 3.9 in 2001. Under intermediate assumptions, the ratio of OASI workers to beneficiaries is expected to decrease to 2.5 in 2030 and to 2.1 in 2080 (U.S. Department of Social Security 2002). In response, taxes imposed on employers and employees to finance the pay-as-you-go OASI system were raised from 1.5% in 1950 to roughly 4.8% in 1983. The rates were revised again under the Social Security Amendments of 1983 and increased incrementally to 5.3% in 2002. Moreover, in anticipation of the baby boom's retirement, the retirement age will rise incrementally to age 67 for people born in 1960 or later.

Health care benefit programs are also affected by the aging of the population. The older generally require more health care than the working-age population. The effects of this trend on medical expenditures are exacerbated by the rapid pace of health care price inflation. Between 1982 and 2000, the price level of medical services and commodities rose 169.0%, compared with a 78.4% increase in consumer prices overall. Propelled by these factors, national health expenditures reached 13.2% of the U.S. gross domestic product in 2000, up from 5.1% in 1960. Between 1960 and 2001, employer spending for health insurance (excluding Medicare) increased an average of 11.8% per year, to $327.4 billion. In response to these developments, employers are taking steps to slow the growth of their health care costs. Increasingly, employers are requiring employees to share the cost of health insurance premiums and/or pay a larger portion of health costs out of pocket. It is hoped that cost sharing and other cost management measures will discourage unnecessary utilization of health care services.

The Medicare program, like OASI, has already been affected by demographic shifts and rapid health care inflation. The employer/employee tax rate for Medicare Hospital Insurance (HI) increased from 0.6% in 1970 on a maximum taxable amount of $7,800 of annual earnings to 1.45% in 2002, with no cap on the maximum amount of annual earnings subject to the tax. In anticipation of further cost increases, Congress changed Medicare's reimbursement system in 1983 to the prospective payment system (PPS) for inpatient hospital care and in 1989 to the resource-based relative value system (RBRVS) for outpatient physician services.

As the population ages, the proportion requiring nursing home care or other long-term care will increase. Currently, private insurance for such health care needs is not widely available, and federal financing for nursing home care is generally available only under the Medicaid program, with eligibility subject to stringent means tests. Many find this situation unacceptable, and pressure is building to make other provisions for financing long-term care, either through expanded provision of voluntary private insurance (perhaps through employers), through a mandatory government program, or both.

Balancing Work and Family. Family structure has changed radically from the days when it typically consisted of a father who was the sole wage earner, a mother who stayed at home, and two children. Today, both husband and wife often work, children are in day care, and there are many single-parent families. The increase in labor force participation by women, especially those with young children, has implications for employee benefits that cannot be overlooked. In 1980, 44.1% of married women with children under age 6 were in the labor force, compared with 70.5% in 2001 (U.S. Department of Commerce 2002). In 1998, out of a total of 68.4 million children, 29.0 million (42.3%) lived in a two-parent family in which both parents worked; 11.7 million (17.2%) lived in a two-parent family where one parent worked; 13.5 million (18.8%) lived in a one-parent family in which the parent worked; and 3.1 million (4.5%) lived in a one- or two-parent family in which the parent or parents were unemployed (U.S. Department of Commerce 2000).

These trends have led to public and private responses that attempt to help workers better balance work and family needs. Legislation has been enacted at the federal and state levels that requires employers to provide a minimum period of parental leave and promotes federal and more state involvement in child care access, affordability, and quality.

Flexibility. Another response to a changing workforce is the growing use of flexible benefit plans. Within such arrangements, employees are permitted choices among benefits and/or benefit levels. Employees thus may exchange benefits that they consider less valuable for others better suited to their needs. Employee benefit programs, whether public or private, that address these and other needs can enhance the economic security of individual workers and their families. The provision of benefits such as child care and parental leave can help smooth career progress, to the overall advantage of labor markets. Thus, these and other benefits can help families and employers reconcile the personal needs of the home with the economic needs of the workplace.

Conclusion

Social Security provides a floor on income protection for those over the age of 62 who choose to retire. The average income replacement rate, however, is near 40%, with the rate being no more than 27% for the 12% of the workforce that earns over $89,000 per year. Unions and employers have sponsored voluntary retirement plans to aid individuals in supplementing Social Security. About 42% of retired Americans report such supplemental income today. Medicare pays for an average of half of health expenses for retirees. Those who have retired from large public and private employers have access to cost-effective supplemental health insurance, and others have access to Medigap policies to purchase. Active workers are most likely to have health insurance from their employer or union, and most workers lucky enough to have short-term disability protection and life insurance have it through employment. Many workers have a wide range of employee-pay-all benefits available to them at work. In short, mandatory programs provide a floor of protection, employment-based voluntary employee benefits add levels of protection, and individual savings and purchased insurance secure a level above what employers and unions provide. (See also DEFINED BENEFIT PENSION PLAN; DEFINED CONTRIBUTION PLAN; EMPLOYEE STOCK OWNERSHIP PLANS [ESOPs]; HEALTH BENEFITS; PENSION PLANS; RETIREMENT PLANS—401(k).)

References

Copeland, Craig. 2001. "Pension Participation: February 2001." *EBRI Notes* 22 (December): 12.

Employee Benefit Research Institute. 1994. *Retirement in the 21st Century . . . Ready or Not. . . .* Washington, DC: Author.

Employee Benefit Research Institute. 1997. *EBRI Databook on Employee Benefits*. 4th ed. Washington, DC: Author.

Fronstin, Paul. 2002. "Sources of Health Insurance and Characteristics of the Uninsured: Analysis of the March 2002 Current Population Survey." *EBRI Issue Brief*, no. 252 (December).

Rosenbloom, Jerry S., ed. 2001. *The Handbook of Employee Benefits: Design, Funding, and Administration*. 5th ed. New York: McGraw-Hill.

U.S. Department of Commerce. Bureau of the Census. 2000. *Statistical Abstract of the United States, 2000*. Washington, DC: GPO.

U.S. Department of Commerce. Bureau of the Census. 2002. *Statistical Abstract of the United States, 2001*. Washington, DC: GPO.

U.S. Department of Labor. 1996. *Employee Benefits in Small Private Establishments*. Washington, DC: GPO.

U.S. Department of Labor. 2000. *Employee Benefits in State and Local Governments, 1998*. Washington, DC: GPO.

U.S. Department of Labor. Bureau of Labor Statistics. 1999. *Employee Benefits in Medium and Large Private Establishments, 1997*. Washington, DC: GPO.

U.S. Department of Labor. Pension and Welfare Benefits Administration. 2002. *Private Pension Plan Bulletin. Abstract of 1998 Form 5500 Annual Reports*. Washington, DC: GPO.

U.S. Department of Social Security. 2002. *Annual Report of the Board of Trustees of the Federal Old-Age and Survivors Insurance and Disability Insurance Trust Funds*. Washington, DC: GPO.

Yakoboski, Paul, and Celia Silverman. 1994. "Baby Boomers in Retirement: What Are Their Prospects?" *EBRI Special Report SR-23/Issue Brief*, no. 151 (July).

Dallas L. Salisbury

EMPLOYEE RETIREMENT INCOME SECURITY ACT (ERISA), statute that federalized the law of employee benefits in the private sector. ERISA substantially modified the federal tax treatment of pension plans, introduced a federal fiduciary law of employee benefit plans, created federal jurisdiction for most employee benefits litigation, expanded disclosure and reporting requirements for employee benefit plans, preempted most state laws relating to employee benefits, vastly extended the scope of Department of Labor regulation of employee benefit plans, and created the Pension Benefit Guaranty Corporation, which insures pension benefits in most defined benefit pension plans.

Congress enacted ERISA in 1974 primarily as a response to grassroots pressure to provide greater federal protection of pension benefits. The statute covers not only pensions but all employee benefit plans. While the statute enhanced federal protection for pensions, it also pushed aside state law protection of employee benefit rights and (as interpreted by the federal courts) extended only limited remedial measures to aggrieved employees, leaving some employees with reduced, rather than increased, rights.

Structure of ERISA

ERISA has four titles. Title I amended the labor laws of the United States. The title includes seven parts: (1) reporting and disclosure, (2) participation and vesting, (3) funding, (4) fiduciary responsibility, (5) administration and enforcement, (6) continuation of health coverage (often referred to as "COBRA," the name of the legislative act (Consolidated Omnibus Budget Reconciliation Act) adding these provisions to Title I); and (7) limitations on preexisting conditions in health plans for employees changing jobs (often referred to as "HIPPA," after the title's name, the "Health Insurance Portability and Accountability Act"). COBRA and HIPPA were added to ERISA by amendment in 1986 and 1996, respectively.

Title II of ERISA amended the Internal Revenue Code (IRC). Certain amendments to ERISA parallel provisions in Title I. For example, Title I and Title II include identical vesting requirements. But other provisions of Title II have no analogue in Title I. These latter requirements reflect tax policy goals rather than employee protection goals. Among these provisions are the rules in IRC Section 415, which restrict the size of contributions to defined contribution plans and benefits from defined benefit plans. The policy basis for this rule is that the tax benefits enjoyed by participants in pension plans should be limited to the creation of reasonable levels of retirement savings. The IRC and regulations also include complex rules requiring tax-qualified pension plans to cover reasonable levels of rank-and-file employees and prohibiting discrimination in favor of highly compensated employees. In addition, some provisions in the Internal Revenue Code provide penalty taxes for violations of provisions that are primarily enforced by the Department of Labor under Title I of ERISA.

There are important differences between Titles I and II. A participant in a pension plan may bring a civil action to enforce any of the rules in Title I of ERISA; actions to enforce Title II generally must be initiated by the Internal Revenue Service (IRS). A plan's failure to follow rules in Title II can lead to the plan's loss of tax benefits, imposition of penalty taxes, or both, depending on the particular rule and its sanctions; no such penalties generally attach to a plan's failure to comply with rules in Title I, although there are certain civil penalties in Title I, especially for certain violations of its fiduciary provisions.

Title III of ERISA includes miscellaneous provisions, statements of primary jurisdictional authority between the IRS and the Department of Labor, and the creation of a certification process for pension actuaries.

Title IV of ERISA establishes the Pension Benefit Guaranty Corporation and the defined benefit plan termination insurance program. There is a separate insurance program for single-employer and multiemployer defined benefit plans. Additionally, Title IV governs other aspects of defined benefit plan termination and, in 1980, was amended to impose "withdrawal liability" on employers who withdraw from underfunded multiemployer pension plans.

ERISA's Vesting and Participation Rules

ERISA's most notable contribution to employee benefit protection was its establishment of minimum vesting standards for retirement benefits. It requires most plans to provide that employees obtain a nonforfeitable right to their benefit at least as quickly as would occur in either of two statutory standards. The first standard provides that employees must have a nonforfeitable right to 100% of their benefits after 5 years of service. The second standard provides that employees must have a nonforfeitable right to 20% of their benefits after 3 years, and then increasing by 20% per year, so that after the seventh year, employees will have a 100% interest in their benefits. The first standard is commonly referred to as "cliff vesting," the latter standard as "graded vesting." (Congress had originally included three alternative vesting standards in ERISA, including a 10-year cliff vesting standard and a 15-year graded vesting standard. In 1986, Congress eliminated another type of vesting, based on the sum of years, service, and age, and which was known as Rule of 45 Vesting. It also reduced the time periods for graded and cliff vesting.)

ERISA also has rules to prevent evasion of the vesting standards. Rules defining service and the accrued benefit to which the vesting rules apply are most important. ERISA also prohibits a plan from conditioning participation on more than one year of service or attaining an age greater than 21.

Title I of ERISA also includes a special rule that prohibits employers from discharging, disciplining, or discriminating against employees for exercising rights under the plan or the statute, or for the purpose of interfering with the attainment of any right to which such participant may become entitled under the plan. An employer violates the statute if it fires employees for the purpose of preventing them from vesting in their benefits. The vesting and participation rules appear in both Title I and Title II of ERISA.

Fiduciary Standards

Title I of ERISA creates an elaborate set of fiduciary rules for most employee benefit plans. ERISA's legislative history indicates that Congress intended to adopt "principles of fiduciary conduct . . . from existing trust law, but with modifications appropriate for employee benefit plans." At the plan level, ERISA Section 403(a) requires that employee benefit plan assets be held in trust, with certain limited exceptions. Moreover, ERISA's substantive fiduciary provisions apply to all plans, even those not structured in trust form.

At the individual level, ERISA defines fiduciaries broadly as persons or entities who exercise discretionary authority or discretionary control over the management, administration, or disposition of plan assets, or render investment advice for a fee. The definition of fiduciary is broadly encompassing, and the courts and the Department of Labor have interpreted the term liberally. As noted, ERISA's legislative history indicates that its fiduciary section "in essence, codifies and makes applicable to . . . fiduciaries certain principles developed in the evolution of the law of trusts." ERISA effects this codification with two related sets of fiduciary standards, the first a series of general trust principles, the second a list of specifically proscribed activities.

The general trust principles provide that plan fiduciaries must discharge their duties solely in the interests of the plan's participants, act prudently, diversify plan investments, and act in accordance with plan instruments. The statute's legislative history indicates an expectation "that courts will interpret the prudent man rule and other fiduciary standards bearing in mind the special nature and purposes of employee benefit plans intended to be effectuated by the Act."

The second set of standards is a more particularized set of prohibitions against fiduciaries causing the plan to enter transactions with parties already related to the plan ("transactional prohibitions"), using plan assets for the fiduciary's own account, or acting on behalf of a party with respect to a transaction involving the plan. The transactional prohibitions are broad and explicit, proscribing dealings with "parties in interest," a term encompassing most individuals and entities with preexisting relations with the plan. ERISA includes statutory exemptions from the prohibited transaction rules and establishes a procedure in which the Department of Labor can create further exemptions administratively.

The Department of Labor, a plan fiduciary, or the participant may bring an action on behalf of a plan against a fiduciary who breaches its obligations under the statute. Moreover, the IRC imposes a tax on a party who has engaged in a prohibited transaction with a plan.

The federal courts, and to a lesser extent the Department of Labor, have been called on to interpret many aspects of ERISA's fiduciary laws. Three judicially developed areas are significant and warrant attention: the recognition of a settlor/fiduciary distinction; the applicability of ERISA fiduciary law to misrepresentations; and limitations on remedies for fiduciary violations.

Settlor/Fiduciary Distinction. ERISA's fiduciary law requires fiduciaries to act solely in the interest of the plan's participants. Many fiduciaries, however, are also the plan sponsor, who are responsible for amending, and terminating, the plan. This raises the question of whether an employer/fiduciary will violate ERISA's fiduciary rules by terminating a plan or amending its provisions in a way that advances the employer's own interests. Courts have resolved this question by recognizing that the fiduciary requirements apply only to employers when they are acting in a fiduciary, as opposed to a settlor, capacity. Decisions to amend a plan or terminate a plan are considered fiduciary functions. Thus, the Supreme Court, for example, held in *Hughes Aircraft Co. v. Jacobson*, 525 U.S. 432 (1999), that an employer's decision to amend a plan could not be attacked in litigation by plan participants as violating the fiduciary rules, even though the amendment advanced the employer's interests over the employees who had been contributing a portion of their compensation to the plan.

Misrepresentations. The Supreme Court, in *Varity Corp. v. Howe*, 516 U.S. 489 (1996), resolved an open question: whether a fiduciary's misrepresentations to a participant in an employee benefit plan violate ERISA. The fiduciary, who was also an employer, argued that making misrepresentations to an employee was not actionable because ERISA's fiduciary provisions were concerned only with actions that harm the plan itself—such as misuse of plan assets—and not with actions that harm individual participants. The fiduciary also argued that its misrepresentations were made in its capacity as employer and not as a fiduciary and thus not actionable for reasons analogous to the justification for the settlor/fiduciary doctrine (see above). The Supreme Court rejected both arguments and held that fiduciary misrepresentations could be actionable under ERISA, at least in certain circumstances.

Remedies. The Supreme Court has held that participants who sue fiduciaries for causing them individual harm (as opposed to harm to the plan itself) may obtain equitable but not legal relief. Because money damages is generally a form of legal rather than equitable relief, this holding has limited the ability of participants to fully remedy some breaches of fiduciary harm.

The basis for the Supreme Court's holding is that the section of ERISA authorizing a participant to bring a civil action to remedy individual harm limits relief to injunctive or other equitable relief. In the most recent of the cases on this subject, *Great-West Life and Annuity Co. v. Knudson*, 534 U.S. 204 (2002), the Supreme Court ruled that money damages would generally be considered "equitable relief" only if it involved the right to a specific item of identified property. In that case, the Supreme Court also reviews the history of its jurisprudence on this subject.

Employee Civil Actions for Benefits and Other Relief

ERISA has by and large federalized jurisdiction over employee benefit claims. Section 502(a)(1) provides that a participant may bring action in federal court to recover benefits under the plan, to enforce rights under the plan, or to clarify future rights to benefits under the terms of the plan. Thus, a participant may bring an action to recover benefits under the plan. Courts, however, have generally refused to award punitive damages or damages to compensate employees for other injuries. Courts have also held that a plan's decision to deny benefits generally is entitled to deference from the courts (if the plan includes language indicating that such deference was intended by the plan's drafters), making it more difficult for employees to recover benefits arguably due them under plan language. A good discussion of this area of law can be found in Kathryn J. Kennedy's "Judicial Standard of Review in ERISA Benefit Claims Cases" (1991).

In addition to providing jurisdiction for benefit claims, ERISA also authorizes participants to bring civil actions against certain parties in other circumstances. Section 502(a)(2) of ERISA, for example, authorizes participants to bring civil actions against fiduciaries whose breaches cause damage to an employee benefit plan. Under this section, a court may order a fiduciary to pay a plan for losses that it suffered, to restore profits earned by the fiduciary using plan assets, and to provide other equitable and remedial relief. The Supreme Court has held that under this section relief must flow directly to the injured employee benefit plan; thus, individuals personally harmed by a fiduciary's behavior may not sue for relief under the section. The Supreme Court has also held that this section applies only to fiduciaries (as defined by ERISA) but does not apply to nonfiduciaries who assist a fiduciary in violating the statute.

Another section of ERISA, Section 502(a)(3), provides for equitable relief when any individual—including someone who is not a fiduciary—violates duties under ERISA. As already noted in this article, however, "equitable relief" includes monetary payments in only limited circumstances.

ERISA Preemption

ERISA preempts state laws that relate, directly or indirectly, to employee benefit plans, with only a few exceptions. The scope of ERISA preemption is broad; courts have held that state law rights to punitive and extra-contractual damages are preempted; that state wrongful discharge law is preempted to the extent the discharge related to an employee benefit plan; that state law actions for misrepresentation are preempted when the misrepresentation involved a plan; that state law garnishment exemptions for employee plan benefits are preempted; and that a state law prohibiting a pension plan from offsetting benefits by a worker's compensation award is preempted.

There are exceptions to ERISA preemption, most notably state insurance law. Thus, a health benefit plan funded through an insurance policy is subject to state insurance law. ERISA has thereby encouraged employers to self-fund health plans in order to escape state regulation. In the area of health care plans, ERISA preemption has been especially problematic, since it has prevented states from attempting to enact health care reforms if they impose conditions or require certain conduct of private sector plans.

It should be said that the judicial approach to preemption has been undergoing an important transition. In the first two decades following ERISA's enactment, courts tended to interpret ERISA preemption literally and thus quite broadly. But a 1995 Supreme Court case signaled a possible change in future preemption cases. The case, *New York State Conference of Blue Cross and Blue Shield Plans v. Travelers Insurance Co.*, 514 U.S. 645 (1995), involved a New York State law that imposed a surcharge on hospital reimbursement served by commercial insurers. The plaintiffs in the case argued that this law imposed an indirect economic cost on employee health care plans, since it skewed the economics of choosing between Blue Cross or a commercial insurer. The Supreme Court, however, held that Congress almost certainly did not intend to invalidate most laws imposing indirect burdens on plans, even though it might be possible to construe the ERISA preemption broadly enough to catch such laws. The case has been regarded by some commentators as taking a more limited and commonsense approach to preemption than it had taken in earlier cases.

Funding and Protection of Defined Benefits

ERISA has attempted to protect employee interests in defined benefit pension plans in two distinct ways. First, ERISA imposes minimum funding rules for pension plans. Employers who fail to fund in accordance with the rules are subject to excise taxes. The minimum funding rules, however, have been criticized as too lenient, particularly in allowing plans to base benefits on past service and then amortizing those liabilities over relatively lengthy periods of time.

Second, Title IV of ERISA established the Pension Benefit Guaranty Corporation (PBGC) to strengthen retirement security by guaranteeing some benefits for defined benefit plan participants. The PBGC insures that payment of a specified portion of promised benefits from private defined benefit plans will be paid to the participants regardless of the status of the sponsor or the level of funds in the pension plan. The PBGC is funded by premiums paid by private sponsors of defined benefit plans, but the agency has been the focus of attention because of potential program deficits and the exposure faced by the PBGC in underfunded plans. Other critics of the PBGC program have contended that the effect of requiring all sponsors to pay premiums, even those whose plans are adequately funded, has the effect of shifting wealth from healthy to unhealthy sectors of the economy. Since ERISA's enactment, the PBGC premium structure has been reformulated to add a component that varied with the amount of plan underfunding and is now partly based on the risk of termination with insufficient assets.

Title IV provides a special program for multiemployer plans that become insolvent. The multiemployer premiums are set lower than the premiums for other plans; the PBGC benefit guarantees are also generally lower than those applicable to other plans. In 1980, Title IV was amended to impose withdrawal liability on employers that cease contributing to an underfunded multiemployer plan. The withdrawal liability equals the withdrawing employer's share of the plan's unfunded vested benefit obligations.

Reporting and Disclosure

Title I of ERISA imposes reporting requirements on employee benefit plans. In addition, Title II imposes reporting requirements on employee benefit plans, and Title IV imposes reporting requirements on defined benefit plans subject to the PBGC plan termination rules. Generally, a plan may satisfy the primary reporting requirements with a single form developed by the Department of Labor, the IRS, and the PBGC. Plans are generally required to prepare a summary annual report. There are also numerous specific reporting obligations imposed by the different ERISA titles.

Plan administrators and sponsors must make disclosure to participants in employee benefit plans. The most important disclosure requirement is that the plan sponsor or plan administrator must prepare a summary plan description and distribute it to plan participants. The summary plan description must be written in a manner that is comprehensible by a participant. On request, the plan must also provide participants with a benefits statement and certain other information. Failure to comply with a request for information within 30 days can lead to a penalty of up to $100 per day.

Spousal Protections

Title I and Title II of ERISA require in certain retirement plans that married pension participants be paid their benefits in the form of a joint and survivor annuity, unless the participant's spouse consents to a different form of distribution. Additionally, retirement plans must provide a preretirement survivor annuity in most cases.

COBRA

In 1985, Congress amended ERISA to provide that sponsors of employee health benefit plans must give former participants and their beneficiaries an opportunity to purchase continued coverage from the plan at the time their coverage under the plan would otherwise end because of death, divorce, termination of employment, loss of dependency status, or reduction of hours. The period of continuation is 36 months, except on termination of employment or reduction of hours, in which case the coverage period is 18 months.

HIPPA

In 1996, Congress enacted the Health Insurance Portability and Accountability Act, which amended ERISA to provide new protections for participants in group health plans. The most important of HIPPA's provisions limits a group plan's ability to impose preexisting limitation conditions on a new enrollee. HIPPA defines preexisting condition as one to which medical advice, diagnosis, care, or treatment was recommended or received during the 6-month period prior to the individual's enrollment. A limitation on preexisting conditions may not generally last for more than 12 months after an individual's enrollment date (18 months for late enrollees), and even that period is generally reduced by the number of days of an individual's prior coverage under a group health plan in which he or she participated within 63 days of the new employment.

Special Tax Provisions

The IRC includes a number of rules that reflect tax rather than employee protection concerns and thus have no analogue in Title I of ERISA. Among these provisions are limitations on benefits from defined benefit plans and on contributions to defined contribution plans; rules requiring that plans cover at least a minimum number of nonhighly compensated employees; rules that prohibit plans from discriminating against non–highly compensated employees; rules imposing excise taxes on certain preretirement distributions from retirement plans or excessive distributions from retirement plans; and rules that require pension plans to begin paying out benefits after employees attain age 70½.

ERISA and Its Critics

Consumer groups have criticized ERISA as not adequately living up to its promise to enhance protection of employee benefits. Such groups argue that a hostile federal judiciary has distorted the statute to dilute employee protections intended by Congress. Among the specific complaints is the deferential standard courts generally use to review plan denials of employee benefits, the restrictive reading of ERISA's remedial provisions, and the broad reading of ERISA's preemption provisions to deprive employees of state law rights they enjoyed before passage in ERISA. In the area of health benefits, where the statute creates few federal rights but preempts most state law rights, employees often find themselves stripped of most rights. In one case, *McGann v. H and H Music Co.*, 946 F.2d 401, 408 (CAS 1991), an employer amended a health plan to cap benefits for AIDS at $5,000. ERISA preempted state law that would have made the cap illegal but provided no federal remedy for the employee.

The business community also is critical of ERISA, whose complexity and compliance costs dampen employer enthusiasm toward sponsorship of employee benefit plans. This is especially the case with ERISA's tax provisions, which have spawned hundreds of pages of detailed regulation that is often unfathomable except to highly trained experts.

ERISA's tax side has also spawned considerable debate. The Joint Committee on Taxation of Congress estimates that the government loses approximately $100 billion in tax revenue each year because of the favorable tax treatment of pension and profit sharing plans. The orthodox explanation for this tax expenditure—the largest in the federal budget—is that it will produce significant retirement savings for individuals who would not otherwise save adequately for retirement. The tax nondiscrimination rules, which require minimum levels of coverage for rank-and-file employees and benefits roughly proportional to pay, is the statutory vehicle to achieve this end. Yet critics have argued that the nondiscrimination rules are too malleable by plan sponsors who wish to skew benefits to affluent employees and do not result in satisfactory levels of coverage for other employees. Others, however, argue that the nondiscrimination rules are too complex as they now stand and thus discourage sponsors from adopting plans at all (see, e.g., Orszag and Stein 2001).

These disparate lines of criticism reflect a fundamental tension in ERISA: Government regulation is necessary to ensure that private law adequately delivers benefits, but too much regulation diminishes the willingness of employers to sponsor plans at all. If this tension is intractable, the next decades may find the nation moving toward either direct government provision of health and retirement benefits or, alternatively, the abandonment of the notion of providing benefits through regulated, tax-subsidized private plans. (See also DEFINED BENEFIT PENSION PLAN; DEFINED CONTRIBUTION PLAN; EARLY RETIREMENT INCENTIVE PLANS [ERIPs]; EMPLOYEE BENEFITS IN THE UNITED STATES; EMPLOYEE STOCK OWNERSHIP PLANS [ESOPs]; PENSION PLANS.)

Organizations

Employee Benefit Research Institute
Pension Rights Center

References

American Bar Association, Section of Business Law. 1994. *ERISA Basics: A Two-Part Primer on ERISA Issues: An ABA Satellite Seminar*. Chicago: American Bar Association.

Kennedy, Kathryn J. 1991. "Judicial Standard of Review in ERISA Benefit Claims Cases." *American University Law Review* 50: 1083.

Orszag, Peter, and Norman Stein. 2001. "Cross-Tested Defined Contribution Plans: A Response to Professor Zelinsky." *Buffalo Law Review* 49: 629.

Salisbury, Dallas L., and Nora Super Jones, eds. 1994. *Pension Funding and Taxation: Implications for Tomorrow*. Washington, DC: Employee Benefit Research Institute.

Stein, Norman. 1993. "ERISA and the Limits of Equity." *Law & Contemporary Problems* 56: 71.

U.S. Congress. Senate Committee on Labor and Human Resources. 1994. *Recent Court Decisions Affecting ERISA and Executive Annuities*. Washington, DC: GPO.

Norman Stein

EMPLOYEE STOCK OWNERSHIP PLANS (ESOPs), an employee benefit plan that is qualified for tax-favored treatment under Section 401(a) of the Internal Revenue Code of 1986, as amended (the "Code"). A plan is qualified under Section 401(a) of the Code if it complies with various participation, vesting, distribution, and other rules established by the Code to protect the interests of employees. An ESOP is a type of deferred compensation plan that invests primarily in stock of the corporation that sponsors the ESOP, as further described in Section 4975(e)(7) of the Code and the applicable regulations thereunder. An ESOP also must comply with various reporting and disclosure requirements and fiduciary responsibility rules of the Employee Retirement Income Security Act (ERISA) of 1974, as amended.

An ESOP is a "defined contribution plan" because the employer's contribution is defined and the employee's benefit is variable. Each participating employee's account is credited with a certain number of shares of company stock and/or cash or other assets over the period of his or her employment. Upon retirement, death, disability, or other termination of service (after partial or full vesting), the employee's account is distributed to him or her (or to his or her beneficiary) in shares of company stock, in cash or a combination of both. The actual dollar amount of the vested benefit to be distributed to the employee is determined by applying the current fair market value of the company stock in his or her account to the number of shares of company stock in such account. The employer also may distribute the employee's account balance in six substantially equal annual installments of company stock and/or cash, or a combination of both, over a five-year period, in which case the actual dollar amount of the vested benefit to be distributed to the employee will vary from year to year based upon the fair market value of company stock. Furthermore, the employer may decide to distribute an employee's vested account balance in one lump sum in the form of company stock, and then the employer or the ESOP trust may repurchase the company stock with a secured promissory note that is adequately secured, bears a reasonable rate of interest, and is payable over a five-year period of time. An employee's benefit, thus, is not defined—as with a defined benefit pension plan—but is dependent upon the fair market value of his company stock.

What Do Employees Receive from an ESOP?

All assets (company stock and other investments) held by an ESOP trust are allocated each plan year to the accounts of all employee participants in the ESOP by a formula usually based on the proportion of an employee's salary to total covered payroll. The ESOP trust's assets are held in an ESOP trust established under a written trust agreement between the employer and the trustee(s) and administered by a board of trustees and/or administrative committee (consisting of employees and/or other individuals) responsible for protecting the interests of employees and their beneficiaries. The ESOP trust sometimes is administered by an institutional trustee.

An employee is not taxed on contributions to his or her ESOP account (or income earned in that account) until the employee's benefits are actually received. Even then, "rollovers" (into an individual retirement account [IRA], for example) or special averaging methods can defer or reduce the income tax consequences of distributions.

An ESOP, like most employee benefit plans, is generally designed to benefit employees who remain with the employer the longest and contribute most to the employer's success. Therefore, an employee's ownership interest in company stock and other assets held in the ESOP trust usually is based on the number of years of employment and amount of compensation. The employee's ownership interest in the ESOP is called his or her "vested benefit," and the provisions that determine the employee's vested benefit are called the "vesting schedule." Although there are various vesting schedules that may be used (extending for periods up to seven years), most are designed so that the longer the employee stays with the employer, the greater his or her vested benefit becomes.

If an employee terminates employment for any reason other than retirement, death, or disability, his or her vested benefit under the ESOP will be determined by referring to the vesting schedule. All company stock (and other assets) in which the employee does not have a vested benefit (because he or she has not worked long enough) will be treated as a forfeiture, which is allocated among the ESOP accounts of the remaining ESOP participants on the same basis as employer contributions. If an employee retires (e.g., at age 65), dies, or becomes totally and permanently disabled, he or she usually will be 100% vested in his or her entire ESOP account balances.

After an employee's participation in the ESOP ends, the employee (or beneficiary) is eligible to receive a distribution of the vested benefit. There are many permissible times and methods for making this distribution. For example, it may be made as soon as possible after an employee's termination of employment, or it may be deferred for a period of up to six years following the plan year in which the employee's employment terminates. Distribution of a former employee's vested benefit must, however, start in the plan year following retirement, total and permanent disability, or death. Distribution may be made in a lump sum or in installments over a period of up to five years (six installments). In a closely held company, distributions are usually made in the form of cash or in shares of company stock that may be sold back to the employer.

How Does an ESOP Benefit Employers?

As a technique of corporate finance, the ESOP can be used to raise new equity capital, to refinance outstanding debt, or to acquire productive assets through leverage with third-party lenders. Because contributions to an ESOP trust are fully tax deductible (within certain limits), an employer can fund both the principal and the interest payments on an ESOP trust's debt service obligations with pretax dollars. Furthermore, an employer that implements an ESOP and combines the ESOP with a broad-based employee ownership culture will likely experience productivity and profitability improvements relative to similarly situated employers that do not do the same. Empirical evidence strongly supports this conclusion.

Federal Income Tax Consequences of an ESOP for the Employer

Employer contributions to an ESOP trust are tax deductible within the limitations of the Code. An employer may contribute to an ESOP trust and deduct up to 25% of covered payroll for each taxable year (provided, however, that such contributions may be allocated to ESOP participants' accounts for the ESOP's corresponding plan year). If the ESOP trust has borrowed and is leveraged, the employer may increase contributions beyond the 25% level to the extent that the excess is used to pay the ESOP trust's interest expense (and the employer is a C corporation). Furthermore, reasonable cash dividends paid on company stock held by an ESOP trust are deductible if applied to the repayment of the ESOP trust's debt or if currently distributed in cash to ESOP participants. Under Section 415 of the Code, the annual additions that may be allocated to the account of an individual ESOP participant each plan year normally may not exceed the lesser of 100% of his or her covered compensation or $40,000 (for plan years beginning on or after January 1, 2002). The annual additions include employer contributions, any employee contributions, and certain forfeitures that are allocated to the employee's account, although contributions used to pay loan interest will usually not be considered annual additions (for C corporations and provided that not more than one-third of employer contributions are allocated to the accounts of highly compensated employees [as defined in Section 414(q) of the Code]).

In a C corporation ESOP, contributions to the ESOP that are used to pay the interest on the ESOP trust's loan from the corporation are fully tax deductible, and they are not included in the 25% contribution limit so long as not more than one-third of the contributions are allocated to the accounts of "highly compensated employees." In a C corporation, reasonable cash dividends on ESOP trust-held company stock also are deductible and not included in the 25% contribution limit if they are passed through directly to ESOP participants, are used to repay a leveraged ESOP trust's loan within the plan/fiscal year of deduction, or are reinvested in company stock at the direction of participants instead of being passed through to them.

In S corporations, distributions on ESOP trust-held company stock are not deductible and may be used to repay an ESOP trust's loan if they are paid on shares of company stock that have not been allocated to ESOP participants' accounts—provided, however, that there is an exception to this rule with respect to distributions of earnings from the company's accumulated adjustments account or accumulated earnings and profits. In no event, however, may distributions of earnings to an S corporation ESOP be passed through to ESOP participants. To the extent that such distributions of earnings are not or may not be used to repay an ESOP trust's loan, they may be used for ESOP distribution purposes.

Under current law, as enacted in 1997 for years beginning on or after January 1, 1998, S corporation ESOPs are exempt from the unrelated business income tax (UBIT); thus, if an ESOP trust owns all of an S corporation, no current tax is imposed on the corporation's income. (That income is eventually taxed because ESOP participants in S corporations are taxed on ESOP trust distributions, as are C corporation ESOP participants.) The Economic Growth and Tax Relief Reconciliation Act of 2001 (the "2001 Act"), which President George Bush signed into law on June 7, 2001, restricts the abuse of this provision by plans designed to benefit only a small number of employees, whether in a very small company or where a small number of employees try to set up an S corporation ESOP just for their own benefit while operating a larger company whose employees are not participants in the ESOP.

The ESOP community of not-for-profit organizations, companies, professionals, and consultants strongly supported the antiabuse S corporation restriction in the Act. In fact, the 2001 Act, which includes H.R. 10 and S. 742, the Portman-Cardin and Grassley-Baucus bills, is landmark legislation for ESOPs, and no prior legislation in U.S. history has been as positive for retirement plans governed by ERISA, including ESOPs. The 1984 and 1986 tax bills, under the guidance of former Senator Russell Long (the first and possibly the strongest-ever ESOP advocate in Congress) and the National Center for Employee Ownership's executive director Corey Rosen, among many others, included the most advantageous specific ESOP legislation ever passed. Those bills, however, included many cutbacks in retirement plan incentives for defined contribution plans in general.

The 2001 Act also includes the first expansion of an ESOP tax incentive for a C corporation (expansion of the deduction for reinvested dividends paid on company stock held by an ESOP trust) enacted by Congress in 15 years. The 2001 Act solidifies the legislative environment for S corporation ESOPs, will help ensure this significant tax incentive for ESOPs, and will make them attractive to a growing number of corporations. This legislation also makes funding defined contribution plans more flexible and attractive to employers and permits substantially more dollars to be added to rank-and-file employees' retirement plan accounts.

Tax Benefits to Selling Shareholders

ESOPs provide a significant tax incentive for a shareholder of a closely held C corporation who plans to sell his or her company and retire. An ESOP trust provides a market for the stock of such a closely held company. Section 1042 of the Code provides a special tax incentive for certain sales of company stock to an ESOP trust, subject to satisfying a number of specific rules. Thus, a shareholder of a closely held C corporation may be able to sell company stock to an ESOP trust, reinvest the proceeds in other debt or equity securities of publicly traded or closely held domestic operating corporations, and defer taxation of any capital gain resulting from the sale. As a result, the retiring shareholder can derive substantial financial security and liquidity for purposes of retirement. Because the tax liability from the sale is merely deferred, however, the shareholder's subsequent sale of the securities purchased with the proceeds from the sale to the ESOP trust will trigger a recapture of the deferred tax. If such securities flow through an estate, the step-up in basis that occurs will help the shareholder and his or her heirs avoid the tax permanently.

The tax deferral has one downside that many selling shareholders focus on in that a subsequent sale of the replacement debt or equity securities will trigger the tax that had been deferred by the sale to the ESOP trust. To address this problem, an investment alternative has been developed and carefully refined in recent years—an innovative security known as an "ESOP Note."

ESOP Notes are publicly registered securities, issued by highly rated companies such as United Parcel Service, AIG, DuPont, and General Electric Capital Corporation. Morgan Stanley Dean Witter, PaineWebber, Merrill Lynch, Wachovia Securities, and other investment advisory firms have helped bring to market a number of similar securities in recent years. These ESOP Notes often have a maturity of 40 to 60 or more years and bear a floating-rate coupon indexed to 30-day commercial paper, LIBOR, or some other floating-rate index. These securities also normally have call protection for 30 to 50 years. ESOP Notes can be margined (without recourse) up to 90% or more of their market value, if properly structured, allowing investors access to a substantial portion of their initial sale proceeds to create an actively managed portfolio without triggering any tax liability on the part of the selling shareholder. The borrowing cost is usually the broker call loan rate (or, in recent years, a much better negotiated rate with institutional lenders such as Bankers Trust) plus a spread (in larger transactions, 50 basis points or lower), which is greatly offset by the income earned on the ESOP Notes. There are a number of traps for selling shareholders who do not properly structure their reinvestments in these securities, so caution and due diligence are warranted.

Voting Rights

In a closely held corporation, unless otherwise determined by the board of directors, employees have voting rights on allocated shares of company stock only with respect to certain major corporate issues, such as merger, certain sales or liquidation of the corporation, and recapitalizations that require the vote of the corporation's shareholders. On other matters, shares of company stock held by the ESOP trust are usually voted in the best interests of the ESOP's participants by the ESOP's board of trustees or administrative committee that has been appointed by the corporation's board of directors to administer the ESOP. Furthermore, unallocated shares of company stock and uninstructed shares of company stock (allocated shares for which the board of trustees or administrative committee do not receive instructions) are normally voted by the ESOP's board of trustees or administrative committee.

Diversification

Unlike other qualified retirement plans, which typically diversify their holdings by investing in various assets, an ESOP trust, by law, must invest primarily in the company stock of the corporation that sponsors the ESOP. Because ESOP trusts must invest in the company stock of such a corporation, there is a higher risk for the employee. Nonetheless, employees approaching retirement age qualify for a limited exception, which permits diversification of their ESOP accounts. Participants who are at least age 55 and have completed at least 10 years of participation in the ESOP (in which they have received allocations in each of 10 plan years) are eligible to make annual elections over a period of 5 years to diversify 25% of their ESOP stock account balance (on an aggregate basis) and at the end of the sixth year to make a final election to diversify up to 50% (again, on an aggregate basis). This does not apply, however, to certain "de minimis" amounts in participants' ESOP accounts.

To meet the diversification requirement, the ESOP must offer at least three investment options other than company stock. Alternatively, the ESOP may satisfy the diversification requirement by distributing to the participant the portion of the account balance that the participant elected to diversify or by allowing a transfer to another plan.

The diversification rules are applicable only with respect to stock acquired by the ESOP trust after December 31, 1986. The ESOP may permit diversification of company stock acquired before that date and may permit diversification of a greater percentage of the participant's ESOP account balance.

Intangible Benefits of an ESOP

For the retiring employee or the selling shareholder, the financial and tax benefits may not be the only important aspects of an ESOP. The retiring employee may derive great satisfaction from receiving evidence (in the form of monetary rewards) of ownership in a company that he or she helped build. The selling shareholder may feel more at ease by placing company stock in the "friendlier" and certainly more familiar hands of the employees. These intangible elements may prove to be as rewarding to the retiring employee and/or selling shareholder as the financial security ESOPs may provide. (See also ASSET ALLOCATION AFTER RETIREMENT; EMPLOYEE RETIREMENT INCOME SECURITY ACT [ERISA]; EQUITY SECURITIES; INFLUENCES ON RETIREMENT INVESTMENT DECISIONS; PROFIT SHARING PLANS.)

Organizations

ESOP Association
National Center for Employee Ownership

References

Howitt, Idelle A. 2001. *Employee Stock Ownership Plan Answer Book.* New York: Aspen Publishers.

Little, Kenneth E. 2000. *Ten Minute Guide: Employee Stock Option Purchase Plans (10 Minute Guides)*. Indianapolis, IN: Macmillan USA.

National Center for Employee Ownership. 1993. *How Small Is Too Small for an ESOP?* Oakland, CA: Author.

National Center for Employee Ownership. 1994. *Employee Ownership Fact Sheet*. Oakland, CA: Author.

Rodrick, Scott, ed. 1999. *Employee Stock Ownership Plans: A Practical Guide to ESOPs and Other Broad Ownership Programs: 2000 Edition*. Orlando, FL: Harcourt Brace.

Rosen, Corey, and Michael Quarrey. 1987. "How Well Is Employee Ownership Working?" *Harvard Business Review* (September–October).

David R. Johanson

EMPLOYER-SPONSORED LONG-TERM CARE INSURANCE, insurance provided as an employee benefit to cover the potentially catastrophic financial impact of an illness or period of frailty where long-term care is required. The market for long-term care insurance exploded during the 1990s and has continued to grow throughout the early portion of the twenty-first century. This market has two key segments: one for individual policies and the other for employer-sponsored and other group products. Sales of employer-sponsored long-term care policies generated premiums of nearly $55 million in the year 2001 according to LIMRA International, while in-force premiums collected posted an increase of 16% (LIMRA International 2002). The number of new employer-sponsored groups grew 10% in the same year, while the average size of these groups declined from 168 participants in 2000 to 147 in 2001, indicating a move toward offering long-term care insurance in the small employer market.

What factors account for growing interest in the employer-sponsored long-term care insurance market? Legislative changes such as the passage of the Health Insurance Portability and Accountability Act (HIPAA) of 1996, which defined tax-qualified long-term care policies, and the Federal Long-Term Care Security Act of 2000, which initiated the sponsorship of long-term care benefits for federal employees, the military, and their families, created market opportunities for employer-sponsored products. Growing awareness of the aging of the U.S. population, as well as increasing numbers of employees with eldercare responsibilities, has also elevated awareness, understanding, and interest in insurance products that could alleviate their financial pressures and facilitate payment for quality long-term care services. A MetLife study found that caregiving by employees impacts employers' bottom line: Informal caregiving costs U.S. employers between $11.4 billion and $29 billion a year due to lowered productivity (MetLife 2001).

Group long-term care insurance has evolved from its early form as nursing home insurance into current policies capable of meeting a variety of consumers' needs. Policies can be explained in terms of eligibility, plan design, and administrative components. Active employees and their spouses, parents and parents-in-law, and retirees and their spouses typically are eligible for coverage; some groups like the federal government plan extend benefits to adult children of employees. Most group long-term care insurance is offered on a voluntary, employee-pay-all basis and is fully portable, and the majority of policies are HIPAA tax qualified, paid through payroll deduction. A key aspect of today's product is that in most plans actively-at-work employees can enroll without medical underwriting, that is, on a guaranteed issue basis, during their initial eligibility period (either when the plan is first offered or as they are newly hired). Family members may be subject to medical exams, although spouses of active employees may go through a simple interview to determine that they have no immediate long-term care needs. Waiting periods for benefits, or an elimination period, are typical and can range from 30 to 180 days.

An employee is typically presented with one of two types of long-term care policies by their employer: one that is a reimbursement model (pays for services covered in the policy after they are delivered) or an integrated policy with "pooled benefits" (policyholders can use the dollars paid for any type of long-term care service that they feel is appropriate). Policies are subject to satisfaction of benefit triggers, which are usually two or three out of five limitations in "activities of daily living" (limits in ability to bathe, dress, transfer, toilet, and eat) or the presence of cognitive deficits such as Alzheimer's or related dementia. Today's policies offer a rich array of benefits coverage for nursing home services, home care (both skilled and custodial), and nursing home alternatives such as assisted living, board and care homes, and adult day care centers. Some plans cover respite and hospice care, and many offer an alternate care benefit, which is designed to provide reimbursement for services of providers not covered by the policy when it may be required by the consumer. Other common benefits are case management services, homemaker or chore services, bed reservation reimbursements, durable medical equipment coverage, home-delivered meals, spousal discounts, survivorship benefits, restoration of benefits, and caregiver training. The range of benefits offered depends on the plan desired by the employer, as well as the needs of the employee population (McSweeney 2002). Benefits may also be supplemented by certain consumer protection benefits, such as inflation protection (adjusts benefits by a fixed percentage in any given year) or non-forfeiture options (employees receive a certain portion of premiums back if they decide to terminate the policy). Other policy models coordinate long-term care insurance with other benefits, such as life insurance or long-term disability coverage. Premium or rate guarantees to protect employees from future increases may also be negotiated by employers for these policies (McSweeney 2002).

Who purchases employer-sponsored long-term care insurance? According to surveys by the Health Insurance Association of America, the average purchaser is age 43, well educated, has more income, plans for the future, and chose to participate in the plan because of employer sponsorship. A survey of 93 large employers conducted by the Lewin Group found that employees enroll in long-term care plans when education and communication about the benefit is clear and when senior management is actively involved in the process (Lutzky, Corea, and Alecxih 2000).

What is the future outlook for employer-sponsored long-term care insurance? According to the 2001 *MetLife Study of Employee Benefit Trends*, 90% of employers surveyed will be introducing a wide array of new work/life benefits, and long-term care insurance is the fastest growing offering in the near term, with 12% of employers expected to add this option within the next 18 months (MetLife 2001). Senior management "championship" of the benefit and comprehensive preenrollment education campaign on the value of long-term care insurance are also key indicators for a successful plan enrollment. While long-term care insurance cannot be offered as part of a flexible benefits program in the workplace, passage of pending legislation in Washington as well as state initiatives to offer tax credits and ultimately full deductibility of long-term care premiums for the consumer will open the market considerably for this employer benefit. (See also EMPLOYEE BENEFITS IN THE UNITED STATES; FRAILTY PLANNING; HEALTH BENEFITS; LIFE PLANNING; LONG-TERM CARE INSURANCE: INDIVIDUAL DISABILITY-ESCALATING ANNUITIES [IDEAs]; LONG-TERM CARE INSURANCE, PRIVATE.)

Suggested Reading

Gajda, Anthony, and Morris Snow. 2001. "Long-Term Care." In *Handbook of Employee Benefits*, ed. Jerry S. Rosenbloom. 5th ed. New York: McGraw-Hill.

References

Coronel, Susan. 2001. "LTC Insurance in the Workplace: A Study of Why Employers Choose to Enroll or Not to Enroll in Long-Term Care Plans." Presentation at the 15th Private LTCI Conference, Miami, FL, August.

LIMRA International. 2002. "U.S. Group Long-Term Care Insurance: 2001 Sales and In-Force." Windsor, CT: LIMRA International, June.

Lutzky, Steven, John Corea, and Lisa Alecxih. 2000. *A Survey of Employers Offering Group Long-Term Care Insurance to Their Employees*. Falls Church, VA: Lewin Group.

McSweeney, Mary Helen. 2002. *Long-Term Care: An Emerging Employer Benefit*. Scottsdale, AZ: WorldatWork.

MetLife. 2001. *2001 MetLife Study of Employee Benefit Trends*. New York: MetLife.

Stucki, Barbara. 2001. "LTC Insurance at Work: The Role of Retirement Planning." Presentation at the 15th Private LTCI Conference, Miami, FL, August.

Mary Helen McSweeney

ENTREPRENEURSHIP, the initiation and assumption of the financial risks of a business and its management. The decision to start a business is often complex. Many factors, including the need for achievement, the need for control over one's destiny, the willingness to take risks, the loss of one's job, and other forms of displacement may prompt a person to start his or her own business. While some writers see no link between age and the decision to start a new business, others have found close links. When age is a significant factor, it is often for psychological reasons.

Entrepreneurial opportunities are most likely to be pursued by people with a college education who are in their late thirties and have established careers. Age is relevant to entrepreneurship, and entrepreneurship is important for the aged. Of those who are employed at age 65 or older, 27% are self-employed (Maddox et al. 1985). It is useful to examine the relationship between entrepreneurship and aging through the internal or psychological aspects of a person's decision to become an entrepreneur.

The Entrepreneur and Hero Compared

Joseph Campbell believed that the entrepreneur was the real hero in our society. Although he never systematically compared the entrepreneur and the hero, it is interesting to do so. Heroes and entrepreneurs are called to take part in an adventure that is a simultaneous journey of self-discovery, spiritual growth, and the personal creativity they make possible. An entrepreneur's journey closely resembles the journey of the hero in mythology as outlined in Campbell's book *The Hero with a Thousand Faces* (1968). There is a strong similarity between the journey that entrepreneurs take and the adventure of heroes. Entrepreneurs and heroes also have similar personality traits. Myths describe the universal human desires and conflicts we see played out in the lives of entrepreneurs. Ian MacMillan and Rita Gunther McGrath (*Wall Street Journal* 1992) of the Wharton School's entrepreneurial center found that entrepreneurs, no matter what country they call home, think alike. Campbell found that the basic pattern in the hero's journey is the same in every culture.

Heroes bring change. Campbell (1968) refers to the constant change in the universe as "The Cosmogonic Cycle" that "unrolls the great vision of the creation and destruction of the world which is vouchsafed as revelation to the successful hero." This recalls Joseph Schumpeter's theory of entrepreneurship as creative destruction. A successful entrepreneur simultaneously destroys and creates a new world, a new way of life. Henry Ford destroyed the horse and buggy age while creating the world of the automobile. Campbell's hero finds that the world "suffers from a symbolical deficiency" and "appears on the scene in various forms according to the changing needs of the race." Changing needs and deficiencies correspond to the changing market conditions or the changing desires for products. The entrepreneur is the first person to perceive changing needs. Campbell believed that people become creative when they engage in an activity, pursue a career or entrepreneurial venture, because it is what one loves to do and because it bestows on one a sense of personal importance and fulfillment. It is not the social system that dictates that it be done; rather, the drive comes from within. It is this courageous action that opens up doors and creative possibilities that did not previously exist.

Relationship of the Hero's Journey to Aging

The hero's goal is now to find a purpose in life. Campbell's and Erik Erikson's (1963) heroes are similar, because the hero's journey is a quest for personal identity that can be found in service to others or to society, or in finding and delivering a boon. During the generativity versus stagnation stage, which comes in the second half of life, in Erikson's eight ages of man, people become willing to take risks in order to be creative or make their mark upon society. Generativity involves establishing and guiding the next generation, but it also includes productivity and creativity, which, along with the willingness to take risks, are essential to entrepreneurship. For Campbell, the act of creating involves the willingness to take a risk and cross a boundary into a new domain of ideas. To be unwilling or afraid to do so is to be controlled by what he calls "the elder psychology" or the unwillingness to strike out on one's own and take risks.

The paradox, then, is that although entrepreneurship may be an important path for people to discover themselves and "do something meaningful for society" as they become older, they must resist this "elder psychology," which Campbell believes blocks risk taking, creativity, and entrepreneurship. When a person is able to champion things becoming, he or she can achieve generativity by making a significant and unique contribution to society. If one is able only to maintain the status quo, he or she will stagnate and will remain self-centered and unable to contribute to society. Almost by definition, entrepreneurs are champions of things becoming.

In counseling and advising older adults in the area of entrepreneurial activity, it is useful to keep these insights from mythology and psychology in mind. They deal with the deepest of needs and forces in the human psyche. For an older person contemplating a new business venture, it will be helpful to recognize that it is not just the potential financial gains or losses involved that are important. The entrepreneurial act may be a life-defining and self-defining act, one with deep personal and perhaps even spiritual implications for the individual and his or her relationship with society. Entrepreneurs are often seen as having different attitudes toward risk: What a nonentrepreneur might view as a great financial risk the entrepreneur may see as a cost of learning and adventuring. The venture is an end in itself, more than the profit. People who start new businesses in the second half of life may view risk in this way, because they feel such a strong need to define themselves and contribute to society. The formation of a viable new business may be one of the finest legacies that anyone can create.

The American growth miracle of the 1990s was largely propelled by entrepreneurs and small business. Even with record growth and stock markets, Fortune 500 companies were largely laying off workers during this time, with small business employment needs sharply surpassing the layoffs. Countries around the world such as Germany and Korea went scrambling for ways to emulate this growth and to find fertile ways to foster entrepreneurship for their own economies. Often, this required a radical change from a dependency on industry and its supporting banks, tax structure, and university education to a concerted search by these institutions to find new ways to nurture young businesses and the technologies upon which they seemed to thrive.

In addition to impressive resources in business and entrepreneurship in printed form at your library or from resources such as common-line bookstores, the Internet has become an impressive resource for starting and building a business. Local community colleges and economic development agencies also will often provide free or low-cost courses on forming a business. (See also BABY BOOMERS AND RETIREMENT; BUSINESS SUCCESSION PLANNING; CONSULTING IN RETIREMENT; GROWTH CAPITAL FOR OLDER ENTREPRENEURS; RISK TOLERANCE; WORKING RETIREES.)

References

Campbell, Joseph. 1968. *The Hero with a Thousand Faces*. Princeton, NJ: Princeton University Press.

Erikson, Erik H. 1963. *Childhood and Society*. New York: W.W. Norton.

Ettenberg, Elliott. 2002. *The Next Economy*. New York: McGraw-Hill.

Jung, Carl G. 1956. *Symbols of Transformation*. New York: Harper Torchbooks/Bollingen Library.

Maddox, George L. et al. 1985. *The Encyclopedia of Aging*. New York: Springer.

Nesheim, John L. 2000. *New High Tech Companies*. New York: Free Press.

Rae, David. 2000. *The Entrepreneurial Spirit: Learning to Unlock Value*. New York: Silver Lake Publishing.

Ries, Al. 1996. *Focus*. New York: Harper Business.

Slywotzky, Adrian J. 1996. *Value Migration*. Boston, MA: Harvard Business School Press.

Smith, Richard L., and Janet Kiholm Smith. 2000. *Entrepreneurial Finance*. New York: John Wiley and Sons.

Vinturella, John B. 1998. *Entrepreneur's Fieldbook*. New York: Prentice Hall.

Wall Street Journal. 1992. February 6, A1.

Cyril Morong
Updated by Ronald Peterson

EQUITY SECURITIES represent shares (stock ownership) in a corporation or in certain designated assets of a corporation or other entity. Shares in investment companies (mutual fund shares) are also broadly referred to as equity securities or equity funds when the investment objectives are to own and hold stocks. Two types of equity securities represent ownership in corporations: preferred stock and common stock. The key distinction between these types of stock ownership is the manner and form in which each class of shareholder participates in corporate earnings.

One advantage of these corporate forms of ownership is that shareholders have limited liability from transactions gone wrong in a corporation. Unlike other forms of business ownership such as sole proprietorships or general partnerships, corporate shareholders are shielded from exposure to loss in the event that firms cannot meet financial or other obligations. In unincorporated businesses, owners may be held personally responsible for payment of unsatisfied claims, for example, and creditors may file claims against owners' personal assets: houses, cars, bank accounts. This is not the case for corporate shareholders. While they can experience a complete loss of their investment, corporate shareholders are protected from further personal liability beyond the value of their investment in the stock.

Common Stock

Unlike general partners in a partnership or an owner in a sole proprietorship, stockholders have little or no control over management decisions affecting the corporation or whether and when they will be paid a return on their investment in the company. Shareholders, in sufficient numbers, elect a board of directors to manage the company for them and through the exercise of voting rights affect management's policy decisions. Elections for board of director positions and amendments to corporate charters are typically done at annual shareholders meetings. Although some shareholders choose to vote in person, most shareholders prefer to vote by proxy. A proxy is a power of attorney appointing a specific agent for the specific purpose of voting at the annual meeting.

Shareholders have a preemptive right to purchase new shares of company stock before they are offered for sale to the general public. If a shareholder currently owns 5% of the outstanding stock of a firm, the preemptive right entitles the shareholder to purchase 5% of the new stock issue. This preemptive right allows shareholders to maintain a fixed percentage of ownership in firms if they wish. If not, their ownership in the firm declines, or is "diluted."

Investors in common stock have a residual claim on earnings distributions and receive their income only after all other claims have been satisfied. Income is either paid out in the form of dividend payments or is reinvested in the business as retained earnings. The immediate cash benefit to dividend payouts is obvious; however, shareholders also benefit when firms retain earnings and reinvest them. By reinvesting earnings, research and new projects can be funded, production capacity increased, facilities built or renovated, and other activities undertaken to increase future value of the stock. These investments in the firm can then result directly in new cash dividends or indirectly in future stock value and increased stock prices.

Additionally, by having residual claims on a firm's income, stockholders have residual claims on the firm's assets in the event of liquidation. This means that if a firm goes into bankruptcy and the courts decree that its assets must be liquidated in order to satisfy outstanding claims, then stockholders end up with whatever is left over after all other claims have been satisfied. The residual value is often only a small fraction of the shareholders' initial investment. One of the benefits of stock ownership is that when the market is doing well the potential returns can be large. However, a disadvantage is that when the market is doing poorly, stock returns can be meager (or even negative if the stock price drops significantly).

The return on an investment in common stock can be broken down into two components: dividend yield and capital gain. The dividend yield is calculated by dividing the dividend paid at the end of the period by the stock's price at the beginning of the period. Although firms do not have to pay dividends, the historical trend has been that once a firm sets a level of dividends, then only in cases of extreme financial distress will it reduce the dividend level. Thus firms where a large percentage of the stock return comes from dividend payments (utilities, for example) can be attractive investments for individuals who rely on investment income for their livelihood.

Capital gain is the other component in the return on a stock investment. Capital gain reflects the appreciation in the firm's stock price: If stock is sold for a price that is higher than the purchase price, sellers realize a capital gain on the investment.

Much has been written about whether shareholders prefer to receive their income from dividends or capital gains. One classic theory is the bird-in-hand theory of dividend payments, which stems from the old adage, "A bird in hand is worth two in the bush." This theory states that shareholders prefer firms to pay out their earnings as dividends rather than retain them, because dividends represent income that is paid out as cash now, whereas capital gains (the result of plowing the income back into the firm) may take a long time, if ever, to be realized. Thus, with dividends there is no risk of the shareholders not realizing their income, while with capital gains there is the risk that the stock price will not appreciate once the money has been plowed back into the firm.

Preferred Stock

Like common stockholders, preferred stockholders receive dividends. However, preferred dividends act like rates of interest. They are set at a specific percentage called the dividend rate, and this rate may be fixed or may float with the market.

It is crucial that before making investment decisions, investors carefully gauge what their time horizon is, how much risk they are willing to take, and whether they need the investment income to finance their daily activities. Investors must also be aware that stocks are risky investments and that they may not be an appropriate investment choice for everyone. As discussed above, when firms go bankrupt, a substantial portion of stockholders' initial investments may be lost. It would therefore be advisable for novice investors to seek the advice of certified financial planners before investing a sizable proportion of their wealth in equity securities. (See also AGENTS AND BROKERS; INVESTMENT CLUBS; INVESTOR EDUCATION; MUTUAL FUNDS; REAL ESTATE INVESTMENTS.)

References

Brigham, Eugene F., and Joel F. Houston. 2000. *Fundamentals of Financial Management*. 9th ed. Mason, OH: South-Western.

Haugen, Robert A. 2000. *Modern Investment Theory*. 5th ed. Englewood Cliffs, NJ: Prentice Hall.

Reilly, Frank K. 2002. *Investment Analysis and Portfolio Management*. 7th ed. Mason, OH: South-Western.

Ben J. Sopranzetti

ESTATE PLANNING, the process of accumulating, preserving, protecting, and transferring wealth from one person or generation to another. The estate planning process begins with a review of an individual's short-range and long-range goals and objectives. These goals are synthesized into a lifetime accumulation and transfer plan that sets forth the steps necessary to accomplish those things that are important to the individual.

Every person's goals are different. Some individuals may not be concerned with transferring large amounts of wealth to family members at death, while others may view this as one of their more important objectives. As the income and standard of living for Americans has risen, a new concern has arisen in the estate planning arena—the possibility of leaving too much to one's heirs. Warren Buffet has been credited with a succinct expression of this goal: "I want to leave enough to my children so that they can do anything, but not so much that they can do nothing." For individuals who have accumulated large amounts of wealth, this may be a very real concern that has to be taken into consideration in developing an estate plan.

A common misconception about estate planning is that estate planning is only important for the wealthy. While it is true that wealthy individuals typically have to pay estate taxes to both the state and federal governments, the estate planning process involves much more than tax planning. At its core, estate planning is the process of achieving one's long-range goals by following an action plan designed to get you where you want to be. No matter what your level of net worth, developing an estate plan is important if you have transfer objectives that you wish to achieve, regardless of the presence or absence of an estate tax impact.

Another misconception about estate planning is that the plan only springs into action when someone dies. Every estate plan will have provisions to deal with what should happen upon an individual's death. Well-designed estate plans, however, include lifetime planning options that will help achieve an individual's goals during life while at the same time minimizing adverse consequences at death. Individuals who do not take advantage of lifetime planning opportunities often find that they cannot easily achieve their transfer goals and objectives.

Basic Planning

In its simplest form, an estate plan is an expression of an individual's goals and objectives concerning property.

Some individuals may decide that the best estate plan is to spend (or give away) everything before they die. This is often expressed in common jokes about estate planning, such as, "My estate plan is to have the check to the undertaker bounce" or "I want to spend my last dime on my last day." Using this approach, there is no need to worry about taxes or fighting heirs. This could be dangerous, though, because if the individual lives longer than expected, he or she may run out of money. Alternatively, if the individual dies before he or she intended, excess assets will have to be dealt with. Even when there is no intent to leave assets to others, it is wise to engage in estate planning to ensure that there will be sufficient assets during one's own lifetime and that anything left after death is dealt with appropriately.

When an individual wishes to leave some property to others, estate planning is even more important. How the property is transferred, as well as how much is transferred to each beneficiary, can become important. A basic understanding of these issues is key to participating in the planning process.

Transfer of Property during Lifetime

Property transfers during lifetime can take two primary forms: the transfer can be a gift or it can be a sale.

If property is transferred by gift, the new owner's basis in the property for purposes of calculating gain or loss at the time of subsequent sale is carried over from the donor. An adjustment can be made if gift taxes were paid on the transfer. Each year, up to a certain amount ($11,000 in 2003) of property can be transferred to each of any number of recipients without triggering gift tax liability. One of the best ways to help reduce the size of an individual's estate is to make regular annual exclusion gifts of surplus property to the intended recipients.

In some circumstances, a sale of the property may be a more appropriate planning technique. If the property is sold to a family member, payments can be deferred under an installment note. Unlike the situation with gifts, a sale of the property allows the purchaser to have a basis equal to what he or she paid for the property (which is usually greater than the seller's basis).

Transfer of Property at Death

Property can be transferred in three ways upon an individual's death: (1) through the probate process, (2) by operation of law, or (3) by contract.

The probate process is a court-supervised procedure whereby ownership of property is transferred from the decedent to his or her heirs. Probate is the "catch all" process, since it governs the disposition of all property that does not pass by operation of law or by contract. Typically, the probate process begins shortly after an individual's death when a petition for probate is submitted to the probate court (called surrogate or orphan's court in some states). Once the petition is filed, the opening of the estate is advertised so that creditors can make claims against the estate. The decedent's property is gathered and recorded and, after the payment of debts, final medical expenses, and funeral expenses, distributed to the heirs. If an individual had drafted a will during his or her lifetime, the will governs the distribution of the property. If no will was drafted or no will could be found, default rules found in the state statutes (called the intestacy laws) take over to determine who will receive the property. Generally, the intestacy laws transfer the property to close relatives of the decedent. In the event that there are no close relatives living at the time the individual dies (no family members closer than the cousins of first cousins under the Uniform Probate Code), the property "escheats," or is transferred, to the state in which the decedent was domiciled at death.

The advantages of probate include court supervision of the disposition of property and the ability to settle all debts of the decedent and extinguish debts that were not submitted to the court in a timely manner. Probate can be costly, however. In some states, the court costs, coupled with executor, attorney, and accountant fees, can be as high as 6% of the value of the probate estate. One way to help avoid probate in high-cost states is to use a revocable trust arrangement (see below) in conjunction with a will. Be aware, though, that while use of a revocable trust will avoid probate, it will not exempt property from federal or state estate or inheritance taxes.

Jointly held assets are the classic examples of property that passes by operation of law. Usually, this form of ownership is associated with real estate. For example, a husband and wife may own their residence as joint tenants with right of survivorship, meaning that, upon the death of the first cotenant, the property passes automatically by operation of law to the surviving cotenant. Any two or more people can own property as joint tenants with rights of survivorship, but in some states, a special form of property ownership is available for spouses only—tenants by the entirety. Tenants by the entirety is simply a joint tenancy with right of survivorship that cannot be severed without the consent of both parties. Property that passes by operation of law does so automatically and is not considered to be part of the probate estate.

The last form of property transfer at death is transfer by contract. Property is transferred by contract in arrangements where beneficiary designations are allowed. Classic examples include death benefits on life insurance policies, pension plan accumulations, and Individual Retirement Accounts (IRAs). These assets will pass directly to the named beneficiary and will not be part of the probate estate. An important reason for frequently reviewing your estate plan is to assure that beneficiary designations are still appropriate.

Common Estate Planning Documents

Estate planning documents include all of the arrangements made to manage property during lifetime or at death. A *will* changes the state default rules (intestacy laws) by directing the distribution of the decedent's property to the individuals or institutions named under the terms specified in the will and appoints the person who will manage the estate (the "executor" or "executrix"). It also allows the appointment of a guardian for minor children, which is perhaps one of the most important issues for young families. Due to the changing nature of client goals and objectives, as well as the levels of wealth achieved or remaining, the provisions contained in a will should be reviewed frequently.

Powers of attorney can be created to allow for the management of property or to provide for medical care when an individual is unable to take care of these items himself or herself. *Premarital (prenuptial) agreements* may have the effect of changing state default rules concerning the disposition of property at death and are often used for estate planning purposes in conjunction with other documents.

A *trust* is a contract between a person (the "grantor") and another person or an institution (the "trustee") to hold and manage property for the benefit of one or more beneficiaries. Trusts are characterized by two sets of adjectives: one that describes when the trust is created and another that describes whether the terms of the trust can be changed. First, a trust can be characterized as a "living" ("inter-vivos") trust or a "testamentary" trust. Living or inter-vivos trusts are created during the grantor's lifetime; testamentary trusts are created at the grantor's death. As used here, "created" refers to when the trust becomes effective, not when it was written. Second, a trust is described as revocable if its terms can be changed during the life of the grantor, and irrevocable if they cannot. Revocable living trusts are often used to avoid probate and to provide for asset management in the event of the grantor's disability but are not effective for avoiding death taxes.

Irrevocable living trusts, often funded only with life insurance policies, may trigger gift taxation upon creation but generally will not be included in the estate of the grantor. Testamentary trusts are often used to help manage the federal estate tax liability that will be faced by a married couple.

Federal Gift, Estate, and Generation Skipping Transfer Taxes

When property is transferred during lifetime, gift taxes generally apply. There are several ways to avoid paying gift taxes, however. The first technique involves the direct transfer (i.e., a transfer that does not involve a trust) of property with a value less than the gift tax annual exclusion ($11,000 for 2003). As long as the total amount of direct gifts made to an individual during a year does not exceed the gift tax annual exclusion, no gift tax will be due. In addition to the annual exclusion amount, an individual can pay educational and medical expenses directly to the provider of the services on behalf of another without triggering gift tax liability. Any gifts made in excess of these amounts, or gifts made through trusts that will not qualify for the annual exclusion, will trigger a gift tax liability. That liability is first offset by the gift tax applicable credit amount (the tax calculated on a value of $1 million for gift tax purposes), and any tax due in excess of the credit will need to be paid by the donor.

Estate taxes apply to property transferred at death. Every individual, however, can leave the applicable estate tax credit amount to his or her heirs without triggering federal estate tax. The first $1 million (in 2003) of taxable transfers during lifetime or at death is shielded by the applicable credit amount. In 2003, the applicable credit for gift and estate tax purposes is the same, and the highest marginal estate tax rate is 49%. If property with a greater value is transferred at death, it will be subject to estate tax. Pursuant to the 2001 Tax Act (Economic Growth and Tax Relict Reconciliation Act [EGTRRA] 2001), beginning in 2004 an individual can leave up to $1.5 million estate tax free at death. Note that this differs (by $500,000) from the amount that can be transferred during lifetime under the applicable gift tax credit.

Any amount that is given to a spouse or to a qualified charity during lifetime or at death will not be subject to either gift tax or estate tax. These are referred to as the Marital and Charitable Deductions for Gift and Estate Tax purposes. Charitable giving is often an important estate planning tool and should not be overlooked in planning the estate. Caution should be exercised in giving too much to a spouse, however. Recall that every person can leave the applicable estate tax credit amount to his or her heirs without triggering a federal estate tax. For example, in a typical situation where a married couple has "I love you wills" (i.e., a will that leaves everything to the surviving spouse), the benefit of the applicable credit of the first spouse to die will be lost. If, instead, the first spouse to die created a trust (called a credit shelter trust) funded with their remaining applicable estate tax credit amount, the assets in the trust will not be included later in the surviving spouse's estate for tax purposes even if the surviving spouse is a beneficiary of the trust. The remainder beneficiaries (usually children) would receive the amounts in the credit shelter trust, plus the surviving spouse's applicable estate tax credit amount, estate tax free at the death of the surviving spouse.

The generation skipping transfer tax applies whenever property is transferred to a "skip person." A skip person is someone more than one generation below the transferor. There are many issues that need to be considered for generation skipping transfer tax planning, and a full discussion is beyond the scope of this entry. Some basic rules regarding the generation skipping tax are important to know, however. Gifts that qualify for the gift tax annual exclusion are exempt from the generation skipping transfer tax. In addition, any payments for medical and educational expenses of another person made directly to the provider of those services will not trigger the generation skipping transfer tax. Finally, each individual has a lifetime exemption ($1.12 million in 2003) that is sometimes automatically allocated to generation skipping transfers. If the exemption is not automatically allocated pursuant to the code, the transferor can allocate a portion of the exemption by filing a notice of allocation with his or her gift tax return. The exemption amount for generation skipping transfer tax purposes will equal the applicable estate tax credit amount beginning in 2004 ($1.5 million).

Asset Protection

Even if taxes are not an issue, a good estate plan will take steps to protect an individual's assets from the claims of judgment creditors and outside parties. While a full discussion of this topic is beyond the scope of this entry, it is important to note that the purpose of asset protection is not to defraud legitimate creditors but rather to protect assets against future claims. If Congress permanently repeals the estate tax (the current repeal sunsets, or disappears, on January 1, 2011), asset protection planning as part of the estate planning process will be even more important.

Asset protection is especially important if assets are being left to a child who may be subject to malpractice claims (physicians, attorneys, accountants, etc.). If an outright bequest is made to the child, those assets are available to a judgment creditor. If, however, the assets are left in a trust that benefits the child and has a strong spendthrift provision, it is unlikely that the child's creditors will be able to access the funds.

At a sophisticated planning level, asset protection techniques can be employed to protect property (and future family members who benefit from that property) from additional transfer taxes. In the normal course of events, an individual will die, leaving assets to the children. If the children haven't spent or consumed the assets prior to their deaths, the assets will be taxed again when they are transferred to the grandchildren. Using this approach, transfer taxes are due at the death of each generation of family members. Use of a so-called Dynasty Trust (a perpetual trust that allows beneficiaries to use assets but not own them) can prevent successive transfer taxes from continuously eroding the value of family assets. Dynasty Trusts must be set up in states that have abolished the rule against perpetuities and require special planning and expert advice.

Cash Needs at Death

When an individual dies, death taxes are due, debts must be paid, medical expenses and funeral expenses must be paid, and there must be some money for the surviving family members to continue to make ends meet. As a result, liquidity planning is very important and should always be considered in estate planning. This is particularly true if an individual holds illiquid assets, such as real estate or business interests. These types of assets are often difficult to liquidate and can cause a liquidity crisis for the estate.

One of the best ways to fund cash needs at death is through the use of life insurance. The proceeds become available at the time when they are needed and can prevent the need to sell illiquid assets to cover estate costs and taxes. There are many types of life insurance, and the best product to use is often determined by the circumstances facing the individual. As a rule of thumb, however, if the life insurance is intended to be in force for ten years or more, it is better to use permanent life insurance contracts (whole life, universal life, variable life, or variable universal life) than term insurance policies.

Charitable Estate Planning

During lifetime and at death, charitable planning is a powerful estate planning tool. Gifts to charities do not result in the imposition of any transfer tax (gift, estate, or generation skipping). Furthermore, giving to charities can help an individual perpetuate those activities he or she feels are important, even after death.

In some circumstances, a gift to charity can be made that benefits the donor. For example, a gift of a remainder interest in a personal residence or farm will generate an immediate income tax deduction for the donor and relieve his or her estate of the costs associated with disposing of the property after death, although it will deny surviving family members enjoyment of the property. Another example would be the contribution of appreciated property to a charitable remainder trust where the donor receives an income stream for a period of time, followed by a transfer of the remainder interest to a charity. *Charitable lead trusts* can be used to reduce estate tax liability as long as an individual is willing to defer the heirs' receipt of the property. At death, a charitable lead trust could be created that would pay an income stream to a charity for a period of years, following which the remainder interest reverts to family members. Only the value of the remainder interest would be taxed for estate tax purposes. This is the technique that Jacqueline Kennedy Onasis planned to use in her estate, which would have removed 98.6% of the value of her estate from estate taxation. Her children, however, decided to forgo the use of the charitable lead trust and take the property directly from the estate, resulting in a large estate tax liability—and illustrating the point that estate planning is about much more than tax savings.

Summary

Everyone should consider estate planning and review estate plans frequently. Estates big and small can benefit from the process. The currently scheduled elimination of the estate tax does not eliminate the need for estate planning but rather emphasizes it. Estate planning is an individually tailored process that looks at the long-term goals of an individual and creates an action plan that can be followed to achieve those goals. Taxes are important to consider but should not be the tail that wags the dog. Considering the tax impact of various estate planning options in conjunction with the long-range goals of an individual may, however, make attainment of the individual's goals more likely.

In developing an estate plan, a team approach works best. Involving the financial planner, attorney, accountant, insurance agent, trust officers, investment advisors, and any other individuals regularly involved in managing the financial affairs of the client often leads to a more attainable, well-rounded estate plan than a plan developed by any one advisor. (See also CHARITABLE CONTRIBUTIONS; ELDER LAW PRACTICE; INHERITANCE; INTERGENERATIONAL CONFLICT AND FINANCIAL ISSUES; TRUSTS; WILLS.)

References

Fontaine, Constance J., ed. 2002. *Fundamentals of Estate Planning*. 6th ed. Bryn Mawr, PA: American College.

Leimberg, Stephan R., Jerry A. Kasner, Stephen N. Kandell, Ralph Gano Miller, et al. 2002. *Tools and Techniques of Estate Planning*. 12th ed. Upper Saddle River, NJ: Prentice Hall.

Thomas P. Langdon

ESTATE TAXES. See Capital Gain; Charitable Contributions; Elder Law Practice; Estate Planning; Inheritance; Wealth Span.

ETHICAL WILL, a method for recording and sharing values, hopes, life lessons, and other personal messages with family and community members.

It is estimated that over the next 20 years more than $6 trillion will pass from one generation to another. This enormous transfer of wealth is likely to occur with little regard for how, and for what purpose, these assets were accumulated or the meaning they represent. Sixty percent (60%) of individuals engage in charitable giving during their lives, yet only 6% bequeath assets to charitable causes after death. How might these assets be leveraged to perpetuate the values of the giver(s) and to improve society?

An ethical will helps answer this question by clarifying one's values and communicating one's life's purpose and meaning to those who survive us. It is both a practical and spiritual tool to use at any stage of life with particular relevance to anyone interested in creating an estate plan or financial plan that perpetuates ideals for generations to come.

What Is an Ethical Will?

People typically write a last will and testament to provide for the distribution of their material assets. Others write living wills, or advance directives, to provide instructions for end-of-life medical treatment in the event of incapacity. Today, an increasing number of people are exploring ways to preserve a different type of legacy, their personal values, for future generations. Ethical wills are a way to share values, hopes, desires, and life lessons with loved ones. An ethical will can also incorporate meaning into a financial or estate plan for the writer.

Historical Context

The tradition of ethical wills is not new. The Hebrew Bible first described ethical wills, and the last testament of Jacob, Genesis, chapter 49, is generally regarded as the first ethical will. They were originally associated with a person's final days of life and were transmitted orally on subjects that included blessings, instructions, advice, and funeral arrangements. There are many examples of this tradition in the Hebrew and Christian Bibles (Deuteronomy, chapters 32–33, and John, chapters 15–18, as additional examples). Over the centuries they became written documents and often were attached to or placed with legal wills (even though they were not considered a legal document).

Classifying these documents as "ethical literature" is reasonable based on their contents and subject matter. However, there is a sharp distinction between ethical wills, which are much more practical in tone, and other modern ethical writings that tend to be more theoretical in nature.

During the past five to ten years, the tradition of creating ethical wills has been experiencing a period of rediscovery and revival. This seems likely to be due to the combination of large numbers of baby boomers entering middle age, the aging of their parents, and a realization that there is more to life than just accumulated assets. At present, ethical wills are more likely to be written at transitional life stages and are usually shared with loved ones while the author is still alive. They are also being written to be used as a foundation for estate planning. Ethical wills can be valuable in articulating the most appropriate financial planning options that leverage the writer's philosophical and spiritual legacy.

Why Write an Ethical Will?

Everyone discovers his or her own motivations for creating an ethical will. This is a partial list of reasons shared by those who have written ethical wills:

- To be remembered for what the person believes and stands for
- To try to insure the continuation of one's values for future generations
- To leave a legacy that is more than material goods or money
- To provide a sense of completion and closure

When to Write an Ethical Will

People will most often be attracted to this idea at turning points and transitions in their lives such as a significant illness, the loss of a loved one, the birth of a child or grandchild, marriage, financial and estate planning, approaching the end of life.

Relevance to Estate Planning

The complexity of estate planning, charitable giving options, and estate tax laws requires a better understanding of one's values in order to consider the most appropriate investment alternatives and strategies. For individuals, and the estate planning professionals with whom they work in collaboration, there will be many opportunities to consider the role of ethical wills in their estate planning. The following are two examples that illustrate the complementary nature of estate planning and ethical wills.

Example 1. A childless couple, both of whom received their Ph.D.s, wanted to bequeath equal portions of their estate to their nieces and nephews. Their planner introduced the concept of ethical wills and encouraged them to complete one before finalizing their plans.

The couple identified the importance of education as a driving value in their lives and quickly agreed on the importance of education for future generations of their families. Consequently, they set up a "memorial trust fund" that would allow current and future family members to apply for and obtain funds to support higher educational pursuits. They did this in addition to leaving individual bequests. They felt they did something very meaningful and significant for themselves and "made an important statement about what they stood for."

Example 2. An attorney encouraged a successful businessman and his spouse to create an ethical will as a means of discovering the couple's important values and to assist the attorney in identifying appropriate estate planning alternatives. Charitable giving and the importance of the family emerged as two high-priority areas. A charitable family foundation was established whereby family members were named as board members of the foundation. Yearly meetings of "the Board" were held at which time family members selected recipients of the charitable gifts from the foundation. This yearly philanthropic activity was designed to convey the importance and responsibility of this family to support institutions that strove to make the world a better place. "The Board" also had the opportunity to get together at least once a year as a family in a setting that allowed for both work and relaxation. (See also ESTATE PLANNING; FINANCIAL PLANNING PROCESS; HEALTH AND LONGEVITY; INHERITANCE; LIFE PLANNING; WILLS.)

Organization

The Legacy Center

Suggested Readings

Albom, Mitch. 1997. *Tuesdays with Morrie*. New York: Doubleday.

Ethical Wills. Available online at http://www.ethicalwill.com. More than 20 modern ethical wills are posted on the only Web site dedicated to the topic of ethical wills.

Remen, Rachel Naomi. 1996. *Kitchen Table Wisdom*. New York: Riverhead Books.

Riemer, Jack, and Nathaniel Stampfer. 1991. *So That Your Values Live On: Ethical Wills and How to Prepare Them*. Woodstock, VT: Jewish Lights Publishing.

Schacther-Shalomi, Zalman, and Ronald Miller. 1997. *From Age-ing to Sage-ing*. Victoria, Australia: Warner Books.

References

Baines, Barry K. 1999. "A Biblical Concept in Estate Planning." *Journal of Retirement Planning* (May–June): 44–49.

Baines, Barry K. 2002. *Ethical Wills: Putting Your Values on Paper*. Cambridge, MA: Perseus Publishing.

Gambone, James V. 2001. *Retirement: A Boomer's Guide to Life after 50*. Minneapolis, MN: Kirk House Publishers.

Barry K. Baines

ETHICS IN FINANCIAL PLANNING, standards or imperatives in dealing with finances in the lives of older adults. Ethical dilemmas range from questions of professional practice to issues of social responsibility and public policy. The published ethical standards of the financial planning industry provide the groundwork for an analysis of principles and rules to help clarify and distinguish acceptable from unacceptable conduct. Many issues remain to be addressed, however, as the field of financial gerontology emerges and matures, and all professionals or entities acting as financial advisors to older persons must grapple with these principles and issues.

Professional Financial Planning

The Financial Planning Association (FPA) and the American Institute of Certified Public Accountants (AICPA) have ethical standards, which are codified. Several of the canons of the FPA are quite straightforward, such as the injunction to put public interest above private gain or the imperative to improve professional skills and knowledge. Other imperatives in the canon seem more obscure; for example, the provision encouraging obedience to the law in order to "avoid conduct or activity which would cause unjust harm" to those relying on financial planners.

Unfortunately, the canons of some associations avoid the most serious dilemmas of financial planning: the need to avoid conflict of interest in giving advice; the requirement for truth-telling and disclosure of options and the level of risk; or the balance between paternalism and autonomy in financial decision making. On the other hand, the ethical standards of the AICPA require that certified public accountants (CPAs) not engage in activities that result in a conflict of interest, "in fact or in appearance." Yet in the majority of states CPAs can legally (and ethically) accept commissions for selling or providing financial products and services to older clients in many situations. The disclosure requirements vary from state to state based upon the laws in effect in each state. However, generally speaking, licensed CPAs must adhere to a policy of full disclosure with respect to fees and conflicts of interest.

Financial Advising

All financial advisors find themselves in a position where advice to an older client could put the client's assets at risk, as financial decisions often do. The risks can be market risks or they can be inflation risk. Regardless of intention, a financial advisor is regarded as an expert. Vulnerable older adults, both those with substantial means and those with modest means, will put their trust in a financial expert. Accordingly, regardless of ethics, codes, or laws, the advisor should assume that the older client believes that the advice being provided is in the client's best interest and unbiased. In light of that trust, what advice is appropriate? Is the idea of a "risk-averse" older adult simply a stereotype to be set aside in favor of customized advice to an individual? It is appropriate to educate clients about all elements of risk. It is also appropriate for advisors to explain risk in a way so that the older client understands the issues that must be considered.

These issues invoke the classic dilemmas of autonomy and paternalism in professional ethics. The pure paternalist position will compel the planner to safeguard the welfare of the older client and to tailor recommendations offered to consider the risk to capital as the primary risk. By contrast, a pure libertarian position will emphasize the complete autonomy of the client and favor complete fact-telling with the ultimate decision left up to the client alone.

Both extreme positions have ethical arguments in their favor. But where a financial advisor has a bias toward one or the other side, it seems imperative to reveal that bias before entering into a contractual relationship to provide financial planning or financial advice.

Social Ethics

Financial advising on behalf of older clients takes place in a public context and therefore requires the vantage point of social ethics. A serious ethical issue for financial advisors concerns the public status and definition of the finance profession itself. Just who qualifies as a "financial advisor" or "financial planner"? In most states, the professional designation is quite loose and ill defined, unlike that for physicians, lawyers, or architects. As a result, financial advisors with very different levels of competence, including those with serious conflicts of interest (e.g., stock brokers), may present themselves as financial planners to a poorly informed public.

Another ethical dilemma in financial planning arises from the interpersonal and multigenerational structure of the family. The financial planner typically encounters older individuals for whom asset protection and estate planning are major issues. The problem arises in Medicaid planning, where financial planners, as well as attorneys in elder law practice, must take account of the need to plan for long-term care expenditures. There has been strong criticism of middle-class seniors who take advantage of spend-down "loopholes" to qualify for Medicaid and safeguard an inheritance for their children. To what extent should a financial advisor take account of such criticism or ethical concerns? There are clearly situations that warrant such planning—particularly when the concern is that the long-term care costs of one spouse could impoverish the other spouse. The ethical concerns could also be difficult to gauge if there is a spouse or offspring with special needs that are to be provided for by the individual seeking this type of planning.

Another area of intersection between individual ethics and social ethics is the realm of financial elder abuse. Does a financial planner have an obligation to protect an older client when the planner sees evidence of exploitation such as occurs when a frail or cognitively impaired older person gives large amounts of money to a younger caregiver or to an affectionate companion? Does it matter if mental competency is in question, or is there a "right to folly?" Guardianship statutes and programs in many states today are wrestling with this dilemma. However, there is an inexorable movement by statute and regulation to stop such abuse of older persons.

With increasing numbers of "oldest old," including many with significant financial assets, the ethical dilemmas of financial planning, financial advising, and aging will surely loom larger. Instead of relying on abstract codes of ethics, it may be more helpful to follow the example of medical ethics in confronting problems of clinical care: namely, to recognize that ambiguity and uncertainty, including ethical dilemmas, are inherent in planning for all stages of life, including old age, and must rigorously and continuously be addressed. (See also CPA ELDERCARE SERVICES; FINANCIAL ADVISORS; FINANCIAL EDUCATION FOR SERVICES; FINANCIAL ELDER ABUSE; FINANCIAL PLANNING PROCESS; MEDICAID PLANNING.)

References

DeGeorge, Richard T. 1990. *Business Ethics*. New York: Collier Macmillan.

Kapoor, Jack R., Les R. Dlabay, and Robert J. Hughes. 2001. *Personal Finance*. 6th ed. Homewood, IL: McGraw-Hill/Irwin.

"Zero in on the Right Financial Adviser." 2003. *Kiplinger's Retirement Report* 10 (February): 2.

Harry R. Moody

F

FEDERAL AGENCY SECURITIES, bonds, debentures, notes, and other securities issued to raise funds in support of public functions. As people approach retirement age, they restructure their investment portfolio. Equity securities tend to become less important and fixed income investments more important. As older persons become less willing to take risks, they try to find investments that provide a satisfactory rate of return and reduce the possibility of principal loss.

The Federal Financing Bank and the Government National Mortgage Association (GNMA) are federal agencies that issue securities backed by the full faith and credit of the U.S. government. Most agencies considered here, however, are government-sponsored enterprises (GSEs); the securities they issue are not guaranteed by the U.S. government but involve federal sponsorship. Government-sponsored enterprises are the largest issuers of agency securities and include the Federal Home Loan Bank (FHLB), Federal National Mortgage Association (FNMA), Farm Credit System (FCS), Student Loan Marketing Association (SLMA), and the Federal Home Loan Mortgage Corporation (FHLMC). SLMA and FNMA are also publicly owned and have stock that trades on the national exchanges.

Agencies were created by Congress to meet the special needs of specific segments of the general economy. They can be divided into three broad categories: (1) agencies supporting the mortgage market—FHLB, FHLMC, FNMA, GNMA; (2) agencies supporting agriculture—FCS; and (3) agencies supporting student loans—SLMA. Several other small agencies sell debt securities for specialized purposes. It is useful to analyze agencies by the type of securities they issue. There are two broad categories: (1) agencies that issue notes, debentures, bonds, or discount notes (FCB, FHLB, FNMA, SLMA) and (2) those that issue mortgage-backed securities, primarily "pass-through" securities (FNMA, FHLMC, GNMA). FNMA issues both types, depending on the financial purpose of the funds being raised. Each of these agencies sells securities to the public through a nationwide group of dealers and dealer banks or through individually negotiated or competitive bid transactions.

Over the years, agency securities have become very popular with older investors. Two reasons for this acceptance are their perceived high quality, which assures investors that their principal is relatively safe, and an active secondary market that allows investors to sell their securities quickly when necessary. The majority of agency issues are debentures or short-term discount notes with set maturity dates from 30 days to 20 years and a set coupon rate, which pay interest every six months. Newer issues have some additional features, such as call options and floating rates, but they are not as popular with individuals since they often require a minimum purchase of $100,000. Typically, agencies issue their debentures in denominations of $5,000 to $10,000.

The fastest-growing segment of the agencies market is for mortgage-backed securities, primarily pass-through securities issued by FNMA, FHLMC, and GNMA. Of these agencies, only GNMA carries the guarantee of the full faith and credit of the U.S. Treasury, and because of this guarantee, GNMA securities are among the most popular fixed income investments in the world.

Government National Mortgage Association

The Government National Mortgage Association was created in 1968 when FNMA was rechartered as a private corporation (privatized). GNMA securities today are the most widely held and actively traded mortgage-backed securities. Through its Mortgage-Backed Securities (MBS) Program, GNMA guarantees securities backed by pools of mortgages, "passing through" the principal and interest payments to the security holder monthly. Since GNMA guarantees the timely payment of principal and interest, the investor takes no risk that the underlying mortgages will become delinquent. Interest paid on mortgage-backed securities is subject to state and local taxes, so investors need to consider this before purchasing them.

Federal Home Loan Bank (FHLB) System

The FHLB was created by an act of Congress in 1932 and amended by the Financial Institutions Reform, Recovery, and Enforcement Act (FIRREA) of 1989. There are 12 district banks comprising the system. These banks operate as a reserve system for the savings and loan and banking industries to stabilize the flow of mortgage credit. They provide a ready, low-cost source of funds to member institutions, which are then made available to the public. Unlike FNMA and FHLMC, which purchase and then pool mortgages, the FHLB makes advances to its members on the security of their mortgages. Since enactment of the FIRREA, the supervisory and regulatory functions of member institutions reside in the Office of Thrift Supervisor within the Department of the Treasury. Owned by member institutions, the FHLBs do not take deposits. Funds are raised by selling FHLB Consolidated Discount Notes and Consolidated Bank Notes. More than $135 billion of consolidated obligations were outstanding at the end of 1993.

Federal Home Loan Mortgage Corporation

The FHLMC was chartered in 1970 as a government-sponsored enterprise. It was established to increase the funds available for residential housing by providing a national secondary market in conventional residential mortgages. The FHLMC accomplishes this by purchasing from bankers mortgages that are not guaranteed by any government agency, putting these mortgages into pools, and selling them as pass-through securities backed by such mortgages. Along with FNMA, FHLMC is responsible for maintaining an active secondary market for home sales. Besides the pass-through securities, FHLMC also issues discount notes and short-term debentures, but pass-through securities constitute the vast majority of outstanding debt. Like GNMA securities, FHLMC securities are not exempt from state and local taxes.

Federal National Mortgage Association

The Federal National Mortgage Association is one of the largest corporations in the United States, based on asset size, and is the largest supplier of funds for home mortgages. It was incorporated in 1938 as a corporation owned by the government. In 1954, it became a mixed public-private corporation, and finally, in 1968, the U.S. Congress split FNMA into two separate corporations, the GNMA, a government agency, and the FNMA, a federally chartered corporation owned by stockholders.

The FNMA supports savings and loan associations, mortgage bankers, commercial banks, and other banks primarily by buying mortgages from them. This availability of funds allows an active secondary market and enables capital to flow to those areas of the country that may need funds. FNMA offers debentures and short-term discount notes and, since 1981, has supported the housing market by purchasing mortgages from originators and generating mortgage-backed securities, which it sells in the capital market. The FNMA has more than $700 billion of outstanding mortgage debt. Income from FNMA securities is subject to state and local tax.

Farm Credit System

The Farm Credit System is a cooperatively owned system of banks and associations that provide both short- and long-term credit to farmers, ranchers, rural homeowners, and agricultural and rural cooperatives. Twelve federal land banks and associations provide the funding for making long-term loans on secured first mortgages by selling debentures and short-term notes in the money and credit markets. The banks are not depository institutions and rely on the Federal Farm Credit Bank Funding Corporation to raise funds for them. The Funding Corporation issues Farm Credit Consolidated Systemwide Discount Notes, Bonds, and Medium-Term Notes. The income derived from these securities is exempt from state and local taxes, which makes them especially attractive to investors on fixed incomes.

Student Loan Marketing Association

The Student Loan Marketing Association, like FNMA, is a government-chartered, publicly held corporation that owns one-third of all U.S. student loans. Chartered in 1972, the SLMA was developed in response to problems in the Guaranteed Student Loan Program of 1965. Originally only educational or student loan institutions were allowed to own stock. This was later changed so that anyone could buy nonvoting stock. As a secondary market for student loans, SLMA lends funds for student loans to qualified institutions. The obligations of SLMA are exempt from state and local taxes and from Securities and Exchange Commission (SEC) regulations. Obligations include discount notes, debentures, and floating rate bonds. Investments in SLMA's securities are without much risk because state and federal authorities bear the brunt of the defaults.

A potential investor in federal agency securities should always talk to a financial advisor before committing funds to this large and complex segment of the financial market. There are numerous types of federal agency securities with varying issuers, terms, liquidity, and tax treatments. Only by closely scrutinizing and understanding both the market and one's particular investment needs can investors navigate toward the retirement years with confidence. (See also ASSET ALOCATION AFTER RETIREMENT; BONDS; MORTGAGE INSTRUMENTS; MUTUAL FUNDS; RISK TOLERANCE.)

References

Bretthorst, Kenneth A. 1988. "Instruments and Markets for Federal Agency Securities." In *The Bankers' Handbook*, ed. William H. Baugh, Thomas I. Storrs, and Charles E. Walker. Homewood, IL: Dow Jones–Irwin.

Rose, Peter S. 1999. *Money and Capital Markets*. New York: McGraw-Hill.

Stuhldreher, Donald J. 1988. "Instruments and Markets for Government Securities." In *The Bankers' Handbook*, ed. William H. Baugh, Thomas I. Storrs, and Charles E. Walker. Home wood, IL: Dow Jones–Irwin.

Kenneth A. Bretthorst

FINANCES OF AGING IN THE GAY COMMUNITY, the perspectives in a wide range of policy debates that affect aging policies and the financial well-being of the gay, lesbian, bisexual, and transgender (GLBT) community in retirement.

Notable improvements have been seen in public opinion toward gay issues, including support for equal treatment of same-sex couples under Social Security benefits (Yang 1999). There has been a dramatic growth in local and state nondiscrimination laws, such that today more than one in three Americans live in a municipality or state with a sexual orientation nondiscrimination law. Increasingly, corporate America is adopting sexual orientation nondiscrimination policies and offering domestic partner benefits to same-sex partners of employees. Same-sex couples, however, are treated unequally under many aging policies, including income support programs. Also, homophobia is a problem in senior services, and gay elders may have particular caregiving needs and experiences that require special attention.

The Particular Barriers Gay Seniors Face

The older GLBT population, currently estimated at 1 to 3 million people, will increase to 4 to 6 million by 2030 (Cahill, South, and Spade 2000). Although gay elders share many of the same human needs and concerns as their heterosexual peers, gay and lesbian seniors often experience particular barriers as well, including discrimination; unequal treatment under Social Security, pensions, 401(k)s, and IRAs (Individual Retirement Accounts); and concerns related to housing, health care, and long-term care. Federal programs designed to assist older Americans can be ineffective or even irrelevant for GLBT elders. Several studies—of both nursing home administrators and directors of Area Agencies on Aging—document widespread homophobia among those entrusted with the care of America's seniors (Fairchild, Carrino, and Ramirez 1996). Even senior centers can be hostile places for gay elders. Many gay elders do not avail themselves of services on which other seniors thrive. Some retreat back into the closet, reinforcing isolation and undermining the possibility of a successful experience of aging. GLBT baby boomers—"out" for most of their lives—are increasingly unwilling to retreat to the closet when they encounter homophobia in aging services.

Long-Term Care Issues

Heterosexism and homophobia are widespread in nursing homes and are symptomatic of a larger sexphobia often associated with those providing services to seniors. In a mid-1990s survey of nursing home social workers, more than half said their coworkers were intolerant or condemning of homosexuality among residents, while most other respondents avoided answering the question. The staff in one nursing home refused to bathe a resident because they did not want to touch "the lesbian," and a home care assistant threatened to "out" a gay client if he reported her negligent care (Cook-Daniels 1997). Many gay elders experience abuse from care providers. Few service providers have instituted policies to address this homophobic behavior, leaving some GLBT elders in hostile and dangerous environments (Parsons 1995).

Gay elders entering assisted living facilities and other institutions are often presumed to be heterosexual and may feel compelled to hide their sexual identity. Long-term relationships may be devalued and unrecognized. Assisted living centers, congregate housing, and home health care services can take proactive steps to minimize discrimination, abuse, and neglect directed at GLBT elders. Caregivers can be trained to be competent in issues of sexuality and gender variance. Nursing homes can include detailed sexuality policies within residents' rights policies and can accommodate the appropriate, private expression of the sexual needs of residents—be they homosexual, bisexual, or heterosexual.

Particular Caregiving Needs

Gay elders may also have particular care and caregiving needs. Since most caregiving in the United States is provided by biological children, and since gays and lesbians are less likely to have children and appear more likely to live alone in old age than heterosexual elders, an urgent question presents itself: Who will care for GLBT elders? In general, the state fails to recognize same-sex relationships. Some studies indicate that GLBT elders may be more likely to live alone, making innovative support networks critical. Often, gay seniors are estranged from their families of origin due to homophobia and/or fear of rejection. Consequently, they may not be able to rely upon traditional caregiving support networks.

GLBT elders are often perceived to be "single" and without family attachments (even though they may have life partners and even children and grandchildren through those relationships) and are disproportionately relied upon by heterosexual siblings to take care of parents, aunts, uncles, and other aging family members (Shippy and Cahill 2002). Despite attempts by some conservatives to construct "family" and "gay" as mutually exclusive categories, one in three gay men and lesbians provides some kind of caregiving assistance—either to children or to adults with an illness or disability (Fredriksen 1999).

Unequal Treatment under Retirement Income Support Programs

In a free market system, income is a critical determinant in the quality of life one enjoys in retirement, including quality of care for those elders in need of caregiving. Those serving GLBT elders need to take into account the impact of the unequal treatment same-sex couples experience under policies regulating retirement income. For example:

- Social Security pays survivor benefits to widows and widowers but not to the surviving same-sex life partner of someone who dies. This may cost GLBT elders $124 million a year in benefits that would otherwise be available (Cahill, South, and Spade 2000).
- Married spouses are eligible for Social Security spousal benefits, which can allow them to receive half their spouse's Social Security benefit if it is larger than their own Social Security benefit. Unmarried partners in lifelong relationships are not eligible for spousal benefits. It is unknown how many millions of dollars a year this costs GLBT elders.
- Medicaid regulations protect the assets and homes of married spouses when the other spouse enters a nursing home or long-term care facility; no such protections are offered to same-sex partners.
- Tax laws and other regulations of 401(k)s and pensions discriminate against same-sex partners, forcing the surviving partner in a same-sex relationship into financially undesirable circumstances and subjecting retirement savings assets to distribution and taxation much earlier than makes sense.

Each of these issues is explored further below.

Social Security

Lesbian, gay, and bisexual people in same-sex partnerships are not eligible for the Social Security spousal benefit or the survivor benefit. This lack of eligibility costs gay elders hundreds of millions of dollars in income per year. The September 11th terrorist attacks illustrated the unfairness of this policy, as same-sex survivors of victims were denied Social Security survivor benefits as well as funds from the victims' compensation fund administered by the U.S. Justice Department.

Social Security survivor benefits allow widows, widowers, and dependent children to put food on the table and provide a sense of fairness when an employee pays into the system his or her whole life but dies before being able to enjoy the retirement benefits. But gay and lesbian survivors are not even eligible for these benefits. In 1998, 781,000 widows and widowers received an average of $442 a month in survivor benefits, a total of $4.1 billion that year. If only 3% of the total population of seniors who survived their life partner are gay, lesbian, or bisexual individuals in same-sex relationships, the failure to pay survivor benefits costs gay seniors about $124 million a year.

The spousal benefit allows husbands and wives to receive an amount equal to 50% of their spouse's monthly Social Security check if that amount is higher than what their own earnings would make them eligible for each month. In marriages where one spouse earns significantly more than the other and/or has a longer work history, taking the spousal benefit instead of the individual's own payment makes sense. However, same-sex partners are not eligible for the spousal benefit.

Unequal Treatment under Pension Regulations

Because GLBT people can still be legally discriminated against in employment in most of the country, and because gay couples are not treated equally under Social Security, pension income is an important policy issue affecting gay elders. Contrary to a widely held stereotype of gay affluence, gay men and lesbians earn no more than heterosexual men and women. In fact, gay men earn about 15% to 20% less than heterosexual men. Lesbians earn the same as heterosexual women, but because women on average earn less than men, lesbian couple households earn significantly less than heterosexual couple households (Klawitter and Flatt 1998). Many transgender people suffer from significant economic hardship.

Same-sex spouses do not receive the legal protections provided married spouses under the Retirement Equality Act of 1984, which prohibits a married worker from taking a life-only pension benefit without his or her spouse's written consent. The design and administration of pension plans vary greatly from employer to employer. Unfortunately, for same-sex couples in retirement, the one aspect most plans have in common is that very few automatically pay benefits to anyone but a legal spouse following the death of a participant. In addition, if a person dies after becoming vested in a pension plan, but before reaching the age of retirement, a legal spouse may be entitled to a cash benefit beginning in the year that the deceased would have started receiving the pension. The surviving spouse receives this benefit until death, but surviving same-sex partners are usually not eligible for this benefit. However, where a pension death benefit requires a beneficiary designation, there is no discrimination.

Unequal Treatment under 401(k) Regulations

If a person with a 401(k) plan dies, the tax implications for the beneficiary depend on whether or not the beneficiary is a legal spouse. If the beneficiary is a legally married spouse, then he or she may roll over the total amount of the decedent's account into an IRA with no tax implications except applicable estate taxes. No distribution must occur; the surviving spouse can maintain the funds in an IRA until April of the year following the year in which he or she turns 70½—the age at which withdrawals from retirement accounts become mandatory. However, if the beneficiary is a same-sex partner who is unable to legally marry, then he or she must begin taking distributions right away, which not only generates current income tax liabilities but also defeats the purpose of the retirement savings.

The Medicaid Spend-Down Provision and Same-Sex Couples

Similar to many heterosexual elders, the lack of coverage for long-term care for most GLBT elders constitutes a crisis in their care as well as personal finances. Often, seniors who enter nursing homes spend all of their assets on their care, then simply apply for Medicaid when they have next to nothing left, a phenomenon known as the "Medicaid spend-down." Medicaid regulations allow one member of a married heterosexual couple to remain in the couple's home for the rest of his or her life without jeopardizing his or her spouse's right to Medicaid coverage. Upon the survivor's death, the state may then take the home to recoup the costs of terminal care. However, since same-sex couples cannot marry, Medicaid regulations do not offer the same protection for same-sex partners, even if they have spent their entire adult lives together. This unequal treatment can force same-sex couples into a Hobson's choice ("an apparently free choice when there is no real alternative"—Merriam-Webster 2003) between getting the medical coverage to meet a partner's health care needs or foregoing medical care in order to avoid giving up the couple's home and life savings. A change in Medicaid regulations to treat same-sex couples equally as married heterosexual couples would be less discriminatory. Same-sex partners should be able to remain in their home without jeopardizing their partners' right to Medicaid coverage (Dean et al. 2000).

Senior Housing Issues

There are now several gay senior housing projects in various stages of development in Seattle, Boston, and Florida. While such developments are welcome, most units will only be accessible to upper-income people. The housing needs of rural, poor and middle-income GLBT elders can best be addressed by making senior housing gay-friendly and either adding sexual orientation and gender identity to the Fair Housing Act of 1968 or passing a federal nondiscrimination law that covers housing as well as employment.

Health Care

GLBT seniors may experience physician bias and often lack access to health coverage from a partner's work benefits. Antigay bias in health care is widespread. A 1994 study by the Gay & Lesbian Medical Association found that two-thirds of doctors and medical students reported knowing of biased caregiving by medical professionals; half reported witnessing it; and nearly 90% reported hearing disparaging remarks about gay, lesbian, or bisexual patients (Schatz and O'Hanlan 1994).

Assuming GLBT seniors can find appropriate care, they must then face the problem of paying for it. For many, Medicare plays a vital role in covering medical expenses and is especially vital for GLBT old people, as lifelong incomes may be lower than similar heterosexual-headed households. One shortcoming of Medicare is that it does not pay for prescription medications. This is especially harmful for the larger proportion of older gay and bisexual men who are living with HIV/AIDS (human immunodeficiency virus/acquired immunodeficiency syndrome) and who need expensive antiretroviral medications. While married spouses often take employer-provided health coverage for granted, most private and public sector employers do not provide such coverage to same-sex partners. These two factors—health care provider bias and lack of access to a partner's benefits—mean many gay people may enter retirement without having accessed health care on a regular basis during their lives. When domestic partner health insurance is available, it is taxed, while heterosexual spouse's health benefits are not. Also, the federal Family and Medical Leave Act does not cover same-sex partners.

Health Care Decision Making

Married heterosexual couples automatically have a right to visit their loved ones in the hospital and to supervise their spouse's funeral arrangements after their death. Additionally, they are commonly, if informally, given deference in terms of their spouse's medical care. These rights and privileges are not automatically granted to same-sex partners.

For example, when a gay man or lesbian is hospitalized, their partner might not be allowed to visit them unless they can present a hospital visitation authorization—a document completed by the hospitalized person specifying who may visit him. Unfortunately, hospital administrators do not always respect these documents, and not all states require hospitals to use these forms. This causes tremendous pain and hardship to members of GLBT families, as it did for Bill Flanigan and Robert Daniel in a Baltimore hospital in October 2000. When Daniel was admitted to the hospital, hospital personnel refused to let Flanigan see his dying partner on the grounds that he was not a family member. They disregarded both Flanigan's durable power of attorney for health care decisions and the fact that he had been recognized as a family member during Daniel's previous hospital stays. Flanigan was not allowed to confer with Daniel's doctors or to let them know that Daniel did not want life-prolonging measures, such as insertion of a breathing tube. Flanigan was finally allowed to see Daniel four hours later—when Daniel's mother and sister arrived. Daniel had already received a breathing tube, contrary to his wishes, and had lost consciousness. Flanigan never had a chance to say good-bye to him (Lambda 2002).

Furthermore, if a gay man or lesbian is incapacitated in the hospital, then his or her closest blood relative will automatically be deferred to for decisions about care unless a medical power of attorney form has been completed empowering the patient's partner to make medical decisions. If this form exists, then the specified health care proxy may act on behalf of the incapacitated person and make decisions as his or her agent. If the incapacitated gay man or lesbian has also completed financial power of attorney forms, then the partner may also act as his or her financial proxy and pay bills or sell assets on behalf of his or her loved one. While completing these forms provides some security to same-sex partners, the cost of writing up legal documents and the requirement that one essentially "out" oneself work to inhibit many gay seniors from taking advantage of this option. State recognition of same-sex couple relationships would provide greater equity in this area.

End-of-Life Issues

Lesbian and gay families are particularly vulnerable when one member of a couple dies. The rituals that inevitably follow death are more challenging for gay families. In order for same-sex couples to ensure that their remains will be disposed of in an appropriate manner, they may need to complete a "consent to autopsy and disposition of remains" form, because some medical power of attorney forms do not cover this subject. This form enables lesbians and gay men to appoint their partners as agents to carry out their final wishes. However, not all states have this form, and the same issues around cost and privacy apply.

When one member of a heterosexual married couple dies without a will, the other member of the couple automatically inherits any property or assets belonging to his or her spouse. However, the same standards do not apply to same-sex couples. An unmarried couple that purchases a house together without putting both partners on the title has no protections if one of them dies. In fact, if a lesbian or gay man dies without a will, then the partner faces the possibility of losing all objects that can be shown to have belonged to the deceased to a biological family member. Wills are the best insurance against a homophobic family member's challenge to a life partner's desire to stay in a house that was not jointly owned and access to other items left by the deceased.

Another way in which surviving same-sex partners are treated unfairly concerns inheritance taxes. When married couples leave property to a surviving spouse, they enjoy an unlimited marital deduction. One hundred percent (100%) of an estate of any size can be left to a legal spouse without diminution by death taxes, and until 2010 at least, assets will be revalued as of the date of death so that the surviving spouse can sell them without income tax consequences. In contrast, when same-sex partners leave property to each other, the value of the estate being bequeathed beyond $1 million is subject to death taxes. Furthermore, married couples are exempt from property tax reassessment upon death of one spouse. An unmarried partner, in contrast, will be subject to a property tax reassessment, even if the property was owned jointly or willed properly. The tax can be so significant that the survivor might be unable to afford to keep the home (Cahill, Ellen, and Tobias 2002).

Conclusion

The documented persistence of homophobia in long-term care environments and senior centers presents barriers to care for GLBT elders and challenges for elder service providers. Elder service and health care professionals can address these barriers by mandating training in the particular issues affecting GLBT elders for all those entrusted with their care. Longer-term, professional development institutions such as schools of social work, health professional training programs, and gerontology programs can incorporate competency in serving GLBT populations into their educational programs. More research is needed to understand the particular caregiving needs and practices of GLBT elders. Unequal treatment of same-sex couples under income support programs should be addressed in the political arena. The Democratic National Committee took an important step in this direction by issuing a resolution supporting equal treatment of lesbian and gay couples under Social Security in January 2002. Such a move also enjoys widespread support among the U.S. public (Yang 1999).

The principle of equal treatment regardless of sexual orientation already enjoys widespread support in the United States. Significant majorities support hospital visitation rights, inheritance rights, and Social Security survivor benefits for same-sex couples (Cahill, Ellen, and Tobias 2002). As America ages and a sizable cohort of gay baby boomers enters retirement, GLBT activists are working with elder service professionals and elder activists to ensure that this principle of equality is realized for elder GLBT people as well. (See also COST OF FAMILY CAREGIVING; LONG-TERM CARE INSURANCE [LTCI]—A CONSUMER'S PERSPECTIVE; MEDICAID; MEDICAID PLANNING; PENSION PLANS; RETIREMENT PLANS—401(k)s.)

References

Cahill, S., M. Ellen, and S. Tobias. 2002. *Family Policy: Issues Affecting Gay, Lesbian, Bisexual, and Transgender Families.* New York: Policy Institute of the National Gay and Lesbian Task Force.

Cahill, S., K. South, and J. Spade. 2000. *Outing Age: Public Policy Issues Affecting Gay, Lesbian, Bisexual, and Transgender Elders.* New York: Policy Institute of the National Gay and Lesbian Task Force.

Cook-Daniels, L. 1997. "Lesbian, Gay Male, Bisexual and Transgendered Elders: Elder Abuse and Neglect Issues." *Journal of Elder Abuse and Neglect* 9(2): 35–49.

Dean, L., I. Meyer, K. Robinson, R. Sell, R. Sember, V. Silenzio, et al. 2000. *Lesbian, Gay, Bisexual, and Transgender Health: Findings and Concerns.* New York: Gay and Lesbian Medical Association and the Center for LGBT Health, Columbia University School of Public Health.

Fairchild, S.K., G.E. Carrino, and M. Ramirez. 1996. "Social Workers' Perceptions of Staff Attitudes toward Resident Sexuality in a Random Sample of New York State Nursing Homes: A Pilot Study." *Journal of Gerontological Social Work* 26(1–2): 153–70.

Fredriksen, K.I. 1999. "Family Caregiving Responsibilities among Lesbians and Gay Men." *Social Work* 44(2): 142–55.

Klawitter, M., and V. Flatt. 1998. "The Effects of State and Local Antidiscrimination Policies on Earnings for Gays and Lesbians." *Journal of Policy Analysis and Management* 17(4): 658–87.

Lambda Legal Defense and Education Fund. 2002. "University of Maryland Medical System to Be Sued Wednesday by Gay Man Prevented from Visiting His Dying Partner at Shock Trauma Center in Baltimore." News Release. Available online at http://www.lambdalegal.org/cgi-bin/iowa/documents/record?record=1011.

Merriam-Webster. 2003. *Merriam-Webster's Collegiate Dictionary*. 11th ed. Springfield, MA: Author.

Parsons, Y. 1995. "Private Acts, Public Places." *Contemporary Long Term Care* 3: 48–52.

Schatz, B., and K. O'Hanlan. 1994. *Anti-Gay Discrimination in Medicine: Results of a National Survey of Lesbian, Gay and Bisexual Physicians*. San Francisco, CA: American Association of Physicians for Human Rights.

Shippy, A., and S. Cahill. 2002. "Family Caregiving among Lesbian, Gay, Bisexual and Transgender Elders in New York City." Paper presented at Third International Family Care Conference, Washington, DC, October 13.

Yang, A. 1999. *From Wrongs to Rights, 1973–1999: Public Opinion on Gay and Lesbian Americans Moves toward Equality*. New York: Policy Institute of the National Gay and Lesbian Task Force.

Sean Cahill

FINANCIAL ADVISORS, a term applied to a wide variety of professional individuals who provide an even wider variety of financial services and products. Among those who may be referred to as financial advisors are financial planners, stockbrokers, life and health insurance agents, bankers, attorneys, daily money managers, and accountants. While each of these categories represents a field of legitimate financial advice, and may involve licensure and regulation, the scope of services offered by any advisor must be measured against his or her particular training and experience, the emphasis of the advisor's practice, and the personal comfort and rapport between the client and advisor. Choosing a financial advisor is similar to choosing any professional in whom a great amount of trust must be placed. Knowing the array of financial advisors and their area of expertise is key, followed by an individual's understanding of his or her own financial needs and knowledge of sources for personal and organizational referrals. Surrendering total responsibility for one's financial affairs to advisors is always unwise. It is especially important for older individuals to learn and to participate actively in as many details of their own financial management as possible, since doing so can improve one's sense of autonomy and increase feelings of personal accomplishment, security, and well-being.

Financial planners constitute a huge and growing population of persons from many different backgrounds with widely varying abilities. Use of the designation "financial planner" requires no specialized license or credential and has been assumed by many stockbrokers, accountants, and insurance salespeople (Savage 1994). However, financial planners who have earned the Certified Financial Planner™ (CFP®) designation are among the most respected in the financial services business. All CFPs have completed a degree course offered at more than 40 colleges and universities around the country or through home study courses. Six core categories comprise rigorous training in subjects ranging from investment advice to tax and estate planning. In addition, to earn the CFP® designation, a ten-hour examination given by the Certified Financial Planner Board of

Standards, Inc., must be passed to demonstrate proof of financial planning–related knowledge.

Creating a financial plan takes both effort and knowledge, and those holding themselves out as financial planners should be compensated for planning. Financial planners are compensated in one of four ways, and persons seeking planning and investment advice should know in advance how they are being charged. Fee-only planners accept no commissions for sales of insurance, annuity, or investment products and are compensated solely by fees charged to their clients for the establishment, implementation, and maintenance of a financial plan, ad hoc advice, and other work performed on either an hourly or fixed-fee basis. Fee-based planners earn most of their income from fees charged to their clients but also earn commissions on sales of insurance and investment products that are recommended to implement the plan. Fee-offset planners also earn commissions but credit them against fees charged to the same client. Commission-based planners charge no fees for their planning work but are instead paid by the companies for which they place, or sell, products. None of these structures *necessarily* poses a conflict of interest, but it is important to take into account a financial advisor's motivation for whatever recommendations are made.

Stockbrokers and commodities brokers are registered representatives or principals of National Association of Securities Dealers (NASD) member firms and are licensed by the NASD after passing the examinations for the particular type of license they wish to hold. Different licenses enable an advisor to sell different types of products or to supervise others who do. In addition, they must pass state examinations and be licensed by the state or states in which they sell securities. The examinations are independent of any specified academic background, so it is not necessary for securities brokers to have any special training beyond what is required to pass the tests. Although some brokers do have advanced academic or other training in financial areas, many do not, and great knowledge of the securities industry is not the same as good financial advice.

Securities—stocks (equity securities), bonds, commodities, mutual funds, and variable annuities—are purchased customarily through brokers who are paid a commission based on the dollar amount of each transaction and the number of securities involved. Brokers should be selected based on their honesty, efficiency, accessibility, and ability to provide clients with information about the investments that are being considered for purchase or for sale, the appropriateness of the investment to the client's situation, and the cost of the transaction.

Insurance agents are licensed to offer life insurance, health insurance (including Medicare Supplement policies), long-term care insurance, and fixed annuity products to their customers on behalf of the insurance companies they represent. Many life insurance companies (but not all) offer extensive training to their agents, and it is not unusual for an insurance agent to also be licensed to sell mutual funds, variable annuities, and securities. Well-trained insurance agents often act as commission-based financial planners and give a broad base of recommendations to their clients. Many insurance agents have obtained additional designations—CFP®, Chartered Life Underwriter (CLU), or Chartered Financial Consultant (ChFC) are three prominent examples—and have taken advanced training that enables them to provide expert advice to their clients. Financial advisors who are also insurance agents may be "career" agents of a particular company, such as the Northwestern Mutual Financial Network or the Mass Mutual Financial Group, and represent only, or at least primarily, that company's products, or they may be independent brokers who offer products from a variety of companies. The extensive support and training provided to a "career agent" must be weighed against access to the great variety of products available in the marketplace.

Attorneys in most states must first obtain a law degree from a law school and then become licensed, after passing the state bar exam, to practice law. Some attorneys have highly specialized backgrounds in taxation and financial consulting, but it is important before engaging the services of an attorney to determine his or her specialized training and area of expertise. No other type of advisor is permitted (by law) to draw some of the instruments that are often a key part of implementing financial advice, such as wills, trusts, and durable powers of attorney. Some attorneys, such as those with an elder law practice, are able to offer very expert advice on the legal issues and instruments most often required in aging, such as advance directives, durable powers of attorney, and wills and trusts, but are inexperienced in investments, pensions, business succession planning, and other areas that impact sound personal financial planning. Even an attorney specializing in the practice of tax law, for example, is likely to have further specialized training within the field of taxation—civil and criminal, personal or corporate—so vast are these and other specialized areas of law. It is the responsibility of a prospective client to ascertain the areas and level of experience that attorneys have, and it is also the duty of an attorney to disclose this information to the client, although many will not volunteer their credentials unless asked.

Accountants and *certified public accountants* (CPAs) have backgrounds in dealing with money and, frequently, in income taxation. This experience often affords them a good basis for advising clients on financial matters, although it does not always extend into every area of financial consulting, such as insurance or investments. The services that accountants are best trained to render as financial advisors are those of tax planning, tax projections, tax return preparation, business valuations, and cash flow projections, although the American Institute of Certified Public Accountants (AICPA) has developed specialized training for CPAs in personal financial planning and eldercare and is even offering a professional designation of Personal Financial Specialist (CPA/PFS) available only to CPAs.

Money managers typically charge a fee to manage large blocks of funds inside investment portfolios. These individuals have credentials and investment experience that vary, and it is always advisable to obtain an investment history for the firms they represent in order to determine their success track record. However, even successful money managers may not be appropriate for some clients, since the minimum amounts they typically accept for investment management are frequently much higher than most individual investors have available.

Areas of knowledge that individuals should seek in their financial advisors include knowledge of people and how they relate to money; how to handle credit, budgeting, and long-range planning; relevant law, estate, and income taxation; life, health, and long-term care insurance; investment management; Social Security, Medicare, and Medicaid; as well as sensitivity to the needs of older persons in general. Two certification programs designed to educate financial advisors and others broadly about issues in the field of aging as well as individual aging have gained many adherents in the last few years, and people with these designations may be better able to serve a retired client than those without them.

The Certified Senior Advisor (CSA) program was founded by the Society of Certified Senior Advisors in 1997 and consists of a national educational program that trains professionals to better understand the health, social, and financial implications of the aging process. More than 9,000 CSAs, many of them financial professionals, are active members of the society. The Certified Financial Gerontologist (CFG) program is new as we go to press, but it is intended to be an academically rigorous program that certifies financial professionals in aging studies. The CFG program was established by the American Institute of Financial Gerontology in partnership with Widener University and the American Society on Aging. Because these matters are diverse and complicated, it is rare that any one individual can satisfy all areas of need for financial expertise, although most people look to one individual as their key advisor.

Perhaps the most common error made by an individual seeking to implement personal financial objectives is to rely on a specialist in one area to provide services, products, or advice outside the specialist's field of expertise. As examples, most attorneys do not prepare tax returns, CPAs are neither trained nor licensed to prepare trust documents or other legal instruments, and investment advisors may not understand estate planning, goals, or techniques. None of these professional experts may be well grounded in Life Planning, which is an essential part of putting financial matters in perspective. Despite these limitations, individuals seeking financial advice should be aware that there is a significant population of financial advisors who do have backgrounds, training, and experience in specialized areas. Once financial objectives are identified, one should seek assistance from more than one professional in order to obtain the range of help needed for financial planning needs.

Financial Advisors Designations

CLU (Chartered Life Underwriter). This designation is awarded by the American College of Bryn Mawr, Pennsylvania, and requires successful completion of ten courses in such areas as law, finance, estate and income taxation, life insurance, and investments. It requires continuing education to maintain the credential.

ChFC (Chartered Financial Consultant). This designation is also given by the American College (see CLU, above) and requires additional, advanced courses in taxation, finance, and investment topics beyond those included in the CLU. The American College primarily trains insurance professionals. It requires continuing education to maintain the credential.

CFP® (Certified Financial Planner). This designation signifies a broad amount of training in financial planning, as discussed above. Financial planners who have the CFP designation must earn continuing education credits in order to maintain the credential.

CPA (Certified Public Accountant). CPAs have significant academic and on-the-job training and must qualify for the designation by passing rigorous examinations. In order to maintain the designation of CPA, a number of continuing education classes must be completed each year.

J.D. (Juris Doctor). The degree conferred by law schools after a three-year academic program. The law school curriculum, at schools jointly accredited by the American Bar Association and the Association of American Law Schools, requires a bachelor's degree from an accredited university and covers the wide range of legal subjects necessary to prepare for the general practice of law.

LL.M. An LL.M. is the Master of Laws, a degree that allows a law school graduate to study areas of specialty within the law, such as taxation, labor law, or patent law. (See also AGENTS AND BROKERS; ATTORNEYS; CPA ELDERCARE SERVICES; DAILY MONEY MANAGERS; ELDER LAW PRACTICE; FINANCIAL COUNSELING FOR MID- TO LATER LIFE; FINANCIAL PLANNING PROCESS; LIFE PLANNING.)

Organizations

AICPA (American Institute of Certified Public Accountants)
American Institute of Financial Gerontology
CFP Board (Certified Financial Planner Board of Standards)
National Association of Financial and Estate Planning (NAFEP)
National Association of Insurance and Financial Advisors (NAIFA)
National Association of Personal Financial Advisors (NAPFA)
Society of Certified Senior Advisors
Society of Financial Services Professionals

References

Jaffe, Charles A. 2001. *The Right Way to Hire Financial Help*. 2nd ed. Cambridge, MA: MIT Press.

Johnson, Dale S. 1988. *Financial Services: Environment and Professions*. Bryn Mawr, PA: American College.

Savage, Terry. 1994. *New Money Strategies for the '90s*. New York: HarperCollins.

Shim, Jae K., and Joel G. Siegal. In press. *Handbook of Financial Planning: An Expert's Guide for Advisors and Their Clients*. Cincinnati, OH: South-Western.

Donald A. Hunsberger
Updated by E. Craig MacBean

FINANCIAL COUNSELING FOR MID- TO LATER LIFE, performed by financial counseling professionals, often employees of a nonprofit organization organized to assist clients in financial difficulty on a one-to-one basis. Clients are helped to resolve problems that impact their financial well-being, to make decisions that have financial implications for life now and in the future, to improve their financial management, to handle difficult transitions, and to improve functioning in the consumer market and/or legal systems by handling financial or consumer collections and other dilemmas. Financial counseling utilizes information and skills to assist clients in changing behaviors in resource management, consumption, lifestyle, and communication in order to obtain and maintain increased financial security. Problems and barriers to change are identified that interfere with meeting unique objectives for various stages of family life. Steps to resolving problems or implementing decisions are individualized and realistic for the particular client's personality, resource limitations, and needs.

Need for Financial Counseling

Reasons that clients seek advice or assistance vary greatly. Some perceive seeking assistance as a weakness, while others perceive it as a sign of strength. Clients may be experiencing financial difficulty such as the possibility of foreclosure, recent unemployment, garnishment of wages, the chronic overuse of credit, or facing some critical life event such as divorce, insufficient funds for retirement, gambling, or other spending addiction.

Psychological reasons may include feeling out of control, being unable "to make ends meet," the inability to say no to a spouse or to children, insufficient income for a chosen lifestyle, continuously paying late fees, lack of confidence to reduce expenses, family fights over finances, or anxiety for the future or some other personal emergency. Some clients simply want assistance with decisions, information, or clarification about the confusing mechanics and financial instruments available to them. Some are in a stage of transition and want to improve their economic security, enhance their wealth, reduce risks, or optimize their resources. Some clients are overly optimistic and set unrealistic goals that are impossible to achieve at their particular education or income level. A common problem is overestimating income and underestimating expenses. Lack of experience, not keeping records, or refusal to face reality may cause this problem.

The need for financial counseling is not always due to mismanagement or lack of information about alternative behavior patterns but may occur because of external events or situations beyond the client's control. An unexpected illness, change in family composition, job loss, car or appliance breakdown, legal problems, business failure, and downturn in the economy are a few examples of circumstances that can precipitate a personal financial crisis and the need for counseling.

Decisions

Decisions in the complex financial arena are difficult: Facing and making decisions is often stressful. Too much information and too many companies, some reputable and others not, cause confusion. Too little information gathered by comparison shopping and experience causes errors and overspending. When people are emotionally disturbed or anxious, they often go in circles and need financial counseling to sort out the priorities, decision-making steps, and the information needed to make good decisions.

Sufficient information is needed for each decision in order to minimize risk or error. The financial counselor can point out the alternatives, the consequences, and steps, but the decision has to belong to the client, who follows through with it. Others in the family who have to implement the decision need to be involved in the decision. Time frames for experimentation or living with a decision and then evaluating can reduce reluctance to try something new.

Process of Financial Counseling

Financial counseling is assisting clients in the development and creative use of all their resources to achieve economic security or well-being by generating alternatives from which the client chooses. Ultimately the client is assisted to improve quality of life with less wasteful resources. The processes are:

1. *Increasing income through exploration of possible sources based on the premise that income, in the economic sense, is a flow of goods and services and not money alone.* Advice and information are presented to mobilize resources through different employment, business expansion, liquidation of assets, government entitlements, rentals, community resources, early inheritance, and exchange in-kind with others.

2. *Reducing some expenses (or wants), maximizing use of money, avoiding additional*

financial burdens, or increasing other expenses after analysis of family needs and recording current spending or observing patterns of various family members. Clients are asked to check a list of alternative ways to reduce expenses, spend less, or practice saying "no" to family members.

3. *Adjusting debts and managing credit and other financial obligations either with a self-administered plan as an assertive consumer or utilizing credit counseling services.* Negotiation theories and skills are applied. Debts are analyzed by how they would hurt the client if not paid: harassment, loss of goods or services, garnishment or court action, and increased costs. Interest rates and legal consequences are noted. Clients are shown the advantages and disadvantages of credit counseling, loan consolidation, bankruptcy, and borrowing from relatives. Forms and addresses are provided for clients to check the accuracy of their credit reports.

4. *Clarifying and prioritizing wants and goals, then planning to meet them sequentially.* This step is listed purposefully after the first three possibilities are explored. Clients are helped to understand the influences and pressures upon them to consume in various ways. They are helped to reconcile wants among family members, to reconcile expenses with income, and to fulfill their wants in less expensive ways; wants are prioritized.

5. *Making decisions after listing them in order of urgency and with time frames for implementation.* Information is given for making the required decisions. Specific steps with time frames and person responsible are written, and clients are asked to clarify what they have heard. In subsequent meetings, clients are asked, "What problems did you have in implementing your decisions (or plans)?" Clients are provided with possible legal consequences of their decisions, financial facts or tax implications, which might be from a referral source or reading material.

6. *Establishing or reorganizing a system of household and financial management.* Appropriate techniques are shown such as necessary record keeping, bill paying on time, tax management, controlling impulsive spending, and communicating effectively with businesses and other family members.

7. *Budgeting or setting up a spending plan with appropriate categories based on individualized needs, personality constructs, and behavior patterns.* The financial counselor provides telescopic vision of possible changes of income from all sources, expenses, and decisions at different stages of the family life. Techniques of "time value of money," cash flow analysis, and net worth analysis are used with some clients in financial counseling but with all in financial planning.

8. *Acting effectively to realize consumer rights, to know the steps for recourse when these rights have been violated, and to effectively resolve a consumer complaint.* The client/consumer can be shown a sample letter for writing an effective complaint letter. The client is motivated and has sufficient confidence to do the research, gather important documents, and communicate effectively to those in authority.

9. *Evaluating programs for meeting past, current, and future needs and protection against risks (insurance).* Areas examined and assessed are housing, transportation, life insurance, health insurance, marital disruption, children's education, investments, and retirement planning. Sources of income and investments can be diversified to increase security. Skills for employment can be enhanced and diversified for transferability and promotion. Drastic changes such as in housing may need to be made for resolving a crisis.

10. *Planning for retirement by reducing current consumption to have income accumulate and generate income for the future.* This acknowledges that the value of money decreases over time, and there is risk in giving up control of current income. The greater the risk, the greater the possibility of income generated. Planning now often includes the necessity of employment after retirement. With a fixed income in retirement, clients have to plan on how they will reduce expenses or be more efficient. The retirement budget plan can include these categories: Years projected, his and her income, fixed expenses, flexible expenses, Social Security, pension, inheritance, sale of property, and liquidation of assets. Some expenses increase, while others decrease. Clients and their children can be creative in sharing housing arrangements. Social Security pamphlets on vital concerns to clients are available. Statements of earnings are checked for accuracy. The temptation for early retirement must be checked with realities, requirements for benefits, and information about pension plans. Changes in other aspects of life to facilitate continued employment can be considered.

11. *Championing change and handling adjustments/crises in lifestyle or family life.* (See also AGING INTO DEBT; BABY BOOMERS AND RETIREMENT; CONSUMER CREDIT; CONSUMER PROTECTION FOR OLDER ADULTS; CREDIT SCORES; FINANCIAL RECOVERY IN LATER LIFE; PREDATORY LENDING.)

Organizations

AARP
Association for Financial Counseling and Planning Education
Attorney General's Office, U.S.
Consumer Information Center
National Foundation for Credit

Flora Williams

FINANCIAL EDUCATION FOR SENIORS. The baby boom generation (approximately 76 million people born between the years of 1946 and 1964) continues to present challenges for educators striving to provide financial education that meets the learning needs of this audience and results in positive behavior changes and increased financial security. Even greater challenges exist in education for the growing cohort of older seniors. In 2000, the number of persons age 65 and older numbered 35 million and represented 12.4% of the U.S. population. The cohort that is 85 or older is growing the most rapidly of all age groups. If mortality rates continue to improve, this group is expected to double in size between 1999 and 2025 and to increase five times by 2050, when the last of the baby boomers enter this age group (Rogers 1999).

The Need for Lifelong Financial Education

The body of evidence documenting the need for lifelong financial education for the senior population of this country is growing. According to the AARP *Beyond 50* report (AARP 2002), there is good news and bad news about the financial situation older generations are presently experiencing. On the positive side, the inflation-adjusted income for Americans over 50 is higher (by 17%) than in 1980, and their wealth has increased even faster than their income (36%). More retirees have pensions, and their pension incomes are up by 35%. There have been marked improvements in the level of education in all age groups in the past two decades, and poverty has dropped to an all-time low for persons 65 and older (9.7%).

On the negative side, income growth has been fairly weak (less than 1% per year after inflation) for this segment of the population, and wealth increases (more than 2% per year after inflation) have been distributed unevenly. "And while poverty in old age at a given point in time is at an all-time low, poverty at some point after age 60 is still a fairly high probability event, as well as a pervasive problem for certain vulnerable groups" (AARP 2002).

The experiences of these vulnerable groups in the nation's older population portray a bleak financial picture. According to the National Association of Consumer Bankruptcy Attorneys (NACBA), more than a quarter of a million Americans aged 55 and older filed for bankruptcy in 2001. Further, the number of Americans 65 and older filing for bankruptcy has tripled in the last ten years, making older Americans the fastest-growing age group in bankruptcy.

> The bankruptcy data suggest that, as the population ages, each new wave of older Americans faces more financial risk than its predecessors. The data reveal substantial economic vulnerability among older Americans, and they indicate this trend is getting worse. (National Association of Consumer Bankruptcy Attorneys 2002)

The 1999 Consumer Bankruptcy Project's nationwide survey of families filing bankruptcy reveals that the financial risk exposure for older Americans stems from a variety of reasons including the following: job loss, large medical expenses, credit card debt, death of a family member, and other financial concerns such as providing financial support for other family members. Job loss was the most frequently listed reason (62.1%) for filing bankruptcy for all debtors aged 50 and older, followed by medical expenses (53.0%).

The study reports that older Americans often used credit cards to supplement their income and that they often charge prescriptions and other medical supplies. "Of those aged 50 and over, 45.5% explain that by the time they file bankruptcy, their credit card debts are completely unmanageable" (National Association of Consumer Bankruptcy Attorneys 2002).

The need for lifelong financial education is great regardless of an older person's place on the "have" or "have-not" wealth continuum. The "haves" need continuing education on how to manage their wealth to ensure financial security throughout their lifetimes, and the "have-nots" need programs tailored to avoiding disastrous results from financial risks they encounter and to ensure financial stability. The complexity of financial products and services, along with rapid changes in technology, information availability, public policy, and increasing cases of consumer fraud, demand a financially literate consumer, regardless of age and economic status.

Education and Successful Aging

Richard Adler (2002), author of "The Age Wave Meets the Technology Wave: Broadband and Older Americans," suggests that in order to age successfully, older adults need to remain engaged in learning throughout later life. He believes lifelong learning is an area of rapidly growing interest among adults and reports that more than 33 million adults over age 45, over one-third of this age cohort, are currently engaged in some form of adult education.

The demand for lifelong learning is currently being addressed by colleges, public schools, Cooperative Extension, and community groups through a variety of formats. Opportunities exist on site at schools and colleges, libraries, museums, public meeting facilities, senior centers, and nursing homes. Alternative media such as newspapers, cable and public television, and educational radio are also utilized. Methodologies include traditional educator-led programs, peer teaching/learning designs, and even instruction provided by regular matriculated students at colleges and universities for an older, non-traditional audience. One example is the "Joining Wisdom with Youth Through Bits and Bytes: Computer Skills Development Through Intergenerational Service Learning" at Clemson University. Residents of a local retirement community are transported to campus where Clemson students teach them how to surf the Internet, scan photos, take digital photographs, and use word processing programs.

One popular lifelong learning environment has been the Elderhostel model. Begun in 1974 at the University of New Hampshire, the Elderhostel concept has expanded to over 1,500 colleges. Once only offered in the summer as one-week programs, Elderhostels are now available all year and may even be international in scope. Seniors typically live on campus, but programs vary and even include 4-H camp environments. The goal is to present older adults with courses that are relevant to their everyday lives and that are enjoyable.

Lifelong Financial Education Programs for Seniors: A Selected Example of a Traditional Format

When following a more traditional education program design, there are special considerations for older adults concerning physical conditions, methodology, and topics presented in these programs. As adults age, they may have special education needs resulting from changing physical status such as impaired vision or hearing and they often develop chronic medical conditions and become increasingly frail. It is suggested that seniors learn best when the material is relevant and interesting to them and programs are structured so that seniors are allowed to learn at their own pace. "To assure that the audience is motivated, planners should make efforts to develop educational sessions stemming from the issues and problems the elderly identify as concerns" (Penn State University 1990).

Clearly, the financial arena contains issues and problems identified as concerns by seniors. Educational programs designed specifically for this audience should be well received. One example of a financial education program for seniors following a more traditional format is the BE SMART program currently being offered in South Carolina. BE SMART is an acronym for Basic Education for Senior Medicare Awareness to Restore Trust, and it is delivered as a cooperative effort of the South Carolina Department of Health and Human Services (SCDHHS), South Carolina Council of Governments (Administration on Aging), South Carolina Department of Consumer Affairs (SCDCA), and Clemson University Cooperative Extension (CES).

The BE SMART program provides information on topics including the SCDHHS's guarding against Medicare fraud, the SCDCA alert on consumer fraud, and CES's update on maintaining organized financial files, medical records, and important documents. The program is delivered by personnel from each of these collaborating partners, and the Council of Governments assists with marketing and arranges physical facilities for the program, usually senior meal sites.

Senior citizens are often thought of as easy prey for a variety of fraudulent activities. Education is the key to insure the financial security of senior citizens and protect them from the dangers of telemarketers and con artists. BE SMART program presentations made to senior audiences empower them to take control of their financial future.

Lifelong Financial Education Programs for Seniors: Utilizing Technology

More and more consumer education, protection, and advocacy groups are utilizing nontraditional, nonformal formats to provide financial education and information. The newest format and one that is expanding exponentially uses personal computers and information posted on the Internet to educate consumers. However, there are limiting factors for seniors in accessing this information. The current "generational digital divide" is documented by statistics that show after age 55 the use of computers declines steadily and falls below 20% among persons age 75 and older (Adler 2002).

Subsequently, the appropriate role of technology in conducting educational programs for the aging population is receiving a great deal of attention. Richard Adler states,

> When a solution is proposed to address a problem of aging that involves the use of technology, the objection is often raised that seniors are "technophobic" and are resistant to adopting any new technology. It is true that older adults do not tend to be "innovators" or the "early adopters" of new technologies—that is, they rarely rush in to be "the first on their block" to try out the latest gadget. But once a technology reaches maturity and its benefits are well understood, seniors are as likely to use it as younger people. The key to the successful introduction of a technology for older adults is to make sure it is affordable, easy to use and delivers significant benefits. (Adler 2002)

Until this technology reaches maturity and seniors adopt it on a large scale, a combination of traditional and nontraditional formats will have to be utilized. Seniors who are early adopters of the technology but do not have access to it within their homes have other opportunities to access this information. It is recommended that they visit local senior centers, libraries, or public schools where librarians or media persons are available to provide aid in searching the Internet and providing alternative ways of obtaining information. The Internet provides a wealth of sites dedicated to a wide variety of benefits for seniors, that is, Medicare, Social Security, prescription drug assistance programs, fraud protection, investment information, public benefits, health, and financial advance planning, to name a few. The time spent to overcome "technophobia" can be very rewarding to seniors seeking information to increase their financial knowledge and skills.

Access to lifelong learning opportunities can be difficult for seniors with limited mobility and stamina. Adler identified several projects designed to deliver educational programs directly to seniors at home. The University without Walls (UWW) project was launched in 1989 in New York City.

> It has provided in-home education to students ranging in age up to 100 and living in places like Florida, Maryland, Utah and Israel. UWW's hour-long classes are delivered by telephone. When a class begins, each student is called and included on a conference line with the instructor and other students. The program now offers a catalog of dozens of courses in the arts and humanities, legal and financial topics, and health. (Adler 2002)

Membership-based organizations are also providing lifelong learning programs for their members. AARP piloted online courses in the summer of 2001. The courses were developed by college and university faculty in the United States and Britain and focused on the following four areas: technology and science, arts and humanities, history and perspectives, and personal management.

Lifelong Financial Education Programs for Seniors: A Selected Example of a Combination Approach

The Cooperative Extension System has launched a national initiative entitled Financial Security in Later Life that utilizes both traditional and technological approaches in the design and delivery of financial education. Curricula, program materials, and resources for Financial Security in Later Life educational efforts are primarily available to educators on the Web site located at http://www.reeusda.gov/financialsecurity. However, this Web site also has pages designed to provide information directly to consumers including the following: online Extension programs, online financial management tools, links to Extension programs across the United States, and educational resources. This format provides the best of both the traditional and technological educational designs. The program impacts will be tracked as the Financial Security in Later Life Initiative continues. The feasibility and usefulness of this design will be assessed along with evaluations by end users to determine the success of this financial education approach.

Conclusions

The need for lifelong financial education programs targeted toward seniors is well documented, the methodologies are varied, and the appeal to this target audience is growing. However, the humble beginning efforts need an influx of creativity and resources. The result will be a generation of older adults who are financially literate and empowered with the knowledge, attitudes, skills, and confidence to practice effective and successful financial management strategies that ensure financial security and stability throughout their lifetimes. (See also EDUCATION OF OLDER ADULTS; FINANCIAL LITERACY; INVESTOR EDUCATION; LIFE PLANNING IN THE WORKPLACE; WORKPLACE FINANCIAL EDUCATION.)

References

AARP. 2002. *Beyond 50: A Report to the Nation on Economic Security*. Washington, DC: Author.

Adler, Richard. 2002. "The Age Wave Meets the Technology Wave: Broadband and Older Americans." SeniorNet. Available online at http://www.seniornet.org/.

Kausler, Donald H., and Barry C. Kausler. 1996. *The Graying of America: An Encyclopedia of Aging, Health, Mind, and Behavior*. Urbana: University of Illinois Press.

National Association of Consumer Bankruptcy Attorneys. 2002. "Bankruptcy and Older Americans." Available online at http://www.nacba.com/older_Americans.html.

Penn State University. 1990. "Planning Education Classes for Older Adults." Available online at http://agexted.cas.psu.edu/docs/21600640.html.

Rogers, C.C. 1999. *Changes in the Older Population and Implications for Rural Areas: Rural Development Research Report.* Washington, DC: Economic Research Service.

Nancy C. Porter

FINANCIAL ELDER ABUSE, improper or illegal use of an elder's assets, property, or income. Policymakers, public and private agencies, law enforcement agencies, and the public at large have become increasingly aware of the phenomenon of elder abuse during the past decade. As awareness has increased, the definitions of abuse have been refined, laws to prevent or address abuse have been introduced, many more stakeholders have been identified, elder abuse prevention programs have been initiated in all states and in many localities, and more rigorous research has been conducted.

Notwithstanding all of these efforts, the available data on the incidence of elder abuse remain highly unreliable because only about 21% of abuse is reported to law enforcement agencies or adult protective services programs. The so-called iceberg theory of abuse postulates that only a small percentage of domestic elder abuse is "visible above the waterline." According to this theory, four out of five incidents of elder abuse remain unreported, have not been noticed by others, and remain unidentified and inestimable at this time (Administration on Aging 1996).

Definitions of Elder Abuse

Definitions of elder abuse vary from state to state, but several broad categories of abuse can be identified, depending on where the abuse takes place or who the abuser is. Domestic elder abuse is abuse that occurs in the elder's home or the home of a caregiver and is perpetrated by someone known to the victim of abuse. Institutional elder abuse occurs in a residential facility and/or was perpetrated by persons that have a legal or contractual obligation to the victim for care and protection. Self-neglect or self-abuse is usually also included in any definition of elder abuse, although this type of abuse is clearly distinctly different from abuse that has been perpetrated by another person. Within these broad parameters, subcategories of abuse can be identified—financial elder abuse being one of seven such subcategories. Financial elder abuse is defined by the Administration on Aging's National Center on Elder Abuse "as the illegal or improper use of an elder's funds, property, or assets."

The Characteristics of Victims and Perpetrators of Financial Elder Abuse

The National Elder Abuse Incidence Study conducted in 1996 by the National Center on Elder Abuse found that 551,000 older adults in domestic settings experienced elder abuse or self-neglect (these data did not include institutionalized persons). The investigators found that among the victims of elder abuse, women are abused at higher rates than men and that the oldest elders, over the age of 80, are abused or neglected at two to three times their proportion of the older population in general. Slightly over 30% of all elder abuse victims experience financial abuse or material exploitation, and most of them (83%) are White, with another 15.5% being African American. Forty-five percent (45%) of all perpetrators of financial elder abuse were under the age of 40, with another

39.5% being between the ages of 41 and 59. Two-thirds (67%) of the abusers were children of the victim, with other relatives and grandchildren constituting 9.7% and 9.2%, respectively. In general, the victims are not the wealthiest among older adults. Based on substantiated incidents of reported financial elder abuse, close to four in five victims had incomes below $15,000 per year. The most prevalent reporters of financial abuse or material exploitation included friends or neighbors of the victim (15%), hospitals (14.2%), and family members (14%).

In recent years, additional types of financial elder abuse have emerged. For instance, in New York State in 2001, investigative reporters for the *New York Daily News* uncovered egregious incidents of financial abuse by guardians of incapacitated persons—people who had been appointed by the courts to manage the financial affairs or the personal well-being of the incapacitated person. Following these exposures, New York State's chief judge appointed two investigative bodies to determine the extent of abuse by duly appointed fiduciaries (the Commission on Fiduciary Appointments and a special inspector general). As a result of the recommendations submitted by these two investigative bodies, the New York State Office of Guardianship Services was established in 2002 within the Unified Court System to offer guidance to guardians and other fiduciaries and to monitor the quality of care given to incapacitated persons.

A study, "Abuse of Powers of Attorney," conducted by the Albany Law School Government Law Center in New York State in 1994 uncovered substantial problems with abuse of powers of attorney; while the Brookdale Center on Aging also noted abuse of joint bank accounts and other surrogate devices.

Other types of financial abuse now reported in the media include credit card fraud, confidence schemes, mail fraud, and telemarketing fraud. Although all Americans are potential victims of these types of abuse, in 2001 the National Fraud Information Center (NFIC) of the National Consumers League found that over 25% of the victims were people over the age of 60.

Factors That Contribute to Financial Abuse

The risk factors that contribute to the potential for financial elder abuse include: advanced age; being a woman; living alone in relative social isolation; having some physical or cognitive impairment; and being dependent on others for care and protection. In addition, financial dependence by the abuser on the victim, substance abuse by the abuser, mental health problems of the abuser, and a history of family dysfunction all contribute to the incidence of financial elder abuse.

Barriers to Addressing Financial Elder Abuse

A major issue in addressing financial elder abuse is the decisional capacity of the victim. Although advanced age cannot be equated with mental impairment, members of the group referred to as the "oldest old" (individuals 85 years or older) are more likely to have some physical or cognitive impairment that manifests in an inability to pay bills or purchase the necessities of daily living. The making of uncharacteristically large gifts may be voluntary and informed but may also be coerced. The belief that it is necessary to hoard or preserve assets to the detriment of personal health and safety may or may not be based on rational concerns or financial obligations. Furthermore, questionable mental capacity of the victim may impede the ability of the criminal justice system to prosecute cases of financial elder abuse because of the victim's inability to testify effectively. Health care facilities, social services providers, and the banking industry complain that the confidential nature of their relationship with the suspected victims of financial elder abuse impedes their ability to report many incidents of abuse to the authorities in the absence of the victim's consent. The banking industry is reluctant to report suspected cases of financial elder abuse when the alleged abuser has a duly executed durable power of attorney or other surrogate authority.

Finally, even when a victim's decisional mental capacity is not in question, it may be impossible to formally address the abuse because victims are often unwilling to report incidents of family dysfunction to law enforcement agencies. Victims of abuse may be dependent on the abuser or be fearful of reprisal. Most are embarrassed, ashamed, and unwilling to admit they were victimized.

Future Directions

Many jurisdictions are in the process of evaluating the use of mandatory reporting requirements. Some states are revising criminal or civil remedies available to the victims of financial abuse; others are in the process of revising power of attorney statutes to build in safeguards and amending guardianship statutes to enable the courts to order limited or onetime interventions so that immediate action is possible pending a full proceeding.

In addition to statutory revisions, there is increased recognition that training programs on elder abuse must be developed and offered to law enforcement agencies, offices of district attorneys, banking institutions, health care facilities, Adult Protective Services, and the aging network. Finally, corporations, human services programs, self-help groups, and attorneys who specialize in elder law practice are increasingly providing preretirement seminars and counseling to middle-aged persons who are looking forward to their own retirement or who are caregivers for their parents or friends. Such consumer education models include information on the positive and negative aspects of various financial surrogate management devices and health care advance directives, in an effort to encourage the public to "plan ahead for incapacity." (See also CONSUMER PROTECTION FOR OLDER ADULTS; CRIME PROTECTION; ETHICS IN FINANCIAL PLANNING; INTERGENERATIONAL CONFLICT AND FINANCIAL ISSUES; PREDATORY LENDING.)

References

Administration on Aging. National Center on Elder Abuse. 1996. "The National Elder Abuse Incidence Study." Available online at http://www.aoa.gov/abuse/report.

Albany Law School. Government Law Center. 1994. "Abuse and the Durable Power-of-Attorney: Options for Reform." New York: Albany Law School.

Brookdale Center on Aging of Hunter College. Jacob Reingold Institute. 1994. "Survey of Financial Institutions." Unpublished manuscript.

National Consumers League. 2002. "National Fraud Information Center, Telemarketing Fraud Statistics." Available online at http://www.fraud.org/02telestats.htm.

New York Daily News. 2001. "Senior Taken for Millions, Lawyers Rack Up Fat Fees as Guardians to the Helpless." May 20.

New York State Commission on Fiduciary Appointments. 2001. Report to the Chief Judge.

Office of the Special Inspector General for Fiduciary Appointments. 2001. "A Report to Chief Judge Judith S. Kaye and Chief Administrative Judge Jonathan Lippman."

Sia Arnason and Debra S. Sacks

FINANCIAL GERONTOLOGY, HISTORY OF, an academic field that embraces multiple perspectives on aging, including population aging, individual aging, and family aging, and focuses on the complexity of relationships among demographic trends, individual attitudes, financial security, and life satisfaction across the life cycle and across generations. An important first definitional concept is to emphasize that *gerontology is not the study of "old people" but is the study of the multiple processes of aging*—including *middle aging*. Consequently, *financial gerontology* focuses not on "old people" but on the financial dimensions of the multiple processes of aging and middle aging. The field pays special attention to how the demographic and financial characteristics of those born from 1946 to 1964 (i.e., the baby boomers) is shaping the social, health, and financial attitudes, hopes, worries, and social policy of the United States in the twenty-first century. The first-born baby boomer will celebrate his or her sixtieth birthday in 2006.

The Origins of Financial Gerontology: The Boettner Research Institute

The origins of financial gerontology are rooted in the vision of two farsighted, charitable men, Joseph Emery Boettner, a successful businessman, and Davis Weinert Gregg, a successful educator. Born in 1903, Joe Boettner entered the insurance business almost accidentally. A star high school athlete, he was recruited to play in the semipro intramural teams of Philadelphia's booming insurance industry. After successful years in insurance sales and education, he and a few friends purchased the failing Philadelphia Life Insurance Company for $1 per share and built it into a successful company. His post–high school education was at the American College of Life Underwriters, the applied life insurance training division of the University of Pennsylvania Wharton School. The college became independent of the university in 1927, and Mr. Boettner earned his Chartered Life Underwriter (CLU) designation in 1934.

Born in 1918, Davis Gregg graduated from the University of Texas and earned his doctorate from the University of Pennsylvania in 1947, where he studied under the legendary Wharton professor of insurance Solomon Huebner, founder of the American College of Life Underwriters. Gregg was on the faculty of Stanford University when Professor Huebner asked him to come back to the insurance college for a short time. Gregg's "short time" spanned four decades, including 1954 to 1983 as the president of the college.

During these years the high school athlete from West Philadelphia and the Wharton Ph.D. from Texas developed a lifelong relationship built on mutual personal affection and professional respect. Boettner began using his wealth to support higher education, endowing professorships at Penn State University, Temple University, and the American College of Life Underwriters, which was moved from the University of Pennsylvania to its own campus in Bryn Mawr, Pennsylvania, in 1961. Although the focus of these gifts was insurance education, as he grew older Boettner's views of the educational needs of the life insurance industry changed. He often reflected on the fact that he was outliving his accountant, his lawyer, his dentist, his doctor, and other important professionals in his life. While his own financial resources allowed him to deal with these changes successfully, he became concerned about how the average older person faces these kinds of challenges and how financial education could be channeled to meet such challenges.

Davis Gregg's intellectual and administrative leadership transformed the nature of the American College of Life Underwriters. Although its professional designation, the Chartered Life Underwriter, focused on life insurance, more elaborate insurance products such as whole life and universal life insurance served a broader insurance-with-investment function. Consequently, under his leadership the college created a second professional designation, the Chartered Financial Consultant (ChFC), in recognition of the need to train students beyond traditional life insurance practices.

By the 1980s Boettner's concerns about old age and consumer education began to merge with Gregg's views on the need for more comprehensive professional education in life insurance and financial services. From these joint concerns came the idea of a new research institute that would focus on the linkages between personal finance and social gerontology.

With a gift from Boettner, Gregg established a Study Committee of nationally known gerontologists to explore the issues. The committee agreed on four organizing principles: (1) that there was indeed a need for a specialized research program combining gerontology with financial planning; (2) that a social gerontology research center could succeed at a small specialized business school; (3) that the permanent director of the institute should be an experienced gerontologist; and (4) that the goal of the new institute would be both to communicate gerontological concerns to insurance and financial professionals and to communicate financial issues to gerontologists.

In 1986 the American College officially established the Boettner Research Institute and in 1989 renamed it the Boettner Institute of Financial Gerontology to more descriptively reflect its focus and recruited Dr. Neal E. Cutler, professor of political science and gerontology at the University of Southern California's (USC) Andrus Gerontology Center, as the director.

From 1989 to 1991 Gregg, Boettner, and Cutler developed a framework for applied research in financial gerontology. As the initial professional and public recognition of the importance of financial gerontology exceeded the expectations of the institute's founders, a broader set of academic skills and interests than originally envisioned was seen as necessary to meet the challenge of this new field. Consequently, in 1992 the Boettner Institute became chartered as a nonprofit charitable educational corporation with an independently appointed board of trustees of prominent business and gerontology academics and practitioners. The trustees then voted to move the Boettner Institute from the American College to the University of Pennsylvania.

Sadly, within a year, on October 27, 1993, Davis Gregg passed away. In the months following the unexpected death, Boettner developed plans for a permanent educational memorial to his lifelong friend: He endowed the Joseph E. Boettner/Davis W. Gregg Chair in Financial Gerontology at Widener University in Chester, Pennsylvania, the university where Boettner was serving as a lifetime member of the board of trustees. Literally one year later, on October 27, 1994, Joseph Boettner also passed away. In keeping with his wishes, Widener University appointed Dr. Cutler in 1994 to be the first holder of the Boettner/Gregg Chair.

At the University of Pennsylvania, the Boettner Institute became the Boettner Center of Financial Gerontology, and in 2003 it was merged into the Wharton School as the

Boettner Center for Pensions and Retirement Security. The Boettner/Gregg Chair in Financial Gerontology at Widener University continues to emphasize interdisciplinary teaching and applied research; Dr. Cutler teaches in both the School of Human Service Professions (e.g., clinical psychology and social work) and the School of Business Administration. In these ways, the vision of applied research and education of two lifelong friends, a businessman and an academic, comes full circle in an institutionalized way that links their insights as well as their names.

The Emerging Literature of Financial Gerontology

One measure of the development of a new field of study is the extent of its professional communication or, in academic parlance, its *literature*. By this measure financial gerontology is indeed becoming a well-established field of study. For example, during its Bryn Mawr years, the Boettner Institute organized a series of annual, published lectures that alternated between nationally prominent gerontology and finance leaders. The inaugural Boettner Lecture was given by Dr. George L. Maddox, director of the Duke University Center on Aging; later lectures were given by sociologist Dr. Matilda White Riley, senior behavioral scientist at the National Institute on Aging, and psychologist Dr. James E. Birren, founding director of the USC Andrus Gerontology Center. Maddox, Riley, and Birren are all former presidents of the Gerontological Society of America. Lectures were also given by Dr. William C. Greenough, chairman and chief executive officer (CEO) of TIAA-CREF; Dallas L. Salisbury, president and CEO of the Employee Benefit Research Institute; and Davis Gregg.

Of greater impact was the development of a regular column on financial gerontology written by Dr. Cutler for the *Journal of the American Society of CLU and ChFC*. Because the journal is received by more than 25,000 financial professionals, the column helps to implement one of Joseph Boettner's central goals: the communication of gerontological insights and research findings to the financial services profession. Beginning in 1990, the subjects of these bimonthly written "minilectures" have ranged from the implications of baby boom demographics for retirement to understanding Alzheimer's disease and the costs of long-term care. This series has featured several guest columnists and from time to time presents serious topics using such less serious titles as "Sex, Asset Allocation, and Rock-n-Roll" (introducing financial planning to younger adults) and "Successful Aging, Willard Scott, and Dental Floss" (the health dynamics of individual longevity). The column continues in the renamed *Journal of Financial Service Professionals* written alternatively by Cutler and Dr. Sandra Timmerman, director of the Mature Market Institute at MetLife.

A hallmark event in the development of financial gerontology "as a field" was the publication in 1996 of the *Encyclopedia of Financial Gerontology*, edited by Dr. Lois A. Vitt and Dr. Jurg K. Siegenthaler. Including over 125 authors and articles, the *Encyclopedia*—the predecessor of the present two-volume edition—both symbolizes and defines the growing scope of the field's research and practice. The editors' list of "Core Topics" into which the articles can be "rearranged" for educational purposes identifies the growing expansiveness of financial gerontology: Income Security, Employment and Retirement, Family and Intergenerational Issues, Consumer Services, Health Care and Insurance, Housing and Housing Finance, Legal Issues and Services, Quality of Life and Well-Being.

Finally, the publication of two "traditional" books also marks the evolution of financial gerontology as an identifiable field of study. In 1992 Springer published *Aging, Money, and Life Satisfaction: Aspects of Financial Gerontology*, edited by Cutler, Gregg, and Dr. M. Powell Lawton, an internationally known psychologist and member of the Boettner Institute Advisory Board. This volume identified a conceptual framework for studying aging in a social, economic, and health context, all directed to the role of financial planning in maintaining economic security and life satisfaction in later life. The book included an early statement of Davis Gregg's model of the "human wealth span."

In 2002 Wiley published *Advising Mature Clients: The New Science of Wealth Span Planning*, written by Dr. Cutler. The book builds on a decade of teaching and applied research suggested by Gregg's model and discusses the wealth span model in terms of such subjects as the changing nature of retirement, the financial psychology of middle age, aging children of older parents, the continuum of long-term care and related decisions, and government health and social service programs relevant to the financial questions typically asked by older and middle-aged clients. The book was published in Wiley's "J.K. Lasser Pro" series that is directed toward financial professionals.

The Future

Over the past decade the phrase *financial gerontology* has become *less unusual* than it was at the beginning. Annual meetings of both practitioners and academics are more likely to see panels and workshops on topics that link aging and money, finance and gerontology. A substantial extension of this bridge-building activity is the recent development of an educational program whose primary goal is to teach a range of gerontological concepts, issues, and data to financial services professionals, the outcome of which is a new professional designation known as the Certified Financial Gerontologist (CFG).

The program is being developed by the American Institute of Financial Gerontology (AIFG) in partnership with the American Society on Aging—a membership organization of 6,000 educators, practitioners, businesspersons, researchers, administrators, and policymakers—and the Widener University School of Business Administration. In keeping with the original vision of a new field of financial gerontology, the goal of the AIFG is to bring gerontology to professionals who are already trained, credentialed, or licensed in their financial profession. Thus, the curriculum leading to the CFG designation emphasizes such subjects as the wealth span model of aging and financial planning; understanding the biology, psychology, and sociology of aging; recognizing and working with the ethical and legal challenges of aging clients and their families; and connecting the variety of age-related health, finance, and social services programs so as to promote financial security and well-being in later life. Thus like the bimonthly columns, the designation reflects the view of financial gerontology as a field that serves as a bridge between gerontological and financial professionals.

In these ways, financial gerontology is moving in the directions that its founders imagined. Starting with the view that researchers should pursue gerontological topics that are of interest and of value to financial practitioners, the field has developed an increasingly important applied research agenda alongside a growing "literature" that reflects and communicates that agenda. Through the meetings and workshops, the articles and the books, and more recently through the establishment of a specialized professional designation, "financial gerontology"—both the phrase and the content—has become increasingly familiar as a central component of both gerontological and financial practice. (See also CPA ELDERCARE SERVICES; FINANCIAL ADVISORS; FINANCIAL LITERACY; FINANCIAL PLANNING PROCESS; RETIREMENT PLANNING; WEALTH SPAN.)

References

Cutler, N.E. 2002. *Advising Mature Clients: The New Science of Wealth Span Planning*. New York: John Wiley & Sons.

Cutler, N.E., D.W. Gregg, and M.P. Lawton, eds. 1992. *Aging, Money, and Life Satisfaction Aspects of Financial Gerontology*. New York: Springer Publishing.

Vitt, L.A., and J.K. Siegenthaler. 1996. *Encyclopedia of Financial Gerontology*. Westport, CT: Greenwood Press.

Neal E. Cutler

FINANCIAL LITERACY, an understanding of a broad range of financial topics, from basic money management—budgeting, saving, insuring, and investing—to economics and how households make decisions within a set of economic conditions and circumstances. The consistent themes running through most discussions of financial literacy include:

1. Being knowledgeable, educated, and informed on the issues of managing money and assets, banking, investments, credit, insurance, and taxes in a given economic environment;
2. Understanding the basic concepts underlying the management of money and assets (e.g., the time value of money in investments and the pooling of risks in insurance); and
3. Using that knowledge and understanding to plan and implement personal financial decisions.

Why Is Financial Literacy Important?

People today are more responsible for their own retirement income security. Over the past 15 to 20 years there has been a shift in responsibility for long-term well-being away from institutions (employers, the government) to individuals. For example, in 1980, 70% of pension plans were defined contribution (DC, as opposed to defined benefit plans; DC plans shift more of the responsibility for the growth of retirement funds to the consumer); by 1997, 92% of plans were defined contribution (Conte 1998). In 1988, one-fourth (25%) of workers were covered primarily by DC plans; in 1998, over three-fifths (63%) were covered by such plans (Copeland 2002). According to Mitchell and Dykes (2001), "[F]uture pension growth will be concentrated in the DC arena, with increasing participant control being exerted over all aspects of the plans—including contributions, investment mix, and payouts."

If families are to make decisions and successfully manage their contributions, investment mix, and payouts, they need to be financially literate. Yet, in one survey, 35% of respondents could not even guess at how much they needed. Of those that did try to provide a savings estimate, on average the number they posed was 44% below their expected needs (Dolliver 2001). In its 2001 Retirement Confidence Survey, the Employee Benefit Research Institute found that only 39% had tried to calculate how much money they will need to save (this was down from 51% in 2000 but up from 32% in 1993) (EBRI 2001).

Using data from the 1998 Survey of Consumer Finances, Montalto (2000) showed that

56% of nonretired U.S. households had fewer assets than they would need to supplement Social Security and pension income throughout their retirement if they planned to maintain their level of living. Level of income, development of a financial plan, and participation in employer-related retirement programs were the most significant factors in determining whether households had saved enough for retirement.

Another possible reason households may be undersaving for retirement could be the complexity of choices offered by employers. In 1994, participants in employers' 401(k) plans had an average of 4.6 investment choices for their funds; by 1998, this had risen to an average of 8.4 (Kochard and Gaumnitz 2000). As the number of choices rise, participants can become frustrated and confused. Madrian and Shea (2000) indicate that employee inertia and procrastination in retirement planning and participation in 401(k) plans may be due to the complexity of choices as well as the lack of information.

Even among households that save, job changes can mean that workers need to move funds from one retirement plan to another. While 60% of payouts made to people changing jobs were rolled over into IRA (Individual Retirement Account)-type accounts, two out of five payouts were spent on consumption. Nearly all payouts over $100,000 were rolled over, while nearly all smaller payouts (under $4,000) were taken as cash (Yakoboski 1997). Small amounts may never have the chance to grow into larger amounts if families don't keep their money invested.

Credit Literacy

As of May 2002, consumers had about $712.2 billion outstanding in revolving credit, up about 6.8% from the previous year. Some of this credit is paid off each month; however, about 60% of U.S. households revolve some portion of their credit card balances. For those that revolve, the Federal Reserve Board reported that their balances were $4,100 in 1998. Other estimates show credit card balances as high as $8,000 in 2000 (McGinn et al. 2001). One out of five families with incomes under $50,000 spend at least 40% of after-tax income on debt servicing (Kennickell, Starr-McCluer, and Surette 2000). Needless to say, money spent on credit card debt is money that cannot go toward retirement savings.

Bankruptcy has also risen over recent years, from 1.27 million households in 1999–2000 to 1.38 million in 2000–2001. Preliminary data for 2002 period show projections of 1.4 to 1.5 million bankruptcies (ABI World 2002).

Another concern among financial planners is the amount of debt held in home equity loans and lines of credit. Housing equity is the major asset in most households' portfolio, but the growth in both the proportion of households with home equity loans and the value of those loans has implications for the use of housing wealth as an asset in retirement. The proportion of households with home equity loans doubled between 1983 and 1997, from 7% to 13% (Canner, Durkin, and Luckett 1998), and the dollar value of home equity loans nearly tripled from $256.4 billion to $725.6 billion between 1991 and 2002 (Federal Reserve Board 2002). Furthermore, roughly one-third of households who refinance their mortgages "cash out" some of the equity in their homes; in 1998–1999, the average amount of this "cash-out" was about $18,000 (Brady, Canner, and Maki 2000).

Beyond these statistics, there is evidence that financially unsavvy consumers are having problems in the marketplace. For example, there is substantial anecdotal evidence of predatory lending that strips home equity from homeowners. Predatory lending has not been explicitly defined, but it can involve loans that carry high costs—either in terms of interest rates or fees—or practices such as "packing" (adding unnecessary insurance coverage) or "flipping" (frequent refinancing of the loan, usually with fees and charges rolled into the refinanced amount), and features such as prepayment penalties, balloon payments, and mandatory arbitration clauses. While most of the focus on predatory lending has been on home-secured loans, there are other high-cost loans in the market, including high-cost auto loans with interest rates ranging from 15% to 25%, credit cards with interest rates ranging from 20% to 40%, payday loans that can carry annual percentage rates of 300% or more, and rent-to-own transactions with implicit interest rates over 100%.

What Financial Literacy Initiatives Are Underway?

There seems to be an abundance of activity on the financial literacy front. Vitt et al. (2000) identify 91 programs offered by schools, Cooperative Extension, colleges (including community colleges), the military, faith-based organizations, community groups, employers, and others. The National Endowment for Financial Education lists over 150 educational resources from a wide range of agencies, organizations, and firms in its Economic Independence Clearinghouse database; many of these materials are available in multiple languages.

Just as there are numerous initiatives, so too are there numerous target audiences. Preretirees, youth, military personnel, low-income families, first-time homebuyers, employees, church members, and women are all targets of one program or another. There are programs targeted to various ethnic groups (e.g., Native Americans or immigrants), various situational groups (including prerelease prisoners), and various demographic groups (such as new parents or preretirees). In essence, it would be difficult for a U.S. consumer not to be part of a target audience for at least one financial literacy initiative.

Adult audiences often connect with financial literacy programs through the workplace. However, they are just as likely to find financial literacy programs via community groups, social service agencies, faith-based organizations, or special interest or affinity groups such as the Parent-Teacher Association (PTA) or AARP.

One task facing human resource professionals, counselors, and educators is finding meaningful learning experiences for audiences. In a recent survey, consumers were more likely to say they learned from the "school of hard knocks" than from formal—or even informal—educational experiences (Perry and Ards 2001). A study of low-income consumers revealed a preference for learning from friends and peers who are successful money managers (Hogarth and Swanson 1993). Thus, traditional "classroom" and lecture-format programs may not succeed with some audiences. Toussaint-Comeau and Rhine (2000) discuss the pros and cons of a variety of delivery strategies, including information seminars, pamphlets and brochures, mass media (newspaper, radio, television), individualized learning (video or DVD), and Web-based delivery. They note that delivery strategy, audience, and topic need to be considered holistically when designing financial education initiatives.

As families become more pressed for time and grapple with increased information loads, educators will need to use alternative strategies—Web or computer based, video/DVD, or audiotapes—to deliver financial education programs. However, the efficacy of these delivery methods has yet to be shown.

Legislative and public policy initiatives are also driving and developing financial literacy efforts. In February 2002, the U.S. Senate Banking, Housing and Urban Affairs committee held two days of hearings on financial literacy with testimony from the Federal Reserve, the U.S. Treasury, and the Securities and Exchange Commission as well as other not-for-profit and private sector participants (see http://banking.senate.gov/02_02hrg/020502/index.htm for an example). In April 2002, the U.S. Department of the Treasury announced a new Office of Financial Education to improve financial education for all Americans by developing and implementing financial education policy initiatives and coordinating Treasury's outreach efforts.

Are Financial Literacy Initiatives Working?

A number of groups (the Consumer Federation of America, the Jump$tart Coalition for Personal Financial Literacy, Americans for Consumer Education and Competition, the American Savings Education Council) have conducted financial literacy quizzes with different audiences. Most of these show that literacy levels are low.

Researchers have just begun to address the question of how literacy and financial behaviors relate. Perhaps the greatest challenge in financial literacy is measuring the efficacy of any program. Getting one's financial house in order can take time, and longitudinal studies to prove that a particular program is effective are costly to conduct. However, there have been some longer-term impact and evaluation studies that show that financial education can make a difference.

Bernheim, Garrett, and Maki (2001) studied the relationship between high school financial curriculum mandates and adult savings patterns and net worth. The study concluded that mandates increase exposure to financial education, and financial education is associated with higher savings rates and higher net worth. They conclude that "education may be a powerful tool for stimulating personal saving".

Money 2000, a Cooperative Extension System program that focuses on participant debt reduction and/or savings accumulation, includes an extended-period behavioral monitoring program. As of the end of 2000, over 13,000 participants in 22 states reported cumulative increased savings of $10,618,271 and cumulative decreased consumer debts of $8,247,219 (a total effect of $18,865,490 (*Money2000* 2000).

Individual development accounts (IDAs) are a relatively new policy initiative designed to help low-income families build wealth. IDAs are meant to improve access to savings institutions for the poor by providing matching funds for savings toward homeownership, higher education, and microenterprise. Financial education is part of the IDA initiative. An evaluation of 2,378 IDA participants showed that average monthly net deposits "increased sharply as hours of general financial [education] attendance increased from zero to 12, after which it leveled off" (Schreiner et al. 2001). This finding seems to confirm Berhneim and colleagues that education is a powerful tool for stimulating savings.

Hirad and Zorn (2001) examined the effectiveness of prepurchase homeownership counseling on reducing 90-day delinquency rates. "Counseling" was defined as "specific and tailored to the particular needs of the individual, while education typically is administered in a generic program". Borrowers receiving counseling had a 19% lower 90-day delinquency rate than those without counseling and lower delinquency rates than those receiving classroom counseling and home study counseling.

The implication for retirement planning education may be to include one-to-one counseling sessions as part of the educational program. In any case, it is important to recognize that information is not the same as education. Benefits counselors, financial counselors, and community educators can help make sure that information leads to education—and the resultant change in behavior that improves the economic security and stability of the family.

These examples provide some concrete evidence that financial education—in various forms—can work to improve the economic status of families. However, it is important to remind ourselves that at the same time these programs are showing positive impacts at the microlevel, we still see evidence of problems with credit and bankruptcy and with a lack of planning and participation in retirement savings at the macrolevel. There is still much room for improvement in the financial literacy levels of U.S. households. (See also AGING INTO DEBT; FINANCIAL EDUCATION FOR SENIORS; INVESTOR EDUCATION; KING LEAR SYNDROME; RETIREMENT PREPAREDNESS; U.S. PERSONAL SAVING RATE.)

References

ABI World. 2002. "U.S. Bankruptcy Filing Statistics." Available online at http://www.abiworld.org/stats/newstatsfront.html.

Bernheim, B. Douglas, D.M. Garrett, and Dean M. Maki. 2001. "Education and Saving: The Long-Term Effects of High School Financial Curriculum Mandates." *Journal of Public Economics* 80: 435–65.

Brady, Peter J., Glenn B. Canner, and Dean M. Maki. 2000. "The Effects of Recent Mortgage Refinancing." *Federal Reserve Bulletin* 86: 441–50.

Canner, Glenn B., Thomas A. Durkin, and Charles A. Luckett. 1998. "Recent Developments in Home Equity Lending." *Federal Reserve Bulletin* 84: 241–51.

Conte, C. 1998. *The National Summit on Retirement Savings: Agenda Background Materials.* Washington, DC: U.S. Department of Labor.

Copeland, Craig. 2002. "An Analysis of the Retirement and Pension Plan Coverage Topical Module of SIPP." *EBRI Issue Brief* 245 (Employee Benefit Research Institute).

Dolliver, M. 2001. "Just Blame It on Ignorance, If Not on Improvidence." *Adweek* 42(11): 45.

Employee Benefit Research Institute (EBRI). 2001. "The 2001 Retirement Confidence Survey Summary of Findings." Available online at http://www.asec.org/2001rcs/01rcses.pdf.

Federal Reserve Board. 2002. "Flow of Funds Accounts of the United States." Table L.218. Available online at http://www.federalreserve.gov/releases/Z1/Current/z1r-4.pdf.

Hirad, A., and Peter M. Zorn. 2001. "A Little Knowledge Is a Good Thing: Empirical Evidence of the Effectiveness of Pre-purchase Homeownership Counseling." Working Paper. McLean, VA: Freddie Mac.

Hogarth, Jeanne M., and Josephine A. Swanson. 1993. "Voices of Experience: Limited Resource Families and Financial Management." American Home Economics Association, *Family Economics & Management Conference Proceedings*, 13–28.

Kennickell, Arthur B., Martha Starr-McCluer, and Brian Surette. 2000. "Recent Changes in U.S. Family Finances: Results from the 1998 Survey of Consumer Finances." *Federal Reserve Bulletin* 86: 1–29.

Kochard, Lawrence E., and Jack Gaumnitz. 2000. "The Transition from Defined Benefit to Defined Contribution Pension Plans in the Public Sector." Kansas Public Policy Institute. Available online at http://www.flinthills.org/Publications/General%20Policy/transition.htm.

Madrian, Brigitte C., and Dennis F. Shea. 2000. "The Power of Suggestion: Inertia in 401(k)

Participation and Savings Behavior." NBER Working Paper. Available online at http://www.nber.org/papers/w7682.

McGinn, Daniel, Adam Bryant, Keith Naughton, Kevin Peraino, Erika Check, Joan Raymond, Ellise Pierce, Jane Spencer, Dori Perrucci, Brian Braiker, and Andrea Cooper. 2001. "Maxed Out." *Newsweek*, August 27, 34–41.

Mitchell, Olivia S., and Erica L. Dykes. 2001. "New Trends in U.S. Pensions." Pension Research Council, Wharton School of Business, University of Pennsylvania. Available online at http://prc.wharton.upenn.edu/prc/PRC/WP/wp2000-1rev.pdf.

Money2000. 2000. "Impact Data and Research Results." Available online at http://www.money2000.org/prac/impact.htm.

Montalto, Catherine. 2000. "New Study: More, than Half of Americans Behind in Saving for Retirement." Press release from Consumer Federation of America, April 20. Available online at http://www.consumerfed.org/nrl5.pdf.

Perry, Vanessa G., and S. Ards. 2001. "The Freddie Mac Consumer Credit Initiative: How Consumers Learn about Credit and Implications for Consumer Education and Policy." Working Paper. McLean, VA: Freddie Mac, April.

Schreiner, Mark, Michael Sherraden, Margaret Clancy, Lissa Johnson, Jami Curley, Michal Grinstein-Weiss, Min Zhan, and Sondra Beverly. 2001. *Savings and Asset Accumulation in Individual Development Accounts*. St. Louis, MO: Center for Social Development, Washington University.

Toussaint-Comeau, Maude, and Sherrie L.W. Rhine. 2000. "Delivery of Financial Literacy Programs." Federal Reserve Bank of Chicago Policy Studies #2000-7/. Available online at http://www.chicagofed.org/publications/publicpolicystudies/ccapolicystudy/pdf/cca-2000-7.pdf.

Vitt, Lois A., Carol Anderson, Jamie Kent, Deanna M. Lyter, Jurg K. Siegenthaler, and Jeremy W. Kent. 2000. *Personal Finance and the Rush to Competence: Financial Literacy Education in the U.S.* Middleburg, VA: Institute for Socio-Financial Studies.

Yakoboski, Paul. 1997. "Large Pan Lump-sum Rollovers and Cashouts." *EBRI Issue Brief* 188 (Employee Benefit Research Institute).

Jeanne M. Hogarth

FINANCIAL PLANNING PROCESS, the process of meeting life goals through the proper management of finances. Financial planning is distinguished from financial counseling by a relative absence of crisis orientation and a relatively higher degree of client affluence. Both involve efforts to increase clients' financial literacy. Financial planning proceeds, generally, along a six-step path: (1) establishing and defining the client-planner relationship; (2) gathering client data, including goals; (3) analyzing and evaluating financial status; (4) developing and presenting financial planning recommendations or alternatives; (5) implementing agreed-upon recommendations; and (6) monitoring the plan and keeping it current.

The professionals who prepare financial plans for clients are known as financial planners and can work in several settings including small financial planning practices, large financial services firms, credit unions, banks, and other financial institutions. The setting, however, is not as important as the match between the client and financial advisor, including how well they are able to communicate and the strength of the personal rapport that is developed between them. Financial planners are compensated in different ways for the services they provide. Some earn commissions on the sale of financial products, and others earn fees only for consulting services. Still others earn a combination of both commissions and fees. It is important for prospective clients to understand the system of payment for financial planners, as the form of payment may constitute a conflict of interest or otherwise color the advice being given. Whether a financial planner is paid by fees or by commissions, particularly if commissions are received per transaction, at least part of the underlying incentive is to earn as much as possible. This can mean trading investments more often than is necessary. While no ethical financial planner would do this consciously, a prospective client should be aware of the possibility of investment churning in light of the system of compensation used by the professional.

While all financial planners are trained to provide comprehensive financial planning services, some specialize in one or more areas or work with specific types of clients. Some are specifically interested in and trained to advise future retirees and older adults. Other specialties include planning for long-term care expenses, including advice on regulations concerning Medicaid eligibility, asset management, or business succession planning. Several candidates should always be interviewed until a prospective client is satisfied that his or her financial planning and investment approach and philosophy and that of the financial planner match.

The financial planning process itself begins with an initial meeting, usually in the financial planner's office. The initial meeting is generally held at no charge and is meant to be an introductory meeting at which the client should be concerned with determining the level of rapport possible with the planner and the extent to which the planner seems capable of doing what the client wants done. The first meeting is the time to get a feel for the communication style of the planner and potential compatibility to the client's own style, as well as the planner's skills and expertise.

In addition, the first meeting should initiate the process of establishing and defining the client's life situation and goals. Financial planners should also be able to explain and document the services that they provide and should give the client an understanding of what is expected from them; the client should obtain the same understanding of the planner. The planner should also fully explain how he or she will be compensated and by whom. Finally, planner and client should agree on how long the professional relationship should last and on how decisions will be made regarding implementation of the financial plan.

Subsequent meetings will begin delving into the facts of the client's situation. The planner will ask the client for all information relevant to the client's current financial situation, as well as any foreseeable financial realities such as inheritance or parental (or sibling) dependency. In addition, the planner will ask more questions about the client's aims and goals and clarify expectations for what the financial advisor will do how to judge whether his or her mutually agreed-upon financial plan is working. Establishing these parameters at this point will forestall potential problems in expectations or communication for both parties and establish a foundation upon which the relationship can work. In terms of a client's financial goals, the more the financial planner can know about what the client wants to happen for himself or herself and family, if applicable, the better both will be able to plan for both short- and long-term concerns. Some planners will use these early meetings to delve into the client's psychological relationship to money and family money history for added insight into the client's life situation.

The advisor will need to gather data such as tax returns, mortgage information, investment assets, company benefit information, insurance documents, wills, trusts, and advance directives to get a better understanding of where the client stands financially and legally. Although this can occur in the first meeting, it is more often a two-step process, with the first meeting promoting understanding of the working relationship and then a second (or even third) meeting to go through the data required to develop the plan. At this point the advisor will begin to analyze and evaluate the client's financial status. The planner will develop an analysis that covers all identified areas of concern, as well as any others the planner identifies while doing the analysis. These could include retirement planning projections, income tax analysis, estate planning issues, investment strategies, protection planning, or financial position planning. All the above may be appropriate, or only one or two areas may need to be covered based on what the client and financial advisor have discussed.

Next, the planner will develop and present the financial planning recommendations and/or alternatives and model the results for the client if the recommendations are implemented. The plan itself should provide specific recommendations that address the client's goals. To the extent that the client's goals have been understood by both the client and the planner, the financial plan is likely to be a success. Once the client and the advisor have reviewed the analysis and the recommendations and agree on the plan, the next step, of course, is to implement the recommendations. The planner will either take responsibility for implementing the plan or instruct the client on how to carry out the recommendations, depending on the terms agreed to in the first meeting.

The final step in the financial planning process is monitoring the financial plan. Once the plan is implemented, life happens, and both situations and objectives are dynamic. A financial plan must be reviewed on a periodic basis, generally at least once a year, to make sure it is on track to achieving the client's goals. (See also BABY BOOMERS AND RETIREMENT; CPA ELDERCARE SERVICES; FINANCIAL ADVISORS; LIFE PLANNING; RETIREMENT PLANNING; RETIREMENT PREPAREDNESS.)

Organization

CFP Board

References

Financial Executives Research Foundation. 2003. *Benchmarking the Planning Process.* Florham, NJ: Financial Executive Research.

Shilling, Dana. 2002. *Financial Planning for the Older Client.* 5th ed. Cincinnati, OH: National Underwriter.

Chip Eubank

FINANCIAL RECOVERY IN LATER LIFE, the process of overcoming a financial setback such as an investment loss or loss of a job. It is often more difficult to recover from financial setbacks as one gets older. There is less time available to invest for retirement, to recoup money lost in the stock market, or to receive "payback" (with a higher salary) from investments in human capital (e.g., college degree). Therefore, it is wise to begin financial planning in early adulthood, in case something goes awry and to increase one's financial resilience.

Financial resilience is the ability to withstand life events, both negative (e.g., loss of a job) and positive (e.g., birth of a child), that impact one's income and/or assets at any age. Some financially stressful events, such as increased family size, unemployment, divorce, widowhood, disability, and health problems, affect people individually. Others, such as layoffs, plant closings, corporate scandals (e.g., Enron), recessions, stock market downturns, and acts of terrorism, affect large groups of people or society as a whole.

Later Life Financial Challenges

Unemployment

Losing a job—at any age—is traumatic, even when a worker receives some severance pay. In addition to loss of income and/or employee benefits, there is a feeling of insecurity as one's way of life is disrupted. Workers faced with involuntary retirement in later life must take stock of their financial resources, marketable job skills, and emotional readiness—or not—for retirement.

The federal COBRA (Consolidated Omnibus Budget Reconciliation Act) law provides an opportunity for continuation of health insurance for up to 18 months, at group rates plus a 2% administrative fee, until an individual policy (or new group coverage) is obtained or a worker is eligible for Medicare. Thus, those who leave a job at age 63½ can use COBRA benefits to tide them over until they are eligible for Medicare at age 65. However, only workers covered by employers with 20 or more employees are eligible for COBRA benefits, and the cost is expensive for someone out of work, often over $600 per month for a family (Von Bergen 2002).

Eight of ten laid-off workers receive severance pay, typically a week of pay per year of service, often with continuation of health insurance benefits while severance pay is received (Siskos 2002). Sometimes it is possible to negotiate for additional perks such as outplacement support, continued benefits, or a larger severance. Another important resource is state unemployment benefits, available to workers who lose a job through no fault of their own. Unemployed workers should file a claim as soon as possible to collect what they are due.

Early Retirement Incentive Offers

Most workers assume they will decide when to retire. Sometimes, however, an employer suggests it in the form of an early retirement (a.k.a. "buyout") offer. An early retirement offer may or may not be voluntary. If it seems likely that employees will lose their jobs anyway with less generous terms (e.g., a specific department is being targeted), taking a buyout is typically advised (Wollan 2002). Buyout offers often include enhanced pension benefits, lump-sum cash payments, and/or continued group health insurance coverage. A typical offer adds two to five years of age and service credit to pension benefit formulas so that workers receive about the same amount they would have received at the employer's normal retirement age.

Employers offer early retirement incentives to save money, usually during economic recessions. They also want to be good to employees and to minimize damage to morale, which is why they provide buyout benefits instead of a pink slip. Many employers require employees who accept a buyout to sign a release saying that they accept the package in exchange for agreeing not to file an age discrimination lawsuit (Mendels 2001). Usually workers have only 45 to 90 days in which to decide to accept a buyout offer. Key factors to consider include attractiveness of a buyout offer, financial stability of the employer, other employment options, access to health insurance, job enjoyment and stresses, emotional readiness for retirement, and payment methods.

Poor or Uncertain Health Prognosis

A life-threatening disease or chronic, debilitating illness prior to or during retirement is a financial wake-up call. Some people accelerate their retirement date to enjoy unstructured time while they can. Others reduce their work hours because they want to or have to (e.g., fatigue). A revised retirement savings analysis that incorporates the health prognosis is in order. Life expectancy estimates and retirement savings plan contributions may need to be adjusted. A poor or uncertain health prognosis may also prompt the drafting of estate planning documents that, ideally, should be in place regardless of health status. These include a will, living will, and durable power of attorney.

Adequate provisions should be made for an ill person's spouse. This includes life and health insurance, pension benefit distributions, IRA (Individual Retirement Account) withdrawals, and/or trust arrangements. Beneficiary designations on insurance policies and tax-deferred retirement savings plans should also be checked to make sure that they are current and don't conflict with the ill spouse's will.

Disability

Three out of ten workers between ages 35 and 65 are disabled, due to accident or illness, for 90 days or longer, and almost one in five will become disabled for 5 years or more (College for Financial Planning 2002). The financial consequences of losing income for many months can be devastating. Not only do many disabled workers not receive a paycheck, but expenses associated with a disability, such as medical bills, create additional financial pressure.

The best defense against potential loss of earning power is disability insurance that replaces lost income. Unfortunately, many workers have minimal, if any, disability coverage. Some mistakenly believe that Social Security or their employer will cover them. In fact, Social Security uses a strict definition of eligibility that disqualifies many workers, and employer group policies are generally short term (e.g., six months). The best individual disability insurance policies have the following features: a liberal definition of disability as the inability to perform the duties of one's current occupation, coverage to age 65, a noncancellable policy form, and monthly benefits equal to about two-thirds of gross income.

Death of a Spouse

Few events can turn a person's financial life upside down as the death of a spouse. In addition to shock, grief, and loss of a spouse's companionship, there is often less household income than before. There are also many decisions to be made (e.g., investing life insurance proceeds), forms to be completed, and suggestions from "helpful" family members and/or financial salespeople. For some survivors, the pressure to do something—anything—becomes unbearable. Decisions are made quickly, much like a "hot potato" that must be tossed away.

Most experts advise surviving spouses to take their time and not make any major financial decisions immediately. Survivors who receive an insurance settlement or other payment can place the funds in a certificate of deposit (CD) or money market mutual fund until they have time to explore longer-term investment alternatives and/or educate themselves about personal finance. Another important step is to identify and secure available resources. Examples include life insurance policy proceeds, employee benefits, and Veteran's benefits.

Divorce

During the process of divorce, two people are expected to make rational and far-reaching decisions at a time of emotional turmoil. This may also be their first experience with the court system and hiring an attorney. Expenses often increase when one spouse moves out and sets up a separate household. Couples must estimate the dollar value of their household property and divide their debts. If either party doesn't pay a jointly held debt, however, creditors may collect from either spouse. Divorce is particularly devastating, financially, for displaced homemakers that lack current employment skills.

If a marriage lasts ten years or longer, divorced spouses can receive Social Security benefits based on the higher of their ex-spouse's earnings or their own. Divorced persons may be entitled to continuing group health insurance for up to 36 months under the federal COBRA law if they lose their status as a dependent spouse. Asset divisions at divorce are not always equal. For example, if one spouse takes sole possession of the family home, he or she also shoulders the burden of future property taxes, repairs, and possible capital gains taxes. If the other spouse receives the same dollar value in a pension, she or he has an asset that will continue to grow tax-deferred: an apparently equal distribution of property is not. Most states apply equitable distribution statutes to divide marital property.

Investment Losses

Prolonged market slumps, such as from 2000 to the present, significantly erode gains made during previous bull markets. Many investment portfolios in early 2003 are a small fraction of their former value. The last time that investors experienced three consecutive years of stock market declines was 1939–1941 (Stewart 2002). Not surprisingly, many investors have discovered that their risk tolerance isn't as aggressive as they thought it was. Some have sold stock at a loss and fled to cash and bonds paying historically low interest rates.

Investment experts preach patience and a long-term perspective. Investors who try to "time the market" often miss the best trading days that inevitably follow days with large losses. History tells us that after a bear market stocks rise quickly. Since 1926, the S&P 500 index has risen an average of 32% in the first six months after a bear market ("Don't Wait" 2002). Bear markets are particularly traumatic for those approaching or in retirement, who may not have the luxury of time to "ride it out." Limiting withdrawals from investment accounts is often required to reduce the risk of outliving one's income.

Financial Recovery Strategies

These strategies can help recover lost income and/or assets following one or more of the life events described above. These strategies can also be used by late savers to make up for lost time and to prepare for a comfortable retirement.

Increase Contributions to Tax-Deferred Retirement Savings Plans. The 2001 tax law increased annual contribution limits for IRAs and employer 401(k), 403(b), and Section

457 plans, at least through 2010. Just a 1% increase in the amount of pay diverted to savings can result in thousands of additional dollars at retirement. Americans contributed an average of $3,514 to 401(k) plans in 2001 (Opdyke and Higgins 2002). The maximum plan contribution limits are $12,000 in 2003, $13,000 in 2004, $14,000 in 2005, $15,000 in 2006, and higher amounts adjusted for inflation thereafter.

Take Advantage of Catch-Up Provisions. Tax law changes also provide workers age 50 and older the opportunity to make additional "catch-up" contributions, above the maximum amounts listed above, to Roth and Traditional IRAs and to employer salary deferral plans. IRA catch-up contributions are $500 for 2003–2005 and $1,000 for 2006 and after. Catch-up contributions for employer plans are $2,000 in 2003, $3,000 in 2004, $4,000 in 2005, and $5,000 in 2006, with amounts adjusted for inflation in 2007 and after. Older workers who take full advantage of the increased contribution limits *and* catch-up contributions will save significantly more than those who invest in taxable accounts or limit their contributions to pre-2002 tax law limits.

Fund Multiple Salary Deferral Plans. If eligible to participate, workers can contribute to more than one type of salary reduction plan. For example, the annual maximum for a Section 457 plan is not reduced by amounts contributed to 403(b), 401(k), SEP (Simplified Employee Pension), or SIMPLE (Savings Incentive Match Plan for Employees) plans. Combined salary reduction contributions cannot exceed $24,000 (2 × $12,000) in 2003.

Accelerate Debt Repayment. Debt payments can be reallocated to retirement savings once creditors are repaid. Specific strategies include paying more than the minimum amount due, requesting a lower interest rate from existing creditors, and transferring balances to lower rate credit cards or loans. Another time- and money-saving strategy is adding the monthly payment from a paid-off debt to remaining debts, in descending order by interest rate.

"Moonlight" for Additional Income. A second job or self-employment, in addition to one's "day job," provides additional income to invest for retirement and access to tax-deferred plans (e.g., SEPs, Keoghs) and tax-deductible business expenses for self-employed persons. It can also serve as a "bridge job" to work following retirement and to provide an opportunity to develop new career skills.

Invest Aggressively. The S&P 500 stock index has averaged about 10% since 1926, compared to under 4% for Treasury bills. The more stock in an investor's portfolio, the higher the average annual return over time periods of ten years or more. The trade-off for aggressive investing is increased short-term volatility. Investment risk is reduced over long holding periods, however, based on a principle called "time diversification." A later life investor's investment time horizon can be reset to their entire life expectancy, not just their retirement date, to take advantage of this principle.

Invest Strategically. Sector investing involves purchasing investments in companies or industry sectors (e.g., health care) that one believes will do exceptionally well and produce superior performance. An example is identifying companies that make products or services of interest to aging baby boomers. There is more risk, however, due to reduced diversification and the potential for poor timing of sector investments.

Maximize Tax Advantages. In addition to making tax-deferred contributions to employer retirement plans, other tax-saving strategies include investing in tax-exempt securities (e.g., municipal bonds) and holding investments for more than a year to take advantage of long-term capital gains rates. Another is investing in tax-deferred annuities with after-tax dollars after maximum contributions are made to an IRA and employer salary reduction plan.

Spend Less in Retirement. If you spend less in retirement, you'll need less of a nest egg. The best way to plan ahead is to track current living costs and to project expenses that will end or decrease and those that will get larger or begin for the first time (e.g., Medigap health insurance premiums). For each $50 that projected monthly spending in retirement can be reduced, the amount of savings needed to fund retirement is reduced by about $10,000, assuming you'll need income for about 30 years (Kristof 2002).

Trade Down. One way to reduce retirement living expenses is to trade down to a smaller home. Proceeds from the sale, minus the cost of new housing, are available to invest. In addition, maintenance, utilities, and property taxes are often lower on a smaller residence. Up to $250,000 of capital gain for singles ($500,000 for couples filing jointly) is exempt from income taxation.

Move to a Less Expensive Location. Taking advantage of differences in housing and other living costs (e.g., property taxes) in different geographic regions is another way to make ends meet. This strategy obviously works only for persons currently living in a high-cost area who can move to an area with lower expenses without other, offsetting negative effects (such as poor access to health care or inability to visit grandchildren).

Delay Retirement Date. Remaining on the job a few more years than originally planned provides additional income to invest and postpones withdrawals from invested assets. Working longer also shortens the time that savings must last and can result in higher pension and/or Social Security benefits than what would be available at an earlier age.

Work After Retirement. Working after retirement stretches retirement assets by providing income that reduces the amount that must be withdrawn. For example, with $200,000 of savings earning 8%, someone could withdraw 5% ($10,000) annually without touching principal and still have a cushion for inflation (ignoring taxation). Viewed another way, however, for every $10,000 of post-retirement earnings, $200,000 of income-providing assets are not required.

Obtain a Reverse Mortgage. Reverse mortgages allow homeowners age 62 and older to borrow against accumulated home equity and receive either a lump sum, monthly payments, or a line of credit. Factors that affect the amount received are the age of the youngest homeowner, the amount of home equity, and current interest rates. The loan is repaid with borrower's equity after the home is sold or the homeowner(s) move or die.

Consider a Sale-Leaseback. Another option to tap home equity for retirement living expenses is to sell a house, typically to a family member, and lease it back. This strategy provides income and tax advantages to the new owner and allows the original owner to remain in the home at a reasonable cost.

Make Tax-Efficient Asset Withdrawals. Retirement savings last longer when invested assets are withdrawn tax-efficiently. Generally, this means tapping taxable accounts or tax-exempt investments first, followed by retirement accounts made with after-tax dollars, and then accounts funded with before-tax dollars. Withdrawals from Roth IRAs should be made last because they have no minimum withdrawal age and earnings grow tax-free.

Rethink the Word "Retirement". The concept of retirement as a prolonged period of total leisure is changing as Americans live longer and healthier lives (Anthony 2001). Studies indicate that a majority of baby boomers plan to work at least part-time when they leave their present job. Many want greater flexibility and stress in the work they perform but desire to remain employed for income, socialization opportunities, and/or daily structure. (See also AGING INTO DEBT; BABY BOOMERS AND RETIREMENT; CONSUMER CREDIT; FINANCIAL COUNSELING FOR MID- TO LATER LIFE; RETIREMENT PREPAREDNESS; U.S. PERSONAL SAVING RATES.)

References

Anthony, M. 2001. *The New Retirementality*. Chicago: Dearborn Financial Publishing.

College for Financial Planning. *Chartered Retirement Planning Counselor Professional Education Program*. 2002. Denver, CO: Author.

"Don't Wait." 2002. *Kiplinger's Personal Finance* (December).

Kristof, K. 2002. "Is It Time for You to Give Up on the Stock Market?" *The Star-Ledger* (Newark, NJ), October [n.d.].

Mendels, P. 2001. "Pay and Perks." *Business Week Online*, February 26. Available online at http://www.businessweek.com/careers/content/feb2001/ca20010226_383.htm.

O'Neill, Barbara. 2002. "Estimates and Tradeoffs: Planning Strategies for Retirement." *Proceedings of the Association for Financial Counseling and Planning Education*.

Opdyke, J.D., and M. Higgins. 2002. "Repairing the Damage to Your Nest Egg." *Wall Street Journal*, October 1, D1–D2.

Siskos, C. 2002. "No Long Goodbyes." *Kiplinger's Personal Finance* (August).

Stewart, J.B. 2002. "Apocalypse Now?" *Smart Money* (September): 43–44.

Von Bergen, J. 2002. "Health Coverage Adds to Unemployed's Peril." *The Star-Ledger* (Newark, NJ), January [n.d.].

Wollan, B. 2002. *Early Retirement Website*. Iowa State University Extension. Available online at http://www.extension.iastate.edu/financial/earlyret/.

Barbara O'Neill

FINANCIAL SECURITY IN RETIREMENT, freedom from fear and anxiety about having sufficient financial resources in later life. Whether considered from an individual perspective or from a societal view, the attainment of financial security in retirement may hold challenges.

From an individual perspective, financial security is subjective, grounded in psychological and spiritual considerations. Many people with adequate, even abundant, wealth may worry about running out of money and experience low levels of well-being. Others, who have little in the way of assets and/or material possessions, may experience a sense of security that includes feelings of material sufficiency.

In the macroview, during the twentieth century important progress was made in the United States toward eliminating poverty for people age 65 and older. Averages, however, can be deceiving, and the twenty-first century presents many unresolved questions. Social Security, Medicare, Medicaid, and employment-based retirement programs all face structural challenges, and few baby boomers can look forward to retirement either with pensions they will not outlive or savings and investments sufficient to finance their current lifestyles.

The financial elements of security in retirement may be addressed as four questions:

1. What sources of income will replace earnings from working?
2. How will the costs of acute medical care and chronic drug therapies be paid?

3. How will the costs for care be covered during periods of frailty?
4. What arrangements have been made for personal or charitable survivors?

Answers to these questions involve the following:

1. Adequate retirement income planning;
2. Medicare and Medicare Supplemental insurance (Medigap);
3. Frailty planning (Simmons and MacBean 2000); and
4. Estate (or legacy) planning.

These elements of financial security, of course, are interrelated, and a response to one is likely to impact the others. A strategy, for example, to maximize retirement income by taking a "life only" pension annuity option has obvious and significant implications for estate planning—especially from a spouse's perspective if the only life for which income is guaranteed is the worker's. A frailty planning strategy that relies on impoverishment (Medicaid) is likely to negatively impact both a retirement income plan and an estate plan. Although it may help to pay for chronic drug therapies, it could also leave a bitter legacy. No choice, however, is free of consequences, and financial security depends primarily upon having made adequate preparation for all four elements.

Retirement Income

Issues around retirement income planning are the most obvious. The traditional "three-legged stool" of retirement income planning—Social Security, pension income benefit, and income from personal savings and investments—is increasingly unsteady. Social Security faces a funding crisis in the first half of the twenty-first century because soon there may not be enough workers paying into the system to support those receiving its benefits. Social Security income lifts more than one in three older persons out of poverty—more than 60% of them women. It is by far the single most important contributor to financial security in old age in America (Porter, Larin, and Primus 1999).

Social Security replaces, on average, almost half of a worker's preretirement income (EPI 2003), or nearly two-thirds of the generally accepted income target for financial security. The prospect of higher income taxes or lower Social Security benefits, however, grows with every year of extended life expectancy and as baby boomers age toward retirement.

In addition, fewer Americans are beneficiaries of pension plans that they cannot outlive. The percentage of workers covered by defined benefit plans (having clearly identifiable monthly benefits upon retirement) has dropped to less than half of those covered in the early 1980s (EPI 2003). For older recipients of proposed cash balance pension plans, this gap is likely to grow.

Beyond these pension benefit trends, "retirement plans," such as 401(k)s and 403(b)s, are really tax-sheltered asset accumulation plans and are largely funded by employees themselves even though they are sponsored by employers. Since both the investment and longevity risks of these plans are borne by individual participants, their future viability for older persons is uncertain. IRAs (Individual Retirement Accounts), whether Roth or regular, present the same investment and longevity challenges. Worse, less than half of all workers participate in any sort of pension (EBRI 2002).

Retirees may be forced to shift their orientation from living on an income they can count on to selling off assets without using them up. Even when retirement planning results in some projected fixed percentage of preretirement income, the difference, psychologically, is between receiving an identifiable amount periodically and confronting the need to harvest assets while preserving the nest egg over a long life—or else run out of money. Analysis has shown that a liquidation rate of 4.5% of assets is sustainable for 20 or more years with better than 95% confidence regardless of investment mix. However, five or ten additional years of life drops that confidence rate to as little as 33% with a conservative portfolio mix of 20% stocks, 50% bonds, and 30% cash (Ameriks, Veres, and Warshawsky 2001). Investment management, then, is becoming a survival skill for some retirees. And those who have the least to manage may have both the greatest need and the poorest prospect of getting expert help.

For those retirees who are likely to need the security of regular monthly income, fixed annuities, including equity-indexed annuities, should be considered. These are financial vehicles that can alleviate fears concerning investment loss and the anxiety of outliving one's money. The popularity of annuities suffered in comparison to the exuberance of the late 1990s when the stock market was considered a much better bet. While sales of annuities are up from $98.5 billion in 1995 to $185.3 billion in 2001, the percentage of investors taking advantage of the guarantees available in these products has nonetheless dropped from 50% to 40%.

Health Care Expenses

The Medicare program still pays for acute health care for all older Americans, although it faces the same structural shifts as Social Security and, therefore, faces the same threats to programmatic stability. Attempts to incentivize health maintenance organizations (HMOs) to expand the traditional Medicare benefits package by providing dental, chronic prescription drug, and other therapies not otherwise included in original Medicare have not worked well and are declining. The expense of most acute care provided to retirees by their own physicians, in hospitals of their own choosing, is still covered by Medicare at rates for which providers are still willing to work.

However, the "gaps" in Medicare coverage can leave unwary older adults unprotected. The Part A deductible of $840 (in 2003) is not wealth threatening for most Americans, but an extended hospitalization with personal liability for deductibles and copays can create medical debts of over $36,000. Medicare Supplement Insurance (Medigap), standardized into ten plans ("Plan A" through "Plan J"), makes it possible for most retirees to obtain insurance that will cover these and other expenses, including limited prescription drug coverage. Still, extended drug therapies such as for arthritis or high blood pressure are not well covered either in Medicare or Medigap policies, and the costs of prescription drugs threaten financial security.

In addition, Medigap itself is expensive and incomplete. By one analysis, an individual may need to have saved between $116,000 and almost $1.5 million *over and above assets needed to generate retirement income* to pay out-of-pocket health care expenses from age 65 to age 100, and twice that for a couple (EBRI 2003).

Frailty Care

The financial aspects of frailty are similar. While the preponderance of long-term care is provided by family members, this shifts the costs from the cared-for to the caregiver. The 1999 *MetLife Juggling Act Study* (MetLife 1999) put the extent of this shift at up to $650,000 for some families. The alternative direct cost is often measured by the cost of moving into a nursing home, which is currently just over $5,000 per month per person on a national average. Full-time care at home, however, may be as expensive as institutional care, depending upon the level of care required.

Taxpayer-funded programs to provide security in the event of frailty are scarce, other than Medicaid, which is designed for the impoverished. Either long-term care insurance or extraordinary wealth are necessary to handle the care that extended frailty requires, so that friends, family, and other members of the community of support remain free to bolster the emotional and spiritual well-being of the frail older person.

Estate Planning

Sense of security in retirement will elude anyone who worries about what will happen to them when someone else dies. Whether the risk is loss of investment expertise, the absolute loss of income (e.g., because a pension benefit has no survivor benefit), the loss of assets to probate and estate taxes, or other circumstance of financial loss, providing for survivors is an element of financial security in retirement.

While money alone cannot provide security, the lack of money can generate insecurity. The key word is *security*, defined in Webster's *Third New International Dictionary of the English Language* as freedom from danger, fear, anxiety, or care. Real security, however, is not measured in currency. It is instead a feeling state: the internal, deep conviction that challenges can be handled as they arise. Information, attention, and intention, along with appropriate answers to the four financial questions, are the foundation of financial security in retirement. The required information is knowledge—and acknowledgment—of the challenges that might lie ahead and of the various tools and techniques to prepare for any that may arise. Information is widely available from employers and from financial services providers, on the Internet, in books and magazines, in financial education classes, and from professional advisors.

Paying attention to the financial details of future living is required over the long term, both before and after retirement. While denial is usually a problem, in retirement, denial is more likely to lead to disaster than to any sense of security. Unwillingness to be proactive about the possibility of frailty is an obvious example. Failure to be mindful creates financial risk, and worse, and the resulting financial problems may be compounded by the human costs of confusion, fear, anxiety, and even shame. Ultimately, financial security in retirement is an individual issue, because security is an individual experience. Government, employer, commercial, and community-sponsored programs and products will support each individual's sense of security to a greater or lesser extent depending upon their relevance and the individual's level of seeking. Collectively, these programs and products have done much to increase the possibility of Americans' financial security in retirement since the days of the Great Depression. (See also FINANCIAL PLANNING PROCESS; LIFE PLANNING; RETIREMENT PLANNING; RETIREMENT PREPAREDNESS; RISK TOLERANCE.)

Suggested Readings

Cutler, Neal E. 2002. *Advising Mature Clients: The New Science of Wealth Span Planning*. New York: John Wiley and Sons.

Needleman, Jacob. 1991. *Money and the Meaning of Life*. New York: Currency Doubleday.

References

Ameriks, John, Robert Veres, and Mark J. Warshawsky. 2001. "Making Retirement Income Last a Lifetime." *Journal of Financial Planning* (December).

Economic Policy Institute (EPI). 2003. *Issue Guide on Retirement Security. DOL Private Pension Plan Bulletin: Abstract of 1998*. Number 11, Winter 2001–2002. Washington, DC: U.S. Department of Labor, Pension and Welfare Benefits Administration. Available online at http://www.epinet.org/.

Employee Benefit Research Institute (EBRI). 2002. "An Analysis of the Retirement and Pension Plan Coverage Topical Module of SIPP." *EBRI Issue Brief* 245 (May).

Employee Benefit Research Institute (EBRI). 2003. "Retiree Health Benefits: Savings Needed to Fund Health Care in Retirement." *EBRI Issue Brief* 254 (February).

MetLife. 1999. *MetLife Juggling Act Study: Balancing Caregiving with Work and the Costs Involved*. New York: MetLife Mature Market Institute.

Porter, Kathryn H., Kathy Larin, and Wendell Primus. 1999. "Social Security and Poverty Among the Elderly: A National and State Perspective." Washington, DC: Center on Budget and Policy Priorities.

Simmons, Henry C., and E. Craig MacBean. 2000. *Thriving after 55: Your Guide to Fully Living the Rest of Your Life*, Richmond, VA: Prime Press.

E. Craig MacBean

FLEXIBLE BENEFIT PLANS, a form of employer-provided fringe benefit that permits employees to pay their share of benefit costs with pretax income and may permit them to choose from among a variety of benefits.

Tax Treatment of Fringe Benefits Led to Flexible Benefit Plans

As a general rule, fringe benefits (such as health insurance) are a form of compensation that is not subject to income tax, Social Security, or Medicare taxes. This is appealing to employers and employees because more of the employer's outlay accrues to the employee than it does when compensation takes the form of wages and is subject to these taxes. If the employee received the money necessary to buy the benefit, say health insurance, in the form of wages, he or she would have to spend more of his/her earnings because it would be "posttax."

The Internal Revenue Service (IRS) lays out specific rules that need to be followed in order for a fringe benefit to be treated as untaxed compensation to the employee. The following benefits are *tax exempt* to the employee if the IRS rules are followed:

- Health coverage (medical, dental, vision, prescription drug)
- Employee life insurance up to $50,000
- Accidental death and dismemberment benefits
- Pretax disability
- Paid time off
- Adoption expenses

The following benefits are always considered *taxable compensation* to the employee:

- Cash
- Employee life insurance greater than $50,000
- Dependent life insurance
- After-tax disability

If the employer offers a benefit package that allows the employee to choose from among different tax exempt benefits—for example, health insurance or life insurance—the plan as a whole is tax exempt because each included benefit is tax exempt. In 1978, the IRS issued new rules that permitted employers to offer a benefit package that offered a choice between taxable and nontaxable benefits without losing the tax exempt status of the former. It is this statute that governs flexible benefit plans.

Types of Flexible Benefit Plans

Several types of benefits fall under the heading of flexible benefit plans. Premium conversion plans, flexible spending accounts, and cafeteria plans all fall into this category of benefit. Identifying these plans can be confusing because they often are known by more than one name.

Premium Conversion Plan. This is the most common type of flexible benefit plan. Also known as a *premium only plan*, this plan option allows employees to make their contributions to group health and/or group term life insurance with pretax dollars. This means that the wages used to pay the employee's share of the premium will not be subject to federal or state income tax, nor is it subject to Social Security and Medicare taxes. Participation in these plans is voluntary but it is usually in the employee's best interest to participate because it can produce significant savings for most people.

Flexible Spending Accounts. The flexible spending account (FSA) allows employees to pay certain medical or dependent care expenses with pretax dollars. The employer may offer a *health care reimbursement account* (HCRA, for medical expenses) or *dependent care reimbursement account* (DCRA, for day care expenses) or may offer both. On an annual basis, the employee elects to have a predetermined amount of salary set aside in these specially designated accounts. Funds from the health care reimbursement account are used to "reimburse" the employee for medical expenses that they have incurred that were not reimbursed by insurance. Likewise, the dependent care reimbursement account would be used to reimburse the employee for day care expenses incurred so that the parent could work.

The amounts contributed to these accounts are not considered taxable income to the employee if certain rules are followed. The most important rule is that any amounts that are unclaimed at the end of the plan year are forfeited—these amounts become the property of the employer. (Typically there is a one- to three-month grace period after the end of the year during which an employee can still file for reimbursement.) This provision is often called the "use it or lose it" provision. There are rules governing what is a permissible expense. For example, day camp for children up to age 13 is a reimbursable expense but sleep-away camp is not. Additionally, the expense needs to be incurred during the year in which the employee is enrolled in the account. Also, these two types of accounts must be kept separate—money cannot be transferred between them. Participation is voluntary, and employees do not need to enroll in both to participate in one.

There are two significant differences between health care and dependent care reimbursement accounts. First, the health care reimbursement account has *no statutory dollar limits* on the amount an employee can contribute. In contrast, in 2002, dependent care reimbursement accounts are limited to the *lowest* of the following:

- The employee's earned income for the plan year
- The spouse's earned income for the plan year (if disabled or a full-time student, income is deemed to be $2,400 if the family has one dependent qualifying for dependent care and $4,800 if the family has two or more qualifying dependents)
- $5,000 (or $2,500 for married employees who file separate tax returns)

A second difference between health care and dependent care reimbursement accounts is that a *uniform reimbursement requirement* applies to health care accounts. This means that the balance that would have been in the account had the full year's contributions been made is available to the employee at any time during the year. Thus, the employee can submit claims at a faster rate than contributions are being collected (although they cannot exceed the total expected contribution for the year). The uniform reimbursement requirement does not apply to dependent care accounts. Unlike health care accounts, employees cannot claim reimbursement from dependent care accounts at a faster rate than they are making contributions.

Cafeteria Plan. Reflecting the original intent of the IRS statute, this type of plan offers an employee a choice between tax-exempt benefits and taxable benefits. For example, within a cafeteria plan, an employer might offer a cash rebate for employees who choose not to take health insurance. The health insurance is not a taxable benefit, but the cash is. Other benefits that might be offered as part of the cafeteria plan include any of those from the tax-exempt and taxable lists above. Some employers will also include things like long-term care and group and homeowners insurance as taxable benefit options. Furthermore, a premium conversion plan or flexible spending accounts can also be offered within a cafeteria plan.

Understanding these flexible benefit plan options can be confusing because an employer could offer any of these plans as a stand-alone plan or a combination of any two or all three. When companies offer both a premium conversion plan and flexible spending accounts, this is sometimes referred to as a *flex plan.* When combined with a cafeteria plan, this is sometimes called a *full flex plan.* In addition, there are closely related plans that are not technically flexible benefit plans—*health reimbursement arrangements*, for example.

One or more of these flexible benefit options is increasingly common among employers. In the 2001 *Hay Benefits Report* (Hay Group 2001) of medium and large employers, 84% of employers surveyed offered a premium conversion plan. The same report found that 78% of employers surveyed offer health care reimbursement accounts, and 83%

Figure 1
Example of Potential Tax Savings

Employee's Annual Contribution to Flexible Spending Account and Premium Conversion Plan		$3,000
Federal Income Tax Savings	(28.0%)	840
FICA Savings	(7.7%)	230
State Income Tax Savings	(5.0%)	150
Total Tax Savings		$1,220

offer dependent day care reimbursement accounts. In contrast, only 22% of employers surveyed offered full flexible benefit plans.

Advantages

It is generally an advantage to employees to have access to these types of plans. As illustrated in Figure 1, the tax savings from employee contributions to premium conversion and flexible spending accounts can be substantial. As a rule of thumb, the higher the employee's marginal tax bracket—shown as 28% in Figure 1—the more valuable the exemption.

In the case of dependent care benefits, however, income tax law permits those below a certain income level to take a tax *credit* for dependent care independent of any employer offering. An employee evaluating whether or not to enroll in their employer's dependent care reimbursement account will have to compare these two options to see which gives them the most tax benefit. A given dependent care expenditure cannot be used for both tax vehicles. Generally, participation in a dependent care reimbursement account reduces your dependent care tax credit dollar for dollar.

An additional advantage of the health care reimbursement account is that the expenses that qualify for reimbursement include several that would not typically be covered by a health insurance plan. In addition to the deductibles, cost share amounts, and copays for medical, dental, or prescription drugs, the following expenses qualify for reimbursement:

- Eyeglasses, contacts, and contact lens supplies
- Orthodontia services (must be able to prove medical necessity)
- Radial keratotomy surgery (laser eye surgery)
- Smoking cessation programs
- Hearing devices and batteries
- Acupuncture
- Buying or renting crutches

In the case of a cafeteria plan, the benefit does not take the form of tax savings but rather the ability to customize the benefit package to suit the employee. A flexible benefit plan allows the employee to direct his or her benefit dollars to the options that he or she values most highly. For example, an employee with health coverage through a spouse might want to forego the health insurance and instead direct those dollars to other benefits that might include additional vacation or cash. A single employee might prefer to purchase the health insurance and forego a different benefit.

Disadvantages

Additional choices also mean more responsibility on the part of the employee. Communications from the employer's human resource department must be studied carefully. Because of the "use it or lose it" rule, particular care must be taken in allocating money to flexible spending accounts. Employees considering this option should know which expenses qualify for reimbursement, and they should understand the procedures that they need to follow to claim reimbursement since documentation of expenses will be required. Finally, they should carefully and conservatively assess their expected expenses.

It is important to remember that, as a general rule, flex plan elections cannot be changed during the plan year unless there is a change in family status such as the birth of a child, marriage, divorce, or death. Of special importance to those considering retirement is the fact that flexible spending accounts are not portable. If an employee terminates or retires before the end of the plan year, he or she will have limited options.

Under COBRA (Consolidated Omnibus Budget Reconciliation Act) provisions, if the employee has not claimed his or her health care reimbursement account balance at the time of retirement or termination, he or she may continue to pay contributions on an after-tax basis for the remainder of the calendar year. This allows the individual to remain eligible to file claims against the account and potentially recover the contributions already made. This would include services received after the date of separation but before the end of the plan year. If the employee chooses *not* to make after-tax contributions, he or she may only seek reimbursement for services received prior to the date of separation. This may be appealing if the employee has already received more health care expense reimbursements than he or she has contributed. In such a case, the employer must absorb the loss.

A *plan year* is any 12-month period of time as determined in the plan's documents. Most often it corresponds with the company's fiscal year. Individuals participating in a dependent care reimbursement account may only seek reimbursement for eligible dependent care expenses incurred during the period of employment. COBRA continuation provisions do not apply to the dependent care account. Since premium contribution plans and flexible spending accounts reduce the salary subject to taxes, they also affect benefits that are based on salary. As a general rule, the advantages of these flexible benefit plans outweigh any effects that might occur for other, salary-based benefits. However, it is wise to review the treatment of these benefits:

Pension. Whether or not pension benefits are affected by these salary reductions will vary from company to company. In those companies where there is an effect, employees close to termination of employment or retirement will be impacted most severely because pension benefits are often based on average salary for the last several years of employment.

Life Insurance/Disability. Life insurance and disability benefit amounts are also typically based on the salary of the employee. The employer has the discretion to determine whether the full or reduced salary is used to compute these benefits. However, because flexible spending accounts are also advantageous to employers, they are usually willing to base these benefit amounts on the full salary to encourage participation.

Workers' Compensation/Unemployment. Workers' compensation and unemployment benefits are based on the average monthly wage. For those who earn above the maximum monthly wage, benefits would not be reduced. However, for lower-income employees, the reduction in potential benefits could be substantial. State law may dictate whether or not these benefits can be based on full salary.

Social Security. Because Social Security benefits are based on salary throughout an employee's career, retirement benefits should not be significantly reduced, particularly if the FSA reduction does not occur over the employee's entire career. However, a young employee who has elected a large reduction and becomes disabled could receive a significantly lower Social Security disability benefit. Likewise, the survivor benefits could be significantly lower.

There is very little in the way of organizations or literature that looks at flexible benefit plans from the viewpoint of the employee. Almost all of it adopts the viewpoint of the employer. Because participation in these plans is voluntary, however, employees should be able to enjoy the maximum benefit and avoid the pitfalls with careful planning. (See also HEALTH BENEFITS; PENSION PLANS; POSTRETIREMENT HEALTH COVERAGE [PRHC]; RETIREMENT PREPAREDNESS; WORKFORCE PATTERNS, CHANGES IN; WORKPLACE FINANCIAL EDUCATION.)

References

Hay Group. 2001. *Hay Benefits Report.* Philadelphia, PA: Author.

Johnson, Richard E., and Sidney Weintraub. 2002. *Flexible Benefits: A How-to Guide.* 6th ed. Brookfield, WI: International Foundation of Employee Benefit Plans.

Morris, Robin C., Mark Manin, Linda Frayling, and Francesca G. Sclandra. 1999. *Flexible Benefits Answer Book.* New York: Aspen Publishers.

Lynn Q. Taylor

FOOD STAMPS. See Elder Law Practice; Gerontological Social Work; Minority Older Adults; Nutrition Programs.

FRAILTY PLANNING, the practice of preparing for all the implications and aspects of frailty before the onset of significant decline. Frailty defies precise definition but encompasses a spectrum of functional limitations of varying severity and has a broad set of implications. It is best defined as the inability to function with complete independence due to either physical or cognitive limitations or a combination of both. Being frail has interconnected consequences and implications in the domains of personal finance, housing, law, health, psychology, spirituality, and medicine. Such a complex problem calls for a complete response. Planning for the possibility of frailty creates a posture of preparedness, which, in turn, enables individuals and those who love and support them to minimize the experience of fear and suffering and to maximize the quality of life—no matter how long frailty may persist—for both the frail and those in their communities of love and support.

Many people resist the notion of frailty planning on the grounds that "it won't happen to me." Certainly, not everyone will live through a period of frailty. Depending on how you define it, statistics are available stating that between one-third and two-thirds of the population—perhaps even more—will experience a period of frailty that may last as long as 10 or 20 years (especially in the event of Alzheimer's or similar dementia). Instead of analyzing the statistics, consider that none of them suggest that frailty is a chance event that will only happen to a few unlucky individuals. Rather, all the statistics tell us that enough of us will live through a period of frailty that to not prepare for it is unwise.

Distinguish from Other Planning Disciplines

Frailty planning is related to but is neither the same as nor a subset of retirement planning, financial planning, or estate planning. *Retirement planning* is the practice of preparing for the financial implications of not working. This is normally focused on generating adequate income for routine living expenses and for supporting lifestyle choices—such as extensive travel—at retirement. Because the pre–baby boomers and the baby boomers are more comfortable with psychological and spiritual issues than were their parents, this field is currently undergoing a transformation that is likely to broaden its scope of inquiry to take in issues of meaning and purpose and to deal with more values-related questions as part of the context for its traditional focus on the financial implications of not working. However, some practitioners, reacting to this trend toward a broader focus, will expand by dealing not with more types of issues related to retirement but rather with more financial issues than just retirement. Those who make this choice will likely deal with some elements of frailty planning (such as long-term care insurance) but may not engage the broader issues and implications.

Financial planning is defined by the Certified Financial Planner™ (CFP®) Board of Standards as "the process of meeting [one's] life goals through the proper management of [one's] finances. Life goals can include buying a home, saving for [a] child's education or planning for retirement" (http://www.cfp.net/learn/knowledgebase,asp?id=1). While it is general in scope, and is often thought to be synonymous with *retirement* planning, in practice financial planning focuses on asset accumulation and investment allocation and is much more attentive to managing investments than the other related planning disciplines. Since being frail is not generally considered a life goal, financial planners are unlikely to deal with frailty planning, although that should not be said of those practicing Financial Life Planning™ or other more holistic approaches to financial planning.

Estate planning is the practice of preparing for the financial implications of dying. That often means minimizing the costs of estate taxes and probate as well as determining who gets what assets or income streams when, how dependents might subsist after the caregiver's death, and how other individuals or institutions that will carry on work or ideas that are important to the decedent will be supported as an aspect of legacy. Because estate planning almost inevitably involves the creation of legal documents (wills and trusts, for example) and frailty planning also involves the creation of legal documents (such as powers of attorney), elder law attorneys are a group of practitioners likely to become involved in frailty planning.

Frailty planning also needs to be distinguished from health care. While not generally considered a planning discipline in the sense of financial, retirement, or estate planning, and while health care is certainly an element of frailty care, one must be careful to avoid the trap of seeing frailty as a purely medical issue. Frailty planning involves health care treatment planning to the extent that it can be predicted prior to the onset of specific conditions, but it also encompasses other disciplines in support of and parallel to health care management issues. Because they may be involved in the sale of health insurance, Medicare Supplement ("Medigap") policies, critical illness coverage or long-term care insurance, life and health insurance agents are another group likely to become involved in frailty planning.

Frailty planning is not yet recognized as a specialty or even a focus area among financial advisors, professional geriatric care managers, ministers, rabbis, imams, or other religious or social services advisors, so getting competent advice can be challenging. However, as the baby boom generation gets older, expect such a focus area to emerge in some service sector. For reasons of expected professional behavior, it appears most likely to come from the financial services arena, although other sectors may prove to be more motivated to serve this population in a proactive, holistic manner.

The Frailty Planning Process

The frailty planning process is neither long nor especially complex, but it requires care. It is multidisciplinary in that it invites input from real estate professionals, lawyers, financial advisors, and medical professionals as well as social workers, life coaches or guides, and religious professionals. Although there are a variety of approaches to frailty planning, those that take pains to assist the client in clarifying her or his values and those of other affected friends or family members (spouse, children) obviously give better results than those that do not. Frailty planning consists of five steps:

1. *Identifying strategic housing choices, clarifying pros and cons and issues around each, and choosing a strategy.* The biggest issue in frailty care is answering the question, "Where will you live when (if) you become frail?" This is the key issue because it may determine treatment and drive decisions that are otherwise undesirable. For example, an individual who has had a stroke but is mobile with the aid of a walker may not be released from the hospital to home if home means living alone with a second-floor bedroom and a basement laundry. Unfortunately, absent frailty planning, this question must be asked reactively in an emotionally charged environment and often leaves both the frail and their families and friends with unsatisfactory choices, guilt, and resentment. Only a proactive, frailty planning approach can provide for a desirable care setting at the appropriate time, support a sense of security, and prevent feelings of guilt and resentment.

2. *Identifying options for support at various levels of frailty and resources available in the community to address them, coordinating resources with strategic housing choices, and projecting costs.* Regardless of one's strategic choice of housing in the event of frailty, there will be identifiable resources to facilitate a plan of frailty care that meets his or her needs. These may be resources such as nonmedical companion and support services or full- or part-time aides to provide in-home intermittent medical care to support the choice to stay there or to move in with a sibling or a child. Others will want to consider moving into a continuing care retirement community (CCRC) with its continuum of independent living activities and care facilities. In the event that one adopts a strategy of moving from care option to care option as the ability to function independently deteriorates, an investigation of adult day care services, assisted living facilities, or nursing homes (among others) would be called for. In almost all cases the opportunity to meet and to get to know a professional geriatric care manager—and to have the care manager

get to know the individual as a fully functional adult prior to the onset of functional decline—is extremely desirable. Identifying these resources proactively not only allows planning for financing frailty care but also facilitates choice and, in some instances, enables a quality of care that is simply unavailable reactively.

3. *Identifying all financial impacts of possible frailty and choosing a financial approach to provide security; coordinating with other financial matters and planning disciplines.* There are only three sources of funds to pay for frailty care: taxpayer dollars (Medicare and Medicaid), personal dollars, and long-term care insurance. Taxpayer dollars are scarce and, except in the case of the impoverished, not designed to provide the breadth of services (medical, social, legal, spiritual) that is required. Even where the government does provide such services, however, resource constraints are such that adequacy of service must be called into question. Personal dollars are usually allocated on a priority basis to generate retirement income and to be held as reserves to provide a sense of financial security, so they are most often either unavailable or inadequate to satisfy the heavy cash demands of frailty care. Some contingency plans are available on a "just in case" basis, such as contemplating the use of a reverse mortgage to free up home equity without the need to move. However, except for those few cases where acquiring long-term care insurance is either not advisable or not available, it is almost always the most satisfactory response to financial aspects of frailty planning.

4. *Identifying desires for treatment options in acute stages of frailty and creating appropriate legal documents; obtaining consent of others to make health care decisions and financial and other life management decisions in the event one is unable to make those decisions oneself and communicating one's desires to his or her community of support and care.* Just as it is necessary to obtain the consent of named guardians for minor children in the event of the untimely death of their parents (an element of estate planning), so it is necessary to obtain the consent of others—family, friends, trusted advisors—to act on one's behalf in making health care decisions and managing one's worldly affairs in the event of acute frailty. However, neither living wills, durable powers of attorney, nor health care powers of attorney are effective if those who will be affected are not aware of their existence or clear about your desires. Organizations such as Last Acts (http://www.lastacts.org/) offer additional information and support for this part of the process.

5. *Identifying strengths and weaknesses in spiritual life and practice as well as community involvement and support; making and implementing plans to build on strengths and minimize weaknesses.* While many of the issues in frailty planning are legal or financial, the greatest impacts of frailty are emotional and spiritual. The proactive approach outlined in the first four steps of frailty planning is important to minimize the practical problems associated with being frail. An equally proactive approach to enhancing emotional and spiritual skills, and to developing appropriate supportive practices, is essential to well-being through the period of frailty, quality of life, and quality of death.

Summary

Frailty planning is a responsible and intelligent response to the increased life expectancies we are all experiencing. It has a place in the same pantheon of planning disciplines as financial planning, retirement planning, and estate planning. It does not fit neatly into any one professional discipline, but rather it requires practitioners with the skills and experience to cut across professional disciplines to create dedicated business entities or professional working alliances. The process is simple but perhaps not easy as it requires enough maturity to be able to tackle issues that carry a significant emotional charge. (See also ACTIVITIES OF DAILY LIVING [ADLs]; CASH FLOW PLANNING FOR RETIREES; CONTINUING CARE RETIREMENT COMMUNITIES [CCRCs]; COSTS OF FAMILY CAREGIVING; LONG-TERM CARE INSURANCE, PRIVATE; REVERSE MORTGAGES.)

Reference

Simmons, Henry C., and E. Craig MacBean. 2002. *Thriving after 55: Your Guide to Fully Living the Rest of Your Life*. Richmond, VA: Prime Press.

E. Craig MacBean

FUNERALS AND FUNERAL FINANCES. Since prehistoric times, people have confronted and transcended death through collective means, including group rituals, collective belief systems, and a variety of aggregated death-related customs and behavior. The funeral, and the more extended process of "funeralization," has always occupied a position of centrality in death-related behavior. The funeral acknowledges death, provides a mechanism for the social transition from life to death, offers a venue for saying goodbye to the deceased, and facilitates group reintegration and community reequilibrium (Hayslip, Sewells, and Riddle 2003).

The American Funeral

During the several centuries of American history, the funeral ritual evolved from a spartan Puritan burial with simple prayers and modest mention of the death at a subsequent church service in the 1600s to a more structured, but still unpretentious, religious service with song, prayer, and sermon in the 1700s. By the 1800s, the funeral service had grown into a lengthy emotional, heavily religious, and complex ceremony involving multiple prayers, numerous songs, strident sermon, and the participation of a large congregation.

By the twentieth century, the United States had become a death-denying society, and the main effort was to avoid confronting death (Stephenson 1985). The deceased was embalmed with the aim of making the body look alive but asleep and peaceful. Bodies were laid out in "slumber" rooms in funeral homes to extend the original aim. Funerals were fashioned so as to aid in insulating the living from the confrontation with death. Funerals became

> increasingly secular, commercial in nature, and seemingly intended to create an aura of an avoidance of death. Funerals are currently shorter than in the past and appear somewhat routine and perfunctory even to the point of being scripted and superficial in manner. (Bryant et al. 2003)

Some services are held in funeral home chapels rather than churches. Many have secular elements mixed with the sacred. Sermons may be brief and quasi-religious, and friends and family members deliver eulogies rather than clergy.

The funeral of the late 1800s, especially the rural funeral, was well integrated into the fabric of community life, and much of the expense of the funeral was borne by com-

Table 1
Funeral Costs

Item	Cost
Casket	$2,330
Embalming	420
Other Preparations (Cosmetology, etc.)	150
Visitation/Viewing	275
Funeral at Funeral Home	350
Transfer of Remains to Funeral Home	154
Hearse (Local)	185
Service Car/Van	85
Professional Service	1,213
Acknowledgment Cards	18
Total	**$5,180**

Source: National Funeral Directors Association, 2001.

munity institutions, especially the church and extended family. Today's funeral, and especially the urban service, is almost exclusively a commercial enterprise with professionals and other outsiders providing a wide array of services with attendant financial costs. Because of the commercial nature of funerals today, the financial burden to the family is not insignificant.

The Economics of the Funeral

The contemporary funeral is one of the more significant expenditures made by American families, generally exceeded only by major economic outlays such as the home, automobile purchases, and college education for the children. The cost of a funeral can range from $1,500 up to levels of $100,000 or more, depending on the economic resources of the family and/or the idiosyncratic inclinations of the deceased individual or the person selecting the funeral.

The vast majority of American families choose a simple, but dignified, funeral of modest cost that involves the full array of services offered by the funeral home. According to the National Funeral Directors Association, the average cost of an adult funeral in 2001 was $5,180. This figure includes the items and services shown in Table 1.

Several of these items and services could be omitted, such as the visitation/viewing, holding the funeral at the funeral home (using a church instead), and the acknowledgment cards, for a savings of $643. A less expensive casket could be selected for a savings of up to another $1,000, and in most instances, the embalming could also be omitted for a total saving of approximately $2,100. By eschewing these items and services, the total cost of the funeral could be lowered to about $3,000.

The average funeral cost of $5,180 does not include the price of a vault (at approximately $950), which is optional but may be required for interment in some cemeteries. This could raise the average funeral price to $6,130. Other costs not included are those for a cemetery plot or space in a crypt/mausoleum, opening or closing the grave, and monument or marker. These considerations may raise the total cost of funeralization by several thousand dollars, depending on choice.

There seems to be only modest variation in the cost of an average adult funeral from state to state. The average cost generally varies by less than 10% between and among the states. Funeral costs in the United States have risen over the years. In 1957, the average cost of an adult funeral (not including vault, cemetery, or grave marker) was $646. By 1977, it was $1,412. By 1985 it was $2,737, and in 1991, it was $3,742. The cost had risen to $4,782 by 1996. It would appear that the cost of an average funeral has only risen annually at about the same rate as that of inflation. Whether or not the average cost of a funeral will rise significantly in the future will likely be a function of both contemporary and future trends in funerals and the funeral industry.

Preneed Funerals

Because of the significant and unexpected economic cost of funerals, financial advisors and funeral directors encourage the public to make provision for preneed funerals. The term *preneed* is a generic term that encompasses both *prearranging* and *prefunding*. Basically this process includes selecting merchandise, planning the service, determining the method of viewing and final disposition of the remains, and selecting persons to be involved in the funeral. In short, an individual can now plan his or her own funeral as he or she wishes it to be. This is said to be desirable from the standpoint of removing the burden from surviving loved ones (Aarons 1999), being able to express and implement one's personal (and even idiosyncratic) preferences in regard to one's own funeral, and making appropriate financial arrangements. Normally, *prefunding* attends *prearranging*. Once personalized funeral plans have been made, they are ideally paid for. This is consistent with good financial planning, and at time of death, funeral costs do not invade the principal assets of the estate. Prefunding can be accomplished after making appropriate arrangements with a funeral director, through the establishment of a trust with the funds put into escrow, the designation of a certain portion of life insurance, or through the purchase of burial insurance. AARP conducted a survey in 1995 and discovered that 7 million people had prearranged their funerals (Leming and Dickinson 2002).

There are, of course, disadvantages to preneed funerals. An individual who made specific funeral arrangements at one point in life may have different preferences later but neglect to change the prearrangement agreement, just as some individuals neglect to alter their living wills as their preferences change. Preneed funerals, in effect, preempt the prerogatives of family members who may have strong emotional concerns about the funeral arrangements that are at variance with the preferences of the deceased.

Preneed funerals have another disadvantage, however. They provide a robust opportunity for consumer fraud (Leming and Dickinson 2002). Now that preneed arrangements have become relatively widespread, instances of abuse and fraud are not uncommon (Geller 2001; Lucia 2001; Stepzinski 2002). In this regard, many states are now moving to regulate preneed funeral arrangements (Alabama, for example) and a few states, such as New York, do not permit preneed funeral insurance but insist that funeral expenses be held in trust (Editors of The Times Union 2001). "Burial" insurance, however, has long been popular with less affluent segments of the population, and some insurance industry representatives have attacked bans on funeral insurance as unfair to poorer consumers (Kryshak 2001). While preneed funerals are not without controversy, such arrangements will no doubt continue to grow in use in the future.

The American Funeral Industry

In 2001, there were 21,757 funeral homes in the United States. The number of funeral homes has remained relatively stable over the past decade or so, although the total number in 2001 is actually down a bit from the 22,153 total in 1996. A total of 34,588 licensed funeral directors operated or worked in these funeral homes in 2001. When embalmers are added, the number of death care professionals rises to approximately 45,000 individuals. There is a curious distribution of funeral homes per state, however. Some sparsely populated states such as Alaska (19) and Nevada (38) have a very small number of funeral homes. Some of the rural states with smaller populations have a disproportionately high number of funeral homes compared to states with much larger populations. Examples here include Alabama with a population in 2000 of 4.4 million and 45,075 deaths and 407 funeral homes, as compared to California with a population in 2000 of 33.9 million and 229,535 deaths and 742 funeral homes, or Mississippi with a population of 2.8 million and 28,671 deaths and 275 funeral homes, as opposed to Texas with a population of 20.9 million and 148,994 deaths but only 1,174 funeral homes (National Funeral Directors Association 2001). This anomaly is likely the result of the fact that the public prefers to patronize a funeral home that is located in their own community, even if quite small. Thus, in rural states like Mississippi, with the population spread about in small communities, there are opportunities for funeral homes to locate in each of these small communities as a matter of convenience. In some of the states with larger populations, the population may tend to be more centralized in a few large urban areas, and a fewer number of large-capacity funeral homes can more readily serve the public's need by virtue of being more centrally located. If the public would be willing to patronize funeral homes that were more centrally located at a greater distance from their home, a significantly fewer number of funeral homes could adequately handle the country's funeral needs.

The funeral industry is economically large. A decade ago in 1993, Americans spent between $9.7 billion and $17.1 billion on funeral, cremation, and cemetery services. According to the National Funeral Directors Association, in 1997 there were 16,031 funeral homes with payroll total receipts of $9,503,010,000. In the same year there were 6,677 cemeteries and crematories with payroll that had receipts of $2,987,878,000. There were also 59,458 cemetery and crematory employees who earned a total of $1,075,090,000 (or an average of $18,082 per employee) (http://www.nfda.org/). Thus, it would appear that the funeral industry generated approximately $13.5 billion. This figure does not include the revenues of other logistical industries that support the funeral industry, such as casket manufacturers, hearse makers, and florists, to mention but some. The figure is higher today and will grow significantly as the number of deaths that occur in the United States rises over time.

Current Trends

Although not widely known, profits on funerals have been declining over the past two decades. Over a 20-year period, the profit on a funeral decreased from 13.73% in 1980 to 8.64% in 2000 (*American Blue Book of Funeral Directors* 2002). This represents a 63% decline in profits and is viewed as a matter of concern by those in the funeral industry. It is believed that this decline in profitability is primarily the result of rising operating expenses for funeral homes, when the cost of funerals has only approximately risen at the annual rate of inflation. Accordingly, the funeral industry has engaged in several efforts at restructuring in an attempt to restore profitability, and "funeral home owners are searching for economies and additional services to provide their clients which might offset these recent declines" (Salomone 2003).

According to one author, these restructuring efforts have included such measures as:

Consolidation. Small, locally owned ("Mom and Pop") funeral homes are increasingly being bought and absorbed into large national funeral corporations that seek to bring an economy of scale to these small mortuaries through improved business practices. Such corporations are also acquiring other types of death-related businesses such as crematoria and cemeteries (Salomone 2003). An example of this practice is Service Corporation International, the largest funeral corporation in the world. Its holdings include 3,611 funeral homes, 193 cemeteries, 55 flower shops, and a number of crematoria (Service Corporation International 2001). This consolidation trend has resulted in four corporations owning approximately 10% of the funeral homes in the United States (Salomone 2003).

Clustering. Funeral homes may acquire and integrate various death-related enterprises such as funeral homes, cemeteries, crematoria, floral shops, tombstone businesses, insurance businesses, and so on, into a unified business entity that can "pool resources, assets, personnel and services in the interest of higher profits" (Salomone 2003).

Preplanning. This practice allows for an individual to design his or her own funeral in advance, choosing the type of funeral service, details such as a particular variety of casket, and method of body disposition, among other concerns. The cost of the funeral is paid in advance, and the money is put into escrow until the death of the client. This represents a profitable arrangement for the funeral home because "preplanning serves the same purpose as burial insurance; it locks in a customer base so as to insure subsequent business eventually" (Salomone 2003).

Other Funeral Practice Trends

Alternative arrangements are another recent trend in funeralization today. Included here are such accommodations as discount or economy funeral homes that provide a minimalist service. Some such funeral homes are now operating in low-rent structures in less desirable locations. They may utilize less expensive makes or used hearses and essentially offer pick-up, embalming, moderately priced caskets, and delivery service to a home and/or cemetery. They frequently do not have space in their facilities for visitation or funeral services. Such businesses can offer relatively inexpensive "essential service" funerals only for families desiring such arrangements (Smith 2002).

Other alternative arrangements include the *memorial service.* Here the body is initially buried, possibly without being embalmed, or cremated without ceremony, and at a subsequent date, family and friends gather in a home or in some larger facility such as a church or lodge hall for a memorial service, without the body of the deceased. Various individuals may present eulogies to the deceased, and clergy may or may not be present. Services may be either religious or secular or a combination. The service may often be followed by a reception or meal. The relevant factor here is the fact that the funeral home is essentially bypassed, other than picking up and delivering the body to the cemetery or crematoria. Some funeral directors now specialize in providing such minimal arrangements.

A related arrangement involves various "do-it-yourself" measures, such as the family purchasing the casket through a discount casket retailer or online and having it delivered to the funeral home. Funeral homes naturally discourage such a practice but, in some instances, are legally required to permit such an arrangement. In such an eventuality, the funeral home may charge a handling and processing fee. Occasionally, especially in the instance of a small casket, such as that used for a child, the family may even request that they transport the body to the cemetery, thereby saving the cost of the hearse.

Because of scattered families living at some distance from each other, and the expense of traveling to a funeral, the use of electronic arrangements, such as closed-circuit television, videotapes, and virtual funerals, are becoming possible and will increase in the future. Rather than the entire family traveling to the funeral, the funeral can take place with only a few of the members (or none) present, and the service can be videotaped for later viewing, or conceivably broadcast on closed-circuit television to other locations where family members are located. The economic benefits and convenience of virtual funerals are such that an increasing number of families may seek such arrangements in the future.

Selling New Services

The funeral industry is actively searching for new services to offer as a means of increasing the profitability of funerals. Among the initiatives in this regard is *aftercare*, which might include memorial services for special dates such as birthdays, weddings, or death anniversaries. Aftercare may also include follow-up services for clients needing support, emotional affirmation, or temporary assistance with the practical necessities of life while they are working through their grief. Funeral homes might ultimately provide licensed staff psychologists or social workers as professional grief counselors.

It has also been suggested that funeral homes could offer *DNA coding*. Here the funeral home might "package and preserve blood and hair samples from a corpse for possible use by consanguineal (blood) relatives of the deceased who might want to know the probably genetic links to certain diseases" (Salomone 2003). Finally, the strategy of using the *Internet* as a digital merchandising system for funeral homes is being tried. The funeral home, its products, facilities, equipment, and services can effectively be shown over the Internet. In effect, funerals can be sold in the home via the computer.

Long-Term Trends in the Funeral Industry

Over the next 75 years the demographics of death in the United States are going to change dramatically, and there are a number of trends and projections that are likely to impact the process of funeralization, the cost of funerals, and the parameters of the American funeral industry.

The current death rate of approximately 8.7 per 1,000 population is projected to rise to 10.9 by 2040 and 13.17 in 2060. It will remain at approximately that level through 2070 and 2080 (Bryant et al. 2003). The rise to 13.17 per 1,000 population from today's 8.7 rate represents an increase of *more than 51.4%*. This is a significant increase in the death rate, which will be the result of increasing life expectancy and a much larger number of persons over 65 years old in the population. This much larger proportion of older adults will, of course, die at some point, pushing the death rate up.

Over the same time period, the overall population of the United States will also increase. This fact, coupled with the much higher death rate, will produce a total annual death figure of 6.5 million persons in 2080, as opposed to only 2.5 million annual deaths, or three times as many deaths as today (Bryant et al. 2003). An annual death total this large would be more than today's 22,000 funeral homes could accommodate. This would suggest that the number of funeral homes in the United States will have to grow at an accelerated pace in order to be able to process that many deaths. Inasmuch as the number of annual deaths may grow at a rate faster than funeral homes can increase, funeral prices may, accordingly, rise in a disproportionate fashion. This cost tendency may be offset to some degree, however, by other long-term trends.

Cremation

For more than two centuries in the United States, burial (or vault interment) was essentially the exclusive mode of body disposition. In the late nineteenth century, however, cremation emerged as a new mode of body disposition. For many years, cremation enjoyed only limited acceptance in the United States, although in Great Britain and Europe, it achieved a much greater degree of acceptance by the mid-twentieth century. From 1876–1884 until the 1934–1938 period, cremation had only achieved a 2.56% of death usage. By 1981, cremation as a choice of body disposition had risen to 11.01% and subsequently to 25.48% in 2000. Cremation has been projected further to rise to 48.65% of body disposition in 2025 (*CANA Report* 2001) and could become even more widespread over the subsequent 50 years, perhaps ultimately reaching a 75% rate or so. Although funeral homes do presently handle arrangements for cremation, there is significantly less profit here than in burials. In time, the funeral home may be bypassed altogether with a delivery service that takes the dead body directly to the crematoria for a minimal fee. In spite of the very large increase in deaths over the next 75 years, the rising trend of cremation utilization, plus other consumer cost-saving behavior trends, may well offset the higher death rate and impact the funeral industry both in terms of funeral profitability and even the viability of the funeral industry itself. (See also ESTATE PLANNING; ETHICAL WILL; FINANCIAL SECURITY IN RETIREMENT; FRAILTY PLANNING, HOME CARE SERVICES FOR OLDER ADULTS; LIVING WILLS.)

References

Aarons, A. 1999. "Prearranging a Funeral Prevents Many Burdens." *Daily News* (New York), June 8.

American Blue Book of Funeral Directors. 2002. 38th ed. Iselin, NJ: Kates-Boylson Publications, Inc.

Associated Press. 2002. "Legislature Passes Bill Regulating Pre-Need Funeral Arrangements." 2002. *Dateline* (Montgomery, AL), January 31.

Banks, Dwayne A. 2003. "On the Economics of Death in the United States." In *Handbook of Death and Dying*, ed. Clifton D. Bryant. Thousand Oaks, CA: Sage Publications.

Bern-Klug, Mercedes, Stanley Deviney, and David J. Ekerdt. 2000. "Variations in Funeral-Related Costs of Older Adults and the Role of Preneed Funeral Contracts and Type of Disposition." *Omega: The Journal of Death and Dying* 41: 1.

Bryant, Clifton E., Charles K. Edgley, Dennis L. Peck, and Kent L. Sandstrom. 2003. "Death in the Future: Prospects and Prognosis." In *Handbook of Death and Dying*, ed. Clifton D. Bryant. Thousand Oaks, CA: Sage Publications.

CANA Report 2001. 2001. Cremation Associates of North America. Available online at http:// www.cremationassociation.org/.

Editors of The Times Union. 2001. "Merchants of Grief: New York State Should Maintain Its Ban on Prearrangement Insurance." *The Times Union* (Albany, NY), October 29.

Geller, Adam. 2001. "Pre-Need Funeral Deals Grow . . . So Does Fraud." *Dayton Daily News*, April 29.

Hayslip, Bert, Jr., Kenneth W. Sewells, and Russell B. Riddle. 2003. "The American Funeral." In *Handbook of Death and Dying*, ed. Clifton D. Bryant. Thousand Oaks, CA: Sage Publications.

Kryshak, Terry J. 2001. "Ban on Funeral Insurance a Denial of Choice." *The Times Union* (Albany, NY), November 11.

Leming, Michael R., and George E. Dickinson. 2002. *Understanding Dying, Death, and Bereavement*. Fort Worth, TX: Harcourt College Publishers.

Lucia, Tony. 2001. "Planning a Funeral without Getting Killed." *The Eagle/Times* (Reading, PA), June 17.

Mclachlin, Mary. 2002. "The Big Business of Death." *The Palm Beach Post* (Palm Beach, FL), February 24.

National Funeral Directors Association. 2001. *NFDA 2001 General Price List Survey*. Brookfield, WI: NFDA Research & Information Department.

Salomone, Jerome J. 2003. "The Evolution of the Funeral Home and the Occupation of Funeral Director." In *Handbook of Death and Dying*, ed. Clifton D. Bryant. Thousand Oaks, CA: Sage Publications.

Service Corporation International. 2001. *2000 Annual Report*. Houston, TX: Author.

Smith, Hilary Groutage. 2002. "The Business of Death: A Look Inside the Funeral Industry." *The Salt Lake Tribune* (Salt Lake City, UT), October 27.

Stephenson, J.S. 1985. *Death, Grief, and Mourning: Individual and Social Realities*. New York: Free Press.

Stepzinski, Teresa. 2002. "Former Coroner Sentenced in Fraud: He Gets 13 Months in Funeral Scam." *The Florida Times Union*, June 1.

Clifton D. Bryant

G

GENERATION X. See Retirement Preparedness.

GERIATRIC CARE MANAGERS (GCMs), practitioners with a graduate degree in a field of human services (social work, psychology, gerontology) or a substantial equivalent (e.g., a registered nurse [RN]). who specialize in assisting older people and their families with long-term care arrangements. Geriatric care managers may be certified by any one of a number of organizations but are not currently licensed by most states.

Increasingly, individuals and families are turning to geriatric care managers to obtain assistance in caring for frail older relatives. If an older person is experiencing difficulty in taking care of daily needs, is isolated from family, neighbors, and friends, is having difficulty knowing where to turn and what services can help, or wants to do preventive planning, the family may want to consider using the services of a geriatric care manager (Polich et al. 1993).

When an older person becomes frail and in need of assistance, families often face the difficult and time-consuming task of negotiating a complex array of public and nonprofit social service agencies, many of which have waiting lists. Other problems may arise in finding a social or medical service, uncertainty about what a service offers, the need to coordinate services for needs unmet even after receiving support from several agencies, refusal of services or claims, considerations of nursing homes versus alternatives, or help with locating a good facility (Polich et al. 1993).

Attempting to understand complicated eligibility requirements and locating the most suitable services for an older family member can create stress and conflict within families. Relevant questions include whether the older family member has trouble making formerly routine decisions or conducting routine financial affairs and whether guardianship or conservatorship should be considered. Adult children or grandchildren faced with career and other responsibilities in addition to their caregiving concerns can seek the assistance of qualified professional care managers.

Possible sources of referral for geriatric care managers are the National Association of Professional Geriatric Care Managers (http://www.caremanager.org/), Area Agencies on Aging, physicians, or home care agencies. Since most family members want to remain involved in a caregiving role, they can use GCMs for initial assessment and periodic consultation. Others, especially those who live far from their aging parent or relative, might retain GCMs to oversee the long-term care plan that has been arranged and to serve as a liaison between the older person and the family members.

When choosing a professional geriatric care manager, a number of points merit consideration. Care managers should have training and experience, usually a nursing or social work background. Knowledge of long-term care services, financing mechanisms, and local community resources should be evident. Good communication skills are important, as is a manageable caseload (probably no more than 50 to 75 clients). References should be requested from the care manager and investigated (AARP 1989).

The process of obtaining GCM services begins with an assessment of the client's situation, needs, and resources. Next, a service plan is designed and implemented. Either services are provided directly by the care manager, the client is referred to another service provider, or the plan is coordinated with other professional resources, such as the family's attorney, investment counselors, insurance specialists, accountants, physicians, and hospital staff. During this period, results are monitored to ensure that the client's needs are met, that services are delivered, and that modifications are made as the client's status changes.

Services provided by GCMs include:

- Conducting care plan assessments to identify problems, eligibility for assistance, and need for services
- Screening, arranging, and monitoring in-home assistance or other services
- Reviewing financial, legal, or medical issues and offering referrals to geriatric specialists to avoid future problems and conserve assets
- Providing crisis intervention
- Acting as a liaison to families, especially families at a distance, making sure things are going well and alerting families to problems
- Assisting with moving an older person to or from a retirement complex, care home, or nursing home
- Providing consumer education and advocacy
- Offering counseling and support

The cost of geriatric care management can be substantial in the initial evaluation stage. Generally, services fall in the range of $60 to $200 an hour—costs vary depending on geographic location and scope of services offered. Once the plan of care is designed, costs recede as the care manager monitors and maintains the services. Payment can be per hour or on a package basis for an assessment, in conjunction with a sliding-fee scale. Most payment for private care management is made directly by the client, family, or caregiver (Parker 1992).

GCMs have joined efforts with the National Academy of Certified Care Managers and the Case Management Institute to establish a credential in geriatric care management, which will ensure to consumers or purchasers a standard of quality, as well as provide care managers greater access to liability insurance. (See also CPA ELDERCARE SERVICES; FRAILTY PLANNING; GERONTOLOGICAL SOCIAL WORK; GUARDIANSHIP; HOME CARE SERVICES FOR OLDER ADULTS; LONG-TERM CARE INSURANCE [LTCI]—A CONSUMER'S PERSPECTIVE.)

Organizations

AARP
Children of Aging Parents
National Aging Information Center
National Association of Professional Geriatric Care Managers
National Family Caregivers Association
National Institute on Aging

Suggested Readings

AARP. 1994. *A Checklist of Concerns: Resources for Caregivers*. Washington, DC: Author.

Amarnick, Claude. 1996. *"Don't Put Me in a Nursing Home!"* Deerfield Beach, FL: Garrett Publishing.

Marcell, Jacqueline. 2001. *Elder Rage, or Take My Father . . . Please! How to Survive Caring for Aging Parents*. Irvine, CA: Impressive Press.

Morris, Virginia, and Robert Butler. 1996. *How to Care for Aging Parents*. New York: Workman Publishing Company.

Rhodes, Linda Colvin. 2000. *Complete Idiot's Guide to Caring for Aging Parents*. New York: Penguin Group.

Wilkinson, James. 1999. *A Family Caregiver's Guide to Planning and Decision Making for the Elderly*. Minneapolis, MN: Fairview Press.

References

AARP. 1989. *Care Management: Arranging for Long Term Care*. Washington, DC: Author.

Cress, Cathy. 2001. *Handbook of Geriatric Care Management*. New York: Aspen Publishers.

Cutler, Neal E. 1994. "Caring for Elderly Parents: Where Do You Look for Help?" *Journal of the American Society of CLU & ChFC* 48: 38–41.

Gray-Davidson, Frena. 2001. *The Caregiver's Sourcebook*. New York: McGraw-Hill.

Parker, Marcie. 1992. "Private Geriatric Care Management: How Families Are Served." *Journal of Case Management* 1: 108–12.

Polich, Cynthia, Marcie Parker, Deborah Chase, and Margaret Hottinger. 1993. *Managing Health Care for the Elderly*. New York: John Wiley & Sons.

Jihane K. Rohrbacker

GERIATRIC REHABILITATION, the process of maintaining function, restoring abilities, and preventing complications, along with administration of palliative care (care designed to relieve symptoms but not to cure), for older adults diagnosed with progressive debilitating diseases.

Functional abilities and capacities vary greatly among adults aged 65 and older. Generally, as age increases, the likelihood of disease, comorbidity (additional, accompanying diseases or conditions), and disability will increase. At the same time, normal effects of aging can confound or complicate existing health problems in older adults. Consequently, older adults are more likely to require the assistance of a variety of caretakers. For most older adults, mild levels of assistance are provided by family and friends, but the onset of debilitating conditions may result in deficits that require anywhere from minimum to maximum levels of assistance. Common problems such as osteoarthritis can negatively affect an older person's function due to pain and joint deformities. According to Resnick and Fleishell (2002), the decline in function among older adults in long-term care settings can range 8% to 32% over a six-month period. Impaired function is particularly prevalent among adults over the age of 85.

Orthopedic and medical disorders that necessitate rehabilitation intervention include diabetes, cancer, and fractures. Diabetes can result in peripheral vascular disease and possible future amputations, necessitating significant rehabilitation. Treatment of cancer also can result in compromised use of limbs, possible amputation, and neurological defects requiring rehabilitation. With an orthopedic fracture, the primary problem is hip fracture, a common result (and cause) of falls. As age increases, the risk for falls increases, as does the risk for hip fracture. Falls are the leading cause of death in the home, taking the lives of 10,700 people in 1998, a 9% increase from 9,200 in 1996. While older adults represent 13% of the population, more than 86% of fatal falls are in people 65 years old or older (National Safety Council 1999). Adverse outcomes go well beyond the injuries sustained as a result of a fall. An injurious fall increases estimated medical costs (relative to nonfallers, in 1996 dollars) by $11,042 in hospitals, $5,325 in nursing homes, $253 in the emergency room, and $2,820 in a home health setting (Rizzo et al. 1996). Therefore, the major focus of rehabilitation efforts should be on patient safety, and of course, all rehabilitation efforts must involve the family and support systems.

Rehabilitation

Rehabilitation is the process of maintaining function, restoring abilities, and preventing complications, along with palliative care for those diagnosed with progressive deteriorating diseases. Rehabilitation in older populations presents particular challenges. The general idea is that older people with functional deficits will be able to increase their ability to perform self-care, and in fact, most research indicates that there are significant rates of recovery among older adults with functional disability. Geriatric rehabilitation, however, is a specialty area that requires that rehabilitation occur across the care continuum, from critical care to community care, and thus occurs within hospitals, nursing homes, community centers, day care centers, and homes.

Rehabilitation Principles

Rehabilitation principles focus on the individual, his or her interaction with the environment, and reintegration into society. Rehabilitation focuses on promoting positive outcomes and independence for older adults. When applied to the individual, rehabilitation programs are designed based on an interdisciplinary assessment of an individual's need. These needs are related to cognitive capacities, physical skills and abilities, and social integration.

Cognitive capacities include a person's ability to receive and to process information, to accurately perceive his/her environment, and to correctly judge and to compensate for problem solving. With aging, these processes can be impacted due to normal visual changes, sensory deficits, and the onset of dementia, among other things.

Physical skills and abilities are focused on a person's ability to bathe, dress, toilet, transfer, and walk. These skills are considered "basic" activities of daily living (ADLs). The first step in rehabilitation is assessment of the person's self-care abilities and needs for personal care assistance. In addition to functioning, rehabilitation focuses on energy conservation, teaching older adults how to redesign activities in order to conserve energy and how to maximize performance. This emphasis can also promote safety, as fatigue can influence a person's ability to complete normal activities and endure the time required to perform them.

Social integration refers to the ability of the older adult to maintain normal social interaction once faced with the changed circumstances brought about by the need for geriatric rehabilitation. Social interaction skills are examined to help the patient maintain or increase his/her ability to be socially appropriate and/or deal with social isolation and to watch for signs of depression.

Primary Care Interventions

Primary care interventions focus on sustaining wellness through a variety of interventions. Education and counseling are primary care interventions that teach patients the facts about aging, along with information and techniques to practice safe behaviors in all settings. Tinetti and colleagues (Tinetti and Powell 1993; Tinetti et al. 1994) and Tennstedt et al. (1998) found that the most effective way to help patients to be safe, prevent falls, and increase confidence in their ability to prevent a fall is through health education and counseling.

As with all primary care, avoidance or delay of disease or debilitating conditions is the primary focus. As a person ages, visual and perceptual changes impact his/her safety. Therefore, rehabilitation efforts should also focus on safety assessment, compensation, and retraining. The most effective intervention for successful aging is exercise. Exercise increases muscle tone, strength, and range of motion, while increasing coordination, balance, and confidence. Designing appropriate exercise interventions that progressively increase a person's strength and endurance, while ultimately increasing one's function, is a prominent intervention in rehabilitation. Yet exercise should be an integral component of all levels of care and all interventions, as older adults have been shown to benefit by even small amounts of regular exercise.

In addition, all primary care practitioners should emphasize primary health behaviors and prevention of disease and disability. For example, assessing a patient's exercise level related to fall occurrence should be as common as assessing one's diet in relation to preventing diabetes and atherosclerosis. Primary prevention strategies include increasing a patient's knowledge of fall risk factors by providing factual information, suggesting ways for the patient to improve his/her level of safety and wellness, and promoting physical activity and exercises.

Secondary Care Interventions

Secondary care has to do with early detection of disease and prevention or slowing of the progression of disease states and disability, once diagnoses have been made. Such prevention programs could include balance training in those with gait irregularities, and strengthening exercises for those who have debilitating diseases with weakness. In older adults, education about diagnoses that place them at risk for further disease or, for example, falls is a major priority for secondary prevention. In addition, patient education about common fall-related home injuries is critical to preventing a fall. Along with the medical information, education on how to modify the home to make it fall-safe is also important. Unfortunately, practitioners often utilize secondary prevention strategies only *after* a fall occurs.

When secondary disease prevention programs are integrated, they focus on disease management. For older adults, the primary diseases necessitating rehabilitation are cardiovascular (carotid artery disease, hypertension), neurological (stroke, transient ischem attack [TIA], Parkinson's disease), or of orthopedic etiology (arthritis, cancer). These diseases require medical management that often involves medication, diet management, and general strengthening exercises.

Tertiary Care Interventions

Tertiary care involves convalescence, rehabilitation, and minimization of the effects of a disabling condition, such as recovery after a stroke, while maximizing the patient's functioning. For example, while primary and secondary care interventions aim to educate older adults on the risks of high blood pressure, benefits of proper diet and exercise (primary), and proper compliance with hypertensive medications (secondary), the tertiary level of treatment is targeted at maximizing the resumption and maintenance of physical and mental functions lost from the stroke. Tertiary prevention in the form of behavioral and environmental modification is very important for the disabled and frail older persons of all kinds. Assisting patients and families in reducing environmental demands and increasing their functional safety are also goals for tertiary care programs.

Tertiary care is needed when persons have actual loss of functions. Usually, disorders necessitating tertiary care are due to neurological diseases necessitating rehabilitation and include stroke and Parkinson's disease. With these diseases, rehabilitation efforts focus on medical management and restoration of functions. With stroke rehabilitation, the efforts focus on restoration of function and prevention of complications. With progressive muscular disorders, geronotological rehabilitation focuses on energy conservation and exercise strategies that increase balance and coordination while titrating and monitoring medication management. Tertiary care can involve a variety of types of therapy, including physical, occupational, social behavioral, and psychological.

Adaptive/Assistive Technology

Rehabilitation needs that are specific to the interface between the person and the environment address the need for technology integration. Technology measures include those that support or substitute for losses or declines in function. These technologies can include *orthotic devices*—those that *support body* functions, such as eyeglasses, hearing aides, braces, and slings. The technology and adaptive equipment used to *substitute* for loss of function are *prosthetic devices*. Prosthetic devices include replacement devices such as artificial limbs (prostheses) and dentures. This aspect of rehabilitation that focuses on modification of the environment is adaptive and supportive in nature. The adaptive strategies enable rehabilitation specialists to redesign the environment by providing older persons with grab bars, shower chairs, raised toilet seats, proper lighting, large print telephones, and more. The older adult uses these devices to increase both independence and safety. Adaptive equipment is needed to accommodate for both normal aging and disability-specific functional loss(es).

Organization of Rehabilitation

Rehabilitation is often provided in acute care hospitals but only on a very short-term basis, as the average length of stay is 72 hours; thus, rehabilitation is generally a secondary intervention following medical stability. Persons are generally transferred to subacute medical units, where the full rehabilitation program can be initiated. Persons may also be referred to acute inpatient rehabilitation programs from either of these settings. Rarely are patients referred to inpatient rehabilitation from progressive cardiac care, but depending on the primary reason for acute hospitalization, or the complications that arise during hospitalization, a person with severe coronary disease will need inpatient comprehensive rehabilitation. The average length of stay in a subacute medical unit is 7 to 14 days, after which a patient will be sent to a nursing home if (s)he is unable to return home. Such referrals are reserved for those individuals who have compromised medical stability and ability to tolerate a comprehensive, intensive exercise program.

Long-term care interventions can extend from one month to six months. For the aging population, these persons are referred to rehabilitation in the skilled care nursing unit, subacute care, a nursing home, or a home health service. Unfortunately, home care is limited to those who are home bound, with limited transportation and social support systems available.

Clinical Pathways/Guidelines

Irrespective of the practice setting, clinicians from a variety of professions and specialty areas have been developing and utilizing clinical guidelines to promote continuity of care, reduce variations in practice, and ensure that practice is evidence based. As a result, more rehabilitation programs are implementing care programs that are based on clinical pathways and guidelines. These strategies maximize outcomes while increasing efficiency and decreasing cost. While these guidelines continue to be developed, clinical practices continue to be evaluated in relation to program effectiveness.

For example, with the Veterans Health Administration, clinical pathways for falls have been developed based on cause of the fall and level of risk. These pathways include (1) initial assessment of level of risk by the Fall Risk Assessment Tools for inpatients and long-term care facility residents; (2) in-depth assessment of risk factors by the Fall Screening clinics for patients scoring in the moderate- to high-risk levels or outpatients having experienced a fall with injury; and (3) standardized interventions based on particular risk factors. Interventions include (1) education to reduce environmental hazards for patients and caregivers; (2) rehabilitative therapy including individualized rehabilitative therapy for patients unable to participate in group therapies, wellness programs for higher-functioning patients or patients who have transitioned from individualized therapy, and referral to Gait/Balance Biomechanics Laboratories when appropriate; (3) medical interventions including reduction in medications, neurological imaging, improvement in vision/hearing, balance testing; and (4) psychosocial interventions including interventions for depression and environmental hazards. These assessment and intervention guidelines increase outcomes of care while decreasing variations and costs.

Summary

Successful aging depends on our society's commitment to and relationship with our elders to promote their independence and confidence in their abilities and to compensate for functional declines. We can demonstrate this commitment and relationship through interdisciplinary interventions that address both the unique intrinsic characteristics of patients and populations as well as through interventions that target extrinsic or environmental factors that impact patient safety. Successful aging is dependent on shared accountability and efforts that involve the patient, family, and care providers, appropriately addressing the unique needs of individual patients along the continuum of care (inpatient, outpatient, home health, long-term care). (See also COMMUNITY-BASED CARE; COST OF FAMILY CAREGIVING; DISABILITY PROGRAMS, FEDERAL AND STATE; HEALTH MAINTENANCE ORGANIZATIONS AND MANAGED HEALTH CARE FOR OLDER ADULTS; LONG-TERM CARE INSURANCE, PRIVATE; OLDER AMERICANS ACT.)

References

Crimmins, E.M., M.H. Hayward, and Y. Saito. 1994. "Changing Mortality and Morbidity Rates and the Health Status and Life Expectancy of the Older Population." *Demography* 31: 159–75.

Dersteine, J.B., and S.D. Hargrove. 2001. *Comprehensive Rehabilitation Nursing*. St. Louis, MO: W.B. Saunders.

National Safety Council. 1999. *Report on Injuries in America*. Itasca, IL: Author.

Quigley, P., ed. 2003. "Program Guide: The Prevention and Management of Patient Falls. A Program Resource Book." In *Veterans Health Administration: VISN 8: Patient Safety Center*. Tampa, FL.

Quigley, P., S. Smith, and J. Strugar. 1998. "Successful Experiences with Clinical Pathways in Rehabilitation." *Journal of Rehabilitation* 64(2): 29–32.

Resnick, B., and A. Fleishell. 2002. "Developing a Restorative Care Program. A Five-Step Approach That Involves the Resident." *American Journal of Nursing* 102(7).

Rizzo, J.A., D.I. Baker, G. McAvay, and M.E. Tinetti. 1996. "The Cost-Effectiveness of a Multifactorial Targeted Prevention Program for Falls among Community Elderly Persons." *Medical Care* 34: 954–69.

Tennstedt, S., J. Howland, M. Lachman, E. Peterson, L. Kasten, and A. Jette. 1998. "A Randomized, Controlled Trial of a Group Intervention to Reduce Fear of Falling and Associated Activity Restriction in Older Adults." *Journal of Gerontology: Psychological Sciences* 53B: 84–92.

Tinetti, M.E., C.F. Mendes de Leon, J.T. Doucette, and D.I. Baker. 1994. "Fear of Falling and Fall-Related Efficacy in Relationship to Functioning among Community-Living Elders." *Journal of Gerontology: Medical Sciences* 49: M140–47.

Tinneti, M.E., and L. Powell. 1993. "Fear of Falling and Low Self-Efficacy: A Cause of Dependence in Elderly Persons." *Journal of Gerontology* 48 (Special Issue): 35–38.

Patricia Quigley

GERONTOLOGICAL NURSE PRACTITIONERS (GNPs), advanced practice nurses who assess health status and functional abilities; diagnose and manage common acute and chronic illnesses; perform and interpret selected laboratory tests; develop and implement treatment plans to promote, maintain, and restore health and maximize functional abilities; promote death with dignity; educate and counsel patients and families; act as advocates for older adults; and collaborate with other members of the health care team. GNPs base decisions on scientific data and interpret and use research as a basis for practice. The unifying theme in all of these functions is a focus on health rather than disease and an emphasis on holistic care to meet the medical, psychosocial, and functional needs of older persons.

Gerontological nurse practitioners, as advanced practice nurses, are licensed and registered nurses who have a graduate degree in a nursing specialty and are certified through a recognized certification program. This training prepares them to provide a full range of health services to older adults and their families. The current expectation is that educational programs for GNPs are at the master's degree level and include academic and clinical practice requirements. Upon completion of an approved educational program, GNPs are eligible to apply for national certification and formal recognition of the nurse practitioner role by state licensing agencies.

According to the government report *The Registered Nurse Population* (Spratley et al. 2002), of the 2.2 million nurses employed in 2000, it was estimated that 196,000 or 7.3% of all registered nurses were advanced practice nurses (APNs). Of that total, an estimated 102,829 were nurse practitioners, but only 58,512, or 64%, functioned under this job title. About 74% had national certification, and 62% had a master's degree. Approximately 10% of APNs came from a racial or ethnic minority background. The minority APNs "were more likely to be found among nurse practitioners than among other APNs" (Spratley et al. 2002). As a subcategory, certified gerontological nurse practitioners numbered 3,390, according to the American Nurses Credentialing Center (personal communication, July 9, 2002).

History, Scope, and Practice Settings

Loretta Ford and Henry Silver at the University of Colorado initially developed the nurse practitioner model in 1965. At first, it was limited to pediatrics but quickly expanded to include other specialties, necessitated by population shifts and health care needs. Likewise, the initial development of the GNP role was intended for primary care settings. However, its expansion and the needs of select populations among older adults have changed this exclusive focus. Gerontological nurse practitioners now practice in long-term care and traditional primary care settings, in community-based clinics, rehabilitation facilities, retirement communities, specialty care clinics, health maintenance organizations (HMOs), or home health care agencies. In 1981, the American Nurses Association established certification for GNPs.

Gerontological nurse practitioners implement practice arrangements in a variety of ways, including collaborative practice with physicians, as a member of a geriatric consult team, through home health agencies, as an employee of a long-term care facility, in an assistive care facility, in an HMO, and in independent nursing practice. In these practice arrangements, GNPs may provide direct care to patients, work with families to improve care or resolve problems, serve as case managers to coordinate a variety of services, consult with or refer to other nurses, physicians, and a variety of health care providers or community agencies, develop or participate in research, or teach students in the health professions. Practice is governed by the laws of the state, by the standards and ethics of the nursing profession, and by standards specifically relating to gerontology and the role of the nurse practitioner.

With the continuing health care crisis and the focus on health care reform at the state level, cost and quality of care have been major issues for many health care providers. Repeatedly, studies have shown that nurse practitioners provide quality health care and perform successfully within an expanded scope of practice. As early as 1986, the Office of Technology Assessment, after analyzing numerous studies of nurse practitioners and other providers, concluded that "within their areas of competence nurse practitioners . . .

provide care whose quality is equivalent to that of care provided by physicians." Further, the study stated that "nurse practitioners . . . are more adept than physicians at providing services that depend on communication with patients and preventive services" (Office of Technology Assessment 1986.) A recent study comparing practice outcomes of nurse practitioners and physicians supported the findings of earlier studies. Mundinger et al. (2000) compared the outcomes for patients in a primary care setting using a large sample size and randomized trial design. The results supported the hypothesis that, using the traditional medical model, outcomes for nurse practitioner and physician care in a primary care setting do not differ.

Barriers to Practice

Barriers to practice have changed little over the years since the inception of the nurse practitioner role. Among the most commonly reported barriers are lack of knowledge about nurse practitioners among the public and other health care professionals, resistance from physicians, reduced or denied reimbursement, limited hospital privileges, inconsistency in legal authority and scope of practice, resistance to practice autonomy, and lack of full prescribing authority. Certain legal restrictions to practice also exist, many of which have direct economic consequences. Professional licensing boards in each state regulate nurse practitioners; consequently, practice restrictions vary greatly. The most common restrictions to practice are in the area of prescriptive authority and third-party reimbursement. Both of these can have significant impact on access to care.

Prescriptive authority for nurse practitioners varies greatly in the type of drugs that may be prescribed and the degree of independence of the nurse practitioner. Twelve states permit prescribing a full range of drugs without physician involvement, while other states permit prescribing with some degree of physician involvement or delegation using protocols or limit the selection of drugs that may be prescribed. All 50 states and the District of Columbia permit some degree of prescribing authority for nurse practitioners (Pearson 2002). These restrictions are considered by some to have detrimental consequences to the advanced practice nurse's professional stature and to the public's access to health care. The need to continually consult with a physician or to seek a physician's signature limits access to care and increases the cost of health care for the public. In one of the largest studies of APN prescribing practices, Hamric et al. (1998) reviewed advanced practice nurses' prescribing practices. They analyzed data from 32 providers that encompassed 1,708 patients. The researchers evaluated the effectiveness of the prescribing practices using patient outcome, patient assessment of outcome, and physician assessment of the APN practice. "By all three of these measures, APN prescribing practices were safe and effective."

Additionally, third-party reimbursement has direct financial consequences that affect the nurse practitioner and the consumer. The federal government, through the Medicaid and Medicare programs, sets standards for reimbursement that are followed by the states and private insurers. Many nurse practitioners are eligible for Medicaid reimbursement. Still, there are common restrictions, such as reimbursement at a discounted percentage of the rate that is paid for the same service by a physician, or the federal rule that permits individual states to determine whether to reimburse services to specialties other than pediatric and family nurse practitioners—that is, GNPs.

The Medicare program also has permitted reimbursement for services performed by gerontological and other nurse practitioners. Nurse practitioners applying for Medicare billing must be certified to receive direct reimbursement from Medicare. Under the Balanced Budget Act of 1997, qualified nurse practitioners may receive direct reimbursement for Medicare Part B services they provide that would normally be provided by a physician. The services are not restricted by site, geographic location, or presence of the physician on site but only by restrictions of state licensing laws. Medicare reimbursement occurs at a percentage of the fee paid to physicians.

Outlook

Given the demographic imperative and the importance of deterring institutionalization and improving the effectiveness of nursing home and community-based care, there is a great need for gerontological nurse practitioners. "Advanced practice nurses are proven providers, and removing the many barriers to their practice will . . . increase their ability to respond to the pressing need for basic health care" (Safriet 1992).

Their role is also an active concern of future research, since HMOs and other managed care settings use GNPs to facilitate effective nursing home and home health care continuity, reduce emergency hospitalization, and monitor medication use. Finally, there is substantial promise in collaborative practice arrangements in which physicians and GNPs no longer relate hierarchically, which allows independent practice for the GNP and permits full reimbursement. A move toward such formalized, customary collaboration is also serving the primacy of patients' needs. As Richard Cooper (2001), a health care policy analyst, states, "Ultimately, the success of each discipline will be judged by how effectively it participates in a continuum of care that meets the needs of patients and of the health care system overall." (See also ASSISTED LIVING; COMMUNITY-BASED CARE; HEALTH MAINTENANCE ORGANIZATIONS AND MANAGED HEALTH CARE FOR OLDER ADULTS; MEDICARE.)

Organizations

American Academy of Nurse Practitioners
American College of Nurse Practitioners
American Nurses Association
National Conference of Gerontological Nurse Practitioners
National Organization of Nurse Practitioner Faculties

References

American Academy of Nurse Practitioners. n.d. "Medicare Regulations." Available online at http://www.acnp.org/medicare.htm.

American College of Nurse Practitioners. n.d. "Medicare & Medicaid Reimbursement for NPs." Available online at http://www.nurse.org/acnp/facts/reimb.shtml.

American College of Nurse Practitioners. n.d. "What Is a Nurse Practitioner?" Available online at http://www.nurse.org/acnp/facts/whatis.shtml.

American Nurses' Credentialing Center. 2002. "Computer-Based Testing for ANCC Certification." Available online at http://nursingworld.org/ancc/certify/cert/catalogs/cbt.pdf.

Cooper, Richard. 2001. "Health Care Workforce for the Twenty-first Century: The Impact of Nonphysician Clinicians." [Electronic Version]. *Annual Reviews of Medicine* 52: 51–61.

Hamric, Ann, Dana Worley, Sharon Lindebak, and Steve Jaubert. 1998. "Outcomes Associated with Advanced Nursing Practice Prescriptive Authority." *Journal of the American Academy of Nurse Practitioners* 10(2): 113–18.

Mundinger, Mary, Robert Kane, Elizabeth Lenz, Annette Totten, Wei-Yann Tsai, Paul Cleary, William Friedewald, Albert Siu, and Michael Shelanski. 2000. "Primary Care Outcomes in Patients Treated by Nurse Practitioners or Physicians: A Randomized Trial." [Electronic Version]. *Journal of the American Medical Association* 283(1): 59–68.

National Conference of Gerontological Nurse Practitioners. n.d. "About NCGNP—What Is a GNP?" Available online at http://www.ncgnp.org/displaycommon.cfm?an=17.

Office of Technology Assessment. 1986. *Nurse Practitioners, Physicians Assistants, and Certified Nurse Midwives: A Policy Analysis*. Washington, DC: GPO.

Pearson, Linda. 2002. "Fourteenth Annual Legislative Update: How Each State Stands on Legislative Issues Affecting Advanced Nursing Practice." *The Nurse Practitioner* 27: 10.

Safriet, Barbara. 1992. "Health Care Dollars and Regulatory Sense: The Role of Advanced Practice Nursing." *Yale Journal on Regulation* 9: 417–87.

Spratley, Ernell, Ayah Johnson, Julie Sochalski, Marshall Fritz, and William Spencer. 2002. *The Registered Nurse Population*. Rockville, MD: U.S. Department of Health & Human Services, Health Resources & Services Administration, Bureau of Health Professions, Division of Nursing.

Linda R. Rounds

GERONTOLOGICAL SOCIAL WORK, a specialty within the profession of social work in response to the increasing health and social service demands of our aging society. Over the last 25 years, social workers in health, mental health, and community development have reshaped their expertise for older adults whose numbers are increasing. It was once uncommon to work with an 80-year-old client at a mental health clinic; now mental health agencies have social workers whose specific jobs are to serve older clients and their families. In the past, nursing homes were the only option when a dependent older person needed more care than the family could provide; now there are many in-home care possibilities and residential options. Thus, a specialized body of social work knowledge and skills in gerontology has emerged, and the demand for gerontological social workers will continue to increase. Gerontological social workers provide clinical services to elders and their families, develop programs to serve older adults and reshape current programs where consumers are aging, administer social and health care facilities, advocate on behalf of older citizens, and participate in the development of social policies. Gerontological social workers are found in health care (health care clinics, hospitals, home health agencies, hospices); residential care (assisted living facilities, nursing homes); mental health services (geropsychiatric units of acute care hospitals, mental health clinics); specialty nonprofit organizations and community development organizations (the Alzheimer's Association; Housing Options Provided for the Elderly, Inc.); and public agencies (State Units on Aging, Area Agencies on Aging).

Social workers are distinguished from other professionals in gerontology by their knowledge of community resources and the range of options available to ameliorate problems; their psychosocial perspective and multidimensional assessment skills; and their skills in engaging the older person, family, and community in aspects of problem solving. In fact, so many elders and their families request help finding solutions to problems associated with aging that many gerontological social workers are opening private practices. These clinicians often help families understand the situation, access in-home services, or make decisions about residential care. Social workers are standard members of interdisciplinary teams working with older adults in clinical settings.

Social work interventions with older adults usually begin with a psychosocial assessment. Due to the close interconnections of the biological, psychological, and social aspects of aging, assessment can be complicated. For example, an older person may lose the ability to drive because of sensory loss; this person may then become socially isolated and eventually depressed; this depression can lead to problems with confusion. If not assessed thoroughly, it could be concluded that this person has an irreversible dementia, when the confusion is a result of other emotional and psychosocial problems that can be addressed. An assessment completed by a gerontological social worker will often be multidimensional and cover physical functioning, health conditions, mental status, emotional health, social resources, physical environment, service use, and financial resources. In order to maximize self-determination and choice, values and preferences of the older adult, especially for care arrangements, need to be determined. Other professionals are involved as needed or permitted by a client. For example, a neurologist should provide the diagnosis of dementia of the Alzheimer's type. A geropsychiatrist or geriatrician should provide the diagnosis of depression. A medical doctor or pharmacist should do the formal review of the medications. However, the social worker often is the professional with the broadest knowledge of the client. Social workers most frequently work with family or friends of the older client.

Financial resources are often an important part of a complete psychosocial assessment. Sometimes this is a sensitive area of questioning, but a good social worker will allay the client's fear regarding misuse of information. The development of service arrangements depends on a client's resources and entitlements, which must be accurately understood. The assessment must also reveal what informal (family and friends) and formal (paid or from an agency) services are already in place for a client. It is often difficult to get a clear picture of what agencies are involved and who is paying, given the various funding sources currently patchworked together to provide assistance to older persons in need. Providers and funding streams are largely invisible in some cases. The client may know that someone comes three times a week to help, but it is difficult to ascertain, for example, that the local Area Agency on Aging is supplying a person to help with personal care through monies from the Older Americans Act. Some older adults and families still mistakenly believe that Medicare is paying for such services. This mistake is being made less frequently, given an increased knowledge about long-term care. A thorough assessment of financial resources is also needed to ensure that older adults are taking advantage of resources available to them. Surprisingly, only 50% of poor older adults who are eligible for Supplementary Security Income (SSI) actually receive those benefits (Hooyman and Kiyak 2002).

Based on information gained from a psychosocial assessment, social workers can choose from a variety of interventions. Clinical case management is often the treatment of choice. Case management is an intervention aimed at organizing an effective and efficient package of long-term care services to a client. Case management functions include case finding (conducting outreach, determining eligibility, and administering the intake process), assessment (identifying current status and problem), care planning (developing a plan based on needs), coordination (arranging delivery of services), follow-up (monitoring client and services), and reassessment (reevaluating). The term *clinical case management* is used because counseling is important in this process; it is more than just arranging services. Some clients present complex psychosocial situations, and some clients are reluctant to accept services. There is also the need to balance family care and assistance from formal sources. Sometimes clients are in degenerative situations, so service needs are continually changing. Thus, social workers' clinical skills are needed to provide effective case management to older clients.

Case management can also have a financial function. There are service models in which social workers authorize funding. Sometimes, these workers must contain the cost of a service package to a predetermined amount of money (which will assure that in-home care is less than nursing home care). There are models in which case managers approve the expenditure of money for a package of client services and monitor this package but have little direct client contact. Different models of case management call for different amounts of client contact and different degrees of authority to purchase and allocate resources. Social workers are most likely to perform case management roles where there is maximum client contact, given their professional expertise in clinical and family work.

The assessment and care arrangement functions are also the key components of discharge planning, and many social workers provide discharge planning services to patients in nursing homes, day treatment programs, and hospitals. Workers assist older adults and families in identifying care needs and options, in making decisions about informal and formal care arrangements, and in establishing such arrangements. Social workers thus play a role in ensuring continuity of care between acute and extended care facilities and home.

Gerontological social workers provide a range of clinical interventions with older adults and their families. They organize and lead therapeutic groups that address all types of challenges posed in later life, such as widowhood, caregiving, or recovering from and adjusting to a stroke or Parkinson's disease. Often membership to these groups is offered free of charge through nonprofit associations such as the Alzheimer's or Parkinson's Association. Social workers also counsel clients individually and assist with problems of depression or adjustment to multiple late-life losses. Families often need assistance in dealing with an aging relative's increasing dependence, and family counseling around issues of aging is a growing demand. Social workers can bill Medicare for psychotherapy services in response to a diagnosed mental disorder (although current reimbursement rates are low and the bureaucratic process very labor-intensive). Many agencies and private clinicians have sliding scale fee schedules.

Understanding who pays for which services is critical and difficult in gerontological social work. There are 50 major public programs that address the needs of the older population through cash assistance, in-kind transfer, and provision of goods and services (Hooyman and Kiyak 2002). Social workers must know the programs that affect their clients. The core policies that affect gerontological social work practice are Social Security, Medicare, Medicaid, SSI, Older Americans Act services, food stamps, and housing subsidies. Medicare is intended to pay for acute care; social workers often help clients understand coverage and work with the bureaucracy to organize bills. Medicaid, the federal-state program that covers medical care for the poor, covers long-term care in nursing homes, in day care centers, and in the home in some states. Social workers assist clients in obtaining Medicaid coverage and using these benefits to meet their care needs. Block grant money and Older Americans Act funds are used at the local level to provide in-home and meal services to elders in need.

Social workers play key roles in accessing these subsidized services on behalf of their clients. Yet most of the money spent on services by elders and their families comes from private funds. Thus, social workers must educate clients and help make decisions about using money to meet care needs. To help them achieve this expertise, the Boettner Center at the University of Pennsylvania, affiliated with the School of Social Work, plans to offer coursework in Financial Gerontology for Social Workers. (See also DAILY MONEY MANAGERS; FINANCIAL GERONTOLOGY, HISTORY OF; GERIATRIC CARE MANAGERS [GCMs]; MEDICARE; MENTAL HEALTH AMONG OLDER ADULTS; WIDOWHOOD.)

References

Barusch, A. 2002. *Foundations of Social Policy*. Itasca, IL: F.E. Peacock.

Butler, R., M. Lewis, and T. Sunderland. 1998. *Aging and Mental Health: Positive Psychosocial and Biomedical Approaches*. Boston, MA: Allyn and Bacon.

Gallo, J., T. Fulmer, G. Paveza, and W. Reichel. 2000. *Handbook of Geriatric Assessment*. New York: Aspen Publishers.

Hooyman, N., and H. Kiyak. 2002. *Social Gerontology: A Multidisciplinary Perspective*. Boston, MA: Allyn and Bacon.

Kane, R.L., and R.A. Kane. 2000. *Assessing Older Persons: Measures, Meaning, and Practical Applications*. New York: Oxford University Press.

McInnis-Dittrich, K. 2002. *Social Work with Elders*. Boston, MA: Allyn and Bacon.

Schneider, R., N. Kropf, and A. Kisor. 2000. *Gerontological Social Work: Knowledge, Service Settings, and Special Presentations*. Belmont, CA: Wadsworth.

Toseland, R., and C. Rossiter. 1996. "Social Work Practice with Family Caregivers of Frail Older Persons." In *Social Work Practice with the Elderly*, ed. M.J. Holosko and M.D. Feit. Toronto: Canadian Scholars Press.

Nancy Morrow-Howell

GOVERNMENT PROGRAMS. See Age Discrimination in Employment Act (ADEA); Disability Programs, Federal and State; Disaster Preparedness and Older Adults; HUD-Assisted Rental Housing; Medicaid; Medicare; Nutrition Programs; Older Americans Act; Social Security Program of the United States; Supplemental Security Income (SSI); Veterans' Benefits.

GROWTH CAPITAL FOR OLDER ENTREPRENEURS, financing available for new enterprises from savings or other funds of the entrepreneur, his or her family, and friends or from a vast number of outside resources. The term *serial entrepreneur* has surfaced to characterize the individuals who are more interested in starting new companies than managing old ones. Simply, there are many people who enjoy the process of developing new companies and expect to stay busy with this very creative process throughout their working lives. While most sources of funds are similar regardless of age, older entrepreneurs may have access to alumni groups, larger networks of friends, established clubs, and so on, that are generally not available to the young. Also, many veterans will have the advantage of career paths that give them impressive credentials to grow new companies.

Sources may include outright grants that may occasionally be obtained from state, local, and federal agencies; bank loans guaranteed by the Small Business Administration or bank equity investments; customer financing; "business angels" (individuals who regularly invest $50,000 to $1 million in speculative new ventures); ethnic groups; social funds; corporate strategic partners; and venture capital. More than 80 different types of capital are available and literally thousands of funding and helping organizations exist, so it pays to do your research. Obtaining such funds often reflects more upon business experience and contacts than it does on the power of an idea, but huge variations in funding criteria exist. Also, in many instances of financing a new company, the entrepreneur may have to give up ownership or otherwise lessen primary control of the business.

A well-thought-out plan is critical to the search for investment funds. The plan will be necessary to detail the purpose and function of the business, as well as to do an examination of such things as competition, markets, risks, personnel, facilities, and the particular niche of the business. Some form of business plan is required for all sources of outside capital today, but the most important single element of planning for a company and being able to convince investors of the merit of investing is a comprehensive and very well thought out marketing plan. A number of templates for writing a business plan can be found on the Internet or in books on just that subject, but the most important thing to remember about a plan is to write down your whole course of action, with some contingencies if critical elements in the plan go awry. You may find that original ideas deviate or that new avenues open up once the business is started.

Once a business plan has been developed and capital sources have been identified, it is important to involve as many people as possible, including business and personal contacts. Involving the local newspaper may be a good place to get the word out to a local community. Finding money is often the most difficult step for any entrepreneur, however, and far too many good business ideas never see the light of day because of failure here. It is important to expect disappointment and that it will be necessary to speak with more potential sponsors than originally thought.

While each of the sources of capital is unique, a perspective on venture capital can be used as a guide for any and all sources of money. If a plan is developed in a form that could be accepted by highly demanding and sophisticated venture capitalists, it should serve well for other sources of capital as well.

Venture Capital

While venture capital funds came into being just before and after World War II, venture capital now exists in all developed countries and takes on a variety of forms. A few funds invest in startups, but most are looking for companies that fit into certain development stages, industry sectors, geographic regions, or size of financing. A very small portion of all new companies actually receive venture capital financing early on. Instead, these are usually financed by friends and family or business angels. Companies have formed their own venture investment funds as well and routinely finance new firms that fit into their own business interests.

It may be difficult for a new business to have success by soliciting large venture capital firms. A big fund may only invest in 5 or 6 proposals each year out of the 15,000 to 20,000 received. In cases where funding is obtained, the venture capitalist will want a professional business plan and may want the entrepreneur to sign a term sheet, an agreement that protects their interests and gives them priority on assets if the new company doesn't make it.

In addition to the traditional business plan, the entrepreneur will need to answer the following questions:

1. What is the market opportunity in this particular niche, and why does it exist? How will this business meet a market need? Just how big is the opportunity and in what direction is it heading?
2. What is the economic model—including revenues and profits? What is necessary to realize a profit, and when can one be expected?
3. What is the market outreach plan? Marketing plan?
4. What and who is the competition? How will it change? What is the company's comparative advantage—what are the competitors' weaknesses and this business's strengths? How will this company differentiate itself from others, and how will it maintain those differences?
5. Who comprises your management team, board of directors, board of advisors, and why should the background of those individuals convey enough confidence that they can do the job? Do they have experience in developing a company and being responsible for investors' money?
6. Can you provide a set of milestones that indicate just what you're going to do, when you're going to do it, what obstacles must be overcome, and when funds are going to be needed? Can you list the risks to your business model and indicate how you intend to overcome them? Can you give investors a feeling that they can monitor your progress and be in control of their money?
7. Have you provided an exit plan to suggest how your investors are going to make money and when? Are there other businesses that are somewhat comparable that you can use as a model for appreciation?

(See also ATTITUDES ABOUT RETIREMENT; BABY BOOMERS AND RETIREMENT; BUSINESS SUCCESSION PLANNING; CONSULTING IN RETIREMENT; ENTREPRENEURSHIP; WORKING RETIREES.)

Suggested Resource

Some sources of venture capital are listed on the Internet and can also be found in pricey annual compilations such as the 2002 *Directory of Venture Capital Firms* (Grey House Publishing, Millerton, NY; http://www.greyhouse.com/).

References

Fichera, Dante, and David Richardson. 2001. *Insider's Guide to Venture Capital, 2002*. Sacramento, CA: Prima Publishing.

Gladstone, David, and Laura Gladstone. 2001. *Venture Capital Handbook: An Entrepreneur's Guide to Raising Venture Capital*. New York: Prentice Hall.

Hill, Brian E., et al. 2002. *Attracting Capital from Angels: How Their Money and Their Experience Can Help You Build a Successful Company*. New York: John Wiley.

Peterson, Ronald. 2003. *When Venture Capitalists Say "No"—Creative Financing Strategies & Resources*. Glen Echo, MD: Comanche Press.

Robinson, Robert J., and Mark Van Osnabrugge. 2000. *Angel Investing: Matching Startup Companies*. Boston, MA: Jossey-Bass.

Ronald Peterson

GUARDIANSHIP, the legal relationship between a ward and a guardian; usually authorized by the probate or equity divisions of a state court. Wards are persons who have been declared by the courts to be incompetent to make particular decisions on their own behalf. Court-appointed guardians act as surrogate decision makers for the ward.

The underlying rationale for guardianship is the legal doctrine of *parens patriae* (literally, "father of the land"), the inherent authority and responsibility of a benevolent society to intervene, even over objection, to protect people who cannot protect themselves. Thus, instead of abandoning cognitively incapacitated individuals to a superficial autonomy to make self-harmful decisions or neglect their own basic needs, the state may exercise its authority to protect even unwilling disabled individuals from their own folly or intellectual deficits.

Every adult is presumed to be legally competent to make individual choices. This presumption may be declared invalid and a substitute decision maker appointed only upon a sufficient showing that the individual is mentally unable to take part in a rational decision-making process. A legal ruling of incompetence signifies that a person, because of a lack of capacity to contemplate and weigh choices rationally, cannot care adequately for his or her own person or property.

Guardianship historically has been a matter of state jurisdiction. Every state has enacted statutes that empower the courts to appoint guardians for decisionally incapacitated persons. Most state guardianship statutes are similar in content because they are based on the Uniform Probate Code (UPC), Article 5, although certain variations in the law and its application exist in the United States, and therefore one's own state statute always must be consulted.

Since the late 1980s, there has been substantial reexamination and revision of existing state guardianship statutes on the part of many state legislatures. Several states have made substantive changes in their guardianship laws by substituting more objective standards for traditional definitions of incompetence that rely heavily on diagnostic labels (e.g., the person is "depressed" or "demented"). These more objective standards are designed to focus on the individual's functional ability to manage personal care or finances on a daily basis. In other words, there is now more focus on the person's ability to meet basic needs rather than just on his or her clinical "condition."

State guardianship statutes today typically contain a two-step definition of competence. First, the individual must fall within a specific category, such as old age, mental illness, or developmental disability. Second, the individual must be found to be impaired functionally—that is, unable to care appropriately for his or her own person or property—as a result of being within that category. Incompetence cannot be equated with a categorical condition (such as advanced years) alone, so the determination of functional, behavioral, or adaptive disability is essential.

A variety of procedural reforms concerning guardianship have been enacted by the states. They are aimed at assuring potential wards greater due process protections against the unnecessary, premature, or improper loss of decisional rights. These procedural reforms deal with such matters as who should perform assessments of capacity, with a marked preference for the multidisciplinary and interdisciplinary perspective; the content of the assessor's report to the court; the appointment of outside visitors to supplement the formal assessment; the right to counsel as advocate; the ward's presence at the hearing; more rigorous requirements with regard to petitions; enhanced notice requirements; formalized hearing procedures and rules; and more specificity in the court's findings and in the order appointing the guardian. Reforms have been passed in the spheres of limited and temporary guardianship as well.

States continue to move away from referring to the legal status of the ward as "incompetent" and toward the language of "decisional capacity," which reflects movement away from emphasis on diagnostic category or label toward more emphasis on an individual's current functional abilities and deficits.

Terminology regarding the judicially created relationship between a decisionally incapacitated person and a surrogate decision maker, however, still varies somewhat among jurisdictions. Although the most common general designation for the court-appointed surrogate is "guardian," some states refer to this entity as a "conservator" (e.g., California). In a majority of states, a court-appointed surrogate with total authority over the ward's personal and financial affairs is called a "plenary" guardian. A surrogate with power over solely financial issues—the disposition of the ward's income and assets—usually is termed a "guardian of the estate" or "conservator." A surrogate decision maker concerning personal (such as medical, residential, and matrimonial) questions only is referred to in most states as a "guardian of the person."

Judicial appointment of a guardian to make decisions on behalf of a person who has been judged incompetent or incapacitated means that the ward no longer retains the legal power to exercise those decisional rights. The legal system historically has treated guardianship as an all-or-nothing proposition, with global findings of incompetence accompanied by virtually complete disenfranchisement of the ward. Plenary guardians ordinarily are awarded total power to control all of the ward's financial and personal matters.

The modern trend, however, has been toward statutory recognition of the concept of limited or partial guardianship and toward the encouragement of judicial deference to this concept. Limited or partial guardianship accounts for the decision-specific, waxing and waning nature of mental capacity for many persons and the ability of some people to make certain kinds of choices rationally but not others. State statutes also have been widely amended recently to permit judges to grant guardianship on a temporary, time-limited basis, rather than the formerly prevalent indefinite orders that shift the burden of proof regarding regained capacity and termination of the guardianship to the ward.

These trends reflect legislative deference to the least-restrictive alternative (LRA) (sometimes called the least-*intrusive* alternative) principle concerning state impingement of an individual's rights to personal autonomy. Under limited, partial, or temporary guardianships, courts fashion their orders to delineate explicitly the particular and exclusive types of decisions that the ward is incapable of making and over which the guardian may exercise proxy authority, with the remaining powers residing with the ward. Limited, partial, or temporary guardianship statutes may be permissive, allowing but not requiring courts to carefully tailor the guardian's power to the ward's needs, or they may mandate that the powers of the guardian be drawn as narrowly as possible. Even in the absence of legislation, state courts have general equity jurisdiction to create limited, partial, or temporary guardianships *sua sponte* (on their own initiative).

A number of policy considerations argue against overuse of the formal legal mechanism of guardianship. Guardianships frequently are expensive, time-consuming, and emotionally draining and result in unnecessary deprivation of basic civil liberties. In many cases, guardianships provide the ward with little meaningful protection against abuse and exploitation. Much attention has been devoted to exploring and developing viable alternatives to guardianship that strike an acceptable accommodation between protection and independence. There has been a significant movement toward greater reliance on these less restrictive and intrusive alternatives to guardianship for older individuals with compromised cognitive and emotional abilities.

Mechanisms that may delay or obviate the need for guardianship to manage one's financial affairs include, but are not limited to, joint bank and other financial accounts, case management, daily money management programs, living or *inter vivos* trusts, durable powers of attorney, and representative payee designations for government benefit checks. (See also ADVANCE DIRECTIVES; ELDER LAW PRACTICE; ETHICS IN FINANCIAL PLANNING; FINANCIAL ELDER ABUSE; FRAILTY PLANNING; TRUSTS.)

Organizations

American Bar Association, Commission on Legal Problems of the Elderly
Center for Social Gerontology
National Academy of Elder Law Attorneys
National Guardianship Association

References

Maddox, George L., ed. 2001. *The Encyclopedia of Aging*. 3rd ed. New York: Springer Publishing Company.

Schmidt, Winsor C., Jr. 1995. *Guardianship: The Court of Last Resort for the Elderly and Disabled*. Durham, NC: Carolina Academic Press.

Symposium on Guardianship Law. 2002. *Stetson Law Review* 31(3) (Spring).

Zimny, George H., and George T. Grossberg. 1998. *Guardianship of the Elderly*. New York: Springer Publishing Company.

Marshall B. Kapp

H

HEALTH AND LONGEVITY, population characteristics with significant social and economic implications as a result of medical advances and improved living conditions and lifestyles.

Life Expectancy and Mortality Patterns

The U.S. population aged 65 and older has grown rapidly, which is attributable to declining mortality rates across the entire life span, improved life expectancy, and improved health care. In 1900, a 65-year-old person could expect to live 11.9 additional years to age 77; by 1999, life expectancy at age 65 increased 17.7 years to almost age 83. Life expectancy at age 65 has increased for all people. Whites have shown the most rapid gains in life expectancy. Between 1950 and 1999, Blacks at age 65 gained 2.1 years compared with 3.9 years for Whites; life expectancy at age 65 for Blacks is 16.0 years compared to 17.8 years for Whites. Comparison of life expectancy at age 65 with other industrialized nations shows that the United States ranked tenth for men and twelfth for women in 1996, suggesting room for even more improvement (National Center for Health Statistics [NCHS] 2001).

In 1998, deaths of persons aged 65 and older totaled 1.7 million, or 75% of all deaths. The leading causes of deaths in older adults are heart diseases, malignant neoplasms, cerebrovascular diseases, chronic obstructive pulmonary diseases, and accidents (NCHS 2000). Death rates for all causes have been declining. Factors responsible for the substantial declines in mortality from heart disease and stroke during the past three decades include improved medical care and interventions, greater availability of coronary care units, advanced surgical and medical treatment of coronary heart disease, improved control of high blood pressure, decreased smoking, modified eating habits, increased exercise, and healthier lifestyles.

Health Status

The health status of older adults can be measured by their own perception of their health, limitations in their usual activities, and restricted-activity and bed-disability days. In 1998, 13% of the noninstitutionalized population reported limitations of activity due to chronic diseases. The rate of activity limitation increases with age, from 6% for those under age 18 to 47% for persons 75 years and over. Among persons aged 75 and older,

30% reported fair or poor health compared with others their age. Almost one out of ten in that age group reported limitations in activities of daily living (ADLs), defined as needing help in bathing or showering, dressing, getting in and out of bed or a chair, using the toilet, and eating; one out of five reported limitations in instrumental activities of daily living (IADLs), defined as needing help in preparing meals, managing money, shopping for groceries or personal items, performing light or heavy housework, and using a telephone (NCHS 2001).

The prevalence of specific, chronic conditions causing limitations of activity among the noninstitutionalized older adults is high. In 1996, 48% of those aged 65 years and over had arthritis, 41% had hypertension, and 24% had heart conditions. Many older adults suffered from impairments: 30% had hearing impairments, 16% had orthopedic impairments, and 17% had cataracts (NCHS 1999). Many suffer from multiple chronic conditions and disabilities. These activity-limiting conditions increase with age. About 27% of persons aged 65 and over have one condition, and 61% have two or more conditions. The United States is estimated to have spent over $500 billion in 2000 (in 1990 dollars) on direct medical care costs for persons with chronic conditions; by the year 2050 the amount is projected to rise to over $900 billion (Institute for Health & Aging 1996).

The numbers of restricted-activity and bed-disability days are significantly affected by the number of conditions. Persons aged 75 years and over with one chronic condition causing activity limitation report 55 restricted-activity days and 26 bed days per person per year. Those with two or more conditions report about twice that amount.

Medical Care Use

Use of health services increases with age, and older adults consume health services in amounts disproportionate to their numbers in the population. They visit physicians and are hospitalized more frequently than younger people. In 1999, persons aged 65 and older comprised 12.7% of the population, but they had 23.3% of almost 1 billion ambulatory visits, 16.3% of 32 million short-stay hospital discharges, 38.5% of 161 million hospital days, and 68.7% of 1.9 million home health patients. About 6% of the population was 75 years and older in 1999, yet this group accounted for 9.9% of all physician visits, 13.9% of hospital discharges, and 20.2% of the hospital days (NCHS 2001).

Older persons who suffer from chronic and disabling conditions heavily utilize medical resources. Noninstitutionalized people aged 75 and over with chronic conditions causing activity limitation saw physicians on average 16.5 times a year, in contrast to 9.6 times for persons under age 18. Multiple chronic conditions for those aged 75 and over cause the number of physician visits to almost double, from 11.3 visits for those reporting one condition causing activity limitation to 21.6 visits for those with two or more conditions.

The number of hospital days also varies with the number of conditions. The older adults aged 75 years and over with two or more chronic conditions causing activity limitation had 47.7 hospitalizations per 100 persons per year, in contrast to 35.9 for those with one condition. Combinations of these use patterns support the hypothesis that multiple chronic conditions create a significantly greater burden than one condition and that the burden increases with age.

According to the 1999 National Nursing Home Survey, about 4.3% of the persons aged 65 and older and 18.2% of persons aged 85 years and older are in nursing homes.

Other chronically ill older adults were in psychiatric or other chronic disease hospitals, Veterans Administration hospitals, and other long-term care facilities. Generally, older residents of nursing homes suffer from multiple chronic conditions and functional impairments.

Long-Term Care Needs

Most older persons who have lost some capacity for self-care require a wide range of social, personal, and supportive services. Long-term care (LTC) is defined as physical care over a prolonged period for those persons incapable of sustaining themselves without such care. Long-term care includes a spectrum of services responding to different needs across a range of chronic illness and disability. To address the multiple and varied LTC needs of the aged population, services must cross the boundaries between income maintenance and health, social, and housing programs. A wide range of organizations, professionals, and paraprofessionals are involved in the delivery of LTC. Long-term care services can be delivered in a variety of settings: a client's own home, community foster homes, multipurpose senior centers, day hospitals, day programs, and residential settings, including sheltered housing, board and care homes, residential hotels, old-age homes, nursing homes, rehabilitation centers, and mental hospitals.

Nearly 80% of older adults requiring assistance with ADLs or IADLs live at home or in community-based settings, while more than 20% live in nursing homes or other institutions. The majority of long-term care is provided by unpaid caregivers to older individuals living either in their own homes or with their families. The availability of home care services often plays a significant role in sustaining the capacity of older and disabled persons to maintain their personal independence and often determines admission into institutions. Caregiving is presumed to be the responsibility of women, because the home has traditionally been considered women's domain and caregiving a natural female characteristic. Women represent seven of ten unpaid caregivers, three-quarters of nursing home residents 65 years and older, and two-thirds of home health care users.

With growing numbers of chronically ill older and disabled adults, increased consideration is being given to alternatives in providing LTC services and preventing the need for high-cost institutionalization. Research and demonstrations in the United States have focused on LTC needs, service systems, and financing for older adults. Recent years have seen the development of a variety of community services such as day care, home health, meals-on-wheels, and respite care. Most of these services are aimed at maintaining the independence of the aged or disabled person at home to avoid institutional placement, often viewed as a measure of last resort.

According to the Agency for Health Care Research and Quality, spending for long-term care (home health, nursing home, and Medicaid spending for home and community-based services) amounted to $134 billion, about 11.4% of the $1 trillion national personal health care expenditures in 1999 (Heffler et al. 2001). Individuals needing care and their families paid for almost one-quarter of these expenditures out of pocket, public programs (predominantly Medicaid and Medicare) funded 61%, private insurance accounted for 10%, and other private sources paid the remaining 5%. These amounts, however, do not include the many hidden costs of long-term care. For example, they do not include wages lost when an unpaid family caregiver takes time off from work to provide assistance.

Financing Medical Care of the Aged

Almost 13% of the noninstitutionalized population was aged 65 and older in 1996, but this group accounted for 33% of all personal health care expenditures. Children and youth under age 18 comprised 27% of the population and accounted for 11% of total spending; adults aged 18 to 64 comprised 59% of the population and accounted for 56% of total spending. For older adults, out-of-pocket funds paid 15%, private health insurance paid 19%, Medicare paid 56%, Medicaid paid 4%, 3% came from other public funds, and the remaining 2% came from other sources (Cohen et al. 2000).

The idea that medical care is a basic right, along with food, clothing, and shelter, was greatly enhanced by the enactment of Medicare and Medicaid in 1965. Medicare is a national health insurance program for the aged and disabled that is administered by the federal government. It is the single largest health insurer in the country, covering virtually all persons aged 65 years and older and certain persons with disabilities or kidney failure. Medicare outlays in 1999 amounted to $214 billion. Over 34 million older persons and 5.3 million persons with disabilities were enrolled in the Medicare program in 1999.

Despite significant protections offered by Medicare, there are gaps in the Medicare benefits package and relatively high deductibles and cost-sharing requirements. To pay for medical deductibles, coinsurance, and uncovered benefits such as prescription drugs and dental care, most Medicare beneficiaries carry some type of supplemental coverage, often at additional cost, to fill the gaps in the Medicare benefit package. In 1999, out-of-pocket spending for health care goods and services and for premium payments by Medicare beneficiaries age 65 and older amounted to $2,430, or 19% of income. These estimates do not include the costs of home care and long-term nursing home care (Gross and Brangan 1999). Older adults experienced higher rates of chronic disease than the younger population and use on average almost four times the number of prescription drugs on average per person. Their prescription drug costs are almost four times that of persons under age 65, $1,378 versus $358, respectively.

Medicaid covers low-income aged, blind, disabled, pregnant, and dependent children and is jointly financed by federal and state governments. Of the 40.6 million Medicaid recipients in 1998, 10% were age 65 and older, accounting for 29% of the $142.3 billion spent under the program (NCHS 2001).

Expenditures in the Last Year of Life

Various studies have shown that older adults approaching death or institutionalization have high expenditures for medical care. About 5% of Medicare beneficiaries die each year, but they account for more than one-fourth of program expenditures. During the period 1993–1998, program outlays for decedents were about six times the amount reimbursed for services provided to survivors. About 38% of beneficiaries had some nursing home stay in the year of death. Hospice was used by half of cancer decedents and by 19% of all Medicare decedents (Hogan et al. 2001). The high medical costs preceding death are not a new phenomenon, and available data do not support the assumption that high medical expenses preceding death are due largely to aggressive, intensive treatment of patients who are moribund. The data suggest that most sick people who die are given the medical care generally provided to persons with severe illness and functional impairment, and sick care is expensive.

Future Morbidity Patterns

Changing morbidity and mortality play an important part in estimating future illness patterns and in developing population projections. Considerable conjecture has arisen about future morbidity patterns and their impact on future Medicare costs. A recent study indicates that the prevalence of chronic disability in older adults declined from 26.2% in 1982 to 19.7% in 1999, or 1.7% per year, more than the 1.5% required to preserve Medicare solvency (Manton and Gu 2001). How closely these observed trends in chronic disability among the older population will correspond to future illness patterns is uncertain. The interaction of future demographic changes and changing disability prevalence is unclear. Whatever else happens, however, the projected growth in the number of very old persons would have a significant impact on the need, demand, and costs of medical and long-term care services. (See also ADVANCE DIRECTIVES; ELDER LAW PRACTICE; ETHICS IN FINANCIAL PLANNING; FRAILTY PLANNING; TRUSTS.)

References

Cohen, Joel W., Steven R. Machlin, Samuel H. Zuvekas, Marie N. Stagnitti, and Joshua M. Thorpe. 2000. *Health Care Expenses in the United States, 1996*. MEPS Research Findings 12. AHRQ Pub. No. 01-0009. Rockville, MD: Agency for Healthcare Research and Quality.

General Accounting Office. 2001. *Long-Term Care: Baby Boom Generation Increases Challenges of Financing Needed Services*. Washington, DC: Author.

Gross, David, and Normandy Brangan. 1999. *Out-of-Pocket Spending on Health Care by Medicare Beneficiaries Age 65 and Older: 1999 Projections*. Washington, DC: Public Policy Institute, Research Group, AARP.

Heffler, Stephen, Katharine Levit, Sheila Smith, Cynthia Smith, Cathy Cowan, Helen Lazenby, and Mark Frieland. 2001. "Health Spending Growth Up in 1999; Faster Growth Expected in the Future." *Health Affairs* 20(2): 193–203.

Hogan, Christopher, June Lunney, Jon Gabel, and Joanne Lynn. 2001. "Medicare Beneficiaries' Costs of Care in the Last Year of Life." *Health Affairs* 20(4): 188–95.

Institute for Health & Aging. 1996. *Chronic Care in America: A 21st Century Challenge*. Princeton, NJ: Robert Wood Johnson Foundation.

Manton, Kenneth G., and XiLiang Gu. 2001. "Changes in the Prevalence of Chronic Disability in the United States Black and Nonblack Population above 65 from 1982 to 1999." *Proceedings of the National Academy of Sciences USA* 98(11): 6354–659.

National Center for Health Statistics (NCHS). 1999. "Current Estimates from the National Health Interview Survey by P.F. Adams, G.E. Hendershot, M.A. Marano." *Vital and Health Statistics* 19(200). Hyattsville, MD: Centers for Disease Control and Prevention.

National Center for Health Statistics (NCHS). 2000. "Deaths: Final Data for 1998 by S.L. Murphy." *National Vital Statistics Reports* 48(11): 1–51. Hyattsville, MD: Centers for Disease Control and Prevention.

National Center for Health Statistics (NCHS). 2001. *Health, United States, 2001*. DHHS Pub. No. 01-1232. Hyattsville, MD: Public Health Service.

Dorothy P. Rice

HEALTH BENEFITS, offered by employers in order to provide workers and their families with protection from financial losses that can accompany unexpected serious illness or injury. They also offer the benefits to promote health, to increase worker productivity, and to provide a form of compensation to recruit and retain qualified workers. Health insurance is the benefit most valued by workers and their families. In a 2001 survey, 60% of workers ranked health insurance as the most important employee benefit (Christensen 2002).

Research illustrates the advantages to consumers of having health insurance and the benefits to employers of offering it. In general, the availability of health insurance allows consumers to avoid unnecessary pain and suffering and to improve their quality of life, and employers offering benefits report that it has a positive impact on worker recruitment, retention, health status, and productivity (Fronstin and Helman 2000).

Employment-based health benefit programs have existed in the United States for more than 130 years. In the 1870s, for example, railroad, mining, and other industries began to provide the services of company doctors to workers. In 1910, Montgomery Ward entered into one of the earliest group insurance contracts for its employees.

Prior to World War II, few Americans had health insurance, and most policies covered only hospital room, board, and ancillary services. During World War II, the number of persons with employment-based health insurance coverage started to increase. When the National War Labor Board froze wages and a shortage of workers occurred, employers sought ways to get around the wage controls in order to attract scarce workers, and health insurance often was used in this way. Health insurance was an attractive means to recruit and retain workers during a labor shortage for two reasons: unions supported employment-based health insurance and workers' health benefits were not subject to income tax or Social Security payroll taxes as were cash wages.

Currently, employment-based health insurance is the most common form of health insurance coverage in the United States. In 2001, 104.4 million workers ages 18 to 64 were covered by employment-based health benefits (Fronstin 2002c). Seventy-seven percent (77%) of these workers had coverage through their own employer, while the remainder had coverage through a family member's employer. The employment-based health benefits system also covers 13.7 million nonworking adults, ages 18 to 64, and 44.2 million children under age 18. In 2002, virtually all employers with 200 or more employees offered health benefits to their workers, while 61% of employers with 3 to 199 employees made the same offering (Kaiser Family Foundation and Health Research and Educational Trust 2002).

Health Insurance Premiums

Under the current tax code, health insurance premiums paid by employers are deductible as a business expense—see Internal Revenue Code (IRC) Section 162(a)—and generally are excluded, without limit, from workers' taxable income.

Employers may choose to pay for the entire health insurance premium, a portion of the premium, or none of the premium, offering the plan but not contributing to its cost. The employee shares of the premiums for both themselves and their dependents generally are paid through payroll deduction and may be paid with pretax dollars under IRC Section 125(a). In 2002, employees paid an average of $38 per month for employee-only coverage (16% of the premium), while they paid an average of $174 per month for family coverage (27% of the premium) (Kaiser Family Foundation and Health Research and Educational Trust 2002).

Benefit Plan Types

According to a 2002 Kaiser Family Foundation study (http://www.kff.org/), 95% of Americans with employment-based health insurance coverage were enrolled in some kind of managed care plan. Health maintenance organizations (HMOs) and preferred provider organizations (PPOs) accounted for 78% of that enrollment. A managed care system typically provides, arranges for, and finances medical services using provider payment methods that encourage cost containment by contracting with select networks of providers.

Before the spread of managed care in the 1990s, insurance coverage was mostly based on a fee-for-service (FFS) system. Beneficiaries in the plan picked their doctors and hospitals at will. Payment was made by the beneficiary when a service was rendered, or the health care provider accepted assignment of the claim from the beneficiary, and afterward claim forms were submitted to the insurance company (or self-insured plan sponsor) for reimbursement. Under managed care, enrollees are often required to follow utilization review and disease management procedures in order to secure coverage for services received.

Other types of employment-based health benefits include different types of accounts through which workers can pay for health care services. Flexible spending accounts (FSAs) allow employees to pay for noncovered or nonreimbursed health care expenses with pretax dollars; they are not taxed on the amount of money that is put into the FSA (see IRC Sections 105(h)(6) and 125(a)). Medical savings accounts (MSAs) allow small employers (with up to 50 employees) and the self-employed to contribute pretax dollars to accounts used to pay for medical expenses, which are coupled with a high-deductible health insurance plan. There are limits on the number of these plans that may be established, and the legislation authorizing MSAs is set to expire in December 2003, unless renewed by Congress. MSAs were instituted originally in the Health Insurance Portability and Accountability Act (HIPAA) of 1996 and have since been reauthorized.

Some employers are considering ways in which they can restructure health benefits. A few employers have turned to, and many others are considering, a trend that started in the 1980s to give employees more choice among different types of benefit arrangements, while at the same time exposing employees more directly to the cost of providing health benefits and health care services. The terms *defined contribution* and *consumer-driven* have been used to describe a wide range of possible approaches to giving employees more incentive to control the cost of either their health benefits or health care and to reduce the size and volatility of employer spending. Many of these plans include tax-advantaged accounts, called *health reimbursement accounts*, *personal care accounts*, and other names, out of which employees pay for their health care needs (Fronstin 2002b).

Employee Cost Sharing

Virtually all covered services in health care plans are subject to payment limitations and require the employee to share in the costs of coverage. These cost-sharing features generally include premium contributions, deductibles, copayments, coinsurance, and maximum caps on benefits. These plan features are intended to reduce plan costs, encourage employee cost consciousness, and lower administrative expenses.

A *deductible* is a specified amount of initial medical costs that would otherwise be treated as covered expenses under the plan, which each beneficiary must pay before any expenses are reimbursed by the plan. Deductibles typically range from $100 to $500 per year per person, although they can be higher.

Copayments are set dollar amounts that a plan participant pays when he or she seeks medical services, such as a $10 payment for seeing their primary care physician or a $20 payment for seeing a specialist. The most common copayment amount for a doctor visit in all types of plans is $10; however, copayment amounts appear to be increasing (Kaiser Family Foundation and Health Research and Educational Trust 2002).

Coinsurance provisions require the plan participant to pay a portion of recognized medical expenses; the plan pays the remaining portion. Commonly, the employee pays 20%, with the plan paying the remaining 80% of recognized charges. Most major medical plans include both deductibles and coinsurance provisions. Thus, once the plan participant pays the deductible (e.g., the first $200 in medical expenses), the plan pays 80% of all other covered charges. Most plans limit beneficiaries' out-of-pocket expenditures for covered services; once a beneficiary has reached the out-of-pocket maximum, covered expenses are reimbursed in full for the remainder of the year.

Most medical plans also impose a *maximum annual* or *lifetime dollar limit* on the amount of health insurance coverage provided. Individual lifetime maximums are usually set at very high levels, such as $1 million or more. Although less common, plans that impose limits may do so on an episodic (or per episode) basis, such as per hospital admission or per disability.

Services Covered

The term *health insurance* refers to a wide variety of insurance policies. These range from policies that cover the costs of doctors and hospitals for general medical and health care services to those that meet a specific need, such as paying for dental or vision care. In the past, health insurance that covered medical bills, surgery, and hospital expenses was typically referred to as a *comprehensive* or *major medical* policy. Today, when individuals talk about an insurance program, instead of using the term *major medical*, they are more likely to refer to FFS (e.g., indemnity), PPO, POS (point of service), HMO, or some other type of insurance program.

Most insurance programs cover medical expenses for hospital and physician fees, surgical expenses, anesthesia, x-rays, laboratory fees, emergency care, and maternity care. Some programs cover physical exams, preventive care (e.g., vaccinations), health screenings (e.g., mammographies), chemical dependency treatment, prescription drugs, dental, vision, mental health or other psychiatric care, and home health, nursing home, and hospice care. For certain services, there may be limits on how much is covered or how many visits are covered annually.

Most health insurance programs do not cover treatment that is experimental or investigational. Insurance programs typically cover only medically necessary care. A typical definition of *appropriate and medically necessary care* is the standard for health care services as determined by physicians and health care providers in accordance with prevailing practices and standards of the medical profession and community.

Medical plans generally exclude services that are not considered medically necessary, including most types of dental, vision, and hearing care. As a result, stand-alone plans providing these benefits are growing in popularity. Because of their highly elective nature, various limits are placed on the benefits provided. When these benefits are offered by or through a vendor other than the health insurer, they are referred to as being "carved out."

Federal Protections, Laws, and Regulations

The Employee Benefits Security Administration (EBSA), formerly the Pension and Welfare Benefits Administration (PWBA), an agency within the Department of Labor (DoL), is responsible for protecting the integrity of pensions, health plans, and other employee benefits for more than 150 million people. The agency assists workers in getting the information they need to protect their benefit rights, assists plan officials to understand the requirements of the relevant statutes in order to meet their legal responsibilities, develops policies and regulations that encourage the growth of employment-based benefits, and deters and corrects violations of the relevant statutes.

Several federal laws affect how workers and their families receive health benefits from employment. Two of the major laws are ERISA and COBRA:

Employee Retirement Income Security Act (ERISA) of 1974. Offers protections for individuals enrolled in health benefit plans sponsored by private sector employers, provides rights to information, and outlines a grievance and appeals process for participants to get benefits from their plans.

Consolidated Omnibus Budget Reconciliation Act (COBRA) of 1985. Contains provisions giving certain former employees, retirees, spouses, and dependent children the right to purchase temporary continuation of group health plan coverage at group rates in specific instances. An employer may charge the departing employee the full cost of the coverage plus 2% to cover administrative costs. In 2002, about 16% of beneficiaries eligible for COBRA benefits actually elected to take the coverage, and claims costs for COBRA were about 150% of active employee claims costs (Charles D. Spencer & Associates 2002).

Both of these laws are administered/enforced by the DoL. Other federal agencies with responsibility for health benefits laws include the Internal Revenue Service, the Department of Justice, and others. Additional laws pertaining to health insurance include the Family and Medical Leave Act (FMLA) of 1993, the Health Insurance Portability and Accountability Act (HIPAA) of 1996, the Newborns' and Mothers' Health Protection Act (NMHPA) of 1996, and the Women's Health and Cancer Rights Act (WHCRA) of 1998. In addition, the Equal Employment Opportunity Commission (EEOC) administers several laws that pertain to employment-based health benefits.

Trends in Health Care Benefits Coverage

In February 2001, 77.4% of workers ages 18 to 64 were offered health insurance by their employer, up from 73.8% in 1993. However, in 2001, 82% of those workers who were offered it took the insurance, down from 85.2% in 1993. As a result, the percentage of workers covered by their own employer remained largely constant from 1993 (62.9%) to 2001 (63.5%) (Fronstin 2002a).

In 2001, rising health benefit costs coupled with the weak economy began to have an effect on health insurance coverage. According to one survey, health benefits costs increased 11% overall in 2001 (Kaiser Family Foundation and Health Research and Educational Trust 2002). As a result of these cost increases, between 2000 and 2001, the percentage of nonelderly Americans with employment-based health benefits declined from 67.1% to 65.6%, the first decline since the early 1990s (Fronstin 2002c). The Kaiser survey found that costs rose even faster in 2002, at a rate of 12.7% overall. This could lead to even further decreases in coverage rates for employment-based health benefits.

Retiree Health Benefits

In addition to health benefits for current workers, some employers offer health benefits to retirees. Retiree health benefits originally were offered on a very limited basis in the late 1940s and 1950s. The number of employers offering these benefits expanded in the late 1960s in conjunction with the creation of the Medicare program. The benefits were provided as part of the health plan for active workers, generally without a separate premium structure or separate accounting. In subsequent years, the changing demographics of the workforce, coupled with increasing life spans and rising health care costs, left many employers with higher retiree-to-active-worker ratios, increasing the costs and liabilities of retiree medical benefits.

In 1989, the Financial Accounting Standards Board (FASB) issued Statement No. 106 (FAS 106), "Employers' Accounting for Postretirement Benefits Other Than Pensions," which required companies to account for these benefits and report liabilities for the future value of all promised benefits on their corporate balance sheets, beginning with fiscal years after December 15, 1992. For the first time, the true cost of the benefits was understood (Employee Benefit Research Institute 1988, 1989). Prior to FAS 106, companies were required to disclose information only on the existence of plans and amounts of benefit outflows.

As a result of FAS 106, and the increasing cost of providing retiree health benefits in general, many employers began a major overhaul of their retiree health benefit programs. Some employers placed caps on what they were willing to spend on retiree health benefits. Some added age and service requirements, while others moved to some type of "defined contribution" health benefit. Some completely dropped retiree health benefits for future retirees, while others dropped benefits for current retirees, although this happened less frequently than other changes. While these changes do not appear to be having much impact on current retirees, they are likely to be felt most by future retirees who are not yet or may never become eligible for retiree health benefits.

Retiree Health Benefits Design and Coverage

There are two basic designs for retiree health benefit plans: one for plans covering retirees under age 65 (early retirees) and one covering retirees age 65 and over. Because of the limited tax preferences of the available funding vehicles, employers are looking to reduce their FAS 106 liability by redesigning their retiree health benefit plans. In general, the percentage of employers offering health benefits to future retirees seems to be declining. An annual survey of employers with 500 or more workers shows that the percentage that currently expect to continue offering health benefits to future early retirees declined from 46% in 1993 to 29% in 2000 (William M. Mercer 2001). The percentage of employers offering health benefits to Medicare-eligible retirees today and planning to offer them to future Medicare-eligible retirees is also declining. A survey that followed a constant sample of employers shows a less dramatic drop of 7% in the likelihood that employers offered retiree health benefits to early retirees and a 9% drop for Medicare-eligible retirees (McArdle et al. 1999).

Most employers continuing to offer retiree health benefits have made changes in the benefit package. Many employers have made modifications to cost-sharing provisions, with employers asking retirees to pick up a greater share of the cost of coverage. Others have tightened eligibility requirements by requiring workers to attain a certain age and/or tenure with the company before they can receive any retiree health benefits. Others have reduced or eliminated the benefits for workers hired (or retiring) after a specific date. Employers have also instituted caps on the total amount of money they are willing to spend on retiree health benefits, either per retiree or on a total aggregate spending basis. In addition to those that have already made changes, more employers also are continuing to consider making changes to retiree health benefits.

It will be a few more years before sufficient data are available to explain how workers and retirees will be affected by cutbacks in retiree health benefits. The accounting requirements of FAS 106 triggered substantial changes to retiree health benefits. However, the changes that employers have made to retiree health benefits do not appear to be having much impact on current retirees. Between 1994 and 2000, the percentage of retirees ages 55 to 64 with retiree health benefits was unchanged at roughly 37%, although it is likely that many current retirees are paying more to maintain retiree health benefits.

The changes that employers have made to retiree health benefits will likely have a greater impact on future retirees. These changes may not have noticeable effects on trends in insurance coverage until a few years after the baby boom generation starts to retire. Retirement behavior patterns may also change as employees nearing retirement age postpone their decision to retire upon learning that, without a job, they may not be able to obtain health insurance coverage. By law, employers are under no obligation to provide retiree health benefits, except to current retirees who can prove that they were promised a specific benefit. In the meantime, it is likely that employers will continue to make changes to retiree health benefits in response to future predicted health care costs and potential federal legislative initiatives.

Conclusion

For many decades, health care benefit plans have played a significant role in employee benefits planning. Modern technology, increased longevity, and a growing emphasis on good physical and mental health make these plans even more important today. The development of managed care plans and dental, prescription drug, vision, and hearing care plans attests to the dynamic nature of this employee benefit area, as does the development of wellness and employee assistance programs. Future innovative efforts in plan design will be influenced strongly by the continuing need for health care cost management, ever-changing medical technology, and constantly changing government regulations.

While an increasing percentage of Americans was being covered by employment-based health plans between 1994 and 2000, this trend has not continued because of the combination of a weak economy and rising health benefit costs. If health care and health benefit costs continue to increase, a greater proportion of the costs may become the responsibility of the employee as employers seek ways to control their spending on health benefits, both for current employees and for retirees. As a result, fewer workers and retirees may become covered by health care benefits through their employers. (See also EARLY RETIREMENT INCENTIVE PLANS [ERIPs]; EMPLOYEE BENEFITS IN THE UNITED STATES; HEALTH AND LONGEVITY; HEALTH MAINTENANCE ORGANIZATIONS AND MANAGED HEALTH CARE FOR OLDER ADULTS; POSTRETIREMENT HEALTH COVERAGE [PRHC].)

Organizations

American Association of Health Plans
American Benefits Council
Blue Cross Blue Shield Association
ERISA Industry Committee
Health Insurance Association of America
Society for Human Resource Management

References

Charles D. Spencer & Associates. 2002. "2002 COBRA Survey: More Were Eligible, Fewer Elected, Cost Was 150% of Active Employee Cost." In *Spencer's Research Reports on Employee Benefits*, no. 329.04. Chicago: Aspen Publishers, October.

Christensen, Rachel. 2002. "Value of Benefits Constant in a Changing World: Findings from the 2001 EBRI/MGA Value of Benefits Survey." *EBRI Notes* 3 (Employee Benefit Research Institute) (March): 1–3.

Employee Benefit Research Institute. 1988. *Measuring and Funding Corporate Liabilities for Retiree Health Benefits: An EBRI-ERF Policy Study*. Washington, DC: Author.

Employee Benefit Research Institute. 1989. *Retiree Health Benefits: What Is the Promise? An EBRI-ERF Policy Forum*. Washington, DC: Author.

Fronstin, Paul. 2000a. "Trends in Health Insurance Coverage: A Look at Early 2001 Data." *Health Affairs* 21(1).

Fronstin, Paul. 2000b. "Can 'Consumerism' Slow the Rate of Health Benefit Cost Increases?" *EBRI Issue Brief* 247 (Employee Benefit Research Institute) (July).

Fronstin, Paul. 2000c. "Sources of Health Insurance and Characteristics of the Uninsured: Analysis of the March 2002 Current Population Survey." *EBRI Issue Brief* 252 (Employee Benefit Research Institute) (December).

Fronstin, Paul, and Ruth Helman. 2000. "Small Employers and Health Benefits: Findings from the 2000 Small Employer Health Benefits Survey." *EBRI Issue Brief* 226 (Employee Benefit Research Institute) (October).

Kaiser Family Foundation and Health Research and Educational Trust. 2002. *Employer Health Benefits: 2002 Annual Survey*. Menlo Park, CA: Henry J. Kaiser Family Foundation.

McArdle, Frank, et al. 1999. "Retiree Health Coverage: Recent Trends and Employer Perspectives on Future Benefits." Report published by The Henry J. Kaiser Family Foundation, Menlo Park, CA, October.

William M. Mercer. 2001. *Mercer/Foster Higgins National Survey of Employer-Sponsored Health Plans 2001*. New York: William M. Mercer, Inc.

Rachel Christensen and Paul Fronstin

HEALTH CARE. See Board and Care Homes; Day Programs for Adults; Drugs and Senior Citizens; Geriatric Care Managers [GCMs]; Gerontological Nurse Practitioners [GNPs], Gerontological Social Work; Home Care Services for Older Adults; Hospice Care; Mental Health among Older Adults; Nursing Homes; Nutrition Programs; Pharmacists; Physician–Older Patient Relationships.

HEALTH INSURANCE. See Health Maintenance Organizations and Managed Health Care for Older Adults; Long-Term Care Insurance, Private; Medicaid; Medicare; Medicare Supplemental Insurance; Postretirement Health Coverage (PRHC).

HEALTH MAINTENANCE ORGANIZATIONS AND MANAGED HEALTH CARE FOR OLDER ADULTS. Managed care has been an option within the Medicare program for almost 20 years. This approach was initiated because of assumptions about the cost savings and care coordination efficiencies associated with this form of service delivery. Opponents of managed care systems for older Americans believe that these plans have often cost the Medicare program more money per beneficiary than if these individuals had been in fee-for-service care. Additionally, they voice concern that there may be unnecessary restrictions on the frequency and length of physician office visits and on the access to tests, procedures, and specialty care. To place these concerns in perspective, this entry reviews studies that have examined the effectiveness and quality of care with managed care systems. Also discussed are two approaches developed within specialty managed care plans that expressly attempt to integrate the care planning and delivery for persons considered at risk for disability or expensive care.

Defining Managed Care

Managed care has many meanings within health care. The most fundamental feature is the management of physician practice. This occurs in various ways: the selection of physicians into provider networks, utilization monitoring and feedback, provider reimbursement and financial risk-sharing incentives, and practice guidelines. Combinations of these procedures are used within any one managed care plan.

Managed care plans include health maintenance organizations (HMOs), preferred provider organizations (PPOs), and point of service (POS) plans. HMOs include arrangements where one or more medical groups may have an exclusive contract with the plan (e.g., Kaiser Foundation Health Plan and the Permanente Medical Group) or the more common network HMOs in which the medical group's relationship is not exclusive. There are some plans where the physicians are employees of the health plan (e.g., Group Health Cooperative).

Providers in PPOs are reimbursed on a fee-for-service basis but at a discounted rate for enrolled members. PPO enrollees come from employer groups, unions, and other groups with which the PPO has negotiated the opportunity to recruit such members. Providers participating in PPOs usually have nonexclusive relationships with each other. Providers participate in PPOs to gain ready access to patients.

POS, or point of service, plans are variations on the provider "lock-in" provisions of both HMO and PPO coverage. The distinguishing feature of a POS is that enrollees can be covered for services outside the HMO or PPO network. When outside providers are used, service copayments and deductibles are usually higher than they would be from a network provider. Managed care in the form of prepaid health plans has existed for decades, but they began to become widespread in the 1980s as employers reacted to high rates of increase in health insurance premiums. By the mid-1990s about 60% of employees covered by health insurance were enrolled in some form of managed care plan. This rate varied greatly by region of the country and even community. Enrollment continued to increase, with more than 80 million workers covered by these programs in

1999, although shifts in the economy during the early 2000s has reduced access to employer-based coverage for many. Within the Medicare program, the development of managed care has been both less extensive and less rapid. The high point of enrollment occurred between 1998 and 2000 when 16% of beneficiaries were enrolled in managed care. That proportion declined to 12% by 2002.

Among the incentives for enrolling in a managed care plan throughout the 1990s was that basic Medicare benefits of hospital, physician, limited skilled nursing facility use, skilled home health, and durable medical equipment were covered with lower monthly premiums and lower copayments and deductibles than Medicare supplemental insurance policies. Additionally, many health plans also offered outpatient prescription drug coverage. Many also offered expanded benefits like routine physical examinations and immunizations, within the basic benefits, and vision, hearing, and dental exams, at discounted prices.

Enrollment in Medicare managed care has declined for a variety of reasons. The most important is that there are fewer providers willing to accept Medicare contracts, with the direct consequence that members must return to fee for service if there is no managed care provider available. Several factors contribute to this. One is that Medicare prepaid payments for enrollees have not kept pace with what providers see as appropriate rates of reimbursement. Another is a continuing uncertainty associated with changes in Medicare reimbursement formulas for health plans. By 2004, these begin phasing in. A third factor is negative media coverage about managed care. Not infrequently these stories are about denials or other restrictions on service or treatment.

Managed Care Practices and Performance

One of the principal ways managed care providers have historically reduced their costs relative to fee-for-service systems is by controlling hospital admissions and lengths of stay. In the mid-1980s before there was preset diagnosis-related hospital reimbursement in fee for service, studies found that managed care hospital days were 10% to 40% lower than fee-for-service reimbursed care. By the early 1990s this difference had reduced, with several studies failing to find differences, even among Medicare beneficiaries.

Findings with respect to physician use are inconsistent. One might expect physician use to be higher if it were preventive or in some manner substituting for hospital use. Staff and group model HMOs tend to have higher physician visit rates, while independent practice plans tend to have similar use as fee for service.

Another means of managed care savings is the possible use of fewer or less costly services. Access to appropriate tests and procedures is both an example of possible cost controls and a presumed indicator of the quality of care within health plans. There is evidence that managed care plans are economical in the use of tests and procedures, while still being attentive to prevention and health promotion. Among Medicare plan members, studies have generally shown equivalent access to routine and preventive care (cancer and hypertension screening tests; breast, pelvic, rectal, and general physical examinations; treatment for congestive heart failure, colorectal cancer, diabetes). The potential for managed care organizations to achieve physician compliance with treatment guidelines and other professionally established standards of care is high. These organizations usually have record systems, which permit them to monitor physician behavior and to know the health conditions affecting members.

While there are likely to have been many occasions when managed care plans and providers have failed to offer or delay tests and procedures, the adverse consequences of this are not reflected in most of the analyses of managed care outcomes: Hospital days are the same or lower in managed care; physician use is the same or higher in managed care. Even studies of health plan satisfaction tend to show that 80% to 95% of members report high satisfaction with their plans, a rate only a few percentage points below the average satisfaction levels of those in fee for service.

Emerging Directions: Chronic Illness Care and Service Integration

A variety of industry and public policy trends are evident in response to the perceived needs and shortcomings of prior efforts to achieve efficient and equitable care within managed care systems. On the policy side are efforts to strengthen quality assurance and performance monitoring and refinement of the reimbursement formula to assure equitable payment for both the plans and Medicare. There are also changes in clinical practice to embrace geriatric care and chronic illness care and interest in exploring and refining approaches to the integration of acute and chronic care.

Two particular approaches to integration deserve special note: The Program of All-Inclusive Care for the Elderly (PACE) and the Social HMO. Both began operating integrated systems of acute and long-term care (LTC) in the mid-1980s as Medicare/Medicaid demonstrations. In 1990 Congress mandated a test of a geriatric model of Social HMOs, and in 1997 Congress made PACE a permanent Medicare program and expressed intention to do the same for Social HMOs. As of February 2003, there were four Social HMO sites serving 110,000 members and 40 PACE sites serving about 8,000 members.

Both Social HMOs and PACE share four features:

1. *Organizational integration.* A sponsor assembles acute care and LTC services into a contracted service network. Sponsors have included HMOs, hospitals, LTC organizations, and joint ventures.
2. *Capitated finance.* Sponsors operate under full-risk, prepaid, limited financing from Medicare and Medicaid.
3. *Voluntary enrollment with lock-in.* Programs must convince beneficiaries to join, and once they join, they agree to obtain all their acute care and covered LTC through the program's managed system of contracted providers.
4. *Service integration.* The full range of acute and LTC services (e.g., personal care and homemaking, adult day health center, nursing facilities) are included in the benefit package, and management systems coordinate service provision.

Social HMOs and PACE differ on five features:

1. *Disabled-only versus broad membership.* PACE services only those who are frail enough to be "nursing home certifiable" (NHC) by state preadmission screening criteria, while Social HMOs serve a broad cross section of the older adults population, including beneficiaries who are frail.
2. *Team versus administrative integration.* PACE sites integrate acute and LTC through a multidisciplinary team based in an adult day health center, which almost all members regularly attend. Most Social HMOs integrate administratively: acute and LTC managers and providers in remote settings work together through communication and coordination protocols. A "second-

generation" Social HMO site begun in 1996 also uses geriatric teams (medically trained persons who specialize in treatment of older persons) to integrate administratively.

3. *Small versus large scale*: PACE sites are designed to serve about 200 members, which is the limit that can be managed in the day health setting. In 2002 the four Social HMOs were serving between 4,400 and 52,000 members and could grow much larger.
4. *Full versus limited LTC benefits*: PACE covers all community and institutional LTC costs for members, while Social HMOs limit community LTC coverage by either dollar limits ($7,500 to $12,000 per year) or time-limited authorizations. If a Social HMO member is permanently institutionalized, he or she can remain in the Social HMO, but LTC coverage ends after several weeks.
5. *Medicaid versus private supplement to Medicare*: PACE premiums for LTC and other supplemental benefits are paid by Medicaid. These averaged $2,422 per month in 2000 (twice the plans' average monthly Medicare premiums). Few individuals can afford this supplemental premium, so almost all PACE members are persons eligible for both Medicare and Medicaid. In contrast, in 2000 Social HMOs' monthly member premiums ranged from no cost to $190, and only 1% to 6% of Social HMO members were Medicaid eligible. Medicare premiums of $560 to $925 per month provided the bulk of Social HMO funding.

One key challenge for Social HMOs and PACE has been marketing/enrollment. PACE sites rely on referrals rather than mass marketing for new members, and their "competition" is the care options available to Medicare/Medicaid eligibles. Despite extensive recruitment, most PACE sites have lagged well behind enrollment targets due to their small market niche and the requirements to switch to the PACE physician and attend day care. Additionally, the PACE providers screen applicants for both program eligibility and the provider's perception of the appropriateness for enrolling them. More than a third of applicants are not accepted. Social HMOs rely on both internal referrals (in HMO-based models) and mass marketing. Their main competition is other private Medicare supplemental plans. Social HMO sites that have sought to grow large have been periodically stopped by federal enrollment caps; but as small plans, they have also faced challenges creating provider networks.

Another challenge faced by both models is changing the system of care for geriatric patients. PACE's integrated service delivery team has achieved dramatic reductions in hospital and nursing home utilization, while increasing the use of ambulatory, preventive, and therapy services. Changes at Social HMO sites have been more difficult to detect, in part due to the lack of reliable comparison groups but also due to the fact that administrative integration is not as strong an intervention as the PACE team. There is some evidence that the team model in the second-generation geriatric Social HMO has reduced acute care utilization. Reductions in institutionalization have also been more difficult to prove in Social HMOs, in part because formal evaluations did not assess this outcome. There is some evidence from nonrandomized studies of reductions in institutionalization. There is substantial variation among both PACE and Social HMO sites in all these utilization areas.

An ongoing policy challenge for both Medicare and Medicaid has been developing prospective payment formulas for health plans like PACE and Social HMOs that enroll disproportionate shares of members with disabilities. Research shows that disability status is an additional risk/cost factor beyond the demographic and diagnostic data that Medicare and Medicaid include in formulas to pay other health plans. Not accounting for disability levels of enrollees would lead to substantial underpayment for PACE (100% NHC) and at least some Social HMOs (which are 20% to 30% NHC). Several generations of formulas that include disability factors have been developed, but research continues.

Formal evaluations of both Social HMOs and PACE have been inconclusive regarding effects on member health status and mortality or Medicare and Medicaid spending. Neither Social HMOs nor PACE have been evaluated with a randomized comparison design, the two Social HMO models were evaluated only in their early operational phases, and evaluation methodologies have been disputed. The comparability of PACE intervention and comparison groups has also been questioned, in part due to PACE sites' rejection of many referrals/applicants.

Conclusions

Managed care raises opportunities for both enhanced coordination and more effective care for the older adults. The experience of Medicare managed care and the Social HMO and PACE programs all show evidence of care outcomes at least comparable to those of fee-for-service delivery. Certainly incentives exist with managed care reimbursement for a balance between the service rationing needed to control costs and the proactive care needed to assure desirable quality of care outcomes. Consolidation of managed care plans, and among medical groups and hospitals, and even the withdrawal of managed care programs from many communities reflect the continuing flux associated with this approach to health care delivery and some of the problems it poses for beneficiary participation. (See also COMMUNITY-BASED CARE; MEDICAID; MEDICARE; MEDICARE + CHOICE; MEDICARE SUPPLEMENTAL INSURANCE; PHYSICIAN–OLDER PATIENT RELATIONSHIPS.)

References

Newcomer, Robert, Charlene Harrington, and Robert Kane. 1999. "Implications of Managed Care for Older Persons." In *Emerging Systems in Long Term Care*, ed. P. Katz, R. Kane, and M. Mezey. New York: Springer Publishing Company.

Williams, Claudia, Justin Treloar, Janet Lundy, Larry Levitt, and Jain Wang. 2002. *Trends and Indicators in the Changing Health Care Marketplace, 2002*. Menlo Park, CA: Henry J. Kaiser Family Foundation.

Robert Newcomer and Walter Leutz

HISTORY OF RETIREMENT, late-twentieth-century, middle-class conventions color images of retirement in the United States. Most of us have attended a party that celebrates an older employee's transition to a new stage of life. Colleagues and supervisors offer kind words about that person's dedicated service. The guest of honor receives a watch, a bowl, or some other token to remember the occasion. The newly retired also fills out the paperwork necessary to obtain a monthly Social Security check and to begin to draw on prior investments to the company's pension plan. Those who were forward looking and/or lucky enough can also count on private savings or support from their children to supplement their retirement income. Ideally, as long as the retiree stays healthy, there should be money sufficient to approximate the standard of living enjoyed in that person's peak earning years. Accentuating the positive, I (like most Americans) look forward to "retirement" as a time for leisure, according us in our golden years the freedom to pursue hobbies and to travel, to volunteer, or just to take it easy.

Such images, accurate as far as they go, tell only a small part of the story—and they are becoming anachronistic. Images of Snowbirds vigorously exercising on the beach and playing their cards shrewdly do not convey many other faces of retirement. For openers, "retirement" only lately has become something older workers of moderate means could hope to attain, much less afford to enjoy. Men and women throughout most of recorded history were expected to work as long as they were physically able to do so, lest they become burdens on their families or their community. In any event, most people born before 1900 died before they reached the age of 60 or 70, so demographic realities in the past did not prompt the easy connection we now make between "retirement" and "old age." Exceptions to these three generalizations are few and far between. There is evidence that Chinese bureaucrats as early as the fourteenth century and certain categories of senior military personnel in Britain and France beginning in the seventeenth century were permitted to quit their posts and to collect a pension drawn from the royal coffers. And of course the very rich could always elect to spend their twilight years as part of the leisure class. The paucity of exceptions underscores the point that "retirement" was not perceived as a social norm until quite recently in world history.

Economic and social trends in the early decades of the American Republic are consistent with patterns elsewhere in the world at the time. "Retirement" prior to the Civil War defined several conditions occurring over the life course, not just events in the latter stages. "The morals of young men, as well as their application to science," wrote Noah Webster in 1790, "depend much on retirement" (Webster, 1828). In addition to students, some classes of middle-aged workers were said to retire under certain circumstances. Almanacs, for instance, noted that farmers "retired" from winter's storms to their family circles. In the first edition of *An American Dictionary* (1828), Webster defined retirement as "1. The act of withdrawing from company or from public notice or station. 2. The state of being withdrawn. 3. Private abode; habitation secluded from much society, or from public life. 4. Private way of life." Each of these definitions might pertain to a senior citizen, but none is exclusively age specific. The only mandatory retirements in early U.S. history are to be found in seven states that imposed upper age limits on holding judicial office. No firms or other government agencies before 1865, however, discharged workers because they had reached a certain age. No public or private institution provided an old-age pension, though a prudent person here and in Europe could purchase an annuity (the word entered the English language in the fifteenth century) as a hedge against the possibility that they might outlive their productive years.

Superannuation was the term that Americans used when they wanted to describe conditions known "to impair or disqualify by old age and infirmity" workers from gainful employment. Advanced age reduced Daniel Boone and Natty Bumppo from hunters to guides. An old horse that trotted was respectable, Hugh Henry Brackenridge reminded readers in *Modern Chivalry* (1804), but one that tried to speed was contemptible. Yet quitting work on account of disability usually was hazardous: Without an ongoing source of livelihood, many aged men and their dependents were reduced to poverty. The older adult poor had to rely on family, friends, and neighbors for essentials. Some took refuge in the county almshouse—a habitat that hardly jibed with Currier and Ives's romantic depiction of "Old Folks at Home."

Transportation businesses inaugurated the first U.S. corporate retirement plans—several decades after banks had established them in England. In 1875, the American Express Company permitted workers past 60 to receive some compensation upon leaving their posts. The retirement program established in 1884 by the Baltimore and Ohio Railroad, which stipulated minimum age (65) and service (10 years) requirements, became the prototype emulated by other firms. But retirement schemes were not as quickly and effectively institutionalized on this side of the Atlantic as in Europe. Of the 150 plans launched in the United States, only 60 of the several hundred thousand corporations offered employee retirement plans by World War I. A few unions and philanthropies as well as municipal, county, and state entities developed pension schemes, but they covered smaller segments of the labor market. Probably less than 2% of the U.S. workforce was potentially eligible for company-sponsored retirement benefits in 1900.

The rationale for late-nineteenth-century pension programs, moreover, did not give priority to the interests of aging workers. Corporate executives generally viewed pensions as an efficient way to weed out inefficient workers. Pensions were not considered part of employee/employer contracts. As a result, not everybody who thought that they qualified for industrial pensions actually got money upon retirement. Treated as gratuities, incentives for productive service, pensions could be withheld and terminated in economic downturns or at management's discretion. Nonetheless, pensions were becoming engrained in American culture. The 1880 edition of Webster's *American Dictionary* helps us to date a key shift in the meaning of *superannuate*—"to give pension to, on account of old age, or other infirmity." Notice the animus against senescence: Old age, like retirement, was deemed a period of obsolescence.

Corporate pensions surely represent an innovation, but it was the federal government that provided the most extensive and generous measure of old-age security through pensions to military veterans and their dependents. In 1818, Congress granted money and/or land to citizens who had served at least nine months in the Continental Army and were "in need of assistance." (By that time, the youngest Revolutionary soldiers were over 55; most veterans already had died.) Similar means-tested provisions were made belatedly for veterans of the War of 1812 and the Mexican-American War. Pension rolls increased dramatically as the Grand Army of the Republic successfully lobbied for assistance for Union soldiers. (Confederate veterans had to turn to their impoverished state officials for relief.) By 1929, more than four-fifths of all beneficiaries of any private or public plan were recipients of war-related pensions; roughly 80% of all money distributed through pensions came from this single source. Congress viewed the military pension system as a reward for risking one's life for the nation; lawmakers steadfastly rejected attempts to draw analogies between compensation for military service and concern for the plight of veterans of productivity. Some reformers drew attention to the growing incidence of old-age dependency, but most Americans were unmoved by the evidence. Few thought that the financial plight of the older adults was a major problem that required a significant public intervention beyond piecemeal efforts.

The Great Depression changed public attitudes. The catastrophe ushered in a new era in the history of retirement in the United States. Older workers were more likely than young men to be discharged from their jobs, to have lost their life savings, and to have anticipated pensions evaporate in corporate bankruptcies. Hard times, not to mention pressure from the Townsendites (a coalition of older Americans demanding generous stipends that would be spent by beneficiaries each month in return for not working) forced Washington to respond to the needs of senior citizens.

The Social Security Act of 1935 was not the New Dealers' first order of business. Nevertheless, the measure became the cornerstone of the U.S. welfare state. Franklin Delano Roosevelt and his advisors designed Social Security to address the unexpectedly widespread predicament of those who were poor and old and to enable future generations of workers to make provisions for their later years. Title I provided a matching federal-state old-age assistance plan, which offered most citizens over 65 in participating jurisdictions to receive on average a dollar a day in support. Title II initially required 60% of the workforce (mainly white-collar employees) to contribute a percentage of their wages, to be matched by their employers, in return for a guarantee of old-age insurance upon their retirement at age 65. The scope of Title II was radically broadened in 1939: The government promised benefits to the dependents of covered employees.

During the 1950s and 1960s compulsory coverage under Social Security was extended to military personnel, agricultural and domestic workers, and the self-employed. A disability program was grafted onto the system; all Title II beneficiaries became entitled to hospital benefits under Medicare (1965). By the nation's bicentennial virtually every U.S. worker was contributing to the Social Security program. Its monthly checks remain the foundation of the average worker's retirement income. Without Social Security, the incomes of roughly two-thirds of all older Americans would fall below the official poverty line.

As anticipated, Social Security made the nation more security conscious in financial matters related to retirement. Unions advocated the establishment of pension funds for their members as a bread-and-butter issue. Human resource managers resisted at first but then realized that they could reduce corporate taxes by liberalizing their firms' pension plans. A 1948 National Labor Relations Board ruling subjected pension plans to collective bargaining. By 1970, more than a third of the civilian labor force could count on corporate plans to supplement Social Security. In 1962 Congress made it possible for the self-employed to set aside funds for their later years through Keogh plans. The Employee Retirement Income Security Act (1974) systematized and liberalized various individual and corporate plans in the private sector, establishing minimum vesting and funding requirements as well as increasing tax incentives for participating. Within three years Americans had created 649,000 Keogh plans, then with assets worth $6.5 billion. No wonder Peter Drucker called workers' concentration of wealth in pension funds *The Unseen Revolution* (1976).

Over the past quarter-century the expansion of pension plans in the public and private sectors has added new wrinkles to the faces of retirement. Age 65 remains the baseline for calculating a contributor's retirement benefits under Social Security, but many workers take advantage of amendments that make it possible to retire at 60 or 62 and receive an actuarially adjusted check. Private funds are free to establish their own age criteria, though they typically are linked to prevailing Social Security triggers. Corporations and universities periodically entice employees to take early retirement with incentives too generous to forego. But many senior citizens prefer not to stop working entirely. Some work part-time; others work part of the year; still others move in and out of the labor force. Voluntary associations, which Alexis de Tocqueville considered the touchstone of *Democracy in America* (1835), nowadays depend on the talents of older men and women to mentor and tutor, to get out the vote, to fill gaps in the social network in their local community.

Despite all of the progress made in shoring up the safety net, retirement in America remains a risky business. Women tend to be more vulnerable financially on average than men, because of their comparative longer life expectancies, interruptions in work histories, and lower aggregate earnings. Minorities and recent immigrants on average qualify for lower monthly benefits than their native-born, White counterparts who remain on the jobs long enough to become vested in pension plans. Prolonged disabilities or the misfortune of mounting prescription bills or doctors' expenses not covered by a health plan can quickly wipe out a person's retirement resources. And while nearly every worker expects to have the option to retire, recent events have shaken virtually all Americans' confidence in existing pension programs. Conservatives have been trying to privatize Social Security for two decades, arguing that workers would do better investing on their own. The political rancor has made Title II an issue on which candidates can sink their campaigns; liberals are chary to recommend any expansion of existing provisions. Nor are people sanguine about recent developments in the private sector. The anguish of middle-class men and women, who lost their retirement funds through the well-publicized bankruptcy of companies such as Enron, has eroded all other workers' sense of security in a roller-coaster stock market. Given the concatenation of historical factors that affect the meanings and experiences of old age in America and the institutionalization of retirement financing, it is safe to predict that more changes are imminent. (See also PENSION PLANS; SOCIAL SECURITY PROGRAM OF THE UNITED STATES.)

References

Achenbaum, W. Andrew. 1978. *Old Age in the New Land*. Baltimore, MD: Johns Hopkins University Press.

Achenbaum, W. Andrew. 1983. *Shades of Gray*. Boston, MA: Little, Brown.

Achenbaum, W. Andrew. 1986. *Social Security*. New York: Cambridge University Press.

Drucker, Peter. 1976. *The Unseen Revolution*. New York: Harper & Row.

Webster, Daniel. 1828. *An American Dictionary of the English Language*. New York: William Collins.

W. Andrew Achenbaum

HOME CARE SERVICES FOR OLDER ADULTS, services provided in the home to promote, maintain, and restore health or to minimize the effects of illness and disability. Home care encompasses a broad continuum of medical, therapy, and social services, ranging from high-technology medical services, such as intravenous therapy and other skilled medical and therapy services, to low-technology, nonmedical services, such as homemaker services and personal care. Home care can be for short-term purposes, such as postacute or rehabilitative care after a hospital discharge or care for the terminally ill, or for long-term purposes, such as assistance with activities of daily living (ADLs) for persons with chronic disabilities.

The Home Care Market

The home care market can be divided into two parts: medically oriented and nonmedically oriented. Medically oriented services are more likely to be covered by insurance, and much of the existing information focuses on this market segment; less information is available concerning nonmedical home care. In the nonmedical service arena, there has been growth in consumer-directed care, where consumers have the opportunity to decide when and where services will be provided and how and by whom the tasks will be performed (http://www.consumerdirection.org/). A number of publicly funded programs, either through Medicaid waivers or state-funded programs, have begun to offer consumer-directed services over the past decade (Benjamin 2001). To provide this wide range of services, there are various types of home care personnel, such as registered nurses, home health aides, social workers, physical, occupational, and speech therapists, personal assistance attendants, and homemaker and chore workers.

A total of $32.4 billion was spent in 2000 on home health care (Heffler et al. 2002), as reflected in the national health expenditures maintained by the Office of the Actuary at the Centers for Medicare & Medicaid Services (CMS), formerly known as the Health Care Financing Administration, or HCFA (Cowan et al. 2001). This expenditure amount includes only freestanding home health agencies (HHAs) and excludes hospital-based HHAs. This amount does not include payments by consumers for nonmedical home care services such as homemaker, daily money management, or social services, nor does it include nursing services from nurse registries that are part of temporary help agencies.

Although home health care accounts for only a small portion of national health expenditures (less than 3%), it was one of the fastest growing categories of personal health care expenditures, averaging 20% growth during the 1993–1996 period (Cowan et al. 2001). The passage of the Balanced Budget Act (BBA) of 1997 resulted in a major transformation of the home health care market due to changes in Medicare reimbursement as well as reinterpretations and changes in benefits. The BBA mandated a new reimbursement system called the Interim Payment System (IPS) until a prospective payment system (PPS) was implemented for Medicare home health in October 2000. The IPS paid the lower of an agency's actual cost, an aggregate cost per visit limit, or an aggregate per beneficiary cost limit. The IPS created incentives to reduce unnecessary expenditures and operate as efficiently as possible. The incentive in the prior reimbursement system was for agencies to keep their costs below national limits but provide more visits since there was no aggregate per beneficiary cost limit. The BBA also reinterpreted intermittent and part-time requirements for the Medicare benefit and specifically excluded patients whose only need for skilled care was for venipuncture. Around the time of the BBA implementation, the government increased its oversight of fraud and abuse activities for the home health benefit and intensified medical review of claims. These expanded oversight initiatives also likely contributed to slowing the growth of Medicare home health (McCall et al. 2001).

As a result of all these changes, there was a sizable contraction in the Medicare home health market between 1997 and 2000, with a 50% decline in expenditures and a one-third reduction in number of providers. The changes in Medicare even spilled over into other payers, with Medicaid home health growth slowing from 8.8% to 7.1% (Cowan et al. 2001).

Under the Medicare home health PPS, begun in late 2000, an agency is paid a fixed amount for each patient for each 60-day episode of care, with adjustment for severity of patient's condition and geographical differences in wages. Since there is no limit to the number of episodes as long as they continue to be authorized by a supervising physician, agencies will not have an incentive to avoid longer-stay patients but might avoid shorter-stay patients with higher costs. The impact of this new PPS on the home health market is still unknown.

Financing

There are several ways for persons to pay for home care: public programs such as Medicare, Medicaid, veterans benefits, private insurance, or out of pocket.

According to data from the National Health Expenditures accounts, which include only medically oriented home care, Medicare and Medicaid and other public sources accounted for 53% of all home health expenditures in 2000 in contrast with 62% of expenditures in 1996, prior to enactment of the BBA (CMS 2002b). During this time period, Medicare declined from 43% in 1996 to 28.4% in 2000, while Medicaid (both federal and state payments) increased from 19% to 24%. Similarly, out-of-pocket spending increased from 15% to 20%. Payment from all private health insurance changed very little, accounting for 26% to 28% of all expenditures.

Medicare. A major public payer of home health services for older adults is Medicare. Its coverage is designed for treatment of acute care conditions and for postacute care and is medically oriented. The main requirements are that the person must be certified by a physician to need skilled nursing services, or skilled therapy (physical, speech/language, or occupational) on an "intermittent" basis, and he or she must be "homebound." In 2000, Medicare home health expenditures were only $9.2 billion, as compared to $14.5 billion in 1996. This decline was in response to several actions taken by the Centers for Medicare & Medicaid Services (CMS) described above (CMS 2002a; Cowan et al. 2001).

Medicaid. Medicaid is also a major public funding source for home care for persons who meet the strict income and asset financial criteria as well as medical/functional requirements. Medicaid spent $22.2 billion in fiscal year 2001 for home care services for all eligible persons, not just for older adults (Burwell, Eiken, and Sredl 2002). There are three main ways in which Medicaid may provide coverage for home care. First, state Medicaid plans must include home health services (i.e., part-time or intermittent nursing services, home health aide services, and medical supplies, equipment, and appliances suitable for use in the home) to Medicaid eligibles entitled to nursing facility services under the state's plan. Second, states can opt to provide other home health services, such as physical therapy, occupational therapy, or speech pathology and audiology services. As of March 2002, states elected to cover the following optional home health services and/or home health–related services under their plans: physical therapy (50 states), speech, language, and occupational therapy (49 states), and personal care services (36 states) (personal communication with K. Blume, CMS, October 2002). In fiscal year 2001, Medicaid spent $2.6 billion for home health care services, $5.3 billion for personal care services, and $8.5 billion for optional other home health services (Burwell, Eiken, and Sredl 2002; K. Blume, CMS, October 2002).

The third Medicaid mechanism is home- and community-based service (HCBS) waiver program authority, which allows states to provide a mix of medical and nonmedical services to help Medicaid recipients stay in the community when they are in need of Medicaid services in an institution. Examples of the types of services provided under these waiver programs are adult daycare, homemaker and chore services, environmental modifications, and respite care. Some of these services like homemaker and chore services can only be provided under waiver programs. The waiver program has permitted states flexibility to cover a broader number of nonmedically oriented services and to extend the benefit package for waiver participants compared to those under the regular state plan. In 2001, all states had one or more waiver programs with $14.4 billion spent on home and community-based waiver services (Burwell, Eiken, and Sredl 2002; K. Blume, CMS, October 2002). It is estimated that three-fourths of these expenditures were allocated to persons with mental retardation and other developmental disabilities. Only 2.4% of HCBS expenditures was specifically targeted for the aged, and another 19% was spent on aged and disabled combined (Eiken and Burwell 2002). The waiver program has doubled between 1990 and 2001 (13% to 29%) as a percentage of all Medicaid long-term care spending, with less emphasis on institutional care at nursing homes or intermediate care facilities for the mentally retarded (ICF-MRs) (Burwell, Eiken, and Sredl 2002). This shift in Medicaid long-term care expenditures is in accord with the recent Supreme Court decision *Olmstead v. L.C.* (June 22, 1999) that unnecessary institutionalization could be a form of discrimination.

The Department of Veterans Affairs (VA). This health system provides noninstitutional long-term care services as part of an extensive continuum of veterans' benefits. The VA's home- and community-based services include the Home-Based Primary Care (HBPC) program, outpatient geriatric care evaluation, home health/homemaker care, home medical equipment, hospice/palliative care, and adult day health care. The HBPC program provides hospital discharge planning and comprehensive primary health care to homebound veterans delivered by a hospital-based interdisciplinary team led by a physician. The HBPC was available at 75 of the 163 Veterans Administration Medical Centers in 2001. Eligible veterans for the HBPC program must be homebound, living within the program service area of the VA medical center, living with a caregiver, have multiple diseases or terminal illness, or be short-term patients needing postacute rehabilitation care. There are no financial eligibility criteria or cost sharing (Department of Veterans Affairs 2002).

Social Services Block Grant (SSBG) or Title XX Program. States may also fund home care services through this program. In 1997, 39 states and the District of Columbia used it to partially finance a variety of home services as well as other services. Appropriations for SSBG have steadily declined, from $2.8 billion in 1993, $2.3 billion in 1996, and $1.7 billion in 2002 (U.S. House of Representatives 2000).

Title III of the Older Americans Act (OAA). This is another funding source for home care, albeit limited. Any person aged 60 and older is eligible for services, but the program targets funds to the most vulnerable older adults. A 1987 amendment to the act authorized in-home services specifically for frail older individuals. Supportive services (in-home services such as homemakers and home health aides, transportation, home-delivered meals, health education and screening, transportation, and information and referral) accounted for one-third of expenditures in fiscal year 1997, or $210 million, for 1.5 million persons served. Spending was greater for congregate meals ($244 million) and served 2.1 million individuals (Kassner 2001). These services are administered through Area Agencies on Aging (AAA) as part of the Administration on Aging (AoA). AoA also supports a nationwide, toll-free information and assistance directory called the Eldercare Locator (1-800-677-1116). The Locator helps individuals to find the appropriate AAA seeking home care and other assistance for older adults. The reauthorization of the Older Americans Act in 2000 appropriated $113 million to create the National Family Caregiver Support Program. This national program provides information, counseling, training, and outreach to caregivers about available services (AoA 2001).

State-Only Long-Term Care Programs. States also devote their own funds to support long-term care services, by allocating funds required by Medicaid and OAA federal matching rules and by subsidizing optional Medicaid services and supplemental services by their own choice. A recent national survey found all but two states provided multiservice home- and community-based programs to older adults. Total expenditures from these state-source programs were more than $1.2 billion in 1996; however, there is substantial variation from state to state (Kassner and Williams 1997). Nearly all these programs cover individuals not meeting the restrictive financial eligibility for Medicaid, and many also serve persons not meeting the Medicaid health and functional eligibility criteria. In addition, some programs supplement services for persons receiving Medicaid services. Nearly all programs cover four core in-home services: personal, homemaker, chore, and respite care. Three-quarters of the programs use cost sharing. Existing state-only programs may decline due to state budget pressures.

Publicly Funded Consumer-Directed Home Care Projects. Public programs have traditionally followed a vendor payment model (i.e., an agency-driven model). They have not permitted direct cash payments to clients, nor have they permitted payment to family members for home care services. With the trend toward consumer or self-directed approaches to the delivery of home care, consumers may receive cash payments or vouchers for authorized services, and family members and friends can be hired as providers. There are a variety of selfdirected approaches ranging from a professional monitoring approach to cash and counseling, where individuals receive the cash equivalent of their benefits through direct payments or vouchers. Several public funding sources (e.g., Medicaid waiver, Medicaid state plan, state funds, OAA, Title XX) finance these projects, usually requiring a Medicaid waiver. Consumer direction models approved by Medicaid are available in over half of the states and in a number of state-only programs. Research challenges and questions remain with respect to appropriateness, cost, quality, and accountability of consumer direction.

Private Sources. Private funding sources for home care include out-of-pocket payments of either the home care recipient and/or family members, private health insurance, long-term care insurance, and Medicare supplemental insurance. Out-of-pocket costs are not an insignificant component of home care expenditures. Based on the national health expenditure data, out-of-pocket expenditures have increased from 15% to almost 20% between 1993 and 2000 (CMS 2002b).

Employer-sponsored postretirement health insurance often provides home health benefits. Long-term care insurance may provide home care benefits in addition to nursing home coverage. The number of persons buying long-term care insurance has grown in recent years. Between 1993 and 1999, the number of policies sold doubled from about 3.4 million in 1993 to almost 7 million in 1999 (HIAA 2002). In addition, four of the ten standard Medicare supplemental insurance plans offer an at-home recovery benefit linked to the Medicare home health benefit. However, a very small percentage of persons purchased policies with this at-home benefit.

Home Care Providers

Providers of home care services can be classified into the following categories: (1) agencies certified by the federal government; (2) uncertified agencies, which may or may not be licensed; (3) home care workers from employment or temporary personnel agencies or nurse registries; and (4) independent providers, either through a formal contract or an informal arrangement. These provider types have differing regulatory requirements, payment arrangements, and service levels. For example, only agencies certified by the federal government can receive Medicare reimbursement. These agencies must provide skilled nursing services and at least one therapy service and meet other conditions of participation. Home health agencies are the market segment typically licensed by states, even if they are not federally certified. Many agencies that are licensed are also certified, but not all; one study estimated that about 59% of licensed home health agencies in 1998 were also certified. Certified agencies may have higher charges than noncertified agencies due to more stringent training and supervision requirements.

Statistics on the first two categories (agency providers) exist but vary depending on the criteria used to define home care; statistics on the other categories, specific to home care, are nonexistent. Using a broad definition to include both medical and nonmedical providers, the National Association of Home Care (NAHC) identified 19,690 home care agencies in the United States in 2000, of which 7,152 were Medicare-certified home health agencies, another 2,273 were Medicare-certified hospices, and the remaining 10,265 were home care providers and hospices not participating in the Medicare program (NAHC 2001). Thus, Medicare-certified agencies account for only 48% of the official home care agency providers using NAHC's definition. Using a stricter definition, the 2000 National Home and Hospice Survey indicates that Medicare-certified agencies are a greater proportion of all home health agencies, accounting for 83% (NCHS 2002a).

In addition to Medicare patients, certified agencies serve Medicaid and private-pay clients, which can account for a sizable percentage of their total patient load. The numbers of Medicare-certified agencies increased from 2,924 in 1980 to a peak of 10,444 in 1997, then dropped to 7,152 partly due to changes in Medicare home health care reimbursement with the passage of the 1997 BBA (NAHC 2001). The IPS may have spurred mergers between old and new agencies since agencies that were in existence prior to 1994 were allowed higher cost limits (Van der Walde 2002).

There are several reasons why an agency may not be certified. It may not provide all or any of the services that Medicare requires. Even if certification requirements are met, noncertified home care agencies may simply choose to serve private-pay, Medicaid, or other public program clients instead of Medicare clients. State programs may reimburse uncertified agencies and independent providers as well as certified providers for home health and personal care services. A recent study of noncertified home health care providers in Ohio found that only 10% of providers were noncertified. Noncertified agencies are smaller and focus more on personal care, home health aide, homemaker services, and companion service. Some of these findings are reiterated in the National Home and Hospice Survey, where noncertified agencies were found more likely to offer companion services and less likely to provide skilled nursing services than agencies certified for either Medicare or Medicaid (NCHS 2002b).

Apart from these agencies, persons may also procure home care workers from employment or temporary help agencies, nurse registries, as individual independent contractors, or through private, informal arrangements. It is not known what proportion of the home care market these sources represent. The informal arrangement is an acknowledged "gray" market, similar to that for child care.

Client Characteristics

The 1998 National Home and Hospice Care Survey (NHHCS) estimated that 7.6 million individuals, or 2.8% of the noninstitutionalized population, receive some type of formal home care service, either medical, nonmedical, or both. Of this number, 69% were aged 65 or older, with the likelihood of use increasing with age. Women, unmarried persons, and persons living alone were more likely to use home health care than men, married persons, and those living with someone. These client characteristics are similar in the 2000 NCHS National Home and Hospice Care Survey. Looking at data only for older adults home health patients, 67% of them received help with either an ADL or IADL, (instrumental activity of daily living) and 59% received help with at least one ADL. Older adult home health clients received the following types of services: skilled nursing services (74%), personal care services (40%), therapy services (29%), and homemaker or companion services (28%) (NCHS 2002a).

Quality Monitoring and Consumer Involvement

There has been a trend for greater accountability in home care, as in other areas of health care. This includes efforts for standardized data collection for monitoring process or outcomes of patients, development of performance measures, and collection of information about patient perspectives on quality of care received. There is also increased emphasis on dissemination of this information to the public as well as to providers for targeting their quality improvement efforts.

The Omnibus Reconciliation Act of 1989 mandated development of client outcome measures for home health care (Hughes 2001). The result was the Outcome and Assessment Information Set (OASIS), which is a uniform set of patient assessment items developed for monitoring and measuring outcomes of care, adjusted for patient factors that might affect those outcomes. Since 1999, all Medicare-certified home health agencies have been required to use OASIS as a part of a comprehensive assessment of most patients at initiation of care and other specific time points during their care; certain patients are exempt from data collection (e.g., pediatric and maternity patients). The primary goal of OASIS is to improve patient care, but it also contains data items that are essential for case mix adjustment for the Medicare home health prospective payment.

The OASIS data collected by the agencies are transmitted to a central source, then outcome, case mix, and adverse event reports are returned to each agency on an annual basis (since February 2002) for targeting their quality improvement activities. With clinical input, 41 measures were derived from OASIS data for an outcomes-based quality improvement program in Medicare. These measures cover (1) functional outcomes, (2) physiologic outcomes, (3) emotional/behavioral/cognitive outcomes, and (4) utilization outcomes. An additional 13 low-frequency adverse patient outcomes were identified and are reported to the HHAs.

The Centers for Medicare & Medicaid Services plans to use a selected subset of the 41 home health quality measures derived from OASIS as part of its public reporting initiative on quality. It is expected that this information will be available in late 2003 to assist consumers, their families, and other intermediaries (e.g., discharge planners) in selecting home health agencies.

There is interest in obtaining patient perspectives on home care services for quality monitoring. CMS has developed a Consumer Experience Survey for voluntary use by state Medicaid programs for the home- and community-based waiver programs. The survey solicits waiver participants' feedback on four aspects of quality: access to care, respect and dignity, community integration/inclusion, and choice/empowerment. There are two survey versions: one for the disabled older adults population and one for persons with developmental disabilities. The survey and user's guide are expected to be issued in 2003 (Bosstick 2002). Outcome measures for quality are not available to individuals and families who directly hire home care workers rather than contracting with a home care agency.

Steps in Choosing and Managing Home Care Services

There are several steps that consumers and their family members should follow to obtain home care services:

Step 1. Assess the Need and Financing for Home Care Services. A consumer and his or her family should first obtain an assessment of:

- The various types, amount, and duration of home care services they will require from formal home care sources;
- The informal assistance available from family members and friends that would complement formal services to provide the appropriate level of care needed; and
- Whether any of the needed home care services can be paid by federal, state, or other programs or insurance, or if one must pay for any or all of the care out of pocket.

To obtain information on and get an assessment, do the following:

- Contact the local Area Agency on Aging (AAA) or the Eldercare Locator for general information on assessments and services available.
- If one is living at home, contact his or her physician, other health care personnel, and social service and home care agencies.
- If one is being discharged from a hospital, patients and family members should contact the discharge planner and receive a written plan of care from their physician for posthospital home care.

Step 2. Finding and Selecting Home Care Providers. For agency providers, lists are available by location from:

- The Eldercare Locator (1-800-677-1116)
- The local Area Agency on Aging.

Additional information sources include hospital discharge planners, other health care and social service professionals, state health departments, as well as telephone directories and the Internet. If one is enrolled in managed care, your primary care physician or care coordinator will be the main gatekeeper for access to formal home care providers.

For independent home care workers not associated with a home health agency, one may check:

- Nurse registries or general employment agencies
- The local newspapers
- Referrals from family or friends
- Posted advertisements for home care assistance

In selecting a particular home care provider, one should consider service reputation and quality. Information on quality of an agency may be obtained through state survey, licensure, and accreditation organizations. The National Association for Home Care's "Consumer's Guide to Home Care" offers a list of questions for help in selecting the right home care provider. For Medicare-certified agencies, one may contact the state health insurance counseling program, the state home health hotline, and the state health department. For privately hired independent home care workers, one needs to interview the prospective care worker, check on references and training, and have a trial work period. With a private arrangement, it is important to have a clear understanding through a signed contract with a home care worker about the work requirements and schedule, taxes, payment, and insurance coverage, expectations about worker performance, and quality of services delivered.

Step 3. Dealing with Service Problems. If there are problems or dissatisfaction with the home care nurse or health care worker, contact the home care supervisor, physician, or the State Department of Health, the Area Agency on Aging, the Long Term Care Ombudsman, or the Home Health hotline in the state or county. If the service is provided under the Medicare benefit, one can contact the state Quality Improvement Organization (QIO) to file a complaint.

If denied care by Medicare-certified home health agencies, a written notice from the agency that the services are not covered, are being reduced, or are being terminated is required. If you believe you are eligible for Medicare coverage, you can ask Medicare for an official decision ("demand bill") and ask the agency to send your claim to Medicare. While Medicare decides if you are covered, you agree to pay the agency privately. If Medicare decides you are covered, the agency must reimburse you. If Medicare denies the claim, you have the right to appeal. However, if you lose the appeal, you are liable for payment. (See also COMMUNITY-BASED CARE; HEALTH MAINTENANCE ORGANIZATIONS AND MANAGED CARE FOR OLDER ADULTS; MEANS-TESTING IN PUBLIC PROGRAMS; MEDICAID; MEDICARE; VETERANS' BENEFITS.)

Organizations

Administration on Aging
Centers for Medicare & Medicaid Services
Consumer Direction, sponsored by National Council on Aging and the National Association of State Units on Aging
Eldercare Locator

Medicare Rights Center: Home Care Channel
National Association for Home Care
Outcome and Assessment Information Set (OASIS)

Suggested Readings

Centers for Medicare & Medicaid Services. 2002. *Medicare and Home Health Care*. Publication #10969. Baltimore, MD: Author. (Call 1-800-633-4227 [available 24 hours a day] for copy of publication.)

Medicare Rights Center, Home Care Channel. Available online at http://www.medicarerights.org/homecare.html.

National Association for Home Care. 1999. *How to Choose a Home Care Provider: A Consumers Guide*. Washington, DC: Author. (Single copies are free by writing to Attn: Publications, 228 7th Street SE, Washington, DC 20003.)

References

Administration on Aging (AoA). 2001. *Family Caregiving Fact Sheet*. Washington, DC: GPO.

Benjamin, A.E. 2001. "Consumer-Directed Services at Home: A New Model for Persons with Disabilities." *Health Affairs* 20: 80–95.

Blume, K. 2002. CMS. Personal communication. October.

Bosstick, S. 2002. CMS. Personal communication. December.

Burwell, B., S. Eiken, and K. Sredl. 2002. "Medicaid Long Term Care Expenditures in FY2001." May 10 Memorandum. MEDSTAT Group, Inc., Cambridge, MA.

Centers for Medicare & Medicaid Services (CMS). 2002a. *Medicare and Home Health Care*. Publication #10969. Baltimore, MD: Author.

Centers for Medicare & Medicaid Services (CMS). Office of the Actuary. National Health Statistics Group. 2002b. Available online at http://www.cms.gov/statistics/nhe/.

Cowan, Cathy, et al. 2001. "National Health Expenditures, 1999." *Health Care Financing Review* 22: 77–111.

Department of Veterans Affairs. Office of Congressional and Legislative Affairs. U.S. Committee on Veterans Affairs. 2002. *Testimony by Robert Roswell*, April 26.

Eiken, S., and B. Burwell. 2002. "Medicaid HCBS Waiver Expenditures, FY1995 through FY2001." May 13 Memorandum. MEDSTAT Group, Inc., Cambridge, MA.

Gwyther, Lisa, Edna Ballard, et al. 2002. *Steps to Success: Decisions about Help at Home for Alzheimer's Caregivers*. Washington, DC: AARP.

Harrington, Charlene, Peter Summers, and Valerie Wellin. 2000. "State Medicaid Home Health Licensing and Certification." *Home Health Care Services Quarterly* 18: 77–104.

Health Insurance Association of America (HIAA). 2002. "Long Term Care Insurance in 1998–1999: Summary of Study Findings." Available online at http://www.hiaa.org/research/research_studies.cfm.

Heffler, Stephen, et al. 2002. "Health Spending Projections for 2001–2011: The Latest Outlook." *Health Affairs* 21: 207–18.

Hughes, S. 2001. "Home Health." In *The Continuum of Long Term Care*, ed. C. Evashwick. 2nd ed. Albany, NY: Delmar Thomson Learning.

Kassner, Enid. 2001. *The Role of the Older Americans Act in Providing Long Term Care*. Washington, DC: AARP Public Policy Institute.

Kassner, Enid, and Loretta Williams. 1997. *Taking Care of Their Own: State-Funded Home and Community-Based Care Programs for Older Persons*. Washington, DC: AARP Public Policy Institute.

McCall, Nelda, H. Komisar, A. Petersons, and S. Moore. 2001. "Medicare Home Health before and after the BBA." *Health Affairs* 20(1): 189–98.

National Association for Home Care (NAHC). 2001. *Basic Statistics about Home Care, 2000.* Washington, DC: Author.

National Center for Health Statistics (NCHS). 2002a. "National Home and Hospice Care Survey, 2000." Unpublished estimates.

National Center for Health Statistics (NCHS). 2002b. "National Home and Hospice Care Survey, 1998 and 2000." Unpublished estimates.

Straker, Jane, and Robert Applebaum. 1999. *A Survey of Non-Certified and Non-Licensed Home Health Agencies in Ohio.* Oxford, OH: Scripps Gerontology Center, Miami University of Ohio.

Super, N. 2002. "Medigap: Prevalence, Premiums and Opportunities for Reform." *NHPF Issue Brief*, 782.

United States General Accounting Office. 2001. *Long Term Care: Implications of Supreme Court*'s Olmstead *Decision Are Still Unfolding.* Testimony before the U.S. Senate Special Committee on Aging, September 24.

U.S. House of Representatives. Committee on Ways and Means. 2000. *Overview of Entitlement Programs. 2000 Greenbook.* Washington, DC: GPO.

Van der Walde, L. 2002. *Health Care Industry Market Update: Home Health.* Baltimore, MD: CMS.

Judith A. Sangl and Linda A. Siegenthaler

HOME MODIFICATIONS FINANCING, mechanisms designed to maximize the safety of disabled and older adults in their own homes through environmental improvements to the residence.

The overwhelming preference of older adults is to age in place in their homes and communities. Modifications to the home can support this preference by helping older adults and their caregivers to perform daily tasks. Home modifications are adaptations to the physical environment that can range from inexpensive railings, rearranged furniture, or extra lighting to more costly ramps, powerlifts, and fully remodeled bathrooms and kitchens. These adaptations address problems such as accessing a home, bathing, and cooking.

Most persons pay for the modifications themselves using savings, assets, or income. According to the 1990 National Health Interview Survey, more than 75% of persons of all ages with home accessibility features paid for these features out of pocket (La Plante, Hendershot, and Moss 1997). However, more extensive and comprehensive modifications, such as elevators and stair lifts, can cost several thousands of dollars. For some people, such changes may be unaffordable, and assistance from outside financing sources may be needed.

Sources of Financing for Older Adults

There is no federal law or program that solely supports or finances home modifications. What exists, however, is a range of public and private financing sources available to both individuals and home modification programs. However, these sources are far from comprehensive, and eligibility requirements are often confusing, which limits the availability of home modifications to those with unmet needs.

Home Equity Financing

Home equity loans or second mortgages are common mechanisms to finance changes to the home. A home equity loan is a line of credit that can be accessed over several years for the purpose of home improvements. In contrast, a second mortgage is a separate loan that can be used for home improvements and must be repaid in addition to the existing mortgage. Alternatively, homeowners may benefit from loans that are given directly to remodeling contractors or suppliers. Many remodelers work directly with finance agencies that specialize in remodeling projects. These loans are available only through remodelers or dealers, but they are more convenient and offer lower closing costs to the consumer.

Different departments within the federal government offer financing programs that can be used to improve home accessibility. The Federal Housing Administration operates two loan guarantee programs: Title 1, which can be used to rehabilitate existing homes; and the 203K program, which can be used for purchasing or rehabilitating a home. For rural or suburban homeowners over age 65, low-interest loans and grants for home adaptations are available through Rural Community Development (formerly Farmers Home Administration). In particular, there is a 504 loan program for very low-income homeowners with disabilities and a 504 grant program for persons with very low incomes over the age of 62.

Disabled veterans can benefit from grant programs administered by the Department of Veterans Affairs. The Home Improvement Structural Alterations program provides grants for home modifications that improve the accessibility of the home as well as electrical and plumbing improvements made necessary due to the installation of medical equipment. This onetime monetary award is available to those who were disabled while in the service and those who have become disabled in their older years. However, persons who were not service disabled receive a smaller award. The Special Housing Adaptation Benefit program provides home adaptations such as special lighting and handrails to those who have lost the use of eyes or hands. The Specially Adapted Housing program benefits those who have experienced significant loss, such as the use of legs or upper extremity. These veterans may qualify for a grant to build an accessible home or remodel an existing home. Eligibility for the latter two programs requires that the veteran must have been disabled while in the service.

Some states operate loan programs to help low- and moderate-income persons pay for home modifications. In particular, state housing finance agencies issue bonds for housing construction and other housing-related projects. These agencies are in an ideal position to create revolving, low-interest loan funds for home repair and adaptation. For example, the Minnesota Housing Finance Agency's (MHFA) Fix Up Fund uses housing revenue bonds to help homeowners increase the livability, accessibility, and energy efficiency of their homes. The low-interest loans are made to homeowners by locally participating banks, credit unions, and housing agencies. The MHFA also has a separate Accessibility Loan program funded by state appropriations targeted at households with one or more persons with a long-term physical disability.

Reverse mortgages help older persons remain in their own homes by allowing them to draw down the cash value through a monthly stipend, a lump-sum payment, or a line of credit. Many of these householders could use reverse mortgages to pay for the long-term care they might need over their lifetimes, home modifications or repair, and other needs. The Home Equity Conversion Mortgage Program and Fannie Mae's Home Keeper Program are examples of programs operated by the U.S. Department of Housing and Urban Development (HUD). However, the acceptance and use of the reverse mortgage have been modest, partially due to its complicated nature, the reluctance of many older persons to tamper with a major asset, and the high closing costs associated with the initiation of the mortgage.

Non–Home Equity Financing

The Fair Housing Amendments Act of 1988 enables renters to request "reasonable" accommodations and modifications that change the physical structure of the individual unit or common areas. However, "reasonable" is a vague term that leaves room for interpretation. Often, "reasonable" depends on whether the changes would present a significant fiscal or administrative burden on the housing provider. In public and federally subsidized housing, the landlord pays for reasonable modifications both to the individual unit and common areas. In the private market, the landlord may or may not be willing to pay for modifications in the common areas and within the individual unit. In such cases, tax credits and tax deductions are available for the expenses incurred for accessibility modifications. However, the landlord is not required by law to pay for changes, and as a result, the tenant may need to assume the cost of the modifications, especially those in individual apartment units. The tenant also has the responsibility of restoring the interior premises to its original condition upon vacating the unit, if such steps can be reasonably performed.

There is anecdotal evidence that some private medical insurers and HMOs (health maintenance organizations) pay for home modifications as a way to reduce the cost of institutional care. While availability is limited, reimbursing for home modifications is consistent with the managed care philosophies of cost-effectiveness and preventative care. Long-term care insurance policies may also provide payouts for home modifications. However, these insurance options are expensive and may not be a viable option for lower-income persons. Unfortunately, Medicare and Medicaid do not reimburse for home modifications. Both programs pay for only medically necessary durable medical equipment and supplies such as hospital beds, crutches, ventilators, and wheelchairs but not for changes to the environment, even those that facilitate the use of such equipment.

Other Financing Mechanisms

Persons receiving Supplemental Security Income (SSI) or Social Security Disability Insurance (SSDI) benefits can take advantage of several options. For SSI beneficiaries, the Plan for Achieving Self-Support program is a savings plan that allows recipients to set aside income for home modifications without jeopardizing benefits. SSDI beneficiaries and, in certain cases, persons who receive SSI benefits can deduct the cost of home modifications from earnings.

Income tax deductions may also help to compensate for the cost of home modifications. The capital expenses incurred in making the modifications can be treated as a medical deduction, provided that a physician certifies the changes as medically necessary. This option pertains only to persons who itemize expenses and pay more than 7% of their income on medical expenses. Examples of deductible expenses include constructing ramps, widening doors, modifying hardware on doors, and modifying electrical outlets and fixtures. In addition, long-term care tax credits are available in certain states to families caring for older adults and persons with disabled adults at home.

Locally, various organizations can provide small grants, loan equipment, and devices or donate their time and manpower. Local chapters of the Multiple Sclerosis Society,

United Cerebral Palsy, and the National Easter Seal Society are possible options to explore. Persons can also contact local chapters of Habitat for Humanity or Rebuilding Together, which build or rehabilitate homes that include accessibility features. Local civic organizations can also provide aid in the form of money, equipment, or time. For example, the Knights of Columbus is particularly interested in helping children with disabilities (Duncan 1998).

The Role of Home Modification Programs

Beyond coordinating the financing of home modifications, persons may need help with assessment of the home environment and installation of the needed modifications. For simple home adaptations, persons with disabilities and their families often self-assess their problems, pay for the home modifications, and carry out the necessary labor on their own. However, more complex changes may require the use of various providers such as occupational therapists, remodelers, contractors, tradesmen, handymen, medical supply companies, and social service agencies.

In an effort to provide home modifications, a number of programs have developed across the country to meet the needs of older adults and persons with disabilities of all ages. These programs can assess the environment, obtain materials and products, and make the adaptations. Such programs can be nonprofit or for-profit. In many nonprofit and governmental programs, these services are provided to low-income older adults at little or no cost. However, nonprofits and governmental programs usually have waiting lists, as the need exceeds their capacity. Budget limitations and a lack of stable sources of funding highly restrict the types of changes programs can make and the amount that can be spent on any individual client. Further, significant gaps exist in the geographical coverage of programs, with rural areas particularly underserved.

Most home modification programs piece together funding from several sources. Funding options, especially from governmental sources, are not stable or guaranteed. Programs continually reapply for funding, and the receipt of funding is not assured. Eligibility requirements for these funding sources can vary by locality. Unfortunately, there are no state or federal entitlement programs dedicated to home modification. Home repair is usually the main mission of housing-related programs, and home modification is a lower priority.

Funding Options for Home Modification Programs

Many programs use Community Development Block Grants (CDBGs) or HOME Block Grants administered by HUD. These funds are passed down from the federal level to states and localities where they can be used for such purposes as community rebuilding, affordable housing, community services, and home repair. Home modifications may be included as part of a home repair initiative. Use of CDBG or HOME funds often requires that homes be brought up to code before a home modification can be installed. For example, broken steps may need to be fixed before special railings can be installed. Such situations represent a significant expense that may raise the costs. In addition, home modification programs are only one of many competing needs that require funding. The primary purpose of CDBG funds is to reverse urban decay and maintain the housing stock in disadvantaged neighborhoods. Nevertheless, CDBG funds are an important source of funds for home modification programs. For example, almost 70% of nonprofit home modification programs in California rely on either city or county CDBG money.

Programs serving older adults, including those with disabilities, may benefit from Title III Older Americans Act funds. These funds are passed down from the federal Administration on Aging to the State Units on Aging and then to local Area Agencies on Aging (AAA). AAAs may have their own home modification program or provide funds to local agencies that provide home modification services. However, home modification is but one of many needs of older adults and may not be of high priority to AAAs. In general, AAAs tend to focus on low-cost items such as grab bars and hand-held showers or more costly but needed items such as ramps.

Medicaid home- and community-based service (HCBS) waivers enable states to "waive" certain federal requirements and develop innovative alternatives to placing Medicaid-eligible persons in hospitals and institutionalized settings. Each state has the flexibility to design a HCBS waiver program that provides services such as case management, home health, respite care, and even environmental modification. Currently, 47 states have in place a Medicaid waiver program that includes environmental modifications. State Medicaid agencies must assure the Centers for Medicare and Medicaid Services that the average per capita cost of providing home- and community-based services will not exceed the cost of institutional care. Furthermore, eligibility is restricted to those who would qualify for Medicaid in an institutional setting, and states can choose to serve all ages or target certain age groups. Medicaid Waiver programs are generally limited to certain geographic areas within states. Those that offer environmental modifications have caps on the amount that can be spent per client.

Home modification programs, particularly nonprofits, also rely on other private funding sources. Many nonprofit programs solicit corporate donations or fund-raising to supplement their budgets. Certain nonprofit programs may require clients to pay a portion of the service cost. Private foundations and voluntary groups such as United Way and Rotary Clubs also provide financial support to home modification programs. Voluntary organizations such as Habitat for Humanity and Rebuilding Together, which build or rehabilitate homes that incorporate basic accessible design features, rely heavily on contributions of supplies and volunteer labor to perform the work.

Conclusion

Despite the range of financing options available, older adults must be diligent because each financing option has different eligibility requirements and other restrictions. Often agencies administering these sources are unaware of other options if an older adult is not eligible for a certain program. Home modifications programs may be helpful because they are able to coordinate assessment and installation while providing these services at low or no cost to low-income older adults. However, these programs are also limited in the number of persons served, the types of persons targeted, and the kind of modifications provided. While older adults prefer to age in place, they face many difficulties in securing the financing needed to make their home environment safer and more supportive. (See also FRAILTY PLANNING; HOME CARE SERVICES FOR OLDER ADULTS; HOMEOWNERSHIP; HOUSING COUNSELING FOR OLDER AMERICANS; MORTGAGE INSTRUMENTS; REVERSE MORTGAGES.)

Organizations

Administration on Aging
Centers for Medicare & Medicaid Services
Habitat for Humanity International
Rebuilding Together
Social Security Administration
U.S. Department of Agriculture
U.S. Department of Housing and Urban Development
U.S. Department of Veterans Affairs

References

Duncan, R. 1998. "Funding, Financing, and Other Resources for Home Modifications." *Technology and Disability* 8: 37–50.

Hyde, J., R. Talbert, and P.J. Grayson. 1997. "Fostering Adaptive Housing: An Overview of Funding Sources, Laws, and Policies." In *Staying Put: Adapting the Places Instead of the People*, ed. S. Lanspery and J. Hyde. Amityville, NY: Baywood Publishing.

La Plante, M.P., G.E. Hendershot, and A.J. Moss. 1997. "The Prevalence of Need for Assistive Technology Devices and Home Accessibility Features." *Technology and Disability* 6: 17–28.

Pynoos, J., P.S. Liebig, J. Overton, and E. Calvert. 1997. "The Delivery of Home Modification and Repair Services." In *Staying Put: Adapting the Places Instead of the People*, ed. S. Lanspery and J. Hyde. Amityville, NY: Baywood Publishing.

Pynoos, J., and C. Matsuoka. 2001. "Housing and the Continuum of Care." In *The Long-Term Continuum of Care*, ed. C. Evashwick. Albany, NY: Delmar Thomson Learning.

Pynoos, J., M. Tabbarah, J. Angelelli, and M. Demiere. 1998. "Improving the Delivery of Home Modifications." *Technology and Disability* 8: 3–14.

Scholen, K. 2000. *Home-made Money: Consumer's Guide to Home Equity Conversion*. Washington, DC: AARP.

Jon Pynoos and Christy Nishita

HOMELESSNESS AMONG OLDER ADULTS. Reforms of the Social Security system undertaken in conjunction with the War on Poverty of the mid-1960s reduced the poverty rate among older Americans to a level somewhat below that of the nation at large. At one time, older adults suffered the highest rate of poverty of any age group; today they have one of the lowest (Wright and Devine 1994). These facts have lulled many commentators into thinking that poverty and poverty-related conditions such as hunger and homelessness have all but disappeared among America's older population. This is not so.

In any given week, there are very roughly a million homeless people in the United States, although the uncertainties around any such estimate are quite large (Burt et al. 2001). Of these, roughly 2% will be over the age of 65, and an additional 6% will be ages 55 to 64. Thus, the older homeless comprise about 8% of the total homeless population. Compared to the percentage of older persons among the larger poverty population (10% ages 55 to 64 and another 16% ages 65 and up), older Americans are severely underrepresented among the homeless, a demographic oddity that has been noted since the 1980s (Burt et al. 2001; Wright 1989). Contrary to a common stereotype, the homeless are relatively young, with an average age in the mid- to late thirties in most studies, a substantial decline from two decades ago when the average age of the homeless was perhaps 20 years higher (Kutza and Keigher 1991).

At the same time, it is likely that the number of homeless older adults will increase in the coming decades as the general population ages and as the demand for affordable housing increases faster than the supply. It is also possible that there are more older homeless right now than studies suggest because they are less likely than the younger homeless to congregate in particular places and are, therefore, less likely to be counted. Thus, attempting to estimate the prevalence of homelessness among older adults is perhaps even more difficult than estimating the precise number of homeless in general.

What accounts for the apparent "deficit" of older adult persons among the homeless? Two hypotheses have been offered. First, a range of benefit programs become available to people once they turn 65 (among which Social Security, Medicare, and various housing subsidies are the most important); these programs may be sufficient in many instances to get otherwise homeless people off the streets (or to allow aging poor people to avoid homelessness). On the other hand, people with sporadic work histories and less access to resources (e.g., women and ethnic minorities) may find that they are not eligible for these programs or that the benefits provided by them are not adequate to keep them housed. Second and more troubling, homeless people may rarely survive to old age. Some half-dozen studies have now reported that the average age of death for various samples of the homeless men is somewhere in the early fifties (e.g., Hibbs et al. 1994; Wright and Weber 1987).

Older homeless were far more prominent in the Skid Row studies of the 1960s and 1970s (Bahr and Caplow 1973; Bogue 1963) than they are today. Wright et al. (1987) reviewed medical charts for homeless men receiving health services at the New York City Men's Shelter, in the very heart of the Bowery, from 1969 to 1984. Among men seen in the early years of this period, the average age was 44; among those seen in the later years, only 36—an 8-year drop in the average age of homeless men in a 15-year period. The average age has apparently stabilized in the mid-thirties in the years since.

People become older *homeless* through two entirely distinct processes. Some homeless people age into this category, and some older persons lose their housing and become homeless. No study of which we are aware has reported evidence on the relative proportions. Either way, the older homeless face all the problems that homeless people face (regardless of age) and many problems that older people face (regardless of their housing situations). There are also significant interactions that make the situation of the older homeless uniquely problematic, for example, an evident need for the vigor and alertness that are important survival skills for all homeless people, coupled with the limited physical capacity and mental acuity that may accompany aging.

What are the living circumstances of the older homeless in America today? The survey by Rich, Rich, and Mullins (1995) in Tampa showed that the single largest group (46%) lived, literally, on the streets, in parks, abandoned buildings, vehicles, or in other outdoor locations. Fewer than a third (30%) lived in homeless shelters, about a tenth (10%) lived in transitional housing, and the rest in rooms or with family and friends. Many older homeless say they avoid the large overnight shelters because the shelters are unsafe (Cohen and Sullivan 1990), as indeed they are, most of all for older homeless people with compromised mental or physical health (who are much more likely to be victimized or injured than other homeless people) or those dealing with other issues of aging such as deteriorating eyesight, hearing, and mobility.

Issues relevant to the homeless in general are also relevant to the older homeless: mental health, alcohol and drug abuse, physical well-being, outreach, access to community resources, and certainly housing. In addition, a range of other factors complicates the situation of the older homeless. One is the intricate patchwork of age restrictions on various service programs. Homeless people, for obvious reasons, tend to age more rapidly than domiciled people. Some programs for older adults become available at age 55, some at age 60, some at age 62, and some at age 65. Even professional caregivers often have trouble keeping all the restrictions and eligibility criteria straight, and so do the older homeless themselves. Program participation is further compromised when they are not aware of services that are available to them or when they are frustrated or dissuaded by the complexities of the application process.

Concerning mental health, older homeless people evidently suffer from the same emotional and psychological problems that younger adults experience, including depression, anxiety, and schizophrenia. Even otherwise stable and well-balanced persons often develop psychological problems once they are without a home and living on the streets. There is a tendency to minimize mental health among older adults in general as the inevitable consequence of aging. The problem is exacerbated by prejudice toward the aged and, even more, against the aged homeless. The use of psychotropic or neuroleptic medication to manage mental illness among the older homeless is also complicated by the material conditions of their existence. The sedative effects of many of these drugs reduce attentiveness and thus increase the already extreme vulnerability of the older adult homeless to robbery or assault. Many psychiatric medications are strongly contraindicated in the presence of alcohol; as among the homeless generally, alcohol and drug abuse is widespread. Some of these drugs increase photosensitivity, which is a much more serious issue for homeless people than for people who have a roof between them and the sun. Other drugs impair thermoregulation (also uniquely problematic for the homeless), increase the probability of hypotensive episodes, disrupt the normal sleep cycle, and have other side effects that interact in uniquely deleterious ways with the conditions of homelessness.

Owing in part to the relative deficit of older persons among the homeless as well as to methods that may inadvertently exclude them, few surveys of homeless people contain enough homeless among older adults to sustain detailed analyses. One important exception is the study by Rich, Rich, and Mullins (1995). In general, this survey of older homeless in Tampa Bay confirms that what is true of homeless people in general is also true of the older homeless. Other details are instructive. For example, nearly 90% of the older adult homeless report having received assistance with their meals, but only 1% say they have received assistance finding permanent housing, as though nutritional issues are relevant to the older homeless but housing issues are not. Even so, three-quarters of the older homeless report eating fewer than three meals a day. Most say they have no close associates (62%), no health insurance (82%), and no income (67%). When asked about the advantages of being a homeless person, nearly 80% saw none. Data such as these should cause us to abandon the hopeful thought that existing programs of assistance to the aged adequately ameliorate the more degrading aspects of a homeless existence.

Why do older people become homeless in the first place? Several researchers have

Table 1
Reasons for Homelessness Cited by a Sample of Older Adults Homeless in Tampa Bay

Reason	Percentage Mentioning Each Reason
Cannot afford rent	76
Cannot afford security deposit	68
Alcohol abuse	38
Lost job	35
Sick, unable to work	28
Left adult family	15
Newly released from jail/other legal reasons	9
Newly released from hospital	8
Divorce	8
Abandoned by spouse/family	7
Asked by family or friends to leave	7
Mental illness	5
Drug abuse	4
Prefers street life	4
Home foreclosed	3
Home condemned	4
Spouse abuse	2
Other	16

Source: Rich, Rich, and Mullins 1995, 121.

attempted to answer this question, including Rich and colleagues (1995) who posed exactly this question to their aged homeless respondents. Results are summarized in Table 1; most other studies have reported similar results. Inability to pay rent or to pay the security deposit necessary to rent a unit were the most commonly mentioned factors by a wide margin and the only factors cited by an outright majority. About two-fifths said their homelessness resulted from alcohol abuse. Other fairly commonly mentioned factors include job loss (35%), physical illness (28%), and familial estrangement (15%). A few were evidently fleeing abusive home situations. Factors such as mental illness or drug abuse (other than alcohol) were mentioned by only about 5%. Similarly, Tully and Jacobson (1994) reported that the three most important factors contributing to homelessness among older adults were poverty, lack of affordable housing, and deinstitutionalization.

Many older adults become homeless for the first time after the death of a spouse or caregiver who formerly provided instrumental or financial support (Rosenheck, Bassuk, and Salomo 2002). Factors such as inadequate income, substance abuse, or mental or physical health problems may become precursors to homelessness only after the loss of a caregiver. Older women and minorities with less experience obtaining formal support as well as older adults who suffer from mental or physical impairment not only may be more vulnerable to homelessness because they have fewer resources. They may also be unable or unwilling to secure appropriate formal support services that would enable them to avoid homelessness.

Recent policy discussions of older Americans have been driven by the image of the "greedy geezer," an image whose inaccuracy is obvious from the very existence of homelessness among older adults. It is, of course, true that the poverty rate among older adults has declined considerably over the past 30 years. Still, there are vast disparities in income among the aged, and their aggregate poverty rate is only very slightly beneath the national rate. Older people become and remain homeless for the same essential reasons that other people do, because they lack the financial resources to live in some other way. From the viewpoint of social policy, the concern is that the declining median age of the homeless population, the relatively lower rate of poverty among older adults, and the widespread but incorrect belief that assistance programs have effectively eliminated poverty among older adults will remove the obvious needs and issues of the older adults homeless from public purview and policy discussion.

A few older homeless report that they actually like being on the streets, but the vast majority in practically every study "express a preference for stable housing and better care settings than they presently experience" (Rich, Rich, and Mullins 1995). It is also apparent that the older homeless are a heterogeneous group. While the group as a whole may be described as being in "double jeopardy," each subcategory has its own resources, problems, and needs. Homeless people do not fit into any single stereotype; nor do the older adults; nor do the older homeless adults. Thus, addressing the problem and providing stable housing and care will remain a challenge. (See also DISABILITY PROGRAMS, FEDERAL AND STATE; MEDICAID; MENTAL HEALTH AMONG OLDER ADULTS; MENTAL HEALTH CARE FINANCING; NUTRITION PROGRAMS; VETERANS' BENEFITS.)

References

Bahr, Howard, and Ted Caplow. 1973. *Old Men, Drunk and Sober*. New York: New York University Press.

Bogue, Donald J. 1963. *Skid Row in American Cities*. Chicago: University of Chicago, Community and Family Studies Center.

Burt, Martha, Y. Laudan, Edgar Lee Aron, and Jesse Valente, eds. 2001. *Helping America's Homeless: Emergency Shelter or Affordable Housing?* Washington, DC: Urban Institute Press.

Cohen, Carl I., Mildred Ramirez, Jeanne Teresi, Margaret Gallagher, and Jay Sokolovsky. 1997. "Predictors of Becoming Redomiciled among Older Homeless Women." *The Gerontologist* 37(1): 67–74.

Cohen, Carl I., Jeanne Teresi, Douglas Holmes, and Eric Roth. 1988. "Survival Strategies of Older Homeless Men." *The Gerontologist* 28(1): 58–65.

Cohen, Neil L., and A.M. Sullivan. 1990. "Strategies of Intervention and Service Coordination by Mobile Outreach Teams." In *Psychiatry Hits the Streets: Outreach and Crisis Intervention for the Mentally Ill*, ed. N.L. Cohen. New York: Guilford Press.

Gilderbloom, John I., and R.L. Mullins. 1995. "Older Adults Housing Needs: An Examination of the American Housing Survey." *International Journal of Aging and Human Development* 40(1): 57–72.

Hibbs, J.R., L. Benner, L. Klugman, R. Spencer, I. Macchia, A.K. Mellinger, and D. Fife. 1994. "Mortality in a Cohort of Homeless Adults in Philadelphia." *New England Journal of Medicine* 331: 304–9.

Kutza, Elizabeth A., and Sharon M. Keigher. 1991. "The Older Adults 'New Homeless': An Emerging Population at Risk." *Social Work* 36(4): 288–93.

Rich, Diane Watt, Thomas A. Rich, and Larry C. Mullins. 1995. *Old and Homeless—Double Jeopardy*. Westport, CT: Auburn House.

Rosenheck, Robert, Ellen Bassuk, and Amy Salomon. 2002. "Special Populations of Homeless Americans." Available online at http://aspe/hhs.gov/progsys/homeless/symposium/2-Spclpop.html.

Tully, Carol T., and Sharon Jacobson. 1994. "The Homeless Older Adults: America's Forgotten Population." *Journal of Gerontological Social Work* 22(3–4): 61–80.

Wright, James D. 1989. *Address Unknown: The Homeless in America*. Hawthorne, NY: Aldine de Gruyter.

Wright, James D., and Joel Devine. 1994. "Poverty among the Older Adults." *Pride Institute Journal of Long Term Home Health Care* 13(1): 5–16.

Wright, James D., Peter H. Rossi, Janet Knight, Eleanor Weber, Richard C. Tessler, Christine Stewart, Marianne Geronimo, and Julie Lam. 1987. "Homelessness and Health: Effects of Life Style on Physical Well Being among Homeless People in New York City." In *Research on Social Problems and Public Policy*, ed. M. Lewis and J. Miller. Vol. 4. Greenwich, CT: JAI Press.

Wright, James D., and Eleanor Weber. 1987. *Homelessness and Health*. New York: McGraw-Hill.

James D. Wright and Tracy Dietz

HOMEOWNERSHIP. Currently, over 84% of older persons live in conventional households, while about 9% live in planned supportive group senior housing facilities, such as congregate living facilities, assisted living, continuing care retirement communities, or nursing homes. Another 7% also live in conventional households, but in dwellings that were owned or rented in the names of younger (under age 65) persons. This entry focuses on the older households (householders or heads of households) who owned their dwelling in their names. Most occupy 1-unit attached or detached structures (86%), but significant proportions occupy 2- to 49 unit (5%), and 50+-unit structures (2%). About 7% are owners of manufactured homes (U.S. Census Bureau 2000).

In the year 2000, over 18.2 million out of 22.8 million older households (80%) owned their dwellings. This rate of homeownership is at a historical high, up from 70% in 1973, 75% in 1983, and 77% in 1990. The rate of older adults' homeownership is projected to increase to 84% by 2020 (Joint Center for Housing Studies of Harvard University 2001).

Selling the home is still the exception rather than the rule, although it is more likely following the death of a spouse or the move to a nursing home. Venti and Wise (2001) offer an economic interpretation of the attraction of homeownership. They argue that most older homeowners are unlikely to draw down their housing equity to obtain greater liquid consumer income. Rather, they contend that most older persons think of their home's equity as touchable only in catastrophic circumstances, for "a rainy day," seek to leave this asset to their heirs, and do not intend to finance their retirement consumption patterns through the sale of their house. Thus, they question the validity of the life-cycle hypothesis of consumption. This predicts that individuals accumulate assets in their middle adult years when their earning capacities are highest, savings are increasing, and housing, family, and other consumer costs are declining, and after retirement, they begin to gradually consume their wealth or dissave.

A psychological explanation of older persons' strong preference to stay put emphasizes their strong emotional and sentimental attachment to their current dwellings that contributes to their social status and positive self-image.

Several government programs that offer cash and in-kind income to poor older Americans also discourage moves by older homeowners. In most states, for example, the Medicaid program's eligibility requirements of having almost nonexistent assets do not include the owned home in their computations. This is similarly true for the eligibility provisions of the Supplemental Security Income and Food Stamp program. Thus, means tests for eligibility for social welfare benefits in the United States infrequently require older people to divest themselves of their homes. A possible, but unestablished, counteracting influence on the residential inertia of older homeowners is their ability to benefit from the capital gains tax exclusion ($250,000 for single and $500,000 for joint tax returns) when they sell their personal residences.

Selling the home is also discouraged because of its increased importance as a setting where a growing population of frail older persons can receive personal assistance and health care services. Because older homeowners live in larger dwellings and are less likely to face occupancy restrictions, they can more easily accommodate a family member, housemate, or live-in who will provide caregiving or home upkeep assistance. There is also a greater prevalence of older adult homeowners who are providing temporary shelter to their unemployed or divorced adult children or who are assuming new and demanding grandparent roles by raising their grandchildren.

Homeowners: A Demographic and Economic Profile

Certain subgroups of older households are more likely than others to own their dwellings (U.S. Census Bureau 2000). The homeownership rate among young-old (age 65 to 74) households is 83%, compared to 77% among old-old households. About 92% of married households compared with 69% of older persons living alone own their homes. African Americans (68%) Asian Americans (53%), and Hispanics (65%) are less likely to own their homes compared with non-Hispanic White older households (83%). Older adults homeowners are also not equally found in all locations. Over 47% of this group is found in the suburbs of metropolitan areas, while 29% is found in nonmetropolitan places, and 24% is located in central cities (U.S. Census Bureau 2000). Older homeowners present a distinctly different demographic profile than older renters. They are more likely to be members of the young-old, married (as opposed to living alone), White, and have a high school education and higher incomes.

About 16% of older homeowners had incomes that placed them below the 100% poverty threshold level; but 30% were below the 150% threshold level. A more complete portrayal emerges when the household incomes of older homeowners are compared with their metropolitan area or nonmetropolitan county's median income and thus reflect cost-of-living differences. About 22% of older households have incomes that are 30% and under of their area's median (extremely low-income group), 44% have incomes that are 50% and under of their area's median (very low-income group), and 66% have incomes that are 80% and under of their area's median (low-income group) (U.S. Census Bureau 2000). Among the group of older homeowners with very low incomes, 41% report no savings, while 26% report savings of less than $25,000. Low incomes are also more prevalent among older households who can be considered "overhoused." An overhoused household has less than 0.5 persons per bedroom (e.g., an older man living alone in a three bedroom dwelling), and over 22% of older households are in this category. About 56% of this group have very low incomes. These households are at greater risk of living in unaffordable housing and to have difficulties paying for their out-of-pocket medical and home care costs, because they are burdened with the upkeep and maintenance of unused dwelling space.

Income differences offer only a partial portrayal of the older homeowner's economic status. Most older homeowners own their homes free and clear (82%). In 1995, of the total home equity wealth ($6.4 trillion) in the United States, 31% (almost $2 trillion) was owned by older households, even as they occupied about 26% of all the owned dwellings (Davern and Fisher 1995). The median equity value of older householders' dwellings (net of mortgage obligations) was $70,000. Including home equity, age 65 and over households had a median net worth of just over $92,000; without it, $24,047. Median net worth, however, declines sharply with age: The median net worth of age 65 to 69 households is $106,408 but only $81,600 for age 75 and over households (Davern and Fisher 1995). These breakdowns still offer an incomplete portrayal of the varied economic circumstances of older homeowners. A substantial share of older homeowners occupy relatively low-valued dwellings. About 13% of older homeowners occupy dwellings valued under $40,000, while about 49% occupy dwellings valued under $100,000 (U.S. Census Bureau 2000). The result is that a significant share of this group is both cash poor and house poor. That is, they have low incomes (80% and under of area median), and they cannot rely on their low-valued houses (less than $100,000) as a financial cushion.

The Affordability of Dwellings Owned by Older Adults

Overall, in 1999 about 27% of older homeowners were paying 30% or more of their monthly incomes on their housing costs, while 13% had 50% or more housing expense burdens. These costs include payments for mortgages or installment loans or contracts, real estate taxes, property insurance, homeowner association fees, cooperative or condominium fees, and utilities. They do not include either the scheduled or unscheduled costs for maintenance and repairs. The prevalence of a higher housing expense burden is far greater among lower-income homeowners. Among very low-income homeowners, 47% were paying 30% or more and 26% were paying 50% or more of their incomes on their housing costs (U.S. Census Bureau 2000).

Even as many older homeowners have very low incomes (cash-poor) and are confronting burdensome property taxes, insurance, and upkeep expenses, they are reluctant to sell their dwellings. Two important types of government programs have helped to alleviate the financial plight of this group: the federally insured Home Equity Conversion Program (HECP) and state-administered tax relief programs.

The Home Equity Conversion Mortgage (HECM) insurance program was created by the 1987 National Housing Act and made it possible for older households (age 62 and over) to obtain a federally insured reverse mortgage. This is a financial instrument designed to allow older homeowners with lower incomes (cash-poor), but who occupy relatively high-valued homes (house-rich), to borrow against the equity in their dwelling and receive tax-free cash payments, either advanced in one or more lump sums, in a steady stream of monthly income payments, in the form of a purchased annuity, or some combination of these payment types. HECM loans are available to all homeowners age 62 and over who have low outstanding mortgage balances or own their home free and clear. The interest on this loan is not tax-deductible until the debt is repaid. This group would otherwise have difficulty obtaining conventional forward mortgages or home equity lines of credit because of their low incomes. Older households can use these funds for any purpose, whether for a vacation or to pay for health care costs. Borrowers do not have to pay back their loans (and the imputed interest) until they die, sell, or permanently move out of their homes.

While the growth of mortgages processed by HECM has steadily grown, nonetheless, through 2001, only 50,000 reverse mortgages had been insured under this program, along with another 10,000 mortgages produced by the private sector. Moreover, the annual number of originating mortgages has never exceeded 14,000. Thus, this program has addressed the needs of an extraordinarily small percentage of older homeowners to date (Eschtruth and Tran 2001).

Experts explain this low demand by emphasizing that most consumers are reluctant to draw down their housing equity to obtain greater liquid consumer income, emphasizing that even when homeowners move, a large share do not reduce their home equity values. Along with the same factors discouraging moves in general, their staying put may be linked to their desire to leave their wealth to their children and their reluctance to take on any forms of new debt. They may also perceive these instruments as too complex or believe up-front loan costs are too high (these can easily represent as high as 15% to 20% of the loan's principal). Moreover, because those older homeowners who most need financial assistance often live in very low-valued homes, most lenders consider them to be unattractive candidates for a reverse mortgage loan.

After mortgage debt service, property taxes are usually the largest dwelling expenditure of older homeowners, and these taxes may be especially burdensome to the poor. Property taxes are often unpopular with seniors because they can increase more quickly than inflation, they can threaten their ability to afford their homes, and they view them as funding projects (e.g., schools) from which they derive few benefits. Older homeowners have higher property tax burdens than younger homeowners, because on average they live in higher-valued homes.

State governments have attempted to reduce the property tax burden of older homeowners (and renters) in several ways. *Homestead exemptions* lower the assessed value of the property subject to taxation for homeowners. *Homestead credit programs* typically offer direct rebates either as a percentage of taxes or as a fixed credit to qualifying owners such as older homeowners. *Circuit breaker programs* provide a direct tax credit on the property tax bill that is typically larger for lower-income households. A fourth approach, *property tax deferral programs*, allows older homeowners to defer payment of property taxes until they sell the home or die. Deferred property taxes become a lien against the value of the taxpayer's home and have similar financial properties as reverse mortgages.

Every state provides some type of property tax relief program, but the benefits vary greatly. Most states favor targeting relief to low-income older adults households, and 44 states and the District of Columbia have at least one property tax relief program that treats older homeowners more generously than younger homeowners. An AARP investigation found that older homeowners were more aware of, and were more likely to apply for, homestead exemption programs (Baer 1998). In contrast, seniors were less likely to be aware of or to use circuit breaker and homestead credit programs. They most infrequently used property tax deferral programs. Significant percentages of the older respondents reported that they did not apply for these programs because they were unaware of these options or needed more information or help filling out the applications. The report concluded that further outreach efforts would be effective.

Despite these programs, property tax burdens remain high for many low-income older adult homeowners, because eligibility is often restricted to homeowners who have very low levels of income or assets and because the participation rate by older homeowners in these relief programs is often low (Reschovsky 1994).

The Physical Condition of the Dwellings Occupied by Older Homeowners

In 1999, less than 5% of older homeowners occupied dwellings that had severe or moderate physical deficiencies in their plumbing, heating, or electrical systems, in their common areas, or in their maintenance or upkeep (U.S. Census Bureau 2000). These physically deficient dwellings were more likely to be found in the central cities of metropolitan areas and in rural or nonmetropolitan areas, especially in the southern United States. Older homeowners who occupied very old dwellings, built 1949 or earlier (29%), were especially likely to have these physical deficiencies (10% of group). Only a small percentage of the older occupants in physically run-down dwellings were found to make improvements and repairs (in a previous two-year period), and they were less likely to engage in these upgrading activities than younger homeowners. Older occupants were also more likely to rely on paid help (U.S. Census Bureau 2001).

The living conditions in these older settings contribute to the poorer economic, physical, and mental health of their occupants. Older homes, for example are often less energy efficient and more expensive to heat than newer homes and result in relatively large home heating costs. Older homeowners may also experience lower psychological well-being and, in the extreme, a sense of helplessness and despair because they cannot change the undesirable features of their dwellings. Older persons who lack the health or energy to maintain their homes may perceive such failings as an unequivocal sign of their inability to live independently. In contrast, renters may delay or avoid such harsh self-assessments, not only because they have fewer or less demanding upkeep burdens but also because when these tasks are necessary, they can often be assumed by a landlord. The property values of undermaintained dwellings may also be depressed. Moreover, when these properties are concentrated in the same location, entire neighborhoods may become physically distressed, resulting in higher rates of property depreciation and lower property tax revenues. Community efforts to revitalize these neighborhoods may be difficult to achieve.

Even homes in good physical condition may prove hazardous to older adult occupants if they have architectural design features that create more difficult to use or unsafe environments, especially when their occupants also suffer from physical limitations. These older adult occupants are at increased risk of having dwelling-based accidents (e.g., falls on stairways, floors, and bathtubs; burns or scalds from fires, hot liquids, and hot surfaces, such as heaters).

Most professionals argue that the home can be physically modified in ways that not only reduce accidents but also enhance the independence of older Americans (Pynoos et al. 1997). Estimates as to what percentage of older homeowners have modified their dwellings to accommodate their frailties vary greatly. The most recent and optimistic analysis found that in 1995 only 42% of older adult homeowners in need of home modifications had actually made some adjustments. The most common modifications included handrails or grab bars by about 27.6% of this group. The next most frequent modifications were specially equipped telephones (7.2%), easy-access bathrooms (7.1%), widened doors or hallways (5.9%), easy-access kitchens (5.0%), and door handles instead of knobs (3.8%) (U.S. Census Bureau 2001). Older persons with more severe disabilities and health problems were more likely to make home modifications (Mutschler 1997).

Older persons report that their most needed home modifications include handrails or grab bars, ramps, easy-access bathrooms, specially equipped telephones, easy-access kitchens, elevators or stair lifts, widened doors or hallways, and modified sink faucets or cabinets. Although relatively small percentages of older persons express these needs, many more are probably unaware of their home's hazards and how modifications would be beneficial. Others are discouraged from making home modifications because of the many obstacles linked with implementation. This is especially true for less educated seniors who find it difficult to apply for financial resources to carry out such work. Home modifications are also less likely by households with incomes below the poverty level, who own low-valued homes, and are Hispanic or African American. Seniors generally fear dealing with contractors or home repair personnel because they often overcharge or do shoddy work. Both consumers and professionals, including home builders, remodelers, and human service professionals, sometimes have inadequate knowledge of the physical attributes of the home that would benefit from modification. The older dwellings occupied by today's older adults only compound an already difficult situation. While they may attend to their most serious maintenance needs, older homeowners may overlook the less visible hazards found in their dwellings (U.S. Census Bureau 2001).

Most studies conclude that older persons would be more likely to modify their dwellings if government programs were more available and effective (Pynoos et al. 1997). The most important federal programs that now fund home modification and repair services are the block grant programs sponsored by the U.S. Department of Housing and Urban Development (Community Development Block Grant) and the Department of Health and Human Services' Social Services Block Grants and Title III of the Older Americans Act. The Rural Housing Services, Section 504 home repair loan and grant program, and the Section 533 Housing Preservation Grant (HPG) program also provide grants to nonprofit organizations for the rehabilitation of homes. Weatherization adaptations are funded under the Department of Energy's Low-Income Home Energy Assistance Program (LIHEAP) and the Weatherization Assistance Program. State-sponsored programs are also increasingly important funding sources. Outside of the government, foundations and charitable organizations are also key sources of funds, but their budgets are small. Advocates argue that these programs are underfunded and are poorly coordinated with the other homemaker and personal care services needed by frail older homeowners.

Future Issues

Traditional assessments of the owned home that are limited to its physical condition and affordability will become increasingly inadequate. Increasing numbers and percentages of older people are opting to age in place in their long-occupied and familiar dwellings. Thus, the dwelling has become not just a source of shelter but also an environment in which older occupants are seeking to cope with physical frailties. The conventional home is increasingly compared with supportive group housing alternatives, such as congregate living, assisted living, continuing care retirement communities, and nursing homes. A central research and public policy issue is the cost-effectiveness of physically and mentally frail older persons receiving shelter and care in their own homes as opposed to relocating to these other settings. (See also CONDOMINIUMS; CONTINUING CARE RETIREMENT COMMUNITIES [CCRCs]; COOPERATIVE OWNERSHIP IN HOUSING; HOME MODIFICATIONS FINANCING; MORTGAGE INSTRUMENTS; REVERSE MORTGAGES.)

References

Baer, David. 1998. *Awareness and Popularity of Property Tax Relief Programs*. Washington, DC: AARP.

Davern, Michael E., and Patricia J. Fisher. 2001. *U.S. Census Bureau, Current Population Reports, Household Economic Studies, Series P70-71, Household Net Worth and Asset Ownership, 1995*. Washington, DC: GPO.

Eschtruth, Andrew D., and Long C. Tran. 2001. "A Primer on Reverse Mortgages." *Just the Facts on Retirement Issues* (October): 1–4.

Joint Center for Housing Studies of Harvard University. 2001. *The State of the Nation's Housing, 2001*. Cambridge, MA: The Joint Center for Housing Studies of Harvard University.

Mackey, Scott, and Karen Carter. 1994. *State Tax Policy and Senior Citizens*. Washington, DC: National Conference of State Legislatures.

Mutschler, Phyllis H. 1997. "The Effects of Income on Home Modification: Can They Afford to Stay Put?" In *Staying Put: Adapting the Places Instead of the People*, ed. Susan Lanspery and Joan Hyde. Amityville, NY: Baywood Publishing.

Pynoos, Jon, Phoebe Liebig, Julie Overton, and Emily Calvert. 1997. "The Delivery of Home Modification and Repair Services." In *Staying Put: Adapting the Places Instead of the People*, ed. Susan Lanspery and Joan Hyde. Amityville, NY: Baywood Publishing.

Reschovsky, Andrew. 1994. *Do the Older Adults Face High Property Tax Burdens?* Washington, DC: AARP.

U.S. Census Bureau. 2000. *Current Housing Reports, Series H150/99, American Housing Survey for the United States: 1999*. Washington, DC: GPO.

U.S. Census Bureau. 2001. *Current Housing Reports, Series H151/95-1, Supplement to the American Housing Survey for the United States in 1995*. Washington, DC: GPO.

Venti, Steven F., and David A. Wise. 2001. *Aging and Housing Equity: Another Look*. Working Paper 8608. Cambridge, MA: National Bureau of Economic Research.

Stephen M. Golant

HOSPICE CARE, specialized care for people during the last phases of illness so that they may live as fully and comfortably as possible. Hospices provide palliative care (pain relief and symptom management) to terminally ill patients and supportive services to patients, their families, and significant others in home- and facility-based settings. Hospice services focus on physical, social, spiritual, and emotional care during the final stages of illness and during bereavement by a clinically directed interdisciplinary team consisting of patients, their families, professionals, and volunteers.

The National Hospice and Palliative Care Organization (NHPCO) estimates there are over 3,100 operational hospice programs (including some with multiple locations) in the United States, including the District of Columbia, the Commonwealth of Puerto Rico, and the territory of Guam. Hospices admitted approximately 700,000 patients in 2000. In 2000, 55% of hospice patients were female and 45% were male; approximately 81% were aged 65 or older. Of all hospice patients, 57% were diagnosed with cancer, 10% had heart-related diagnoses, 6% had dementia, 3% had end-stage kidney disease, 2% had end-stage liver disease, and 16% had other diagnoses. The average length of time a patient received hospice services in 2000 was 48 days (NHPCO 2001).

Hospice provides a coordinated program of services in a variety of home- and facility-based settings. The primary setting for hospice care is the patient's home. The Medicare Hospice Benefit includes a comprehensive set of services in all settings. Covered services include nursing care, which may be continuous during periods of crisis to maintain a patient at home; medical social service; physician service; counseling service; pastoral care; short-term inpatient and respite care; medical appliances and supplies; drugs for symptom management and pain control; home health aide and homemaker services; physical, speech, and occupational therapies; and bereavement counseling. These services are coordinated by an interdisciplinary team of professionals and delivered according to the patient's individualized plan of care. Volunteers are also fundamental to the hospice philosophy and play an integral role in providing care. In a requirement unique to hospice programs, Medicare asks hospices to use volunteers in administrative or direct patient care roles equal to 5% of the total patient care hours of all paid hospice employees.

Hospice care is financed through a number of sources, including Medicare, Medicaid, private insurance plans, patients, and charity funds. In 2000, Medicare and Medicaid accounted for approximately two-thirds of hospice revenues. Medicare reimbursement for hospices is on a prospective, per diem basis, at four different rates relating to the level of home or inpatient care provided. Medicare also imposes an annual aggregate cap on hospice care; for the fiscal year ending October 31, 2001, it was calculated on a per patient basis of $16,650.85.

Medicare covers hospice services when the beneficiary elects the Medicare Hospice Benefit, where the patient is certified by two physicians as terminally ill with a life expectancy of six months or less, and when care is provided by a Medicare-certified hospice program. Once hospice is elected, the beneficiary waives traditional Medicare coverage for the terminal illness, and the hospice benefit covers the four levels of care routine: home care, continuous home care, respite, and general inpatient care. All services are covered with the exception of the patient's attending physician, who bills directly to Medicare Part B. Hospices may require coinsurance from Medicare beneficiaries only for drugs and inpatient respite care. Coinsurance may not exceed 5% of the cost of a prescription (up to a $5 maximum) or 5% of the payment made by Medicare for an inpatient respite day (Lewin-VHI, Inc. 1995).

Interest in hospice care has grown because of its cost-effectiveness relative to conventional care. As has been widely publicized, 28% of all Medicare expenditures (more than $40 billion in 1992) are for people in their last year of life, and almost 50% of these costs are expended in the last two months of life. The federally sponsored evaluation of the first three years of the Medicare Hospice Benefit (Kidder, Merrell, and Dohan 1989) found significant savings for hospice care compared with conventional care. For example, for every dollar spent on hospice care, Medicare saved $1.26. During the last month of life, hospice care averages $3,069, while conventional care costs $4,071 (Lewin-VHI, Inc. 1994). A 1995 Lewin-VHI study, commissioned by NHPCO, showed that for every dollar Medicare spent on hospice, it saved $1.52 in Medicare Part A and Part B expenditures. The 1995 study also showed that in the last year of life, hospice patients incurred $2,737 less in costs than those not enrolled under the Medicare Hospice Benefit. These savings totaled $3,192 in the last month of life, as hospice home care days often substituted for expensive hospitalizations. Other data indicate that hospice patients paid significantly fewer out-of-pocket costs than conventional care patients. According to the National Hospice Study, hospice patients receiving waived medical services under the hospice demonstration project paid about $6 per day in out-of-pocket costs, while hospice patients not receiving waived services under the demonstration project paid $23 per day, and conventional care patients spent $46 per day (Mor, Green, and Kastenbaum 1988).

A recent NHPCO study indicates that the cost to provide aggressive, comprehensive end-of-life care is outpacing Medicare's payments to the hospices that provide the care. The study reveals an average 10% to 20% shortfall between the costs of delivering hospice care and Medicare's reimbursement for the nation's hospice care providers. Particularly striking are the rising costs for prescription medications and outpatient therapies (NHPCO and Milliman 2001).

Research on hospice care also has focused on quality. There is reasonably strong evidence that hospice care provides better quality of life for patients and caregivers. Although it is difficult to evaluate quality of life scientifically, based on available data, significant differences were found in five quality-of-life measures for hospice and conventional care patients. These include measures of pain, satisfaction with interpersonal care, satisfaction with involvement with care, quality of care, and patient's social involvement with the support system. Significant differences were also found to favor hospice in four measures used to evaluate the quality of life of the primary caregiver. Hospice primary caregivers were less anxious and were more satisfied with their involvement in care than the conventional caregivers.

Hospice has been successful in today's health care environment because it addresses people's fears about dying in pain, alone, and without personal dignity. Hospice is particularly important because of its strong emphasis on coordination of services, patient participation in care planning, and patient choice. While the growth of hospice care has been steady over the last decade, its value is becoming more widely known and will undoubtedly increase as the population ages. A recent Gallup Poll suggested that almost 90% of Americans would prefer to use the services commonly associated with hospice care if they were terminally ill rather than undergo multiple hospitalizations, nursing home placements, or disorganized home care treatment. Hospice provides a choice to the terminally ill patient for whom a traditional medical model, with its technological imperative, may no longer be appropriate. (See also ADVANCE DIRECTIVES; HEALTH MAINTENANCE ORGANIZATIONS AND MANAGED HEALTH CARE FOR

OLDER ADULTS; HOME CARE SERVICES FOR OLDER ADULTS; LIVING WILL; MEDICAID; MEDICARE.)

Organizations

Hospice Association of America
National Hospice and Palliative Care Organization
National Hospice Foundation

Suggested Readings

Health Care Financing Administration. 2000. *Medicare: Hospice Benefits*. Publication No. HCFA 02154. Baltimore, MD: Author.

National Hospice Foundation. *Hospice Care: A Consumer's Guide to Selecting a Hospice Program; Communicating Your End-of-Life Wishes; The Medicare Hospice Benefit*. Available online at http://www.hospiceinfo.org/.

References

Gallup Organization. 1996. "Knowledge and Attitudes to Hospice Care." Alexandria, VA: National Hospice Organization.

Kidder, D., K. Merrell, and D. Dohan. 1989. *Medicare Hospice Benefit Program Evaluation: Final Summary Report*. Cambridge, MA: Abt Associates, Inc.

Lewin-VHI, Inc. 1994. *Hospice Care: An Introduction and Review of the Evidence*. Arlington, VA: National Hospice Organization.

Lewin-VHI, Inc. 1995. *An Analysis of the Cost Savings of the Medicare Hospice Benefit*. Arlington, VA: National Hospice Organization.

Mor, V., D.S. Greer, and R. Kastenbaum. 1988. *The Hospice Experiment*. National Hospice Study. Baltimore, MD: Johns Hopkins University Press.

National Hospice and Palliative Care Organization (NHPCO). 2000. *NHPCO Standards of Practice for Hospice Programs*. Alexandria, VA: Author.

National Hospice and Palliative Care Organization (NHPCO). 2001. "NHPCO Facts and Figures." Available online at http://www.nhpco.org/.

National Hospice and Palliative Care Organization and Milliman USA. 2001. *The Costs of Hospice Care: An Actuarial Evaluation of the Medicare Hospice Benefit*. Alexandria, VA: Author.

Christine Cody

HOUSING COUNSELING FOR OLDER AMERICANS, educational and counseling services for seniors who are experiencing changes or problems with their present housing situation. While housing counseling is offered to the entire population, there are many types of counseling that address the problems that are specific to the older population. The following sections will explore the background of housing counseling; the present status of the industry; the basic elements of the housing counseling process; and the types of counseling services specifically offered to seniors.

Background of Housing Counseling

The housing counseling industry came into existence through the passage of the 1968 Housing and Urban Development (HUD) Act. Under this legislation, HUD could authorize public and private organizations to provide counseling to mortgagors under its basic single-family mortgage insurance program. Other legislative milestones continued to shape the industry in later years. A 1969 amendment to the original legislation allowed HUD to authorize additional entities to provide counseling and even expanded counseling to include topics such as money management and child care. In 1971, HUD set up a system to approve housing counseling agencies that could serve low- and moderate-income home buyers. The following year, HUD required approved counselors to help implement the assignment program, largely due to an epidemic of defaults that had begun to occur on FHA (Federal Housing Administration)-insured mortgages. In 1972, Congress appropriated $2.5 million to fund the housing counseling work of 31 private agencies in 19 cities nationwide (Feins et al. 1980).

Also during 1972, HUD initiated a two-year demonstration program to assist mortgagors who were delinquent under its Section 235 and Section 237 programs (U.S. Department of Housing and Urban Development 1983). It was only in 1974 that legislation authorized HUD to fund counseling efforts. Section 801 of the 1974 Housing and Community Development Act authorized HUD to grant funding for housing counseling agencies. Funding for HUD's Housing Counseling Program (HCP) has been a source of controversy since its inception, however. Over a period of several years covering many administrations, both HUD and Congress have exhibited alternating strategies for funding the HCP. While Congress agreed philosophically with the notion that counseling prior to homeownership would assist marginally creditworthy, lower-income families in developing the skills to become a successful homeowner, funds were not appropriated continuously for housing counseling until 1977 (U.S. Department of Housing and Urban Development 1983). It was even suggested during the mid-1970s that some housing counseling programs shifted roles from educating the housing consumer to consumer advocacy in light of documented abuses by the housing industry and HUD in its housing counseling programs (Organization for Social and Technical Innovation 1974). During the 1977 fiscal year, funding for counseling efforts began to be appropriated regularly, and the funds set aside for counseling efforts grew from $3 million in 1977 to $12 million in 1993. In 1977 and 1987, HUD legislation broadened counseling to include all of its various single-family homeowner programs, emergency homeownership situations, and home equity conversion programs (Quercia and Wachter 1996). From 1968 to 1982, the percentage of agencies that participated in the HCP and were funded by HUD fluctuated but averaged roughly 16% per year. Nevertheless, funding through HCP was never a consistent or substantial source of funding for most counseling agencies. Other sources of funding included dollars from Community Development Block Grant programs and those from various other federal state and local service delivery programs, which appear to have been utilized to a far greater extent (U.S. Department of Housing and Urban Development 1983). In the spring of 1983, Congress called upon HUD to document "reasonable" housing counseling practices as well as counselor training procedures.

By 1983, of the approximately 600 certified agencies nationwide, approximately 240 received HUD grants in that year (Heintz, Schare, and Turner 1984). After the mild recession and credit crunch of 1989–1991, the industry began to grow precipitously. It was during this period that the industry began to see a large number of housing counseling providers being established. By the end of 1993, it is estimated that over 1,000 counseling agencies and organizations were receiving some form of financial support from both states and the Fannie Mae Foundation (Quercia and Wachter 1996). Perhaps the most significant change within the industry that occurred during the late 1980s and early 1990s is that there was a marked change in the industry's orientation, shifting from primarily a postpurchase default prevention to a prepurchase homeownership program (McCarthy and Quercia 2000).

Present Status of the Housing Counseling Industry

Despite the fact that the housing counseling industry has been around for decades, the industry has not received much attention until recently. Affordable homeownership programs are expanding across the country, however, and they include homeownership education and counseling as a fundamental component of their strategies. As a result, there are literally thousands of organizations and entities that provide housing counseling services to low- and moderate-income borrowers.

To some in the housing field, counseling is seen as a wasteful, time-consuming, or unnecessary exercise. Rather than embracing the housing counseling concept, some realtors and mortgage bankers have tried to avoid dealing with potential borrowers who state that they are interested in participating in some of the homeownership programs that require a borrower to undertake housing counseling. Furthermore, the fragmented and diverse nature of counseling across agencies, along with the lack of regulation, has many within the housing industry worried about the quality of services delivered by housing counseling and education agencies. This question of quality has become even more important to the banking community in recent years, as the number of commercial banks shrinks through mergers and acquisitions and the local community bank becomes less common in today's society. Slowly, however, the attitudes and feelings toward housing counseling have begun to change, thanks to a proliferation of first-time homebuyer programs and various other initiatives by federal and local governments to help spur participation in the industry by those living in underserved markets. For example, HUD decided in 1996 to reduce user costs of the FHA single-family mortgage insurance program for those home buyers who undergo homeownership counseling. In this arrangement, HUD would cut the up-front mortgage insurance premium from 2.25% to 1.75% of the mortgage amount for home buyers who successfully completed the counseling programs *before* settlement on their home (McCarthy and Quercia 2000). HUD does not, however, require a minimum amount of counseling, nor does it specify a particular type of course curriculum for counselors and educators to follow. The training may be received in either a classroom or in a one-on-one setting.

Today, HUD's Housing Counseling Program has three strategic goals: (1) to improve the quality of renter and homeowner education; (2) to develop a reliable stream of funding and resources for homeownership counseling agencies; and (3) to enhance coordination among local housing providers. In its capacity, HCP funds HUD-approved local housing counseling agencies; national, regional, or multistate intermediaries; and state housing finance agencies that provide counseling and education services. Aside from providing basic counseling services, HUD-approved housing counseling agencies are permitted and even encouraged to conduct community outreach activities with the objective of increasing awareness of homeownership opportunities and improving low- and moderate-income households' access to sources of mortgage credit.

There have even been some social and professional changes related to the industry occurring during the past few years that are worth noting. There has been tremendous growth of personal financial literacy programs in the United States since the mid-1990s. For those populations in which the home-buying process is seen as unfamiliar, formidable, and unattainable, financial literacy programs may be the only remedy available to the underserved market (Vitt et al. 2000). Encouraging steps have been taken by public policy practitioners to help improve the general financial knowledge of people young and old.

Basic Elements of the Housing Counseling Process

Although housing counseling organizations differ greatly in their structure and function, there are roughly four essential elements of the housing counseling process that most agencies seek to follow. These elements are described in more detail below.

First, counselors seek to establish a working relationship with the housing client in need. It is important that the counselor conveys the message to the client that the counseling experience is essentially a partnership in which both parties understand each other's objectives clearly. The housing counselor must also be supportive of the client's efforts to realize his or her objectives. A standard of confidentiality is therefore crucial in cementing this partnership relationship. Above all, it is imperative that clients who seek counseling, especially those who are experiencing trouble in meeting their bills on time, do not feel as if they are being judged by counselors. Judgmental and subjective behavior on the part of the housing counselor could stigmatize these people from receiving help by a housing counselor in the future, which in the long run could worsen the delinquency problem. In immigrant populations, the housing counselor can also play a vital role by providing low-cost information and consumer outreach in nontraditional markets. This allows counselors to cross cultural and linguistic barriers and helps build community trust in local lending institutions and in the mortgage marketplace.

The second element of the counseling experience is the ability to successfully analyze the problem. A client's problems may be myriad, such as a borrower's lack of familiarity with the housing market; lack of a preplanned budget; lack of understanding of what kinds of features should be available in a standard single-family home; inability to recognize potential hazards such as lead-based paint; overcoming a bad credit rating; familiarity with rights of renters; and a lack of understanding of one's own fair housing rights. Of course, in delinquency counseling, the problems become a little more obvious as people enter the counseling relationship after realizing that they need to improve their personal budgeting habits, especially after a personal financial crisis.

The third part of the housing counseling process involves setting goals for the client. After analyzing the problem, it only makes logical sense that the counselor be involved in the client's setting reasonable, actionable, specific, and tangible goals for the client to reach with the hopes of eradicating the existing or potential delinquency problem. By working together to set and establish these goals, this phase allows the client to further realize that the counselor's relationship with him or her is indeed a partnership, while still realizing that the eradication of the problem in its most fundamental forms still must come from within the person seeking help. The culmination of this particular phase will involve the implementation of a corrective action plan to which the client must adhere.

The final phase of the counseling experience involves the evaluation of the client's results. This process should be a continuous one for the counselor and the client and really just encompasses a follow-up of the client's progress. In order to be effective in this phase, the counselor should be open to reevaluating the goals of the client and his or her corrective action plan as the situation changes. If the client is having troubles in meeting his or her goals, then a new corrective action plan may be formulated.

While the elements of the housing counseling and education intervention are roughly the same for all housing counseling agencies, the program content may in fact vary across agencies. With limited funding available to counseling agencies and local housing issues dominating the efforts of counseling providers, a wide variety of counseling approaches have emerged. Many counseling providers develop their own curriculum and educational materials, yet programs differ according to the topics covered, the breadth and depth of instruction, and the specific goals of the counseling agencies.

Types of Counseling Services Offered to Seniors

Much of the recent attention on housing counseling services has been focused on counseling efforts tied toward first-time homebuyers. While this is not likely to be an area that seniors utilize often, there are still a wide variety of situations in which seniors feel it is wise to seek the services of a housing counseling agency or provider.

Reverse Mortgage Counseling. By far the most common situation in which homeowners seek out the services of a housing counselor is when they are interested in making a reverse mortgage transaction or a Home Equity Conversion Mortgage (HECM). While reverse mortgage counseling services are offered in many areas nationwide, this type of counseling service is perhaps most commonly utilized in areas that serve older neighborhoods containing predominantly "house-rich but cash-poor" older residents with homes of moderate to high value. Many times, counselors will meet with such clients to discuss the advantages and disadvantages of taking on a reverse mortgage. Effective counseling measures on this topic will usually advise the client on (1) the realistic payment streams, tax consequences, and overall financial implications that he or she can expect to receive from entering into a reverse mortgage transaction; (2) other types of financial options that might be available to the homeowner, other than the reverse mortgage; (3) the most reputable lenders of the reverse mortgage product in the area; and (4) possibly even detailed suggestions for legal assistance to ensure favorable contract terms for the client. Currently, FHA and Fannie Mae require reverse mortgage counselors to be certified before offering counseling services on their respective products. FHA goes even further by requiring seniors to receive counseling, in order to be eligible for a federally insured HECM. In many cases, counseling providers are also given educational materials developed in the 1990s by the AARP. Because of the growing popularity of the reverse mortgage and the increasing rise in age of the population, one can expect that reverse mortgage counseling services will grow in magnitude and importance in the future.

Predatory Lending. Because older adults are often targets for fraud and abuse (along with low-income and minority populations) by financial services companies, many counseling entities are devoting more attention to the topic of predatory lending. In low-income communities, seniors are especially at risk for becoming victims of predatory lenders, because of the lack of available mainstream banking options available to them. As a result, "subprime" lenders have proliferated throughout these communities, all the while operating under a largely unregulated environment. Although predatory lending has been hard to define in specific terms, housing specialists and public policy officials usually define predatory lending activities as including such practices as (1) steering to high-rate lenders, (2) lending to people who cannot afford the loan, (3) offering exceedingly high interest rates and/or points, (4) inflating appraisal costs, and (5) requiring excessive prepayment penalties, just to name a few. Aside from these situations, seniors may find themselves particularly at risk from predatory lenders in situations involving unnecessary refinancings and unscrupulous reverse mortgage lenders. Housing counselors provide information and education that many mainstream banks and financial service centers can and will provide mortgage services to borrowers at more favorable terms than subprime lenders, regardless of where one is located.

Fair Housing/Tenant Counseling. This type of counseling service is offered in many counseling agencies nationwide. Because of the myriad issues that renters face both during their search for housing and after they have moved in, many counseling agencies classify types of tenant counseling into pre- and postoccupancy counseling services. Among other things, tenant counseling helps to (1) explain tenant and landlord legal rights, as well as rights under the Fair Housing Laws; (2) make suggestions about disputes; (3) advise renters on how to handle potential situations involving housing discrimination by age and race; and (4) inform counselees on how to deal with federal and local government assistance programs. Many housing counselors even go so far as to intercede on behalf of the client if he or she is in default on rent payment and is in danger of being evicted from his or her property.

Other Types of Counseling. Because there are many things that occur during one's housing situation, it is understandable that a variety of other housing counseling services are available to older clients who have special needs. Seniors are as much in need of default counseling as other members of the general population. Default counseling involves intervening on behalf of a homeowner client who is in arrears on his or her mortgage payments and who may be later thrust into a foreclosure situation as a result. Similarly, a wide array of counselors also provide homelessness prevention counseling. Because homelessness is a growing problem in many areas where housing is unaffordable, counselors can work with older clients to determine how best to avoid homelessness. In heavily populated older immigrant communities, counselors also provide many valuable services. These agencies cater specifically to immigrant populations by providing language services and advice on neighborhoods in which the new immigrants can live. In some situations, older immigrants get caught up in experiencing the "American Dream" of homeownership and decide to purchase a home for the first time—a goal that might have been impractical in their birth nation. Prepurchase housing counselors can certainly help older immigrants navigate the complicated and cumbersome process of applying for a mortgage. Also, there are housing counselors in progressive seniors communities that provide relocation services for older Americans. These specialty counselors provide information on assisted living options and facilities available to seniors as well as information on rental communities for seniors who are interested in downsizing living conditions for their retirement years. Finally, as the older population becomes increasingly more active over time, housing counseling agencies may offer an abundance of home improvement workshops that are led by local area experts. (See also CONTINUING CARE RETIREMENT COMMUNITIES [CCRCs]; GERIATRIC CARE MANAGERS [GCMs]; GERONTOLOGICAL SOCIAL WORK; HOME MODIFICATIONS FINANCING; HOMEOWNERSHIP; REVERSE MORTGAGES.)

References

Feins, Judith, D. Bain, Jr., L. Dixon, and John A. Kirlin. 1980. *Results of the Prepurchase Homeownership Counseling Demonstration*. Cambridge, MA: Abt Associates, Inc.

Heintz, Kathleen G., Ann B. Schnare, and Margery A. Turner. 1984. *Report on Housing Counseling Agencies*. Washington, DC: Urban Institute.

McCarthy, George W., and Roberto G. Quercia. 2000. *Bridging the Gap between Supply and Demand: The Evolution of the Homeownership Education and Counseling Industry*. Washington, DC: Research Institute for Housing America.

Organization for Social and Technical Innovation. 1974. *An Evaluation of the HUD Concentrated Default Counseling Program*. Newton, MA: Author.

Quercia, Roberto G., and Susan M. Wachter. 1996. "Homeownership Counseling Performance: How Can It Be Measured?" *Housing Policy Debate* 7(1): 175–201.

U.S. Department of Housing and Urban Development. 1983. *Report to Congress on Housing Counseling*. Washington, DC: Author.

Vitt, Lois A., C. Anderson, J. Kent, Deanna M. Lyter, Jurg K. Siegenthaler, and J. Ward. 2000. *Personal Finance and the Rush to Competence: Financial Literacy Education in the U.S.* Middleburg, VA: Institute for Socio-Financial Studies.

Andrew Carswell

HUD-ASSISTED RENTAL HOUSING, programs enacted under the National Housing Act (NHA) of 1937, as amended, and administered by the U.S. Department of Housing and Urban Development (HUD). Financial help is provided for older Americans through a variety of public, private, and nonprofit sponsorships where rent is based on a rent-to-income ratio for eligible tenants. Three HUD programs have provided the rent-subsidized housing units that serve the U.S. older population (aged 62 and older): Conventional Low-Rent Public Housing, Section 202 Program, and the Section 8 Program.

Shelter is a basic need that can consume the major portion of a monthly budget. For older people on fixed incomes, housing costs can be overwhelming. Although regulations, requirements, and financing arrangements concerning housing development and tenant subsidies vary, the financial impact on older persons who participate in these rental assistance programs is essentially the same. It is this impact, rather than the subtle differences between programs, that is valuable to understand.

Approximately 1.5 million older families are helped through various HUD-assisted housing programs. According to HUD's 1998 *Picture of Subsidized Households*, HUD housing programs served approximately 37% of older American households with some form of their housing assistance. The Section 8 New Construction and Substantial Rehabilitation program, where most of the property is owned and operated by nonprofit sponsors, provides the bulk of assisted housing to seniors. The Public and Indian Housing Authorities provide the second largest number of apartments to the senior group.

Of major interest to the financial issues of our current and future seniors is their income distribution. This information was developed for the Commission on Affordable Housing and Health Facility Needs for Seniors in the 21st Century, published in 2002. See Figure 1.

Income distribution is an important factor in determining eligibility for assistance in HUD-assisted housing programs. In some instances, those with incomes of less than 80% of their area's median income are eligible for housing assistance. Those seniors with incomes of 50% or less of area median income (AMI) are more likely to apply for such

Figure 1
Income Distribution of 65+ Population, by Area Median Income, 2000

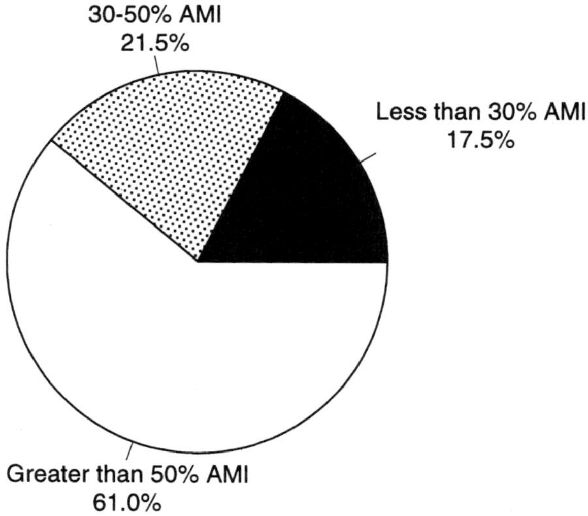

Source: Commission on Affordable Housing and Health Facility Needs for Seniors in the 21st Century 2002.

assistance. According to the commission's study, the Current Population Survey classifies 39% of current seniors falling into this "less than 50% category of area median income" and being eligible for HUD-assisted rental programs.

Conventional public housing projects for older adults in most communities are high-rise or garden complexes that are owned, operated, and maintained by local public housing agencies. There are about 3,000 agencies in various U.S. communities, not including American Indian housing authorities. These agencies may acquire, construct, modernize, or lease low-income housing for older individuals and husband-wife couples. Local agency-owners strive to make their developments appear no different from those offered by private owners at market rates. Financial assistance to subsidize operations and maintenance of these properties is funded by HUD to the local agency. In some areas (often large cities) housing supported under these programs is poorly regarded. It sometimes is badly managed and has received negative press. In other areas, particularly small- and medium-sized communities, local agencies provide quality programs, and the housing developments they manage are favorably regarded.

The Section 202 Program, enacted under the NHA in 1959, finances construction by nonprofit sponsors of low-rent apartment developments for older persons and the non-older disabled populations. Originally intended to serve older persons with incomes somewhat higher than Public Housing tenants, 202-funded apartment projects were combined with the Section 8 housing assistance program in 1974, making the units available to lower-income older adults. Tenants spend 30% of their incomes on rent and utilities. Operating deficits are covered by monthly subsidies from HUD. Many of the developments built under Section 202 contain community rooms and recreational services and are outfitted with ramped entries, grab bars, and other design features necessary for older adults residents.

Under the Section 8 Certificate Program, an older adult person or family is issued a certificate attesting to their qualification for rental assistance. An eligible older adult person or family finds suitable housing in the private marketplace and can choose either 202-funded housing run by nonprofit sponsors for older adult persons or privately owned and operated houses or apartments. The Section 8 Certificate represents a commitment to the landlord in either case to pay the difference between what the individual or family can afford to pay and the market rent. Market rents are determined and approved for housing unit types located within particular geographic areas or regions. They represent the maximum rent that would be charged for an apartment by a private landlord. The local housing authority maintains a schedule of approved fair market rents.

The Section 8 Program also includes nonprofit or limited profit, privately owned, and managed housing for older adult residents. The difference from the Certificate approach is that the subsidy is allocated to the individual units, and if a family qualifies, application is made directly to the owner or manager of the privately sponsored, assisted housing development. Services geared to the needs and concerns of an older community may also be provided. They may include free, on-site medical screening, transportation services, meals-on-wheels, and recreation activities at low or no additional cost to residents.

A Case Illustration

John and Mary Jones are former homeowners now in their late sixties. When their children were grown and gone, they sold their home and rented a two-bedroom apartment for $650, plus utilities that averaged $100 per month. A working-class family, home equity was their only asset, and the amount cleared from the sale of their home was $95,000. They gave their son $15,000 toward a downpayment on his own house and saved $75,000, which now earns interest in a combination of certificates of deposit and passbook savings rates of 3%. Their second-story, walk-up apartment consumes approximately 50% of their monthly income, and their health costs are rising. Mary's arthritis is making it difficult for her to climb stairs. Rents, however, are increasing in the community, and John and Mary can find no affordable ground-level alternative—even a smaller apartment.

To learn whether John and Mary are eligible for federal assistance, their total annual income must be calculated. From combined Social Security and pension payments, they receive income of $15,096 plus $2,350 in interest income, for a total of $17,446. Although the Jones's own a car, jewelry, and other personal effects, these are not counted within the asset definitions, which include only the $75,000 in savings.

Income is the major criterion that qualifies older persons for rental assistance. Amounts are based on the median income for the standard metropolitan statistical area in which the housing is located. Therefore, differences exist in income eligibility criteria throughout the United States. Eligibility income for New York City, for example, would be considerably higher than for Brownsville, Texas. Eligibility is based on personal income in relation to others' personal incomes in their geographic location. Conventional Public Housing apartments allow a family to earn as much as 80% of median income for their area and remain eligible. The Section 8 Housing Assistance Program limits eligibility to 50% of median income for the area.

In almost all geographic areas, John and Mary Jones would qualify under the Conventional Public Housing Program. In many areas, they also would qualify for the lower-income eligibility requirements of the Section 8 Program. John and Mary would be eligible, under federal rules, for a one-bedroom apartment, and a rent-to-income formula would be used to determine the rent they must pay. Rent is based on a family's total annual income, less deductions for individual circumstances. Since most older people do not have children and are not working, two types of deductions are most applicable. The first is an Older Adults Family deduction of $400 for a family head or spouse over age 62. The second is for excessive medical costs. Medical expenses must be substantiated and not reimbursed by medical insurance or other sources.

Mary's arthritic condition is likely to satisfy the excessive medical cost requirement, since she incurs out-of-pocket, nonreimbursed expenses of $750 a year for medical insurance, doctor visits, physical therapy, prescription, and over-the-counter drug purchases connected to her arthritis. After the medical deduction allowance is calculated, the Jones's may deduct $227 for allowable medical expenses plus the $400 allowance for older adult families. Their adjusted income is $16,319.

The formula that must now be applied to determine whether the family's rent is the greater of 30% of monthly adjusted income ($436) or 10% of monthly annual income ($145). In a federally assisted apartment, John and Mary would be expected to pay $436 a month as rent. Since both the Conventional Public Housing and Section 8 Programs, under statute, must provide both shelter and utilities in the total tenant payment, this would reduce the Jones's housing and utility cost by approximately 40% per month.

The Joneses could explore the availability of housing under the Conventional Public Housing, Section 8 Program or private, nonprofit-sponsored housing program using Section 8 federal assistance. In the case of Conventional Public Housing, the Joneses would submit their application to the local housing authority in their community.

Under the Section 8 Certificate Program, the housing authority or agency administering the Section 8/Voucher program establishes the maximum local rent (market rent) for a one-bedroom apartment. Apartments owned by private landlords who meet the Housing Quality Standards set by HUD, who are willing to accept the established market rent established for the local area, would be another option for the Joneses. Private nonprofit organizations who have developed Section 8 New Construction are also another option for John and Mary.

Conventional Public Housing developed and managed by local agencies, together with Section 202 and Section 8 New Construction developed and managed by local nonprofit groups, provide a wide range of ancillary support services to their older adult residents. Common services could include a Senior Center where lunch is available at minimal cost, as well as blood pressure checks and other health screening services. They also may organize social events, trips, and transportation services.

In March 2002, HUD competitive funding became available for the Assisted Living Conversion Program for Eligible Multifamily Developments. This Notice of Funds Availability and the Commission on Affordable Housing and Health Facility Needs for Seniors in the 21st Century are clear indicators that current levels of assistance will not support the needs of the future. In the year 2020, the number of senior households is expected to grow by nearly 53%. The number of seniors in need of affordable housing will also increase at a steady pace. The Seniors Commission Report projects that in 2020, 730,000 additional rent-assisted units will be needed to accommodate the senior households age 65 and older who are likely to have housing problems at the same 5.8 to 1 ratio at which they are accommodated today (Commission on Affordable Housing and Health Facility Needs for Seniors in the 21st Century 2002).

Further information on available federally assisted public housing in a particular locality can be obtained from the local housing authority, the municipal government, or the local HUD field office. (See also FINANCIAL COUNSELING FOR MID- TO LATER LIFE; HOMEOWNERSHIP; HOUSING COUNSELING FOR OLDER AMERICANS; MEANS-TESTING IN PUBLIC PROGRAMS; OLDEST OLD.)

References

Commission on Affordable Housing and Health Facility Needs for Seniors in the 21st Century. 2002. *A Quiet Crisis in America: A Report to Congress*. Washington, DC: Author.

Foulest, E., and D. Yeas. 1994. *Housing the Aging Population*. New York: Garland Publishing.

Gloat, Stephen M. 1992. *Housing America's Older Adults*. Newbury Park, CA: Sage Publications.

National Association of Housing and Redevelopment Officials. 1981. *Public Housing Management Resource Manual*. Washington, DC: Author.

U.S. Department of Housing and Urban Development. 1989. *Programs of HUD, 1989–1990*. Publication 214-PA(17). Washington, DC: Author.

U.S. Department of Housing and Urban Development. 1994. *Report to the Congress on Older Adults Families, Families with Children, and Disabled Families Served by Federal Housing Programs*. Washington, DC: Author.

U.S. Department of Housing and Urban Development. 1998. *A Picture of Subsidized Households in 1998: United States Summaries*. Washington, DC: Author.

U.S. Senate. Special Committee on Aging. 1993. *Developments in Aging: 1993*. Publication 103-403. Washington, DC: GPO.

Veronica M. Bukowski and Richard H. Stanton

I

IDENTITY THEFT, occurs when the identifying information of a person—name, Social Security number, mother's maiden name, or other personal information—is used to commit fraud or to engage in other unlawful activities. It is a silent, invisible crime.

Identity theft headed the top ten consumer fraud complaints in 2001, according to the Federal Trade Commission. This type of theft can be used for a myriad of illegal activities. According to Norman A. Willox, Jr. and Thomas M. Regan of NFC, Inc. (2001):

> Identity fraud is a drug trafficking problem. It is also a cyber crime problem as Eastern European criminals assume or make up passwords and user IDs to steal sensitive consumer data in order to extort unsuspecting companies. It is an alien smuggling problem, a gun-running problem and money-laundering problem. It is, as law enforcement officials have confirmed, a problem at the core of many different types of organized crime, committed locally, nationally and globally.

In the course of setting up bogus accounts, identity thieves typically provide banks and creditors with a false name and address to which bills are then routed. Victims are usually unaware that someone is exploiting their credit until months later when creditors call, demanding payment on fraudulent accounts. Though not responsible for the actual charges a thief runs up, victims must contend with harassing creditors and closed doors as they watch expenses accumulate in their name. In the end, it is consumers who absorb the considerable expense and damage wrought to the merchants, credit issuers, and the financial industry—as much as $11.9 billion a year, but they could actually be greater when law enforcement, criminal justice, attorney time, and merchant losses are tallied.

This is also a costly crime for its scope and breadth. Thefts average $17,000 per victim, with multiple victims exploited simultaneously. According to the Federal Trade Commission, identity theft topped the list of consumer fraud complaints in 2001. That year catalogued between 500,000 and 1.1 million victims. It is also growing at an alarming rate, making it the fastest-growing and most expensive consumer fraud in the country (Gregoire 2002). This explosive growth is catalogued daily; in November 2002, ringleaders of one of the largest identity theft rings victimized more than 30,000 people. Identity theft may also be used in conjunction with other criminal activity such as prostitution, drugs, and terrorism. According to Willox and Regan (2001), identity theft is an integral and indigenous part of most criminal attacks. It is suspected that the terrorist attacks of September 11, 2001, were orchestrated by a well-financed, highly motivated, and resourceful terrorist group who may have taken advantage of ineffective, or nonexistent, identification systems.

The emotional cost to victims is considerable as well. Financial loss, even when temporary, can result in wage garnishment, tax refund withholding, or property liens. Furthermore, there can be problems finding employment, renting or purchasing a home, obtaining credit, or drawing from government benefits (Beales 2002). Everyone is vulnerable, as identity thieves may be in positions to have access to highly personal information. In May 2002, Ford Motor Credit Co. notified 13,000 people that their credit reports had been obtained through unauthorized inquiries by thieves who had gained access to Experian credit files. In many cases, an employee who has access to this sensitive information will steal and distribute thousands of consumers' personal files. In March 2002 a former employee of the Prudential Insurance Co. was arrested for selling names he extracted from a database of more than 60,000 policyholders (Fries 2002). In November 2002, a Teledata Communications Inc. employee was arrested for downloading and exploiting the personal identification records of more than 30,000 people (Masters 2002).

A study undertaken by Gartner, Inc. and the National Fraud Center found that 11.6% of consumers who earn $100,000 or more annually had their identities stolen, and 37.5% were victims of credit card fraud. Online shoppers are also vulnerable, according to another Gartner study, which reported that 5.2% of respondents were credit card victims in 2001, and 1.9% were identity theft victims. Gartner further reported that 1 in 12 online consumers has experienced identity theft. Holidays are a prime time for identity thieves. As Americans become more comfortable making purchases online, especially during holiday shopping seasons, they must be aware of the potential dangers on the other side of the modem.

State governments, through their Computer Crimes Units, are becoming increasingly aware of and attuned to this problem. Repercussions can include draining an entire bank account with just a few mouse clicks in the course of a few minutes. There are several problems with tracking and prosecuting identity theft crimes. It is often difficult for law enforcement agents to prosecute identity thieves. Agencies have difficulty exchanging information across state lines because of the ease, fluidity, and legality of selling and trading identification numbers. It is legal, for instance, for Internet companies to sell Social Security numbers and other personal identifying information to a third party. Despite proposed legislation to make this practice illegal, it is still commonly practiced.

Identity Theft Detection

Evidence of identity theft will often first appear in a person's credit report. Three major companies maintain credit records and issue credit reports: Equifax, Experian, and TransUnion. The information tracked by these companies is a combination of data from banks, brokerage firms, insurance companies, debt collection agencies, courts, and local/regional credit bureaus. Not all companies collect the same information on each person; therefore, a person's credit information may vary from company to company. Approximately 4.5 billion individual bits of data are processed each month to create these individual credit histories (Forster 2002). These reports are then sold to organizations such as banks, brokerages, employers, landlords, utilities, hospitals, doctors, dentists, insurance companies, credit unions, finance companies, retailers, department stores, credit card companies, car dealers, mortgagors, investigators, lawyers, and courts. It is this massive exchange of information, which is easily bought and accessed, that in part has led to the rise in occurrences of identity theft.

Protective Measures Against Identity Theft

Given that almost anyone who can offer a credit bureau a valid reason can order a person's credit history, financial experts urge consumers to regularly check their credit reports to ensure that no one's tampering with their files. They also recommend enrolling in a monitoring service that alerts them to any updated information. These services let customers know when any credit or identification activity occurs, when a new account is opened, or an inquiry is made into their credit file. By routinely monitoring their credit reports, or having an organization do it for them, consumers can become aware of possible problems before the problem is unmanageable.

There are also other measures consumers can take to protect themselves. Common preventative measures include shredding all documents that have personal identification information on them, limiting the use and disclosure of Social Security numbers, destroying credit offers, avoiding Web sites that ask for too much credit data, and reporting missing bills. Most experts, legislators, and industry leaders agree that there's no easy answer to the problem of identity theft. However, processes are being implemented that will make it more difficult to obtain a person's identification information.

Some proposed ideas include biometrically based "signatures" (verification of identity such as those based on hand or fingerprints) and authentication (use of uniquely identifying information). The private sector has also been enlisted in helping to prevent identity theft. Merchants have access to a wide range of tools, including address verification systems, fraud detection systems, and more consistent identity verification on check and credit card transactions. Overall, the best system will be one with several levels of identity verification. Yet the difficulty in this is that it is often easier and less costly for a merchant to write off a theft than it is for them to implement any of these systems.

Contact Information

Credit reports are available directly from the credit bureaus: Equifax Inc., 1-800-685-1111; Experian (formerly TRW), 1-800-682-7654; and TransUnion, LLC, 1-800-916-8800. Some companies market three-in-one credit reports: Intersections, Inc., based in Chantilly, Virginia. (1-800-777-9700; http://www.intersections.com/), also offers a monitoring service that lets people know when information on their credit report changes. The better services offer live support that can help consumers differentiate errors from misunderstandings and out-and-out fraud.

Actions to Take if a Victim of Identity Theft

1. Consumers should contact the three credit bureaus' fraud units, report the theft, and ask that a "fraud alert" be placed on their file and that no new credit be granted without their approval. Consumers should also keep a record of all communications. If enrolled in a monitoring program, contact its Fraud Protection Unit.

2. Consumers should notify all creditors and financial institutions, in writing and by phone, that their name and accounts have been used without permission. Accounts that

are thought to be the objects of theft should be closed, and new credit cards, checks, and account numbers should be issued. Any questionable or fraudulent activity should be reported to the issuing company immediately.

3. Consumers should file a police report with either local police or with the police in the community where the identity theft took place. Consumers should have a copy of this report in hand, as it may be necessary to send a copy to credit card companies, banks, and credit bureaus.

4. Crimes should also be reported to the Federal Trade Commission's ID Theft Clearinghouse toll-free at 1-877-IDTHEFT. The Identity Theft Hotline and the ID Theft Web site (http://www.consumer.gov/idtheft) also provide information and guidelines for those who are victims of identity theft. (See also CONSUMER CREDIT; CONSUMER PROTECTION FOR OLDER ADULTS; CRIME PROTECTION; FINANCIAL ELDER ABUSE; INTERNET USE BY SENIORS.)

Organizations

Federal Trade Commission Response Center
Identity Theft Resource Center (ITRC)
Intersections, Inc.

References

Beales, J. Howard. 2002. Senate Committee Hearing, March 20.

Bernstein, Jodie. 1999. "Financial Identity Theft." Prepared Statement for Presentation to the Subcommittee on Telecommunications, Trade and Consumer Protection and Subcommittee on Finance and Hazardous Materials of the House Committee on Commerce, April 22.

Forster, Stacy. 2002. "If Credit Report Firms Can Flag Errors, Why Not Do It for All?" *Wall Street Journal*, July 26.

Fries, Jacob H. 2002. "Worker Accused of Selling Colleagues' IDs Online." *New York Times*, March 2.

Gregoire, Christine O. 2002. *Identity Theft: Restoring Your Good Name*. Testimony to the U.S. Senate Committee on the Judiciary, March 20.

Masters, Brooke A. 2002. "Arrest Made in Identity Thefts." *Washington Post*, November 26.

Willox, Norman A., Jr., and Thomas M. Regan. 2001. "White Paper on Identity Theft." National Fraud Center, October 17.

Louisa Woodville

INDIVIDUAL RETIREMENT ACCOUNT (IRA), a personal retirement savings plan providing tax benefits and available to anyone regardless of age who receives taxable compensation during the year. For IRA contribution purposes, compensation includes wages, salaries, fees, tips, bonuses, commissions, taxable alimony, and separate maintenance payments. There are no minimum or required IRA contributions. Withdrawals at retirement may be in one lump sum, in the form of an annuity in installments over remaining life expectancy, or as a series of periodic withdrawals. Husbands and wives may each have an IRA, even if one person in that marriage is not working.

Traditional IRA

A traditional IRA is an IRA available to those under age 70½ who have earned income (i.e., job compensation). Earnings within the traditional IRA are tax-deferred until withdrawal. Contributions to a traditional IRA may or may not be deductible in the tax year

Table 1
Traditional and Roth IRA Annual Contribution Limits

Year	Normal Contribution	Catch-up Contribution
2002	$3,000	$500
2003	$3,000	$500
2004	$3,000	$500
2005	$4,000	$500
2006	$4,000	$1,000
2007	$4,000	$1,000
2008	$5,000	$1,000
2009+	Indexed*	$1,000

*Normal contribution limits are indexed in $500 increments.

made, depending on the owner's income tax filing status, adjusted gross income (AGI), and eligibility to participate in a tax-qualified retirement plan through employment. A person's annual contribution, whether made to just one or to multiple IRAs, is limited to the lesser of total taxable compensation or to the normal yearly amount shown in Table 1. Individuals over the age of 50 may make an additional catch-up contribution in the amount indicated for the year concerned.

If the traditional IRA owner participates in an employer's qualified retirement plan on any day in the tax year, the deductibility of contributions declines to zero between certain AGI ranges as shown in Table 2.

A working spouse not covered by a retirement plan through employment may make a tax-deductible contribution to a traditional IRA of up to the applicable annual limit shown in the contribution limits table despite the other spouse's coverage under an employer-provided retirement plan. When the couple's AGI reaches $150,000, deductibility for such contributions begins to decline, and it reaches zero at a joint AGI of $160,000.

Money may be withdrawn from an IRA at any time, but on withdrawal it may be taxed and/or penalized. Withdrawals from a traditional IRA will always be taxed, either in whole or in part, at ordinary income tax rates, except for the nondeductible part of contributions. Withdrawals from a traditional IRA prior to age 59½ will result in a 10% excise tax as well as an ordinary income tax. Mandatory distributions for traditional IRAs must begin no later than April 1 of the year after the IRA owner reaches age 70½. Failure to take required minimum distributions at that age results in a 50% excise tax on the amounts not distributed.

Roth IRA

In contrast to the traditional IRA, a Roth IRA is one in which contributions to the account are not deductible for tax purposes, but contributions and earnings on contributions grow tax free, and "qualified" distributions (i.e., withdrawals) from the account

Table 2
AGI Phaseout Limits for Deductible Traditional IRA

Year	Single Filer	Joint Filer
2002	$34,000–$44,000	$54,000–$64,000
2003	$40,000–$50,000	$60,000–$70,000
2004	$45,000–$55,000	$65,000–$75,000
2005	$50,000–$60,000	$70,000–$80,000
2006	$50,000–$60,000	$75,000–$85,000
2007+	$50,000–$60,000	$80,000–$100,000

are not taxable. A "qualified" distribution from a Roth IRA is a withdrawal that meets one or more of the following:

1. Made after the taxpayer attains age 59½
2. Made to a beneficiary after the taxpayer's death
3. Made because the taxpayer is disabled
4. Made by a first-time homebuyer to acquire a principal residence.

Earnings on the account are taxable and subject to an early withdrawal penalty only when a withdrawal is not a "qualified" distribution.

Annual contributions to a Roth IRA are subject to the same contribution limits as a traditional IRA (shown in the contribution limits table), as reduced by any contribution made to a traditional IRA. Contributions to a Roth IRA may be made even after the owner reaches age 70½. The annual contribution limit is phased out as AGI increases from $150,000 to $160,000 (married filing jointly) or $95,000 to $110,000 (single filer).

Amounts in traditional IRAs may be transferred to Roth IRAs provided the taxpayer's AGI (married or single) for the transfer year is $100,000 or less. Transferred amounts must be included in that year's income, but the money transferred will be exempt from the 10% excise tax for a withdrawal prior to age 59½. No withdrawal allocable to earnings on the transferred amounts is considered to be a qualified distribution unless it is made more than five tax years after the transfer.

Education IRA (EIRA)

An Education IRA, also called the Coverdell Education Savings Account (ESA), is an account established to provide funds that will allow a beneficiary to attend a program of higher education. There is no tax deduction allowed for the contribution, but all deposits and earnings may be withdrawn free of tax and penalties if used to pay for the costs of higher education. Beginning in 2002, allowable contributions are $2,000 per year with phaseouts beginning at $150,000 for joint filers and $95,000 for single filers. Contributions may be made regardless of the beneficiary's income but cannot be made on or after the beneficiary's eighteenth birthday. Plan proceeds may also be used free of tax and penalty to pay for the qualified expenses for kindergarten through twelfth grade education in public, private, and/or religious schools. If distributions exceed the education expenses, the earnings must be included in gross income and are subject to the 10% excise tax to the extent of the excess. The EIRA, if unused on or before age 30, may be transferred to another qualifying family member as the new beneficiary for educational use. Such transfers must occur before the beneficiary reaches age 30.

Rollover (Conduit) IRA

A rollover IRA is a traditional IRA set up by an individual to receive a distribution from a qualified retirement plan. Distributions transferred to a rollover IRA are not subject to any contribution limits. Additionally, the distribution may be eligible for subsequent transfer into a qualified retirement plan available through a new employer. (See also CASH FLOW PLANNING FOR RETIREES; EARLY RETIREMENT INCENTIVE PIANS [ERIPs]; ESTATE PLANNING; FINANCIAL ADVISORS; KEOGH PLANS; MEDICAL SAVINGS ACCOUNTS (MSAs) AND MEDICAL IRAs; PENSION PLANS FOR THE SELF-EMPLOYED; RETIREMENT PLANNING; RETIREMENT PREPAREDNESS; WEALTH SPAN.)

References

Gitman, Lawrence J., and Michael D. Joehnk. 2002. *Personal Financial Planning*. 9th ed. Mason, OH: South-Western/Thomson Learning.

Keown, Arthur J. 2001. *Personal Finance*. Upper Saddle River, NJ: Prentice-Hall

The Motley Fool: Personal Finance Web site. Available online at http://www.fool.com/.

Ganas K. Rakes and Rajesh Narayanan

INFLATION. See Asset Allocation after Retirement; Bonds; Cash Flow Planning for Retirees; Cost-of-Living Adjustments (COLAs); Economic Hardship Measures in the Older Population; Equity Securities; Homeownership; Savings Investments.

INFLUENCES ON RETIREMENT INVESTMENT DECISIONS can be grouped into four categories: (1) retirement plan characteristics, (2) employee demographic characteristics, (3) psychological biases, and (4) social effects. Understanding this view of retirement investment influences may benefit plan sponsors, employees, researchers, and others interested in retirement investment behavior.

Increasingly, people are being asked to manage their own retirement savings. Over the past two decades, employee retirement plans have largely shifted from defined benefit plans predominantly managed by professionals to defined contribution plans (such as 401(k) plans) predominantly managed by employees. Yet most employees have difficulty reaping the benefits of managing their own retirement savings and, on average, do not make optimum investment decisions.

Retirement Plan Characteristics

The more successful defined contribution benefit packages have several characteristics in common, all designed to encourage employee participation and build employee loyalty. These include a substantial contribution match, a greater number of investment options available to employees, the ability to make changes to the plan as often as the employee wishes, and access to targeted investment education programs and/or financial planning services (Hansen 1999).

Employee participation levels for 401(k) plans with employer matching contributions are 18% higher than for plans with no match (Hansen 1999). Most employers do offer some level of matching contributions; 69% of employers that offered 401(k) plans had a contribution match of at least 50%, according to KPMG's *Retirement Benefits in the 1990s: 1998 Survey Data* (1998).

However, while there may be greater participation levels when there is some level of employer match, the *amount* employees contribute decreases slightly when employers make matching contributions (Holden and VanDerhei 2001a). Nevertheless, the total contributions (employer and employee combined) are higher for employees who have employer contributions. It is therefore beneficial to the employee, and to the employer in terms of employee loyalty, for a company to offer some level of matching contribution, especially if it is equal to or greater than 50 cents to the dollar.

In addition, choice in investment options is important to employee participation in benefit plans. Fund types may include international funds, income (bond) funds, money market funds, growth funds, value funds, large cap funds, and mid/small cap funds. This range of choices is especially important to companies who have a heterogeneous and diverse workforce, as there are more options to accommodate the retirement needs of a greater range of employees. There are several reasons why companies may not offer a broad range of investment options. Of increasing importance is the unwillingness of companies to open themselves up to potential legal action by employees who have lost significant amounts of their retirement benefits due to unwise or uninformed asset allocation decisions. Companies may feel that their workforce is not substantially informed on how to invest wisely, and offering more options (especially higher-risk, higher-yield options) has the potential to be more damaging than beneficial over a given time period. Furthermore, a large number of investment choices may serve more to confuse employees than to assist them.

The ability for employees to make changes and adjustments to their retirement plans provides another way for employers to add value to their benefits packages. While it is mandated by law that there must be an "appropriate" number of periods during the year in which an employee is permitted to change his/her retirement plan's asset allocation, recent technological advances now enable many employers to offer employees daily access (and with it the ability to make daily changes) to their account. Interestingly, employees who have access to this type of system tend to take a fairly conservative view of their investments, preferring to take a longer-term view and not engage in daily trading (Hansen 1999).

Finally, educational programs for employees are also seen as a factor for increased employee participation in their company's retirement benefit plan. According to the 1998 KPMG study, participation rates in 401(k) plans are 5 percentage points higher (71% compared to 66%) when employers offer investment education programs than when they don't. Companies have become quite innovative in the programs offered to their employees. Examples include offering intra- and extra-net computer programs, models, and simulations by which employees can see "firsthand" the projected consequences of investment decisions, toll-free telephone investing for employees that spend a majority of their time on the road, and culturally sensitive, targeted programs for diverse work groups. When companies make employee participation in their benefit plans easy, accessible, and personal, employees are more willing to take advantage of benefit plans—thereby helping to build a strong, mutually reinforcing employer-employee relationship.

Other Factors Affecting Retirement Plan Participation

Retirement plans that are structured with automatic enrollment have higher levels of participation than plans requiring employees to opt in (Madrian and Shea 2000, 2001). Other characteristics of the automatic enrollment plan, namely, the rate of contribution and fund allocation, can also influence investment behavior because there is a strong tendency by employees to maintain rates and allocations set as the plan's default options.

Although employees often use the default rates instead of actively choosing contribution amounts and allocations, many prefer *flexibility* in their retirement accounts. They fully expect to work for several different organizations during their working careers. As such, they desire the ability to control their retirement accounts through portability features (Dulebohn, Murray, and Sun 2000). A second flexibility characteristic is the option to borrow from one's 401(k) account. Holden and VanDerhei (2001a) find that participant contribution rates increase in plans that give employees the option to borrow from their accounts. There is a hidden danger, however, in this option. In the event of termination, downsizing, or leaving a position, the borrower may be required to pay back immediately the loan from his or her retirement account. If unable to do so, and if the holder is under 59½ years of age, he or she may be subject to a tax liability for the withdrawn amount, plus a 10% penalty. According to David Wray, president of the Profit Sharing Council, "[Someone] might be obligating [himself] to pay back that loan at one of life's worst times" (Smartmoney.com 2003).

Employee Demographic Characteristics

Employee demographic characteristics (such as age, income, and job tenure) influence 401(k) participation rates, contribution rates, and allocation preferences. An employee's *age* is associated with several 401(k) plan investment decisions. First, participation rates increase with age. Second, participants who are older tend to contribute more. However, the relationship between employee asset allocation decisions and age appear to be more complicated. Financial advisors usually recommend that the portion of investments allocated to equities decline as the employee's investment horizon declines. A common rule of thumb is that the portion of a portfolio allocated to equities be 100 minus their age. Accordingly, the 30-year-old employee "should" have 70% in equities, and the 60-year-old "should" have 40% in equities. Indeed, younger employees tend to allocate larger portions of their accounts and contributions to equity funds, and older employees tend to allocate more to fixed income securities and bonds. This is somewhat complicated by the fact that employees rarely change their asset allocation after making the initial decisions. Therefore, the realized allocation to equities is mostly a function of the initial decision and the realized returns over time of each asset class.

The most important determinant of participation in an employer-sponsored 401(k) plan may be the employee's *income*. Participation rates are about 35% for employees with an income of less than $15,000, and over 80% for employees with an income of at least $75,000. Also, employees with higher income levels allocate larger portions of their accounts to equity funds (Holden and VanDerhei 2001b). Employees with greater *job tenure* participate more than employees with less job tenure. Likewise, contribution rates tend to increase as job tenure increases.

Psychological Biases

The human brain is constantly being stimulated with information. To decrease the amount of information received, the brain filters out some information and uses shortcuts to decrease the complexity of other information. These shortcuts allow the brain to make judgments and decisions before fully digesting all the available information. This process causes several psychological biases for the investor.

People often prefer the familiar, and because of this, investors tend to believe that the stock of familiar companies is less risky than that of unfamiliar companies. This misconception is referred to as the *familiarity bias*. The company most people are most familiar with is the company for which they work. In large firms, about 32% of plan assets are invested in the sponsoring companies' stock (Benartzi 2001). The familiarity bias contributes to employees' desire to own the company stock.

Another psychological bias that can affect some investors is the *representativeness bias*. The brain makes the assumption that things sharing similar qualities are alike. The representativeness bias causes investors to buy stocks that represent desirable qualities. That is, they mistakenly believe that a good company is a good investment. Good companies are ones that have a good workforce, or have good management, or have high sales growth. Good investments are stocks that increase in value. The former does not always imply the latter.

Investors also make this error when examining past stock returns. A common misconception is that past returns are representative of what can be expected in the future. This causes investors to chase the winners and buy funds or asset classes that have trended upwards in price. Employees often compound the familiarity bias error described earlier by succumbing to the representativeness bias. That is, they buy more of their company's stock after its price increases.

People have a tendency to do nothing when faced with many choices. *Status quo bias* involves preferring the default choice, which is often the do-nothing option. Indeed, when an employee is participating (or not) in a retirement savings plan, there appears to be an inertia effect such that the participation remains at that given level (Madrian and Shea 2001). Put another way, many employees do not take an ongoing active role concerning their retirement savings. Rather, once a contribution level and fund allocation have been set, it is easiest to put aside further analysis and decision making in favor of maintaining the status quo.

Social Effects

The effects of social interactions on individual behavior have been modeled, tested, and applied to a wide variety of events. Acknowledging that social interaction may affect financial decisions simply recognizes that people receive and process information through interaction with others. Peer effects influence retirement savings decisions because many people have not thought carefully through the advantages and disadvantages of their plan strategy and may lack their own reasoned information for making retirement investment decisions.

Investing conversations are an important part of gathering information and becoming comfortable with decisions. Because information is obtained and decisions formed through talking with others, sociable people may learn more about investing than less sociable people. As a consequence, highly sociable people are more likely to invest in the stock market or participate in their 401(k) plan (Hong, Kubik, and Stein 2001).

The participation rate of an employee's peers has a large impact on whether he or she decides to participate. The social norms of each peer group develop over time. Some social norms develop to value retirement plans, while others do not. The likelihood that an employee will decide to contribute to a retirement plan is low if his or her peers do not contribute.

Conclusions

There are many influences on employee retirement investment decisions. This entry summarized some of the research investigating the influences of plan characteristics, employee demographic characteristics, social influences, and psychological biases. Increased understanding of the broader view of retirement investment influences should benefit plan sponsors, employees, researchers, and others interested in retirement investment behavior. (See also BABY BOOMERS AND RETIREMENT; FINANCIAL ADVISORS; FINANCIAL EDUCATION FOR SENIORS; INVESTMENT ADVICE; INVESTOR EDUCATION; RISK TOLERANCE.)

References

Benartzi, S. 2001. "Excessive Extrapolation and the Allocation of 401(k) Accounts to Company Stock." *Journal of Finance* 56: 1747–64.

Dulebohn, J.H., B. Murray, and M. Sun. 2000. "Selection among Employer-Sponsored Pension Plans: The Role of Individual Differences." *Personnel Psychology* 53: 405–32.

Hansen, F. 1999. "401(k)—How Good Is Yours?" *Management Review* 88: 55–60.

Holden, S., and J. VanDerhei. 2001a. "Contribution Behavior of 401(k) Plan Participants." *ICI Perspective* 7: 1–19.

Holden, S., and J. VanDerhei. 2001b. "401(k) Plan Asset Allocation, Account Balances, and Loan Activity in 2000." *ICI Perspective* 7: 1–27.

Hong, H., J.D. Kubik, and J.C. Stein. 2001. "Social Interaction and Stock-Market Participation." *Journal of Finance*.

KPMG. 1998. *Retirement Benefits in the 1990s: 1998 Survey Data*. Washington, DC: Author.

Madrian, B.C., and D. Shea. 2000. "Peer Effects and Savings Behavior in Employer-Sponsored Savings Plans." Working Paper, University of Chicago.

Madrian, B.C., and D. Shea. 2001. "The Power of Suggestion: Inertia in 401(k) Participation and Savings Behavior." *Quarterly Journal of Economics* 116: 1149–87.

SmartMoney.com. 2003. "5 Things You Should Know about Your 401(k)." Available online at http://www.smartmoney.com/retirement/401k/index.cfm?story=5things.

John R. Nofsinger

INHERITANCE, the disposition of one's property upon death. Historically, inheritance was the passing of one's estate to his or her heirs. Who would inherit was strictly predetermined by established law, usually designating the decedent's eldest son. Today, there is a wide degree of latitude in one's options for disposing of property after death. Although most states guarantee a share to a surviving spouse, a person is otherwise free to dispose of his or her property as he or she chooses. Inheritance now applies to any disposition of property after death, whether by will, trust, or operation of law. There are a number of tools available to control who will inherit one's estate. They vary in complexity, cost, and the degree of control the deceased can exercise from the grave.

The History of Inheritance

Records of inheritance date back as far back as the Book of Genesis. Consider the account of Esau selling his birthright (inheritance) for a bowl of lentil stew. Records of inheritance in the Roman Empire also exist. Seeking a source of revenue for a permanent military, Caesar Augustus imposed what may have been the first "estate tax." The tax was imposed only on assets valued at around 50 pieces of gold or more and was only imposed on inheritances from distant relations.

The modern inheritance system emerged from feudalism, in the early stages of which the strong man extorted or confiscated the land of the weak in return for protection. The lord then "lent" it back to his vassal as long as certain obligations were faithfully performed. After the Norman Conquest of 1066, William the Conqueror confiscated all land owned by the Saxons, redistributing it to his own barons. The king remained the true owner, and the barons held the land as "tenants in chief" as long as they remained obedient. These feudal tenures originally terminated upon death, but it soon became customary to regrant the land to the decedent's eldest son, although, of course, a fee was required. The system provided stability and predictability and by the end of the twelfth century had "crystallized into a 'common law right of inheritance' " (Cribbet et al. 1996). The system was so stable and predictable, however, that the wishes of the deceased were unable to alter the scheme.

In England, where American law originated, the transfer of land (real property) by will was not allowed until 1540, although transfer of personal property by will was more or less unrestricted. In fact, the ecclesiastical courts had jurisdiction over the probate of wills for personal property, and by convincing the flock of believers that a will was necessary for salvation, the Church guaranteed itself substantial fees. Though lawyers have replaced priests, remnants of the Church's probate scheme remain today.

The Social Merits of Inheritance

The social merits of inheritance have long been debated. Thomas Jefferson, in a letter to James Madison, said "that portion occupied by an individual ceases to be, and reverts to the society" (1789). The Soviet Union went so far as to ban inheritance, but the policy was abandoned as a failure after only four years because it was felt that inheritance encouraged savings and incentives to work and relieved the state of providing for dependents (Dukeminier and Johanson 2000). While a ban on inheritance has proven to be counterproductive, it is not unreasonable to expect a decedent to "pay his tab to society." The nation's estate tax policy is an attempt to balance these competing factors.

While defending the vast wealth he and other industrialists had accumulated, Andrew Carnegie was equally adamant that disparities in wealth should not be perpetuated through inheritance. The industrialists had earned their wealth, after all, but the social utility of leaving great wealth to family members who made no significant contributions to its accumulation was questionable. Does inheritance of wealth encourage the hard work, thrift, and initiative that helped to create it in the first place, or does it perpetuate a class of unproductive ingrates? Carnegie encouraged the altruistic use of one's excess wealth, funding projects that would benefit the public generally. To encourage such altruism, the government should impose severe estate taxes, said Carnegie. While people may argue, "My family is my preferred charity," if asked whether higher taxes on income today or higher taxes after death is preferable, who doubts the likely response?

Intestacy

A person dying without a will or other estate plan leaves the state to determine who will inherit and prompts the involvement of a probate court, with its attendant costs and delays. Although "intestate succession" laws vary from state to state, they generally distribute specified shares to the spouse and children if they survive the decedent or to other designated relatives if they do not. These laws entail a series of presumptions about how the decedent wanted his or her estate to be distributed—presumptions that may be entirely inconsistent with a person's wishes. After the estate is reduced by probate costs, attorney's fees, and estate taxes, the residue is distributed with no regard to what the decedent really wanted.

For all but the most meager estates, some form of estate planning is needed to ensure that the estate passes according to the decedent's wishes, that estate taxes are minimized, and that probate may be avoided. Traditional estate planning tools include wills and inter vivos ("living") trusts.

Wills

The will is the backbone of traditional, conservative estate plans. Through a will, one leaves his or her instructions for the distribution of his or her estate. While it does provide a means for expressing one's wishes, those wishes can only be executed by authority of the probate court. Being a judicial proceeding, probate is lengthy, costly, and intrusive. The costs of a simple probate vary, but the AARP found that they can deplete the average middle-class estate by as much as 10%, and costs can skyrocket if the will is challenged.

Living Trusts

For many people, an inter vivos trust (living trust) is a better option: trusts offer something for everyone. A primary benefit of a living trust is probate avoidance. Because the title to property is transferred into the trust *during the life* of the decedent, court involvement is usually not required. Living trusts have been used for centuries but have only become popular as will substitutes since the middle of last century. The up-front costs of a trust are greater than for a will, since the trust is a more complex document than a will, and title to assets must be transferred. However, the costs of settling a trust estate are generally much less than the costs of probate. Generally, trusts are cost-effective for estates of about $100,000 or more (Wasik 1993). Provisions can be included in a trust that can reduce the impact of estate taxes, though similar provisions can also be added to a will. While probate of a will is a matter of public record, a trust estate can generally be settled privately.

There has been a concern in recent years over the "selling" of living trusts by non-lawyers, and several states have taken measures to curb this "unauthorized practice of law" (Wasik 1993). In his 1993 *Consumer's Digest* article, John Wasik also cautioned that "most of the fraudulent products were being sold by agents or financial planners, not lawyers." People should exercise care when preparing legal documents or taking advice from nonlawyers. A telephone call or letter to the state bar association is a good referral source for qualified estate planning attorneys.

Most people prefer to leave some sort of legacy to those they love: an inheritance. At the personal level, inheritance law offers the tools for a well-informed transfer. At the societal level, the magnitude of inheritance is growing rapidly. The $84 billion of wealth transferred per year at present will increase to $336 billion in the year 2015 and will have a significant impact on the American economy.

Estate Taxes

Between now and the year 2040, baby boomers will inherit some $10 trillion: an average of roughly $90,000 (Stern 1993). This staggering sum will reshape the nation's social and business fabric and may even become a potential source of revenue for politicians seeking solutions to the budget deficit. Legislators may look increasingly to estate taxes for a solution to counter the mounting deficit, since raising rates on income taxes is an increasingly unpopular move, and budget cuts seem even more elusive. As the debate over deficit reduction continues, society may ask, "Why not let parents and grandparents pay the deficit by increasing estate taxes?" Inheritance, after all, has always been subject to the debts of the decedent.

Current Law

The government has not, however, exacted an onerous burden on estates. The estate tax has recently undergone extensive changes, which will be phased in over the first decade of the twenty-first century. Under the current system, between now and 2009, the estate tax rate will decline from 50% to 45%, and the amount of one's estate that is effectively exempt from taxation will rise from $1 million to $3 million. In 2010, the estate tax will be repealed altogether, so even Bill Gates's estate would pay no estate tax if he dies in 2010; however, in 2011 the estate tax is revived, with only $1 million being effectively exempt. This may all change, however, depending on politics. A married couple who plans properly may continue to double the estate tax exemption.

While the federal government theoretically will take a substantial share of the nation's largest estates, the vast majority of estates are passed estate tax free to heirs. Current capital gains tax is also structured to favor heirs. If an exempt $1 million inheritance is composed of real estate purchased many years earlier for $100,000, and sold immediately by the heirs, the capital gains tax that would otherwise be owed on the $900,000 appreciated value would be avoided by the heirs. This too will change in the year 2010.

There are several types of mechanisms available to reduce the size of one's estate, but only qualified attorneys and accountants should be consulted for such planning.

Charities

When considering the sale of a highly appreciated property where capital gains taxes are daunting, people consider giving it away. By using a Charitable Remainder Trust, the appreciated property may be sold now, free of capital gains, and a guaranteed income for life retained from the proceeds. In addition, a current tax deduction is available for gifting the remainder to charity. These tax breaks, coupled with income from the untaxed proceeds of the sale, could pay for or exceed the actual gift to charity. Although the gift must go to the charity at death rather than to one's heirs, the overall tax consequences may dramatically improve the amount of one's net estate.

Life Insurance

Finally, life insurance is a tool many people use to provide an estate for their family or to fund the ultimate estate tax bill. It is important to realize, however, that insurance proceeds may dramatically increase your estate tax bill if not handled properly. Insurance proceeds can be sheltered from estate taxes through use of an irrevocable life insurance trust.

Estate Tax Planning

If an estate is large enough that estate taxes could be a potential problem, it is imperative to consult an attorney who specializes in estate planning. Shop carefully, however, because it has been estimated that only 1% of all attorneys can properly draft a living trust (Faltermayer 1991). And even fewer are capable of drafting the more advanced estate planning tools. Spending a little extra now for an attorney who is an expert on estate planning can save a family thousands of dollars later. (See also BUSINESS SUCCESSION PLANNING; CAPITAL GAIN; CHARITABLE CONTRIBUTIONS; ELDER LAW PRACTICE; ESTATE PLANNING; FINANCIAL LITERACY; HEALTH AND LONGEVITY; INTERGENERATIONAL CONFLICT AND FINANCIAL ISSUES; TRUSTS; WILLS; WEALTH SPAN).

References

Cribbet, John E., Corwin W. Johnson, Roger W. Findley, and Ernest E. Smith. 1996. *Cases and Materials on Property*. 7th ed. Westbury, NY: Foundation Press.

Dukeminier, Jesse, and Stanley M. Johanson. 2000. *Wills, Trusts and Estates*. 6th ed. Boston, MA: Little, Brown.

Esperti, Robert A., and Renno L. Peterson. 1999. *Protect Your Estate: Definitive Strategies for Estate and Wealth Planning from Leading Experts*. New York: McGraw-Hill.

Faltermayer, Edmund. 1991. "The Financially Perfect Death: Adroit Moves While You're Still Around Can Shrink Estate Taxes and Spare Your Heirs the Long Wait of Probate." *Fortune*, February 25.

Gibbon, Edward. 1988. *The Decline and Fall of the Roman Empire*. Vol. 1. Chicago: Encyclopedia Britannica.

Jefferson, Thomas. 1789. "Letter to James Madison, Paris, September 6, 1789." In *Social and Political Philosophy*, ed. John Somerville and Ronald E. Santoni. Garden City, NY: Doubleday.

Stern, Linda. 1993. "Inheritances: Next Boom for Boomers." *Seattle Post-Intelligencer*, December 28.

Wasik, John F. 1993. "Living Trusts vs. Wills: Estate Planning Guide." *Consumer's Digest* (September–October).

Scott A. Miskiel

INSURANCE. See Accident Insurance; Liability Insurance; Long-Term Care Insurance (LTCI)—A Consumer's Perspective; Long-Term Care Insurance: Individual Disability Escalating Annuities (IDEAs); Long-Term Care Insurance, Private; Medicaid; Medicare; Medicare Supplemental Insurance; Postretirement Health Coverage (PRHC).

INTERGENERATIONAL CONFLICT AND FINANCIAL ISSUES, tensions and disagreements between family members over financial matters, including the distribution of financial assistance between aging parents and adult children. Family and gerontology researchers have only recently turned their attention to the issue of intergenerational conflict, and the subject of how family conflicts impact financial matters has rarely been explored.

What Is Intergenerational Conflict?

In the contemporary literature on family relations, moderate family conflict is often viewed as a normative aspect of family relationships and has been discussed as a functional and even necessary element for maintaining family harmony (Clarke et al. 1999). It is unclear how much conflict exists between aging parents and adult children. Some studies conducted using quantitative measures reported fairly low levels of intergenerational conflict (Suitor and Pillemer 1988), but Clarke et al. (1999) report a surprisingly high level of intergenerational conflict when examining open-ended qualitative responses. About two-thirds of their sample of aging parents and adult children reported conflicts, tensions, or disagreements. While conflict is typically thought to be highest between parents and their children during adolescence, it is now clear that these earlier conflicts may resurface at later stages in the life course. The literature is mixed regarding whether aging mothers or fathers experience more frequent conflicts with adult children.

How parents and adult children "fight" has also been of research interest. In a study examining the relationship between aging mothers and adult daughters, Fingerman (1995) found that mothers and daughters equally used "constructive" techniques to try to resolve conflicts that arose. However, Fingerman also cited research showing that older individuals have fewer overt conflicts with others, and she suggested that as parents age and adult children mature, they may practice avoidance tactics to prevent conflict over issues that they know will generate tensions. While the most extreme and violent way to resolve conflicts with aging parents may take the form of elder abuse, for the purposes of this discussion the focus is on milder and more constructive forms of conflict and tensions that do not involve physical aggression toward another person.

What Are the Topics of Intergenerational Conflict?

Very little research has identified the focus of intergenerational conflicts. A qualitative study of conflict and tensions between adult children and their aging parents identified six types of issues that generate conflicts in families (Clarke et al. 1999):

1. Communication and interaction style
2. Personal habits and lifestyle choices
3. Child-rearing practices and values
4. Politics, religion, and ideology
5. Work orientation
6. Household maintenance

The type of conflicts mentioned most by both parents and adult children were the first three. Concerns and conflicts over the allocation of financial resources were included in the "habits and lifestyles" type, and these centered on adult children not saving their money, having spending patterns and priorities that differed from the parents' expectations, and concern over "continued dependency" either because the adult child had not become financially self-supporting or because the aging parent was relying on the adult child for financial assistance.

How Do Intergenerational Conflicts Impact Exchanges of Financial Support?

Research findings indicate that a strong sense of duty can override other intergenerational relationship qualities, such as low affection or past conflicts, and lead to the exchange of help and support between the generations (Parrott and Bengtson 1999; Whitbeck, Hoyt, and Huck 1994). Retrospective accounts of the quality of intergenerational relationships in the past (both as adolescents and younger-aged adults) can influence the propensity of adult children to give help and support to aging parents (Whitbeck, Hoyt, and Huck 1994). However, this finding varied based on type of help and support given and the level of intergenerational affection and sense of obligation felt. Some studies show no relationship between recent or past conflicts and the exchange of financial support between parents and adult children. Using prospective accounts of family relationships, Parrott and Bengtson (1999) found that earlier conflict in parent–adult child relationships did not interfere with contemporary exchanges of help and support, including financial support to/from a parent/adult child.

Silverstein, Parrott, and Bengtson (1995) identified gender differences in what motivates the supportive behaviors of adult children toward their aging parents, including whether or not financial assistance is given. Intergenerational affection most motivated adult daughters to provide support to parents, while adult sons were motivated by filial obligation, expectation of an inheritance, and frequency of contact with parents. They noted that the anticipation of a financial reward (i.e., an inheritance) could be an incentive to an adult child to provide help and support to aging parents.

However, Parrott and Bengtson (1999) found that levels of financial exchanges between parents and adult children were relatively low, occurring infrequently compared with other types of instrumental support, and the predictors of financial support were related to the need and age of the adult child. In this study, affectionate bonds were not necessary for parents to aid their adult children. On the other hand, affectionate bonds increased the likelihood of financial assistance being given to aging mothers.

The "intergenerational stake hypothesis" also sheds some light on the mixed findings regarding the impact of conflict on financial exchanges of intergenerational support. This theory holds that the older generation perceives more similarity and closeness to the younger generation than the younger generation perceives and reports. Said differently, parents report "less distance" or gaps in their relationships with adult children (Lynott and Roberts 1997). From this interpretation, parents would also be expected to report fewer conflicts and disagreements with their adult children than the adult children report because the parents have more of an investment or "stake" in the relationship over time. This means that adult children may be more affected by the conflicts and differences between the generations than are parents who have a tendency to "view things through rose-colored glasses." Some research backs this up, suggesting that parents perceive relationship characteristics and the meaning of them differently than do their adult children.

Fingerman (1995) found that "older mothers underestimate daughters' negative behaviors and feelings in conflict situations."

Do Financial Issues Cause Intergenerational Conflict?

For decades, research has shown that financial matters are consistently a source of marital disagreement and conflicts. Thus, it is not surprising that financial issues can also generate conflicts in intergenerational relationships. For example, in families with more than one child it is not uncommon for one child to receive more assistance than another. Those children who need the most (due to divorce, for example) typically get more compared with children who are doing well and do not require financial assistance from parents. This financial dependency tends to create tension between the giver and the receiver. Moreover, sibling conflicts may also arise due to differential financial support from parents to the adult children and perceived inequalities in parental treatment of siblings. It has been shown that perceived feelings of preference for one sibling over another can impact later exchanges of help and support with aging parents (Whitbeck, Hoyt, and Huck 1994).

Financial planners find that adult children often second-guess the investment decisions of their parents. Further, adult children who expect an inheritance may feel angry over spending decisions their aging parents make, such as opting to spend their savings while they are alive versus leaving an inheritance. As Clarke et al. (1999) demonstrated, financial issues can be the object of conflict and tension between parents and adult children when one generation does not approve of how the other is spending their money. Disapproving adult children may take measures to protect their inheritance, including obtaining decision-making authority for the estate of an aging parent or encouraging estate planning practices that ensure savings are not spent down to cover the costs of long-term care for the aging parents. All of these tactics can undermine the autonomy and decision-making ability of the parent and can generate additional intergenerational conflicts.

The financial drain of caring for an aging parent—due to purchasing in-home community-based care or taking time off from work—can lead to conflicts and tensions in the intergenerational relationship as well. This is particularly true if the caregiving costs are competing with the cost of college for a child or the adult child's own retirement plans. In such situations, the dependency of the parent on the adult child may play a role in the level of conflict the adult child experiences, partly because the adult child may feel uncomfortable with the change in parent-child roles or because the adult child may resent the drain of caregiving on financial and emotional family resources.

How Can Social Exchange Theory Explain Conflict and Financial Support in Families?

A number of studies have focused on the causes of intergenerational conflict and the determinative effect of financial support. Economists would suggest that parents strategically make "investments" in children in anticipation of needed support in old age. They can, for example, withhold or extend financial resources to ensure greater interaction or future assistance (Silverstein et al. 2002). Sociologists tend to point to social exchange theory and reciprocity norms to explain supportive behaviors in families. They suggest that "delayed" or "lagged" reciprocity norms account for the behaviors observed, even in the face of poor-quality relationships. From a life course perspective, it is clear that there is a typical flow of exchanges of support over the life course of individuals in families as their roles, life stages, needs, and resources change. The middle generation typically gives the most to the younger and older generations, while the younger and older generations are net recipients of assistance (Morgan and Kunkel 2001). Why families help each other in this patterned way has been examined in the empirical literature.

Silverstein et al. (2002) "defined lagged reciprocity as the circumstance when the provision of support to older parents was the fulfillment of an obligation to repay a social debt based on that parent's earlier transfers to the child." Looking over a 26-year time period and using six data points, they found that financial transfers were similar to an insurance model, where investments in adolescent and young adult children had a return in the future when the aging parent exhibited a need (defined as a functional impairment) for assistance. Silverstein and colleagues described this as one example of an implied social contract between family members that works to ensure reciprocity in the long term when an aging parent has a need for help. This study found that even when there had been very little or no financial support received from parents at an earlier age, there was still increasing support given to parents as they got older. Thus, some level of altruism was also at work.

Given that there may be a link between income and levels of family violence, it may also be true that the likelihood of nonaggressive conflicts arising in families is higher when an adult child or older parent has limited resources because he/she would have fewer resources to bring to an exchange and reciprocate. This can lead to dependency and may create feelings of tension. Conversely, having few resources may make individuals less likely to generate conflicts because they are dependent on the other for assistance. The same self-interested motivation may be true for individuals in poor health. For example, an aging parent needing assistance due to health problems may be willing to overlook things an adult child does or says that they disagree with because they need the adult child to provide assistance. In situations where the assistance is duty driven, we might expect more expressions of conflict as well, because the behavior is motivated by obligation rather than affection.

What Impact Will Family Diversity Have on Family Conflict and Financial Issues?

Divorce, step-parent relationships, grandparents raising grandchildren, childlessness, and other family diversity issues further complicate attempts to understand the relationship between intergenerational conflict and financial matters. When there are adult stepchildren and biological children, who receives more financial assistance? How does divorce relate to the amount of conflict between the generations in later life? Does it alter financial assistance between the generations? Do childless individuals have conflicts with other family members who they treat "like a child," and do these have the same impact on financial assistance, or is financial assistance given in these cases based solely on reciprocity rather than obligation? Since research on grandparent-grandchild relations has not focused to date on intergenerational conflicts, it is unclear what impact such conflict might have on financial assistance between the generations. These are questions that must be addressed in future research to better appreciate the complex nature of intergenerational conflict and the implications for financial issues. (See also ELDER

LAW PRACTICE; ESTATE PLANNING; FRAILTY PLANNING; GUARDIANSHIP; KING LEAR SYNDROME; LIFE PLANNING.)

References

Clarke, Edward J., Mar Preston, Jo Raksin, and Vern L. Bengtson. 1999. "Types of Conflicts and Tensions between Older Parents and Adult Children." *The Gerontologist* 39(3): 261–70.

Fingerman, Karen L. 1995. "Aging Mothers' and Their Adult Daughters' Perceptions of Conflict Behaviors." *Psychology and Aging* 10(4): 639–49.

Lynott, Patricia Passuth, and Robert E.L. Roberts. 1997. "The Developmental Stake Hypothesis and Changing Perceptions of Intergenerational Relations 1971–1985." *The Gerontologist* 37(3): 394–405.

Morgan, Leslie, and Suzanne Kunkel. 2001. *Aging: The Social Context.* 2nd ed. Thousand Oaks, CA: Pine Forge Press.

Parrott, Tonya M., and Vern L. Bengtson. 1999. "The Effects of Earlier Intergenerational Affection, Normative Expectations, and Family Conflict on Contemporary Exchanges of Help and Support." *Research on Aging* 21(1): 73–105.

Silverstein, Merril, Stephen J. Conroy, Haitao Wang, Roseann Giarrusso, and Vern L. Bengtson. 2002. "Reciprocity in Parent-Child Relations over the Adult Life Course." *Journal of Gerontology: Social Sciences* 57B(1): S3–S13.

Silverstein, Merril, Tonya M. Parrott, and Vern L. Bengtson. 1995. "Factors That Predispose Middle-Aged Sons and Daughters to Provide Social Support to Older Persons." *Journal of Marriage and the Family* 57: 465–75.

Suitor, Jill, and Karl Pillemer. 1988. "Explaining Generational Conflict When Adult Children and Elderly Parents Live Together." *Journal of Marriage and the Family* 50: 1037–47.

Whitbeck, Les B., Danny R. Hoyt, and Shirley M. Huck. 1994. "Early Family Relationships, Intergenerational Solidarity, and Support Provided to Parents by the Adult Children." *Journal of Gerontology: Social Sciences* 49B(2): S85–S94.

Tonya M. Parrott

INTERNET USE BY SENIORS. Seniors make up roughly 13% of the U.S. population but in 2001 comprised just 4% of the U.S. Internet population. According to the National Telecommunications and Information Administration (U.S. Department of Commerce 2000), Internet use by individuals in the 50+ age group from December 1998 to August 2000 experienced the highest rate of growth (53% compared to a nationwide Internet use growth rate of 35% for the same period). Despite this increase in use, seniors are among the least likely to be Internet users—and those seniors who do go online are less likely than Internet users in other age groups to explore many of the uses of the Internet.

Fifty-six percent (56%) of all Americans go online. Fifty-one percent (51%) of Americans 50 to 64 have access to the Internet and are active Internet users, while only 15% of Americans over the age of 65 have access to the Internet. One factor in this use pattern is that few individuals now over age 65 were in the workforce or attending classes in the 1990s, so their exposure to the World Wide Web and other Internet-based pursuits is limited. Those seniors who were in the labor force are almost three times as likely to be Internet users than those who were not (U.S. Department of Commerce 2000).

Although women outnumber men among senior citizens, senior men outnumber senior women online. The gender ratio of today's online senior population is about 60% male and 40% female. Thirty-two percent (32%) of those senior men who are online have had three or more years of experience with Internet use compared to only 14% of similar senior women. However, seniors (especially senior women) are coming online at faster rates, and the gender gap in Internet use is disappearing (Fox et al. 2001).

Online seniors are more likely to be male, married, highly educated, and enjoying relatively high retirement incomes. Eighteen percent (18%) are widows or widowers (compared to 39% of all seniors). Eighty-one percent (81%) of the Internet senior users only have access at home, in contrast to the 50 to 64-year-old group who are more likely to have access both at work and at home (Fox et al. 2001).

Barriers to Internet Use

Overall, persons with disabilities are only half as likely to have access to the Internet as those without. Over one-half (52.1%) of the population age 65 and older has a disability (U.S. Department of Commerce 2000). Individuals in this age group account for only 15.6% of the population as a whole but over one-third (37.4%) of the total number of people with a disability. Disabilities common among seniors such as impaired vision (11.4%) and problems with manual dexterity (9.4%) further reduce the likelihood of computer use (U.S. Department of Commerce 2000).

Income is a barrier to Internet use for people in all age groups. Many seniors are on fixed or limited incomes and cannot afford a computer or the monthly fees associated with Internet access. According to U.S. Census information, the median income of older persons in 2001 was $19,688 for males and $11,313 for females. Households containing families headed by persons 65+ reported a median income in 2001 of $33,938 ($34,661 for Whites, $26,610 for African Americans, and $24,287 for Hispanics). For all older persons reporting income in 2001 (32.9 million), 31.8% reported less than $10,000. Only 31.2% reported $25,000 or more. The median income reported was $14,152.

Although education level, specifically literacy, can be a limiting factor in computer and especially Internet use, surveys show a 93% rate of growth in Internet use by individuals age 50 and over who were in the labor force with only an elementary level education and a 53% increase in use among those who did not graduate high school (U.S. Bureau of the Census 2000).

Most Frequently Used Internet Applications

Although seniors are the least likely group to use the Internet—and those seniors who do go online are much less likely to have sampled all that the Web has to offer—recent studies have identified the Internet applications that are used by the majority of online seniors.

E-mail for communication with friends and relatives is the most heavily used application (92.6%) by online seniors. On a typical day, seniors are more likely to send e-mail than the average Internet user. Many seniors now online were encouraged to go online by family members. Nearly three in five online seniors say that the Internet has improved their connections with family (Fox et al. 2001).

The next highest Internet use among seniors is for research. Research topics include information concerning hobbies and pastimes (most frequent), health and financial information, and current news and events. Senior Internet use, however, differs from that of the average Internet user. While many wired seniors (44%) search for financial news online and seem to enjoy managing online portfolios, few seniors do their banking on the Internet (8%) (Fox et al. 2001).

As a group, online seniors seem to be as engaged as the general Internet population in researching medical information and advice online. Although studies show that senior women are more likely to seek health information online than men, neither education nor income level seem to make much difference in whether or not seniors seek out health information.

Future Senior Internet Use

According to recent studies, most of the strongest Internet holdouts are older Americans. They are ambivalent about the Internet or distrust it and often do not feel there are any benefits to be had from its use. They are more wary of possible privacy invasions and online tracking of their activities and are more concerned than the average American about businesses and people they do not know getting personal information about them or their families.

Despite these attitudes, the future of Internet use by seniors is changing. There is some evidence that the hesitant senior who may currently just dabble in e-mail will eventually become confident enough to begin exploring more activities online. The more experience a wired senior has, the more likely he or she is to begin to fit the pattern of use seen in the general online population. Internet users with several years' experience typically spend more time in an online session and tend to explore new applications (Fox et al. 2001).

Another factor changing senior Internet use is the "silver wave" of individuals in the 50 to 64 age group who are mostly Internet users now and are likely to keep their Internet access after retirement. An American between the ages of 50 and 64 is three times more likely to have Internet access than someone over the age of 65.

Sites for Older Americans

In February 1995, in "Internet and E-mail Resources on Aging," the U.S. Administration on Aging (AoA) listed two sites in the field of aging. In the next two years, that grew to approximately 2,500 sites (Post 1997). Today, the "Internet and E-mail Resources on Aging" Web page is no longer maintained. There are currently so many sites related to aging that the AoA, in attempting to keep up with the rapid growth of these sites, has developed a directory of aging-related links in key areas to major Web resources on selected topics and issues from Alzheimer's disease to workforce and aging. There are also links on the AoA Web site to state and area agencies on aging, federal agency consumer Web sites of interest to older adults, metasites (sites with links to many aging sites), and related resources within the AoA Web site. (See also AGING AMERICA; ATTITUDES ABOUT RETIREMENT; BABY BOOMERS AND RETIREMENT; BANKING SERVICES FOR THE MATURE MARKET; INVESTOR EDUCATION; LEISURE.)

References

Fox, S., et al. 2001. "Wired Seniors: A Fervent Few, Inspired by Family Ties." *Pew Internet & American Life Project.* Washington, DC. Available online at http://pewinternet.org/.

Post, J.A. 1997. "Internet Resources on Aging: Sites to Start With." *The Gerontologist* 37(6).

U.S. Administration on Aging. 2003. "Internet and E-mail Resources on Aging." Available online at http://www.aoa.gov/.

U.S. Bureau of the Census. 1998. *Current Population Surveys*. Washington, DC: GPO.
U.S. Bureau of the Census. 2000. *Current Population Surveys*. Washington, DC: GPO.
U.S. Bureau of the Census. 2001. *Annual Supplement to the Social Security Bulletin*. Washington, DC: GPO.
U.S. Bureau of the Census. 2002. *Money Income in the United States: 2001. Current Population Reports P60–218*. Washington, DC: GPO.
U.S. Department of Commerce. Economics and Statistics Administration. National Telecommunications and Information Administration. 2000. *Falling Through the Net: Toward Digital Inclusion*. Washington, DC: GPO.

Jamie Losikoff-Kent

INVESTMENT ADVICE, recommendations about how to invest savings taking into account an individual's financial goals, tolerance for *investment risk* (change in the value of the investment), and *time horizon* (length of time until the money is needed).

Only the very wealthy used to need—or were able to afford—investment advice and other financial planning services. Most workers expected to spend their careers with one company and retire with a gold watch and a guaranteed pension, which, in addition to Social Security payments, would give them a secure retirement income. No longer. Social Security payments alone can't provide a standard of living equal to that during one's working life, and the future of Social Security is less than certain. What's more, fewer and fewer workers have guaranteed pension plans.

Individuals increasingly have been forced to take on responsibility for managing their own retirement savings, whether through employer-sponsored plans such as 401(k)s or through Individual Retirement Accounts (IRAs). Yet the average worker may lack the necessary expertise and time to make informed investment decisions. This has become apparent since 2000, as the declining market has destroyed the savings of many individuals who hadn't followed accepted investing principles such as diversification (dividing money among different kinds of investments) and rebalancing (ensuring that the mix of investments remains appropriate). Having available and affordable investment advice has become essential to the future retirement security of the general population, and making this information available to a wider audience has become a key market niche for many investment firms.

Why Advice Is Necessary

Defined contribution employer-sponsored plans such as the 401(k) were introduced in the 1980s and became increasingly popular in the 1990s. Before then, most companies that offered retirement plans offered "defined benefit" plans, which are managed by employers and provide a regular pension check to retired employees who qualify based on length of employment. By contrast, "defined contribution" plans, including 401(k) plans (and their equivalents, 403(b) and 457(b) plans, for employees of nonprofit and governmental entities, respectively), require the *employee* to decide how much to contribute and how to invest it. The benefit paid out at retirement depends on employee savings, matching employer contributions (if any), and investment performance. Defined contribution plans have overtaken defined-benefit plans. As of 1998, 58 million private-sector workers participated in defined contribution plans compared with 42 million in defined benefit plans (EBRI 2002d). Forty-two million households had IRAs as of May

2002 (Investment Company Institute 2002). Individuals may have IRAs in addition to either a defined contribution or defined benefit plan.

Employees don't forfeit defined contribution plans and IRAs when they change jobs (except, in some cases, unvested employer matching contributions). This is an advantage over defined benefit plans for an increasingly mobile workforce. However, defined contribution plans present a major challenge by putting the burden of saving and investing on workers rather than employers. Many workers don't save as much as they should for retirement, either through ignorance or because they can't afford to. On limited incomes, many workers may have to make income appropriations decisions, and the short-term expenses, including college expenses and mortgage payments, are very often addressed before saving for retirement.

Misperceptions about retirement and investments may be contributing to the low savings rates. Common mistakes include overestimating investment returns, and consequently over-withdrawing funds in retirement; underestimating the needed income to preserve an active lifestyle; expecting too much from Social Security; depending on an inheritance or a spouse's pension; and underestimating longevity. ("The 2002 National Summit on Retirement Savings" 2000)

Women are particularly at risk of not saving and investing properly for retirement. On average, women live longer than men but earn lower wages. Consequently, they receive lower Social Security payments and lower pension benefits (if they even qualify), and they save less in their retirement accounts. Women also tend to put family financial needs before their own retirement saving, which can hurt them financially in the long run, although it is not clear that they do so to any greater degree than men at comparable income levels.

When people *do* save for retirement, they often don't invest the money appropriately. During the bull market of the 1990s, many individuals with little or no investing experience thought investing was easy. All they had to do was put money in a stock and watch it grow. However, once stock values began to tumble in 2000, individuals who hadn't followed accepted investing principles watched their account balances dwindle and realized they needed help. The 2002 Merrill Lynch "Retirement Survey" found that only 25% of Americans are confident in their investment skills, and over 44% of Americans said they were more likely to seek professional help with their retirement portfolios *after* the economic downturn began. Unfortunately, this realization comes too late.

In addition to the stock market tumble, two other factors created a need for widely available investment advice. First, retirement plan account balances have grown substantially over the last two decades. A five- or six-figure account balance demands more attention than a smaller one. Second, the number of investment choices available in defined contribution plans has increased. When these plans were first introduced in the early 1980s, they generally offered only three investment options. Now, most companies offer at least ten (Cerulli Associates 2002). Some plans offer a "brokerage window" that lets investors choose from the entire universe of mutual funds, and in some cases even individual stocks and bonds. This is quite a large choice, even for experienced investors. With IRAs, the investment choice depends on what is offered by the financial institution housing the account and is generally quite broad.

Why Employers Hesitate

Many individuals hope to receive investment advice through their employer. In a 2002 study by CIGNA Retirement & Investment Services, 89% of employees said they would "welcome personalized financial-planning advice from their employers." However, only 22% of 401(k) plans surveyed in 2001 by PSCA (Profit-Sharing/401[k] Council of America) offered investment advice.

Why do employers hesitate? The employer is a plan fiduciary, which means it is responsible for ensuring that the plan is administered in the best interests of the participants. This includes selecting reasonable plan investments and performing due diligence on any third party involved with the plan, including an investment advisor. The Employee Retirement Income Security Act (ERISA) of 1974 imposes certain requirements on employers that sponsor retirement plans for their employees. For example, plan sponsors themselves are not allowed to give investment advice to employees, nor are financial companies that sell investment products (such as mutual funds) that are offered by the retirement plan, because of the potential conflict of interest. However, employers are allowed to hire an independent company to provide investment advice. In the PSCA study, employers said they hesitated to make such advice available to their employees because they feared they would be held liable if the advice resulted in an investment loss. They also expressed concern about their ability both to select and to monitor a competent provider in accordance with ERISA.

ERISA also requires retirement plan sponsors to provide employees with enough information about the plan investment options and the plan rules, as well as general investment principles, to enable them to make reasonable investing decisions. Most employers fulfill this obligation through newsletters, company-sponsored investment seminars, or access to investment materials on the Internet. Employers may also offer investment "guidance," which gives individuals an asset allocation recommendation based on their financial goals, time horizon, and risk tolerance. (An asset allocation recommendation details how much to invest in different asset classes—for example, 60% stocks, 30% bonds, and 10% cash—but doesn't recommend specific investment products within those asset classes.)

Investment *advice* goes a step further than guidance and recommends a mix of specific investment products (such as particular mutual funds) in which to invest money. The Department of Labor ruled in 2001 that employers may hire an independent company to provide advice to employees, and even manage their accounts, as long as the advice provider/manager is selected using due diligence and prudence. Some experts even argue that providing independent advice is in the employees' best interests and that *not* doing so increases employers' liability exposure. At the time of writing, Congress was considering proposals to address employers' concerns about liability, but it was not clear what action, if any, would be taken.

Who Gives Advice?

Many financial institutions offer some form of investment advice or guidance to their clients. Some have developed asset allocation software internally, while others have partnered with independent advice providers such as Financial Engines, Morningstar, or mPower (which was acquired by Morningstar in July 2003) to provide advice on retirement plans. When an individual logs on to an advice Web site through his or her financial institution or employer, information such as the retirement account balance generally is already entered. This data integration makes the process less time-consuming for the individual, meaning that he or she may be more likely to take advantage of the service. Data integration likely will become more prevalent in years to come (Punishill 2003).

A fairly small number of participants with access to purely online advice are actually using it—generally fewer than 25% (Deloitte and Touche 2002). They may be hesitant to put sensitive financial information on the Internet or be confused about the process and not know where to seek help. Increasingly, financial institutions are offering Internet advice combined with human advisors whom employees can phone or meet in person to further discuss their financial plans (Cerulli Associates 2002).

Another option that should be mentioned is that an individual may choose to consult a financial planner on his or her own. Financial planners generally look at the entire household financial situation and determine whether the client is saving enough in the right types of accounts to have a good chance to meet his or her financial goals. If not, the financial planner advises the client on how to save more. After reviewing the client's financial situation and goals, the planner will generally recommend specific investments. Individuals should choose a financial planner carefully, as some receive commissions for selling certain investment products. The Certified Financial Planner Board of Standards publishes a helpful guide to choosing a financial planner, titled "10 Questions to Ask When Choosing a Financial Planner."

How Good Is Advice?

To paraphrase an old saying, what you get out of advice depends on what you put into it. Advice can only be as good as the assumptions it is based on. These include such things as projected length of life, projected investment performance and interest rates, projected rates of inflation and taxation, salary, and so on. A surefire way to know exactly how much money an individual will have at retirement simply does not exist. Results from any planner online or human will provide an indication, not a guarantee.

The more personal and financial information an individual provides to the advisor, the more the investment advice can be tailored to the individual's situation. This is true whether the advisor is an online program or a live person. Investment advice should, at a minimum, be based on the individual's time horizon until retirement, tolerance for investment risk, and retirement income goals.

Sophisticated advice tools use a technique called Monte Carlo simulation to forecast returns and future values of investments. This computerized technique runs hundreds of scenarios to arrive at a likely result for a mix of investments over a certain period of time. Monte Carlo simulation has been criticized for providing unrealistic results (Harris 2002). However, it also is defended by those who argue that it can give a realistic picture if the right assumptions are used—those that take into account the unpredictable nature of investment returns (Goerz 2002). It has also been suggested that guaranteed return investments should be introduced for retirement accounts to take away the uncertainty of volatile investments such as stocks and high-risk bonds (Bodie 2003).

Many sources of investment advice and guidance available to the mass market via the Internet focus on the accumulation stage—in other words, how to invest money while one is working and accumulating savings. Less attention has been paid to advising people on how to manage their money once they retire and no longer receive a salary. This phase requires a "drawdown" or "retirement income" strategy, with considerations different from the accumulation phase. These include health issues and long-term care insurance and an emphasis on investments that preserve capital and generate income (Cerulli Associates 2002). Advice programs designed for the accumulation phase aren't appropriate for the drawdown phase. Even programs designed specifically for the drawdown phase may have their limitations. The Society of Actuaries studied a number of such software programs. It concluded that, in general,

> their value is in helping people estimate income, retirement needs, and spending . . . [but] the programs are generally not developed to address retirement risks. Instead, the tools mainly mask risk by using averages. This means their results [advice] may not be appropriate for an individual's own situation. (Society of Actuaries 2003)

For example, the effect of a bear market on a retirement account depends in part on its timing. If the market slumps just when retirement is beginning, the effect may be harsher than if it hits later in retirement. This risk, along with many others, must be managed (EBRI 2002b). As baby boomers approach retirement, they will most likely demand this type of planning.

Conclusion

Individuals are increasingly responsible for saving and investing their retirement nest eggs, and they need help from professionals in the form of advice and/or investment management. This is true both for workers accumulating savings and those near retirement. Each group, and each individual, has different needs that must be addressed if they are to successfully endure stock and bond market fluctuations. The situation is becoming more urgent as the U.S. retirement system increasingly shifts toward accounts that are managed by individuals (who are not necessarily equipped to properly manage investments) and as the baby boom generation approaches retirement. (See also FINANCIAL ADVISORS; FINANCIAL EDUCATION FOR SENIORS; INFLUENCES ON RETIREMENT INVESTMENT DECISIONS; INVESTOR EDUCATION; RETIREMENT PLANNING; RETIREMENT PLANS—401(k).)

Organizations

Employee Benefit Research Institute (EBRI)
Financial Engines, Inc.
Financial Planning Association (FPA)
Investment Company Institute
Morningstar, Inc.
National Association of Personal Financial Advisors (NAPFA)
Women's Institute for a Secure Retirement (WISER)

Suggested Readings

Benna, Ted, and Brenda Watson Newmann. 2003. *401(k)s for Dummies*. New York: Wiley Publishing, Inc.

Women's Institute for a Secure Retirement (WISER). 2002. *Your Future Paycheck®: What Women*

Need to Know About Pay, Social Security, Pensions, Savings and Investments. Washington, DC. Available online at http://www.wiser.heinz.org.

References

Bodie, Zvi. 2003. "An Analysis of Investment Advice to Retirement Plan Participants." In *The Pension Challenge: Risk Transfers and Retirement Income Security*, ed. Olivia S. Mitchell and Kent Smetters. New York: Oxford University Press.

Certified Financial Planner Board of Standards. n.d. "10 Questions to Ask When Choosing a Financial Planner." Available online at http://www.cfp-board.org/cons_10qs.html.

Cerulli Associates. 2002. "Demographics Portend Change." In *The Cerulli Edge U.S. Edition.* Profit-Sharing/401(k) Council of America (PSCA) 45th Annual Survey of Profit-Sharing and 401(k) Plans. Boston, MA: Author.

Deloitte and Touche, LLP. 2002. *Annual 401(k) Benchmarking Survey.*

Employee Benefit Research Institute (EBRI). 2002a. "An Evolving Pension System: Trends in Defined Benefit and Defined Contribution Plans." *Issue Brief* 249 (September).

Employee Benefit Research Institute (EBRI). 2002b. "Can 401(k) Accumulations Generate Significant Income for Future Retirees?" *Issue Brief* 251 (November). Available online at http://www.ebri.org/ibex/ib251.htm.

Goerz, David. 2002. "Crystal Balls and Forecasting the Future with Monte Carlo." *mPower Café*. Available online at http://www.mpowercafe.com/investing/analysis/analysis.3.3.3_12182002.html

Harris, Elizabeth. 2002. "In Search of Better Odds in Retirement Planning." *New York Times*, October 8.

Investment Company Institute. 2002. *Investment Company Institute Fundamentals* 11(3) (September).

Merrill Lynch. 2002. "Retirement Survey." Press release January 2002. Available online at http://www.ml.com/about/press_release/10092002-1_retirement_plans_pr.htm.

Punishill, Jaime. 2003 "Wealth Management 2003: Five Predictions." Forester Research Brief. Available online at http://www.forrester.com/ER/Research/Brief/0,1317,16282,FF.html.

Society of Actuaries. 2003. "Retirement Planning Software." Available online at http://www.soa.org/library/monographs/retirement_systems/m-rs03-1/m-rs03-1_tableofcontents.html.

"The 2002 National Summit on Retirement Savings." 2002. Delegate Resources, Washington, DC. International Foundation of Employee Benefit Plans, Inc. Available online at http://www.ifebp.org/PDF/SummitBackFinal.pdf.

Brenda Watson Newmann

INVESTMENT CLUBS, small groups of individuals who pool their efforts and resources to invest in the common stocks of publicly traded corporations. Investment club members meet regularly to learn about investing, study publicly traded companies, and reach consensus decisions about the merits of particular stocks. Although investment club structure can vary, participants typically pay a small, set amount each month into a joint account for purchasing stocks. The membership of an investment club generally consists of acquaintances, friends, neighbors, relatives, coworkers, fellow church members, or other like-minded individuals. Investment clubs can provide opportunities to socialize, and members often enjoy a strong sense of camaraderie as they work together on the club's portfolio.

For many Americans, purchasing shares in publicly traded corporations has proven to be the best way to meet long-term goals such as buying a home, paying for education, and funding retirement. During the second half of the twentieth century, the Standard & Poor's 500 stock index increased at an average annual rate of 12.8%. In contrast, long-term corporate bonds had annualized average returns of 6.2%, and U.S. 30-day Treasury bills averaged only 5.2%. The percentages may be somewhat different depending on which periods and indexes are compared, but throughout the past century, the pattern remained the same—stocks delivered higher average returns than other varieties of financial assets.

No guarantee exists that these patterns will continue, of course. But given the historical record, people who include common stocks in their investment programs may have more success increasing the total value of their assets throughout their lives. That will be required to cope with the rising cost of living. Some degree of growth is especially important in retirement when inflation can erode the purchasing power of a fixed income. For example, concern is widespread over evidence that increases in the cost of health care—especially for prescription drugs—may continue to exceed the rate of inflation. And retirees typically are the biggest consumers of medical products and services. In addition, Americans are retiring earlier and living longer on average, so many retirees may have to depend on their nest eggs for longer periods than was true of their parents' generation.

Everyone is aware that stock values rise and fall—sometimes at an alarming pace. Over sufficiently long periods, however, the peaks and valleys cancel each other out, and historically the trend in prices has been upward. The most successful investors tend to be those who invest in high-quality, profitable, growth-oriented companies that they identify through dogged research and purchase when attractively priced. They don't "invest in the market" or view stock shares as commodities they can trade to get rich quickly. They ignore media coverage of the stock market that dwells on the concerns of short-term traders rather than addressing the information needs of long-term investors.

Regardless of how people structure their investments, one key to achieving their goals is to harness the power of compounding. Over long periods, even small investments can grow into substantial sums. Therefore, the younger the investor, the more benefit from compounding. Suppose someone starts investing $2,000 a year at age 19 and stops after 8 years. At a 9% average rate of return, the portfolio would grow to $692,796 by the time the investor reaches age 65. (For the sake of simplicity, this example does not factor in taxes or transaction costs.) The amount invested would total $16,000. To achieve a comparable amount at the same rate of return, another investor who begins contributing $2,000 a year at age 27 would need to continue for 39 years until age 65. The late starter would have invested a total of $78,000—almost five times more—but accumulated only $673,765.

Choosing individual stocks has several advantages over one popular alternative—mutual funds. Deregulation and the resulting competition have helped lower brokerage commissions for stock trades, for example, and many companies now sell shares directly to individual investors at minimal cost. In contrast, mutual funds—particularly those funds that are actively managed—charge a variety of fees and commissions that in recent years have been rising. Fund managers may engage in relatively frequent trading, raising costs, increasing tax liabilities, and eroding the ultimate return to shareholders. Those costs help account for the fact that most actively managed funds fail to generate rates of return that even match the growth rates of major stock indexes.

Mutual funds remain attractive partly because investors can simply pay a fee to have their portfolios managed professionally. But individuals who invest in stocks exclusively through mutual funds miss out on the opportunity to learn how to make their own investment decisions. That's especially true when investors choose index funds—"baskets" of stocks that closely match those constituting indexes such as the Standard & Poor's 500 index, the Dow Jones industrial average, and the NASDAQ composite index. A fund's rate of return therefore will closely follow movements of its index, minus the impact of fees, of course. Index fund investors benefit from the relentless upward movement of the market long term, but they miss the opportunity to become more knowledgeable and informed investors that can come with investment club membership.

Investment club advocates maintain that investors who choose individual stocks through diligent research often can exceed the average returns offered by index funds, especially when they buy shares in quality growing companies at attractive prices and hold them over long periods. Achieving results that are even slightly higher than the market averages can produce much larger portfolios over time, given the mathematics of compounding. For example, over 30 years an initial investment of $10,000 that produces a 12% average annual rate of return—just under the recent 50-year record of the S&P 500—would grow to $299,597. But with an average annual return of 15%, the same $10,000 would produce more than double the result, as it grows to $662,118.

For many people, joining a club is one of the most efficient ways to invest in individual stocks. By pooling their money, members have more to invest. That makes it easier for them to diversify, that is, reduce risk by holding shares in a variety of companies. Participating in a group effort and receiving moral support makes it easier for the average person to stick with a program of disciplined, long-term investing through the ups and downs of the broader market. Also, members can divide up the work of researching companies, which makes stock picking more practical for those who are short of time. And members benefit from sharing their investment knowledge and experience as they develop a disciplined approach to studying stocks and investment.

Small groups of investors had banded together previously, but the second half of the last century saw the investment club movement blossom. The National Association of Investors Corporation (NAIC), a nonprofit membership organization, was founded in 1951 to provide educational services and promote the growth of investment clubs. As of mid-2002, 30,349 investment clubs belonged to the association. The average club membership was 11. A total of 389,174 people belonged to the educational organization, including individual members with no investment club affiliation.

The late George A. Nicholson, Jr., father of the investment club movement, believed in "people's capitalism"—the economic freedom and opportunity that flows when a large portion of the population owns common stocks. He believed that investment clubs were the best means to provide three necessary ingredients for people's capitalism. To foster individual stock ownership—and thereby support modern capitalism and free enterprise—Nicholson and other pioneers of the movement founded NAIC to spread their message and provide members with ways to become educated investors. They taught that investors can stay motivated by establishing clear long-term financial goals, and they developed a set of simple guiding principles.

NAIC advocates a disciplined approach to investing. The nonprofit corporation recommends investing in growth stocks—stocks of companies whose sales and earnings are growing at rates that are consistently higher than the growth rates of their industries or the overall economy. One of the chief characteristics of such a company often is a management team that values growth very highly and makes it a guiding principle for the business.

Another principle that the NAIC teaches is to invest regularly and to reinvest dividends and any capital gains from the sale of shares. Investors are encouraged to seek out corporations that display signs of quality such as consistent growth in sales and profitability. Another principle is to diversify—to build portfolios that include corporations from different size categories, economic sectors, and industries. Investors also are encouraged to remember the "rule of five"—on average, long-term investors can expect three of every five carefully selected holdings to perform as expected or close to expectations, one to prove a major disappointment, and one to exceed original projections by a significant margin.

A club membership of around 16 is considered ideal: with more members, finding a large enough meeting place may prove difficult; with fewer, each member has to take on a larger workload. The members of a new club need to appoint officers, agree upon a structure—a partnership, usually—and file the necessary paperwork. They also must agree upon an investment approach such as the long-term growth strategy the NAIC recommends. They must select a brokerage service to handle their portfolio transactions. The members decide where and how often to meet—monthly meetings are typical—and establish how much each member will contribute regularly to the portfolio.

In some clubs, however, members only consult about stocks—they don't pool their money. While they may reach a consensus about a particular stock, individual members decide whether to buy or sell shares for their own portfolios. This approach is found among "virtual" clubs whose members often live in different areas and confer online.

Each member is responsible for tracking the progress of a few businesses. At meetings they take turns profiling individual corporations. Following such presentations, they vote on whether to purchase or sell some of those companies' shares. Members also give educational presentations, and they may invite outside speakers such as local stockbrokers or financial planners. Discussions of portfolio accounting and other club business are part of most meetings.

Club members in many parts of the country can attend educational seminars and investment fairs sponsored by volunteers in NAIC's 115 regional chapters. NAIC also holds nationwide conferences such as its annual congress, where attendees can go to seminars, meet representatives of publicly traded companies, and talk shop with other investors. (See also EQUITY SECURITIES; FINANCIAL EDUCATION FOR SENIORS; INFLUENCES ON RETIREMENT INVESTMENT DECISIONS; INVESTMENT ADVICE; INVESTOR EDUCATION; MUTUAL FUNDS.)

Organizations

American Association of Individual Investors
FoolMart
National Association of Investors Corporation

Suggested Readings

Maranjian, Selena. 1998. *Investment Clubs: How to Start and Run One the Motley Fool Way.* Alexandria, VA: Motley Fool Books.

O'Hara, Thomas E., and Kenneth S. Janke, Sr. 1998. *Starting and Running a Profitable Investment Club: The Official Guide of the National Association of Investors Corporation.* Royal Oak, MI: NAIC.

References

National Association of Investors Corporation. 2002. *Introducing Teenagers to . . . Investing the NAIC Way!* Royal Oak, MI: Author.
T. Rowe Price Investment Services, Inc. 2001. "Historical Returns for Different Investments." Available online at http://www.troweprice.com/retirement/historical.html.

Kevin J. Lamiman

INVESTMENTS. See Annuities; Bonds; Commodities; Derivatives; Equity Securities; Mutual Funds; Savings Account Trusts; Savings Investments.

INVESTOR EDUCATION, knowledge designed for individuals preparing to invest or already having holdings in the capital markets to help them make informed investment decisions. A generation ago, retirees who had worked for a company that provided a retirement benefit could look forward to receiving a pension check every month for the rest of their lives. Workers who are retiring currently are less likely to have a traditional pension plan, and they must be aware that Social Security benefits will typically fall far short of meeting all their retirement needs. Income to supplement Social Security increasingly comes from periodic distributions from a defined contribution plan, IRA (Individual Retirement Account), or another type of planned retirement savings where workers must make their own investment decisions. Unlike a traditional pension plan, the ultimate payout value of these retirement plans will fluctuate, depending upon the investment choices made, and they may or may not provide adequate income for retirement. Even if a worker uses a financial advisor or other investment expert, he or she must take ultimate responsibility for the investing choices that are made, both before and after retirement.

The dramatic growth of 401(k)-type retirement plans that pay retirement benefits in lump-sum distributions rather than annuities, and the increasing payment of lump sums from defined benefit pension plans, means that individuals are increasingly responsible for decisions that will determine their future retirement. According to Dallas Salisbury, president and chief executive officer of the Employee Benefit Research Institute (EBRI), workers who change jobs or otherwise trigger the distribution of retiree savings must decide whether to spend it immediately, whether to save the lump sum and roll it over, how to invest it, and how fast they can spend it in retirement and not outlive the money (seniorjournal.com 2003).

Investing for retirement requires many assumptions, such as the annual rate of inflation, the after-tax return investments will earn, estimated life expectancy, and expected retirement expenses. Faced with more complex decisions about retirement—from choosing long-term care insurance to asset allocations, from taking distributions from IRAs to selecting stocks, bonds, or mutual funds, from charitable giving to estate planning—today's retirees must learn to make financial decisions that will have long-lasting effects. To make those decisions, workers must become educated even though they may choose to work with a financial planner or other expert. "Don't assume that retirement is a stage of life that will simply take care of itself," say Robert J. Garner and Robert Coplan, authors of the *Ernst & Young's Personal Financial Planning Guide* (1995).

There are several sources of reliable, up-to-date investor information. Local libraries carry traditional print resources—magazines, books, and computers for searching Internet resources. A local senior citizen center may offer classes on Internet use. Senior centers may also offer seminars and workshops on investing, estate planning, and making the most of financial resources. If they do not, individuals may organize programs and invite guest speakers from the community who are qualified to address such topics as the financial markets, diversification, risk management, estate planning, charitable giving, and investing after retirement. Community colleges or universities are good resources for speakers, classes in investing, or financial planning courses. Many offer discounts for seniors who want to take classes, and many others permit seniors to audit courses at reduced tuition rates. (See also DEFINED CONTRIBUTION PLAN; EDUCATION OF OLDER ADULTS; FINANCIAL ADVISORS; FINANCIAL EDUCATION FOR SENIORS; RETIREMENT PLANS—401(k); RETIREMENT PLANS—403(b); RETIREMENT PREPAREDNESS; RISK TOLERANCE.)

Organizations

American Association of Individual Investors
Bond Market Association
CNN Money
Dow Jones & Co. Online Investing
FinanCenter, Inc.
International Association of Financial Planners
Intuit
Investment FAC
Investors Guide
Mutual Fund Education Alliance
National Association of Investors Corporation
Office of Investor Education and Assistance
Senior Journal
Smart Money University

References

Gard, Jim. 1996. *The Small Investor*. Berkeley, CA: Ten Speed Press.

Garner, Robert J., and Robert Coplan. 1995. *Ernst & Young's Personal Financial Planning Guide*. New York: John Wiley & Sons.

Lynch, Peter. 1989. *One Up on Wall Street*. New York: Simon and Schuster.

O'Hara, Thomas E., and Kenneth S. Janke, Sr. 1995. *Taking Control of Your Financial Life*. Burr Ridge, IL: Irwin Press.

Seniorjournal.com. 2003. "Baby Boomers to Face Financial Challenges in Retirement." July 25. Available online at http://www.seniorjournal.com/NEWS/Retirement/04-30-01BoomRetirmntThreat.htm.

Tobias, Andrew. 2002. *The Only Investment Guide You'll Ever Need*. San Diego, CA: Harcourt Brace & Company.

Jo Ann Linck and Karen Brelsford